THE CAMBRIDGE COMPANION TO
THE FEDERALIST

The eighty-five *Federalist* essays written by Alexander Hamilton, John Jay, and James Madison as 'Publius' to support the ratification of the Constitution in 1787–88 are regarded as the preeminent American contribution to Western political theory. Recently, there have been major developments in scholarship on the Revolutionary and Founding era as well as increased public interest in constitutional matters that make this a propitious moment to reflect on the contributions and complexity of *The Federalist*. This volume of specially commissioned essays covers the broad scope of Publius' work, including historical, political, philosophical, juridical, and moral dimensions. In so doing, they bring the design and arguments of the text into focus for twenty-first century scholars, students, and citizens and show how these diverse treatments of *The Federalist* are associated with an array of substantive political and constitutional perspectives in our own time.

JACK N. RAKOVE is William Robertson Coe Professor of History and American Studies and Professor of Political Science, Emeritus, at Stanford University. He is the author of seven books, including the Pulitzer Prize-winning *Original Meanings: Politics and Ideas in the Making of the Constitution* (1996).

COLLEEN A. SHEEHAN is Professor of Politics and Director of the Matthew J. Ryan Center at Villanova University. Her publications include *James Madison and the Spirit of Republican Self-Government* (2009) and *The Mind of James Madison: The Legacy of Classical Republicanism* (Cambridge, 2015).

OTHER VOLUMES IN THE SERIES OF CAMBRIDGE
COMPANIONS TO PHILOSOPHY

Continued at the back of the book

The Cambridge Companion to
THE FEDERALIST

Edited by

Jack N. Rakove
Stanford University

Colleen A. Sheehan
Villanova University

CAMBRIDGE
UNIVERSITY PRESS

CAMBRIDGE
UNIVERSITY PRESS

University Printing House, Cambridge CB2 8BS, United Kingdom

One Liberty Plaza, 20th Floor, New York, NY 10006, USA

477 Williamstown Road, Port Melbourne, VIC 3207, Australia

314–321, 3rd Floor, Plot 3, Splendor Forum, Jasola District Centre,
New Delhi – 110025, India

79 Anson Road, #06–04/06, Singapore 079906

Cambridge University Press is part of the University of Cambridge.

It furthers the University's mission by disseminating knowledge in the pursuit of
education, learning, and research at the highest international levels of excellence.

www.cambridge.org
Information on this title: www.cambridge.org/9781107136397
DOI: 10.1017/9781316479865

© Cambridge University Press 2020

First published 2020

A catalogue record for this publication is available from the British Library.

ISBN 978-1-107-13639-7 Hardback
ISBN 978-1-316-50184-9 Paperback

Contents

Contributors

Jack N. Rakove is William Robertson Coe Professor of History and American Studies and Professor of Political Science, Emeritus, at Stanford University. His many books include *Original Meanings: Politics and Ideas in the Making of the Constitution* (1997), which won the Pulitzer Prize in History.

Colleen A. Sheehan is Professor of Political Science and Director of the Matthew J. Ryan Center at Villanova University. She is the author of *James Madison and the Spirit of Republican Self-Government* (2009) and *The Mind of James Madison: The Legacy of Classical Republicanism* (2015).

Max M. Edling is Reader in American History at King's College London. He is the author of *A Revolution in Favor of Government: Origins of the U.S. Constitution and the Making of the American State* (2003) and *A Hercules in the Cradle: War, Money, and the American State, 1783–1867* (2014).

Jon Elster is Robert K. Merton Professor of the Social Sciences at Columbia University. His many books include *Alexis de Tocqueville: The First Social Scientist* (2009); *Securities Against Misrule: Juries, Assemblies, Elections* (2013); and *Explaining Social Behavior: More Nuts and Bolts for the Social Sciences* (2007, 2015).

John Ferejohn is Samuel Tilden Professor of Law at New York University and Carolyn S. G. Munro Professor of Political Science, Emeritus, at Stanford University. His writings include *Pork Barrel Politics: Rivers and Harbor Legislation, 1947–1968* (1974) and (with William Eskridge) *A Republic of Statutes: The New American Constitution* (2010).

Alan Gibson is Professor of Political Science at California State University, Chico. His works include *Interpreting the Founding: Guide to the Enduring Debates over the Origins and Foundation of the American Republic* (2009) and *Understanding the Founding: The Crucial Questions* (2010).

David M. Golove is Hiller Family Foundation Professor of Law at New York University. He is the author of "Treaty-Making and the Nation: The Historical Foundations of the Nationalist Conception of the Treaty Power," and (with Bruce Ackerman) *Is NAFTA Constitutional?* (1995).

Roderick Hills is William T. Comfort, III Professor of Law at New York University. He is the author of numerous articles on the current state of American constitutionalism and federalism.

Daniel J. Hulsebosch is Charles Seligson Professor of Law at New York University. He is the author of *Constituting Empire: New York and the Transformation of Constitutionalism in the Atlantic World, 1664–1830* (2005) and (with David M. Golove) "A Civilized Nation: The Early American Constitution, the Law of Nations, and the Pursuit of International Recognition."

Larry D. Kramer is President, William and Flora Hewlett Foundation, and formerly Richard E. Lang Professor of Law and Dean at Stanford Law School. He is the author of *The People Themselves: Popular Constitutionalism and Judicial Review* (2004) and "Madison's Audience."

Harvey C. Mansfield is William R. Kenan, Jr. Professor of Government at Harvard University, where he has spent most of the past seven decades. He is the author of numerous works in political theory, notably including *Machiavelli's Virtue* (1996) and *Taming the Prince: The Ambivalence of Modern Executive Power* (1993).

Eric Nelson is Robert M. Beren Professor of Government at Harvard University. He is the author of four books, including *The Greek Tradition in Republican Thought* (2004) and *The Royalist Revolution: Monarchy and the American Founding* (2014).

Paul A. Rahe is Charles O. Lee and Louise K. Lee Chair in the Western Heritage, Hillsdale College. His many works include *Republics Ancient and Modern: Classical Republicanism and the American Revolution* (1992), *Against Throne and Altar: Machiavelli and Political Theory under the English Republic* (2008), and *Montesquieu and the Logic of Liberty: War, Religion, Commerce, Climate, Terrain, Technology, Uneasiness of Mind, the Spirit of Political Vigilance, and the Foundations of the Modern Republic* (2009).

David J. Siemers is Professor of Political Science at University of Wisconsin-Oshkosh. He is the author of *Ratifying the Republic: Antifederalists and Federalists in Constitutional Time* (2002) and *The Myth of Coequal Branches: Restoring the Constitution's Separation of Functions* (2018).

Quentin Taylor is Professor of History and Political Science at Rogers State University and a former Resident Scholar at Liberty Fund. His publications include a number of articles and chapters on *The Federalist*.

William M. Treanor holds the newly established Paul Regis Dean Leadership Chair at Georgetown Law Center, where he has served since 2010. He is the author of numerous essays on the origins of judicial review and problems of constitutional interpretation.

Greg Weiner is Associate Professor of Political Science and Provost at Assumption College. He is the author of *Madison's Metronome: The Constitution, Majority Rule, and the Tempo of American Politics* (2012) and *The Political Constitution: The Case Against Judicial Supremacy* (2019).

Michael Zuckert is Nancy R. Dreux Professor of Political Science Emeritus at the University of Notre Dame and Professor at Arizona State University. He is the past editor of *American Political Thought* and the author of *Natural Rights and the New Republicanism* (1994).

Acknowledgments

The editors wish to extend their thanks, first, to all the contributors, for responding to our suggestions and for tolerating the various delays that accompanied the preparation of this volume; and second, to Brenda Hafera, John Guerra, and Ann Riddle, for their valuable assistance.

Abbreviations

DHRC   John P. Kaminski et al., eds., *The Documentary History of the Ratification of the Constitution* (Madison: State Historical Society of Wisconsin, 1976–)

Fed.   Jacob Cooke, ed., *The Federalist* (Middletown CT: Wesleyan University Press, 1961)

RFC   Max Farrand, ed., *The Records of the Federal Convention of 1787* (New Haven, CT: Yale University Press, 1911, 1937, 1966)

PAH   Harold C. Syrett and Jacob E. Cooke, eds., *The Papers of Alexander Hamilton* (New York: Columbia University Press, 1961–87)

PJM   William T. Hutchinson, William M. E. Rachal et al., eds., *The Papers of James Madison: Congressional Series* (Chicago: University of Chicago Press and Charlottesville, VA: University of Virginia Press, 1961–91)

Introduction

Jack N. Rakove and Colleen A. Sheehan

THE PROBLEM OF AUTHORSHIP

For well over a century, the authorship of the individual essays of *The Federalist* was a matter of great uncertainty. The initial source of this uncertainty simply reflected the conventional practices of eighteenth-century political writing, when most polemical pieces, especially those appearing in newspapers, were published pseudonymously. When Alexander Hamilton, the instigator and chief author of *The Federalist*, chose Publius as the penname, he was paying homage to Valerius Publius Publicola, the sixth-century BCE aristocrat who was a chief founder of the Roman republic. His two co-authors, James Madison and John Jay, would have welcomed his choice. Madison in particular would have saluted Publius's distinguished republican credentials. A major part of Madison's preparations for the Federal Convention of 1787 involved his comparative study of "ancient and modern confederacies" and his thorough assessment of the failings of popular government recorded in his famous memorandum on the "Vices of the Political System of the United States." Madison returned to that project shortly after the Convention adjourned on September 17, 1787. Within the next few years, he developed an even more ambitious plan – apparently never fulfilled – consulting writings either from antiquity or about it to provide the framework for a study of modern republican government.[1]

The early readers of *The Federalist* would not have cared which author wrote any particular essay. The great cause of ratification was what dominated their concerns. But as political party tensions emerged and quickly escalated in the early 1790s, the question of individual authorship did begin to matter, first to Hamilton and Madison, then to a larger audience. A critical turning point came in 1804, which led to the deeper confusion over the authorship of individual essays that persisted for nearly a century and a half afterward. Shortly before his fatal duel with Aaron Burr on July 11, Hamilton compiled a short list identifying the authors of the eighty-five essays, and he conspicuously deposited this document in the bookshelf of Egbert Benson, his friend, supporter, and fellow New York City lawyer. Benson was no stranger to the identity of Publius. Back in June 1789, when Representative William Loughton Smith of South Carolina cited *Federalist* 77 to argue that the consent of the Senate would be necessary for the removal of cabinet officers, Benson let their colleagues in the House know "that *Publius* had informed him since the preceding day's debate, that upon mature reflection he *had changed his opinion* & was now convinced that the President alone should have the power of removal at pleasure." There should be no doubt who wrote *Federalist* 77, Smith wrote John Rutledge: "He is a candidate for the office of Secretary of Finance!"[2] Though Madison and Hamilton had both let George Washington know of their involvement in *The Federalist* as soon as the first essays began appearing, the first published confirmation of authorship occurred only with the French translation of 1792.

In his list, Hamilton allotted five essays to Jay, gave Madison credit for twelve others, noted that he and Madison had co-written the three papers devoted to the history of other confederacies, and claimed the remaining sixty essays for his own pen. Madison survived Hamilton by a near third of a century, and he stated his own counter-claims to the authorship of twenty-nine essays in the Gideon edition first published in 1818. This discrepancy remained largely unresolved until 1944, when Douglass Adair published a famous essay on "The Authorship of the Disputed Federalist Papers."[3] Reviewing the entire controversy, Adair concluded that the twenty-nine essays Madison had claimed as his own in 1818 were indeed justly his. Nearly every scholar writing since then has accepted Adair's analysis. His findings were further vindicated by a pioneering work in the quantitative analysis of literary material published in 1964.[4]

The problem of the authorship of *The Federalist* takes a different face, however, when modern scholars have to decide which name they wish to use when identifying a particular *Federalist* essay. Should one speak of Publius as a coherent intellectual personality, the collective author of all eighty-five essays? Or is it more appropriate to identify the individual author of any particular essay or set of essays? How one answers these questions may reflect the distinctive emphases of scholarly disciplines. Political theorists are more comfortable speaking of Publius when their underlying concern is to articulate the core ideas they associate with the founding in general, or to distinguish an eighteenth-century science of politics from the modern academic discipline of political science, or to understand Publius on his own chosen terms. Historians, by contrast, are born contextualists, and naturally incline to be as specific as they possibly can. Why make Publius the author of *Federalist* 10 when that essay was the culminating statement of a set of ideas that Madison had been developing for the past eight months, perhaps longer, and which he was still actively musing over four years later? Why not explicitly recognize Hamilton as the author of *Federalist* 78, with its defense of the judicial review of the constitutionality of legislation, when we know that Hamilton had argued the precursor case of *Rutgers v. Waddington* in 1784 and would play the same role in the seminal case of *US v. Hylton* in 1796?

The diverse concerns and approaches of the disciplines of history and political science are reflected in this volume. Seeing *The Federalist* through a multifaceted lens contributes to bringing the text and its arguments into focus for twenty-first-century readers. Yet this difference in perspective on how one identifies the author(s) of *The Federalist* also reflects concerns more fundamental than the mere accident of scholarly discipline. It is also, to borrow a phrase used in the first paragraph of *Federalist* 1, a matter of "reflection and choice," and that choice has important implications for the ways in which we analyze the philosophical, political, juridical, historical, and even moral dimensions of *The Federalist*. Thus, as conventional as the diverse disciplinary treatments of *The Federalist* have become in our time, it is critical to recognize that they also illustrate an array of substantive political and constitutional perspectives.

The importance of scholarly perspective on *The Federalist* is paralleled by the important place that the founding and the revolutionary era – rival terms for the same general phenomenon – occupy in American political culture. The more one regards *The Federalist* as the best exposition of the original meaning of the Constitution, the more weight one might give to the political consensus that permitted its approval at a precise historical moment. That view is also consistent with the originalist theory of constitutional interpretation, which argues that the meaning of the text is derived from the general understanding of the sovereign authority that approved it – the people themselves, acting through the state conventions that ratified the Constitution. Respect for the sovereignty of the people requires attention to the constitutional compact proclaimed by the will and authenticated by the seal of the sovereign people, as a matter of republican right and public trust.[5]

Many historians would view this question differently. They could appreciate the ingenious tactics that allowed the framers and their Federalist supporters to produce an unequivocal decision in favor of ratification a bare ten months after the Federal Convention adjourned. Yet they would also skeptically question whether or how well the ratification decisions of 1787–88 accurately reflected the real state of public opinion. Even more important, they would doubt whether the ideas prevailing at any set moment of historical time can definitively ascertain or fix the meaning of a document, even if *The Federalist* is read as an exemplary commentary, an authoritative *midrash*, on the original sacred text. The legal fiction of originalism might have its uses within the courts of constitutional jurisprudence, but it could never provide an adequate way to assess the true meaning of the Constitution.

For historians the clock of constitutional time never stops running. The expectations that shaped the agenda of the Convention, the debates at Independence Hall, the rhetoric of ratification, the early decisions about implementing (or in Madison's phrase in *Federalist* 37, liquidating) the meaning of the text: these represent the four successive phases of the development of constitutional ideas and practices, and each has to receive its due to obtain a just result. Such an approach will prefer treating the two main authors of *The Federalist* individually, and will ask how their concerns and ideas evolved over time. Publius may make an occasional appearance (especially during a putative Act III, the ratification struggle) and even have a prolonged soliloquy now and then. But Hamilton and Madison, those two "young men of the Revolution," remain the central characters. Their contributions to *The Federalist* matter not only in their own right, but also as key moments in the continuing evolution of their political thinking and purposes.

Originalists are often criticized for holding that the textual meaning of the Constitution was locked into the document at the moment of its adoption. Yet many originalists regard its interpretation as a dynamic process, but one that has to recognize the Constitution's unique status as fundamental law anchored in a unique expression of popular sovereignty. To use the historians' clock metaphor, because the doctrine of "constitutionalism" is derived from and justified by the sovereign authority of the people, it might be said that the strike of midnight has a special significance for originalists. It is the start of the day and the point that sets the instrument's measure. Like the ratification of the Constitution, it is both a beginning point in time and the setting of a principle – *ab initio* and *a principio*.[6] Certainly, time brings novel challenges and may require new applications of constitutional powers, or perhaps new and different constitutional measures, but the legitimacy of the latter is contingent on adhering to the constitutionally prescribed modes of alteration. This is requisite not because the Constitution is fixed in time, but because changes in the fundamental law must be sanctioned by the sovereign authority.

These two perspectives characterize many of the essays that comprise this volume, and they thus invite readers to ask which stance they find more convincing. Of course, one might well choose to take seriously both the historical and the constitutional considerations that inscribed the work of Hamilton, Madison, and Jay. In doing so, we are led to ask further if *The Federalist* still has meaning for us today, and if so, what is the guidance it provides us. Should we perhaps take Publius seriously when he pronounced that the "prudent enquiry in all cases, ought surely to be not so much *from whom* the advice comes, as whether the advice be *good*" (*Fed.* 40, 267).

THE AGENDA OF REFORM

In making this comparison between the one-voice Publius and the multifaceted author, it is also helpful to consider how the authors divided their labors. There are two obvious ways to divide or categorize the contents of *The Federalist*. One approach would divide the eighty-five essays into two somewhat uneven halves. The first thirty-six essays make the case for a reconstituted union and a national government fully capable of pursuing its delegated duties and responsibilities. The remaining forty-nine papers are devoted to an exposition of the Constitution itself, with subseries of essays devoted to the federal structure, separation of powers, the legislature, the executive, and the judiciary. The McLean edition of 1788 followed this division exactly, treating Hamilton's *Federalist* 1 and Madison's *Federalist* 37 as parallel introductory essays to its two volumes. This division of labor conveniently reflected the particular interests and experiences of the two main authors. Madison was first and foremost a student of legislative deliberation and a critic of the potential misuse of legislative power. It made sense therefore that he focused on Article I and on the separation of powers. Hamilton was a greater enthusiast for executive power and already, barely past the age of thirty, one of the nation's ablest attorneys. It was similarly appropriate that he should take charge of the essays devoted to Articles II and III.

Yet there is another way to distinguish Madison's and Hamilton's respective contributions to *The Federalist*. Madison was an avowed "votary" of the cause of republican or "popular" government. On the eve of the Convention, while analyzing what he entitled the Vices of the Political System of the United States, he had fretted that the evils of the "multiplicity," "mutability," and (worst of all) "injustice" of state legislation were calling "into question the fundamental principle of republican Government, that the majority who rule in such Governments, are the safest Guardians both of public Good and of private rights." He self-consciously saw his constitutional labors of 1787–88 as an effort to discover, as the final paragraph of *Federalist* 10 declared, "a republican remedy for the diseases most incident to republican government." Any constitution that was not "strictly republican," *Federalist* 39 announced, would not "be reconcilable with the genius of the people of America; with the fundamental principles of the Revolution; or with that honorable determination which animates every votary of freedom, to rest all our political experiments on the capacity of mankind for self-government." The animating spirit of his twenty-nine essays was his effort to explain how the new Constitution truly represented a superior form of republican government. On this point, Madison was an enthusiast – and so we read his essays still, even if many modern commentators often emphasize the cautions he raised about the dangers of popular misrule.

Hamilton's enthusiasms lay elsewhere. His accommodation with republicanism, if not grudging, rested on the same recognition Madison voiced in *Federalist* 39: this was the genius of the American people. But the admiration for the British constitution that he expressed in his Convention speech of June 18, 1787, was hardly an affirmation of republican principles. Hamilton's deeper admiration for the British system was grounded less in some lingering affection for a balanced constitutional monarchy than in his frank appreciation of the advantages wielded by the British fiscal–military state, a state that had developed the mechanism of public credit needed to mobilize the nation's resources with the aim of projecting enormous economic and political power abroad. That admiration in turn rested on the harsh lessons that Hamilton and his fellow officers in the Continental Army had learned from waging a long and costly war. While the Continental

Congress and the states struggled from one year to the next to keep their army in the field, General George Washington's military "family" – his closest aides and subordinates – chafed at the feebleness of the American republics. By the early 1780s, Hamilton and many of his fellow officers were becoming proponents of constitutional reform. In their view the real challenge Americans faced was not to find republican remedies for republican diseases, but to give the national government the legal authority it needed to project American power effectively, converting the revolutionary confederation into a modern nation-state. As Hamilton once put it, if America is a Hercules, she is yet "a Hercules in the cradle."[7]

Yet Hamilton also took constitutional ideas quite seriously. The conceptions of executive and judicial power that he expressed in essays like *Federalist* 70 and 78 were visionary, and they accurately anticipated important developments in the workings of the Constitution. Still, Hamilton was more a state-builder than a constitutionalist. Some of his best insights as Publius appear in essays, now little studied, discussing the military priorities of the nation or methods of raising revenue and establishing public credit. When these essays are set against Madison's famous statements of the theory of the Constitution and his ideas of republican government, they demonstrate that Publius had a broad array of political purposes. Although we reject Alpheus T. Mason's suggestion that Publius had "a split personality,"[8] we are vividly aware that Madison and Hamilton did have their particular concerns and distinct viewpoints. In Hamilton's coldly realistic perspective, there was nothing ambiguous about the international challenges that Americans faced in a dangerous Atlantic world where the empires of Britain, France, and Spain wielded enormous power. Creating a continental republic and forming a modern nation-state were two sides of one common project.

LASTING LEGACIES

Yet the dominant strain in the modern interpretation of *The Federalist* remains far more Madisonian than Hamiltonian, far more concerned with the creation of a federal republic than with the institutional organization of an internationally powerful American nation-state. *Federalist* 10 and 51 remain the ur-texts of American constitutional theory, and the prevailing supposition that the United States still lives under a Madisonian constitution rests largely upon those two essays. That does not mean that Madison got every aspect of the story right. It is easy to criticize the famous hypotheses of *Federalist* 10 and 51. The existence of a multiplicity of factions in an extended republic can make it easier for particular or "special" interests to lobby their way to success, because the majority will, if it exists at all, lies dormant and inert.[9] So, too, the idea that the separation of powers will work when the "interest of the man … [is] connected with the constitutional rights of the place" assumes a commitment to institutions that is often overpowered by the loyalty that officials feel to their political party.[10] Even so, when modern commentators stipulate that Americans live under a Madisonian constitution, the famous passages of these two essays retain their paradigmatic authority.

That conviction in turn justifies the enormous scholarly labor that has gone into recovering the sources of Madison's ideas and in tracing his ongoing reflections on American constitutionalism. One significant question involves the intellectual origins of Madison's key positions. Like other members of the founding generation – Thomas Jefferson, John Adams, John Dickinson, George Mason, James Wilson, and of course Hamilton – he was deeply learned, spending long hours reading history, politics, law, and theology. In the utter quiet of his Montpelier study, with its commanding view of the Blue Ridge, Madison's preparations for the Federal Convention included working his way through the "literary cargo" of political and historical works that Jefferson, the American minister to the court of Louis XVI, had shipped him from Paris. The notes on ancient and modern confederacies that he began compiling in 1786, which later provided the basis for *Federalist* 18–20, mark one notable illustration of his scholarly temperament.

As Publius, Madison applied the conclusions of his intense studies to the models of the most influential political writers of his age: Charles Secondat, Baron de Montesquieu and David Hume. As the author of *The Spirit of the Laws*, arguably the greatest work of eighteenth-century political science, Montesquieu was associated with two principles or convictions that *The Federalist* had to address. One was the familiar idea that stable republics had to be small in extent, socially homogeneous, and peopled with citizens who shared a common sense of civic virtue. The other involved Montesquieu's flattering portrait of the eighteenth-century mixed British constitution and its doctrine of separation of powers, which he studied closely during his visit to England in 1731. Montesquieu was the first thinker to clearly distinguish judicial and executive power and thus to imagine a modern moderate government resting on the trifold existence of legislative, executive, and judicial authority.

"The celebrated Montesquieu," as Madison referred to him, was thus the source of a conventional wisdom about republicanism and separated powers that *The Federalist* (and Federalists more generally) had either to challenge or coopt. Some writings of David Hume, the great Scottish philosopher and historian, potentially provided solutions to that challenge. Hume was much less a scientist of politics than Montesquieu, but he wrote with a facility, clarity, and a breezy familiarity with British history that the baron lacked. Beginning with two enormously influential articles by Douglas Adair on the origins of the Tenth *Federalist*,[11] many scholars have debated the extent to which Hume's political essays, most notably including "Idea of a Perfect Commonwealth," inspired Madison's theory of the extended republic. On another side of the equation, one could also ask whether Hume's candid discussions of "The Independency of Parliament" supported a Hamiltonian approach to the Constitution that recognized that executive influence over Congress – patronage or, in eighteenth-century terms, "corruption" – was essential to making the whole system of government work.

Emphasizing and assessing the influence of Montesquieu and Hume can affect our reading of *The Federalist* in several ways. First, it helps us to identify the central eighteenth-century conceptual challenges that Publius had to answer: What was the orthodoxy that *The Federalist* had to contest, refute, or adapt, and what strategies did Publius deploy toward these ends? Second, what role did prior authorities play in shaping Madison's and Hamilton's underlying ideas? As Douglas Adair told the story, it was Madison's discovery or recovery of Hume's ideas that enabled him to resolve a daunting problem he might otherwise not have mastered. Reading Hume gave Madison a sudden *aperçu* that led directly to the Virginia Plan and the broader argument that *Federalist* 10 and other related texts elaborated. Yet we also know that neither Madison nor Hamilton believed that his political thinking was frozen during the period when they collaborated as Publius. Their engagement in constitutional politics did not end in July 1788, when Virginia and New York became the tenth and eleventh pillars supporting the ratified Constitution. That ongoing engagement required a further rethinking of the Constitution that occasionally led them to call each other out, indirectly, on their prior statements as Publius.

Our critical reading of *The Federalist* thus has to balance the intellectual influences that shaped its arguments with the recognition that Madison and Hamilton were deeply practical thinkers who continued to examine the consequences of events and their own actions. The question of *how* the Constitution would be interpreted itself became one of the great issues of American politics in the 1790s, and all three authors of *The Federalist* – including John Jay, the first chief justice – contributed to the development of new modes of interpretation. These modes of interpretation certainly drew upon the existing conventions of Anglo-American common law. Yet because the idea of a written constitution as supreme fundamental law was one of the great innovations of the founding era, so too the question of its interpretation was dynamic as well.[12] In distinct yet comparable ways, the authors of *The Federalist* were critical participants in this process, not only in 1787–88, but throughout the next decade.

The essays of *The Federalist* need to be read with these considerations in mind. On the one hand, there is no question that its eighty-five essays provide the most comprehensive and systematic assessment of the Constitution at the moment of its adoption. No other writer on either side of the debate was as thorough and insightful in exploring the multiple facets of the text or the political situation that Americans faced. Nor could one identify two more insightful and powerful thinkers than Hamilton and Madison. In Thomas Jefferson's early, highly enthusiastic judgment, *The Federalist* was "the best commentary on the principles of government which was ever written."[13] Countless commentators since have echoed that opinion, or at least treated Publius as the best interpreter of the original meaning and underlying theory of the Constitution.

Yet as the distinguished historian Bernard Bailyn has observed, "a strange and important paradox" is embedded in this continuing "near-religious veneration for a series of arguments that emerged from a frantic political struggle" over the ratification of the Constitution. *The Federalist* was written for a "preindustrial world" vastly different from our own, Bailyn notes; "yet it is seen now, and increasingly, as not merely relevant in some vague way to our postindustrial world but instructive, even prescriptive, on specific problems of the twenty-first century." Its relevance cannot rest solely on the prescience of its authors, because in so many respects they simply could not anticipate the then-unimaginable conditions that we take for granted. The continuing authority of *The Federalist* rests elsewhere. "[I]mpelled by the urgency they felt and the complexity of reconciling radical ideals of political liberty with the present need for power," Bailyn concludes, the authors of *The Federalist* "went beyond the range of familiar problems to reach a level of thought deeper and more original than that of any of the other pamphleteers and essays" engaged in the struggle over ratification.

In that depth and originality, *The Federalist* developed many of the central concepts that still inform our understanding of the Constitution. There is, after all, quite a gap between the dry language of its clauses and the conceptual richness of *The Federalist*. It is through the essays of Publius that we glimpse "the specific political process that unfolded during the founding," the political theorist William B. Allen has observed. But "where in the Constitution," Allen also asks, "does one find the separation of powers mentioned? Where does the expression 'checks and balances' occur in the Constitution?" The same concern covers other concepts that dominate our accounts of the constitutional system: the extended republic sketched in *Federalist* 10 and reprised in *Federalist* 51; the complexities of the federal system mapped in *Federalist* 39; the novel doctrine of judicial review laid down in *Federalist* 78; even the ideal of constitutional veneration alluded to in *Federalist* 49 (an essay that receives recurring consideration in this volume). We evoke these terms and concepts because they formed the grounds of agreement for the acceptance of the Constitution. Yet these concepts and the clauses they explicate are not the sole sources of constitutional liberty. We often presume that it is "free governments that make free peoples," Allen notes. Yet the cause of *The Federalist* is to prove the opposite: *"Free people make free governments*. The trick of *The Federalist*," he concludes, "is to demonstrate how that is done."[14]

The production of *The Federalist* "amid a bedlam of conflicting voices" reveals one final truth about its authority, demonstrated vividly in the harmonious judgments drawn by Bailyn and Allen: *The Federalist* illustrates the remarkable and unprecedented nature of the political experiment that Americans conducted in 1787–88. No prior example existed of a nation conducting a sustained public debate over the adoption of a constitution, or having more riding on the capacity of a people to prove themselves up to the task. Accordingly, Hamilton opened *The Federalist* with its stirring and memorable proclamation:

> It has been frequently remarked that it seems to have been reserved
> to the people of this country, by their conduct and example, to
> decide the important question, whether societies of men are really
> capable or not of establishing good government from reflection and
> choice, or whether they are forever destined to depend for their
> political constitutions on accident and force.

Only recently, thanks to the painstaking efforts of platoons of documentary editors, have we come to appreciate the richness of this debate or acquired a master narrative of the complexity of its politics.[15] The idea of popular sovereignty, before 1787, was at best an abstract device for imagining or conjecturing how governments, in theory, could have originated. The founding generation moved well beyond this mythologized notion of a state of nature and instead developed a set of specific procedures for determining how constitutions could be written, not by an inspired "lawmaker" but through processes of collective deliberation. Further, they worked out, in a process of trial and error beginning with the state constitutions, how such documents could be ratified and established as supreme law, not by simple referendum, but again through acts of collective deliberation resting on the consent of the governed

Publius, and the founding generation generally, conceived of the political project they were engaged in as the world's great experiment in self-government. Its success was contingent on the practical working out of the principles of the American Revolution and the demonstration of mankind's capacity for self-rule. The eyes of the world were upon the American people – they were "Actors on a most conspicuous Theatre," as they charted a "new and more noble course."[16] In Madison's 1792 assessment, the ideas Publius had begun developing in the pages of *The Federalist* constituted a republican constitution that was indeed unprecedented, and which was substantially superior to anything formerly devised by eighteenth-century political philosophers or by those who preceded them. The American republican model, he declared, is "the government for which *philosophy has been searching, and humanity* been *sighing*, from the most *remote ages.*"[17] And so, although many scholars rightly remain cautious in measuring the actual influence *The Federalist* exerted over ratification decisions in the several states, there is no question that its essays remain the highest expression of this debate, and thus of the potentialities of the creation of an American – and an improved – science of politics.

A NOTE ON THE CONTENTS

In organizing the contributions to this volume, the editors have roughly followed the logic of *The Federalist*. After an introductory essay explaining how Publius responded to the various charges leveled by the Anti-Federalists, the volume presents three chapters examining how *The Federalist* approached issues of national security. The next seven essays deal with the classic questions about federalism, republicanism, and popular politics developed primarily in James Madison's celebrated essays, with special attention to *Federalist* 10, 39, and the discussion of separated powers in papers 47–51. We then turn to interpretive chapters analyzing how Publius described the essential character of the three departments of government. The volume closes with two reflections on the form of political science (or the science of politics) that Publius practiced.

The editors wish to extend their thanks, first, to all the contributors, for responding to our suggestions and for tolerating the various delays that accompanied the preparation of this volume; and second, to Brenda Hafera, John Guerra, and Ann Riddle, for their valuable assistance.

NOTES

1 Colleen A. Sheehan, *The Mind of James Madison: The Legacy of Classical Republicanism* (New York: Cambridge University Press, 2015).

2 William Loughton Smith to John Rutledge, June 21, 1789, in Linda Grant De Pauw et al., eds., *The Documentary History of the First Federal Congress of the United States of America* (Baltimore, MD: Johns Hopkins University Press, 1976–), XVI, 831–34.

3 Douglass Adair, "The Authorship of the Disputed Federalist Papers," *William and Mary Quarterly*, 1 (1944), 97–122.

4 Frederick Mosteller and David Wallace, *Inference and Disputed Authorship: The Federalist* (Reading, MA: Addison-Wesley, 1964). A handful of scholars still suggest that Hamilton wrote *Federalist* 62 and 63, but the editors of this volume find that speculation unpersuasive.

5 See James Madison, "Charters," in *PJM*, XI, 191–92.

6 For an excellent discussion of this distinction in respect to constitutionalism, see William B. Allen, "The Constitution: Not Just a Law – A Dissent from Misspelled Original Intent," in Edward B. McClean, ed., *Derailing the Constitution: The Undermining of American Federalism* (Wilmington, DE: ISI Books, 1995), 61–85.

7 Alexander Hamilton to George Washington, April 14, 1794, in *PAH*, XVI, 266–79.

8 Alpheus T. Mason, "The Federalist – A Split Personality," *The American Historical Review*, 57 (1952), 625–43.

9 See the seminal critique of *Federalist* 10 in Robert A. Dahl, *A Preface to Democratic Theory*, expanded edition (Chicago, IL, and London: University of Chicago Press, 2006 [1956]), 4–33, 152–72.

10 For an extended analysis, see Daryl J. Levinson and Richard H. Pildes, "Separation of Parties, Not Powers," *Harvard Law Review*, 119 (2005–06), 2312–86.

11 Douglas Adair, "The Tenth Federalist Revisited," *The William and Mary Quarterly*, 8 (1951), 48–67; "'That Politics May be Reduced to a Science': David Hume, James Madison, and the Tenth Federalist," *Huntington Library Quarterly*, 20 (1957), 343–60; both are reprinted in Trevor Colbourn, ed., *Fame and the Founding Fathers: Essays by Douglas Adair* (Chapel Hill: University of North Carolina Press, 1974).

12 Jonathan Gienapp, *The Second Creation: Fixing the American Constitution in the Founding Era* (Cambridge, MA: Harvard University Press, 2018).

13 Jefferson to Madison, November 18, 1788, in *PJM*, XI, 353. Thanks to Madison and some other correspondent, Jefferson already knew who the three authors were, but he appears to have concluded that Madison wrote the bulk of the essays.

14 William B. Allen, "The Constitution of The Federalist Papers," *The Imaginative Conservative*, January 1, 2017, https://theimaginative

conservative.org/2017/01/constitutionalism-federalist-papers-william-allen-timeless.html; see also Allen, *The Federalist Papers: A Commentary* (New York: Peter Lang, 2004).

15 *The Documentary History of the Ratification of the Constitution*, ed. John Kaminski et al. (Madison, WI: State Historical Society of Wisconsin, 1976–); Philip Kurland and Ralph Lerner, eds., *The Founders' Constitution*, 5 vols. (Indianapolis: Liberty Fund, 2000); Pauline Maier, *Ratification: The People Debate the Constitution, 1787–1788* (New York: Simon and Schuster, 2010).

16 George Washington, "Circular to the States," in *George Washington: A Collection*, ed. W. B. Allen (Indianapolis: Liberty Fund, 1988), 240; *Fed.* 14.

17 James Madison, "Spirit of Governments," in *PJM*, XI, 233–34.

1   Publius and the Anti-Federalists:

"A Satisfactory Answer to all the Objections"?[1]

David J. Siemers

The very existence of *The Federalist* is due to the roiling dissents that greeted the Constitution in the weeks following its publication. By late September 1787, informed Americans knew that three prominent members of the Philadelphia Convention – Elbridge Gerry, George Mason, and Edmund Randolph – had refused to sign the document and that they would likely make the reasons for their opposition public. The fiery "Centinel" began publishing essays in the *Philadelphia Independent Gazetteer* on October 5. Two weeks later, the articulate defender of the middle class, "Brutus," started a series of essays in the *New York Journal* arguing the Constitution threatened self-government. This is close to the date that Alexander Hamilton wrote *Federalist* 1. Critics of the Constitution appeared in nearly every state. James Madison worried in a November 18 letter to George Washington that initial enthusiasm about the Constitution in Virginia had starkly subsided, "giving place to a spirit of criticism".[2] Madison's first contribution to the collaboration, the now-famous *Federalist* 10, appeared in print only four days later.

The authors of *The Federalist* were almost uniquely poised to counter the Anti-Federalists' "spirit of criticism." Madison, Hamilton, and John Jay were well versed in the art of governing and the defects of the Confederation, having spent a combined eleven years serving in the Continental Congress. Jay had been its president in 1778–79. Madison and Hamilton knew the Constitution and the proceedings of the Convention as well as anyone. Writing in New York City, their work could be published quickly and distributed widely. They viewed ratification as the only viable means of forging an effective nation. Rejection of the proposed government, revision before ratification, or even a second convention would jeopardize the opportunity to make a true nation of the United States, perhaps forever.

There was no parallel collaborative series written by any of the nationally known figures who opposed ratification. Such a work would have been difficult to compile, as the Constitution was opposed for many different reasons that were often specific to states, regions, and individuals. This diversity aided Anti-Federalists in a certain way: they could tailor their argument to particular audiences. Yet it also gave Publius substantial ammunition, as he had myriad, often contradictory arguments to critique. Other critical writings were poorly made or overwrought, and the cumulative effect meant that Hamilton, Madison, and Jay could easily suggest that the Anti-Federalists were sloppy, confused, and inconsistent, as *Federalist* 38 explicitly argued. They could also plausibly claim that the critics had no viable alternative to the proposed Constitution, even though many individual Anti-Federalists did offer coherent positions about how to structure politics.

This chapter examines three aspects of how Publius's work relates to the Anti-Federalists. First, though the authors of *The Federalist* endeavored to present a learned and workable republican theory of government, they also aggressively attempted to discredit their opponents. Barbed critiques of the Anti-Federalists undermined the work's status as a well-informed, unbiased, and careful commentary. It is important to realize how Publius approached his task and how *The Federalist* was received by its audience. The harshness of its approach to the Constitution's critics was what its audience most likely knew from the series, not its innovative political theories. Second, *The Federalist* offered confident appraisals of how politics works and what the new government would bring about that are not strongly validated by subsequent experience. Madison, Hamilton, and Jay believed that they were on the cutting edge of "political science" and they explained why the Constitution reflected a superior understanding of politics than that of their opponents. Their key differences are described here, and the issues about which they were most confident are compared against Anti-Federalist views and lived experience. The high epistemological and ontological confidence displayed in the writings of both groups seems unwarranted. The study of politics itself is less of a science than the authors of *The Federalist* portrayed it to be, a lesson that has rather profound implications for constitution-making. Third, discrediting Anti-Federalists meant delving into a kind of politics that many of the Federalists hoped to avoid – where the favor of public opinion is actively fought over by factions and political leaders who not only mold public opinion, but also shape their own arguments to resonate with it. Cultivating a politics of public opinion was necessary to effect ratification. This development indicates how difficult it would be for political leaders to consistently stand above or "refine and enlarge" public views, as many Federalists argued the president and Senate should do. What Publius had to do to effect ratification called into question the workability of their project – crafting fundamental law that would put substantial brakes on popular politics. The strengths of *The Federalist* are well chronicled. However, attention to the series' approach to the Anti-Federalists exposes a weaker side of the work and the philosophy of government that accompanied it.

THE GRUMBLETONIANS

In *The Federalist*, Hamilton, Madison, and Jay pushed for ratification not only by touting the Constitution's benefits but also by undercutting the Anti-Federalists and their claims. This dual focus shaped *The Federalist* in a number of ways. Most importantly for its contemporary audience, it presaged a certain kind of reception for the work. Instead of a dispassionate, reasoned analysis that stood far above others, *The Federalist* stood squarely in the fray – a devoted partisan document with a tendency to vilify opponents, to shade and to spin as much as to inform.

Publius leads from strength, reframing the argument by emphasizing the benefits of a working national government and the defects of the Confederation rather than simply refuting the constitutional criticisms already rendered. Many Anti-Federalist criticisms of the Constitution were broached in the eighty-five essays and ardently critiqued, but they were also redefined. Additionally, Publius moved beyond the opponents' arguments to discuss their personal attributes. The three authors felt no obligation to treat opponents gingerly. Many Anti-Federalists crafted arguments to make their opponents look bad, and Publius returned fire in kind. *The Federalist* occasionally acknowledged that some critics of the Constitution were well intentioned, though misled. Only once, in *Federalist* 82, did Publius grant that some who have expressed questions about how the new Constitution would work in practice – not necessarily Anti-Federalists – have a worthwhile thought. Publius's primary approach to the Anti-Federalists was to treat them as selfish, hypocritical, mistaken, overly negative, and naïve. In sum, Publius struck a strongly combative pose.

From *Federalist* 1, where Hamilton suggests that self-interested state politicians are engaged in a whisper campaign to destroy the Union, to *Federalist* 85, where he notes that the aspersions they cast should "inspire the disgust of all sensible men" (*Fed.* 85, 589), the Anti-Federalists, not just their arguments, take a beating. In other words, the authors performed the job they set out to do. Yet this line of argument came at a cost. It significantly compromised the parallel attempt to provide an authoritative, measured, and convincing approach to constitutionalism that might significantly aid the cause of ratification. The vast majority of the contemporaneous commentary on Publius's work was entirely predictable: Federalists praised it as an excellent defense of the Constitution and Anti-Federalists treated it as verbose and misleading. Few who were truly "neutral" commented on *The Federalist*. Its essays were not viewed as fundamentally different from other commentaries, except perhaps in their length. Partisan commentary may also obscure how it was really thought of by critical readers. Among the few truly neutral observers was Louis Guillaume Otto, the French chargé d'affaires. In a dispatch home he noted that *The Federalist* "is not at all useful to educated men and it is too scholarly and too long for the ignorant."[3] Otto's dismissal of the work hints at *The Federalist*'s equivocal approach to its goal, simultaneously attempting to tar opponents *and* offer learned commentary. The educated did not need eighty-five essays or such aggressive partisanship to take a position on the new government. Others were either uninterested by it or confused.

The leading Anti-Federalists were well known to the three authors of *The Federalist*. Their acquaintance added a critical dimension to the work. Jay and Hamilton had long engaged in political battle with Governor George Clinton in New York. As Hamilton privately observed, "obstinacy" was "the prevailing trait in his character."[4] All three knew Elbridge Gerry from concurrent service in the Confederation Congress. Gerry spoke more than a hundred times at the Philadelphia Convention, shaping the document in ways large and small, but in the end, he would not be satisfied. The same contrarian spirit that made him an early antagonist of the British during the Revolution induced him to oppose the Constitution. An unknown correspondent of Thomas Jefferson called Gerry a "Grumbletonian" at the Convention and noted that he was "of service by objecting to everything he did not propose" himself.[5] James Madison thought Patrick Henry's refusal to participate in the Philadelphia Convention was utterly self-serving. He wrote to George Washington that Henry wished for the Constitution to "receive its destiny from [Henry's] omnipotence" in Virginia politics.[6] Hamilton, Madison, and Jay found the leading Anti-Federalists, each in their own way, to be difficult people. They believed that Anti-Federalist writings generally reflected such distempered views.[7] Some were overly suspicious. Others were selfish and duplicitous. Few approached the Constitution in good faith. Nor did they give Federalists any credit for their yeoman efforts at helping the American nation to succeed.

These feelings were not softened or obscured by the authors of *The Federalist*. On the contrary, Publius wanted to publicize the Anti-Federalists' bad faith. Contemporary readers did not examine *The Federalist* as modern scholars do, explicating its most learned passages. The essays were serialized, and read as they came out in New York and a few other places.[8] During the ratification debate, *Federalist* 10 had no special status over any other essay. "It took twentieth-century scholarship to rescue Madison's essay from obscurity," Larry D. Kramer has observed. "In its original context, however, Madison's theory of the extended republic was an insignificant detail, an unappreciated ingredient in the larger sweep of events."[9] Those who read the essays during the ratification debate came away with a very different view of the series than we have today. The commentary that deeply questioned the motives and character of Anti-Federalists was almost surely the most memorable argument that *The Federalist* made. The Hamilton–Jay line of reasoning that began the series – that the Anti-Federalists aimed to split up the Union – likely had a bigger impact on how the series was perceived than anything else Publius wrote. Critics of the Constitution dealt with this initial argument as a transparent attempt to mislead the public. In subsequent writings they made clear that they favored a federal union, and the authors of *The Federalist* moved to other lines of attack.

All this was quite in keeping with the tenor of political discourse at the time. Anti-Federalists punched and counterpunched, too. Read in the context of the time and essay by essay, *The Federalist* intentionally and aggressively joined a factional fight already in progress – in most states consisting of elite, commercial, and coastal interests being at odds with more agrarian and less affluent ones away from the coast. The series could have struck a less aggressive stance, patiently explaining the Constitution's benefits while holding out an olive branch to win over independent thinkers and those with mild qualms. But the authors of *The Federalist* chose, with few exceptions, to insist on the Constitution's correctness and the critics' unreasonableness. Publius attempted to move the political public toward the position he saw as undeniably true: The Constitution as written was much better than the status quo. His flattening out of political discourse, limiting choices to a take-it-or-leave-it proposition, was what Publius felt would best serve his cause. However, it was not to be.

Doubts about the Constitution's approach were too pervasive to effect ratification this way. Most of the later state conventions forwarded recommendatory amendments to be considered by the First Congress, a development that turned out to be necessary to achieve ratification. Eventually some form of compromise was devised, but *The Federalist* itself maintained an uncompromising insistence on the Constitution's reasonableness and its opponents' unreasonableness that did not set it apart from and above the writings of others.

"INFLAMMATORY RAVINGS OF INCENDIARIES"[10]

Hamilton in particular offered up personal critiques of Anti-Federalists. In *Federalist* 29, for instance, he transformed his response to concerns about militia clauses into an assessment of his opponents' minds. Two clauses in Article I, Section 8 pertain to state militias – one gave the national government the power to call up the militia to enforce federal laws, "suppress insurrections and repel invasions"; another empowered Congress to "provide for organizing, arming, and disciplining" the militia. Anti-Federalists expressed fear that these powers could be used by the national government to take over the militias and employ them in enforcing its alien will on people in the individual states.[11]

Hamilton suggests that the Anti-Federalists' fears are barely worth refuting. Why have a militia if it is poorly trained and equipped? A state would not stand for a large swath of its workforce being taken from productive activity to train for military service. What danger could be posed from a corps taken directly from among the people of a state anyway? And marching militias across country to put down people of other states would be absurd. Anti-Federalist arguments on this subject were "so far-fetched and so extravagant" that he doubted whether they should be taken seriously (*Fed.* 29, 185). So he turned to alternatives. Perhaps theirs was "a mere trial of skill, like the paradoxes of the rhetoricians," a trick of language engaged in for sport. Or perhaps they knew these were sham arguments, but were willing to engage in "a serious artifice to instill prejudices at any price." The only other option was "political fanaticism" that blinded critics to the obvious benefits of the militia clauses (*Fed.* 29, 185).

All of these scenarios deeply troubled Hamilton. Discerning readers would understand how needlessly negative the Anti-Federalists were being. Their work would also lead a reader of Anti-Federal tracts to

> imagine that he is perusing some ill-written tale or romance, which, instead of natural and agreeable images, exhibits to the mind nothing but frightful and distorted shapes – "Gorgons, hydras, and chimeras dire"; discoloring and disfiguring whatever it represents, and transforming every thing it touches into a monster.
> (*Fed.* 29, 185–86)

The embedded quote came from Book II of John Milton's *Paradise Lost*, where a frightful conclave of devils has just disbanded that had discussed how to continue their battle against Heaven. The devils had made the decision to corrupt humankind, ranging across Hell afterward, seeing its monsters in their travels. To Hamilton's way of thinking, this was an apt description of the Anti-Federalist project. They portrayed the Federalists as devils and the landscape imposed by the Constitution as monstrous and denuded. Their criticisms were not "sober admonitions of discerning patriots" but rather "the inflammatory ravings of incendiaries" who were protecting their own status within the states (*Fed.* 29, 187). And, again quoting Milton, theirs was "vain wisdom … and false prophecy."

In a nation where state-led militias had fought and bled to resist British rule, the argument seems tone deaf. Many Americans still believed in the efficacy of militias and that they needed to remain under state control to preserve freedom. Sensitivity to this audience might have been in order, including a more patient explanation of why the federal government could be trusted with training, equipping, and deputizing the state militias. What Hamilton offered instead was an exasperated screed. His speculations have the merit of letting the reader decide which unsavory reason is the cause of the Anti-Federalist opposition. However, his detour into psychology, motive, and literary allusion could not have won over many who were not already in favor of substantially increasing national power.

The tenor of *Federalist* 29 and other references to the Constitution's critics threatened to undercut the moderate, statesmanlike rationalism that Publius touted as an advantage for the Federalist side. Indignant exasperation overshadowed argument in a number of installments. Publius describes the Anti-Federalists as "bigoted idolizers of state authority" (*Fed.* 80, 538), as "distempered enthusiasts," (*Fed.* 29, 187) and as men with a "talent for misrepresentation" (*Fed.* 67, 452). They are found by him to employ "devices, not less weak than wicked . . . contrived to pervert the public opinion" (*Fed.* 67, 453), they offer some arguments "too absurd to merit a refutation" (*Fed.* 83, 561), and they possess "a rage for objection, which disorders their imaginations and judgments" (*Fed.* 78, 522).

Hamilton takes pains to explain his ardent tone in the final essay, writing that he was whipsawed between a desire to accurately characterize the critics' arguments and a wish to maintain moderation. He admits that his zeal for accuracy "occasionally betrayed me into intemperences of expression which I did not intend" (*Fed.* 85, 589). This is no apology. Hamilton believes that the Anti-Federalists fully deserved every blow delivered and more. But it is also an admission that the better strategy might have been to smooth over the rough, personal tone of the work. The explanation occurs in an essay where he notes that he has been "provoked" and suggests that the Anti-Federalist charges of an aristocratic conspiracy should "excite the indignation . . . and disgust of all sensible men" (*Fed.* 85, 589). Hamilton's pique is real and it is personal. Indeed, he confesses in *Federalist* 85 that his own strong words may have gotten in the way of his effectiveness in arguing for the Constitution.

Predictably, Madison strikes a more measured tone. He may have been thinking of this difference of tone between himself and Hamilton as much as their differences on politics when he noted that each had allowed the other simply to have his say without comment or editing.[12] His approach suggests more pity and less condemnation.

In a revealing letter to Edmund Randolph, Madison relates that the vast majority of people are led, and often misled, by just a few opinion leaders. Anticipating an important line of modern public opinion research, he speculates that support in Virginia would have been unanimous had not a few key leaders like Henry and Mason taken a strong stance against the Constitution.[13] Madison views most Anti-Federalist sympathizers as ignorant, culpable only in being misled. Thus, he sets out on a number of educational projects in *The Federalist*. Large republics are possible (*Fed.* 10); confederations are almost inevitably short-lived and fail because of the weakness of their coordinating power (*Fed.* 18–20); legislatures need to be internally and externally checked to keep from accumulating power (*Fed.* 51). A regime that mixes and divides the functions of government is not to be feared but actually of great benefit (*Fed.* 39).

Yet Madison was just as willing to criticize as he was to educate. Anti-Federalist leaders "scanned the proposed Constitution, not only with a predisposition to censure, but with a predisposition to condemn" (*Fed.* 37, 232). They chose to put the worst construction on every aspect of the Constitution and made spurious arguments. In their zeal they misinterpreted key authorities, got historical facts wrong, and made claims that were not true. One of the reasons that Madison was so willing to take on the task of public education resulted from his faith that a "bad cause seldom fails to betray itself" (*Fed.* 41, 274). And the Anti-Federalist cause appeared quite bad to Madison. He reserved his most accusatory language to rebut the idea that the national government might destroy the states. These views are either the "incoherent dreams of a delirious jealousy, or the misjudged exaggerations of a counterfeit zeal, [rather] than ... the sober apprehensions of genuine patriotism" (*Fed.* 46, 321).

Jay's few essays stress the shockingly cavalier nature of Anti-Federalism supposedly unearthed by Hamilton in *Federalist* 1: they are ready to split up the Union. In Hamilton's telling, these were secret whispers. In Jay's essays, it is simply a fact that Anti-Federalists endorse three or four separate confederacies (*Fed.* 8, 12, 15). The editors of the definitive *Documentary History of the Ratification of the Constitution* cite this as an example of Publius "deliberately misrepresenting the position of the Anti-Federalists."[14] Immediately after the Constitution was released, some New York Anti-Federalists may have intimated that the state would do just as well without the others or at the head of a regional confederation. These were almost surely loose speculations rather than expressions of preference.[15] The suggestion that many critics of the Constitution wished to split the United States into several confederacies founders on a lack of evidence. To the contrary, almost all Anti-Federalists acknowledged that the existing Union needed to be strengthened and preserved. Even those who wished to retain state sovereignty wanted to strengthen the Confederation. Publius acknowledges this position in *Federalist* 15, and critiques it as nonsensical. The likely reason that Jay and Hamilton leaned so heavily on the argument about three or four confederacies, at least initially, was that it was an easy way to make the Anti-Federalists look bad.

When there is praise for Anti-Federalists in *The Federalist* it is sparing and qualified. In all instances, the Anti-Federalists still come out wanting. The "perverted ambition" of many is leavened by the acknowledgement that others are "actuated by upright intentions" (*Fed.* 1, 4). The latter are simply confused, making "honest errors" rather than dishonest and dishonorable ones. Even the "moderate and more rational adversaries" of the Constitution are not willing to give the national government the power it needs to succeed (*Fed.* 22, 145). The Federalists' "more intelligent adversaries" are willing to dedicate tax revenue to the nation, but they are unwilling to grant it enough for it to work (*Fed.* 30, 190).[16] The "more respectable adversaries to the Constitution" want a strict separation of legislative, executive, and judicial powers, but they are utterly mistaken that such a thing is needed, possible, or that it was endorsed by Montesquieu (*Fed.* 47, 324–27). The ardent cry of Anti-Federalists for explicit protection of individual rights is dismissed mostly by omission. Only the penultimate essay treats the topic in any depth. In *Federalist* 82 Publius finds a concern about the Constitution spoken "in the mouths of men of sense," but not necessarily Anti-Federalists: how to set up concurrent jurisdictions for state and federal courts will require serious attention in the First Congress (*Fed.* 82, 553). Active in politics nearly their whole adult lives, the authors of *The Federalist* knew the character of their leading opponents. These men exasperated them and, counter-productively, they let their feelings show. The dedication of later jurists and scholars to mining the more theoretically rich material in *The Federalist* is what has created its high reputation, a reputation it did not enjoy during the ratification debate.

"A ZEAL FOR LIBERTY MORE ARDENT THAN ENLIGHTENED"

Over the course of many essays the authors of *The Federalist* contrasted their philosophy of government with that of the Anti-Federalists. In short, Publius believed that the critics of the Constitution stressed liberty too much, a view that would prevent effective governance. Greater authority, expert representation, and mechanisms to promote institutional stability must be placed alongside liberty to make popular government work. Publius also observed that the Anti-Federalists were relying on plausible but spurious political theories. *The Federalist* takes pains to refute and revise these ideas, presenting a new republican political theory in the process.

The Federalist has supported and defended a living government for more than two centuries. This alone places it among the most successful projects of political theory ever written. However, as with any political theory, the work is a product of its time. Most late eighteenth-century thinkers possessed far different assumptions about the nature of political knowledge than ours. They had confidence in the robustness of theories about politics that more recent generations do not. Publius did recognize that his knowledge of politics was imperfect (*Fed.* 37). Yet he was also very confident that his work constituted a significant improvement on anything that had gone before (*Fed.* 9; *Fed.* 48), and that his major theoretical contributions were sound. That confidence aided setting up a workable national government and has helped endow it with significant public support. Yet many of Publius's axioms are not strongly vindicated by lived experience.

Madison articulates the essential difference between the rival camps in *Federalist* 37, his first installment about the work of the Convention. A vital interest of those who gathered in Philadelphia was to "combin[e] the requisite stability and energy in government, with the inviolable attention due to liberty and the republican form" (*Fed.* 37, 233). Without striking this balance, a nation would be prone to upheaval, either from domestic disturbances or from external threats. Power is required to effect the "prompt and salutary execution of the laws." It is part of "the very definition of good government" and it is what the Articles of Confederation lacked (*Fed.* 37, 233). Formulating law is not enough; a government must possess enough power to effectively execute the law under its purview. This conviction colors Publius's view of every specific power contained in the Constitution. Broad provisions for taxation are necessary and useful in effecting the public will. So is an independent and effective judiciary. So too, particularly in the last resort, is a nation's military. A provision recognizing the supremacy of a central government and acknowledging that it may do what is "necessary and proper" to carry out its prerogatives would create a government with usable powers rather than hollow ones. Madison's was a pro-government argument. He argued that the Constitution would set up an effective republic.[17]

Hamilton had earlier made similar observations about balancing these multiple braces of good government, as had Jay. Both stressed that liberty had been overemphasized in forming governments during the revolution (*Fed.* 26; *Fed.* 2). Disarray resulting from the Articles of Confederation's weakness was a matter of everyday experience to them, placing the union of states in jeopardy, risking civil discord and external interference. Already in *Federalist* 1, Hamilton calls a zeal for liberty a "noble enthusiasm," but warns that it "is apt to be infected with a spirit of narrow and illiberal distrust" (*Fed.* 1, 5). Publius believes that the Anti-Federalists repeatedly fall into this trap, blinded by a mania for freedom from centralized control. In Hamilton's pithy phrase, they possess "a zeal for liberty more ardent than enlightened" (*Fed.* 26, 164). Their over-emphasis on freedom threatened to "utterly unfit the people of this country for any species of government whatever" (*Fed.* 26, 165).

As a counterpoint Hamilton and his co-authors promised to add "an enlightened zeal for the energy and efficiency of government." This is something he knows "will be stigmatized as the offspring of a temper fond of despotic power and hostile to the principles of liberty," but it is, in truth, the only way to maintain popular government through time (*Fed.* 1, 5). Madison and Hamilton famously disagreed on just how much power the national government should have, as well as the internal placement of that power.[18] Jay, too, had his distinctive views. Yet they were all clearly on one side of a divide. If there was to be a United States, there would have to be a national government with significant powers effectively wielded. Such a national government promised large advantages: better external defense, improved internal stability, commercial success, enhanced preservation of human rights and additional policy advantages that a strict confederation of states could not deliver. The Anti-Federalists, of course, disputed their characterization by Publius. They were guardians of liberty, true, but they also believed they were protecting popular government.[19] Most believed that effective government could only be had on the state level because each state's politics was distinctive, and each state's politics fit that state. Consolidating all of the states together threatened self-determination.

To the Federalists, effective representation required expertise. One legislative House would be directly elected, but state officials would select the members of the Senate. This did not make it unrepresentative or aristocratic. Each state would be represented by two citizens chosen by the people who were entrusted to make the state's most important decisions. Their mechanism for electing the president was similar: Trusted citizens in each state would favor candidates known for knowledge, character, and judgment.

Anti-Federalists were more concerned with representation being an accurate reflection of the public's will rather than a refinement of it. Good representation was likely to occur when legislators remained physically close to constituents and shared their identity, such as in middle-class occupations. If representatives lived in a distant capital, they would come to identify less with constituents. Congressional constituencies were also so large that only renowned figures, typically the wealthy and powerful, would be elected. Almost all the Anti-Federalists granted that the Confederation should have additional powers, but the necessary and proper clause combined with the supremacy clause promised to be a blank check for these unrepresentative national officials. Over time, they would exert ever more power, resulting in the annihilation of the states.

Most Anti-Federalists harbored "Whiggish" views, wary of the concentration of power, especially in the executive.[20] Good government could only be sustained through the greater representativeness of legislatures. This thinking had been useful to the colonists. It justified the work of colonial assemblies, and yielded suspicion of the British Empire with its distant centralized power headed by King George III. The governments set up during the Revolution reflected this philosophy, generally having weak executives and predominant legislatures. Most Anti-Federalists believed they were upholding this standard.

The authors of *The Federalist* rejected Whig views. The history of England offered empirical proof that popular legislatures tended to gather power rather than lose it. Hamilton noted that the House of Commons had "raised themselves to the rank and consequence of a co-equal branch of the legislature" over the centuries (*Fed.* 71, 485). There was every reason to believe that it would continue gathering power at the expense of the House of Lords and the crown. Rather than the executive coming to predominate, it was "the tendency of the legislative authority to absorb every other" power (*Fed.* 71, 483). In Madison's poetic words, "the legislative department is everywhere extending the sphere of its activity, and drawing all power into its impetuous vortex" (*Fed.* 48, 333).

This induced Publius to tout the Constitution's "auxiliary precautions," institutional contrivances that would keep the legislature from swallowing up the executive and judiciary. The legislature itself had been split in two to check it. Power was shifted away from the legislature and toward the executive through a variety of mechanisms: the veto, an administrative apparatus that reported directly to the executive, the presidential power to make appointments, and the expectation that the president would recommend measures to Congress. Anti-Federalists protested these perceived violations of the separation of powers.[21] The executive, they stressed, should not participate in the legislative process. Madison easily batted aside the argument that the division of legislative, executive, and judicial power needed to be "orthodox," with only the legislature involved in the legislative process and the executive only executing laws. No state operated like this. Even the great authority Baron de Montesquieu, who was cited by Anti-Federalists as being in favor of this position, had not really endorsed it. The sharing of governing responsibilities was actually a more effective check on institutional encroachments (*Fed.* 48).

Publius took on the idea that there could be no large republics. First, Hamilton reexamined Montesquieu. The small republics he had envisioned were significantly smaller than the states, meaning that the Anti-Federalists were not following Montesquieu's precepts to begin with. Additionally, Montesquieu had suggested that the size of popular governments could be substantially increased by creating a "compound" or "federated republic" (*Fed.* 9). In truth, the sage that critics used to dress up their argument in fancy intellectual clothes was no help to them at all. Madison offered his idea of the extended republic several times, not just in *Federalist* 10 (there is a shorter version included in *Fed.* 51 and a brief recapitulation in *Fed.* 14).[22] A large republic would produce better policies and be more stable than small ones. Publius reassured readers that the states were not going away. They would be much more active in the lives of citizens than the federal government because states would retain all the powers not specifically granted to the nation (e.g. *Fed.* 14; *Fed.* 27; *Fed.* 39; *Fed.* 83).

There was a good deal dividing Publius and the Anti-Federalists. Because the government proposed had not yet been implemented, the debate centered on how politics under the new Constitution would work – and both sides were drawn to theorizing. The implementation of the Constitution would provide a practical test of their diverse theories.

"THE ABLEST ADEPTS IN POLITICAL SCIENCE"

Despite their differences, Federalists and Anti-Federalists both had an abiding faith that social phenomena are highly patterned and that governments should be constructed with those patterns in mind. The Anti-Federalists believed certain precepts of politics had been long established and that they were faithfully adhering to them. The authors of The Federalist thought great improvements in political knowledge had been made recently. Their own work was an act of exploration and discovery. They had faith that the understandings presented in The Federalist were more advanced than any other yet produced.

Today we call what they wrote political theory. However, the authors of The Federalist described their work as "political science."[23] That Publius used the term "science" to describe what we call "theory" is telling. It suggests that we do not share his confidence in what can be known or demonstrated as true. "Science" is considered more solid, more prone to demonstration, and more useful in application than "theory"; "theories" are considered more abstract, more difficult to translate to practice, perhaps even the province of ideologues, yielding endless, counterproductive wrangling. The professionalization of the field of political science in the years after Publius wrote and its more systematic approach to evidence has made us (if not politicians themselves) much more wary of broad, reductive theories of politics.

Among the most robust conclusions produced by modern political science is "the softness and historical boundedness of political theories," as Gabriel Almond has described it.[24] Political science is not a hard science. It is not characterized by "clocklike" precision and the infinite replicability of findings across time and place. There can be predictable outcomes, but even in its most data-rich fields, social phenomena defy reduction to permanent and universal axioms. New developments often surprise us. The social and legal conditions that yield certain results are unlikely to be permanent. Contexts change, humans learn through time, they adjust behaviors, strategies, and goals. All this produces new results, which may hold for a time, only to be superseded by something new.[25]

The government the Federalists adopted has been long-lived. But can we confidently conclude that their political theory is more correct than the Anti-Federalists' political theory? Publius observed that legislatures tend to gain power through time; most Anti-Federalists thought that executives almost inevitably do. Given the complex nature of social reality it is apparent that neither group is simply correct. In other words, both are mistaken in the confidence with which they presented their case. The better question to judge between them may be "which group has been more correct over the long run?" A systematic discussion of this matter would require observations over vast periods of time and a great deal of comparison at the national and sub-national levels. The result of such an inquiry would likely mirror what we would find in the American national government. At times Congress has exerted greater power than the president and at times the opposite is true.[26] Partly this may be chalked up to the flexibility within the system of institutions that the Federalists created. However, these fluctuations are not just a matter of institutional flexibility. Most Federalists were hoping to stave off the migration of power from one institution to another and from one level of government to another through the system of checks and balances. Institutional boundaries are stretched by the actors who occupy them, sometimes beyond what seems authorized by the Constitution. This has been particularly true with the modern presidency, substantially extending executive power and defying *The Federalist*'s stated expectation that institutional dynamics favored legislatures. Does this indicate that the Federalists were wrong about legislatures? It does not with anything approaching finality, but it does seem that executive power more often has the upper hand, not only in the United States, but in modern nation-states more generally.

Have states eroded national power more than the nation has encroached on the states? Here too, there is no simple answer. At times, and on certain issues, the states have been very effective in leading and even eclipsing federal rules and initiatives. This dynamic may describe the development of racial policies during the Jim Crow era, for instance. The resistance of states led the way in vacating the meaning and intent of the Fourteenth Amendment's due process and equal protection clauses. Yet no description of American politics could possibly ignore the substantial and more general expansion of national power vis-à-vis the states over time. The states have not withered and died. On the contrary, they are far more active and powerful than they were during the early republic. However, if our question is confined to the relative power and reach of state and nation, the national government has clearly gained more power than the states, and it has often done so at the expense of the states. There is also cooperation between levels of government, something that Publius foresaw, as well as a substantial provincial bias built into our national politics (best treated in *Fed.* 45 and 46). Yet the power dynamic that Publius predicted would hold between the nation and the states has been far from axiomatic.

Anti-Federalist concerns about representativeness are still alive today. The descriptive representativeness of Congress has never been very high, particularly in terms of race and gender. Anti-Federalists confined their concern about descriptive representativeness to wealth and professional interests. Their argument was that Congress would never adequately represent citizens in these regards. What might be called the "permeability" of Congress – how readily its elective positions may be accessed – varies substantially through time. At times more middle-class members are elected. At other times, it is easier for the well-off to get elected. Incumbency advantage fluctuates, as does the ability of members to enrich themselves through or after their public service as they transition to lobbying and other lucrative work in Washington. The Anti-Federalist complaint that the wealthy would dominate Congress and produce policies beneficial to elites is not easily dismissed. Publius responded simply by saying that those who would be elected *are by definition* the legitimate representatives of the people (*Fed.* 57). The power of this stance to dissolve Anti-Federalist concerns is sharply diminished by such environmental factors as gerrymandered districts, war chests filled with the money of political action committees, and the unlimited use of personal wealth in campaigns. A recent study by Martin Gilens and Benjamin I. Page concluded that the American government is not a democracy but an oligarchy; this was the precise fear articulated by many Anti-Federalists. In creating favorable conditions for a vibrant commercial republic where the "better sort" would exert substantial political influence, the Federalists helped point the American polity in this direction. Social mobility is lower, and disparities of wealth are higher in the United States than in most other developed nations; this is a validation of Anti-Federalist views that they would not have wished for. Is American politics inevitably tinged with aristocracy or oligarchy? No. One can imagine a series of laws, a set of Supreme Court decisions, or amendments to the Constitution that would change this context significantly, giving less rather than more credence to Anti-Federalist predictions about how representation and wealth interact in the United States. Nevertheless, the disproportionate influence of the well-off is a recurring theme in American politics and one that is certainly timely today.

The most prominent axioms offered by both the Anti-Federalists and Publius turn out not to be invariably true. Institutional power, federalism, and representation are all buffeted on the tides of context and human choice, what Almond calls "systems of plastic controls."[27] There are regularities rather than hard truths, persisting for a time and then melting away, replaced by new regularities with different characteristics. The authors of *The Federalist* were hardly naïve. They knew of the indeterminacy of politics firsthand. Yet their arguments exhibit a confidence about how politics works that experience has not validated.

The creation of a long-lasting national government is an immense accomplishment. So is the invention of a thought-provoking and enduring political theory. To accomplish both of these things in one's lifetime is an extraordinary achievement. No other collaborators in human history have done this quite as successfully as Hamilton, Madison, and Jay did. But it is far from clear that Publius was more right in certain parts of his political science than the Anti-Federalists. At present, the case for the Anti-Federalists being more correct about certain matters seems strong.

The Federalists were sufficiently confident in their political science to make amending the Constitution very difficult. They did not want backsliding on enhanced national power or on their complicated institutional structure of checks, or on their shift of power toward the executive, or on the mechanisms designed to refine and enlarge public opinion. Sanford Levinson observes that the United States' Constitution is the most difficult constitution in the world to change.[28] In the time since the ratification era, a great deal has been learned about politics, including that there seem to be no universal laws about institutions, parties, and public opinion. Working democracies can have unicameral legislatures. Parliamentary systems can be as effective as presidential systems and may often be more effective. Direct elections seem not to produce outcomes worse than indirect elections. Changing the United States government significantly is not absolutely precluded by the high bar set in Article V, but it is made much more difficult. In a world of plastic controls, the American government is not suitably lithe, which is increasingly of concern as it moves well into its third century.[29] In an age of political impasse, complaints about the multiplicity of constitutional veto points seem well taken.

The political theories of the founding era are often thought to be rationalizations or cover for the pursuit of interests. Interests were understandably downplayed, and principles given center stage during the ratification debate. Yet the earnestness with which most of these theories are presented and their consistency with the demonstrated thinking of the individuals presenting them suggests that key axioms were more a matter of belief than of show. Hamilton, Madison, and Jay were more sophisticated and knowledgeable than most of the writers active during the ratification debate. In *The Federalist* they were putting the best face on a set of institutions they were unsure would work. However, they did believe that legislatures tended to gather power to themselves, that federal governments were in danger of failing due to centrifugal forces, and that elected offices could not be instruments of aristocracy. These positions would be controversial today, just as they were controversial when written into *The Federalist*. The major difference is that we have more than two centuries of additional experience that substantially challenge assumptions around which the Constitution was built.

"THE CURRENT HURRIES US AWAY"

The Federalist predated Alexis de Tocqueville's *Democracy in America* by nearly fifty years, but both rest on a similar assumption: there is a kind of relentlessness to democracy. Tocqueville calls the advance of citizen equality that is a necessary prerequisite for democracy a "Providential fact."[30] It has crossed borders, it has seeped into every societal institution and practice, and this trend has proved robust over the centuries. Tocqueville chided those who resisted this tide. He imagined France in his own day as being swept away by a rapidly rushing stream. In this perilous position, Tocqueville's fellow aristocrats "obstinately fix [their] eyes on the ruins which may still be described on the shore we have left, whilst the current hurries us away."[31] Their wish was to return to this former home, but the force of the waters was too strong. The better approach to the current was not to fight it, but to work with it. French aristocrats should not long for what could not be restored. Rather, they should aim to effect the best possible democratic condition. Democracy could bring great benefits to the world, as long as it was channeled and moderated. Tocqueville embraced widespread participation, popular devotion to values (especially those found in religion), and preservation of local political control to channel the democratic impulse toward positive ends.

Publius is not one of those looking longingly back. He soundly rejects the hereditary aristocracy of old Europe in favor of a much more popular regime, dedicated to human rights and the general well being of citizens. But if we are to place the authors of *The Federalist* in Tocqueville's river metaphor, we would also not find them paddling hopefully (if also somewhat fearfully) downriver, working with the current to land at a new and better democratic shore. Instead, Publius struggles mightily to remain in place, attempting to fight the strong current of public opinion and democratization through constitutional checks.

The large constituencies and indirect elections set up by the Constitution are designed to produce government with a healthy dose of trusteeship exerted by national officeholders. The founders were particularly "worried that the dynamics of mass politics would at best produce poorly qualified presidents and at worst open the door to demagoguery and regime instability."[32] Thus, they created the electoral college, to allow individuals who knew the leading candidates' characters to select the chief executive. The presidents chosen, it was hoped, would stand above the fray of politics, cancelling problematic flights of fancy from the more representative legislative branch. Judges insulated from politics with life terms would police the constitutional order and restrain fickle public impulses with legal expertise. Many Federalists believed that senators were indirectly selected and given long terms so that they could serve as an "American House of Lords."[33] Though "enlightened statesmen" would not always be "at the helm," the Federalists attempted to create a more expert-oriented politics than existed in the states. National officials were expected to moderate and direct public opinion toward beneficial ends.

The challenge Publius sets for himself is to overcome the fears stoked by Anti-Federalists that would lead the public to oppose this new brand of politics. This was a fitting cause for three experienced and learned politicians. They understood that politicians who intentionally promote fear and mislead the public are always present and that leaders frame the political options that citizens consider. In this regard the ratification fight possesses the characteristics of virtually every other significant political fight.

Yet by strongly denigrating the Anti-Federalists, Publius resorts to tactics that look like the very kind of wrangling he wishes the nation to rise above. Popular resentment is stoked in an effort to dampen the power of popular resentment. Public opinion is marshaled in an effort to put limits on the power of public opinion. With a great deal at stake, it is understandable that Publius would make every effort to win converts. There were legitimate frustrations about Anti-Federalist arguments, which may have couched self-serving motives as principled stands. However, delving deeply into the politics of personality, encouraging doubts and fears about the Anti-Federalists as people rather than just criticizing their ideas calls into question whether a more genteel, expert-led politics could succeed. If the Federalists themselves could not "refine and enlarge" public opinion in trying to effect ratification of the Constitution, could the president, the Supreme Court, and senators be expected to do so with very important decisions to be made about taxation, the conduct of foreign affairs, and slavery?

It is telling that Madison and Hamilton themselves would so quickly and inexorably plunge into the maelstrom of party politics after ratification. They both had well considered reasons to support the kind of politics they did. Yet in seeking to advance their separate causes, they and their political allies cultivated public opinion and created party structures to help their vision prevail. They were not only present for the creation of a more popular and divisive brand of politics than what they were comfortable with in theory, they effected it.[34] This outcome was predictable because the ratification battle itself had this dynamic. Not content to offer just a republican theory of government, The Federalist helped to draw and reinforce partisan lines that would help to define what politics would be like after ratification. Unfortunately, it was a brand of politics they did not favor. Most of those who had been Federalists believed the

Constitution failed to produce the kind of politics they wished, as public opinion was too powerful a force in the new nation.[35]

Both the president and the Senate also quickly became entangled in the popular and party politics that the Federalists hoped they had insulated these institutions from. George Washington and John Adams attempted to govern above the fray, but their administrations inevitably favored the nascent Federalist Party. Thomas Jefferson changed the presidency forever by being elected as the recognized leader of a political party and coordinating that party.[36] "The Constitution's prescription ... that the executive would stand apart from and subdue factions proved to be chimerical, a dream shattered by fundamental conflict over the very meaning of the fundamental law."[37] The figures who loom largest in the history of American politics – Andrew Jackson, Abraham Lincoln, Theodore Roosevelt, Woodrow Wilson, and Franklin Delano Roosevelt – are known for tightening linkages between the presidency and public opinion. No modern president could possibly stand aloof from the democratic tide that Publius wished that office to check.

The same story can be told for the Senate. The body quickly came to play a primary role in national politics, with its most prominent figures being nationally known presidential hopefuls and party leaders. Its smaller numbers led to correspondingly greater attention and prestige for its members. This enabled senators like Henry Clay, John C. Calhoun, and Stephen A. Douglas to cultivate public opinion rather than resist it. The Progressive era produced a democratic impulse sufficiently strong to alter how members of the body are selected. The Seventeenth Amendment's direct election confirmed that the Senate's job was not to refine and enlarge public opinion so much as cultivate it and follow it. The body's ability to do this may have been compromised away during the Philadelphia Convention anyway, in the agreement to represent states.[38] For those who clung to the view that long terms would allow senators to act as trustees, the operation of the Senate proved to be a disappointment in practice.[39] Both institutions designed to beneficially filter public opinion were drawn into the center of a more modern and more democratic style of politics than the Federalists hoped would prevail.

Publius was frustrated by the ease with which Anti-Federalists could win converts. Critics of the Constitution played on pre-existing beliefs and fears to make their case that state governments were more likely to preserve popular rule. It was easy to portray the states as being more representative and thus superior. This was part of a larger democratic impulse that the authors of *The Federalist* repeatedly acknowledged. The public was likely to place more faith in states than the nation. Legislatures tended to gain power at the expense of executives, precisely because they were closer to the people (*Fed.* 48 and 49). Because representatives were popularly elected and could mingle more closely with their constituents, the House would likely come to overshadow the Senate (*Fed.* 58). The House of Commons had become more powerful than the House of Lords and the king because it was the popular branch (*Fed.* 71). Publius thus viewed democratization as a durable tendency of modern political development, but also one that would have to be constantly fought.

Hamilton's substantially underappreciated essay *Federalist* 17 squarely acknowledges how difficult it would be to get the national government to succeed.

> It is a known fact in human nature, that its affections are commonly weak in proportion to the distance or diffusiveness of the object. Upon the same principle that a man is more attached to his family than to his neighborhood ... the people of each State would be apt to feel a stronger bias toward their local governments than towards the government of the Union.
>
> (*Fed.* 17, 107)

Only a "much better administration" of the federal government than the state governments could overcome this natural tendency. An accompanying challenge was that the national government's daily responsibilities were unlikely to be noticed by many Americans. As a result, Hamilton set himself to providing a better administration for the new government with unusual energy as secretary of the Treasury, an indication that he believed the national government would fail otherwise. Obscured by the agreement of the three authors to ardently support the Constitution are their own grave fears about its likely success.

With a relentless democratic impulse bearing down on them, the stark remove at which a continent-wide national government would have to operate, demagogic voices always present on the political stage, and an easily manipulated public, it would be very difficult for the new national government to work as intended. If their hopes for the national government did not fully materialize, at least they were aware of why this would occur. They had anticipated a hard slog to successfully implement the new government. What neither Madison nor Hamilton suspected is that they themselves would help produce the change that favored a more popular, partisan, democratic, and public-opinion-oriented form of politics.

The list of American politicians who have made their name by complaining about the national government is long and rapidly lengthening. It is commonplace for citizens to rail against the national government, all the while enjoying its benefits. There have been times when the American public expressed substantial faith in its national government, but we are not in such a time. Barring unforeseen events, we are unlikely to have such confidence return any time soon. This is proof enough of the validity of Hamilton's theory about local bias in *Federalist* 17. It is a testament to the strength of their convictions and their deep patriotism that Hamilton, Madison, and Jay attempted what they did. They were valiant oarsmen, but the current of politics has long since hurried us away from the kind of nation that they considered ideal.

CONCLUSION

As Hamilton was wrapping up the full series, he blamed New Yorkers' "first impressions" for being too much for the collaborators to overcome. The ratification convention elections in his state had produced an Anti-Federalist rout.[40] Put more bluntly, *The Federalist* had not been persuasive. As a whole, the work simply offered too many words to be easily digested and its theories were often expressed in a complex manner that blunted their impact. Furthermore, its clear partisanship and the pique expressed toward Anti-Federalists dampened attention to those carefully developed theories. Publishers outside of New York were reluctant to reprint *Federalist* pieces and Anti-Federalists did not feel a pressing need to refute them, except in a few particular points. It could more easily be mocked as a waste of paper that fatigued readers, as it was by Centinel, who wrote that Publius, "mistaking sound for argument, has with Herculean labour accumulated myriads of unmeaning sentences, and mechanically unleashed a torrent of misplaced words."[41]

Hamilton's original plan seems to have been for the series to run to about twenty to twenty-five essays.[42] A great deal would have been lost to posterity had *The Federalist* been limited to this size. A somewhat less ambitious scope and pace might have allowed the trio to edit, to compress, to hone, and to cut out the needless invective. Yet had this happened, the project would no longer have been characteristic of the famously loose-penned and scrappy Hamilton. It may not have helped anyway. The Constitution's likely effect on New Yorkers seemed pretty clear to most. Commercial New York City stood to benefit, while most of the rest of the state, at least in the near term, stood to lose. The state's ratification convention voters reflected this understanding almost perfectly.

The nation needed reform, but there were serious reasons to object to the Constitution as it came out of Philadelphia. The absence of a bill of rights, the potential for a strong upper-class bias among national representatives, the difficulty of amending the Constitution, and the fuzzy nature of the federal relationship topped the list. In short, Americans were not willing to place full faith in the Federalists' theories about government. And they were wise not to do so. The Constitution was designed to create a more perfect union. Many Anti-Federalists hoped for that end, too.

Nationally, many Americans came to the conclusion that the Constitution could use some changes. It would take recommended amendments to induce enough states to approve of the Constitution and begin preparations for a new government. In New York, the logic of not being left behind by the new nation, along with the salve of recommended amendments and a call for a second convention would accomplish what Publius could not. Even if *The Federalist* was not terribly persuasive during the ratification era, it would offer Americans enduring lessons about the Constitution. Its stark dismissal of the Anti-Federalists would also help consign the critics of the Constitution and their thinking to obscurity well into the twentieth century. Though their historical reputation is much higher, one cannot clearly conclude that the Federalists won the ratification debate. The elite-corrected popular politics that they hoped to effect has rarely characterized the American polity. It did not even characterize the Federalist efforts during the ratification debate.

Did Publius have a satisfactory answer to all the objections of the Anti-Federalists? He did offer many well-reasoned, plausible, and ingenious answers that are worth examining at length. He did have ideas at the ready to help bandage together a highly imperfect federal union. He did possess more learning in politics than any Anti-Federalist. Yet like a professor who does not quite know when to stop, Publius relentlessly backed the Constitution. It is understandable that Publius took this tack – it is what he believed was needed to aid the cause. Yet the three individuals who wrote *The Federalist* did not come close to believing that the Constitution was without flaw. Publius did have an answer to all the objections to the Constitution, but a good number of them are not entirely satisfactory. Their defense of the Constitution was timely and necessary, but it was not sufficient to craft a nation. Though it might have turned out much differently and much worse, it was the struggle between the Federalists and Anti-Federalists that created a nation. This dialogue produced a better government than what would have been created by either group alone. What genius there is in the United States' national government lies in the embrace of a more collective wisdom than even what could be provided by Alexander Hamilton, John Jay, and James Madison.

NOTES

1 *Fed.* 1, 7.

2 *The Papers of George Washington*, ed. W. W. Abbot, Confederation Series (Charlottesville: University Press of Virginia, 1997), V, 444.

3 *DHRC*, XIII, 494.

4 Hamilton to Gouverneur Morris, May 19, 1788, *PAH*, IV, 651.

5 October 11, 1787, in John P. Kaminski, ed., *The Founders on the Founders: Word Portraits from the American Revolutionary Era* (Charlottesville: University of Virginia Press, 2008), 177.

6 March 18, 1787, in *Papers of Washington*, V, 95.

7 Publius almost always refers to Anti-Federalists obliquely, as "adversaries of the new Constitution," or "those who object," or "the writers on the other side," as if naming their opponents would grant them a dignity that was not deserved. Not identifying opponents allowed more leeway in argumentation. It freed Publius to characterize arguments in ways that reflected negatively upon the Anti-Federalists. This pattern is broken somewhat toward the end of the work. In *Federalist* 67 an Anti-Federalist is mentioned by pseudonym for the first time. Cato is accused of mistakenly claiming that the president would be filling vacancies in the Senate (*Fed.* 67, 454n.). Only one Anti-Federalist is mentioned by name: Abraham Yates, who defends the veto power in New York (*Fed.* 73, 499n.). The highly adversarial dissent of the Pennsylvania Minority is mentioned in two essays. In *Federalist* 78 Hamilton points out that they are effectively objecting to the "right of the people to alter or abolish the established Constitution, whenever they find it inconsistent with their happiness" (*Fed.* 78, 527). In *Federalist* 83 he disputes their position that the right to jury should be the same "as heretofore," a nonsensical stance in a nation without a federal judiciary. This constitutes the entirety of Publius's references to specific Anti-Federalists.

8 Having not garnered as many reprints outside of New York as they might have hoped because of the speed of their production, the authors arranged to have the work bound and distributed in two volumes, the first coming out in late March and the second in late May.

9 Larry D. Kramer, "Madison's Audience," in *Harvard Law Review*, 112 (1999), 611–79, at 679.

10 Cooke, *The Federalist*, 187.

11 E.g. Aristocritis #3, Federal Farmer #17.

12 *DHRC*, XIII, 487–88.

13 Madison to Randolph, January 10, 1788, *PJM*, X, 355–56; see John R. Zaller, ch. 9. *The Nature and Origins of Mass Opinion* (Cambridge: Cambridge University Press, 1992).

14 *DHRC*, XIII, 488.

15 Hamilton later reported to Madison that a spy in Clinton's inner circle reported to him that Governor Clinton had suggested New York could easily live outside of the Union – that was in May of 1788, six months after the initial charges were leveled. This stance simply reflected what was reality: as a state with the best harbor in the region, goods would continue to flow into New York, and other states would still pay excise taxes on them, subsidizing state operations. Patrick Henry went further than Clinton, at times openly suggesting that Virginia would be just fine on its own, but that had not yet occurred when *The Federalist* began its run. It is also unlikely that either Clinton or Henry wished for that outcome as an optimal choice. Hamilton to Madison, May 19, 1788, *PAH*, IV, 649–50; Jürgen Heideking, *The Constitution before the Judgment Seat: The Prehistory and Ratification of the American Constitution, 1787–1791* (Charlottesville: University of Virginia Press, 2012),139; Ralph Ketcham, *James Madison: A Biography* (Charlottesville: University of Virginia Press, 1971), 235.

16 Many Anti-Federalists were willing to give the national government a dedicated source of revenue in the form of taxes on imports and exports. States, meanwhile, would maintain their exclusive right to raise taxes from "internal" sources. This arrangement would have been highly problematic. If war threatened or occurred, the nation's revenue could dry up, even if the United States was not a participant. Even after ratification, many American leaders clung to this belief. As president, Thomas Jefferson dismantled the nation's internal taxes, relying almost exclusively on revenue from imports and exports. When Britain and France became embroiled in a war for control of the Atlantic, American revenue dwindled and the nation suffered from a deep recession.

17 However, see David Brian Robertson's argument that delegates to the Philadelphia Convention ultimately wanted to construct failsafe mechanisms, protecting them from national power. The resulting institutional structure and distribution of powers grew intentionally

cumbersome. David Brian Robertson, *The Constitution and America's Destiny* (Cambridge: Cambridge University Press, 2005).

18 Douglass Adair, "The Authorship of the Disputed Federalist Papers: Part II," *William and Mary Quarterly*, 1 (1944), 255–60; Lance Banning, *The Sacred Fire of Liberty: James Madison and the Founding of the Federal Republic* (Ithaca, NY: Cornell University Press, 1995), 198–202, 296–98; Alpheus Thomas Mason, "The Federalist – A Split Personality," *The American Historical Review*, 57 (1952), 636–41; David, J. Siemers, *Ratifying the Republic: Antifederalists and Federalists in Constitutional Time* (Stanford, CA: Stanford University Press, 2002), 74–86.

19 The diversity of Anti-Federalist thought is important to keep in mind and is covered extensively in Saul Cornell's *The Other Founders: Anti-Federalism and the Dissenting Tradition in America, 1788–1828* (Chapel Hill: University of North Carolina Press, 1999) and David Siemers's *The Antifederalists Men of Great Faith and Forbearance* (Lanham, MD: Rowman & Littlefield, 2003).

20 See e.g. Gordon S. Wood, *The Creation of the American Republic, 1776–1787* (Chapel Hill: University of North Carolina Press. 1969), 523; Jack N. Rakove, *Original Meanings: Politics and Ideas in the Making of the Constitution* (New York: Alfred A. Knopf, 1996), 146–52; Heideking, *The Constitution before the Judgment Seat*, 109–11.

21 With the Senate empowered to approve treaties and appointments, they speculated that the president, the Senate, or both combined would predominate, producing an aristocracy or a tyranny. See e.g. Address of the Pennsylvania Minority, Federal Farmer #3, Luther Martin's *Objections*, and Brutus #16.

22 Madison had earlier written a version into his "Vices" memo, which he prepared in advance of the Convention, and he also summarized the argument in his well-known letter of October 24, 1787, to Thomas Jefferson. This was an elaboration and refinement of an idea of the Scottish Enlightenment skeptic David Hume: the wide range of interests and values in a large nation would prevent any one group from dominating and tyrannizing over others. Douglass Adair, "'That Politics may be Reduced to a Science': David Hume, James Madison, and the Tenth *Federalist*," *Huntington Library Quarterly*, 20 (1957): 343–60.

23 Publius used the term "science" to describe the systematic study of politics in six separate essays, always with a confidence that there were axioms that could be derived from systematic observation (*Fed. 9; Fed. 18; Fed. 31; Fed. 37; Fed. 47; Fed. 66*).

24 Gabriel A. Almond, with Stephen Genco, "Clouds, Clocks, and the Study of Politics," in Gabriel A. Almond, *A Discipline Divided: Schools and Sects in Political Science* (Newbury Park, CA: Sage, 1989), 37.

25 Ibid., 35–40.

26 Charles O. Jones, *Separate but Equal Branches: Congress and the Presidency*, 2nd ed. (Chappaqua, NY: Seven Bridges Press, 1999), chs. 1 and 2; Stephen Skowronek,*The Politics Presidents Make: Leadership from John Adams to George Bush* (Cambridge, MA: Belknap Press of Harvard University Press, 1993), ch. 2.

27 Almond, "Clouds, Clocks, and the Study of Politics," 35–37.

28 Sanford Levinson, *Our Undemocratic Constitution: Where the Constitution Goes Wrong (and How We the People Can Correct It)* (New York: Oxford University Press, 2006), 160.

29 Mancur Olson, *The Rise and Decline of Nations: Economic Growth, Stagflation, and Social Rigidities* (New Haven, CT: Yale University Press, 1982); Jonathan Rauch, *Demosclerosis: The Silent Killer of American Politics* (New York: Three Rivers Press, 1995); Larry J. Sabato, *A More Perfect Constitution: 23 Proposals to Revitalize Our Constitution and Make America a Fairer Country* (London: Bloomsbury, 2007); Levinson, *Our Undemocratic Constitution.*

30 Alexis de Tocqueville, *Democracy in America*, ed. Richard D. Hefner (New York: Mentor, 1956), 29.

31 Ibid., 30.

32 Jeffrey K. Tulis, "The Two Constitutional Presidencies," in Michael Nelson, ed., *The Presidency and the Political System* (Thousand Oaks, CA: SAGE Publications, 2018), 6.

33 Elaine K. Swift. *The Making of an American Senate: Reconstitutive Change in Congress, 1787–1841* (Ann Arbor: University of Michigan Press, 1996), ch. 1.

34 Gordon S. Wood, "Interests and Disinterestedness in the Making of the Constitution," in Richard Beeman et al., eds., *Beyond Confederation: Origins of the Constitution and American National Identity* (Chapel Hill: University of North Carolina Press, 1987), 69–109.

35 See Linda K. Kerber, *Federalists in Dissent* (Ithaca, NY: Cornell University Press, 1970); Edmund Morgan, *Inventing the People: The Rise of Popular Sovereignty in England and America* (New York: W. W. Norton, 1988); Stanley Elkins and Eric McKitrick, *The Age of Federalism: The Early American Republic, 1788–1800* (Oxford: Oxford University Press, 1993); James Roger Sharp, *American Politics in the Early Republic* (New Haven, CT: Yale University Press, 1993).

36 John Patrick Diggins, *John Adams* (New York: Times Books, 2003), 11–15.

37 Marc Landy and Sidney M. Milkis, *Presidential Greatness* (Lawrence, KS: University Press of Kansas, 2000), 237.

38 Daniel Wirls and Stephen Wirls, *The Invention of the United States Senate* (Baltimore, MD: Johns Hopkins University Press, 2004), ch. 5.

39 Swift, *The Making of an American Senate*, chs. 1 and 5.

40 Hamilton to Madison, May 19, 1788, *PAH*, IV, 649–50.

41 Centinel XI, *DHRC*, XV, 388.

42 Ron Chernow, *Alexander Hamilton* (New York: Penguin, 2004), 248.

2 John Jay, *The Federalist*, and the Constitution

Quentin P. Taylor

On October 22, 1787, five days before the appearance of the first *Federalist* paper, John and Sarah Jay hosted a dinner party in New York City whose guests included Alexander Hamilton and James Madison.[1] Hamilton had recently returned from Albany, where he had pled before the state supreme court, while Madison was attending the moribund Continental Congress. John Jay's hosting duties represented the social side of his official role as secretary for foreign affairs under the Articles of Confederation, but on this occasion his guests were all men of affairs, and politics could hardly be avoided in the charged atmosphere created by the recently proposed Constitution. While it is tempting to picture Jay, Hamilton, and Madison – the future Publius – finalizing their plans over Madeira and rum punch, the secrecy of the project makes it unlikely that it was openly discussed.

The authors' concern for anonymity has clouded the precise origins of *The Federalist*. While Hamilton is universally credited with the idea for the series, the evidence is circumstantial. He did pen the first number – according to legend on a Hudson sloop returning from Albany – which outlines the plan of the work. Shortly thereafter he is believed to have recruited Jay and then Madison as contributors to the project. Madison later reported that he was courted by Hamilton *and* Jay, but there is no direct evidence that Hamilton recruited Jay.[2] In light of their decade-long friendship and shared political views, it is likely that *The Federalist* owed its origins to a degree of collaboration between the two men unsuspected by most scholars.[3]

Jay was not only older, but more politically experienced than Hamilton. When Hamilton was penning his first political essays (1774–75), Jay was serving in the Continental Congress, as well as in his native New York, whose first Constitution (1777) was largely his work. In the years that followed, Jay served as president of the Continental Congress (1779) and undertook diplomatic missions to Spain and France (1780–84). In Paris he played a key role in negotiating the treaty (1783) that recognized America's independence and borders. Upon his return to the United States, Jay learned that he had been appointed secretary for foreign affairs, a position he accepted once Congress agreed to strengthen the authority of the office. In this capacity, Jay was, in effect, the chief executive officer of the federal government and arguably its most important official.

If Jay was senior in age and stature to both Madison and Hamilton when *The Federalist* was written, he would in time be eclipsed in fame by his younger colleagues. And because the latter's reputations owe a good deal to their performances as Publius, Jay's meager contribution (he wrote but five of the eighty-five papers) has done little to elevate his reputation.[4] In the massive body of scholarship on *The Federalist*, Jay has been largely ignored, mainly for the paucity of his effort, but also for his failure to make any original contribution to the theory of federalism, separation of powers, or republican government. Only in his final paper, *Federalist* 64, did he touch on aspects of institutional design for which Hamilton and Madison are so well known. Jay's first four papers (*Fed.* 2–5) emphasize the advantages and promise of a strong union of states under the Constitution and warn of the ominous perils sure to follow from its rejection. Although rich in style and analysis, Jay's five papers are dwarfed in number and scope by his collaborators', reducing Jay to a "junior partner" in the project. As a biographer of Hamilton has written, "[a]n accurate title page of *The Federalist* would thus have to read: 'By Alexander Hamilton and James Madison, with Contributions by John Jay.'"[5]

Jay's role as the "lesser Publius" was neither part of the original plan nor owing to a lack of effort. He possibly expected to contribute a good deal more to the series, an expectation shared by Hamilton, who yielded his pen to Jay after the first number. A larger role for Jay is also suggested by Hamilton's pledge in the lead essay to illustrate the proposed Constitution's *"analogy to your own state constitution"* (*Fed.* 1, 7). As the principal author of the latter, it is likely that Jay would have contributed to this part of the plan. Yet with Jay sidelined, it fell to Hamilton (a fellow New Yorker) to draw the analogy. In doing so, he undermined many objections to the Constitution by noting that these same charges could be leveled against the much-admired state constitution.[6] Students of *The Federalist* have largely overlooked the analogy to the New York Constitution in the argument of Publius (although it was one of six topics originally slated for discussion) and its indirect yet tangible contribution to the work.

It was not a lack of industry but a severe bout of rheumatism that felled Jay after his run of four numbers. By the time he recovered, the series was well advanced, with Madison now bearing much of the load. Jay would contribute only one more essay before turning to a parallel project that possibly had a greater impact on public opinion in New York than all the *Federalist* essays combined. The *Address to the People of the State of New York* was published as a pamphlet in mid-April 1788, shortly after Jay suffered another shock to his system: this time a severe head wound from a missile thrown in a riot.[7] The *Address* was a further plea for union, a patriotic call to give the Constitution "a fair trial." Opposition to the Constitution ran high on the eve of elections for the state ratifying convention, and Jay hoped a reasoned address to a broad audience might convince the undecided and convert its detractors. Many contemporaries – including Washington and Franklin – believed he had admirably succeeded. Jay's biographer calls the *Address* "the single most persuasive paper in the blizzard of paper produced in New York about the Constitution."[8] Yet for all its eloquence and good sense, a large majority of Anti-Federalists were elected to the state convention.

By mid-June, Jay was well enough to attend the New York ratifying convention in Poughkeepsie, joining Hamilton as a fellow delegate. Both worked indefatigably to secure ratification on the convention floor and behind the scenes, but Jay – respected by supporters *and* opponents of the Constitution – was the more effective of the two.[9] While external events, viz., ratification by New Hampshire and Virginia, were perhaps more compelling than Federalist arguments, the Eleventh Pillar was duly raised to the federal edifice, and John Jay had been the chief architect.[10]

With the Constitution ratified and elections for the new government under way, Jay retained his post as secretary for foreign affairs to provide a degree of continuity during the transition. After Washington was inaugurated in April 1789, Jay served as acting secretary of state until Thomas Jefferson assumed the office in May 1790. During this period and beyond, he advised the president, who gave Jay his choice of cabinet positions in the new administration. Jay, a skilled lawyer, preferred the bench – perhaps grasping the importance of establishing national authority through the federal courts – and was appointed first chief justice of the Supreme Court. From this position he continued to shape national policy and civic culture, until called upon by Washington to negotiate a treaty with Great Britain to avoid a war which America was ill-prepared to fight. Jay knew his acceptance of the mission would prove controversial and damage his political fortunes regardless of the outcome. Widely regarded as a possible successor to the presidential chair, the treaty (1795) that bears his name had the predicted result. He was, however, still popular in his home state, and Jay rounded out a distinguished public career as a two-term governor of New York (1795–1801). His subsequent retirement and withdrawal from politics produced neither a memoir nor a history of the Revolution. By the time of his death in 1829, with the exception of Madison, he was the last of the Fathers.

Given the many high offices he occupied and his vital contributions to the American founding, it is rather remarkable that John Jay is so little known or discussed. He does of necessity occupy a notable position in many histories of the founding, but he has received only a fraction of the scholarly attention or popular notice of other top-tier founders. For many years his association with the venerable *Federalist* papers kept his name alive, if only to place him in the shade of its towering co-authors. For two decades historian Richard B. Morris almost single-handedly kept Jay from further oblivion with a series of studies and two volumes of edited papers. In order to restore this "forgotten founder" to his rightful position, Morris placed Jay alongside Franklin, Washington, Adams, Jefferson, Madison, and Hamilton as among the "seven who shaped our destiny."[11] Other scholars, notably John Kaminski[12] and Herbert Johnson,[13] would contribute to this revival of interest and reputation, while Walter Stahr has provided a much-needed modern biography. More recently, historian Joseph Ellis has grouped Jay with Madison, Hamilton, and Washington in "the Quartet" that rescued America's foundering experiment in self-government under the Articles.[14] More promising still is the ongoing project to make Jay's papers widely available in a critical edition.[15]

Given the virtuoso performances of Hamilton and Madison as Publius, there is little cause to regret Jay's minor role in the production. It was not the first time fate had intervened to limit his place in history. A few months before the Declaration of Independence was signed in Philadelphia, he was called back to New York to help organize provincial defenses. Later, as work was being completed on the state constitution, the sudden death of his mother required that he leave the Convention before he could offer key amendments and oppose others he disapproved of. His mission to Spain proved frustrating and fruitless; he was never even officially recognized by the host government. His subsequent effort to negotiate a commercial treaty with Spain led to a sharp sectional controversy that tarnished Jay's reputation in the South. Most fateful, however, was the defeat of his nomination to the Federal Convention in the New York legislature. A leader in every assembly in which he had served, Jay is likely to have played an active role in the proceedings. How might history look upon John Jay had he been both a signer of the Declaration of Independence and a framer of the Constitution?

But "history" is made by historians, and Jay's notable absences were more apparent than real. While the signers of the Declaration were declaring war from the safety of Philadelphia, Jay was fighting a war in New York. When news of independence arrived on July 9, Jay drafted the state's response – a ringing if fatalistic endorsement. His absence from the Federal Convention is more significant. Would he have served to moderate Hamilton or joined in his high-toned, consolidationist scheme? The latter is most unlikely. Jay had given hints of a remarkably similar plan in his correspondence in the months preceding the Convention, yet he was no "monocrat" and was soon disabused of any idea of consolidating the states. It is probable that Jay would have been an influential delegate on the floor and in committee, but any further speculation is vain. The complicated and difficult task of framing the Constitution hardly begs for an alternative scenario or a more successful issue.

Jay's chief contribution to the Constitution occurred before the Convention met and after it adjourned: First, through the dissemination of nationalist and continentalist ideas among elites during the Confederation era, and next, by his role in securing ratification in New York. As chief justice he would defend the independence of the judiciary and upheld the supremacy of the Constitution. A robust nationalism, tempered with republican prudence and crowned with a sober vision of American greatness, would remain hallmarks of Jay's thought to the end. When he left federal office in 1795, he was arguably the most experienced and accomplished – if not the most popular – statesman in America. If any founder was "present at the creation," it was John Jay.

Years later John Adams identified Jay as "of more importance than the rest" in paving the road to Philadelphia and securing adoption of the Constitution.[16] Perhaps an exaggeration, yet, as president, Adams reappointed Jay chief justice of the United States, an honor Jay declined. By this time, Jay's public life had traversed the entire arc of the revolutionary era – from the First Continental Congress to the "Revolution of 1800." Washington had just passed into glory, and Hamilton had but a few gloomy years remaining. Jay would live to see the triumph of Andrew Jackson. Politically, he (like James Madison) may be said to have outlived himself.

From the existing scholarship on Jay it is possible to piece together his contribution to the Constitution both before and after its adoption, but there is still no focused account of the source of this contribution in the evolution of Jay's *nationalism*. Nor have Jay's *Federalist* essays received the close reading lavished on those of Hamilton and Madison. The former is well beyond the present scope, but the latter may fill a sizable gap in the literature on *The Federalist* and contribute to the broader prospect.

One striking feature of *The Federalist* is its unity: its continuity of style, singleness of purpose, and consistency of argument. The fiction of a single author is maintained throughout and only modern statistical analysis has been able to establish the authorship of certain disputed numbers. Whatever their private reservations regarding the merits of the Constitution, the three authors agreed to speak with one voice in explicating its meaning and supporting its ratification. The systematic execution of the plan, the smooth transitions from author to author, the references to earlier numbers, and the repetition of key themes all contribute to the impression that it was the product of a single mind.

Jay's five essays fit seamlessly into the broader plan, and it is largely through our knowledge of his authorship that we may discern his distinct contribution to the series. His first four essays (*Fed.* 2–5) appeared between October 31 and November 10 in the *Independent Journal*, the New York City daily in which most of the *Federalist* papers initially appeared. In the first bound volume of the complete series, Jay's four numbers fall under the heading of "Concerning Dangers from Foreign Force and Influence" and constitute a subset of "*The Utility of the UNION to your Political Prosperity*" (*Fed.* 2–14). In the lead essay, Hamilton had already linked the fate of the American Union to that of the proposed Constitution, an ingenious if disputable equation that raised the stakes of the ratification contest dramatically. For "Publius," the people were not being asked to choose between the Constitution and the existing government, but between "an adoption of the new Constitution or a dismemberment of the Union" (*Fed.* 1, 7). Adopting the Constitution meant preserving the Union, "the safest course for your liberty, your dignity, and your happiness" (*Fed.* 1, 6). Rejecting it meant courting danger, disunion, and the loss of freedom.

Was it not then "superfluous to prove" the truth of this syllogism when "the utility of the Union" is engraved upon the hearts of "the great body of the people in every State" (*Fed.* 1, 7)? Sadly, Hamilton observes, the debate over the Constitution will unleash "[a] torrent of angry and malignant passion" (*Fed.* 1, 5) "little favorable to the discovery of truth" (*Fed.* 1, 4). The proposed plan of government simply "affects too many particular interests, innovates upon too many local institutions" to expect a calm and candid examination of its merits. No less "formidable" to a fair hearing is "a certain class of men in every State" who will oppose the Constitution out of narrow self-interest, and "the perverted ambition of another class" who look to a break-up of the Union as an opportunity for advancement. The former, Hamilton avers, hope to retain the advantages they possess under current state establishments, while the later aim at "the subdivision of the empire into several partial confederacies" (*Fed.* 1, 4).

This "subdivision" of the Union – not the persistence of Union under the current or an alternate system – was for Publius the inevitable corollary of a rejection of the Constitution. In addition to the "perverted," who welcome such a division, there are others who maintain "that the thirteen states are of too great extent for any general system, and that we must of necessity resort to separate confederacies of distinct proportions of the whole" (*Fed.* 1, 7). Whatever the motives or rationale for opposing the Constitution, its defeat will spell disunion, and with it disaster. Hence it was not "superfluous" to "begin by examining the advantages of that Union, [and] the certain evils, and the probable dangers, to which every State will be exposed from its dissolution" (*Fed.* 1, 7).

As America's leading foreign policy expert and a confirmed nationalist, John Jay was uniquely qualified to examine "the value and blessings of Union" (*Fed.* 2, 10) and the "dangers from *foreign arms and influence*" (*Fed.* 3, 14). He was also a skilled polemicist and practiced in the art of persuasion.[17] Jay's talent and experience converged in *The Federalist* to produce a powerful argument on behalf of Union, which for Jay (as for Hamilton) was synonymous with ratification. As suggested above, the equation of Union with adoption of the Constitution (and its rejection with disunion) was a shrewd rhetorical move that not only raised the stakes of the ratification contest to a referendum on the fate of popular government, but cast the Constitution's opponents as de facto disunionists. If this move was peremptory and unfair, it had the advantage of putting the Anti-Federalists on the defensive. Conversely, by framing the question in zero-sum terms – the Constitution or Chaos – Hamilton placed the Federalists on the high moral ground of patriotic (and pragmatic) unionism. From this citadel, Jay would assail those unnamed "Politicians," who in defiance of "the received and uncontradicted opinion ... of the people of America ... and the wishes, prayers, and efforts of our best and wisest Citizens," now look "for safety and happiness ... in a division of the States into distinct confederacies or sovereignties" (*Fed.* 2, 8).

It goes without saying that the opponents of the Constitution did not view its rejection as the occasion for disunion. Nor did leading Anti-Federalists advocate the formation of separate confederacies in lieu of its adoption. Virtually all Anti-Federalists were committed to an American Union and favored some type of reform that would strengthen the national government. Most simply objected to specific provisions in the Constitution and the absence of others, viz., a bill of rights. Their formal objections were expressed in proposed amendments to the Constitution that were submitted with several of the states' articles of ratification. Yet as the great contest commenced in the fall of 1787, there was no predicting what might follow a rejection, and many Federalists were loath to renounce any strategy or tactic that might secure ratification.

While Jay did not impugn the motives of certain "classe[s] of men" who opposed the Constitution, he did assume with Hamilton that its defeat would result in disunion. Yet for Jay the specter of "three or four confederacies" (*Fed.* 2, 12) or even "thirteen separate states" (*Fed.* 3, 15) assumes the character of an *idée fixe* in his brace of four papers. In light of the unanimity of opinion – both popular and elite – regarding the advantages of Union, it is no surprise that Jay looked upon the prospect of disunion with dismay and trepidation. Disunion and the attendant "division of the States into distinct confederacies and sovereignties" (*Fed.* 2, 8) not only defied "received and uncontradicted opinion," but would appear to frustrate "the design of Providence" itself (*Fed.* 2, 9). Without resort to religion per se (and Jay was the most religious of the leading founders), Publius invokes a beneficent Deity whose handiwork had "blessed" the continent with natural riches "for the delight and accommodation of its inhabitants." This same Providence "has been pleased to give this one connected country, to one people, a people descended from the same ancestors, speaking the same language, professing the same religion, attached to the same principles of government, [and] very similar in manners and customs" (*Fed.* 2, 9).

The informed reader – then as now – must pause at this portrait of a racially, linguistically, religiously, and politically homogeneous America. The reality, of course, was far more complex, and Jay knew it. As Walter Stahr observes, "Jay knew well that Americans were descended from various ancestors and practiced various religions. But Jay's purpose was not description but *persuasion*."[18] As such, the actual differences counted for little when set against the common heritage of "our western sons of liberty" and the experience of the "band of brethren" who "by their joint councils, arms and efforts, fighting side by side throughout a long and bloody war, have nobly established their general Liberty and Independence."[19] Geography and history would appear to have conspired under a benign Providence to place the American people under "one nation" (*Fed.* 2, 8) – one people "united to each other by the strongest ties," who "should never be split into a number of unsocial, jealous and alien sovereignties" (*Fed.* 2, 9).

In Jay's patriotic tableau, the realities of American diversity – political, religious, and ethnic – are dissolved in a mytho-poetic haze of providential history. If unity was the key to America's "political salvation," as Publius believed, the rough knots of pluralism – its tensions, contradictions, and conflicts – had to be sanded, smoothed, and varnished. Accordingly, "[t]o all general purposes ... [Americans] have uniformly been one people," and, as such, quickly recognized "the value and blessings of Union" under one central government (*Fed.* 2, 10). Unfortunately, but not surprisingly, the government created in the fog of war – the Articles of Confederation (1777) – proved "greatly deficient and inadequate" to the ends of Union. The American citizenry at large – "[t]his intelligent people" – felt the defect and sought a remedy "in a national Government more wisely framed," and summoned, "as with one voice," the Federal Convention of 1787. This august body, many of whose members were "highly distinguished for their patriotism, virtue, and wisdom," "passed many months in cool uninterrupted and daily consultations" and, uninfluenced by any passion but "love for their Country," produced a plan through "their joint and very unanimous counsels" for the consideration of the people (*Fed.* 2, 10–11).

Jay was correct regarding the origins and imperfections of the Articles, but his account of the origins and deliberations of the Convention was itself imperfect. Defects in the Articles were widely perceived among the politically informed, but the Convention owed its birth more to the persistent efforts of a handful of elite leaders (e.g. Jay, Hamilton, Madison) and recurring crises (e.g. Shays' Rebellion) than to popular pressure. Far from summoning "as with one voice" the gathering in Philadelphia, "the people" played no direct role in the process. (Interestingly, Jay was one of the few to advocate popular election of convention delegates.) Nor did the state legislatures act with unanimity: some selected delegates before Congress approved the Convention, others dragged their feet after the fact, and Rhode Island refused to participate altogether. Although the assembly was exceptional in terms of the experience, intelligence, and talent of its members, Jay's characterization of its deliberations as "cool [and] uninterrupted," and its delegates as motivated by no other interests but "love of Country," neither accords with the history of deliberative bodies nor the records of the Convention. Even at the time it was widely known that some delegates had left the Convention in opposition while a few others had refused to sign the final document – a far cry from the "very unanimous counsels" he ascribed to the delegates. Moreover, it was known to all that the Convention's deliberations had been conducted in secrecy. How then was Jay in a position to describe its proceedings with accuracy?

As noted, Jay-cum-Publius was less interested in strict accuracy than in persuasive effect, and if that required a selective use of the past or creative embellishment he was willing to sacrifice little truths for the larger goal of union. He also had to explain opposition to the Constitution – which was widespread in New York – in terms that did not impugn the character or judgment of "the people."[20] Jay did this by invoking the factional politics of the Continental Congress to illustrate how ambitious, self-interested, and parochial politicians attempted to mislead the public. Yet owing to the good sense and patriotism of the American people such efforts had ultimately failed. "Many indeed were deceived and deluded, but the great majority of the people reasoned and decided judiciously" (*Fed.* 2, 11). And if this "great majority" came to place its trust in the relatively untried and unknown members of Congress, how much more should they "respect the judgment and advice of the Convention," which included "some of the most distinguished members of that Congress" (*Fed.* 2, 12). Both bodies contained men "tried and justly approved for patriotism and abilities," and both "invariably joined with the people in thinking that the prosperity of America depended on its Union."

Jay's contention that a legislature empowered to achieve national independence (the Congress) and an assembly authorized to maintain it through constitutional reform (the Convention) had both identified American prosperity with American Union may appear self-evident, even redundant. This redundancy only made sense if the alternative to ratification was disunion, if "the rejection of [the Constitution] would put the continuance of the Union in the utmost jeopardy" (*Fed.* 2, 13). Jay concluded it would and pitted the good sense of "the people" who "have always thought right on this subject," against "some men" who "deprecate the importance of Union" and suggest "that three or four confederacies would be better than one" (*Fed.* 2, 12). The populist strain in Jay's argument is unmistakable and clearly calculated to court if not flatter the average sensual man. Conversely, he implicitly linked opposition to the Constitution with disunion, and disunion with disaster, thus casting doubt on the judgment if not the character of the plan's adversaries.

Jay also appealed to the hopes, and particularly the fears, of readers, ending each of his first four papers on an ominous note of foreboding.[21] In number two he quotes from Shakespeare (*Henry VIII*) to underscore the consequences of American disunion: "Farewell, a long farewell to all my greatness" (*Fed.* 2, 13). In the next number a divided America is faced with the prospect of "humiliation from Spain, or Britain, or any other *powerful* nation" (*Fed.* 3, 18), thus illustrating the lesson that "when a people or family so divide, it never fails to be against themselves" (*Fed.* 4, 23). In time a divided America would likely become the playground of foreign powers, teaching the further lesson of "how much more easy it is to receive foreign fleets into our ports, and foreign armies into our country, than it is to persuade or compel them to depart" (*Fed.* 5, 27). In each case, Jay's logic is inexorable: The defeat of the Constitution will spell disunion; disunion will engender three or four separate confederacies; separate confederacies will spawn intersectional rivalries, invite foreign intervention, and effectively end American independence. This gloomy forecast was a potent draught, and Jay served it up without a chaser.

He did, however, brighten this bleak prospect with the promise of union. For every reference to the dreaded "separate confederacies," Jay counters with an appeal to "one good national government" to which "the people of America have so long and uniformly entertained ... the importance of their continuing firmly under" (*Fed.* 3, 13). Just such a government – "vested with sufficient powers for all general and national purposes" – was embodied in the proposed Constitution, and Jay translates the people's "universal and uniform attachment to the cause of the Union" (*Fed.* 2, 12) into popular support for its ratification.

The American people – "intelligent and well-informed" – "have always thought right on this subject" and cannot but find in the Constitution the means to preserve it.

Persuaded that the people's "reasons" for Union are "cogent and conclusive," Jay proceeds to illustrate its foremost utility: securing the "*safety* of the people" – particularly "against dangers from *foreign arms and influence*" (*Fed.* 3, 14). As America's diplomat-in-chief, Jay was well-placed to address these dangers and to determine "whether the people are not right in their opinion that a cordial Union under an efficient national Government affords them the best security that can be devised against *hostilities* from abroad." Such a government, with exclusive authority over foreign affairs will prevent treaty violations and other wayward acts by the states, and thus forestall the two principal causes of "just" wars. It will also have the advantage of superior leadership, for it will attract and draw upon the talent of the entire nation. "[O]nce an efficient national government is established, the best men in the country will not only consent to serve, but will also generally be appointed to manage it" (*Fed.* 3, 15). Here Jay anticipates Madison's contention that in an extended republic – with "the widest field of choice" – the national councils will be populated with "fit characters" (*Fed.* 10, 63). He also anticipates Hamilton's corollary that the national government will likely be better administrated than the states (*Fed.* 17, 107; *Fed.* 46, 317). Given the presence of the "best men" in the former, Jay avers, "the administration, the political counsels, and the judicial decisions ... will be more wise, systematical, and judicious, than those of individual States" (*Fed.* 3, 15).

Jay even foreshadows Madison's famous discussion of factions. While the "passions and interests" of individual states – or groups therein – may be prompted to violate treaties and other acts of defiance, a "good national government," composed of members drawn from the entire Union, will rarely exhibit such tendencies. Moreover, the latter will have the authority and incentive to prevent or punish those who do. "[T]he national Government, not being affected by those local circumstances, will neither be induced to commit the wrong themselves, nor want power or inclination to prevent, or punish its commission by others" (*Fed.* 3, 16). And should a rogue state start a war, the national government will be able "to accommodate and settle [it] amicably" (*Fed.* 3, 17). National officials "will be more temperate and cool" than their prideful counterparts in the states: "[t]he national Government in such cases will not be affected by this pride," and with "moderation and candour" address and resolve the difficulties.

The argument for the capacity of Union to prevent the "just" causes of war applies with equal force to unjust or "*pretended*" ones. With a realism gleaned from history and confirmed by direct experience, Jay observes that "nations in general will make war whenever they have a prospect of getting anything by it" (*Fed.* 4, 18–19). In the case of nations governed by absolute monarchs (France and Spain) the motives for war may be entirely personal and arbitrary. Yet there are additional "inducements to war" rooted in America's "relative situation and circumstances" (*Fed.* 4, 19). Foremost among these are *commercial* rivalries, e.g. over rights to the fisheries in the North Atlantic, control of the St. Lawrence and Mississippi rivers, and access to the India and China trade. Moreover, America's comparative advantage – "the cheapness and excellence of our productions ... the circumstances of vicinity, and the enterprise and address of our merchants and navigators" – "cannot give pleasure" to those European rivals with interests in the New World: France, Britain, and Spain. As a budding commercial and continental power, it is far more likely that the European governments will come to look upon a united America with "jealousies and uneasiness" than "with an eye of indifference and composure" (*Fed.* 4, 20).

These and other considerations – including those unforeseen – point conclusively in favor of "Union and a good national Government" as the best means to "repress and discourage" war instead of "*inviting*" it (*Fed.* 4, 20). In addition to presenting a common front to a would-be foe, "one good Government" will have several advantages in the event of actual hostilities, and in their successful termination. As in peacetime, such a government may draw upon "the talents and experience of the ablest men" from across the nation and coordinate the parts for the defense of the whole, including the state militias. Conversely, if one part is attacked will not the others "fly to its succor, and spend their blood and money in its defence" (*Fed.* 4, 22)? Will not a single government of a united people negotiate treaties in the interest of the whole (*Fed.* 4, 21)? Finally, can any of these palpable advantages be expected to accrue to an America divided into "thirteen, or if you please three or four independent Governments"?

Such questions were, of course, largely rhetorical, yet shrewdly to the purpose. For united or disunited, "foreign nations will know and view it exactly as it is; and they will act towards us accordingly" (*Fed.* 4, 22). If united, "they will be much more disposed to cultivate our friendship, than provoke our resentment," but if not, they will soon hold America in "contempt" and "outrage" (*Fed.* 4, 23). Nowhere in *The Federalist* is the polarity between union and disunion more starkly cast. On one hand, Jay paints a picture of "our national Government ... efficient and well administered – our trade prudently regulated – our militia property organized and disciplined – our resources and finances discreetly managed – our credit reestablished – our people free, contented, and united" (*Fed.* 4, 22). Juxtaposed to this earthly heaven is a political nightmare – an America "either destitute of an effectual Government (each State doing right or wrong as its rulers may seem convenient) or splitting up into three or four independent and probably discordant republics or confederacies, one inclining to Britain, another to France, and a third to Spain, and perhaps played off against each other by the three" (*Fed.* 4, 23).

In his final essay on the "Dangers from Foreign Force and Influence," Jay retains this Manichean method of contrast, but he also provides an historical analogue that endows his prior speculations with a probative weight. Earlier, Jay had drawn upon the past to illustrate such dangers, but the examples used were either too obscure – Genoa's submission to France (*Fed.* 3, 17–18) – or too remote – the fatal *stasis* of ancient Greece (*Fed.* 4, 22) – to support the sweeping conclusion that "what has so often happened, would under similar circumstances happen again." Nor did these examples provide a *positive* corollary to political division and disaster. Both defects could only be supplied by an historical parallel at once familiar to readers and relevant to America. Queen Anne's letter on the unification of England and Scotland (1706) fit the bill fetchingly.

John Jay, like Madison and Hamilton, was a practical statesman who turned to history for "useful lessons" in guiding statecraft. Their applied use of the past – so characteristic of the Enlightenment – is a hallmark of the *Federalist* papers. The two passages Jay reproduced from Queen Anne's letter could not have been more deftly selected. The first touts the blessings of "an entire and perfect Union" between the two kingdoms: peace, prosperity, stability, security. Remove a word or two ("Island," "kingdoms") and it would be indistinguishable from a passage in *The Federalist*. The second passage requires no such emendation and uncannily mirrors the tone, style, and substance of Publius's calls for ratification: "We most earnestly recommend to you calmness and unanimity in this great and weighty affair, that the Union may be brought to a happy conclusion, being the only *effectual* way to secure our present and future happiness; and disappoint the designs of our and your enemies, who will doubtless, on this occasion, *use their utmost endeavors to prevent or delay this Union*" (*Fed.* 5, 24).

The parallel to America was so close and its lesson so clear that Jay had little need to belabor the point. He does, however, remind readers that for many ages the people of Britain had paid a high price for their division into three separate nations (England, Scotland, Wales) when their insular position and mutual interests dictated that they "should be but one nation" (*Fed.* 5, 24). Once more Jay turns from the light of American unity to the darkness of division, a descent in which "envy and jealousy" blot out "confidence and affection" and the "partial interests of each confederacy" smother the "general interests of America." So divided, America will come to resemble a Hobbesian state of nature: its "three or four nations" will "always be either envolved [sic] in disputes and wars, or live in the constant apprehension of them" (*Fed.* 5, 24–25).

But might not "three or four confederacies" serve to balance one another (*Fed.* 5, 25)? Might not "alliances offensive and defensive ... put them and keep them in a formidable state of defence against foreign enemies" (*Fed.* 5, 26)? Jay demolishes these "arguments" with a combination of logic, history, and psychology. Assuming an initial balance of power, it is unlikely that an equilibrium could be maintained over time. In addition to variations in "local circumstances," there is the strong probability "that superior policy and good management [will] ... distinguish the Government of one above the rest" (*Fed.* 5, 25). (Here again Jay anticipates Hamilton's emphasis on "good administration" as the mark of "good," i.e., *strong*, government.) The manifest superiority of one confederacy would trigger the Hobbesian cycle of "envy" and "fear" among the others, and end in the mutual distrust of all. Jay even predicts that in such a divided state, the northernmost confederacy would soon predominate, and be sorely tempted to encroach upon its "more delicate [southern] neighbors" (*Fed.* 5, 26). "[N]eighbors," in fact, is the wrong word to describe parties who "neither love nor trust one another, but on the contrary would be a prey to discord, jealousy and mutual injuries," the very condition in which "some nations doubtless wish to see us, viz., *formidable only to each other*" (*Fed.* 5, 26).

As for a system of alliances among confederacies to preserve their independence, Jay is no less dismissive. Did divided Spain or Britain ever effectively unite against a foreign foe? And like England and Scotland, "[t]he proposed confederacies will be *distinct nations*," with distinct *commercial* interests, which will in turn create distinct *political* attachments with the European powers (*Fed.* 5, 26). Reversing the logic that led Americans to unite against imperial Britain, Jay maintains that the individual confederacies would be more fearful of one another than of the trans-Atlantic powers, and thereby more inclined to seek "foreign alliances, than to guard against foreign dangers by alliances between themselves" (*Fed.* 5, 27). The reversal is all the more striking when viewed against the patriotic panegyric that marked Jay's initial essay as Publius. What has become of the "one connected, fertile, wide spreading country" blessed by Providence? It has been unnaturally severed and divided. And what of the "one united people," sharing a common tongue, religion, principles, and manners? They have been turned against each another and rendered "enemies." And what of the "the band of brethren" who gave their nation "Liberty and Independence"? They have been eclipsed by political opportunists presiding over petty republics.

If Jay's speculative "reversal" betrayed a moral inconsistency, it was largely a function of the logic he adopted as an advocate of ratification. Publius identified the failure to ratify the Constitution with disunion, and disunion with separate confederacies along with all their attendant horrors. Jay drew upon his considerable knowledge, experience, and skills to render the consequences of the Constitution's defeat in the starkest hues. (His appeal to the *rational* fears of readers would prove a recurrent theme of the series.) And while Anti-Federalists might charge Publius with setting up a straw man (or a scarecrow) others may have found the image sufficiently lifelike to err on the side of caution. "Let candid men judge then whether the division of American into any given number of independent sovereignties would tend to secure us against the hostilities and improper interference of foreign nations" (*Fed.* 5, 27).

With this Publius concludes his brief on foreign dangers and turns to the "Dangers from Dissensions between the States." Here the division of labor and expertise required that Hamilton once more take up his pen. It is unknown if Jay expected to contribute additional numbers to the project – perhaps on the New York Constitution – but illness prevented his active participation for nearly four months. When he returned to contribute his next (and last) number, Madison had just completed his final paper, and Hamilton had arranged for the first thirty-six *Federalist* essays to be published in a bound volume. On March 5, Jay's *Federalist* 64 appeared in the *Independent Journal* as a continuation of Publius's treatment of the proposed Senate. Jay's isolated performance has often been looked upon as something of an anomaly – a second act that turned out to be a one-night-stand. In reality, it was a scripted cameo with America's chief diplomat cast in the role of defender of the Constitution's treaty-making power.[22]

Under the Articles of Confederation, treaties had been negotiated by agents appointed by Congress, including the secretary for foreign affairs, while ratification required the approval of nine of the thirteen state delegations. Under the proposed Constitution, treaties would be negotiated by the president (or his agents) and ratified with the "advice and consent" of two-thirds of the Senate. If Jay found the treaty-making power among "the most unexceptionable articles" (*Fed.* 64, 432) in the Constitution, critics had raised doubts as to its wisdom. Jay preempts these objections with a defense of the prescribed method of selecting the officials who will exercise this power: the president and senators. Few could doubt that this "important" trust should be vested with "men the best qualified for the purpose," and exercised "in the manner most conducive to the public good." The framers appear to have had this thought in mind when they placed the selection of the president with state-chosen electors and that of senators with the state legislatures. Just as these elective bodies will "in general be composed of the most enlightened and respectable citizens," so too will their choice fall to "those men ... the most distinguished by their abilities and virtue" (*Fed.* 64, 433). In contrasting this method with election "by the people in their collective capacity" (*Fed.* 64, 432), Jay echoes Madison's "filtration" argument in *Federalist* 10.

The framers were also wise to vest the treaty-making power in men of approved age and holding offices of sufficient duration to gain the experience and information necessary for "the attainment of those great objects" of national interest (*Fed.* 64, 434). Conversely, placing this trust in a "large popular assembly" marked by high turnover and a lack of secrecy "must necessarily be inadequate" to the task (*Fed.* 64, 435, 434). An additional safeguard is provided by the staggered terms of senators, which "obviate the inconvenience of periodically transferring those great affairs entirely to new men" who lack the qualifications vital to sound diplomacy. In conclusion, "the constitution provides that our negociations [sic] for treaties shall have every advantage which can be derived from talents, information, integrity, and deliberative investigation on the one hand, and from secrecy and dispatch on the other" (*Fed.* 64, 436).

To the objection that treaties are *laws* and should be made solely by *legislative* bodies, Jay replies with a primer on constitutional theory. "All constitutional acts of power, whether in the executive or in the judicial departments, have as much legal validity and obligation as if they proceeded from the Legislature" (*Fed.* 64, 436). Disabusing those who still adhered to the exploded doctrine of "legislative supremacy," Jay observes that all such acts are equally "act[s] of sovereignty." He also reproves those who object to the legal *supremacy* of treaties and maintain they should, "like acts of an assembly ... be repealable at pleasure." Treaties, unlike laws, are a species of contract or a "bargain" between two parties. They may be modified or abrogated by common consent, but not by mere "legislative acts" (*Fed.* 64, 437).

As for "apprehensions" of bias, corruption, or perfidy through abuse of the treaty-making power, Jay explains why these "fears" are misplaced. First, each state is represented in the Senate and a treaty requires two-thirds approval, greatly reducing the chances of a pernicious agreement becoming law. Second, the treaty-makers themselves, as well as "their families and estates," will be subject to the same odious measure – hardly an incentive to malfeasance. And in the highly unlikely case of a treaty obtained by fraud, the "law of nations" will render it "null and void" (*Fed.* 64, 438). Finally, if "neither honor, oaths, reputation, conscience, the love of country, and family" are insufficient "security for their fidelity," there is always "fear of punishment and disgrace" – impeachment and removal.

With these assurances, Jay concludes his defense of the treaty-making power and his performance as Publius. It is doubtful that he expected (or was expected by Hamilton) to contribute further to the series. Jay had already begun work on a related project that would prove far more notable than his five newspaper essays. With elections for the New York Ratifying Convention swiftly approaching, Jay's efforts on behalf of the Constitution were only just beginning. In mid-April, two weeks before he was chosen as a delegate, he published *An Address to the People of the State of New York*, a nineteen-page pamphlet that leading Federalists hailed as a masterstroke. Washington praised the *Address* for its "good sense, forcible observations, temper and moderation," and judged it well-calculated to make "a serious impression on the antifederal mind." Franklin urged Jay to give the meritorious but unsigned work the "additional Weight" of his name. Noah Webster, editing the *American Magazine*, was no less effusive in praise and concurred with those who found Jay's "arguments against appointing a new general Convention, for the purpose of altering or amending the constitution, ... altogether unanswerable."[23]

Calls for "a new general Convention" are likely to have prompted Jay's *Address*, for rejecting such calls is the stated purpose of the essay. Some critics of the Constitution hoped to make its ratification conditional on the adoption of "necessary" amendments by a second convention. Since the first convention had worked in secrecy and left the people with an all or nothing choice, the flawed document, it was argued, should be subject to amendment based on public discussion and scrutiny. Interestingly, this argument had first been made in the Federal Convention before the Constitution had even been signed. In the final days of the proceedings, Edmund Randolph moved that the state conventions be permitted to propose amendments to the Constitution, and that a second convention be authorized to consider these before it was adopted. The motion was seconded by another Virginian, George Mason, and supported by Elbridge Gerry of Massachusetts. The remaining delegates were unmoved or hostile, and despite the appeals of Franklin for unanimity, Randolph, Mason, and Gerry refused to sign the Constitution.[24]

As more states adopted the Constitution the idea of a second convention burned less brightly, but it continued to flicker. It was only with reluctance that Randolph abandoned his pet scheme in the Virginia Ratifying Convention, although the state legislature had pledged to reimburse delegates' expenses in the event of a second convention.[25] In New York, however, the idea flared up again. As elections for the ratifying convention approached, a number of Anti-Federalists urged a second convention in the interest of correcting the "dangerous errors" in the Constitution.[26] The most substantive argument appeared in a pamphlet under the pseudonym "Plebeian" and bearing the title *Address to the People of the State of New York*. While published two days after Jay's *Address*, it anticipates his arguments so closely that one almost suspects "Plebeian" was working from an advance copy. The suspicion is piqued – if not substantiated – by the "Postscript" added to Plebeian's *Address* just two days after Jay's appeared: quite a remarkable turnaround under the circumstances. Here, "Plebeian" says nothing about Jay's objections to a second convention, having already provided "a satisfactory answer in the preceding remarks."[27]

Just who was "answering" whom was of little concern to Federalist leaders, who quickly seized upon Jay's *Address* and had it widely distributed in New York and elsewhere. Despite the testimony of contemporaries and the judgment of posterity, it probably appeared too late in the process to influence the outcome of the election. In any event, it did not prevent a large Anti-Federalist majority from gathering in Poughkeepsie or dissuade its leaders from attempting to make New York's ratification contingent on a second convention. In the end, the Federalists were required to compromise in order to secure adoption, and then only by a three-vote margin. As part of the agreement, New York would "recommend" a convention in the form of a "circular letter" to its sister states. Ironically, the letter was largely the work of John Jay.[28]

With ratification secured and the Constitution adopted, Jay's *Address*, along with the flood of campaign literature penned during the contest, receded into ephemera. In time, Jay would be identified as a co-author of *The Federalist*, but his minor contribution did little to enhance his reputation as a political writer on a scale with Madison and Hamilton. The distance would only widen in time, in no small part due to the high-profile roles played by Madison and Hamilton in the new government. Jay's role as chief justice was necessarily less conspicuous, while the 1795 treaty he negotiated in England blackened his name with half the nation. He outlived Hamilton by twenty years and matched Madison's longevity, but he neither sought nor received the accolades of a grateful nation. Nor did he, like Jefferson and other fame-conscious founders, take great care to preserve his correspondence and private papers. Finally, Jay's moderate temper, public probity, and personal integrity have given posterity little fodder to generate the controversy and partisanship that has marked the reputations of Jefferson, Hamilton, and (to a lesser degree) Madison.

This said, Jay deserves better. It was largely by accident that he was neither a signer, a framer, nor an equal partner in the *Federalist* project. Any doubt that he could have approached or even matched Madison in depth and range of analysis is belied by his outpouring of correspondence and state papers prior to ratification. Moreover, he had been the principal architect of the "justly celebrated" New York Constitution, which Publius would repeatedly draw upon to illustrate its analogy to the federal Constitution – a boast neither Madison nor Hamilton could make. And though limited in scope and number, Jay's *Federalist* essays are no less cogent or penetrating than those of his collaborators. And it was Jay, no less, who set the lightning pace of three or four papers a week.

An appreciation of these neglected aspects of Jay's contribution to *The Federalist* may serve to place the "lesser Publius" in a greater light, but there has been an additional oversight of even greater significance that has further dimmed his performance. Scholars invariably identify Jay's *Address* as the "most ... effective," the "most successful," and the "most persuasive" appeal among the "blizzard of paper produced in New York about the Constitution,"[29] but have had little more to say about it. This is all the more puzzling in view of the acknowledged praise it received from the likes of Washington, Franklin, and Noah Webster. Whatever influence the *Address* may have had on public opinion, it was a masterpiece of political prose.

Nearly the length of Jay's five *Federalist* essays combined, the *Address* betrays no signs of the haste that periodically marked the efforts of Publius. Nor does it match in dire urgency Jay's earlier productions, although the *Address* is no less solicitous of ratification and union. And if the author is not entirely at ease, neither is he rushed, for the object of the address is the "calm and dispassionate" reflection on the momentous subject at hand. After a sweeping if synoptic account of how the nation arrived at its present crisis – the first half of the address – Jay reveals the work's design: to consider the wisdom of a second convention. His arguments in opposition may have been "unanswerable,"[30] but he appears to have shifted the terms of the debate. Proponents like "Plebeian" viewed a second convention as a forum for making amendments to the Constitution *before its ratification*, yet Jay makes his case against a *de novo* convention should the Constitution be *rejected* – two very different things.

If Jay played fast and loose with the idea of a second convention, he did so with such style and finesse that the distinction was all but lost. Indeed, the *Address* stands out among the productions of the time no less for its felicity of expression than its forceful reasoning. As such, it suggests that Jay's literary gifts were equal, perhaps even superior, to those of Madison and Hamilton. It was also a grand summation of the case for union that surpassed any single *Federalist* paper in scope and grace. As Joseph Ellis has observed, Jay "actually outdid Publius in making the most comprehensive argument for what was at stake, in language that was, even more than that of Publius, simultaneously accessible and lyrical."[31] Yet Jay did not so much outdo Publius – for the *Address* is but an extension of *The Federalist* essays – as crown the work with a command performance.

NOTES

1 Walter Stahr, *John Jay: Founding Father* (New York: Continuum, 2005), 248.

2 In a letter enclosed with volume two of *The Federalist*, Madison informed Jefferson (then residing in Paris) that the papers were the work of "*Jay, Hamilton, and myself. The proposal came from the two former.*" Madison to Jefferson, August 10, 1788, in *PJM*, XI, 227. Three decades later, Madison recalled that "[t]he undertaking was proposed by A. H. (who had probably consulted with Mr. Jay & others) to J. M. who agreed to take part." Madison also revealed that "[t]he papers were originally addressed to the people of N. Y.," but the signature was "changed for that of 'Publius'" since Madison was not a New Yorker and some of the papers had been reprinted in other states. Madison to James K. Paulding, July 23, 1818, in *PJM, Retirement Series*, I, 310.

3 An early biographer is among the few to hint that Jay played a more forward role in the origins of *The Federalist*. "It is not clear whether the suggestion came from Hamilton or from Jay, nor is there any certainty when the design was formed. It is probable that it arose from one of the many conferences of Jay and Hamilton, possibly early in October 1787." Frank Monaghan, *John Jay: Defender of Liberty* (New York: Bobbs-Merrill, 1935), 289.

4 As Robert A. Ferguson writes, this "robbed 'the third Publius' of his authorial due" and served to "cast him in the role of figurehead for the more creative energies and strategies of his younger colleagues." Ferguson's article admirably attempts to restore Jay's "intellectual ascendency in 1787," "by taking the writer himself seriously." "The Forgotten Publius: John Jay and the Aesthetics of Ratification," *Early American Literature*, 34 (1999), 223.

5 Jacob E. Cooke, *Alexander Hamilton* (New York: Charles Scribner's Sons, 1982), 53.

6 Hamilton deployed his expert knowledge of the New York Constitution – "justly celebrated both in Europe and America as one of the best of the forms of government established in this country" (*Fed.* 26, 167) – to full effect in *The Federalist*. It is notable that he concludes the series with an argument based on its analogy to the federal Constitution. "It is remarkable, that the resemblance of the plan of the convention to the act

which organizes the government of this state holds, not less with regard to many of the supposed defects, than to the real excellences of the former. Among the pretended defects are the re-eligibility of the executive, the want of a council, the omission of a formal bill of rights, the omission of a provision respecting liberty of the press: These and several others, which have been noted in the course of our inquiries, are as much chargeable on the existing constitution of this state, as on the one proposed for the Union. And a man must have slender pretensions to consistency, who can rail at the latter for imperfections which he finds no difficulty in excusing in the former" (*Fed.* 85, 587–88).

7 The injury Jay received in the so-called Doctors' Riot proved a source of confusion for his early biographers. George Pellew believed the injury had "interrupted Jay's work on the 'Federalist'" (*John Jay* [Boston, MA: Houghton Mifflin, 1890], 254), while Monaghan claimed Jay "began to write his *Address*" as "soon as he had sufficiently recovered" from his wound (*John Jay*, 291). As noted above, Jay's long hiatus as Publius was aggravated by a serious case of rheumatism which occurred some five months prior to the incident. Moreover, the *Address* was completed before the riot erupted on April 13, and published on April 15, a day after Jay sustained his injury.

8 Stahr, *John Jay*, 254.

9 This has not prevented Hamilton from receiving much of the credit in traditional accounts of the Poughkeepsie Convention, a tradition reinforced by the famous image of the federal ship *Hamilton*, a miniature but fully rigged frigate that figured conspicuously in New York City's celebration of July 23, 1788, when New York State had not yet ratified the Constitution. For a corrective to the "exaggerated role" afforded Hamilton, see Richard B. Morris, "John Jay and the Adoption of the Federal Constitution in New York: A New Reading of Persons and Events," *New York History*, 63 (1982), 133–64.

10 See Linda Grant De Pauw, *The Eleventh Pillar: New York and the Federal Constitution* (Ithaca, NY: Cornell University Press, 1966), and Stephen L. Schechter, ed., *The Reluctant Pillar: New York and the Adoption of the Federal Constitution* (Troy, NY: Russell Sage College, 1985).

11 Professor Morris's scholarship on Jay includes "John Jay and the Radical Chic Elite," in *Seven Who Shaped Our Destiny: The Founding Fathers as Revolutionaries* (New York: Harper & Row, 1973), 150–87; *John Jay, the*

Nation, and the Court (Boston, MA: Boston University Press, 1967); "The Jay Court: An Intimate Portrait," *Journal of Contemporary Law*, 5 (1979), 163–79; *Witness at the Creation: Hamilton, Madison, Jay and the Constitution* (New York: Harper & Row, 1987); and "John Jay and the Constitution," https://dlc.library.columbia.edu/jay/jay_constitution.

12 John P. Kaminski, chief editor of *The Documentary History of the Ratification of the Constitution* (Madison: University of Wisconsin Press, 1976–) is a leading authority on Jay. See his essays, "Honor and Interest: John Jay's Diplomacy during the Confederation," *New York History*, 83 (2002), 293–327; "Shall We Have a King?: John Jay and the Politics of Union," *New York History*, 81 (2000), 31–58; and, with C. Jennifer Lawton, "Duty and Justice at 'Every Man's Door': The Grand Jury Charges of Chief Justice John Jay, 1790–1794," *Journal of Supreme Court History*, 31 (2006), 235–51.

13 The legal historian Herbert A. Johnson has contributed a number of important works on Jay. See *John Jay: A Colonial Lawyer* (New York: Garland, 1989); *John Jay, 1745–1829* (Albany: University of the State of New York, 1970); "John Jay and the Supreme Court," *New York History*, 81 (2000); "John Jay: Lawyer in Time of Transition, 1764–1775," *University of Pennsylvania Law Review*, 124 (1976), 1260–92; and "John Jay: Federalist and Chief Justice," in *Well Begun: Chronicles of the Early National Period*, ed. Stephen L. Schechter and Richard B. Bernstein (Albany: New York State Commission on the Bicentennial of the United States Constitution, 1989), 91–95.

14 Joseph J. Ellis, *The Quartet: Orchestrating the Second American Revolution, 1783–1798* (New York: Alfred A. Knopf, 2015).

15 Under the editorship of Elizabeth M. Nuxoll, the University of Virginia Press has published five of the projected seven volumes of *The Selected Papers of John Jay* (2010–).

16 Adams to James Lloyd, February 6, 1815, quoted in Morris, "John Jay and the Adoption of the Federal Convention in New York," 138.

17 After graduating from King's College (now Columbia), Jay studied for the bar and steadily advanced in the legal profession before he was chosen by the provincial assembly to serve in the first Continental Congress. While just twenty-eight and unknown outside of New York, Jay emerged as a leader of the moderate faction and distinguished himself with the *Address to the People of Great Britain*, an eloquent defense of American rights and

conduct unanimously adopted by Congress. While often at odds with the
more radical delegates, Jay was able to "hold his own with the best
debaters and writers of the colonies." Stahr, *John Jay*, 42.

18 Ibid., 249–50.

19 "In so eloquent a plea," writes Morris, "Jay might be pardoned for
stretching the facts." *Witness at the Creation*, 49.

20 The suspicion that Jay self-consciously walked a fine line between elitism
and populism is suggested by many of the corrections he made to his
Federalist essays. Based on an examination of Jay's drafts – the only ones
that survive – Professor Morris concludes that Jay was not only
"constantly seeking a crisper style," but routinely "deleting evidences of
anti-democratic thought." "John Jay and the Adoption of the Federal
Constitution in New York," 144.

21 As Supreme Court Justice Harry A. Blackmun observed, "Jay knew how to
conclude his essays." "John Jay and the Federalist Papers," *Pace Law
Review*, 8 (1988), 243.

22 There is every reason to "suspect that Jay must have been asked
specifically to write this one." Ibid., 244.

23 See editorial note to the *Address* in DHRC, XX, 922–27.

24 Pauline Maier, *Ratification: The People Debate the Constitution,
1787–1788* (New York: Simon and Schuster, 2010), 45.

25 Ibid., 261, 228.

26 See ibid., 336–39, and DHRC, XXIII, 2501–04.

27 "A Plebeian," *Address to the People of the State of New York*, DHRC, XX,
959. Scholars suspect "Plebeian" was Melancton Smith, an Anti-Federalist
leader who would square off in debate with Jay and Hamilton in
Poughkeepsie, but who ultimately voted for ratification.

28 The revival of the idea of a second convention and New York's "circular
letter" provided an interesting coda to Publius's efforts on behalf of the
Constitution. When the Anti-Federalists proposed to make the state's
ratification conditional on calling a convention to consider amendments,
Hamilton wrote to Madison (now back in New York as a member of
Congress) for his opinion on the matter. Hamilton would read Madison's
reply on the floor of the Convention in order to reinforce Jay's argument
that "conditional" ratification was no ratification at all. Yet when
Madison learned that New York had "recommended" a convention to
consider amendments he was livid. Terrified that a second convention

would "mutilate the system," Madison bemoaned "the most pestilent tendency" of New York's example, particularly in Virginia. His obsession was carried into the First Congress where his hectic efforts to add a bill of rights to the Constitution were largely aimed at forestalling a second convention. Jay would inform Washington that Madison's fears were exaggerated, even in the unlikely event a convention was called. Maier, *Ratification*, 401–03; 425–29; Stahr, *John Jay*, 262–66. According to Morris, "Madison would never quite forgive Jay for proffering as a peace gesture the prospect of another convention, the very idea Jay had himself denounced both in his *Federalist* letters and in his *Address to the People of New York." Witness at the Creation*, 251.

29 E. Wilder Spaulding, *New York in the Critical Period, 1783–1789* (New York: Columbia University Press, 1932), 8; Maier, *Ratification*, 336; Stahr, *John Jay*, 254.

30 In the last *Federalist* essay, Hamilton would pay tribute to Jay's "excellent little pamphlet," and concur with Noah Webster that its arguments against a second convention were "unanswerable" (*Fed.* 85, 591).

31 Ellis, *The Quartet*, 188.

3 "A Vigorous National Government": Hamilton on Security, War, and Revenue

Max M. Edling

Alexander Hamilton's essays in *The Federalist* on the need for an energetic central government have long stood in the shadow of James Madison's essays on interest-group conflicts, the structure of government, the perils of majority rule, and the protection of minority rights. This privileging of Madison over Hamilton in the interpretation of both *The Federalist* and, by extension, the founding began more than a century ago, when Charles Beard presented *Federalist* 10 as the essence of Federalist political philosophy. In his *Economic Interpretation of the Constitution*, Beard even claimed that his own view of the Constitution as the outcome of clashing economic interest groups, ultimately rooted in "the various and unequal distribution of property," was "based upon the political science of James Madison."[1] The central thrust of Madison's intervention, *The Federalist*, and the Constitution, Beard said, was to promote material gain by providing greater safeguards for private property rights.

Many scholars rejected Beard's economic interpretation but nevertheless accepted his hypothesis that the primary aim of the Constitution was to check the "excess of democracy" running rampant in the state legislatures after the American Revolution. Where they disagreed with Beard was over his uncritical endorsement of majoritianism. To these scholars, it seemed essential that a stable liberal democracy had to protect minority rights by introducing institutional mechanisms of checks and balances that could prevent temporary populist passions from being translated into oppressive policies.[2] Madison's concerns with majority faction, the extended republic, and minority rights all speak precisely to this issue and so the perception remained that *Federalist* 10 was the core exposition of the political principles informing the Constitution. Consensus has long reigned that the Constitution is best interpreted as a means to impose limits on government in order to temper socio-economic conflict among domestic interest groups.

In the last few decades this view of the Constitution's origins has been significantly challenged, as historians and political scientists have come to analyze the American founding through the combined perspective of federalism and international relations rather than social conflict and minority rights. Peter Onuf and David Armitage have written about the international and global history of the Declaration of Independence. David Golove and Daniel Hulsebosch have interpreted the Constitution as "a fundamentally international document": not a counter-revolutionary negation of the promise of the Declaration, but a continuation of its attempt to secure international recognition of the fledgling United States. Eliga Gould has explained how the founders' main concern was to make the United States a "treaty worthy" nation that could be trusted to uphold international agreements, thus gaining acceptance by "the powers of the world." Robbie Totten has argued that the Constitution was the solution to the two-sided problem of how to work out the relationship between the thirteen new American state-republics, on the one hand, and their collective relationship to foreign powers, on the other. Leonard Sadosky has shown that in addition to establishing a framework for relations with the European states and empires, the new nation had to come to terms with its American Indian neighbors to secure the promises of independence. Similarly, Gregory Ablavsky has interpreted the Constitution in part as a response to the need to deal with the obstruction to territorial expansion by the "savage" nations inhabiting the United States' borderlands.[3]

Central to this shift in perspective is the recognition that the Declaration of Independence and the Articles of Confederation created the United States as both a sovereign nation in the international system of states and as a union among thirteen republics that transferred part of their powers to a common central government but retained the right to govern most of their internal affairs. In its incorporation as a sovereign nation, the United States faced the problems of securing international recognition by other nations in the international state system and of defending its territorial integrity and commercial interests against competitors. In its incorporation as a union, the United States faced the problem of creating a North American interstate regime that guaranteed the security of the member states and thereby ensured that they would continue as popular republics. To address these problems, the new polity created governmental institutions. The Confederation Congress was thus designed to be both a council for peaceful conflict resolution among the state republics that formed the American union and a government that could represent the American nation in the international arena.

The Philadelphia Convention presented the substitution of the Constitution for the Articles of Confederation as an act of popular sovereignty. It was the people, whose will was expressed in the ratifying conventions of their respective states, not the state governments, which adopted the Constitution. The renewed American union was thereby founded on a popular grant of power. The Constitution also erected a national government capable of acting independently of the states. But the rationale behind union did not change. Nor was the Constitution intended to deprive the states of the authority to order their domestic affairs as they saw fit. The polity that came out of the Founding was a complex construct in both conceptual and institutional terms, and latter-day interpreters have struggled with how to best characterize this new political organization. Part of its complexity is captured by David Hendrickson's description of the United States as "an American system of states inside a larger [international] system of states," at the same time a union and a nation. An equally vital aspect is captured by Michael Zuckert's description of the United States as a "compound system" containing "two sets of governments ruling over the same population and territory, dividing up the objects of concern between them with each set of governments possessing perfectly self-contained instrumentalities for effectuating its objectives without the involvement of the other set."

Institutionally separate, the state and the federal governments had different roles to fulfill. The "objects of concern" of the federal government were the management of foreign affairs, including international commerce and relations with Indian nations within the national domain; the administration of the federal territories in the trans-Appalachian West; and the regulation of intra-union relations between the member states. Other governmental concerns were left to the states.[4]

The shift in the study of the founding toward a "unionist paradigm" or "federalist interpretation" makes it possible to take a fresh look at *The Federalist* to emphasize themes presented in some of the essays that have been overshadowed by the predominant emphasis on Madison's *Federalist* 10 and 51. Almost the entire first half of *The Federalist* focused on the questions of how the United States would be able to maintain its independence against the threats of predatory European great powers and promote its interests in the Atlantic marketplace and the western borderlands. Central to this ability was the creation of a greater military and fiscal capacity in the central government than what existed under the Articles of Confederation. But in order to develop such capacity it was necessary to reform the federal union.

A careful reading establishes the overwhelming concern with security in *The Federalist*, and with the importance of the military and fiscal powers needed to achieve it. After Hamilton's opening essay, the next nine explain how the Constitution will provide effective protection against security threats arising from international war (*Fed.* 2–5), civil war (*Fed.* 6–8), and domestic insurrection (*Fed.* 9–10). The three essays then following show how the adoption of the Constitution and the creation of a national government would improve commerce, increase government revenue, and save on the cost of government. Madison's *Federalist* 14, a defense of the viability of the geographically extended republic, rounded off the first part of the work, which aimed to demonstrate the benefit of the American Union to the states and their citizens (*Fed.* 1, 6). The second part of *The*

Federalist, essays 15 to 22, investigates the deficiencies of the Articles of Confederation. Here, too, security, commerce, and international recognition loom large in the analysis. With *Federalist* 23, Hamilton begins the third part of the work, a series of fifteen essays dealing with the military and fiscal powers of the proposed national government. This part of the work demonstrates the necessity of an energetic central government to the preservation of the Union. It is highly revealing that Hamilton discusses only the proposed fiscal–military powers here. In the final essay of this third part of *The Federalist*, he merely notes that "I have passed over in silence those minor authorities which are either too inconsiderable to have been thought worthy of the hostilities of the opponents of the Constitution, or of too manifest propriety to admit of controversy" (*Fed.* 29).[5]

There is no deep mystery why these themes feature so prominently in Hamilton's thinking and in the pages of *The Federalist*. All too often scholars have confused the original American Union with the modern federal government. *The Federalist* was an argument for a reformed federal union. Although the modern federal government ranges very broadly, the original union had a limited and clearly defined remit. "The principal purposes to be answered by Union are these," Hamilton explained in *Federalist* 23: "The common defence of the members – the preservation of the public peace as well against internal convulsions as external attacks – the regulation of commerce with other nations and between the States – the superintendence of our intercourse, political and commercial, with foreign countries" (*Fed.* 23, 147). Much of what the federal government does today was the sole concern of the states in the early national period.

Once the significance of these themes of union and international relations in *The Federalist* is established – and consequently the role of the central government's military and fiscal capacity in realizing the benefits of Union by the joint management of the member states' international relations – it becomes difficult to justify the neglect that Hamilton's writings on these topics have suffered for so long. This neglect distorts our understanding not only of *The*

Federalist but, much more important, of a main rationale behind the creation of the Constitution and some of its main consequences. When the framers' intentions are interpreted through a Madisonian lens, it is hard not to conclude that the Constitution fell considerably short of their aspirations. In particular, a key element of the Madisonian vision, i.e. constitutional protection of national individual rights from overbearing legislative majorities in the states, had to await the adoption of the Fourteenth Amendment after the Civil War and the development of the incorporation doctrine in the twentieth century. In fact, it was only when the Supreme Court began to actively strike down southern laws of discrimination after the Second World War that the Madison vision was fully realized in the United States.

Interpreted through Hamiltonian eyes, the record of the Constitutional Convention looks much more successful. To Hamilton, the Constitution was the means to create a government that could act with energy and "vigour", a favourite word of his, on the international scene where the most pressing threats to the survival and success of the American federal union arose from foreign competitors on the Atlantic Ocean and in the continental interior. What Hamilton envisioned for the new nation in fact came to pass quite soon after the ratification of the Constitution. Under his leadership as secretary of the Treasury, the federal government put its financial house in pristine order, and on that basis could begin to build a small army and, later, a small navy. From modest beginnings, the federal government grew in power, and already by the mid-1790s it had managed to score considerable diplomatic successes in agreements with Britain and Spain and was making fast progress in subjecting Native American nations and confederacies, thereby opening the western borderlands to European American settlement.

I

In *Federalist* 3, John Jay notes that "[a]mong the many objects to which a wise and free people find it necessary to direct their attention, that of providing for their *safety* seems to be the first" (*Fed.* 3, 13–14).

The Constitution has been insightfully described as "the solution to two diplomatic crises, that amongst the units (states and regions) of the Confederation and that amongst the units of the Confederation with foreign powers."[6] In other words, the "more perfect Union" promised by the adoption of the Constitution would allow Americans to deal effectively with security threats in the form of both international and civil war. In addition to these two threats, the Constitution also promised protection against a third security concern, which sprang from "domestic faction and insurrection" (*Fed.* 9, 50). A modern reader has no difficulty understanding how political union, just like a military alliance, can better position a state to deal with external threats. But the other two security threats challenge modern conceptions of American politics. It is far from obvious why, in 1787, Pennsylvania had cause to fear an attack from Virginia, or why Massachusetts had reason to fear domestic insurrection. Yet to Publius these were real concerns and union was their solution.

The *Federalist* presented its audience, the "citizens of New York," with the stark choice of accepting the Constitution or facing the consequences of disunion when the United States disintegrated into thirteen sovereign states or, more likely, into two or more regional confederacies. According to this logic, Publius smeared the critics of the Constitution as "Anti-Federalists," or advocates of disunion (*Fed.* 2, 8). It mattered little that few, if any, Anti-Federalists supported either disunion or regional confederacies. To no avail one critic called the argument of *The Federalist* a "hobgoblin" created by "the deranged brain of *Publius.*"[7] The rhetorical strategy of Publius effectively foreclosed any discussion of more limited reforms of the Articles of Confederation, which was the Anti-Federalists' real aim. The strategy also drew attention away from the fact that the Philadelphia Convention had overstepped its mandate by proposing a completely new compact of union rather than merely amendments to the Articles. With great consistency, throughout *The Federalist*, Publius juxtaposed the blessings of Union with the dangerous consequences of disunion.

With the Declaration of Independence, the colonies claimed a place among the European "family of civilized nations" and thus the power to do all "Acts and Things which Independent States may of right do." To the Declaration's contemporaries, what an independent state "may of right do," and how it was expected to interact with other independent states, was stipulated by the law of nations. A nebulous body of doctrine grounded in the abstract theories of natural law, it found expression in early modern legal treatises and in bi- and multilateral international agreements, such as the Peace Treaty of 1783 that recognized the United States as a sovereign nation.[8] For this reason, *The Federalist*'s analysis of security threats arising from international war, the topic of essays 2–5, took the form of a discussion of "just" and "unjust wars." Encroachments on the law of nations gave cause for just war and Jay argued that a united America would be able to prevent the states and their citizens from committing such violations. The states already had a proven record of sidestepping the rights of Loyalists and British creditors that had been guaranteed by the Treaty of Paris. Meanwhile, on the frontier, white settlers, acting alone or in collusion with their state governments, had frequently violated the occupancy rights of Native Americans. By monopolizing diplomatic power and by creating the ability to police states and citizens, the federal government would be in a much better position than "thirteen separate States" or "three or four distinct confederacies" to minimize the causes for just war (*Fed.* 3, 14–15).

The law of nations represented an attempt to regulate the inherently anarchic international system of interest-maximizing states. But without a police force to hold offenders to account, conflicts of interest between states were often settled by international war. This unprincipled pursuit of self-interest was the source of unjust, as opposed to just, wars. According to Jay, there was tension in the American Union's relationship to European powers over both North American territory and international commerce. Union made possible the projection of military power and the creation of effective commercial regulations that would protect American interests and prevent

foreign aggression. "If they see that our national government is efficient and well administered – our trade prudently regulated – our
militia properly organized and disciplined, our resources and finances
discreetly managed – our credit re-established – our people free, contented, and united," Jay explained, "they will be much more disposed
to cultivate our friendship, than provoke our resentment" (*Fed.* 4, 22).

Historians of the founding have long tended to make light of
security concerns because they see the long period from 1783 to 1941
as an age of free security. But this view rests on a failure to appreciate
that the greatest security risk to the American Union came not from
the outside but from within. Despite the Civil War and the intermit-
tent sectional crises that preceded it, scholars find it difficult to accept
just how fragile the American Union was. All too often the national
identity, and by extension the national existence, of the United States
has been taken for granted, as if the nation emerged fully formed out
of the Declaration of Independence at the stroke of Jefferson's pen. But
as Hendrickson has recently forcefully reminded us,

> the sense of common nationality was more a consequence of
> mutual entanglement and exiguous necessity than a sense of
> common peoplehood. At the beginning, in 1776, Americans
> constituted not a body politic but an association of bodies politic,
> readily recognizable to eighteenth-century taxonomists of political
> forms as a "league of firm friendship," a "*république fédérative*," or
> as a "system of states."

The Articles of Confederation bound the independent American
states together in "a firm league of friendship." But the American
Union nevertheless remained "a system in which the danger of war
lurked in the background as a potential way in which state and
sectional differences could get resolved."[9]

Civil war was presented as a pressing reality rather than a
distant possibility by Publius. Hamilton, who authored the essays
on interstate war, rested his case that disunion would inevitably be
followed by war on a passage from Abbé de Mably's *Des principes*

des négociations, to the effect that "NEIGHBOURING NATIONS ... are naturally ENEMIES of each other" (*Fed.* 6, 35). In the American context, this argument ran counter to a version of what is now known as the "democratic peace theory," but which eighteenth-century writers, had they settled on a technical term, would have thought of as the "commercial republican peace theory." Thinkers such as Thomas Paine and the Baron de Montesquieu had popularized the idea that a state's tendency to go to war depended on its regime type. Whereas monarchies were war-prone, republics were inherently peaceful. Commerce, which fostered increased interaction between nations, was also conducive to peace. Montesquieu believed that "[t]he natural effect of commerce is to lead to peace. Two nations that trade with each other become reciprocally dependent; if one has an interest in buying, the other has an interest in selling, and all unions are founded on mutual needs."[10] In other words, disunion might not lead to war if only the American states remained commercial republics.[11]

Faced with this line of argument, Hamilton pointed out that history disproved the thesis that commercial republics were more peaceful than other regime types. Republics were in fact as "addicted to war" as monarchies, and the growth of commerce had done no more than "change the objects of war." From the middle of the seventeenth century, few nations had been engaged in more wars than the world's principal trading nations, the Dutch republic and Britain, including the four wars they fought against each other. Frequently aimed at commercial advantage, these wars had more often than not found popular support (*Fed.* 6, 31–32). Based on this observation, there was no reason to think that the disunited states of America would be spared competition and war. "To look for a continuation of harmony between a number of independent unconnected sovereignties, situated in the same neighborhood, would be to disregard the uniform course of human events, and to set at defiance the accumulated experience of ages," Hamilton tersely noted (*Fed.* 6, 28).

Numerous instances of conflicts of interest between the states had in fact already appeared in the short period that had passed since independence. Landed and landless states contended over the future of the trans-Appalachian territories. Pennsylvania and Connecticut had been engaged in border disputes in the Wyoming Valley, as had the government of New York and settlers from New England, supported by their home states, in Vermont. In a future state of disunion, competition over commerce was certain to be a "fruitful source of contention" when states with busy ports made less fortunate neighbors "tributary to them." Yet another source of conflict was the public debt that had been contracted to fight the War of Independence. "The apportionment, in the first instance, and the progressive extinguishment, afterwards, would be alike productive of ill humour and animosity." Hamilton ended his list of potential conflicts between the states with the violation of private contracts between citizens of different states (*Fed.* 7, 39–41; see also *Fed.* 5, 23–27).

If history demonstrated the universality of interstate conflicts of interest, it also demonstrated that such conflicts sooner or later escalated into interstate war. Publius further argued that frequent war would lead to the downfall of republican rule. In America, a war between the states would be attended with greater horrors than in Europe. In contrast to Europe, there were no "disciplined armies" or fortifications in the American states that would confine military operations to border regions. Instead, open and defenseless borders would make conquest and plunder the norm in American warfare. When the people tired of their exposed situation they would follow in the footsteps of the peoples of Europe and accept the need to maintain standing armies and other military preparations in time of peace. As Hamilton said,

> [t]he violent destruction of life and property incident to war – the continual effort and alarm attendant of a state of continual danger, will compel nations the most attached to liberty, to resort for repose and security, to institutions, which have a tendency to destroy their civil and political rights. To be more safe they, at length, become willing to run the risk of being less free.
>
> (*Fed.* 8, 44–45)

Early modern political theorists believed that war led to government expansion and the centralization of power. Hamilton shared this view, noting that "[i]t is of the nature of war to increase the executive at the expence of the legislative authority" (*Fed.* 8, 46).

It is necessary to pause briefly at this stage in Publius's argument because today most Americans believe that a strong military capability is a precondition for, rather than a threat to, the preservation of their system of government and the defense of their liberties. The authors of *The Federalist* nowhere fully spell out the precise reasons why military might is incompatible with republican rule. But Publius's views on this matter were far from original and can be inferred from *The Federalist* and other contemporary statements. In part, the reason was that war, as Hamilton observed, strengthened the executive. This point was developed more fully by the Anti-Federalists, who criticized the Constitution's failure to prohibit standing armies in peacetime. Doing so, they drew on the rich anti-army argument of the British Country Whig tradition, which claimed that, if given half a chance, the executive would not hesitate to implement narrow, self-serving policies at the point of a bayonet. But war and freedom were also held to be incompatible because frequent wars and their attendant preparations impoverished the people. Wars and armies undermined the material position of economically independent, property-owning citizens, who constituted the necessary backbone of the republic and whose welfare was its reason for being. Military preparations were seen as part of an entangled complex that also contained growing taxes and an increasing public debt. Together they formed what one perceptive historian has called "a trinity of evils." "Of all the enemies to public liberty war is, perhaps, the most to be dreaded because it comprises and develops the germ of every other," Madison wrote a few years after the Constitution had been adopted. "War is the parent of armies; from these proceed debts and taxes; and armies, debts, and taxes are the known instruments for bringing the many under the dominance of the few."[12]

The authors of *The Federalist* come closest to explaining the threat from the "trinity of evils" in their repeated calls to Americans to beware the fate of Europe. In *Federalist* 8, Hamilton repeated a common claim that Britons had retained their freedom because their island kingdom did not need to fear an invasion and consequently had no cause to keep up a large standing army. "If, on the contrary, Britain had been situated on the continent, and had been compelled, as she would have been, by that situation, to make her military establishments at home co-extensive with those of the other great powers of Europe, she, like them, would in all probability, be at this day a victim to the absolute power of a single man" (*Fed.* 8, 49). But as Jay had pointed out in *Federalist* 5, the internal peace of Britain was in fact a relative novelty. In the past, the island had frequently been rent asunder by wars between its different kingdoms. The union between England and Scotland in 1707 changed this and ushered in an island-wide Pax Britannica. Both Hamilton and Jay made the point that the American states could repeat British history if they had the sense to stay united. Madison picked up this theme in *Federalist* 41. In a dramatic passage he argued that disunion would herald "a new order of things." From the moment of disunion "the face of America will be but a copy of that of the Continent of Europe. It will present liberty every where crushed between standing armies and perpetual taxes" (*Fed.* 41, 272).

According to *The Federalist*, union offered the best protection from international and civil war. But the "utility of a confederacy" also served "to suppress faction and to guard the internal tranquility of States" (*Fed.* 9, 52), the third security threat identified by Publius. Hamilton made this case in *Federalist* 9 and Madison developed it further in the following essay. Despite the manifold uses to which *Federalist* 10 has been put by scholars, this was the essay's original context of origin. It was widely accepted among early modern political writers that republics were inherently unstable forms of government subject to domestic faction and turbulence, which frequently fell victim to unrest and rebellions leading to regime change (*Fed.* 9, 50–52). Protection from such a destiny was of central importance to the long-term success of the American republics.

Hamilton argued that modern developments of statecraft had come a long way to counter this particular threat to the security and stability of republics. He listed the distribution of power between government branches, checks and balances in the legislature, an independent judiciary, and representative government as some of the "powerful means, by which the excellencies of republican government may be retained and its imperfections lessened or avoided." To these well-known changes to the structure of republican government Hamilton added the new idea that "the ENLARGEMENT of the ORBIT" of the republic or confederacy could bring stability (*Fed.* 9, 52). Madison of course took this idea further in *Federalist* 10, which served to demonstrate how domestic factions and ensuing insurrections were less likely to appear in the extended republic than in the geographically confined polity idolized by the Anti-Federalists.

Despite such institutional precautions, insurrections would inevitably happen, and union was the best means to contain the damage. The Constitution guaranteed to "every State in this Union a Republican Form of Government, and shall protect each of them against Invasion; and on Application of the Legislature, or of the Executive (when the Legislature cannot be convened), against domestic Violence."[13] Historians frequently read this clause as an anti-democratic measure that allowed for the military suppression of popular protests. But to the authors of *The Federalist* it was foremost a security measure. Madison went to great lengths to demonstrate that factions were contrary to the common good and therefore a danger to the republic. Knowing well the reverence with which his opponents read *The Spirit of the Laws*, Hamilton no doubt enjoyed citing Montesquieu's words about the role of confederation in securing the domestic tranquility of the member states. "Should a popular insurrection happen, in one of the confederate States, the others are able to quell it," Montesquieu had written. "Should abuses creep into one part, they are reformed by those that remain sound" (*Fed.* 9, 54).[14]

Although the guarantee to uphold republican government in the states may seem to concern solely the domestic arrangement of the member states, it also had a bearing on interstate security and the danger of civil war. Montesquieu had explained that confederations should consist of states of similar regime type. It was impossible for republics and monarchies to coexist in a stable confederacy. "The spirit of monarchy is war and expansion; the spirit of republics is peace and moderation. The only way these two sorts of government can continue together in one federal republic is by force." Referring to the ancient Greek Amphictyonic League, Montesquieu warned that in "Greece all was lost when the Macedonian kings gained a place among the Amphictiones."[15]

II

In the third part of *The Federalist* Hamilton discussed the institutions and policies needed to meet the security threats facing the American states in an effective manner. Here he favored centralizing virtually unlimited powers over the military and fiscal policy in Congress. To Hamilton, the competitive nature of the Atlantic world and the strength of European "fiscal–military states," but also Americans' own ambitions, left no doubt that these powers were necessary. He believed that under the Articles of Confederation the Union suffered from fundamental structural flaws that could not be repaired by mere amendments but demanded complete overhaul of the Articles. Yet despite the call for a stronger central government with virtually unlimited powers in certain defined areas, Hamilton never envisioned the bloated and intrusive state that his Anti-Federalist opponents feared. The demands of the federal government on citizens would be kept to a minimum. To the people, the reform of the Union would therefore result in reduced burdens of taxation and military service. It is also clear that Hamilton believed that the federal government would be much smaller than contemporary central governments in the Old World. Indeed, union was held out to be the best means to avoid the growing armies, taxes, and debts that crushed the European peoples under the burdens of government and the surest way to keep

American government at both federal and state level lean. The ideas about American federalism and modern statecraft that Hamilton presented in *Federalist* 23–36 take on particular importance because they served in many ways as a blueprint for the governmental institutions and policies that the Federalists launched after the first federal Congress met in the spring of 1789.

The most striking premise of Hamilton's argument was his conviction that wars would be a recurrent feature in the national life of the United States (*Fed.* 30, 193). History showed that "the fiery and destructive passions of war" dominated over peaceful dispositions in mankind and that "to model our political systems upon speculations of lasting tranquility" would be "to calculate on the weaker springs of the human character" (*Fed.* 34, 212). Mostly, wars would arise from external aggression. The United States was a weak and peripheral power in a hostile trans-Atlantic state system, where predator nations were always ready to take advantage of nations that appeared "naked and defenceless" (*Fed.* 25, 161). But Hamilton conceded that war might also spring from the nation's own ambitions. If the United States meant to continue as "a commercial people, it must form part of our policy, to be able one day to defend that commerce." This meant building a navy and engaging in naval wars (*Fed.* 34, 211).

Hamilton's keen understanding of modern war and statecraft is revealed in his stress on finance rather than the military as the key factor determining state power. In April 1781, Hamilton had written to the newly appointed superintendent of finance, Robert Morris, that independence would be secured "not by gaining battles" but "by restoreing [sic] the public credit."[16] Six years later, his views had not changed. Wars, troops, and naval vessels were prohibitively expensive and by far the most important reason why governments had to possess adequate fiscal powers (*Fed.* 34, 211–12; *Fed.* 30, 187–88). Although he did not present a detailed plan for financing future contingencies in the pages of *The Federalist*, Hamilton made clear that public credit would be instrumental. "In the modern system of war," he said, "nations the most wealthy are obliged to have recourse to large loans." Ever since

Hamilton first began to think seriously about public finance, he had treated public credit as a crucial resource of the modern state, of "immense importance" to "the strength and security of nations." A state able to borrow money could mobilize resources far beyond what its tax base alone allowed. A state unable to borrow, in contrast, would be left to the mercy of stronger states (*Fed.* 30, 192).[17]

Public credit also allowed governments to raise money in ways that were less painful to the people and less disruptive of the economy than alternative means of resource mobilization. In modern wars, Hamilton wrote in one of his Treasury reports, "the current revenues of a nation do not ... suffice. Plunder or Credit must supply the deficiency." Since the first alternative was clearly unacceptable and entailed "a subversion of all social order," credit was the only option.[18] This did not mean that taxes were unimportant. To the contrary, because an adequate system of taxation was a prerequisite for borrowing, the transfer of fiscal powers from the states to Congress was critical. As Hamilton explained, the "power of creating new funds upon new objects of taxation by its own authority, would enable the national government to borrow, as far as its necessities might require" (*Fed.* 30, 192–93). But when lenders had "to depend upon a government, that must itself depend upon thirteen other governments for the means of fulfilling its contracts" they would hesitate to offer their money to Congress (*Fed.* 30, 193).

The cost of war and the need to maintain public credit required virtually unlimited fiscal powers in the national government. In his discussion of both the military and taxation, Hamilton again and again returned to the fundamental maxim that a government's means had to be commensurate to its ends. The power needed to care for the Union's defense ought to exist without limitation

> *Because it is impossible to foresee or define the extent and variety of national exigencies, or the correspondent extent & variety of the means which may be necessary to satisfy them.* The circumstances that endanger the safety of nations are infinite; and for this reason no constitutional shackles can wisely be imposed on the power to which the care of it is committed. (*Fed.* 23, 147)

The most forceful statement of this logic is found in *Federalist* 31. Hamilton's starting point was the familiar idea that a "government ought to contain in itself every power requisite to the full accomplishment of the objects committed to its care." The Articles of Confederation gave to the national government the duty to protect the nation from external aggression and to preserve the public peace against domestic violence. This duty involved expenditures "to which no possible limits can be assigned," and therefore the ability to meet them "ought to know no other bounds than the exigencies of the nation and the resources of the community." Because revenue was "the essential engine" that would allow the government to respond to the exigencies of the nation, its power over taxation had to be without limits. Consequently, a change in the organization of the federal union was necessary. Both theory and practice demonstrated that "the power of procuring revenue is unavailing, when exercised over the States in their collective capacities" and it followed that "the Federal government must of necessity be invested with an unqualified power of taxation in the ordinary modes" (*Fed.* 31, 195–96).

An important part of Hamilton's defense of the Constitution's fiscal clauses therefore rested on the inefficiency of the requisitions system under the Articles of Confederation, which forced Congress to apply to the states for the payment of common expenses. Requisitions were an "*ignis fatuus* in finance," a will-o'-the-wisp without substance or reality, which had offered "ample cause, both of mortification to ourselves, and of triumph to our enemies" (*Fed.* 30, 189). The problem was structural and therefore the solution had to be, too. "The great and radical vice in the construction of the existing Confederation is in the principle of LEGISLATION for STATES or GOVERNMENTS, in their CORPORATE or COLLECTIVE CAPACITIES and as contradistinguished from the INDIVIDUALS of whom they consist." This vice could only be overcome by investing the national government with an unlimited power to tax individuals without interference by the states (*Fed.* 15, 93).

Hamilton presented a parallel argument about the need to trust Congress with the power to determine defensive preparations. "[I]f we are in earnest about giving the Union energy and duration, we must abandon the vain project of legislating upon the States in their collective capacities," he wrote in *Federalist* 23. "We must discard the fallacious scheme of quotas and requisitions, as equally impractical and unjust" (*Fed.* 23, 148). In the previous essay, he had criticized the quota system used during the War of Independence when states had outbid each other for recruits and potential enlistees had waited for increased compensation "till bounties grew to an enormous and insupportable size." Insufficient numbers of recruits had come forward to serve in the army, leading to "oppressive expedients for raising men." Quotas also distributed the burden of war unfairly between the states. States close to the theaters of war had contributed much, others little. Hamilton therefore dismissed the method for raising men and money under the Articles of Confederation as "a system of imbecility in the union, and of inequality and injustice among the members" (*Fed.* 22, 138). The remedy was to invest Congress "with full power to levy troops; to build and equip fleets, and to raise the revenues, which will be required for the formation and support of an army and navy, in the customary and ordinary modes practiced in other governments" (*Fed.* 23, 148–49).

Anti-Federalists did not object to the creation of a professional army in the event of war, but they did oppose standing armies in time of peace. Although it might have made better sense to leave this issue alone, Hamilton attempted a full vindication of the need for unfettered federal power over the military also in peacetime. First, he pointed out that, true to the British tradition, the Constitution vested control over the army in the legislature. Whereas the Anti-Federalists denied that Congress could ever properly represent the American people, Hamilton did not agree. Like Madison he believed that the federal legislature would attract better men than the state assemblies and that the power over the army could be safely left in their hands (*Fed.* 26, 164–65; *Fed.* 23, 150–51). Second, Hamilton pointed to security concerns that made any restriction on peacetime troops dangerous. Britain and Spain possessed colonies north and south of the United States that could be easily supported from across the ocean. Perhaps the most serious concern was what Hamilton called the "savage tribes on our western frontier," the "natural enemies" of the United States and the "natural allies" of Britain and Spain. The reach of European maritime powers and the "ravages and depredations of the Indians" called for "small garrisons" on the Atlantic seaboard and the western frontier. In the West in particular "[t]here are and will be particular posts the possession of which will include the command of large districts of territory and facilitate future invasions of the remainder" (*Fed.* 24, 156–57). In *Federalist* 28, Hamilton also defended the use of military force against "seditions and insurrections" within the states, an argument that hardly won him any converts, except possibly in the slaveholding south (*Fed.* 28, 176).

III

The Federalist nowhere offers a detailed plan for the United States peace establishment. Alarmed Anti-Federalists claimed that the friends of the Constitution contemplated an army of 100,000 or even 200,000 men, representing an extreme level of militarization relative to the American population of less than four million people.[19] Hamilton and Madison had both been members of a congressional committee to consider the future of the army after the War of Independence. When that committee presented its proposal in 1783, Congress ignored it. But after the Constitution was ratified, the committee's plans would be gradually realized in the 1790s. There is no reason to think that Publius's ideas about defense deviated significantly from that of the 1783 committee on the peace establishment.

Hamilton, who drew up the committee's report, was well aware that neither public opinion nor the public finances allowed for a large peacetime army. Hence he suggested that Congress establish a small force of about 3,000 men. Part of the force would be made up of a corps of engineers, to which would be attached instructors in mathematics, chemistry, natural philosophy, and civil architecture. The peace establishment had two major functions. The first was to police the western frontier in order to contain Britain and Spain and to preserve peace with the Indian nations. The other was to ensure the future military capability of the United States by preserving the skills and traditions of the Continental Army and by training future officers in the military sciences. Organized as a "skeleton" force designed for rapid expansion, the army could quickly transition to a wartime footing. With twice the number of officers and companies of wartime regiments, it would be possible to double the manpower without the need for reorganization. Hamilton also proposed that the regular army be complemented by a select reserve of part-time volunteer soldiers.[20]

The 1783 committee faced the same principled aversion to a standing army that Publius did in 1787–1788. The American political creed held that the only proper defensive force of a republic was the militia, an organization in which every white male between the ages of sixteen and forty-five was required to serve. Like most officers in the Continental Army, Hamilton believed that the War of Independence had conclusively demonstrated that the militia was unable to combat trained regulars. The notion that the militia was the "natural bulwark" of the republic, he wrote in *Federalist* 25, "had like to have cost us our independence. It cost millions to the United States, that might have been saved." Hamilton never doubted that "[t]he steady operation of war against a disciplined army can only be successfully conducted by a force of the same kind" (*Fed.* 25, 161–62).

Hamilton's conviction that "[w]ar, like most other things, is a science to be acquired and perfected by diligence, by perseverance, by time, and by practice" represents an endorsement of military professionalism that was influenced by the luminaries of the Scottish Enlightenment (*Federalist* 25, 162). To these thinkers, who made social progress their core concern, governments could only function if they were in harmony with the wider society. The militia became an important issue to Scottish eighteenth-century social theorists for, while it seemed an institution that fostered civic virtue, it was hopelessly at odds with modern societies characterized by commerce and manufacturing. Smith's *Wealth of Nations* explained how the division of labor, the defining feature of modern society, had now made the citizen-soldier of the ancient republics an anomaly. When the workforce was employed in manufactures, a laborer who quit his workplace to take up arms in defense of his country would find his income "completely dried up." The rapid development of the modern military profession also made it "necessary that it should become the sole or principal occupation of a particular class of citizens, and the division of labour is as necessary for the improvement of this as of every other art." A government could counteract the division of labor either by forcing its subjects to undertake extensive military training, or it could employ "a certain number of citizens in the continual practice of military exercises," thereby rendering "the trade of a soldier a particular trade, separate and distinct from all others."[21]

Hamilton fully embraced Smith's notion of modernity and the division of labor. Any policy "contrary to the natural and experienced course of human affairs, defeats itself." Singularly unimpressed by the ancient republics, he summarily dismissed those who held them up as models for modern America as men "who hope to see realized in America, the halcyon scenes of the poetic or fabulous age" (*Fed.* 30, 193). Already in his *Continentalist* letters from the early 1780s, Hamilton had complained about the tendency among American politicians to turn to ancient Greece rather than modern Europe for models. It was vain to think that the American polity could be built on civic virtue and selfless service to the public good. This ran counter to the instincts of modern man. American citizens would no sooner reconcile themselves to disinterested civic duties than they would

> to the Spartan community of goods and wives, to their iron coin, their long beards or their black broth. There is a total dissimulation in the circumstances as well as the manner of society among us, and it is as ridiculous to seek for models in the simple ages of Greece and Rome, as it would be to go in quest for them among the Hottentots and Laplanders.[22]

In America "the industrious habits of the people of the present day, absorbed in the pursuits of gain," were "devoted to the improvements of agriculture and commerce" (*Fed.* 8, 47). If militiamen were employed to do the job of regular soldiers there would be aggregate economic losses to society. Even if they could be prevailed upon to garrison the western posts, "the increased expence of a frequent rotation of service, and the loss of labor and disconcertion of the industrious pursuits of individuals, would form conclusive objections to the scheme." Similarly, the time taken to train the citizens to become adequate soldiers would amount to a serious "annual deduction from the productive labour of the country." And to "attempt a thing which would abridge the mass of labour and industry to so considerable an extent would be unwise." In short, depending on the militia for peacetime defense "would be as burthensome and injurious to the public, as ruinous to private citizens" (*Fed.* 24, 156; *Fed.* 29, 184).

In his approach to taxation, too, Hamilton argued that the best regime was one that respected the traditions of society and imposed the least possible burden on the citizenry. If the demand for unfettered fiscal powers was part of a warning against the dangers of a weak union, Hamilton was also keen to point out that the new system promised to reduce the tax burden on the people. This promise was made in the context of eighteenth-century ideas of taxation and political economy and the common distinction between direct and indirect taxes. The former fell on property, chiefly land, and persons, through so-called poll or capitation taxes. The latter were duties on trade, either internal duties, or excises, on the production, retail sale, and possession of goods, or external duties on exports, imports, and tonnage. In the postwar period, state governments had relied mostly on direct property taxes to raise revenue. It had not been a happy experience. "Tax laws have in vain been multiplied," Hamilton noted, "new methods to enforce the collection have in vain been tried – the public expectation has been uniformly disappointed, and the treasuries of the States have remained empty." Direct taxes would never produce much revenue in the United States. But neither would excise duties. Their administration required inspections and assessments of the citizens' property that were highly unpopular. This left the government with duties on imports and tonnage as the most acceptable forms of taxation (*Fed.* 12, 75).

Adoption of the Constitution did not promise to reduce the total amount of taxes paid. As Hamilton put it, the "quantity of taxes to be paid by the community" would be the same whether or not the plan were adopted. But adoption nonetheless offered the possibility to shift the burden of taxation from land to trade, thereby easing the pressure on most taxpayers. A national government would be able to make more money from trade duties than the state governments for several reasons. It would promote trade more effectively, thus increasing the tax base. It would be more efficient at tax collecting. And its monopoly on import duties meant that it could raise customs duties to higher levels than thirteen states in competition could (*Fed.* 12, 75; *Fed.* 36, 227–29). To Hamilton the key to a functioning fiscal system was always to minimize friction, to employ methods of taxation that were considered legitimate by the taxpayers and therefore gave rise to no opposition. "It might be demonstrated," Hamilton said at one point, "that the most productive system of finance will always be the least burthensome." Duties on trade constituted such a system as long as they avoided taxing basic consumer items. The citizen-taxpayers could then choose either to buy an item and pay the duty levied on it or abstain from consumption and not pay the tax. In other words, there was a voluntary element to such tax administration, which accorded well with republican ideas of rule by consent. By targeting luxury items, the tax would fall on those who could best afford to pay. The ideal system of taxation was therefore one that rested lightly on the citizens and in particular on the members of the community with the least ability to contribute to the common good. "Happy it is when the interest which the government has in the preservation of its own power, coincides with a proper distribution of the public burthens, and tends to guard the least wealthy part of the community from oppression," as Hamilton so nicely put it (*Fed.* 35, 221; *Fed.* 26, 228–29).

IV

In December 1795, President Washington sent his seventh annual address to Congress. It was an optimistic message, and it struck a tone very different from the gloomy predictions that had prevailed between the Peace of Paris and the adoption of the Constitution. "I have never met you at any period, when more than at present, the situation of our public affairs has afforded just cause for mutual congratulations," Washington said. In the West, the Indians in the Ohio country had been defeated by General Anthony Wayne's American Legion and made to conclude the Treaty of Greenville. In retrospect, Wayne's victory at the Battle of Fallen Timber and the ensuing treaty was the turning point that opened up the Ohio and Mississippi River Valley to European American settlement by displacing the American Indian residents.

Of no less importance to the future development of the trans-Appalachian West was the conclusion of negotiations between the United States and European colonial powers. At Madrid, Washington reported, Thomas Pinckney was about to sign a treaty "securing amicably very essential interests to the United States." Although the existence of a new treaty with Britain had been known for months, the president now officially disclosed that John Jay, the author of the four *Federalist* essays on international war, had concluded "a Treaty of Amity, Commerce and Navigation" in London. Pinckney's Treaty kept the Mississippi open to American trade, a prerequisite to realize the full economic potential of the West and retain the loyalty of European American residents there. Jay's Treaty, too, was of great significance to the future of the West, as Britain at last agreed to evacuate strategic military posts it had occupied in breach of the 1783 peace treaty. These forts controlled the fur trade and the transport routes in the Old Northwest and held the key to the subjection of the Indian nations living there. Without control of the posts, the Treaty of Greenville's cession of territory to the United States would have been little more than a dead letter. Together, the treaties amounted to "the extinguishment of all the causes of external discord, which have heretofore menaced our tranquility."

Turning to domestic affairs, Washington pointed out that whereas Europe was again suffering from the hardships and distress of war, the United States was at peace. The economy was singularly prosperous, to no small degree thanks to the benefits of neutrality. Diplomatic and military success and the protection of the nation's neutrality were all due to the vigorous actions of the federal government. Nevertheless, this government rested so lightly on the shoulders of the citizenry that its burdens were "scarcely to be perceived." Otherwise the president said little about internal matters. By far the most important intervention of the federal government in the nation's domestic affairs was the suppression of the so-called Whiskey Rebellion, a protest against the federal exercise on distilled spirits, in western Pennsylvania. Washington could report that "[t]he misled" had now "abandoned their errors, and pay the respect to our Constitution and laws which is due from good citizens to the public authorities of the society." Of course, the "misled" had also paid their sullen respect to an army of more than 10,000 men that had marched across the mountains from the seaboard. At roughly the same size as the Continental Army that laid siege to Yorktown in the final stages of the War of Independence, this was an enormous undertaking by the new government. The overwhelming response to the rebellion shows the administration's determination to exert its sovereignty in the interior regions of North America and to ensure that the taxes levied on the citizens were duly collected. The predominant focus of the federal government on foreign rather than domestic concerns and on the continued centrality of security was also evident in Washington's call to Congress to attend to the army and naval establishments, militia reform, American Indian relations, harbor fortifications, arsenals and military stores, and the public debt.[23]

The Federalist had promised that the Constitution would deliver the benefits of union to the member states and their citizens by means of a central government that would reduce rather than increase government impositions on the citizenry. By staying united, the American states would be able to deal much more efficiently with security threats in the form of international war, American civil war, and domestic disturbance than they could hope to do on their own or as members of regional confederacies. The verity of that proposition was never tested for the simple reason that the American Union prevailed. But in the years that followed on the adoption of the Constitution, the reorganized Union and the federal government did begin to address the major security threats that Publius had identified. As Washington's message indicates, its efforts were largely successful.

The first achievement of the Washington administration was to keep the United States out of the Wars of the French Revolution. This would hardly have been possible without the centralization of diplomatic and military power in the federal government effected by the Constitution, which allowed the government to both police American citizens who committed crimes against the law of nations and to offer a credible threat of retaliation against foreign powers that interfered with American rights. However, as Washington admitted, the government had been less successful in preventing frontiersmen from committing violence and murder against the Indians. In the century that followed, the federal government would continue to side with its citizens against the American Indian population.

The Union also diffused the causes that Hamilton had identified as the principal causes of conflict among the American states. The landed states gave up their trans-Appalachian land claims to Congress, which assumed the direct rule over the western marches. The defeat of the Northwest Confederacy and the suppression of the Whiskey Rebellion demonstrated that this rule was no longer merely nominal. The federal monopoly on commercial regulation and taxation of imports created a customs union that removed the tension between the states over commercial restrictions. As Treasury secretary, Hamilton consolidated the public debt by settling state accounts and providing for regular interest payments to the public creditors. In the handling of the Whiskey Rebellion, the federal government

demonstrated its readiness to clamp down hard on domestic disturbance that the administration perceived as a threat to law and order and
the stability of a republican system of government.

The Washington administration also lived up to the promise
that the Constitution would reduce rather than increase the burdens
on the citizens. The claim that these burdens were "so light as
scarcely to be perceived" was not empty rhetoric. In 1795, the federal
government looked remarkably similar to the ideas that Hamilton
had outlined in *The Federalist*. To a modern observer it appears a
government trimmed to its bare bones. The central executive departments in Philadelphia were only three – State, War, and Treasury –
and small in size. The field services they oversaw were on a scale to
match. The revenue service was essentially a waterfront operation.
Customs duties accounted for over nine-tenths of the government's
income. There was also an excise service levying internal duties that
were accepted along the seaboard but unpopular west of the mountains. Thanks to the federal assumption of their debts, state governments could dramatically reduce or altogether discontinue taxes on
property and persons that had generated much hardship but little
money during the Confederation era. The Constitution thereby made
possible a seventy to ninety percent reduction of direct taxes nationwide. But Hamilton's tax reforms led not only to reduced taxes but
also to the restoration of public credit. This allowed the federal government to borrow rather than tax when faced with extraordinary
expenditure. As secretary of the Treasury, Hamilton borrowed to
finance both Indian wars and the expedition against the Whiskey
Rebellion. His successors would use public credit to pay for
international wars and territorial purchase.[24]

The army, too, looked much like Publius had promised. Secretary of War Henry Knox's ambition to introduce extensive military
training for the militia came to naught. Instead, the federal government left the states at liberty to neglect their militia at their leisure
and concentrated on building a small professional army. During
Washington's administration the troops were stationed in the west;

later on the army would be divided between the federal territories and the coastal fortifications that guarded the Atlantic seaboard. In the west, the main task of the army was to police the so-called Indian frontier, which was the government's attempt to maintain peace in the borderlands through the physical separation of American Indians and European Americans. It remained small, just as Hamilton had suggested in *The Federalist*. In peacetime it rarely exceeded 10,000 men before the mid-1850s. When the exigencies of war demanded it, the regular army was reinforced by short-term volunteer soldiers.[25]

The Federalist is largely a negative argument about the dangers of disunion. But in one of the essays, Publius allowed himself to speculate about a glorious future for America. *Federalist* 11 begins rather conventionally with America's commercial prospects. If power were to be centralized so that the federal government could formulate commercial policy and if the government acquired the means to build and command a navy, the United States would be in a strong position to further its material interests in the trans-Atlantic state system. "A price would be set not only upon our friendship, but upon our neutrality," Hamilton said, and "we may hope ere long to become the Arbiter of Europe in America; and to be able to incline the ballance of European competitions in this part of the world as our interest may dictate" (*Fed.* 11, 68).

Toward the end of the essay the discussion unexpectedly broadens to take in European cultural and economic imperialism. Despite his versatility, we are not accustomed to cast Hamilton in the role of postcolonial theorist battling against the global dominance of Old World maritime empires. Yet in *Federalist* 11 he lashes out at the ways in which Europe, "by her arms and by her negociations, by force and by fraud," has come to rule the world. "Africa, Asia, and America have successively felt her domination." In their arrogance European navigators, merchants, politicians, and men of letters have come to think of their continent as "the Mistress of the World, and to consider the rest of mankind as created for her benefit." But Hamilton's postcolonialism was wedded to a belief that the United

States was an emerging empire in its own right, and his America soon shapeshifts from downtrodden colonies to leader of the New World. And here we witness the unfortunate confusion of the national interest of the United States with the universal interest of mankind:

> It belongs to us to vindicate the honor of the human race, and to teach that assuming [European] brother moderation ... Let Americans disdain to be the instruments of European greatness! Let the thirteen States, bound together in a strict and indissoluble union, concur in erecting one great American system, superior to the controul of all trans-atlantic force or influence, and able to dictate the terms of the connection between the old and the new world!
>
> (*Fed.* 11, 72–73)

These were words that would echo down the ages as a once fragile union of thirteen republics came to dominate the world.

NOTES

1 Charles A. Beard, *An Economic Interpretation of the Constitution of the United States* (New York: Macmillan, 1935 [1913]), vi, 14–15 (quotation); Alan Gibson, *Interpreting the Founding: Guide to the Enduring Debates over the Origins and Foundations of the American Republic* (Lawrence: University Press of Kansas, 2006), 7–12.

2 Alan Gibson, *Understanding the Founding: The Crucial Questions* (Lawrence: University Press of Kansas, 2007), 46–52.

3 Peter S. Onuf, "A Declaration of Independence for Diplomatic Historians," *Diplomatic History*, 22 (1998), 71–83; David Armitage, *The Declaration of Independence: A Global History* (Cambridge, MA: Harvard University Press, 2007); David M. Golove and Daniel J. Hulsebosch, "A Civilized Nation: The Early American Constitution, the Law of Nations, and the Pursuit of International Recognition," *New York University Law Review*, 85 (2010), 932–1066 (quotation at 934); Daniel J. Hulsebosch, "The Revolutionary Portfolio: Constitution-Making and the Wider World in the American Revolution," *Suffolk University Law Review*, 47 (2014), 759–822; Eliga H. Gould, *Among the Powers of the Earth: The American*

Revolution and the Making of a New World Empire (Cambridge, MA: Harvard University Press, 2012); Robbie J. Totten, "Security, Two Diplomacies, and the Formation of the US Constitution: Review, Interpretation, and New Directions for the Study of the Early American Period," *Diplomatic History*, 36 (2012), 77–117; Leonard J. Sadosky, *Revolutionary Negotiations: Indians, Empires, and Diplomats in the Founding of America* (Charlottesville: University of Virginia Press, 2009); Gregory Ablavsky, "The Savage Constitution," *Duke Law Journal*, 63 (2014), 999–1088.

4 David C. Hendrickson, *Peace Pact: The Lost World of the American Founding* (Lawrence: University Press of Kansas, 2003), quotation at 22 ("system of states"); Michael P. Zuckert, "A System without Precedent: Federalism in the American Constitution," in Leonard Levy and Dennis J. Mahoney, eds., *The Framing and Ratification of the Constitution* (New York: Macmillan, 1987), 132–50, quotation at 141 ("compound system", "two sets of government"); Max M. Edling, "A More Perfect Union: The Framing of the Constitution," in Edward Grey and Jane Kamensky, eds., *The Oxford Handbook of the American Revolution* (New York: Oxford University Press, 2012), 388–406.

5 *Fed.* 29, 187, 626 n. 22. For reasons explained in his footnote, Cooke omitted the final paragraph of the original essay from his text.

6 Totten, "Security, Two Diplomacies, and the Formation of the US Constitution," 79.

7 Centinel *DHRC*, XV, 388.

8 See Armitage, *The Declaration of Independence*; Golove and Hulsebosch, "Civilized Nation"; Gould, *Among the Powers of the Earth*; Hulsebosch, "Revolutionary Portfolio"; Onuf, "A Declaration of Independence."

9 Hendrickson, *Peace Pact*, ix–x.

10 Montesquieu, *Spirit of the Laws*, ed. Anne M. Cohler, Basia Carolyn Miller, and Harold Samuel Stone (Cambridge: Cambridge University Press, 1989), pt. IV, bk. 20, ch. 2, 338.

11 On the origins of the democratic peace theory before Immanuel Kant's famous *Zum ewigen Frieden* (1795), see David M. Fitzsimons, "Tom Paine's New World Order: Idealistic Internationalism in the Ideology of Early American Foreign Relations," *Diplomatic History*, 19 (1995), 569–82, and Thomas C. Walker, "The Forgotten Prophet: Tom Paine's

Cosmopolitanism and International Relations," *International Studies Quarterly*, 44 (2000), 51–72.

12 Quoted in Herbert E. Sloan, *Principle and Interest: Thomas Jefferson and the Problem of Debt* (1995; repr., Charlottesville: University of Virginia Press, 2001), 86.

13 US Constitution, art. IV, sect. 4.

14 The passage quoted is from Montesquieu, *Spirit of the Laws*, pt. II, bk. 9, ch. 1, 132.

15 Ibid., ch. 2, 132–33.

16 Alexander Hamilton to Robert Morris, April 30, 1781, *PAH*, II, 606.

17 Alexander Hamilton, "Defence of the Funding System," ibid., XIX, 60.

18 Alexander Hamilton, "Report on a Plan for the Further Support of Public Credit," ibid., XVIII, 125. In *Federalist* 30, 188, Hamilton presented the alternatives to credit as either the "continual plunder" of the people or the "fatal atrophy" of the government.

19 Max M. Edling, *A Revolution in Favor of Government: Origins of the US Constitution and the Making of the American State* (New York: Oxford University Press, 2003), 120.

20 "Continental Congress Report on a Military Peace Establishment," June 18, 1783, *PAH*, III, 378–97; Edling, *Revolution in Favor of Government*, 121–24.

21 Adam Smith, *An Inquiry into the Nature and Causes of the Wealth of Nations*, ed. R. H. Campbell, A. S. Skinner, and W. B. Todd, 2 vols. (Oxford: Oxford University Press, 1976), II, 695, 697, 698. On the militia in the Scottish debate, see John Robertson, *The Scottish Enlightenment and the Militia Issue* (Edinburgh: John Donald, 1985).

22 Alexander Hamilton, "The Continentalist No. VI," *PAH*, III, 103.

23 George Washington, "Seventh Annual Address," in *A Compilation of the Messages and Papers of the Presidents, 1789–1908*, ed. James D. Richardson, 11 vols. (New York: Bureau of Art and Literature, 1909), I, 182–86.

24 Max M. Edling, *A Hercules in the Cradle: War, Money, and the American State, 1783–1867* (Chicago, IL: University of Chicago Press, 2014), 50–107.

25 Richard H. Kohn, *Eagle and Sword: The Federalists and the Creation of the Military Establishment in America, 1783–1802* (New York: Free Press, 1975).

4 "The Known Opinion of the Impartial World"

Foreign Relations and the Law of Nations in The Federalist

David M. Golove and Daniel J. Hulsebosch

> *It is the reason of the public alone that ought to regulate the government.*
> *The passions ought to be controlled and regulated by the government.*
>
> (*Fed.* 49, 343)

INTRODUCTION

Conventional accounts of *The Federalist* tend to overlook a critical and uncontroversial fact about the Constitution: the principal function it assigned the proposed new government was the conduct of the Union's foreign affairs. By neglecting this simple point, readers too often miss the forest for the trees. The central task of *The Federalist* was not to offer a general blueprint for republican government but rather to demonstrate the depth of the Confederation's failures in foreign affairs and to explain why the new federal government would govern more effectively in that realm without imperiling the republican commitments of the Revolution. This insight in turn reveals another: Even when *The Federalist* focuses on other, very different themes – whether in analyzing the general principles of federalism or the separation of powers, the importance of energy in the executive or independence in the judiciary, or the deficiencies of popular assemblies – foreign affairs remains its ultimate subject. These explorations were so many arguments to demonstrate that the federal government would neither repeat the Confederation's foreign affairs blunders, nor pose a threat to the states and the republican principles upon which they were founded.

The tension between productive foreign relations and domestic republicanism that emerged during the Revolution had not been anticipated at its outset. The Declaration of Independence assumed that these were harmonious ends when it announced as twin goals of the Revolution independent republican government in the states and peaceful commercial relations with the larger world, governed by the principles of the law of nations.[1] By the time the Philadelphia Convention met, however, it was widely agreed that the weak institutions of the Confederation had failed on the latter front. State violations of treaties and the law of nations, which Congress could neither control nor redress, combined with its dependence on the states for financial and military resources, left the Confederation incapable of conducting the nation's diplomatic relations, ensuring its security, promoting its commerce, or even paying its bills, not least the foreign loans that had helped finance the fight for independence. The ensuing foreign policy fiascos, combined with a mounting sense of impugned honor among American elites – rather than a quixotic effort to reform internal governance within the states from the ground up – provided the main impetus for constitutional reform.

Although there was consensus on the need to reform the Confederation, sharp controversy remained over how many and what sort of amendments to seek. The framers provided their collective if negotiated answers to these questions in the proposed Constitution. *The Federalist*'s improved "science of politics" was designed to answer Anti-Federalist critics by demonstrating that the proposed reforms were the minimum necessary to preserve the Revolution's goals of robust republican government at home and full integration of the United States into the Atlantic world of "civilized nations."[2] According to the authors' diagnosis, the Confederation's dysfunctional foreign relations resulted from the failure to manage the tension between these goals properly. At the root of the problem were the twin early decisions to concentrate largely unchecked power in the states' legislative assemblies and, conversely, to construct only weak federal institutions to unite them. Experience demonstrated that the revolutionaries had struck the balance defectively. To preserve republicanism while managing foreign affairs effectively and honorably, it was necessary to adopt the Constitution's innovative structural arrangements, which, *The Federalist* argued, would resolve the tension between republicanism and international legitimacy without jeopardizing either.

It was in developing a theory adequate to respond to Anti-Federalist criticisms and justify the Constitution that the authors of *The Federalist* were led to their deepest insights. Borrowing from Scottish Enlightenment ideas – which they filtered through their political experiences under the Confederation – they rooted their argument in theories of human nature and the social psychology of governance, which they then applied not only to diagnose the causes of the Confederation's failings but also to explain the institutional arrangements that could overcome them. The resulting account explained how the new federal government would be able to limit the influence of the destructive passions over the making of foreign policy and thereby take advantage of the bounded possibilities of peaceable, productive international relations.

Central to this vision was the law of nations. Not simply a collection of black letter rules, the law of nations embodied a system of principles, maxims, practices, and procedures that was supposed to guide an enlightened nation's foreign policy. Alexander Hamilton, James Madison, and John Jay were not naïve or utopian about international relations. Rather, they followed a main line of Enlightenment thought in believing that a balance of powers among nations would make it possible for each nation – if it was willing to invest prudently in its own self-defense and to commit itself to adhering to treaties and the law of nations – to reap the benefits of international engagement without becoming overly vulnerable to its perils. *The Federalist* accordingly emphasized the importance of the Constitution's innovative institutional arrangements that were designed to encourage the United States to become that sort of nation and thereby enable it to participate credibly in the Atlantic world of trade and commerce. Especially in the later essays, *The Federalist* began to sketch out a vision of a world in which nations, capable of maintaining mutual respect with one another, could engage in beneficial international relations, guided by treaties and the customary rules of engagement in times of both war and peace. The new federal government would be able to gain that respect, conclude those treaties, enforce them at home and abroad, and generally "possess that sensibility to the opinion of the world." Above all *this* opinion, what Madison called "the known opinion of the impartial world," was the "best guide" to, as well as the reward for, wise national decision-making (*Fed.* 63, 423). For all their apparent realism, the belief that public reason was possible – a collective national reason constituted in part through dialogue with the civilized world – reveals the profoundly hopeful premise of *The Federalist*.

INTERNATIONAL RELATIONS IN THE CONFEDERATION

Alexander Hamilton was not mincing words when he declared in *Federalist* 15 that "something is necessary to be done to rescue us from impending anarchy." His critique of the "insufficiency of the present Confederation to the preservation of the Union" remains a classic account of the so-called "critical period" before the Constitution. Strikingly, nearly every count in his indictment concerned foreign affairs. Charging that the Union had "reached almost the last stage of national humiliation," Hamilton offered an extended bill of particulars demonstrating that collective security and commercial prosperity were both at risk. In violation of the Treaty of Paris, British troops occupied several key forts along the Union's western boundary. But Congress lacked the military capacity to negotiate seriously for their withdrawal or even the moral authority to make the attempt, given "[t]he just imputations on our own faith, in respect to the same treaty." Notwithstanding the political and economic importance of the American claim "to a free participation in the navigation of the Mississippi[,] Spain excludes us from it." Nor could Congress pay its foreign or domestic debts, though these had been "contracted in a time of imminent peril, for the preservation of our political existence." Indeed, Congress had seemingly abandoned the cause of restoring public credit "as desperate and irretrievable." The most promising source of revenue, customs duties, lay in the hands of the states.[3] Even had Congress possessed that authority, it would have made little difference, because it could not convince the leading Atlantic powers, especially Britain, to enter into negotiations for beneficial commercial treaties, bringing the nation's commerce to its "lowest point of declension" (*Fed.* 15, 91–92). As Hamilton bemoaned in *Federalist* 22, "No nation acquainted with the nature of our political association would be unwise enough to enter into stipulations with the United States" when its "engage-ments," they knew, "might at any moment be violated by its members; and while they found from experience that they might enjoy every advantage they desired in our markets without granting us any in return." A leading figure on the British Board of Trade had accordingly advised Parliament to avoid developing a long-term commercial policy "until it should appear whether the American government was likely or not to acquire greater consistency" (*Fed.* 22, 136).

The Confederation's predicament, according to Publius, was fundamentally one of governmental structure. Famously, Publius maintained that it was the weakness of the Confederation and the centrifugal forces the Revolution had unleashed that were the major sources of the problem. The states had the de facto power to override Congress's decisions simply by refusing to carry out its resolutions, and they had regularly done so to serve local interests and satisfy momentary passions, drummed up by populist demagogues. Because Congress could not rely on the states to provide either soldiers or revenues, the Confederation lacked an effective military force, its coffers were empty, and it could not control the behavior of the states nor their citizens (*Fed.* 15, 91). As Hamilton succinctly observed, "[w]e have neither troops, nor treasury, nor government" (*Fed.* 15, 91).

The parochial perspectives of the states, moreover, had produced immoral as well as self-defeating policies. Hamilton's first indictment went directly to this point: "Are there engagements, to the performance of which we are held by every tie respectable among men?" he asked. "These are the subjects of constant and unblushing violation" (ibid.). The British cited the states' violations of the treaty to justify their continued possession of the posts, and, because those charges were true, the Confederation was not even in "a condition to remonstrate with dignity." The predictable result was a state of "national humiliation ... degrad[ing to] the character ... of an independent nation" and rendering the Confederation incapable of even acting the part of a civilized nation: "Is respectability in the eyes of foreign powers a safeguard against foreign encroachments? The imbecility of our government even forbids them to treat with us. Our ambassadors abroad are the mere pageants of mimic sovereignty" (*Fed.* 15, 92). At home, so, too, was Congress.

Hamilton's coauthors offered similar indictments in their essays. John Jay wrote only five numbers but the contributions of the Confederation's secretary of foreign affairs memorably focused on the inefficacy of the states' diplomacy near and far. Sounding a central theme of *The Federalist*, he observed that the Confederation's wounds were largely self-inflicted, and he counseled that the best defense against foreign aggressions was preemptive discipline over the American states and citizens. Belligerent Americans, not foreign belligerents, posed the greatest threat to American security: Opportunist state legislators and unruly western settlers risked exposing the United States to recriminations for their breaches of treaties, violations of the law of nations, and provocations against other powers in the American "neighborhood" – namely, British and Spanish colonies surrounding the States and, within and around them, Native American nations (*Fed.* 3, 17).[4] The thrust of Madison's essays was similar. "Every nation ... whose affairs betray a want of wisdom and stability, may calculate on every loss which can be sustained from the more systematic policy of their wiser neighbors." This was not just an abstract lesson derived from philosophy and history, he argued. Instead, "the best instruction on this subject is unhappily conveyed to America by the example of her own situation. She finds that she is held in no respect by her friends; that she is the derision of her enemies; and that she is a prey to every nation which has an interest in speculating on her fluctuating councils and embarrassed affairs" (*Fed.* 62, 420–21). The painful truth was that responsibility for the Confederation's failings lay not so much in the overreaching of neighboring powers as in the opportunities for such that the Confederation's structure made inevitable.

Nor was this assessment especially original to *The Federalist*. Everyone, Hamilton noted with only some exaggeration, "opponents as well as the friends of the new Constitution," agreed that the Union required reform, pointing to the same set of failures. Samuel Bryan and the other twenty "Dissenters" in the Pennsylvania Ratifying Convention, for example, admitted that "the federal government" should have the power to negotiate treaties of foreign commerce and to lay indirect taxes and that the purpose of those powers would be to bolster the nation's international reputation. "[O]ur national character," the Dissenters acknowledged, "was sinking in the opinion of foreign nations," because, among other things, "congress could make treaties of commerce, but could not enforce the observance of them."[5] Many other Anti-Federalists similarly conceded that Congress needed more control over foreign affairs. "That the present confederation is inadequate to the objects of the union," Centinel wrote in the Philadelphia Independent Gazette, "seems to be universally allowed. The only question is, what additional powers are wanting to give due energy to the federal government?"[6]

Centralization of the foreign affairs powers – war, peace, diplomacy, and commerce – was the common denominator. With consensus on the need to reform the states' diplomacy with the rest of the world, the key issue in the ratification debate quickly became not whether change was needed but how much change and of what sort.[7] "[T]here should be a confederated national government," proclaimed one Anti-Federalist, "but that it should be one which would have a control over national and external matters only, and not interfere with the internal regulations and police of the different states in the union. Such a government, while it would give us respectability abroad, would not encroach upon, or subvert our liberties at home."[8] Embracing the goal of respectability, Anti-Federalists often drew the line, familiar from pre-Revolutionary debates within the empire, between internal and external powers. The distinction, however, was of little help, as Hamilton had recognized in his *Phocion* essays of 1784.[9] Given its essential ambiguity, it served mostly as a cover for fundamental disagreements about how the competing goals of the states should actually be balanced: Should the states retain exclusive power to execute the Confederation's decisions and resolutions, or should the federal government be empowered to operate directly on all citizens? The former ensured state autonomy but risked undermining the ability of the federal government to carry out its foreign affairs responsibilities. Similarly, should the federal government's measures be subject to the states' bills of rights, because, as Patrick Henry asserted in Virginia's Ratifying Convention, treaties could threaten the liberties of individual Americans?[10] Or did state limitations on federal policymaking unduly threaten the uniformity and supremacy of federal law and treaties throughout the Union? (*Fed.* 44, 299)

These questions shaped the main themes of the ratification debate. Anti-Federalists feared that the federal government's enhanced powers to act directly on citizens and not through the sovereignty of the states would overly constrict the hard-won local, popular sovereignty won in the Revolution. In response, the authors of *The Federalist* turned the tables, maintaining that it was the susceptibility of the states' popular institutions to demagoguery and the cacophonous pursuit of local interests that accounted for the ineffectiveness and injustice of their own governments and, more importantly, for the foreign policy failings of the Confederation itself.[11] Nor was it sufficient merely to augment the federal government's foreign affairs powers and further limit the de jure powers of the states over international affairs. The Articles of Confederation had already granted most of those powers and imposed many of the necessary limits – but to no avail. What was crucial was to reaffirm those powers and re-impose those limits and, simultaneously, to make all of the federal government's powers, and all of the corresponding limitations on the states, effective. That required an overhaul of the principles of the federal Union. Most urgent of all was to eliminate the dependence of Congress on the states for implementing its decisions, from raising troops and money to executing treaties. Only then could the national government ensure the effective implementation of federal policy, by maintaining consistency and reining in both state and private provocations. "[A] cordial Union under an efficient national Government, affords them the best security that can be devised against hostilities from abroad," Jay maintained. Why? Because "the Union tends most to preserve the people in a state of peace with other nations" (*Fed. 3, 14*). An effective state was a peaceful one, able to harmonize national policy and the interpretation of treaties and the law of nations, as well as to enforce both within the United States.

The relationship between the states and the federal government was not, however, the only issue. Once the federal government was freed from dependence on the states, the question of the proper structuring of the relationships among its various branches came into view, a subject to which the authors devoted even more pages of text and about whose importance they were equally emphatic. The complex institutional structures embodied in the text, which were nowhere more in evidence than in the context of foreign affairs, necessitated an equally complex defense.[12] Among their core concerns was that the more democratic House of Representatives, like the state legislatures, would be especially susceptible to the sway of local passions and partial interests in international controversies. *The Federalist* accordingly emphasized the Constitution's institutional strategies for curbing those excesses, including the exclusion of the House from many of the most important elements of diplomacy, like treaty-making and the implementation and enforcement of treaties and the law of nations. The Constitution assigned those matters instead principally to the more insulated president and Senate and also to the independent judiciary. There were good reasons to exclude the House from any role "in the formation of treaties," Hamilton explained in *Federalist* 75.

> The fluctuating and, taking its future increase into the account, the multitudinous composition of that body, forbid us to expect in it those qualities which are essential to the proper execution of such a trust. Accurate and comprehensive knowledge of foreign politics; a steady and systematic adherence to the same views; a nice and uniform sensibility to national character; decision, secrecy, and despatch, are incompatible with the genius of a body so variable and so numerous. (*Fed.* 75, 507)

Madison, more pointedly if more abstractly, noted that "the more numerous an assembly may be, of whatever characters composed, the greater is known to be the ascendency of passion over reason." The larger the representative body, "the greater will be the proportion of members of limited information and of weak capacities. Now, it is precisely on characters of this description that the eloquence and address of the few are known to act with all their force" (*Fed.* 58, 395–96). Paradoxically, larger representative assemblies would prove more susceptible to the demagogic entreaties of a "few." Simply put, there was a mismatch between the revolutionary faith in popular assemblies and what the authors of *The Federalist* saw as the universal and enduring psychological and institutional truths of politics. Americans could only ignore those truths at the cost of undermining the promise of republicanism.

Given the consensus on the Confederation's foreign affairs failures, the authors of *The Federalist* were notably restrained in specifying the state legislation that had violated treaties and the law of nations and thereby generated Congress' diplomatic travails.[13] In other documents and venues too numerous to cite, Hamilton, Jay, and Madison had developed these criticisms at great length and in granular detail. Instead, here they developed a theory for why the problems had emerged and provided a positive account of the promise that their "science of politics" held for a future in which foreign affairs were deftly managed. Standing back from the negotiated document that they had helped craft but that had wholly satisfied none of them,[14] the authors largely ignored the compromises that went into the Constitution's making, portraying it instead as a coherent scheme of government to be defended in broad theoretical terms. It was this move that enabled them to make their most original contribution to the ratification debate and to American political theory. Everyone felt the symptoms. Publius provided a new diagnosis in support of a novel prescription.

HUMAN NATURE AND AMERICAN REPUBLICANISM

The theory of politics at the heart of *The Federalist* was polemical in its origin – there was after all an election to win in New York (which the Federalists, in fact, lost). In the course of defending the Constitution, however, the authors' ambition grew – along with the number of essays they penned, expanding from about twenty, as originally planned, to eighty-five (and leaving their printer financially distraught[15]). This evolving project led them to root their argument in a theory of the nature of the human personality and of the social psychology of governance that mixed Enlightenment ideas with their lived political experience. The result produced some of *The Federalist's* most innovative and profound theoretical insights, as well as an extended account of how the new federal government's institutional arrangements would facilitate productive international relations.

The fundamental defect of the Confederation, Publius argued, was that its structure had left the nation's foreign affairs subject to the passions and interests of local lawmakers and consequently to their short-term thinking, expedience, and frequently belligerent instincts. Reform required that the Union be restructured in such a way as to maximize reasoned rather than impassioned decision-making, long- rather than short-term calculations, and sociable rather than belligerent inclinations. The authors' analysis in this respect derived substantially from Scottish common sense philosophy and faculty psychology, but they arranged these familiar ideas in new and controversial ways.

For Hamilton and Madison, in particular, political theory began with an account of human nature and proceeded to analyze how effectively alternative institutions, interacting with that universal psychology, would achieve the ends of republicanism. Hamilton was perhaps being overly polemical in suggesting that political theory must rest on the premise that "men are ambitious, vindictive, and rapacious" (*Fed.* 6, 28). It was a notion, however, that he borrowed from Scottish psychological realism, and what was supposedly "real" about eighteenth-century realism was its unsentimental conception of human nature. According to David Hume, it was "a just *political maxim, that every man must be supposed a knave*; though, at the same time, it appears somewhat strange, that a maxim should be true in *politics* which is false in *fact.*"[16] All men were not in fact knaves, but the careful institutional designer had to take seriously this deflating maxim. As Madison explained in his famous excursus in *Federalist* 51 on the connection between individual human nature and government structure: "what is government itself, but the greatest of all reflections on human nature? If men were angels, no government would be necessary" (*Fed.* 51, 349).

In fact, however, the authors recognized that republicanism was inconsistent with a rigid adherence to Hume's most pessimistic dicta. Humans are capable of being virtuous, public-regarding, and even wise, but their passions, prejudices, and interests also leave them susceptible to biased judgments and unjust, and self-defeating, conduct. "As there is a degree of depravity in mankind which requires a certain degree of circumspection and distrust," Madison observed, "so there are other qualities in human nature which justify a certain portion of esteem and confidence. Republican government presupposes the existence of these qualities" (*Fed.* 55, 378). Hamilton, too, understood this essential feature of republicanism: "The supposition of universal venality in human nature is little less an error in political reasoning than the supposition of universal rectitude." Departing from the more pessimistic portrait of human nature in his earliest contributions, he observed that "[t]he institution of delegated power implies that there is a portion of virtue and honor among mankind, which may be a reasonable foundation of confidence" (*Fed.* 76, 513–14). To be sure, as Madison insisted, if men were angels, no government would be necessary. Equally, if they were all devils, no government could succeed. Because they were neither, the task of constitution-making was to supply the deficit, identifying the institutional arrangements that would bring virtue to the fore, minimize the occasions in which deleterious passions and interests would work their poison, and channel self-interested impulses to promote the public good. Having revealed the springs of politics, *The Federalist* sketched a psychological account of human behavior that purported to explain how humans made short- and long-term decisions and why some people, under the right conditions, were better able than others to assess correctly, and then pursue, their own and collective interests and moral duties.

The challenge posed for republican government by the human passions was especially severe in the conduct of foreign affairs. Many of *The Federalist's* most characteristic themes reflect an assessment of the obstacles that human nature posed for carrying out this critical task. The inevitable partiality of national viewpoints in the rivalries of international relations, exacerbated by the dynamics of internal political competition, rendered popular opinion especially susceptible to parochial perspectives and to the appeal of demagogues, whose "brilliant appearances of genius and patriotism," as Jay gently put it, "like transient meteors sometimes mislead as well as dazzle," or who "flatter [the people's] prejudices to betray their interests," as Hamilton more pointedly explained (*Fed.* 64, 433; *Fed.* 71, 482). Events since 1776 had demonstrated that foreign affairs suffered acutely when government was incapable of constraining popular or demagogic passions and local interests. The great difficulty, Madison explained, was the prospect that "[t]he *passions,* ... not *the reason,* of the public," would be the arbiter. "But it is the reason of the public alone that ought to control and regulate the government. The passions ought to be controuled and regulated by the government" (*Fed.* 49, 343).

For nations as for individuals, the authors argued, gaining respect in the world required internal self-discipline. Historians over the past generation have examined how *The Federalist* deployed Enlightenment philosophy, in particular the Scottish realism of Francis Hutcheson, David Hume, and Adam Smith.[17] They have not, however, analyzed how faculty psychology proved especially useful when the authors sought to explain the Constitution's complicated structures of power. Despite, and perhaps because of, the many compromises that went into its making, the authors reframed the Constitution as a comprehensive blueprint for a new kind of federal government and sought to lay its foundations on fundamental psychological premises, rather than on more transient or even casuistic grounds. That was not a matter of explicating the meaning of particular clauses to help future generations resolve constitutional disputes. The point, rather, was to persuade voters to accept the Constitution by demonstrating how its structures would enable the Union to foster reasoned decision-making and limit the influence of the destructive passions over government, especially in foreign affairs. It was for this purpose that they presented their vision, inspired by the Scottish writers, of each branch of the new government as both a faculty and a composite of faculties, each with its own roles, virtues, and weaknesses. Publius's goal was to elucidate how the Constitution's complex institutional arrangements would simultaneously enhance public reason and control popular passions.[18]

Self-discipline was the answer. A recurring motif in *The Federalist* (as in much Enlightenment thought) was the modeling of states on individuals – not on an organicist notion but as a reflection of the fact that states are just collections of individual persons.[19] States, like individuals, were comprised of momentary passions, long- and short-term interests, an inclination toward sociability, and a deep concern for reputation and respect. Taking these crosscutting faculties and impulses as given, political institutions – a constitutional system – could help minimize the most destructive features of human psychology while maximizing the best, meaning those most productive, virtuous, and honorable.[20] The complexity of the federal Constitution created firewalls against impulsive, short-term decision-making and would thereby foster more reasoned and long-term choices. Although Hamilton in *Federalist* 78 famously ascribed to each of the three federal branches faculties of the mind – force in the executive, will in the legislature, and judgment in the courts – the authors generally tended to treat each branch as possessing the full range of inputs (passions, interests) and psychological faculties for making decisions: reason, understanding, and will.[21] The gravamen of *The Federalist* was that the proposed Constitution would generate respectable national policymaking by arranging these institutions in a way that fostered reasoned decision-making in each branch acting alone and together. In some contexts that required including a particular branch in decision-making in order to play a checking function. In others, it meant excluding that same branch in order to channel decision-making into the more suitable institutions. For example, in the context of making, interpreting, and enforcing international obligations, the prospects for reasoned decision-making depended, the authors argued, on the exclusion of the more democratically-responsive elements in the American system, particularly the House of Representatives and the state legislatures, in favor of the president, the Senate, and the courts.[22] Officials in these more electorally insulated branches would have not only the motive but the "time and opportunity for more cool and sedate reflection," Hamilton argued, so that they could "withstand the temporary delusions" and recall the people to their true interests (*Fed.* 71, 482–83). In this context, the Constitution's careful division of powers – between the federal and state governments and among the branches of the former – would work together to promote more effective, and more just, decision-making.

Given the psychological foundations of their theory, it was quixotic to believe that the exceptional virtue of the American people and the revolutionary states would somehow exempt them from the ordinary pitfalls of human nature. "Have we not," Hamilton asked, "already seen enough of the fallacy and extravagance of those idle theories which have amused us with promises of an exemption from the imperfections, weaknesses and evils incident to society in every shape?" To so believe "would be to disregard the uniform course of human events, and to set at defiance the accumulated experience of ages" (*Fed.* 6, 35). It was this supposition of psychological universalism that lends *The Federalist* much of its cosmopolitan character, motivating, for example, the authors' reliance on the experiences of other nations, ancient and modern, as well as of the states themselves. The fact that human nature was everywhere the same, however, did not imply that people everywhere acted the same way or that one set of institutions was appropriate for all polities. As Montesquieu had taught, climate, geography, size, religion, economic development, and a host of other factors were relevant to the analysis.[23] Taking human nature as given, it was the task of constitution-makers to identify the institutional arrangements that best fit their particular polity. That, *The Federalist* claimed, had been accomplished at the Philadelphia Convention.

The authors observed that some people are more public-spirited and possessed better reasoning capacities than others. That notion supported repeated assertions that "the best men" would be elected and appointed to the federal government. But that assumption was in no way inconsistent with *The Federalist's* basic premise of psychological universalism. There were, and would always be, differences among individuals, the sources of which were traceable to both nature and nurture. As Madison explained most famously in *Federalist* 10, the Constitution's institutional arrangements were self-consciously designed to take full advantage of this unavoidable feature of human society by ensuring that government officials would be most likely "to centre on men who possess the most attractive merit and the most diffusive and established characters" and "whose wisdom may best discern the true interest of their country, and whose patriotism and love of justice will be least likely to sacrifice it to temporary or partial considerations" (*Fed.* 10, 63). Nonetheless, individuals were only better or worse at managing the internal conflict between reason and passion. No one was immune from the affliction.

REASON AND STRUCTURE IN FOREIGN AFFAIRS

The authors of *The Federalist* were not Pollyannaish about international relations. They had a sober view of human nature and of history, especially the history of international relations of the European states, and they doubted that laissez-faire international relations would be free of conflict and war, or that the good motives of other nations would naturally yield mutually beneficial and fair terms of international commercial exchange. They recognized, moreover, that the absence of a sovereign institution that could adjust disputes among nations – what Hamilton referred to as a "superintending power" or an "umpire or common judge" (*Fed.* 7, p. 38; *Fed.* 15, p. 95) – meant that other mechanisms were necessary to achieve peace and stability. The problems of international relations were therefore especially delicate. They would require informed and skillful management, for which the maxims, doctrines, and institutions of public law provided guidance.

Like many eighteenth-century thinkers, the authors looked to the balance of powers as part of the solution to the problem of international relations. Although today that concept has realist connotations, in the eighteenth-century Enlightenment it was closer to an ideal, counterpoised to the alternative of universal monarchy, and was a crucial part of the eighteenth-century jurisprudence of the law of nations with which the authors were intimately familiar. Grotius, Pufendorf, Vattel, Bynkershoek and many other European jurists were required reading not only for lawyers but for all men of affairs, and all three authors had pored over their treatises as part of their education.[24] Far from merely listing natural law bromides, these volumes elaborated on the principles and maxims governing the conduct of international relations and offered detailed accounts of diplomatic institutions like treaties, embassies, admiralty courts, and arbitral tribunals; parsed the customary and treaty-based rules for going to war and waging it; and analyzed the conventions of peacetime commercial relations between nations. Nor were these treatises just textbooks for students; they remained guides that Hamilton, Madison, Jay, and countless others consulted, analyzed, and argued about throughout their careers.

The ideal of balance in this literature held that a nation counterbalanced by other nations would be less opportunistic, more hesitatant about risking war, and more inclined to resolve disputes peacefully under the law of nations. It would not willfully impose its interests on other states in violation of their acknowledged rights. Likewise a world balanced in power and interlocked by commercial connections would not only reduce the likelihood of war but also generate new opportunities for trade.[25] Many of the eighteenth-century thinkers who aspired to this world did not naïvely believe that commerce would produce permanent peace. Commercial rivalry could be intense and generate new jealousies. However, the jealousies caused by shifting commercial balances were different from those caused by imbalances of political power. They were less predictable, more shifting and unstable, and subject to the imperatives of an international economy that tended toward equilibrium. As a result, they were thought less threatening than the lopsided power relations caused by skeins of military alliances.[26]

If the literature of the law of nations provided instruction for the conduct of foreign affairs, it also offered a rich theoretical model that helped the authors of *The Federalist* elucidate the dynamics of federal-state and inter-branch relations under the Constitution. Just as there was no "superintending power" to resolve international disputes over the rights of nations, so too there would be no such power that could ultimately "umpire" disputes between the federal and state governments, or among the three branches of the federal government, over their respective rights and powers. The burden on *The Federalist* was thus to demonstrate why this structural feature of the Constitution, which reiterated the structural dilemma of international relations, would not leave the states vulnerable to abuse by the federal government, and leave the weaker branches of the federal government – the courts and the executive – defenseless against the overbearing power of Congress. Publius devoted a series of essays to answering this critical challenge, which drew from the law of nations literature and similarly rested on the principle of the balance of powers, only now transposed into the domestic context. It was this balance that explained why the Constitution's limits would generally be respected, and how defections would be policed, just as it elucidated in the international context the circumstances under which nations could establish and maintain peaceful and law abiding relations. In this respect, the Constitution, as the public law of the Union, would serve the same function internally that the law of nations, as the public law of "civilized states," served for the wider society of nations. As William Grayson declared in the Virginia Ratifying Convention, the Constitution was to be "the law of nations in America."[27]

Given the states' resistance to federal treaties and their repeated violations of the nation's international legal duties, it was not surprising that the Constitution recognized the law of nations as part of the supreme law of the land and that the two bodies of public law intertwined in the former. The authors of *The Federalist* associated the states' cavalier attitude toward their international duties with selfish, parochial perspectives that only confirmed the European view of the former colonists as lacking in both sophistication and moral rectitude. Hamilton, in particular, resented this European sense of "superiority." But he also had to acknowledge that "Facts have too long supported these arrogant pretensions of the Europeans" (*Fed.* 11, 72). His frustration reflected a still fresh sense of wounded honor occasioned by the disparaging treatment that the Confederation's diplomats had experienced in Europe. The most memorable came at the hands of the British Ambassador to Paris, the Duke of Dorset, who summarily dismissed American entreaties to negotiate a commercial treaty, remarking with artful contempt: "The apparent determination of the respective States to regulate their own seperate [sic] Interests renders it absolutely necessary, towards forming a permanent system of commerce, that my Court should be inform'd how far the Commissioners can be duly authorized to enter into any engagements with Great Britain which it may not be in the power of any one of the States to render totally fruitless and ineffectual."[28] Dorset's dismissal cut so deeply because it was so undeniably reasonable under the circumstances.

In part, the authors of *The Federalist* focused on the instrumental benefits of compliance with the law of nations – for example, as protection against the hostile policies of foreign powers and as a prerequisite to obtaining favorable commercial privileges. Hamilton underscored this point, at first discreetly, by subtly alluding to Congress's failure even to begin negotiating a commercial treaty with Great Britain, and then more frankly, by observing that "[t]he imbecility of our government even forbids [foreign nations] to treat with us" (*Fed.* 11, 67; *Fed.* 15, 92). A "requisite sense of national character," Madison likewise insisted, was a condition for admittance on an equal footing into the European state system, a status that was essential to the nation's interests after the rupture with Great Britain. International respectability was valuable not only for its instrumental benefits, but also for its own sake, to ensure that the nation's conduct would appear to foreign powers "as the offspring of a wise and honorable policy" (*Fed.* 63, 422–23). Experience had taught, however, that preserving "good faith and justice" towards other nations could not be achieved without the proper constitutional arrangements, as the states' attitude to treaties and the law of nations had demonstrated. "The case of the treaty of peace with Britain," Jay noted with considerable understatement, "adds great weight to this reasoning." Without a government that could prevent "each State [from] doing right or wrong, as to its rulers may seem convenient ... what a poor, pitiful figure will America make in [the] eyes [of foreign nations]! How liable would she become not only to their contempt, but to their outrage?" (*Fed.* 4, 22–23).

Notwithstanding these commitments, *The Federalist* seems at first blush to have had a schizophrenic perception of international relations and law. The early essays drew a shocking portrait of relations among the American states in a hypothetical future in which the Constitution was rejected. If the Confederation's centrifugal tendencies were already apparent, the authors insisted, they would only intensify if the constitutional project failed. The inevitable result would be the collapse of the Union into two or three regional confederacies or possibly into thirteen separate sovereigns. At that stage, relations among them would be essentially no different from international relations.[29] Yet, although the authors were at pains to emphasize how the federal government under the Constitution would be able to participate productively in a world of sovereign nations, meeting its international obligations, preserving peace with the rest of the world, and fostering prosperity through beneficial trade, the states would face a radically different prospect. They would "be a prey to discord, jealousy, and mutual injuries" and risk devolving into "an infinity of little, jealous, clashing, tumultuous commonwealths, the wretched nurseries of unceasing discord, and the miserable objects of universal pity or contempt" (*Fed.* 9, 52–53).

Hamilton was especially strident, and also brilliant, in playing out the inevitable dynamics, painting a dark picture of international relations and uncharacteristically denigrating the force of treaties and the law of nations. "The genius of republics (say they) is pacific," Hamilton wrote, capturing an optimistic strand of Enlightenment thinking embraced by many Anti-Federalists, who argued that the independent and sovereign American states would always enjoy peaceful, productive relations, no matter the form of their association. Unfortunately, he observed in *Federalist* 6, the history of the classical republics proved otherwise. So did the recent history of the Netherlands, which, though a republic, had taken "a leading and conspicuous part in the wars of Europe." The claim that republics would avoid war because the people would vote against belligerent representatives was simply untrue, for history showed that there were "almost as many popular as royal wars." Nor would continuing commercial relations among the states promise greater success. Reflecting Montesquieu's notion of *doux commerce*, many Anti-Federalists claimed that "the spirit of commerce has a tendency to soften the manners of men, and to extinguish those inflammable humors which have so often kindled into wars. Commercial republics, like ours, will never be disposed to waste themselves in ruinous contentions with each other. They will be governed by mutual interest, and will cultivate a spirit of mutual amity and concord" (*Fed.* 6, 31). But, Hamilton countered: "Is not the love of wealth as domineering and enterprising a passion as that of power or glory?" and the jealousy of trade as powerful as the thirst for land or glory (*Fed.* 6, 33).

This claim was no less belied by experience. Although Britain was no republic, "commerce has been for ages the predominant pursuit of that country. Few nations, nevertheless, have been more frequently engaged in war; and the wars in which that kingdom has been engaged have, in numerous instances, proceeded from the people." Similarly, the recent controversies over paper money between the most tightly linked commercially of American states, Rhode Island and Connecticut, revealed the fallacy of this kind of utopian thinking. Summing up his indictment of the naïve belief that the special combination of republican government and commercial pursuits would yield peace, Hamilton invoked an especially grim version of Scottish theory as applied to international relations:

> Has it not, on the contrary, invariably been found that momentary passions and immediate interest have a more active and imperious control over human conduct than general or remote considerations of policy, utility or justice? Have republics in practice been less addicted to war than monarchies? Are not the former administered by *men* as well as the latter? Are there not aversions, predilections, rivalships and desires of unjust acquisition that affect nations as well as kings? Are not popular assemblies frequently subject to the

impulses of rage, resentment, jealousy, avarice, and of other irregular and violent propensities? Is it not well known that their determinations are often governed by a few individuals, in whom they place confidence, and are of course liable to be tinctured by the passions and views of those individuals? Has commerce hitherto done anything more than change the objects of war?

(*Fed.* 6, 31–32)

Nor was Hamilton through. Anti-Federalists were also wrong to think that an interlocking web of treaties of alliance among the newly independent American states would maintain the peace. The history of multilateral alliances, he continued in *Federalist* 15, shows that such "fondly hoped for benefits were never realised." The celebrated treaties of Utrecht "were scarcely formed before they were broken, giving an instructive but afflicting lesson to mankind how little dependence is to be placed on treaties which have no other sanction than the obligations of good faith; and which oppose general consider-ations of peace and justice to the impulse of any immediate interest and passion" (*Fed.* 15, 94).

There was a deep tension between this gloomy diagnosis of relations among the American states, were they to become fully independent, and the confidence with which Publius asserted that the federal government would be able to navigate international rela-tions effectively and foster trans-Atlantic peace and prosperity. If nations really did regard their obligations as cavalierly as Hamilton suggested in *Federalist* 6, the authors' emphasis on the importance of national character, good faith, and earning the confidence of foreign nations seems baffling. What purpose would law-abiding conduct serve if the rapaciousness of foreign nations rendered any assumption of reciprocal good faith unrealistic and national charac-ter beside the point? Why would the framers have developed so many innovative institutional mechanisms for promoting strict compli-ance with the nation's international obligations? Why would Publius have begun the essays by emphasizing the "high importance to the

peace of America" of "observ[ing] the law of nations towards" foreign powers? (*Fed.* 3, 14)

One obvious and compelling answer is that *The Federalist* was
an argumentative text that sounded its most polemical in these early
essays. The authors felt a great sense of urgency as they sought to
influence the election of delegates to the New York ratifying convention. Federalists had insisted that the only option for the states was
either to accept or reject the new Constitution in full. The nature of the
election as a take-it-or-leave-it referendum affected the tone and, at the
outset, the substance of *The Federalist*. Given the daunting electoral
prospects, the authors began by wielding their most fearsome weapon:
a warning that rejection of the Constitution would mean the end of the
Union, devastating conflict and war among the states, and ultimately
the undermining of their republican institutions. Hamilton offered a
kind of Hobbesian argument in which Union was the only viable option
because the available alternatives were catastrophic. It was only as the
number of essays expanded and the authors turned to their positive
account, that the emphasis shifted toward the advantages of the new
Constitution in the international realm.

It also matters that Hamilton and Jay were both successful
attorneys and that Madison had studied law intensely. A good
common lawyer's tactics often change subtly over the course of litigation in ways that are superficially reconcilable but also reveal theoretical inconsistencies. The authors never committed themselves to
theoretical consistency and, at least in the early essays, deployed what
they believed were the most rhetorically effective claims. It would be
reasonably simple to discount the *bona fides* of these arguments,
which, in any event, were responding to postulated Anti-Federalist
arguments of dubious provenance.[30]

Beyond this strategic motive, a close reading of the text reveals
more subtle explanations for the inconsistency between the authors'
dour view of the prospects for relations among the states should the
Constitution be rejected and their hopeful prognosis for the Union's
international affairs should it be adopted. Some of *The Federalist*'s

most penetrating insights derived from the authors' recognition of the inextricable link between domestic and international politics. Publius maintained that a nation's international environment inevitably influences the character of its domestic politics, and, conversely, that the character of its domestic politics inevitably shapes the quality of its international relations. For the authors, this self-reinforcing dynamic underscored the importance of adhering to treaties and the law of nations and of the Constitution's institutional arrangements designed to achieve that result. Republican institutions could not long survive amidst the constant threat of war. Not only security, but republicanism itself, therefore, depended on an effective law of nations to mitigate the dangers of unregulated interstate interactions. At the same time, the effectiveness of the law of nations in maintaining peaceful and productive international relations depended on domestic institutions that simultaneously promoted the observance of national duties and the capacity to defend national rights.

This theoretical framework – positing the interdependence of municipal and international public law – underwrote the authors' radically different prognoses for federal and state management of international relations. Hamilton assumed that in the event the Confederation were to dissolve, the states would retain their constitutions essentially intact, including their commitments to legislative dominance, popular politics, weak executives, and no standing armies. It was the states' inability to grasp the interlocking character of international relations and domestic political institutuions – and the tension between effective international diplomacy and republican institutions – that rendered their prospects so grim. International diplomacy under the Constitution would be more auspicious, in contrast, because it would be conducted under radically different constitutional principles.

Hamilton was emphatic that doctrinaire republicanism would doom the states to especially brutal wars. European nations had, in fact, mitigated the most devastating consequences of conflict in part by embracing standing armies, an institution that, if it could not solve the problem altogether, at least kept it in check. "The disciplined armies always kept on foot on the continent of Europe," he observed,

> though they bear a malignant aspect to liberty and economy, have, notwithstanding, been productive of the signal advantage of rendering sudden conquests impracticable, and of preventing that rapid desolation which used to mark the progress of war prior to their introduction. ... The history of war, in that quarter of the globe, is no longer a history of nations subdued and empires overturned, but of towns taken and retaken.
>
> (*Fed.* 8, 44–45)

In contrast, the unwillingness of the American states to countenance standing armies or other means of discouraging the predatory behavior of neighboring states would leave them dangerously vulnerable.

> War between the States, in the first period of their separate existence, would be accompanied with much greater distresses than it commonly is in those countries where regular military establishments have long obtained ... The jealousy of military establishments would postpone them as long as possible. The want of fortifications, leaving the frontiers of one state open to another, would facilitate inroads ... Conquests would be as easy to be made as difficult to be retained. War, therefore, would be desultory and predatory. PLUNDER and devastation ever march in the train of irregulars.
>
> (*Fed.* 8, 44–45)

Aiming to protect liberty at home, the disunited states would unwittingly provoke cruel war and collective ruin. Unfortunately, these horrors would only be the beginning. Under the pressure of insecurity and war, the states' republican institutions would begin to weaken, until ultimately they would be abandoned altogether. "The violent destruction of life and property incident to war, the continual effort and alarm attendant on a state of continual danger, will compel nations the most attached to liberty to resort for repose and security to institutions which have a tendency to destroy their civil and political rights. To be more safe, they at length become willing to run the risk of being less free." The result would be an embrace of "standing armies and the correspondent appendages of military establishments," because, parchment constitutional barriers notwithstanding, "[f]requent war and constant apprehension ... will infallibly produce them." That necessity, in turn, would force the states "to strengthen the executive arm of government, in doing which their constitutions would acquire a progressive direction toward monarchy. It is of the nature of war to increase the executive at the expense of the legislative authority." In the end, the continual need for the military would "enhance[] the importance of the soldier, and proportionably degrade[] the condition of the citizen," until finally, "the military state becomes elevated above the civil" (*Fed.* 8, 45, 46, 48). The logical endpoint of not ratifying the Constitution would thus be the fiscal-military state, on the early modern European model, and the recapitulation in America of the darkest periods of European history.

If doctrinaire republicanism would thus perversely undermine the very republican commitments that the states had set out so jealously to defend, the new international environment in which the states would interact would be a ready source of conflict to set these devastating dynamics in motion. In part, Publius emphasized the special problem of geography as a source of conflict among the states. Montesquieu had famously argued that geography and climate explained much about a nation's destiny. Hamilton pursued this theme, focusing on "neighborhood" as the explanation for why the states would be locked in a cycle of conflict and violence. It was unrealistic to expect "a continuation of harmony between a number of independent, unconnected sovereignties in the same neighborhood," he wrote, as it was "a sort of axiom in politics, that vicinity or nearness of situation, constitutes nations natural enemies." The problem of neighborhood would be especially severe for the states, Hamilton claimed, because of geographical features that would enable certain states, like New York, to exploit their favorable geography to the detriment of their neighbors. "The opportunities which some States would have of rendering others tributary to them by commercial regulations would be impatiently submitted to by the tributary States" (*Fed.* 7, 35–36). Such domination would soon breed resistance. Even more inauspicious, however, would be the states' commitment to granting a large share of influence over the management of their foreign affairs to popular assemblies. Under these circumstances, unavoidable conflicts of interest among the states – over territorial claims to the western lands, the allocation of the existing public debt, commercial policy and foreign alliances, to name but a few – would be "productive of ill-humor and animosity," leading "citizens of the States interested [to] clamour" and *"denominate injuries those things which were in reality the justifiable acts of independent sovereignties consulting a distinct interest."* The hostile measures that would ensue "would naturally lead to outrages, and these to reprisals and wars" – ultimately, "not of *parchment,* but of the sword" (*Fed.* 7, 40–42).

With British and Spanish colonies surrounding the states, moreover, the states' larger neighborhood portended conflict with Europe's imperial powers. Here, too, the Union, as an extended republic, had the advantage over the states. Jay argued that a national government would be able to tamp down impulsive state responses to problems in America's continental "neighborhood" that would otherwise be the source of conflict. "The neighborhood of Spanish and British territories, bordering on some States and not on others, naturally confines the causes of quarrel more immediately to the borderers," Jay explained. "The bordering States, if any, will be those who, under the impulse of sudden irritation, and a quick sense of apparent interest or injury, will be most likely, by direct violence, to excite war with these nations; and nothing can so effectually obviate that danger as a national government, whose wisdom and prudence will not be diminished by the passions which actuate the parties immediately interested" (*Fed.* 3, 17). In the absence of a federal government able to alleviate their sense of insecurity, the states would inevitably enter into conflicting European alliances – "one inclining to Britain, another to France, and a

third to Spain, and perhaps played off against each other by the three"
– and, when conflict arose, out of a sense of desperation they would
feel compelled to invite foreign intervention. "And here let us not
forget how much more easy it is to receive foreign fleets into our
ports, and foreign armies into our country, than it is to persuade or
compel them to depart" (*Fed.* 5, 27). The result would be that "by the
operation of such jarring alliances, [the states would] be gradually
entangled in all the pernicious labyrinths of European politics and
wars; and by the destructive contentions of the parts into which [they
were] divided, would be likely to become a prey to the artifices and
machinations of powers equally the enemies of them all" (*Fed.* 7, 43).
Principled adherence to small-state republicanism would thus yield
yet another perverse effect: re-colonization.

The Atlantic coast provided another important factor favoring
the Union over the disunited states. "There is a wide difference,"
Hamilton maintained in *Federalist* 8, "between military establishments in a country, seldom exposed by its situation to internal invasions, and in one which is often subject to them, and always
apprehensive of them." Nations insulated from others by maritime
borders, like Great Britain, and, on the east coast, the United States,
had less reason to fear invasion by armed forces. Water formed a
natural defensive border because it limited the practical access of an
invading army. Its "insular situation" enabled Britain to discourage
foreign invasion by maintaining a "powerful marine" and thereby
avoiding the necessity for a large standing army. This favorable geographical position was one source of British liberty (*Fed.* 8, 49). If the
states were united under the Constitution, Hamilton wrote,

> we may for ages enjoy an advantage similar to that of an insulated
> situation. Europe is at a great distance from us. Her colonies in our
> vicinity will be likely to continue too much disproportioned in
> strength to be able to give us any dangerous annoyance. Extensive
> military establishments cannot, in this position, be necessary to
> our security.
>
> (*Fed.* 8, 49)

In contrast, if disunited into separate nations or "thrown together into two or three confederacies," the states would lose this providential blessing and find their security "prey to the means of defending ourselves against the ambition and jealousy of each other" (*Fed.* 8, 49).

Finally, many of Hamilton's most skeptical remarks are best interpreted as exaggerated expressions of traditional balance-of-powers theory rather than an anticipation of modern international relations realism. Hamilton delighted in ironies like the Scottish thinker he essentially was. To avoid war, a nation had to prepare for one. This maxim, which always shocked his opponents, was a clear implication of balance-of-powers reasoning. Once prepared, a nation ought to go as far as possible to avoid conflict (something his opponents also never fathomed). Every nation, Hamilton insisted, needed some minimum state capacity to be taken seriously and to ward off foreign hostility. Without some plausible means of naval self-defense, he warned in *Federalist* 11, "our commerce would be a prey to the wanton intermeddling of all nations at war with each other; who, having nothing to fear from us, would with little scruple or remorse supply their wants by depredations on our property" (*Fed.* 11, 68). Hamilton was not denying the importance of the international law of neutrality, any more than *The Federalist* was questioning the importance of the Constitution by insisting that institutional arrangements, rather than the force of law or morality alone – "the weaker springs of the human character" – were necessary means to ensure compliance with its principles (*Fed.* 34, 212). He was simply observing that, to be effective, the law of nations, like other legal restraints, must be backed by some capacity to impose costs on those whose interests would otherwise incline them to disregard their duties. "The rights of neutrality will only be respected when they are defended by an adequate power." Thus, to obtain the benefits of neutral rights, the Union would need to establish a modest navy, one "which, if it could not vie with those of the great maritime powers, would at least be of respectable weight if thrown into the scale of either of two contending parties." Any nation that neglected its own defense and was thus

"despicable by its weakness, forfeits even the privilege of being neutral." That would be especially tragic for the United States, because
guaranteeing extensive commercial opportunities would only require
the maintenance of a small navy (*Fed.* 11, 68–69).

In these early essays, Hamilton and Madison borrowed – more
than has been recognized – from the writings of the Abbé de Mably,
the "intelligent writer" to whom Hamilton referred in *Federalist* 6
and whom Madison explicitly invoked in *Federalist* 18 and 20.
Mably's well-known volume on "the principles of negotiation"
appears to have provided an inspiration for some of the authors'
fundamental ideas about the conduct of foreign affairs, as well as a
model for their use of historically-grounded comparative analysis.[31]
Like Hamilton, Mably was unsparing in his realism about human
nature. Emphasizing how the passions and interests of Europe's ruling
elites drove international diplomacy, Mably eschewed basing his
advice on moral "maxims which are ill-suited with beings who have
our passions. My morality has so little austerity in it, that I desire not
to have virtuous but ambitious men, who make some use of their
reason, for my readers." Nevertheless, again like Hamilton, Mably
was a hard-boiled idealist who held that "justice, moderation, and
kindness [we]re the soul" of an enlightened foreign policy. Obeying
law and duty were in principle the right things to do, but they were
also prudent policy. "[A] republic, which respected not the law of
nations," he observed "but disturbed its neighbours, and waged every
day unjust wars, in order to extend its dominions" would ultimately
be "forced ... to yield to the efforts of conjured enemies, whom [its]
ambition would have raised against [it]; deprived of any other advantage, but that of burying [itself] under the ruins of [its] country."
Although indulging unjust, aggressive passions was thus self-
defeating, that did not mean that nations should refrain from maintaining an adequate military capacity. Once again like Hamilton,
Mably insisted that to ensure that its rights were respected, a state
had to have the means to defend itself: "I own, that virtue, divested of
strength, passes only for weakness; and that a state which defends

itself against powerful neighbours, only with justice and moderation, must soon or late be oppressed." However "vicious" men might be, Mably added, they will "place their confidence in the moderation of [a potential rival] ... when these qualities are accompanied with power and courage." Mably acknowledged that European nations and elites were not yet prepared to accept his guidance, given their constitutions, manners, and passions, but, as if anticipating the authors of *The Federalist*, he dared "to hope, that my reflections may persuade some man, who raised, one day, to the government of affairs, might be led away by vulgar prejudices. But when, on the contrary, he is guided by maxims drawn from the purest sources, he may be the cause of his own nation's happiness, by not disturbing that of his neighbors."[32] *The Federalist* embraced a similar view of international affairs. The authors remained hopeful and committed to the principles of the law of nations. At the same time, they eschewed naïve optimism about human nature and its implications for the behavior of nations. Proper institutional design would vindicate their hopeful realism by mitigating threats to the United States and enhancing the prospects for peaceful, productive international relations.

SEPARATING POWERS TO ENFORCE THE LAW OF NATIONS

As the number of essays expanded, and the authors turned from their polemical diagnosis of the consequences of disunion to their affirmative defense of the Constitution, they offered a strikingly different vision of international relations and the possibilities for the Union's diplomacy under the reformed Constitution. In this account – as in their critique of the states under the Confederation – they emphasized the critical importance of law and of institutional design in promoting compliance with the nation's duties and thereby ensuring its "respectability," "character," and "honor." At the outset, Jay declared that "It is of high importance to the peace of America, that she observe the laws of nations," a point that the authors recurred to frequently (*Fed.* 3, 14). Their focus, however, was not simply on the need to adhere to black-letter rules but also on the importance of deftly managing ongoing relations. Law was for them a managerial mode as much as a collection of rules. Of course there were also rules governing international relations, and the place where they would most often be applied would be in federal institutions.

The federal judiciary was to play a critical role in this respect. As Jay explained, it would fall to the courts to ensure that the law of nations "will always be expounded in one sense and executed in the same manner" (*Fed.* 3, 14), which was one reason why, two years later, he chose to become Chief Justice of the Supreme Court rather than continue on as foreign secretary (under a new title). The federal judiciary's independence would enable it to counteract "the effects of those ill humors, which the arts of designing men, or the influence of particular conjunctures, sometimes disseminate among the people themselves" (*Fed.* 78, 522). Several of the classes of cases to which Article III extended the judicial power were drawn with the goal of enabling the federal courts to enforce the law of nations in mind. Indeed, Hamilton noted, Article III had gone further, granting the federal courts jurisdiction over "all causes in which the citizens of other countries are concerned." Although "a distinction may perhaps be imagined between cases arising upon treaties and the laws of nations and those which may stand merely on the footing of the municipal law," he explained, "it is at least problematical, whether an unjust sentence against a foreigner, where the subject of controversy was wholly relative to the *lex loci,* would not, if unredressed, be an aggression upon his sovereign, as well as one which violated the stipulations of a treaty or the general law of nations." Accordingly, federal court jurisdiction in all such cases was "not less essential to the preservation of the public faith, than to the security of the public tranquility" (*Fed.* 80, 536).

Even more critical, was the role of the federal judiciary in applying the international law of admiralty, especially when determining prize cases during war, a subject of great delicacy, as wartime experience had taught those responsible for conducting the Confederation's diplomacy. Admiralty matters "so generally depend on the laws of nations, and so commonly affect the rights of foreigners," that "the most bigoted idolizers of State authority have not thus far shown a disposition to deny the national judiciary the cognizances of maritime causes" (*Fed.* 80, 538). Notwithstanding the wartime practice of some of the states, moreover, it was necessary to exempt prize cases from the ordinary right to a jury trial in order to ensure strict adherence to the law of nations. "Juries cannot be supposed competent to investigations that require a thorough knowledge of the laws and usages of nations," Hamilton explained, "and they will sometimes be under the influence of impressions which will not suffer them to pay sufficient regard to those considerations of public policy which ought to guide their inquiries." Indeed, "[i]t will add great weight to this remark, in relation to prize causes, to mention that the method of determining them has been thought worthy of particular regulation in various treaties between different powers of Europe, and that, pursuant to such treaties, they are determinable in Great Britain, in the last resort, before the king himself, in his privy council" (*Fed.* 83, 568).[33] Even a fundamental right, like the vaunted right to a jury trial, had to be harmonized with the law of nations.

Article III also charged the federal courts with responsibility for enforcing the nation's treaty obligations. To aid in the task, the Supremacy Clause further declared treaties to be supreme law of the land, since "to have any force at all, [treaties] must be considered as part of the law of the land." This explicit declaration addressed the problem, so damaging to the Confederation, of conflicting and bad faith interpretations of international obligations in the states. "The treaties of the United States, under the present Constitution, are liable to the infractions of thirteen different legislatures, and as many different courts of final jurisdiction, acting under the authority of those legislatures," Hamilton observed in *Federalist* 22. "The faith, the reputation, the peace of the whole Union, are thus continually at the mercy of the prejudices, the passions, and the interests of every member of which it is composed." State officials were ill-prepared to take the broader and longer view; they were handicapped by parochial perspectives, local interests, and the influence of whipped up passions. Foreign audiences, moreover, were fully apprised of the problem. "Is it possible that foreign nations can either respect or confide in such a government? Is it possible that the people of America will longer consent to trust their honor, their happiness, their safety, on so precarious a foundation?" The federal courts, in contrast, would produce "true" and uniform interpretations, which ultimately required that treaty issues "be submitted, in the last resort, to one SUPREME TRIBUNAL" (*Fed.* 22, 143–44).

At the same time, the nature of the judicial process, which confined courts to cases of a "Judiciary Nature," imposed limits on their capacity to ensure the compatibility of American law and diplomacy with federal treaties and the law of nations. As a result, a large share of responsibility for enforcing international law would fall to the political branches, necessitating the deep involvement of federal officials in interpreting and applying the law of nations. Indeed, even members of the House, who were charged, for example, with setting commercial policy, would have a role. They had to be acquainted, Madison declared, "not only ... with the treaties between the United States and other nations, but also with the commercial policy and laws of other nations." In addition, in a subtle reminder both of the importance of the law of nations and of the limited role the House was to play in the area, even a representative serving only two years "ought not to be altogether ignorant of the law of nations; for that, as far as it is a proper object of municipal legislation, is submitted to the federal government" (*Fed.* 53, 364). More importantly, Congress had the power to declare war, which included the power of determining when war was justified or necessary, and thus depended on a proper understanding of treaty commitments and the law of nations.

In contrast to the House, the Senate was supposed to play a more central role in foreign affairs. Accordingly, its role proved controversial in Philadelphia and remained so during the ratification debates. The authors of *The Federalist* defended the upper house not primarily because it represented the states as integral communities but rather because they imagined the Senate acting as a repository of reason. With their longer term, fewer numbers, and more discriminating selection process, senators would be more broad-minded, less susceptible to impulse, and less interested in satisfying a vengeful populace than representatives in the House. In addition, once in office together, the small body of senators would identify their service with the national interest in a way not possible for the larger, more mutable, and more locally accountable members of the House. "Those who represent the dignity of their country in the eyes of other nations," argued Madison, "will be particularly sensible to every prospect of public danger, or of a dishonorable stagnation in public affairs" (*Fed*. 58, 395). They were therefore institutionally well suited to participating in treaty-making.

The Senate was designed with this purpose in mind. It would take the long view, consider ramifications for the whole nation and not just localities, and consult other guides than the loudest constituents. The indirect and mediated selection process for senators would guarantee, Jay argued in *Federalist* 64, that the Senate would be "composed of the most enlightened and respectable citizens ... who have become the most distinguished by their abilities and virtue ... and whose reputation for integrity inspires and merits confidence." Six-year terms, moreover, would afford senators "sufficient time to become perfectly acquainted with our national concerns, and to form and introduce a system for the management of them" (*Fed*. 64, 433–34). Their superior qualifications also included the constitutional age requirement: 30, as opposed to only 25 for the House. This was necessary, Madison argued, because the Senate's greater role would require "greater extent of information and stability of character." In addition, their longer term of office would help prevent "the mischievous effects of a mutable government," the foremost of which was that "it forfeits the respect and confidence of other nations, and all the advantages connected with national character" (*Fed*. 62, 420).

Madison's reference to foreign opinion echoed similar warnings by Jay and Hamilton in their essays, but Madison went farther in elaborating structural reasons why the Constitution would send positive signals to the rest of the world. Though less well known than *Federalist* 10 and 51, Madison's final two essays, 62 and 63, are imbued with a Humean social psychology that, along with Madison's characteristic concern with countervailing powers and institutional design, applied directly to the Senate's role in foreign affairs. Madison's goal in these essays was to explain how the Constitution's division and specialization of powers would foster wise diplomacy. Everyone, he noted, would immediately apprehend how an "inconstant" individual is "a speedy victim to his own unsteadiness and folly." Friends will "pity" him while enemies will take the "opportunity to make their fortunes out of his." The same held for nations. "Every nation, consequently, whose affairs betray a want of wisdom and stability, may calculate on every loss which can be sustained from the more systematic policy of their wiser neighbors." This was not just an abstract lesson derived from philosophy and history, he argued. Instead, "the best instruction on this subject is unhappily conveyed to America by the example of her own situation. She finds that she is held in no respect by her friends; that she is the derision of her enemies; and that she is a prey to every nation which has an interest in speculating on her fluctuating councils and embarrassed affairs" (*Fed.* 62, 420–21). Once again, Americans had primarily themselves to blame for their dismal record in international relations.

Critically, the Constitution would create more stable institutions for the conduct of foreign affairs. There were two objects of government, Madison argued in *Federalist* 63: those producing measures with "immediate and sensible operation" and those "depending on a succession of well-chosen and well-connected measures, which have a gradual and perhaps unobserved operation" (*Fed.* 63, 424). While Madison implied that the House was adequate to the first, it was only the Senate that had "sufficient permanency to provide for such objects as require a continued attention." It could similarly protect the polity from those

> particular moments in public affairs, when the people stimulated by some irregular passion, or some illicit advantage, or misled by the artful misrepresentations of interested men, may call for measures which they themselves will afterwards be the most ready to lament and condemn. In these critical moments, how salutary will be the interference of some temperate and respectable body of citizens, in order to check the misguided career, and to suspend the blow meditated by the people against themselves, until reason, justice and truth, can regain their authority over the public mind?
>
> (*Fed.* 63, 425)

Institutions like the Senate had historically proved to be a beneficial checks on popular assemblies because they maintained "the cool and deliberate sense of the community" against fleeting passions and local interests that tended to infect not only popular assemblies but also "the people themselves" (*Fed.* 63, 426). In those moments, a smaller, durable upper house acted as a brake protecting "the people against their own temporary errors and delusions" and marking time "until reason, justice truth, can regain their authority over the public mind" (*Fed.* 63, 425).

Federalist 63 represents Madison's most penetrating application of his counterbalancing theory of interests and institutions to the Senate and House, and particularly to the former's expected role in formulating foreign policy. It was also his last *Federalist* essay, written just as he was readying to return to Virginia. Nearly a decade of service in the Virginia assembly and in Congress stood behind his deep skepticism about deliberative assemblies. His analysis of this problem takes up a good portion of his writings in the 1780s and indeed his analysis of this problem was almost a preoccupation of his writings in the 1780s.[34] After the Convention, notwithstanding his reservations about the principle of equal state representation, he retained a deep belief in the importance of a separate, upper house with a capacity for deliberation and cool-headed discernment. *Federalist* 63 represents the culmination of his thinking about democratic legislatures. It came as he applied his theory of countervailing institutions to the conduct of foreign affairs. Without a senatorial check, Madison warned, "the esteem of foreign powers will not only be forfeited by an unenlightened and variable policy, proceeding from the causes already mentioned; but the national councils will not possess that sensibility to the opinion of the world, which is perhaps not less necessary in order to merit, than it is to obtain its respect and confidence" (*Fed.* 63, 422).

Why, however, was "the opinion of the world" so crucial? "An attention to the judgment of other nations is important to every government for two reasons," Madison explained. First, "independently of the merits of any particular plan or measure, it is desirable, on various accounts, that it should appear to other nations as the offspring of a wise and honorable policy." These states would respect a nation that made wise rather than foolish decisions. The wise decision-maker thereby gained twice: once by the decision itself, and further by the respect other nations would then extend. The second reason, Madison continued, was that "in doubtful cases, particularly where the national councils may be warped by some strong passion or momentary interest, the presumed or known opinion of the impartial world may be the best guide that can be followed" (*Fed.* 63, 423). That opinion of "the impartial world," in other words, could help policy-makers navigate through the shoals of popular opinion in politically fraught times and on the most politically sensitive questions involving the nation's foreign affairs.

This was a deep point in manifest tension with the more pessimistic portrait of international relations that Hamilton and Madison had painted in the early essays. In elucidating the benefits of the Constitution's structural design, a different picture emerged. Faced with impassioned impulse, national decision-makers should consult "the opinion of the impartial world." Although Madison did not elaborate on how that opinion was to be ascertained, his method shows that he repeatedly recurred to ancient and modern history and the known rules of international relations. His axiom that "all very numerous assemblies" tend to become "mob[s]," in which passion never fails to wrest the sceptre of reason," applied especially to conducting relations with the rest of the world (*Fed.* 55, 374). Jay and Hamilton were of the same mind and looked even more explicitly to the law of nations as a guide to international decision-making. The authors of *The Federalist* contrasted the traditional customs of international public law to transient domestic politics and found in the former truths that had been tested over time.[35] Those known and conventional rules, tried by history and supported by reason, would offer a better guide to foreign policy than factional or even majoritarian impulses.

Of course, neither Madison, nor Hamilton, nor Jay would have denied that nations sometimes acted unjustly and disregarded the law of nations. To follow suit, however, would be self-defeating. Each nation actually stood to gain more by conducting itself honorably. "What has not America lost by her want of character with foreign nations," Madison asked, "and how many errors and follies would she not have avoided, if the justice and propriety of her measures had, in every instance, been previously tried by the light in which they would probably appear to the unbiased part of mankind?" (*Fed.* 63, 422–23). Notwithstanding the hard-boiled skepticism about human nature and collective politics that they sometimes expressed, the authors retained the belief that there was an "unbiased" perspective on national behavior available in the larger world, measured across time and space, which could serve as a kind of global impartial spectator. It was this opinion that ought to guide a nation's foreign policy.

Similar considerations stood behind the institutional features of the presidency, the most original of the Constitution's institutions and one that was also structured primarily to improve American foreign policy. The novel system of presidential electors would identify "characters pre-eminent for ability and virtue," Hamilton assured his readers in *Federalist* 68. "Talents for low intrigue and the little arts of popularity may alone suffice to elevate a man to the first honors in a single state; but it will require other talents and a different kind of merit to establish him in the esteem and confidence of the whole union." Virtue and efficiency would combine to produce "good administration" (*Fed.* 68, 460–61). The single executive that many Anti-Federalists thought dangerous would actually assure the "perfect *secrecy* and immediate *dispatch*" for diplomacy that a council could not (*Fed.* 64, 435. See also *Fed.* 70, 472). Combined with the Senate when making treaties, "the constitution provides that our negotiations for treaties shall have every advantage which can be derived from talents, information, integrity, and deliberate investigations on the one hand, and from secrecy and dispatch on the other" (*Fed.* 64, 436). The executive possessed other virtues than efficiency, however. Because of his independence from the legislature, the president would not be subservient to all its desires. Instead he could, and should, exercise his own reason and judgment. "The republican principle demands that the deliberate sense of the community should govern the conduct of those to whom they entrust the management of their affairs," Hamilton explained, but "it does not require an unqualified complaisance to every sudden breese [sic] of passion, or to every transient impulse which the people may receive from the arts of men, who flatter their prejudices to betray their interests" (*Fed.* 71, 482).

In addition, while a four-year term would give the president "firmness," that tenure was not so long as "to justify any alarm for the public liberty" (*Fed.* 71, 485). Nor was he restricted to a single term, because that limitation might "occasion a disgraceful and ruinous mutability in the administration of the government" (*Fed.* 72, 487). Finally, the president's qualified veto gave the executive more than mere "parchment delineation" from Congress; it supplied "constitutional arms" to provide for effective self-defense, as well as "to encrease the chances in favor of the community, against the passing of bad laws, through haste, inadvertence, or design." Having more eyes reviewing each bill, would, in Hamilton's words, increase "the diversity in the situations of those who are to examine it." "It establishes a salutary check upon the legislative body, calculated to guard the community against the effects of faction, precipitancy, or of any impulse unfriendly to the public good, which may happen to influence a majority of that body" (*Fed.* 73, 494–95).

The treaty power fell to another "distinct department" that likewise was structured to enhance the ability of the nation to interact effectively with other nations. As Hamilton and Jay explained in their parallel essays on the treaty power, a treaty was a contract or "bargain" with a foreign nation and, as such, was neither purely executive nor legislative in nature. Its negotiation required a capacity for secrecy and flexibility, as well as the "wisdom" and "integrity" of individuals "the most distinguished by their abilities and virtue" and who "best understand our national interests" (*Fed.* 64, 433). These traits marked out the executive as the most suitable branch. On the other hand, "the vast importance of the trust, and the operation of treaties as laws" strongly suggested the necessity of a participation by a part of the legislature (*Fed.* 75, 504–05).[36] It was true that the president would have the qualities "indispensable in the management of foreign negotiations" in the highest degree, but *The Federalist*'s social psychology explained why adherence to strict Enlightenment separation-of-powers theory would nevertheless be unwise in this context.[37] In Britain, the king had the sole power of making treaties because his hereditary status gave him "personally too much at stake in the government to be in any material danger of being corrupted by foreign powers." In a republic, however, the president would be "raised from the station of a private citizen," have only a modest fortune, and would expect to return to private life. These different conditions were a recipe for temptation, corruption, and even "aggrandizement, by the aid of a foreign power" (*Fed.* 75, 505).

It would, however, go too far in the opposite direction to empower the Senate alone to make treaties, because an agent appointed by the Senate to negotiate – even were it the president himself – "could not be expected to enjoy the confidence and respect of foreign powers in the same degree with the constitutional representative of the nation." Nor could he operate with the same "weight or efficacy." Moreover, involving the House would be folly in view of the defects of popular assemblies in conducting foreign affairs. As Jay explained,

> They who wish to commit the power under consideration to a popular assembly, composed of members constantly coming and going in quick succession, seem not to recollect that such a body must necessarily be inadequate to the attainment of those great objects, which require to be steadily contemplated in all their relations and circumstances, and which can only be approached and achieved by measures which not only talents, but also exact information, and often much time, are necessary to concert and to execute.
>
> (*Fed.* 64, 433–34)

Hamilton added: "An accurate and comprehensive knowledge of foreign politics; a nice and uniform sensibility to national character, decision, *secrecy* and dispatch; are incompatible with the genius of a body so variable and so numerous" (*Fed.* 75, 505–07).[38] In view of the defects of the House, the Supremacy Clause wisely made treaties "part of the law of the land" (*Fed.* 75, 505–06). This explicit declaration carried forward, and virtually completed, the elimination of the most popular branch from the treaty process by empowering the federal courts, the most insulated branch, to enforce treaties directly, without involving the House. As a result, "[t]heir true import ... must, like all other laws, be ascertained by judicial determinations" (*Fed.* 22, 122). Indeed, Jay added, the Supremacy Clause went so far as to place treaties "beyond the lawful reach of legislative acts" (*Fed.* 64, 437). The need to insulate treaty compliance from the winds of popular opinion was, all three authors maintained, a crucial lesson of history – not least the American states' own short history.

CONCLUSION

We began with Hamilton's indictment of the Confederation's international woes in *Federalist* 15. He did not end that essay, however, on a dark note. Instead he sought to remind his readers of what, he thought, was the large consensus about the very point of inter-state cooperation, at home and abroad: "impelled by every motive that ought to influence an enlightened people, let us make a firm stand for our safety, our tranquillity, our dignity, our reputation," because the present course "has too long seduced us from the paths of felicity and prosperity" (*Fed.* 15, 92). What made the United States special, Hamilton argued in *Federalist* 1, was not that it was a republic or collection of republics, nor that it sought commercial engagement with the rest of the world rather than conquest. Instead, what made it special was its experiment with new forms of self-governance, and prominently with institutional mechanisms that would maximize effective, just, and honorable decision-making, while minimizing wasteful, unjust and ineffective decision-making. When Hamilton proclaimed that the United States could become a model for the world, he did not merely mean that people in other nations might copy the American constitutions and enjoy better states at home. Rather, he was observing that the benefits of reformed American constitutionalism would increase as other nations followed the American lead in "establishing good government from reflection and choice," instead of relying for their constitutions "on accident and force." This is what he meant by adding "the inducements of philanthropy to those of patriotism" in making his case for ratification (*Fed.* 1, 3). The world itself would become better governed, each nation, starting at home, and then all together.

NOTES

1 "[T]hese united Colonies are, and of Right ought to be Free and Independent States," the Second Continental Congress declared, and "as Free and Independent States, they have full Power to levy War, conclude Peace, contract Alliances, establish Commerce, and to do all other Acts

and Things which Independent States *may of right do.*" Simultaneously, Congress was drafting its Model Treaty to promote free trade and provide the foundation of the United States' relations with the European world. Daniel J. Hulsebosch, "The Revolutionary Portfolio: Constitution-Making and the Wider World in the American Revolution," *Suffolk University Law Review*, 47 (2014), 759–822.

2 David M. Golove and Daniel J. Hulsebosch, "A Civilized Nation: The Early American Constitution, the Law of Nations, and the Pursuit of International Recognition," *New York University Law Review* 85 (2010), 932–822.

3 Max Edling, *A Revolution in Favor of Government* (New York: Oxford University Press, 2003); Roher H. Brown, *Redeeming the Republic: Federalists, Taxation, and the Origins of the Constitution* (Baltimore, MD: Johns Hopkins University Press, 1993).

4 See also James E. Lewis, *The American Union and the Problem of Neighborhood: The United States and the Collapse of the Spanish Empire* (Chapel Hill: University of North Carolina Press, 1998).

5 *The Address and Reasons of Dissent of the Minority of the Convention of the State of Pennsylvania, to their Constituents*, in *DHRC*, II, 619. The language here about trade retaliation was controversial, but some Federalists, notably Jefferson and Madison, believed that trade retaliation was a valid weapon in diplomacy.

6 Centinel IV, *Independent Gazetteer*, November 30, 1787, *DHRC*, *XIV*, 317.

7 See Frederick W. Marks III, *Independence on Trial: Foreign Affairs and the Constitution* (Baton Rouge: Louisiana State University Press, 1973), and Jack N. Rakove, "From One Agenda to Another: The Condition of American Federalism, 1783–1787," in *The American Revolution: Its Character and Limits*, ed. Jack P. Greene (New York: New York University Press, 1987), 80–103. For analyses of the Confederation reaching different conclusions about its viability absent substantial reform, compare Merrill Jensen, *The Articles of Confederation: An Interpretation of the Social-Constitutional History of the American Revolution, 1774–1781* (Madison, WI: University of Wisconsin Press, 1940), with Jack N. Rakove, *The Beginnings of National Politics: An Interpretive History of the Continental Congress* (New York: Knopf, 1979),

and Richard Morris, *The Forging of the Union, 1781–1789* (New York: Harper & Row, 1987).

8 An Observer, *New-York Journal*, December 3, 1787 (responding to Jay's *Fed. 5*), *DHRC, XIX*, 268, 270.

9 Alexander Hamilton, A Letter from Phocion to the Considerate Citizens of New York (January 1–27, 1784), Harold C. Syrett, ed., *The Papers of Alexander Hamilton* (New York: Columbia University Press, 1961–1987), *PAH*, III, 483–97. For an intellectual history of this attempt to separate state from national powers, see Alison L. LaCroix, *The Ideological Origins of American Federalism* (Cambridge, MA: Harvard University Press, 2010).

10 Patrick Henry, June 18, 1788, in *DHRC*, X, 1384–85.

11 See Gordon S. Wood, *The Creation of the American Republic, 1776–1787* (Chapel Hill: University of North Carolina Press, 1969); Jack Rakove, *Original Meanings: Politics and Ideas in the Making of the Constitution* (New York: Alfred A. Knopf, 1996).

12 A leading modern scholar famously described the Constitution's allocation of foreign affairs powers as "not so much 'separated' as fissured, along jagged lines indifferent to classical categories of governmental power." Louis Henkin, *Foreign Affairs and the United States Constitution*, 2nd edition (Oxford: Oxford University Press, 1996), 27.

13 Many of these had only recently been described in luxurious detail in John Jay's report to the Confederation Congress on state violations of the Treaty of Paris. Worthington C. Ford et al., eds., *Journals of the Continental Congress* (Washington, D.C.: Government Printing Office, 1904–1937), XXXI, 781–874.

14 Madison, for example, had wanted Congress to exercise a federal negative over state legislation. Hamilton favored lifetime appointments for the president and the senators. Jay, like his two colleagues, wanted proportional representation in both houses of Congress.

15 Although the essays were originally published in New York newspapers, early in the process Hamilton planned to compile them into a book for wider distribution. When submitting his bill in late 1788, the printer recalled that "[w]hen I engaged to do the work, it was to consist of twenty Numbers, or at the utmost twenty-five, which I agreed to print for thirty pounds, five hundred copies." However, as the number of essays

increased from 25 to 85, he was obliged to print three times the number of estimated pages, across two volumes. By the fall of 1788, after the ratification debate was all but over, he was left with "several hundred copies on hand" and expected that he "would not clear five pounds on the whole impression." Archibald McLean to Robert Troup, 11 Oct. 1788, in Allan McLane Hamilton, *The Intimate Life of Alexander Hamilton* (New York: Charles Scribner's Sons, 1910), 82.

16 David Hume, "The Independency of Parliament," in *Essays, Moral, Political and Literary* (new edition, London and Edinburgh, 1764; revised edition, Indianapolis: Liberty Fund, 1987), ed. Eugene F. Miller, 42–47; and see Morton White, *Philosophy, The Federalist, and the Constitution* (New York: Oxford University Press, 1989), 95–99.

17 Daniel Walker Howe has effectively argued that Scottish realism informed "the psychology of *The Federalist*" and, in particular, that the authors "used" Scottish faculty psychology realism to justify and explain the workings of the three branches. Daniel Walker Howe, "The Political Psychology of *The Federalist Papers*," *William and Mary Quarterly*, 44 (1987), 485–509; Howe, "The Language of Faculty Psychology in *The Federalist Papers*," in Terence Ball and J. G. A. Pocock, eds., *Conceptual Change and the Constitution* (Lawrence, KS: University Press of Kansas, 1988); Howe, "Why the Scottish Enlightenment Was Useful to the Framers of the American Constitution *Comparative Studies in Society and History*, 31 (1989), 572–87. Other commentators, including Morton White, Forrest McDonald, and Garry Wills, have parsed the essays to discover just what the authors might have known about Scottish philosophy and which currents of thought were most influential in their thinking.

18 The Scottish thinkers actively debated the relationship between reason and passion. Hume juxtaposed the two in his early essays, for example, but later categorized reason as a special, socially useful kind of passion. Publius by contrast simply contrasted the two. For an analysis of these two concepts in Hume's writings and elsewhere, see Stephen Holmes, *Passions and Constraint: On the Theory of Liberal Democracy* (Chicago, IL: University of Chicago Press, 1995), 42–68.

19 Golove and Hulsebosch, "Civilized Nation," 972–75.

20 As Howe has observed, "the art of governing was a decision-making process analogous to that of an individual; the institutions of government

were analogous to the individual's faculties of mind. In both cases, reaching a right decision required a careful act of balancing. Precipitate, ill-advised action was to be avoided; long-term prudence and morally right actions were desired." Howe, "The Political Psychology of The Federalist," 499–500. See also Colleen A. Sheehan, "The Politics of Public Opinion: James Madison's 'Notes on Government,'" ibid., 49 (1992), 609–27.

21 In order for the separation of powers to function, which "is admitted on all hands to be essential to the preservation of liberty, it is evident that each department should have a will of its own." *Fed.* 51, 349.

22 Golove and Hulsebosch, "Civilized Nation," 989–1015.

23 See Paul M. Spurlin, Montesquieu in America, 1760–1801 (University, LA: Louisiana State University Press, 1940).

24 For the connection between the law of nations literature and the Scottish Enlightenment, see Knud Haakonssen, *Natural and Moral Philosophy: From Grotius to the Scottish Enlightenment* (New York: Cambridge University Press, 1994), 322–27.

25 Felix Gilbert, *Toward the Farewell Address: Ideas of Early American Foreign Policy* (Princeton, NJ: Princeton University Press, 1961).

26 For Enlightenment debates about the effect of commerce on international relations, see Istvan Hont, *Jealousy of Trade: International Competition and the Nation-State in Historical Perspective* (Cambridge, MA: The Belknap Press of Harvard University Press, 2005).

27 William Grayson, speech of June 18, 1788, *DHRC*, X, 1383. See also David Hendrickson, *Peace Pact: The Lost World of the American Founding* (Lawrence, KS: University Press of Kansas, 2003). Grayson was an Anti-Federalist who was not satisfied that the Constitution would establish the appropriate law of nations for the Union.

28 Dorset to the American Commissioners, 26 March 1785, in Julian Boyd, ed., *The Papers of Thomas Jefferson* (Princeton: Princeton University Press, 1950–), VIII, 55, 56, 59.

29 Hendrickson, *Peace Pact:* and see also Peter S. Onuf, "Anarchy and the Crisis of the Union," in *To Form a More Perfect Union: The Critical Ideas of the Constitution*, ed. Herman Belz, Ronald Hoffman, and Peter J. Albert (Charlottesville: University Press of Virginia, 1992).

30 An Observer, New-York Journal, November 19, 1787, *DHRC*, XIX, 268, 270 (denying Publius's suggestion that Anti-Federalists were

complacent about the prospect of the Union dividing into multiple confederacies and confessing "that I have not seen, in any of the pieces published against the proposed constitution, any thing which gives the most distant idea that their writers are in favor of such governments ... and from hence it must evidently appear, that the design of Publius, in artfully holding up to public view such confederacies, can be with no other intention than wilfully to deceive his fellow citizens").

31 Gabriel Bonnot de Mably, *The Principles of Negotiations: or, An Introduction to the Public Law of Europe Founded on Treaties, &c.* (Printed for James Rivington and James Fletcher, at the Oxford-Theatre in Pater-noster Row, 1758). Notably, Publius's essays on ancient and modern confederacies also explicitly rely on Mably. See also Madison, Federalist 18 and 20, pp. 114, 127. Mably's prominence in America was heightened by his printed debate with John Adams over the principles of government. See Abbé de Mably, *Remarks Concerning the Government and the Laws of the United States of America: In Four Letters, Addressed to Mr. Adams* (London, 1784).

32 Mably, pp. 38, 40, 41, 42, 46.

33 For prize cases in the state courts during the Revolution, see Henry Bourguignon, *The First Federal Court: The Federal Appellate Prize Court of the American Revolution, 1775–1787* (Philadelphia: American Philosophical Society, 1977).

34 See Rakove, *Original Meanings*, esp. 23–56; and see also Jack N. Rakove, *A Politician Thinking: The Creative Mind of James Madison* (Norman, OK: University of Oklahoma Press, 2017).

35 See Michael P. Federici, *The Political Philosophy of Alexander Hamilton* (Baltimore, MD: Johns Hopkins University Press, 2012), 117.

36 This explanation calls to mind John Locke's "federative power," although Hamilton did not invoke Locke. See John Locke, *Second Treatise of Government*, in *Two Treatises of Government*, ed. Peter Laslett (Cambridge: Cambridge University Press, 1988), ch. XII.

37 On the transformation from a social to political conception of the separation of powers, see M. J. C. Vile, *Constitutionalism and the Separation of Powers* (Indianapolis: Liberty Fund, 1998); William B. Gwynn, *The Meaning of the Separation of Powers: An Analysis of the*

Doctrine from Its Origin to the Adoption of the United States Constitution (New Orleans, LA: Tulane University Press, 1965).

38 He applied the same logic for excluding the House from the appointment of officers, including ambassadors. Hamilton, *Fed.* 77, 519 ("A body so fluctuating, and at the same time so numerous, can never be deemed proper for the exercise of that power").

5   *The Federalist's* New Federalism

Michael Zuckert

Judging from the title that Publius gave his collection of essays, the label that defenders of the proposed Constitution took for themselves, and the label that became attached to their opponents, federalism seems to have been *the* central issue in the debate over the proposed Constitution. Yet the labels themselves are often the source of confusion when speaking of the debate over its ratification. One form the confusion takes is the puzzlement that derives from the fact that the Constitution's opponents, the Anti-Federalists, are usually characterized as a group who sought a more federal constitution than the nationalist-leaning document the so-called Federalists were sponsoring. It might seem that the parties were strangely mislabeled, a feeling shared not only by many modern readers, but by some of the participants in the debate themselves. So Melancton Smith, a leading Anti-Federalist, was reported to have said in the New York Ratifying Convention, in reply to a speech by a leading Federalist: "He hoped the gentleman would be complaisant enough to exchange names with those who disliked the Constitution, as it appeared ... that they were Federalists, and those who advocated it Anti-Federalists."[1] The confusion over names was certainly a natural one, but the names that have stuck were not so inappropriate or so much a usurpation as critics like Smith averred. All the parties to the debate, even Anti-Federalists like the Federal Farmer, thought by many to be Smith, agreed that a federal system had two major components: member states and a "federal head" or general government for the whole.[2] Since a federal system was normally contrasted with a unitary or consolidated system like France, the federal system was thought to be the one with decentralized authority, that is, with more authority in the member states relative to the greater authority in the general or central government of a unitary system. Thus, one could plausibly be labeled a federalist if one were in favor of greater authority in the member units relative to the federal head (as the Anti-Federalists were). But one could just as well be a federalist for favoring the strengthening of the federal head or central government (as the Federalists did). Given the circumstances of the debate over the Constitution, its advocates even had a somewhat stronger claim to the label, despite the understandable ambiguities. The pro-Constitution forces came before the country with a proposal to strengthen the federal head and thus were in this sense Federalists.

We cannot, however, begin to understand federalism in *The Federalist* if we approach the issue with only our contemporary understanding of federalism in mind. As Martin Diamond put it over fifty years ago, the generally accepted terminology as understood in the post-founding era is that "there are three kinds of government – confederal, federal and unitary (national) – and that the United States exemplifies the middle term."[3] But founding-era Americans did not divide the political world into these three types of government. As Diamond also pointed out, "For them, there were but two possible modes: – confederal or federal, as opposed to unitary or national."[4] He cited eighteenth-century dictionary definitions to reveal that federal and confederal were considered synonymous at the time. Likewise, Diamond used his discovery of the two- rather than three-part classification scheme to make sense of James Madison's summary statement on the topic in *Federalist* 39. As Madison put it, "The proposed Constitution . . . is in strictness neither a national nor a federal constitution; but a composition of both (*Fed.* 39, 257)." Leading Anti-Federalist writers also described the system established by the new Constitution in ways that conform to Diamond's findings regarding eighteenth-century usage rather than in terms like our twenty-first-century three-part classification. Like Madison, the Federal Farmer called the proposed constitution "partly federal."[5] He also described it as a "partial consolidation," which he understood to be a mixture of the two pure forms, "federal" and "complete consolidation," the latter being equivalent to what Diamond called unitary or national government.[6] What the founding generation saw to be a combination of the two forms is seen by us to be a third form, a terminological change that we must keep in mind when we read *The Federalist*.

In a paper "A Sketch Never Finished nor Applied," that Madison worked on during his retirement years of the 1830s, he spoke of the Constitution's "combination" of federal and national or consolidated union as a remarkable innovation: "It remained for the British Colonies, now United States, of North America, to add to those [earlier] examples [of 'confederal associations'], one of a more interesting character than any of them: which led to a system without a [sic] example ancient or modern, a system ... so combin[ing] a federal form with the forms of individual Republics, as may enable each to supply the defects of the other and obtain the advantages of both."[7] What we have come to call the federal elements of the new constitutional system were not only a major innovation, but were also in Madison's mind the glory of the new system. The intention of this essay is to take Madison's judgment as its theme: to examine his claims for the novelty and for the greatness of the new federalism as developed in *The Federalist*.

I   ON THE ENDS OF THE FEDERAL UNION

The topic of federalism is so central to *The Federalist* that important discussions of it appear and, in some cases, dominate all the major sections of the book. In every case the author attempts to show that the proposed system is a new kind of federalism, that is, that it is a species of the genus "federal" or "confederal" system, but a species that breaks with established modes of federal construction. Recall that Madison, in the document quoted earlier, referred to the new order as a type of "confederal association." That is also the way in which Publius saw it, an insight often lost to view when we look back at the founding with twenty-first-century eyes.

"The utility of union," the first section of Publius's defense of the Constitution, is remarkably effective at presenting both the traditional and some of the innovative aspects of the proposed Constitution. As Madison emphasizes in his "Sketch," which he meant to stand as a preface to his notes on the Constitutional Convention, American federalism may be entirely novel, but federalism itself is not: "feeble communities, independent of each other, have resorted to a Union ... with common Councils, for the common safety ag[ainst] powerful neighbors, and for the preservation of justice and peace among themselves."[8] Defense against powerful neighbors was the core of the traditional understanding of the purpose or, in Publius's term, "utility of union." It was widely believed in the eighteenth century (and before) that republics necessarily had to be small, a view especially powerful among the Anti-Federalist opponents of the Constitution, and, they alleged, in the French political philosopher Montesquieu's classical study, *The Spirit of the Laws* (1748). Accordingly, in *Federalist* 2–5, Publius begins his presentation of "the utility of union" with the widely accepted idea that it is prudent and even necessary for small republics to form a union of some sort in order to safeguard themselves against "foreign force and influence." In beginning here, Publius is not only aligning himself with the most traditional defense of federation, but striking a note that Anti-Federalists were least likely to find objectionable.

Publius's ever fertile brain does not stop with the standard argument for the utility of union for defense against foreign threats, however, but extends it in novel directions. One such extension is an emphasis on the dangers that the American states will pose to each other, a less explored theme of traditional federal theory. This theme was pertinent in the context in two ways. First, in the initial eight papers Publius speaks on several occasions of the likelihood that if this new plan for union fails, the union as the Americans have hitherto known it would fail as well, perhaps to be replaced by two or three smaller confederacies. Although there is little evidence of scheming going on toward this end in 1787–88, such an outcome was a very plausible resultant of a failure to ratify the Constitution. One of the central grounds of opposition to the Constitution was that as a confederation of republics that itself aspired to be a republic, the general government under the new Constitution would be too large to remain free and would despotize over the member states. Nonetheless, all agreed that some sort of defensive union was desirable. Smaller confederacies are a plausible solution to the dual imperatives the American republics faced – the need to unite for the sake of defense and the need to not be too large, because of the incompatibility between largeness and republicanism. By emphasizing the dangers of war among the Americans, Publius was preemptively speaking to the temptation toward partial confederacies. He attempted to head off the view that a number of smaller confederacies can be just as effective as the one large union proposed in the new Constitution. Because closer in proximity, the danger posed by the states as independent polities or partial confederacies might well be as great as or even greater than the danger of foreign force.

Publius feared that many Americans may have been lulled into thinking that partial confederacies or even no confederacies would suffice perfectly well in North America because the new states were all commercial and republican. The theory was that commercialism and modern republicanism worked to make states more pacific due to intertwined interests and a moral tone in accordance with commercial (rather than martial) life. A continent of commercial republics would thus be naturally peaceful. So far as that is true, union for the sake of defense is less necessary, especially when joined to a sense that foreign danger was far away. In one of the rare moments when he turns against Montesquieu, ordinarily his political mentor, Publius forcefully addressed and refuted this theory. The French thinker had declared that commerce fosters peace because it weaves bonds of mutual interest among nations, softens the mores, and makes the peoples of the world more tolerant.[9] Republicanism, Montesquieu maintained, could also work for peace. He certainly knew that the ancient republics tended to be martial, but he believed that in the modern context republics were less likely than monarchies to pursue war as a policy. In the latter, the incentives were such that monarchs derived most of the benefits of (successful) war – increase in wealth, territory, glory – while the people bore the costs in blood and gold. In republics the incentives were arrayed so as to favor war to a much lesser degree, for the people both paid the price and reaped the rewards of war. The people, therefore, are more likely to weigh carefully the costs and benefits of war than princes are.

Federalist 6, one of the classic essays of the series, responded head-on to Montesquieu's analysis. Publius not only pointed to well-known bellicose republics like Rome, but also appealed to history to demonstrate that commerce cannot be relied on to quell armed conflict among nations. Indeed, as commerce spread in the world, warfare caused by commercial rivalries also increased. It would be unrealistic and therefore imprudent to believe that distance from Europe or the character of the American states would protect them against aggression from foreign forces or continental neighbors (*Fed.* 6, 28–36). The relevance of *Federalist* 6 to federalism is thus clear: the classic goal of federation as a means to strength and security cannot be achieved in any way short of an effective federation comprised of all the existing states. Such an effective federation, having to a much greater degree the character of a national republic than traditional federations or the Articles of Confederation, would require, in turn, facing squarely the fear that republicanism and largeness are simply incompatible.

This theme runs throughout the remainder of *The Federalist*, but Publius turns to a particularly important aspect of it in the immediate sequel when he expands considerably upon the accepted notions of "the utility of union." A union, the nature of which is still unspecified at this point in the argument, can serve not only the defensive purposes of traditional federal theory, but can also contribute positively to certain imperatives of good governance within the member states. In the most famous essay in the book, *Federalist* 10, Publius purports to show how a large republic can help resolve the tension between republican government and "the very principles of civil liberty" that could lead "the enlightened friends to liberty" to disfavor the republican form (*Fed.* 10, 51). Alternatively put, the extended or large republic, so far from being a threat to liberty, can provide a solution to the hitherto insoluble and even mostly unrecognized problem of majority tyranny. That problem appears to be insoluble because a republic is precisely the government that arms majorities with the power to govern, and perforce lacks a check on tyrannous majorities. As Alan Gibson details in his essay in this volume, Publius argues that the large republic can solve this problem in a wholly republican way, i.e. not by appealing to any non-republican ruling power (like a hereditary monarch). Conversely, the small republic favored by Anti-Federalists did not offer a solution to the problem of majority tyranny. Publius takes the momentous step of claiming that a union of the states can constitute a non-tyrannous government, thus accomplishing not only external defense but also internal good governance for the member states. It must be noted, however, that Publius does not here specify how far this proposed Constitution goes in providing this benefit. The discussion in the first section of the book is very abstract – what the utility of union can be; it does not yet include a discussion of whether this union achieves these advantages, especially the good of non-tyrannous republican governance.

In affirming such an extension of the ends union may serve, Publius indicates, without yet explaining just how, that the new federalism he is promoting must be very different in its structure, powers, and mode of operation from the old federalism (such as the Americans possessed in the Articles of Confederation). In part to encompass the newly identified end of union and in part to diagnose the much experienced failure of the Articles of Confederation, Publius turns in the next set of papers (*Fed.* 15–22) to his second topic: "The insufficiency of the present confederation to preserve that Union."

II   ON THE INSUFFICIENCY OF THE PRESENT CONFEDERATION

The "present confederation" is an instance of the old federalism that Publius hopes to supplant. Publius could take for granted that his audience would be sufficiently familiar with the Articles of

Confederation that he did not need to describe it in detail. In fact, he describes it only as far as he parades before his readers those defects that make it incapable of preserving the Union: it is incapable of achieving even the traditional ends of the old federalism, to say nothing of its being unable to achieve the novel end of solving *the* republican problem that Publius introduced in *Federalist* 10.

It is worth sketching the main features of the government established under the Articles of Confederation. With apologies to Abraham Lincoln, we might characterize the Articles as establishing government of the states, by the states, and for the states. The "citizens" of the Articles' government were the states, each of which was declared in Article II to retain "its sovereignty, freedom, and independence, and every Power, Jurisdiction and right, which is not by this confederation expressly delegated to the United States." Government was *for the states* in the sense that its purposes were purposes only of the states as states: "their common defence, the security of their [the states'] Liberties, and their [the states'] mutual and general welfare" (Art. III). It established government *by the states* in that its only agency of governance was an assembly of representatives of the states; the representatives acted as delegates from their states rather than as holders of seats in an assembly. They were in this sense more like present-day delegates to the United Nations than like representatives or senators in the current Congress. The states could control their delegates through their power of appointment, removal, very short terms of office, and setting of salary. The Articles' Congress had the power to make only requests or requisitions on the member states, who then had the duty, the power, and the agency to effectuate – or not – those requests. In this sense too, we had government *by the states*. The states stood between the general government and the humans who were their citizens. So far as we can speak of the government under the Articles as having any governing authority, it is government *of the states*. Its resolutions, requisitions, and recommendations went to the states and directed the states as such to do or not do. Accordingly, Publius doubts whether the Articles' government can rightly be said to have any genuine governing power at all.

Publius announced in the very first sentence of his very first essay that he considered the government under the Articles to have demonstrated only its own "inefficacy" (*Fed.* 1, 3). By the time he came to *Federalist* 15, he asserted that this judgment is not unique to him or to men of his party; it is a judgment "which is not either controverted or doubted, to which the understandings and feelings of all classes of men assent" (*Fed.* 15, 90). Even those who oppose the new Constitution agree. Where they disagree is on what is to be done in response to this nearly universally perceived "inefficacy." Publius will argue that what is needed is the new federalism; the Anti-Federalists, for the most part, wish to stick closer to the old federalism, but even they – or the most insightful of them – were willing to adopt some version of the new federalism. The Federal Farmer, for example, conceded that a plan of a partial consolidation "is ... the only one that can secure the freedom and happiness of this people."[10]

In *Federalist* 37 Publius summarized the results of his inquiry into the causes of the "insufficiency" of the Articles' government for achieving the ends of the Union: "It has been shewn in the course of these papers, that the existing Confederation is founded on principles which are fallacious; that we must consequently change this first foundation, and with it, the superstructure resting upon it" (*Fed.* 37, 233). It is no mere detail of construction of the Articles' system that is defective, but rather the "first foundation" itself. And this foundation is not unique to the Americans' effort to construct a federation: "It has been shewn, that the other confederacies which could be consulted as precedents, have been viciated [sic] by the same erroneous principles, and can therefore furnish no other light than that of beacons, which give warning of the course to be shunned, without pointing out that which ought to be pursued" (ibid.). The error in the Articles is universal to *all* previous confederacies: Publius's new federalism must be without example.

Publius straightforwardly identified the chief defect of the Articles – and by extension of all previous federations – as "the principle of LEGISLATION for STATES or GOVERNMENTS, in their CORPORATE or COLLECTIVE CAPACITIES" (*Fed.* 15, 93; capitalization in original). This is another way of saying that the problem is treating the member states of the federation as its citizens. The alternative is legislation for "the INDIVIDUALS of whom [the member states] consist" (ibid.). Acting on the member states or governments as collective or corporate entities was known as acting according to "the federal principle"; acting on human individuals was known as acting on the national principle.

The pervasiveness of the federal principle in previous federations seems to be a natural (if mistaken) consequence of the generic character of federations. As Publius says, "The definition of a *Confederate Republic* seems simply to be, an 'assemblage of societies' or an association of two or more States into one State" (*Fed.* 9, 55). Publius is adapting his definition from Montesquieu's discussion of the subject: A federal republic, said the French philosopher, "is an agreement by which many political bodies consent to become citizens of the larger state that they want to form. It is a society of societies that make a new one."[11] As the product of pre-existing independent societies or states, entered into for protection against aggression by larger neighbors, it is natural to treat the member states as citizens of the larger new state and to deal with them "in their collective capacities."

Publius's major analytic innovation is to reveal why this foundational principle of federations dooms them to ineffectiveness and failure, and his major practical innovation is to invent another mode of federal construction that promises much more success. It must be noted, however, that Publius's innovative adoption of a new national mode of operation and construction is nonetheless a *means* to the effectuation of the traditional end of producing a federation. It is not meant to be the establishment of a national system per se, because it is a system in which the states remain independent and political entities in their sphere of operation, and continue to possess the lion's share of powers.

Publius's most pressing task is to make clear to his audience why breaking with the traditional federal principle is necessary to make an "efficacious" government for the Union, because it is that break that most obviously characterizes and raises fundamental questions about the proposed Constitution. The core of Publius's defense of his innovation is, perhaps surprisingly, an analysis of the necessary role of coercion in politics. Recent political philosophy had emphasized the role of coercion in politics, as is visible in John Locke's definition of political power as "*a Right* of making Laws with Penalties of Death, and consequently all less Penalties ... and of employing the force of the Community, in the Execution of such Laws."[12] The central motif of the social compact account of the origin of government, a narrative Publius accepts, is precisely to explain how an entity with the power to rightly coerce comes to be and why that power to coerce is necessary (*Fed.* 21, 129–30; *Fed.* 44, 301). Just as coercion is needed in ordinary governance, so it is needed in federal systems, but the customary federal systems fail to recognize that fact or to provide properly for it.

The Articles of Confederation made no provision for the exercise of coercive power by the government of the Union at all. This was not an unintentional omission. "There was a time," Publius tells us, "when we were told that breaches, by the States, of the regulations of the federal authority were not to be expected; that a sense of common interest would preside over the conduct of the respective members, and would beget a full compliance with all the constitutional requisitions of the Union" (*Fed.* 15, 96). The thought, which many Anti-Federalists still clung to, seemed to be that if the government of the Union was indeed pursuing policies in the common interest, then the states would voluntarily comply, because it would be to their benefit to do so. Publius finds this expectation not to have stood the test of experience, for the states had regularly neglected to perform their duties under the Articles. He presents at least three reasons why this neglect of duty might be expected. First, it is generally acknowledged that governments require coercive authority, and what reason is there to think that this would be different in a federation than in an ordinary government? The reason coercion is so central a part of government, as it is for Locke, is that despite whatever common interest human beings may have in peaceful cooperation, coordination, and justice, the need for government derives from the fact that "the passions of men will not conform to the dictates of reason and justice, without constraint" (*Fed.* 15, 96).

Moreover, in dealing with collective bodies like political communities, one has reason to expect even more reluctance to obey non-coercive authority: "there is in the nature of sovereign power an impatience of controul, that disposes those who are invested with the exercise of it, to look with an evil eye upon all external attempts to restrain or direct its operations." This "spirit" leads to "a kind of eccentric tendency in the subordinate or inferior orbs, by the operation of which there will be a perpetual effort in each to fly off from the common center." This "spirit" finds its origin in a yet more primitive feature of human nature – "the love of power." As Publius explained, "Power controuled or abridged is almost always the rival and enemy of that power by which it is controuled or abridged" (*Fed.* 15, 96–97).

Finally, Publius noticed a phenomenon very akin to what has come to be called the "free-rider problem." It is not merely wayward passion, but reason itself, that can lead member states to fail to comply voluntarily with their duty in a non-coercive situation. If the other members are complying so that the collective good sought from the federation is in fact supplied, then it may be rational for any given member to scant its contributions, for it can receive the benefit without paying its share of the cost. On the other hand, if the others are not contributing their share, it remains rational for any given member not to do its part either, for, if it did so, it would bear the cost without the offset of receiving the benefit. Either way, then, it is rational for a member state to scant its contributions or conformity to federal rules (*Fed.* 15, 97–98).

In ordinary governments coercion is needed to overcome these various disincentives to obedience. But, as already noted, the Articles' government has no resources to apply coercion against its member states. On the eve of the Constitutional Convention, many astute political leaders from the different states were becoming aware of the need for coercion, and proposals to add that to the powers of the Articles' government were not uncommon. Indeed, an important part of the Virginia Plan introduced at the opening of the Constitutional Convention was its Sixth Resolution, which provided, in part, that the legislature of the Union should have the power "to call forth the force of the Union ag[ainst] any member of the Union failing to fulfill its duty under the articles thereof."[13] Thus there would be coercion, and, according to Publius's analysis, the Union could, for the first time, be said to have "the power of making laws," for "it is essential to the idea of a law, that it be attended with a sanction; or, in other words, a penalty or punishment for disobedience." Without such a sanction, "the resolutions or commands which pretend to be laws will in fact amount to nothing more than advice or recommendation" (*Fed.* 15, 95). Arming the Articles government with the authority and capacity to sanction would for the first time actually make it a government, for "government implies the power of making laws," i.e. commands with sanctions.

While the power to sanction or coerce is necessary for the very existence of government and law, to say nothing of their effectiveness, the approach taken by the Sixth Resolution of the Virginia Plan amounts to the same as not providing for coercion at all. The Virginia Plan's resolution contemplates what Publius calls "COERTION [sic] of arms" (rather than "COERTION [sic] of the magistracy"), but coercion of arms is ineffectual as well as dangerous. When one collective body (the government of the federation) attempts to enforce its laws on other collective bodies (the states), "every breach of the laws must involve a state of war, and military execution must become the only instrument of civil obedience" (*Fed.* 15, 95–96). If civil war is the price to be paid for every effort to enforce the law in "the federal manner" of government on government, then the most likely result is that the government of the federation will forgo efforts to sanction disobedient states, and the system will succumb *in practice* to the same ineffectiveness under which it suffers when it lacks any enforcement authority whatever.

In order to have an effectual federal system, the federation must thus abandon the federal principle and have recourse to the national mode of operation – governing of citizens via "coercion of the magistracy." The government of the federation must operate directly on and have direct relations with the human beings who compose its member states. This shift in the mode of operation is related again to the theme of coercion. For there to be government and law, there must be coercion, but for coercion to be effective it must not be applied to collective entities like states, which are themselves armed, but against individuals, against whom coercion may be applied at much lower cost and with much less danger – and therefore far more effectively. In a word, individuals are much weaker and less able to resist the power of the federal government than states are. But what Publius has in mind is nowhere near as dramatic as the talk of coercion might suggest. He means the ordinary, garden-variety sort of coercion that occurs through the use of courts, magistrates, and other officers of the law. Less dramatically put, Publius means that the government of the federation must reach the human citizens of the federation directly, using its own agents of enforcement as well as legislation. The old model of federalism, where the member states stood in all governance between the government of the federation and individual citizens, must be jettisoned. That is the simple but very far-reaching thought behind the new federalism Publius is promoting.

There is one other aspect of coercion in relation to the new federalism that must be noticed. According to Publius the threat of coercion is not only a stick, but can also be a carrot. Speaking of the reasons that citizen attachment under the new federalism will remain primarily to the states, Publius points out that the latter, having in their custody "the ordinary administration of criminal and civil justice," will be "the immediate and visible guardian[s] of life and property ... regulating all those personal interests and familiar concerns to which the sensibility of individuals is more immediately awake." The ordinary administration of justice is "the most powerful, most universal and most attractive source of popular obedience and attachment," because it has "its benefits and its terrors in constant activity before the public eye." The benefits supplied though coercive enforcement of the law, as well as the terrors aroused by the display or presence of coercion, contribute "more than any other circumstance to impressing upon the minds of the people affection, esteem and reverence towards the government" (*Fed.* 17, 107). The states may be the primary beneficiaries of the attachment that the possession and exercise of coercive power produces, but arming the federal government with similar powers will almost certainly have the positive effect Publius outlines of fostering esteem, affection, and attachment to the federal government. Changing the principle of operation of the government of the federation gives it some resources to attract the affections of the people in a way that governments operating under the principles of the old federalism could never do. Although Publius does not call attention to the fact, the psychic mechanism he describes can also serve as an incentive for the government of the federation to attempt to increase the scope of its powers and activities so as to be yet more present to the people and more likely to be seen as the source of benefits and terrors.

More than 250 years before *The Federalist*, Machiavelli pronounced in his *Prince* that a prince, in order to rule effectively and to remain in power, must depend on his own arms and influence and not on the arms and influence of others. Publius seems to have taken Machiavelli's maxim to heart in affirming that the federation, in order to achieve its own ends, must possess the power to supply sanctions for its own laws and thus have direct relations with its human citizens. This small change had immense implications for federal theory and practice. Where the government under the Articles of Confederation had no executive or judiciary (with a very few relatively slight exceptions) and, according to Publius, did not even have a proper legislature, since it lacked the power to make proper laws, the new kind of federal arrangement called for the creation of a "full service government." The new federation would have its own executive and judiciary, the possession of which enabled it to have a proper legislature as well. Since the new government is to operate directly on its human citizens, it must also derive its officers via a direct relation to those citizens. To take the clearest reason: the new type of federal government is to have power to raise its own revenue and not to depend on the states. But if the government has the power to tax, it must also properly represent those whom it taxes; Americans fought a revolution, after all, in part to vindicate the principle "no taxation without representation." The new kind of federal government requires a robust two-way relation with its citizens, both acting on and derived from them. The newly modeled government of the federation thus becomes government of the people, by the people, and for the people.

In line with the dominant understanding of political legitimacy, this new government must be republican – that is, it must meet the standards of republicanism. If one half of Publius's task was to depict the nature of the new federalism, so his second task was to teach his countrymen the true principles of republicanism and to demonstrate that the proposed Constitution met them.[14] Publius undertook this crucial task in *Federalist* 39, where he proposed a definition of republicanism requiring more popular involvement in governance and in the selection of governors than many of the standard definitions of the day required, but flexible enough to permit the many instances of indirect popular involvement provided for in the proposed constitution.

As Tocqueville noted, the new federalism leads to an extremely complex governmental system, one with two sets of governments where citizens are simultaneously citizens of both governments. Each of the governments is more or less self-contained and independent, with its own powers and responsibility for its own objects. One implication of this structure is that neither government is generally subordinate to the other. As Publius said, possessors of power are resistant to being subordinated to others, and the best way to avoid the kind of expected friction that might easily arise when two governments exercise authority over the same populations is to allow the two governments to touch as little as possible. Thus, the federal government does not depend upon the states to execute its policies, except, as we will see, in the particular relations the judiciaries of the two sets of government have with each other. Under the Constitution of 1787, almost nothing remained of the "government of the states, by the states" character of the Articles of Confederation.

Two governments governing the same population. It sounds like the very definition of the dreaded *imperium in imperio* – an empire within an empire, a clash of authorities that promises anything but peace and public order. Publius was convinced that this would not be the fate of the new federal system for two reasons: first, the constitutive principle of the new federalism was a division of powers such that each government had its own objects and sphere of action, thus minimizing the possibility of outright clashes of authority; second, where overlapping authority was unavoidable, a relatively clear decision rule for determining which government has supreme authority existed within the Constitution. Put simply, the government of the Union would be supreme in its sphere. To effectuate this decision rule, however, there was also needed a body to pronounce how the rule would apply in any given case. That body in the new Constitution would ultimately be the Supreme Court. Thus, *the* federalism-related topic most in need of further treatment in the remainder of *The Federalist* is the division of powers and the maintenance of the proper spheres for each government.

III   THE NECESSITY OF A GOVERNMENT AT LEAST EQUALLY ENERGETIC WITH THE ONE PROPOSED

The nature of the powers granted to the new government is thus the most urgent question remaining for treatment. As Publius sees it, two aspects of this question have special cogency: First, what powers must be vested in the new government of the federation for it to be able to achieve the ends sought from it? And second, how to minimize and resolve potential clashes of authority between the different govern-ments. In order to begin his treatment of these issues, Publius turned to his third major topic: the necessity for a government at least as energetic as the one proposed. The topic as announced is extraordin-arily abstract in that it does not so much deal with the powers actually contained in the proposed Constitution, but with the nature of the powers that would have to be granted in any constitution of the new federal type.

Though Publius's treatment in this set of papers, numbers 23–36, is abstract, the powers he discussed were among the most emphasized and controversial topics in the entire debate over the Constitution. The most politically insightful of the Anti-Federalists saw the problem as follows: the new government does not on paper establish a unitary or consolidated government for the entire United States, but the powers granted and the way in which they are to operate nearly guarantee that it will become a consolidated govern-ment. As such, the Constitution will destroy the free, republican character of American governance and usher in one or another form of despotism.

Two aspects of the title of this section of *The Federalist* are particularly worthy of note. First, Publius turns to the issue of powers under the rubric of "energy." Both "power" and "energy" are terms from the science of physics. Energy in the political context seems to refer to the governmental ability to act effectively. In physics the expenditure of energy is required to set matter in motion or to hinder motion. So what Publius seems to have in mind by energy is what can induce change (or motion) and what can hinder externally imposed change. The sources of energy as developed by Publius are twofold: the powers possessed by the government and the mode of operation by which those powers act. In turning to the issue of powers, Publius thus has two aspects in mind: First, the division and allocation of authority between the two sets of government, and second, the provi-sion of energy. Both are necessary to make the new federalism suffi-cient to its purposes.

Publius – here Hamilton – also speaks of the need for a government *at least* as energetic as the one proposed. While he does not assert that the proposed government is insufficiently energetic, Publius's discussion does leave this possibility open.

The powers discussed in the set of papers on energy are those that are indispensable for supplying the capacity for effective action to any government and thus to the new federal government. These powers are two: the power to raise and spend money and the power to raise and deploy arms, the powers of the purse and the sword. We might think of these as the powers that more than any others impart motion to a government. Sensing the importance of these two powers, the Anti-Federalists were more fearful of the grant of these powers to the general government than they were of any other aspect of the new Constitution. More precisely, they wanted these powers granted in a more limited way and with the inclusion of some form of state agency in the exercise of them. Many of the Anti-Federalists saw that a return to the old requisition system for raising revenue for the general government would be unwise, and so they supported some power in the government to raise revenue without the intercession of the states. But they also feared the unlimited power of the general government to raise revenue, as provided in the new Constitution. They feared that such an unlimited power would lead to the general government grabbing all the important sources of revenue, leaving the states without adequate funds and thus in effect transferring governance increasingly to the general government. They also feared that the open-ended empowerment of that government to spend money would allow it to expand its actions beyond the realm of the enumerated powers, thereby greatly enlarging the sphere of federal governmental action. As a response to these concerns, many Anti-Federalists proposed changes in the Constitution that would limit its possible sources of revenue; for example, by allowing the new government the power to tax imports, but requiring any revenue beyond that to be raised via something like the old requisition system. This modification would limit the direct ability to raise revenue and at the same time build in state agency, thereby insuring that the states possessed the ability to control or limit the revenue of the federal government and guarantee their own sources of revenue. One can easily understand the Anti-Federalist concerns from the perspective of the twenty-first century and the growth of central governmental power. One could understand their concern even better if one imagined a system in which the United Nations was empowered to directly raise revenue from its member states with no limitations set on the source of the revenue and with no provision for the ongoing consent of the member states. That was the potential the Anti-Federalists saw in the proposed general government.

Nonetheless, given the general consensus on the need to defend the Union against foreign danger, the Anti-Federalists accepted government's ability to deploy force in dealings with foreign nations. But they also feared granting such control over armed force to the central government, because they recognized that control of the coercive powers in a society can be used against the home population, as well as against foreign enemies. Ever wary of threats to their liberty, the Anti-Federalists sought limitations on the military power parallel to those they sought to place on the revenue power, while at the same time preserving state agency through greater reliance on state militias.

Publius strongly opposed all efforts to modify the Constitution in the direction of these energy-robbing proposals. In developing his opposition, Publius launched one of the most probing discussions of constitutionalism in the history of political thought. In doing so, he raised the possibility that the new government and any government constructed along the lines of the new federalism might always lack sufficient energy to accomplish its ends.

Publius invokes "axioms as simple as they are universal. The *means* ought to be proportioned to the *end*; the persons, from whose agency the attainment of any *end* is expected, ought to possess the *means* by which it is to be attained" (*Fed.* 23, 147). In this case, there is agreement that the general government has as one of its purposes "the common defence of the members" (*Fed.* 23, 146). That decision made, "it will follow, that that government ought to be cloathed with all the powers requisite to the complete execution of its trust" (*Fed.* 23, 147). Since we cannot say in advance what the source and nature of threats to "the public safety" might be, "it must be admitted, as a necessary consequence, that there can be no limitation of that authority, which is to provide for the defence and protection of the community" (*Fed.* 23, 147–48). Therefore, the various Anti-Federalist schemes are self-contradictory: they *will* a certain end but not the means necessary to achieve it. The consequence of this half-heartedness is most likely even greater damage to the cause of constitutionalism and limited government than could be inflicted by the robust notion of power and energy that Publius is advocating:

> Nations pay little regard to rules and maxims calculated in their very nature to run counter to the necessities of society. Wise politicians will be cautious about fettering the government with restrictions, that cannot be observed; because they know that every breach of the fundamental laws, though dictated by necessity, impairs that sacred reverence, which ought to be maintained in the breasts of rulers towards the constitution of a country, and forms a precedent for other breaches, where the same plea of necessity does not exist at all, or is less urgent and palpable.
>
> (*Fed.* 25, 163)

Although Publius does not expand on the issue in this context, his discussion of the need for energy *at least* equal to that provided by the proposed Constitution strongly implies that this government is not energetic enough. Consider Publius's argument: (1) certain objects are entrusted to the general government; (2) powers that are means to the object are then granted to the general government; these *powers* must be granted without limit, as we have seen. But are these granted powers all the powers that may be needed to achieve that object? If the needs imposed by the object are unpredictable, how can one ever say in advance that these are all the powers needed? Is it not a fundamental error to think that one can identify a finite set of powers as sufficient for achieving a given object, especially an object like defense? Can one ever predict in advance what powers will be needed?

Might it not follow from this line of thinking that the federal scheme itself, that is, the division of objects and then of powers, is misguided? Would the real consequence of the argument about energy be the necessity for what one of the Publii argued for at the Constitutional Convention: that the federal government, entrusted with purposes like defense, must possess full sovereign power, and not an unworkable sliver of power? We come at this point to a place where the two chief persons who compose Publius may disagree, with Hamilton, from the outset, much more dubious than Madison about the new federalism. It is on this and related issues, I would suggest, that Hamilton and Madison only a few years later came to part ways over the nature of the new Constitution, with Hamilton persuaded that the Constitution must be interpreted in such a way as to make it as energetic as it needed to be, but Madison more committed to the viability of the federal system as embodied in the Constitution as ratified.

IV   THE CONFORMITY OF THE PROPOSED
     CONSTITUTION TO THE TRUE PRINCIPLES
     OF FEDERAL GOVERNMENT

When Publius completed his discussion of energy, he turned to his next and last major set of papers as outlined in *Federalist* 1, aiming to show the conformity of the institutions of the new government to republican principles. This is a major turning point in *The Federalist*, for it marks a turn to *this* actual proposed Constitution rather than the abstract matters hitherto discussed. The main theme of this large group of papers will be the institutions of the general government, but despite the title Publius gives to these essays, they also return to and complete the discussion of federalism. As Publius puts it in *Federalist* 39, the adversaries of the Constitution charged that its authors "ought ... to have preserved the *federal* form, which regards the union as a *confederacy* of sovereign States; instead of which, they have framed a *national* government, which regards the union as a *consolidation* of the States" (*Fed.* 39, 253).

In responding to this charge, Publius provided a truly brilliant analysis of the new federalism. The premise of his response is a denial of the binary classification his Anti-Federalist opponents deployed in their critique of the Constitution. Instead of holistic categories Publius proposed that the Constitution must be viewed in its various aspects – what one can call federalism variables – according to whether each aspect is federal or national in character. That is to say, Publius looked at the Constitution in terms of its federal or national principles and character, with federal understood as an aspect in which the government of the Union relates to the states as states, and national understood as those where the government of the Union relates directly to the people as individuals. It is on this basis that Publius concludes that the system proposed is "partly federal, and partly national" (*Fed.* 39, 257). So, to take a particularly telling example, Publius distinguishes between the *operations* of the new governmental powers and the *extent* of those powers. This distinction allows him to clarify an ambiguity in the Constitution that served to confuse observers then and even now: the *operation* is national in character, but in extent of powers it is federal. As he says, "The idea of a [fully] national [or consolidated] Government involves in it, not only an authority over the individual citizens; but an indefinite supremacy over all persons and things, so far as they are objects of lawful Government. Among a people consolidated into one nation, this supremacy is compleatly vested in the national Legislature" (*Fed.* 39, 256). The new government cannot properly be considered a consolidated one "since its jurisdiction extends to certain enumerated objects only, and leaves to the several States a residuary and inviolable sovereignty over all other objects." So, with regard to its powers, the new government is rightly seen as neither wholly federal (in the sense of the Anti-Federalist usage) nor wholly national.

Publius also considers the foundation of the new government, the sources from which it draws its ordinary powers, and the amendment process. In his consideration of these factors, there is no doubt some rhetorical ingenuity at work, sometimes enabling Publius to overstate the federal character of the variable in question. So, for example, when he inquires into the "foundation" of the system he looks to the procedure for ratification, according to which the Constitution is to go into effect when nine states, acting via popularly elected ratifying conventions, agree to it. Publius calls this a federal feature, for the "ratification is to be given by the people, not as individuals composing one entire nation; but as composing the distinct and independent States to which they respectively belong" (*Fed.* 39, 542). Publius adds that only those states that ratify are part of the Union, further revealing the federal character of the ratification. However, he downplays the significance of the popular ratification within the states, for this mode of proceeding is different from the traditional federal ratification process in which the state governments decided the issue, as occurred under the Articles of Confederation. Under the traditional federal mode, the states, constituted through popular sovereignty, were of higher authority than the government of the Union, itself the product only of the state governments and not of the people of the states. The ratification procedure outlined in the new Constitution does not justify calling it wholly national in its foundation, but it does establish a juridical equality (at least) between the government of the Union and the governments of the states in that both derive from the authority of the people. Thus the foundation, as expressed in the ratification procedure, is better described as Publius described the whole – partly federal and partly national. The other two aspects of the system, the sources of its ordinary powers and the amendment procedure, are both also best described as mixed national and federal, as Publius admits.

In identifying the "federalism variables," in seeing that unions can be created using various combinations of the federal and national principles, and in laying out the particular combination embodied in the Constitution, Publius has revolutionized the political science of federalism and created a system "without example" in world history.[15] The variables that most decisively define the new federalism are first, the foundation, which puts the government of the federation on the wholly new footing of embodying popular sovereignty and gives it unprecedented dignity and status, and second and third, the operation and extent of its ordinary powers. Operating as it does, it is no longer a purely federal system; dividing and allocating powers as it does, it is not a truly or wholly national system.

So far as the system remains a federal one, the decisive aspect is the division of objects and powers between the two sets of government. In *Federalist* 37 Publius had remarked as particularly "arduous ... the task of marking the proper line of partition, between the authority of the general, and that of the State Governments" (*Fed.* 37, 234). It is always difficult, Publius claims, to "discriminate objects, extensive and complicated in their nature" (*Fed.* 37, 234–35). This certainly applies to the attempt to draw proper lines between state and federal powers.

The task is complicated by the further distinction between objects and powers. As Publius indicated in a passage already quoted, the first task in allocating powers is to identify the objects to be assigned to each level of government. But a constitutional government, or the American government at least, is not simply granted custody over objects or purposes. The powers required to effectuate those objects are also identified and granted to the general government in an explicit enumeration, as occurs in Article 1, section 8 of the Constitution. In the set of *Federalist* essays, numbers 41–46, Publius examined the various classes of powers granted to the general government in relation to the objects of that government. These identified objects are six in number: "1. security against foreign danger – 2. regulation of the intercourse with foreign nations – 3. maintenance of harmony and proper intercourse among the States – 4. certain miscellaneous objects of general utility – 5. restraint of the States from certain injurious acts – 6. provisions for giving due efficacy to all these powers" (*Fed.* 41, 269).

We have not the space here to follow Publius's complete discussion of the relation between the enumerated powers and their objects, other than to note that although the objects guide the lawgiver in identifying and allocating powers, what is granted to the government by the Constitution are powers, not objects per se. However, as we have seen when Publius quietly raised the question whether the Constitution is energetic enough, the relation between objects and powers raises some difficult problems: Can one be sure we have identified the powers actually necessary to achieve the objects or ends sought? But if we were to grant to the general government the objects rather than powers with the understanding that it has all powers plausibly related to the objects, do we not challenge the commitment to constitutional, i.e. limited, government, and do we not especially call into question the federal, i.e. non-consolidationist, character of the system? There seem to be costs and drawbacks to either solution, enumerating powers or granting custody of objects. It appears from the text of the Constitution itself and from Publius's account of the matter that the Americans opted for the solution most compatible with a federalist constitutional system, i.e. granting powers to government rather than defining the objects of governmental action.

Within the Constitution this issue is critically highlighted in the necessary and proper clause: "Congress shall have Power ... to make all Laws which shall be necessary and proper for carrying into Execution the foregoing Powers, and all other Powers vested by this Constitution in the Government of the United States, or in any Department or officer thereof." This power was one of the most controversial of those assigned to the general government during the ratification debate. As Publius says, "Few parts of the Constitution have been assailed with more intemperance than this" (*Fed.* 44, 303). Publius attempts to defang the opposition by arguing that "without the *substance* of this power, the whole Constitution would be a dead letter." That is because no constitution could possibly contain all the subordinate powers that will be required to run a government. For example, Congress is granted power to raise an army; to accomplish this, Congress may have to establish local recruiting stations, or it may have to offer bounties to enlistees, or it may have to take any other of a large number of possible acts. No constitution contains and no constitution makers could anticipate all the means required to effectuate the power to raise an army. So there *must* be powers implied as means to the powers that are expressly granted. That much is clear. Difficulties arise when one adds in the consideration that the granted powers are themselves means to objects: In determining what powers are implied in the necessary and proper clause, is it proper to find implied powers, arguably necessary and proper to the effectuation of the objects, or only necessary and proper to the effectuation of the express powers? That has perhaps been the most difficult and recurrent question in American constitutional history, with the two chief pens of Publius dividing on this issue from almost the moment the new government began. In the debate over the Bank of the United States as proposed by Secretary of the Treasury Hamilton and opposed by Congressman Madison, the former took the position that the objects provided grounds for implied powers, a proposition the latter denied.

In Publius's list of the objects of union, two others are eminently worth noting. Both concern the states and indicate that the new federalism aims for more than the old federalism tended to do. On the one hand, it was to maintain harmony among the states, and on the other it was to prevent the states from "certain injurious acts," many of which are acts against their own citizens. The new federalism is thus not limited to the defensive ends that traditionally form the core of the federalism portfolio.[16] As Publius explains, the prevention of injurious acts is to be accomplished by such features of the Constitution as the prohibitions in Article 1, section 10 of certain actions by the states, such as the passage of *ex post facto* laws. This part of the Constitution is part of that expanded range of purposes the Union can serve that Publius brought out in *Federalist* No. 10. The larger republic of the Union will prevent the smaller republics of the states from engaging in some of the acts that Publius saw as typical of the majority faction-inspired acts of legislation that marred the performance of the states under the Articles of Confederation.

Here is a place where one of the defining features of the new federalism is waived, for in this case the general government is to act on the states to prevent these injurious acts from occurring, or to overturn them when they do. Some action of government on government is thus a part of the new federalism, and indeed in principle a fairly large part, for the general government is granted powers that can overlap and even conflict with state legislation. For example, the general government is given the power to regulate commerce among the several states, but the states retain their own powers over commerce, so that potential conflict is built into the system. In case of conflict, one or the other must prevail, else we have the dreaded evil of *imperium in imperio*. Publius makes the case that supremacy in such a case must lie in the general government, for otherwise we would have "a monster" where "the authority of the whole society [is] every where subordinate to the authority of the parts ... in which the head was under the direction of the members" (*Fed.* 44, 306). So the general government must act on the states both to enforce the limitations on the states and to secure the supremacy of valid federal law. The instrumentality of that action is located in two features of the Constitution acting in conjunction. Article VI declares the Constitution, laws, and treaties to be "the supreme Law of the Land," taking priority over conflicting state laws and constitutions and binding all officers, but especially state judges, to an oath to the Constitution with its declaration of federal supremacy.

Yet the Constitution does not depend only on the conscientiousness of state officers in maintaining federal supremacy where warranted. It also provides that cases involving the Constitution, law, or treaties of the United States are appealable to the judiciary of the federation, which presumably has a greater incentive to uphold federal supremacy than the state judges do. As Publius so well said in *Federalist* 51: "The interest of the man," in this case the judge, "must be connected with the constitutional rights of the place" (*Fed.* 51, 349). The appeal to ambition to maintain the independence and powers of the officeholder applies as much to the judges in the general government as it does to the president with his veto power or the Senate with its various powers. This arrangement – the supremacy of the federal government in its sphere as enforced by the federal courts – should be considered the keystone holding the pieces of the new federalism in place. As does the keystone in architecture, so this keystone completes the structure and holds the disparate elements in place. Operating through the judiciaries of the two sets of government, it minimizes the friction that necessarily arises when, as finally here, the two levels of government must touch in a potentially friction-laden manner. It is the finishing touch on a system truly without example and produces an edifice capacious and not without beauty. Publius supplied a lucid and judicious defense of this new type of structure and at the same time showed a deep awareness of the potential fault lines of the structure, including especially the potential the system has toward both centripetal and centrifugal development. Centrifugal dangers arise because the system builds in state actions and shared state sovereignty, traits Publius knew to be fraught with potential for the emergence of greater state autonomy and even independence. Centripetal dangers arise because the promise of more effective governance at the center might tempt the people to tip the delicate balance of powers toward the general government, to say nothing of the potent analysis Publius provided of the tension between objects and powers and, consequently, the potentially expansive character of the federal government's powers. Subsequent constitutional history has revealed the potential for both possibilities, first in the antebellum crisis of federalism and then in the twentieth-century movement toward greater centralization of government.

NOTES

1 Melancton Smith, Speech of June 20, 1788, in *The Anti-Federalist Writings of the Melancton Smith Circle*, ed. Michael P. Zuckert and Derek A. Webb (Indianapolis: Liberty Fund, 2009), 291.

2 See e.g. Federal Farmer, "Letter I," ibid., 25.

3 Martin Diamond, "What the Framers Meant by Federalism," in *As Far as Republican Principles Will Admit: Essays by Martin Diamond*, ed. William A. Schambra (Washington, DC: AEI Press, 1992), 95.

4 Ibid.

5 Federal Farmer, "Letter I," 25.

6 Ibid., 25–26.

7 James Madison, "A Sketch Never Finished Nor Applied, 1830?," in *James Madison: Writings*, ed. Jack N. Rakove (New York: Library of America, 1999), 828.

8 Ibid.

9 See Montesquieu, *The Spirit of the Laws*, trans. and ed. Anne M. Cohler, Basia Carolyn Miller, and Harold Samuel Stone (Cambridge: Cambridge University Press, 1989), XX.2, 338–39.

10 Federal Farmer, "Letter I,"26.

11 Montesquieu, *The Spirit of the Laws*, IX.1, 131.

12 John Locke, *Second Treatise*, in *Two Treatises of Government*, ed. Peter Laslett (Cambridge: Cambridge University Press, 1988), 1.3, 268.

13 James Madison, *Notes of Debates in the Federal Convention of 1787* (Athens: Ohio University Press, 1984), 31.

14 See Michael Zuckert, "The Political Science of James Madison," in *History of American Political Thought*, ed. Bryan-Paul Frost and Jeffrey Sikkenga (Lanham, MD: Lexington Books, 2003), 149–66; and Michael Zuckert, "James Madison in *The Federalist*: Elucidating 'The Particular Structure of This Government,'" in *A Companion to James Madison and James Monroe*, ed. Stuart Leibiger (Malden, MA: Wiley-Blackwell, 2013), 91–108.

15 For other possible combinations, see Michael Zuckert, "Federalism and the Founding: Toward a Reinterpretation of the Constitutional Convention," *Review of Politics*, 48 (1986), 166–210.

16 On this theme, see ibid., esp. 187–97.

The Political Psychology of Publius

Reason, Passion, and Interest in The Federalist

Jon Elster

I   INTRODUCTION

A common perception of the arguments in *The Federalist* may be stated as follows. In designing the Constitution, the framers were motivated by *reason*. Their task was to limit the influence of *interest* and *passion*, and perhaps enhance the role of reason, in the future political agents whose choices the Constitution would guide and constrain. In a more compact version, to paraphrase Friedrich Hayek, the American Constitution – like constitutions quite generally – was a tie imposed by Peter when sober on Peter when drunk.[1]

The ancient moralists, notably Aristotle and Seneca, viewed much of human behavior as based on an ongoing struggle between passion and reason. Needless to say, they were well aware of the role of interest, especially material interest, in human affairs. (Seneca was the richest man in the Roman world at his time.) Yet they never attempted to assess the strength of interest compared to passion and reason in the way they explicitly compared the latter two motivations. Only in the seventeenth and eighteenth centuries was the idea of interest elevated to a conceptual status comparable to those of passion and reason. "Once passion was deemed destructive and reason ineffectual," Albert Hirschman observed, "the view that human action could be exhaustively described by attribution to either one or the other meant an exceedingly somber outlook for humanity. A message of hope was therefore conveyed by the wedging of interest in between the two traditional categories of human motivation."[2]

Hirschman has two references to *The Federalist*. Citing the claim in *Federalist* 72 that for a president lacking the prospect of re-election "his avarice would be likely to get the victory over his caution, his vanity, or his ambition" (*Fed.* 72, 489), Hirschman comments that the passage shows "real virtuosity" in the handling of the idea of countervailing powers. Commenting on *Federalist* 51, Hirschman suggests that Publius confused the checks and balances among the organs of government with the countervailing powers "within the arena of a single soul."[3] There is indeed a striking verbal similarity between the two passages. In *Federalist* 72, Publius says that given the prospect of re-election, the president's "avarice might be a guard upon his avarice" (*Fed.* 72, 489). In *Federalist* 51, he asserts that to prevent encroachments of one organ of government on another, "[a]mbition must be made to counteract ambition." The first statement refers to the motivation of "a *single* soul," the latter to that of different individuals. Yet the similarity is only verbal, and Hirschman's charge of confusion seems groundless.

In an outstanding study of *The Federalist*, Morton White offers a two-pronged analysis of the arguments of Publius. On the one hand, he shows how Publius consistently argues that actions can be caused or blocked by various *combinations of motive and opportunity*. On the other hand, he also shows that Publius appealed to three kinds of motive: reason, interest, and passion.[4] "[A]ll the motives [Publius] mentions seem to fall into three main categories that were commonly distinguished by British moralists of the eighteenth century, namely reason, passions, and interests." White emphasizes notably the writings of David Hume and of Bishop Butler. Although much has been written about the extent of Hume's influence on Publius (White has dozens of references to Hume in his book), in fact Publius mentioned Hume only once in his final essay, as a "solid and ingenious writer." (In Madison's notes from the Federal Convention, the only reference to Hume is Hamilton's approval of Hume's defense of corruption as maintaining "the equilibrium of the constitution.")[5]

Publius does not mention Butler, but White conjectures that Madison's teacher, John Witherspoon, may have exposed him to Butler's views.[6]

White does not mention the French moralists, and Publius does not cite them. Yet the most clear-cut and explicit statement about the relations among reason, passion, and interest occurs in a maxim by the seventeenth-century French moralist La Bruyère: "Nothing is easier for passion than to overcome reason, but its greatest triumph is to conquer a man's own interests." The second part of this statement is echoed by Hume: "Who sees not that vengeance, from the force alone of passion, may be so eagerly pursued as to make us knowingly neglect every consideration of ease, interest, or safety?"[7] We might add, as a corollary to the maxim, that nothing is easier for interest than to overcome reason, except when reason allies itself with passion. The name of this alliance is *enthusiasm*, which I discuss at some length in Section II.

The succeeding sections of this essay discuss these three motivations of reason, passion, and interest. The discussion of interest is the briefest, as it poses fewer conceptual difficulties. The motivations, which pertain to the *ends* of the agents, must be seen in conjunction with the beliefs about the proper *means* and *conditions* for attaining them. In addition to causal beliefs about means, action may require factual beliefs about the conditions for action, e.g. about the present and future size of the population. Publius adopted as a matter of course this "folk" model of human behavior, as based on the desires of the agents and their beliefs about how to achieve them.

For rational agents, desires and beliefs are, to a first approximation, independent of each other. An irrational agent may, however, be subject to wishful thinking and other mechanisms of irrational belief formation. For normative purposes, the appropriate definition of reason would include instrumental rationality in the choice of means. For the explanatory purposes adopted here, I shall assume that when reason dictates the choice of ends, it can (by a causal mechanism discussed later) fail to discern the appropriate means.

White did not apply the reason–passion–interest schema to the authors of *The Federalist*, perhaps because he thought Publius was moved only by reason. I shall address this assumption only briefly. The Constitution that Publius defended was, however, the product of a convention where interest and passion were in play. In *Federalist 62*, Publius seems to admit the role of interest when he describes the compromise between proportional and equal modes of representation as a "lesser evil" brought about by bargaining. The observation in *Federalist 37* that the struggle between the small and the large states "could be terminated only by compromise" is ambiguous, as the compromise might lie either between different particular interests or between different conceptions of the public interest (*Fed.* 37, 237). There is no recognition of any role of passion at the Convention, although in *Federalist 49* Publius cites "[t]he danger of disturbing the public tranquility by interesting too strongly the public passions" as an objection to Jefferson's proposal of "a frequent reference of constitutional questions to society as a whole" (*Fed.* 49, 340).

II   REASON

Publius was not a philosopher and did not practice conceptual analysis. No formal definition of reason is found in *The Federalist*, hence any attempt to excavate an implicit definition from these essays must be conjectural. Nevertheless, certain passages provide a great deal of useful material. Consider the following examples (here as elsewhere, italics in quotation are added unless otherwise noted).

(1) By a faction I understand a number of citizens, whether amounting to a majority or a minority of the whole, who are united and actuated by some common impulse of passion, or of interest, adverse to *the rights of other citizens, or to the permanent and aggregate interests of the community* (*Fed.* 10, 57).

(2) [I]ndirect and *remote considerations* ... will rarely prevail over the immediate interest which one party may find in disregarding *the rights of another or the good of the whole* (*Fed.* 10, 60).

(3) To those who do not view the question through the medium of passion or of interest, the desire of the commercial States to collect, in any form, an indirect revenue from their uncommercial neighbors, must appear not less impolitic than it is unfair; since it would stimulate the injured party, by resentment as well as interest, to resort to less convenient channels for their foreign trade. But the mild voice of reason, pleading the cause of an *enlarged and permanent interest,* is but too often drowned, before public bodies as well as individuals, by the clamors of an *impatient avidity for immediate* and immoderate *gain* (*Fed.* 42, 283).

(4) But in a representative republic, where the executive magistracy is carefully limited; both in the extent and the duration of its power; and where the legislative power is exercised by an assembly, which is inspired, by a supposed influence over the people, with an intrepid confidence in its own strength; which is sufficiently numerous to feel all the passions which actuate a multitude, yet not so numerous as to be incapable of pursuing the objects of its passions, *by means which reason prescribes;* it is against the enterprising ambition of this department that the people ought to indulge all their jealousy and exhaust all their precautions (*Fed.* 48, 333–34).

(5) An appeal to the people by a convention "would inevitably be connected with the spirit of pre-existing parties, or of parties springing out of the question itself. It would be connected with persons of distinguished character and extensive influence in the community. It would be pronounced by the very men who had been agents in, or opponents of, the measures to which the decision would relate. The *passions,* therefore, not the *reason,* of the public would sit in judgment. But it is the reason, alone, of the public, that ought to control and regulate the government. The passions ought to be controlled and regulated by the government (*Fed.* 49, 342–43; italics by Publius).

(6) [Commenting on the Council of Censors in Pennsylvania]: In all questions, however unimportant in themselves, or unconnected with each other, the same names stand invariably contrasted on the opposite columns. Every unbiased observer may infer, without danger of mistake, and at the same time without meaning to reflect on either party, or any individuals of either party, that, unfortunately, *passion,* not *reason,* must have presided over their decisions. When men exercise their reason coolly and freely on a variety of distinct questions, they inevitably fall into different opinions on some of them. When they are governed by a common passion, their opinions, if they are so to be called, will be the same (*Fed.* 50, 345–46; italics by Publius).

(7) [I]n all cases a certain number at least seems to be necessary to secure the benefits of free consultation and discussion, and to guard against too easy a combination for improper purposes; as, on the other hand, the number ought at most to be kept within a certain limit, in order to avoid the confusion and intemperance of a multitude. In all very numerous assemblies, of whatever character composed, *passion never fails to wrest the scepter from reason.* Had every Athenian citizen been a Socrates, every Athenian assembly would still have been a mob (*Fed.* 55, 374).

(8) [I]n all legislative assemblies the greater the number composing them may be, the fewer will be the men who will in fact direct their proceedings. In the first place, the more numerous an assembly may be, of whatever characters composed, *the greater is known to be the ascendency of passion over reason* (*Fed.* 58, 395–96).

(9) As the cool and deliberate sense of the community ought, in all governments, and actually will, in all free governments, ultimately prevail over the views of its rulers; so there are particular moments in public affairs when the people, stimulated by some irregular passion, or some illicit advantage, or misled by the artful misrepresentations of interested men, may call for measures which they themselves will afterwards be the most ready to lament and condemn. In these critical moments, how salutary will be the interference of some temperate and respectable body of citizens, in order to check the misguided career, and to suspend the blow meditated by the people against themselves, *until reason, justice, and truth can regain their authority over the public mind?* What bitter anguish would not the people of Athens have often escaped if their government had contained so provident a safeguard against the tyranny of their own *passions?* Popular liberty might then have escaped the indelible reproach of decreeing to the same citizens the hemlock on one day and statues on the next (*Fed.* 63, 425).

Although statements (1) and (2) do not explicitly refer to reason, statement (3) leaves no doubt that this idea is intended. There is, however, an important difference between (1) and (2) on the one hand and (3) on the other. The last, taken by itself, suggests that *reason is concerned with the long-term public good,* an idea succinctly stated by La Bruyère: "To think only of ourselves and of the present time is a source of error in politics."[8] Broadly speaking, this is a consequentialist conception of reason. It need not be purely utilitarian, but can also include distributive concerns.

The reference to *rights* in (1) and (2), however, points, to a non-consequentialist idea. In *Federalist* 84, Publius enumerates the rights that are guaranteed by the Constitution: habeas corpus, the prohibitions on bills of attainder and *ex post facto* laws, trial by jury. The rights protective of property have an implicitly consequentialist justification: it is in the collective long-term interest of society that they be respected, since otherwise people would hesitate to trade and invest. The intellectual property rights guaranteed by the Constitution have an explicitly consequentialist justification, rather than a non-consequentialist justification based on the principle of finders-keepers. The rights protective of liberty have a non-consequentialist justification. Overall, however, the reasoning in *The Federalist* seems overwhelmingly consequentialist. Publius repeatedly attempts to tease out or speculate about the incentive effects of various institutional arrangements, and recommend those that on balance seem more likely to promote the long-term public good.

Although conceptions of the public good vary, let us suppose that institutional designers adopt one specific version of the idea. The question then shifts from a normative to a causal one, or from reason to rationality: Which are the institutions that are more likely to promote the public good? This way of phrasing the issue immediately excludes purely *possibilistic* (as distinct from probabilist) arguments, based on worst-case or (at least in theory) best-case scenarios. Publius is mostly skeptical of possibilism. "In reading many of the publications against the Constitution, a man is apt to imagine that he is perusing some ill-written tale or romance, which instead of natural and agreeable images, exhibits to the mind nothing but frightful and distorted shapes [...], discoloring and disfiguring whatever it represents, and transforming everything it touches into a monster" (*Fed.* 29, 185–86). Or again, "Whatever may be the limits or modifications of the powers of the Union, it is easy to imagine an endless train of possible dangers; and by indulging an excess of jealousy and timidity, we may bring ourselves to a state of absolute skepticism and irresolution" (*Fed.* 31, 197). In the Virginia debates on ratification, Henry Lee observed that "I have heard suspicious against possibility, and not against probability." Madison, too, objected to the supposition that "the general legislature will do every thing mischievous they possibly can."[9] Although Publius at one point does refer to the sheer "constitutional possibility" of a worst-case scenario, the issue is marginal and contrived (*Fed.* 59, 399).

We must ask, then, how good are the *probabilistic* arguments in *The Federalist*? Some of them are a posteriori, that is, based on experience. The long discussions of earlier political regimes are justified by the statement that "[e]xperience is the oracle of truth" (*Fed.* 20, 128). More specifically, Publius claims that "it is a truth, which the experience of ages has attested, that the people are always most in danger when the means of injuring their rights are in the possession of those of whom they entertain the least suspicion" (*Fed.* 25, 159). The claim does not seem to be obviously true; to my knowledge, it has not – then or later – been systematically examined. In a passage to which we will return, Publius writes that

> The people can never err more than in supposing that by multiplying their representatives beyond a certain limit, they strengthen the barrier against the government of a few. Experience will forever admonish them that, on the contrary, after securing a sufficient number for the purposes of safety, of local information, and of diffuse sympathy with the whole society, they will counteract their own views by every addition to their representatives. The countenance of the government may become more democratic, but the soul that animates it will be more oligarchic. The machine will be enlarged, but the fewer, and often the more secret, will be the springs by which its motions are directed.
>
> (*Fed.* 58, 396)

Again, I know of no empirical studies of this claim.

Other arguments are a priori, based on the likely incentive effects of institutions. In defending the three-fifths rule for counting slaves both in the representation to the lower house of Congress and in assessing direct taxes, Publius writes that

> the establishment of a common measure for representation and taxation will have a very salutary effect. As the accuracy of the census to be obtained by the Congress will necessarily depend, in a considerable degree on the disposition, if not on the co-operation, of the States, it is of great importance that the States should feel as little bias as possible, to swell or to reduce the amount of their numbers. Were their share of representation alone to be governed by this rule, they would have an *interest* in exaggerating their inhabitants. Were the rule to decide their share of taxation alone, a contrary *temptation* would prevail. By extending the rule to both objects, the States will have opposite interests, which will control and balance each other, and produce the requisite impartiality.
>
> (*Fed.* 54, 371–72; emphasis added).

Although stated in the context of slavery, the argument can be applied to any political system based on taxation and representation. In a scheme proposed in France by Dupont de Nemour just before the Revolution of 1789, "those who wished to exercise the full measure of their vote in the assembly would have to declare the entire net product of their land, information which could then be used for purposes of tax assessments."[10] In making this incentive argument, both Nemour and Publius assume that economic and political agents will report their situation honestly only if it is in their interest to do so. Neither author explains, however, why the two opposed interests should "control and balance each other." Even if they work in opposite directions, one might prove much stronger than the other.

Publius makes another important incentive argument when discussing the design of the Senate. This one concerns a perennial and largely unresolved problem of democratic politics: how to reconcile the short tenure of parliaments and governments with the need to take measures that will bear fruit only in the distant future. As Publius notes, no "steward or tenant, engaged for one year, could be justly made to answer for places or improvements which could not be accomplished in less than half a dozen years," nor would he have an incentive to undertake them. His solution is to have an upper house in the legislature "which, having sufficient permanency to provide for such objects as require a continued attention ... may be justly and effectually answerable for the attainment of those objects," and hence have an incentive to undertake them (*Fed.* 63, 424). The extended tenure of senators will not only motivate them to pursue good (or at least long-term) *ends*, but also, by virtue of the opportunity for learning that it offers, enable them to choose good *means*. In the language of *Federalist* 62, the Senate will favor heads as well as hearts.

Note, however, that *a long-term goal rationally pursued is not ipso facto one that promotes the public good.* Although as *Federalist* 72 observed, prudent or farsighted avarice may guard against a short-sighted form of greed, one cannot assume that self-interest properly understood will always mimic a concern for the public interest. Publius claims, nevertheless, that senators will be not only prudent, but also virtuous: because "the State legislatures who appoint the senators will in general be composed of the most enlightened and respectable citizens, there is reason to presume that their attention and their votes will be directed to those men only who have become the most distinguished by their abilities *and virtue*" (*Fed.* 64, 433; emphasis added). No mechanism that would justify this presumption is specified, however. In the language of La Bruyère, institutional design can induce political agents to think beyond "the present time," but it is less clear how it can make them think beyond "themselves."

In retrospect, one can make the opposite argument. Small bodies whose members have long tenure tend to develop practices of logrolling that may not be in the public interest. The club-like nature of the Senate, as shown in various forms of "senatorial courtesy," provides an illustration. Another suggestive fact is that on four occasions, the Senate did not perform its supposed role as a break on the allegedly more impulsive House of Representatives. In 1798, the Sedition Acts passed the Senate by a wide margin, but obtained a bare majority of 44 to 41 in the House. In 1964, the Gulf of Tonkin Resolution passed the House by 416 votes to 0 and the Senate by 88 to 2. In 2001, the Patriot Act passed 98 votes to 1 in the Senate and 357 to 66 in the House. In 2002, the "Authorization for use of Military Force against Iraq Resolution" passed the House by 297 votes to 133 and the Senate by 77 votes to 23. Although these examples by themselves prove nothing, they suggest the need for a systematic analysis of the effects of bicameralism on decision-making in crises. Until the analysis has been done, the constitutional dogma of the virtues of upper houses remains a cliché.

The motive of "approbativeness" – the desire to be approved by others for promoting the public good – may induce agents to promote it.[11] For some, this satisfaction is good enough. Hume claimed that "To love the glory of virtuous deeds is a sure proof of the love of virtue."[12] Publius similarly described "the love of fame as, "the ruling passion of the noblest minds" (*Fed.* 72, 488). Douglass Adair wrote that the American framers were "drunk with the hope of fame," just as the framers of the first revolutionary French constiution were "drunk with disinterestedness" when, on May 16, 1791, they declared themselves ineligible to serve in the first ordinary legislature.[13] Yet, others might argue, these motivations only *mimic* reason: they do not constitute it or imply its presence in the agent. As Michel de Montaigne observed, "If that false opinion" of being concerned for what other people think "serves the public good by keeping men to their duty ...then let it boldly flourish and may it be fostered among us as much it is in our power... Since men are not intelligent enough to be adequately paid in good coin, let counterfeit coin be used as well." He went even further: "The more glittering the deed the more I subtract from its moral worth, because of the suspicion aroused in me that it was exposed more for glitter than for goodness; goods displayed are already halfway to being sold."[14] Whatever stance one takes on this issue, it seems clear that framers cannot by institutional design inculcate in later generations of political agents the desire to be *seen as* disinterested any more than they can drum up the desire to *be* disinterested.

Other examples of probabilistic reasoning in *The Federalist* seem to be based neither on a posteriori nor on a priori premises, but on rough intuitive assessments.

In his discussion of the presidential veto, Publius anticipated a possible criticism and tried to refute it as follows:

> It may perhaps be said that the power of preventing bad laws includes that of preventing good ones; and may be used to the one purpose as well as to the other. But this objection will have little weight with those who can properly estimate the mischiefs of that inconstancy and mutability in the laws, which form the greatest blemish in the character and genius of our governments. They will consider every institution calculated to restrain the excess of law-making, and to keep things in the same state in which they happen to be at any given period, as much more likely to do good than harm; because it is favorable to greater stability in the system of legislation. The injury which may possibly be done by defeating a few good laws, will be amply compensated by the advantage of preventing a number of bad ones.
>
> (*Fed.* 73, 496)

How does he know? Publius does not tell us. Nor does he point to the fact that the veto of the president comes on top of the veto of the Senate and of the Supreme Court (assuming that the idea of judicial review stated in *Federalist* 78 was intended to apply to federal legislation and not merely to state law). The joint effect of these veto points could well be undesirable, and arguably has been.

Concerning next the role of the senators in trying impeached officials, Publius considers the objection that "they would be too indulgent judges of men, in whose official creation they had participated" (*Fed.* 66, 448). The objection is well-founded in the pervasive influence of *self-love*, which undermines, for instance, the common proposal to substitute repeated votes in one assembly for bicameralism. People do not like to change their mind, and especially to be seen to do so, as Publius observes in *Federalist* 70. Although Publius acknowledges that the objection has some purchase, "in the main" he rejects "the supposition that the Senate, who will merely sanction the choice of the executive, should feel a bias towards the objects of that choice strong enough to blind them to the evidences of guilt so extraordinary as to have induced the representatives of the nation to become its accusers" (*Fed.* 66, 449). How does he know? He does not tell us.

A third example of such rough intuitive assessments concerns the re-eligibility of the president, an issue that was hotly debated at the Federal Convention. The Virginia Plan, which strongly reflected the views of one of the authors of *The Federalist*, stated flatly that the national executive should be "ineligible a second time" (*RFC*, I, 21). Yet Publius asserts that "There is an excess of refinement in the idea of disabling the people to continue in office men who had entitled themselves, in their opinion, to approbation and confidence, the advantages of which are at best speculative and equivocal; and are overbalanced by disadvantages far more certain and decisive" (*Fed.* 72, 492). How does he know? He does not tell us.

In all these cases, it would have been intellectually more honest to assert that the issues were indeterminate, but that some choice had to be made and that the proposals of the Convention were not demonstrably worse than the alternatives. Publius might have applied to himself statement (6), in which he proposes an interesting test to determine the absence or presence of reason (or rationality) in a deliberating body. In matters as complex as devising or revising a constitution, reasonable men not only can but will differ. Politically, however, the acknowledgment of ignorance and indeterminacy would have undermined the efficacy of *The Federalist*.

Publius was very concerned with the optimal size of deliberating bodies, that is, with *the relation between size and reason*. In statement (7) above, he stipulates an upper limit to the size above which "passion wrestles the scepter from reason." (Implicitly, he also stipulates a lower limit below which *interest* takes hold of the scepter.) His famous comment on Socrates ("Had every Athenian citizen been a Socrates; every Athenian assembly would still have been a mob") (*Fed.* 55, 374) is uninformed, though, and ignores the fact that on the occasion when the Athenian assembly was at its most mob-like, the illegal trial of the generals after the Battle of Arginusae, Socrates was the only one among the prytanes who refused to act against the law.[15] Incidentally, his question in statement (9), what "bitter anguish would not the people of Athens have often escaped if their government had contained so provident a safeguard [as the American Senate] against the tyranny of their own passions?," is also misleading. Douglas MacDowell observes that "after the turmoil of 403 the Athenians ... wanted to make it difficult for themselves to introduce changes in the laws." Martin Ostwald similarly writes that these reforms "show that law was to be supreme in the new democracy and that the demos could no longer regard whatever it pleased as valid and binding." As a further comment on the classical scholarship of Publius, the highly negative comments on Pericles in *Federalist* 6 contrast strongly with Ostwald's assessment that "Pericles' intelligence and psychological and political insight prevented unreason from dominating policy."[16] Finally, the comments on the Athenian Council of the Five Hundred in *Federalist* 63 contain three substantive mistakes, notably the statement that its members were elected. Even if some of these erroneous statements accorded with the best scholarship at the time, their existence cautions us to scrutinize the many other classical references in *The Federalist* with great care.

Statement (4), also concerned with size, is puzzling. Here Publius seems to imagine two size thresholds, one beyond which the *ends* of the assembly tend to be given by passion rather than by reason, and a higher one beyond which the assembly is incapable of choosing the appropriate *means* to pursue these ends. As the next section will show, passion tends very generally to induce suboptimal choice of means. In other words, the two thresholds coincide. This proposition is consistent with statement (8), where Publius affirms that larger assemblies generate stronger passions. Also note the claim made in *Federalist* 58 that a large body will ultimately become an effective if secret oligarchy, which is presumably animated by interest rather than by passion. Given statement (8), also from *Federalist* 58, Publius distinguishes between the motivations that are quantitatively the most important and those that are causally the most efficacious. The larger the assembly, the stronger the passions of the many and the easier it is for the few to manipulate them. Thus oligarchy arises and interest dominates at both ends of the numerical continuum.

Two millennia apart, Aristotle and Bentham identified another pernicious effect of large decision-making bodies, that "What's everybody's business is nobody's business."[17] The authors of *The Federalist* were aware of this free-rider problem from their experience during the Revolutionary War, in which many decisions were delegated to boards rather than entrusted to one person.[18] Publius criticizes the twelve-member collective executive in Pennsylvania on the grounds that it is "exempt from the restraint of an individual responsibility" (*Fed.* 48, 337), but recommends the prospective twenty-six-member federal senate on the grounds that it has "a number so small that a sensible degree of the praise and blame of public measures may be the portion of each individual" (*Fed.* 63, 423). The inconsistency seems blatant, but does not affect the overall argument: whether the aim of the individual members of the body was to make a good decision (as Bentham assumed) or to achieve fame (as Hamilton assumed), the multiplication of their number would reduce their incentive to make an effort.

Publius was also concerned with the optimal size of electoral districts. In *Federalist* 10, he argues by purely statistical reasoning that a large republic is more likely to produce a high proportion of "fit characters" among the representatives than a smaller one. As White demonstrates, the argument shows only that the large republic has enough "fit" candidates to fill an assembly, not that they will be elected.[19] The voters will have the opportunity to choose "fit" representatives, but not necessarily the motive. Publius does not try to establish a motive, but focuses instead on the difficulty for unfit characters to be chosen: "Extend the sphere," *Federalist* 10 declares, "and you take in a greater variety of parties and interests; you make it less probable that a majority of the whole will have a common motive to invade the rights of other citizens; or if such a common motive exists, it will be more difficult for all who feel it to discover their own strength, and to act in unison with each other" (*Fed.* 10, 64). Here, "fitness" must mean concern for the public interest, since Publius explicitly opposes it to factional interests.

Publius argued for a golden mean with respect both to the size of assemblies and to the size of electoral districts. The defects of the extremes are not the same in the two cases. Small electoral districts, as in the state legislatures, will be more vulnerable "to local prejudices and to schemes of injustice." Large districts will prevent the representatives from possessing the requisite know-ledge of local circumstances. Small assemblies are vulnerable to cabals of interest, and large assemblies to the dominance of passion (and perhaps even of interest). Publius does not discuss the inter-action of the two issues: the possibility that electoral districts of optimal size might not generate an optimal-size assembly. On this point, he wisely admitted some indeterminacy: "no political prob-lem is less susceptible of a precise solution than that which relates to the number most convenient for a representative legislature" (*Fed.* 55, 373).

Did Publius try to design institutional means that could ration-ally be counted on to promote the long-term public good? Did he succeed? The answer to both questions is a very qualified Yes. Publius defended a long term for senators by the dual effect on their capacity to plan for the long term and on their intellectual ability to choose good means for their long-term ends. He did not, however, consider that their long tenure might undermine their commitment to the public good, nor did he specify a plausible mechanism by which public-spirited senators would be elected in the first place. The argu-ment that large electoral districts would promote the election of public-spirited members of the House of Representatives is perhaps more convincing, but still remains somewhat tenuous. As the Convention had abstained from imposing any qualifications on voters or representatives, Publius had no need to defend the argument for wealth as an imperfect proxy for wisdom or virtue that he probably held in private.

III   PASSIONS

Where Publius used the word "passion," today we say "emotion" to denote the same phenomenon, or rather phenomena. There are indeed many passions, at least several dozen that can be clearly distinguished from each other and whose effects on behavior vary a great deal.[20] Publius often uses the term without specifying which passion he has in mind. To cite only one example among many, he refers in generic terms to the "sudden and violent passions" that may animate the lower house of a legislature (*Fed.* 62, 418). Sometimes he is more specific, as when he cites the "mutual jealousies, fears, hatreds, and injuries ended in the celebrated Peloponnesian war; which itself ended in the ruin and slavery of the Athenians who had begun it" (*Fed.* 18, 112) or the "suggestions of wounded pride [and] the instigations of irritated resentment" that might induce the states to take up arms against the Union "to avenge the affront, or to avoid the disgrace of submission" (*Fed.* 16, 100–01). He also asks, "Are not popular assemblies frequently subject to the impulses of rage, resentment, jealousy, avarice, and of other irregular and violent propensities?" (*Fed.* 6, 32). In a key passage quoted below he also refers to enthusiasm. Altogether these passages list about ten distinct passions.

The Federalist is no more a tract of political psychology than of political philosophy. In *Federalist* 37, Publius affirms as much:

> The faculties of the mind itself have never yet been distinguished
> and defined, with satisfactory precision, by all the efforts of the
> most acute and metaphysical philosophers. Sense, perception,
> judgment, desire, volition, memory, imagination, are found to be
> separated by such delicate shades and minute gradations that their

boundaries have eluded the most subtle investigations, and remain
a pregnant source of ingenious disquisition and controversy

(Fed. 37, 235)

Publius does not hesitate to refer to the love of wealth as a "passion,"
whereas in its non-pathological forms, when it is ultimately oriented
toward consumption or acquisition, it is a paradigm of interest. *Federalist* 41 makes a potentially interesting distinction between "the
passions of the unthinking" and "the prejudices of the misthinking"
(Fed. 41, 268–69), but does not bother to spell it out. Sometimes, in
fact, the duo of "passions and interests" is replaced by a trio of
"passions, interests, and prejudices" *(Fed.* 22, 144; *Fed.* 31, 195; *Fed.*
85, 591). By and large, however, his language is consistent and his
reasoning as clear as the subject matter allows. *(Federalist* 37, in
particular, provides a catalogue of obstacles to precision.)

Before we consider the explanatory and analytical import of the
passions in *The Federalist*, some preliminary remarks on their causes,
nature, and effects may be useful. Passions are triggered by a belief;
anger, for instance, is triggered by a belief that another has done me an
injury, envy by the belief that another has a good that I want, in both
senses of that term, and so on. They are directed toward an object, be
it a person or a cause. They have *valence*, that is, are intrinsically
pleasant or unpleasant; shame, for instance, is aversive and pride
enjoyable. They generate physiological *arousal* and have characteristic physiognomic expressions. Valence as well as arousal can vary in
strength: they are stronger, for instance, when a person is injured by
another than when he sees another injuring a third party. Publius
refers to some passions as "violent" *(Fed.* 6, 32; *Fed.* 62, 418).

If valence and arousal are absent, as when a person takes an
umbrella because she is "afraid" that it might rain, there is no passion.
She suffers a simple prudential fear, not the visceral fear she might
experience in the face of acute danger. When Publius refers to fear, as
he often does, it can be hard to tell whether he is imagining the
prudential or the visceral form. It is likely that the "chimerical fears"

that he ascribes to certain alarmist defenders of the state governments (*Fed.* 46, 323) are of the visceral variety, whereas the "fear of powerful neighbors" (*Fed.* 19, 122) could be of either kind. The important point for my purposes is that none of Publius's many discussions of the sudden and impulsive passions of assemblies refer unambiguously to visceral fear. He might have cited, for instance, the panicky reactions of several state legislatures which adopted debt relief measures in 1786–87 as evidence of the impact of passion on decision, but he does not.[21]

Passions have two main effects. First, they generate *action tendencies*, incipient actions that may turn into actual behavior or be nipped in the bud by prudential concerns or by counteracting passions. The angry man who wants to hit out and the envious one who feels an urge to destroy the envied object may pull their punches if the risk or cost is too high. Fear can induce a flight tendency in soldiers, unless kept in check by the shame they would feel before their comrades. Second, passions distort rational belief formation, by two distinct mechanisms. On the one hand, the *urgency* of passion – the desire to act immediately rather than take one's time – can induce suboptimal gathering of information (Elster 2009 b). On the other hand, passions can induce *bias*: the wish can be the father of the thought. Anger, in particular, tends to induce excessive optimism (Lerner and Kellner 2001), as does enthusiasm (Jennifer Lerner, personal communication). Urgency and bias can reinforce each other, if the agent first forms the belief she would like to be true and then uses it as premise for action before gathering more information.

Publius often refers to the *transient* nature of passions. They are not standing attachments, but arise suddenly and abate quickly. *Federalist* 16 talks about "sudden and occasional ill humours" (*Fed.* 16, 104). The "necessity of a senate is not less indicated by the propensity of all single and numerous assemblies to yield to the impulse of sudden and violent passions" (*Fed.* 62, 418). Referring to the Spanish and British territories, Publius writes that the

> bordering States ... will be those who, under the impulse of
> sudden irritation, and a quick sense of apparent interest or injury,
> will be most likely, by direct violence, to excite war with these
> nations; and nothing can so effectually obviate that danger as a
> national government, whose wisdom and prudence will not be
> diminished by the passions which actuate the parties immediately
> interested
>
> (*Fed.* 3, 17)

Recalling the political situation of 1774–1776, Madison observed in
Federalist 46 that, "after the transient enthusiasm for the early Congresses was over ... the attention and attachment of the people were
turned anew to their own particular governments" (*Fed.* 46, 316). Or
again, the

> republican principle demands, that the deliberate sense of the
> community should govern the conduct of those to whom they
> entrust the management of their affairs; but it does not require an
> unqualified complaisance to every sudden breese of passion, or to
> every transient impulse which the people may receive from the arts
> of men, who flatter their prejudices to betray their interests.
>
> (*Fed.* 71, 482)

The proposition that passions have a *short half-life* is widely accepted
in the psychological literature. It must be distinguished from the
proposition that many agents have *a short time horizon*. Publius
makes this very distinction in *Federalist* 6, when he asks, "Has it
not ... invariably been found, that *momentary passions* and *immediate interest* have a more active and imperious control over human
conduct than general or remote considerations of policy, utility or
justice?" (*Fed.* 6, 31). In *Federalist* 42, Publius deplores the "impatient
avidity for immediate and immoderate gain" in individuals as well as
public bodies (*Fed.* 42, 283). "[R]emote considerations," Madison
observed in *Federalist* 10, "will rarely prevail over the immediate
interest" that particular factions may feel (*Fed.* 10, 60). These and
other statements refer to psychological dispositions, not to the

institutional fact of short tenure of elected officials that I discussed earlier. As Morton White emphasized in his interpretation of Publius, individuals will not act in the public interest (nor against it) unless they have both the motive and the opportunity to do so. Since passions induce a high rate of time discounting,[22] institutional designers can extend the subjective time horizon of the agents by creating a setting that is unfavorable to the emergence of passion. There are limits, however, to what can be achieved in this respect, since even individuals in a dispassionate state discount the future more heavily than what can be justified by mortality tables.

The claim that passions have a short half-life is grounded in evolutionary considerations. "It is not only adaptive for emotions to be capable of mobilizing the organism very quickly (onset), but for the response changes so mobilized not to last very long unless the emotion is evoked again."[23] It is far from clear, however, that all passions have evolved to mobilize the organism. Envy, for example, does not serve any obvious evolutionary purpose. Unless the agent succeeds in destroying the envied object, it can persist indefinitely. Publius recognizes one "standing passion," which he variously calls "pride" or "self-love," and which I shall call "pridefulness." It stands in the same relation to pride as shame does to guilt. Guilt is triggered by the belief that one has done a bad action, shame by the belief that one is a bad person. Similarly, pride is triggered by the belief that one has done a good action, pridefulness by the belief that one is a good person. Whereas pridefulness does not have an obvious action tendency, it can still shape our beliefs. The books I buy or the meals I cook must be good because they are *mine*; my friends must be in some respect outstanding because they are *mine*; the institutions to which I belong must be important because *I* belong to them. My opinions and decisions must be right, too, because they are *mine*.

Publius often appeals to these effects of pridefulness. "The pride of states, as well as of men, naturally disposes them to justify all their actions, and opposes their acknowledging, correcting, or repairing their errors and offenses" (*Fed.* 3, 17). (For some reason he thinks the national government will be exempt from this tendency, or more resistant to it, but presumably it might be animated by it in its relation to other states.) At the level of the member states of the Union, one effect is that "The inordinate pride of State importance has suggested to some minds an objection to the principle of a guaranty in the federal government, as involving an officious interference in the domestic concerns of the members" (*Fed.* 21, 131). At the level of individuals, Publius observes that "Men often oppose a thing, merely because they have had no agency in planning it, or because it may have been planned by those whom they dislike. But if they have been consulted, and have happened to disapprove, opposition then becomes, in their estimation, an indispensable duty of self-love. They seem to think themselves bound in honor, and by all the motives of personal infallibility, to defeat the success of what has been resolved upon contrary to their sentiments" (*Fed.* 70, 474–75). More subtly, he notes that

> As long as the reason of man continues fallible, and he is at liberty to exercise it, different opinions will be formed. As long as the connection subsists between his reason and his self-love, his opinions and his passions will have a reciprocal influence on each other; and the former will be objects to which the latter will attach themselves.
>
> (*Fed.* 10, 58)

The opinions of a reasonable person are like putty-clay: initially, he forms his beliefs by a rational assessment of the evidence, but once formed and hardened, these beliefs are less open to rational adjustment.

As noted, the members of an assembly or another political organ may feel institutional pridefulness: theirs must be an important institution simply because they belong to it. This thought might, for instance, induce members of constituent assemblies, "working themselves up into infallibility,"[24] to make it excessively difficult to amend the constitution that they are writing. If the institution has the power to exercise a veto on other organs, its pridefulness will make it seek occasions to do so.[25] Publius points to a positive effect of this passion. In cases of impeachment, "So far as might concern the misbehavior of the Executive in perverting the instructions or contravening the views of the Senate, we need not be apprehensive of the want of a disposition in that body to punish the abuse of their confidence or to vindicate their own authority. We may thus far count upon their pride, if not upon their virtue" (*Fed.* 66, 451). At the same time, as noted earlier, Publius did not think that the pride of the senators would prevent them from impeaching an official they had endorsed.

Publius often refers to envy and jealousy to suggest that these passions would destabilize the country if it devolved into several confederacies. The most striking statement is the following: "Whenever, and from whatever causes, it might happen; and happen it would, that any one of these nations or confederacies should rise on the scale of political importance much above the degree of her neighbours, that moment would those neighbours behold her with envy and with fear. Both those passions would lead them to countenance, if not to promote, whatever might promise to diminish her importance; and would also restrain them from measures calculated to advance, or even to secure her prosperity" (*Fed.* 5, 25). This statement seems to refer to what psychologists sometimes describe as "white envy": a desire to reduce the wealth or power of a rival without necessarily suffering any costs oneself. Publius never appears to invoke the alternative concept of "black envy": the willingness to cut off one's nose to spite one's face, in a triumph of passion over interest. Even had he suggested that one confederacy might have been willing to suffer an economic loss in order to impose even greater losses on others, its motivation would not necessarily be envy. In relations among states, relative advantage often counts for more than absolute gain.

A main theme of *The Federalist* is, of course, that both passion and interest can override reason. Yet the relation *between passion and interest* is a problem that Publius does not discuss at any length.

Consider first the impact of interest on passion. Although *Federalist* 72 briefly acknowledges that "avarice" can get the "victory" over "vanity," the general theme of "interest as tamer of the passions" that Hirschman emphasized so strongly does in fact not occupy a prominent one in *The Federalist*.[26] In *Federalist* 6, Publius asks a number of rhetorical questions that challenge the idea of "le doux commerce":

> Has commerce hitherto done anything more than change the objects of war? Is not the love of wealth as domineering and enterprising a passion as that of power or glory? Have there not been as many wars founded upon commercial motives since that has become the prevailing system of nations, as were before occasioned by the cupidity of territory or dominion? Has not the spirit of commerce, in many instances, administered new incentives to the appetite, both for the one and for the other?
>
> (*Fed.* 6, 32)

Consider next the impact of passion on interest. Unlike La Bruyère and Hume, Publius never says that passion can induce agents to neglect their own interest. He was probably aware of this possibility, but from his point of view it was of secondary importance. The repeated use of the expression "passions and interests" and similar conjunctions suggests that he saw them as co-equal threats to reason, and that the replacement of one by the other did not hold out any hope of improvement. The reference to "momentary passions and immediate interest" in *Federalist* 6 is consistent with the idea that passions could *modulate* interest, by inducing a shorter time horizon. They can also do so, of course, by causing the agents to hold irrational beliefs – "temporary errors and delusions" (*Fed.* 63, 425) – about how best to promote their interest. By contrast, La Bruyère and Hume referred to the fact that passions can make people act against their interest *as they perceive it at the time of acting.*

I conclude this section by commenting on the reference to *enthusiasm* in *Federalist* 49. Psychologists do not acknowledge enthusiasm as a passion. Numerous handbooks and textbooks on emotions, as well as the usual data bases, lack any reference to enthusiasm as a specific emotion. Yet its importance in dramatic instances of political change is beyond doubt, providing a striking instance of the gap between academic psychology and psychological reality. It is probably not easy to generate enthusiasm in the laboratory.

If we adopt the definition of enthusiasm used in the *Oxford English Dictionary*, the principal current sense of the word is "Rapturous intensity of feeling in favor of a person, principle, cause, etc.; passionate eagerness in any pursuit, proceeding from an intense conviction of the worthiness of the object." Although psychologists have not studied this passion, Kant offers brief and penetrating analyses.[27] Broadly speaking, he affirms that enthusiasm induces good ends but (like other passions) a bad choice of means. Whereas other writers then and since have used the term in a pejorative sense, to denote a kind of idling sentimentality, Kant reserves the term "Schwärmerei" for that phenomenon and distinguishes it explicitly from enthusiasm, without which, he wrote, "nothing great can be accomplished." Hume's essay on "Superstition and enthusiasm" is consistently negative in its judgments of the effects of the latter, probably because he had in mind the excesses of religious fanaticism in recent English history. The American framers, though, acknowledged that it could have positive effects and might even be indispensable.

One example of political enthusiasm has already been cited: the framers of the French constitution of 1791 who were "drunk with disinterestedness." The story is complicated, but it is likely that some of the twelve hundred framers who voted to make themselves ineligible did so because they did not see what was obvious to sober observers: that the consequence of their decision would be a legislature filled with inexperienced members who would be easily dominated by the radical Jacobin clubs. The outcome was disastrous. It should be added, however, that when the same framers in a moment of self-sacrificial enthusiasm (mixed with fear) abolished feudalism on the night of August 4, 1789, they achieved a profound reform that sober minds could never have accomplished. As one of them said about another of their reforms, "Anarchy is a frightening yet necessary passage, and the only moment one can establish a new order of things. It is not in calm times that one can take uniform measures."[28] The making of the Norwegian constitution of 1814 provides another example of political enthusiasm with – as in America – an accidentally happy outcome.[29]

Some passages from David Ramsay's insightful *History of the American Revolution*, published in 1789, illustrate the point. In his opinion, the actions of the American revolutionaries were largely based on wishful thinking. Their "ignorance of the military art, *prevented their weighing* the chances of war with that exactness of calculation, which, if indulged in, might have damped their hopes." They were "buoyed above the fear of consequences by an ardent military *enthusiasm*, unabated by calculations." Concerning the use of paper money to fund the war, he wrote that although it inevitably led to "a general wreck of property," a "happy ignorance of future events, combined with the ardor of the times, *prevented many reflections* on this subject, and gave credit and circulation to these bills of credit." Moreover, their passion was not an idling sentimentality, but generated *action*: "such was *the enthusiasm of the day*, that the colonists gave up both their personal services and their property to the public, on the vague promise that they should at a future time be reimbursed."[30]

Publius echoes the last comment when he refers to "those oppressive expedients for raising men which were upon several occasions practiced, and which nothing but the enthusiasm of liberty would have induced the people to endure" (*Fed.* 22, 138). Among his other comments on this passion, I have already cited his observation on its transient character. In *Federalist* 83 Publius refers to its distorting effect on rational belief formation, when he asserts that those who propose jury trials in all cases, and not merely in criminal trials, are "blinded by enthusiasm" and "men of enthusiastic tempers" (*Fed.* 83, 565, 572). In *Federalist* 1 he suggests that "the noble enthusiasm of liberty is apt to be infected with a spirit of narrow and illiberal distrust" (*Fed.* 1, 5), leading to what has been called "libertarian panics."[31] The most striking reference, however, occurs when *Federalist* 49 argues against Jefferson's proposal of revising the constitution by a constitutional convention whenever two-thirds of the members of two of the three branches of government call for it. In the continuation of a passage cited earlier, Publius wrote that

> We are to recollect that all the existing [state] constitutions were formed in the midst of a danger which repressed the passions most unfriendly to order and concord; of an *enthusiastic confidence of the people in their patriotic leaders, which stifled the ordinary diversity of opinions on great national questions;* of a *universal ardor* for new and opposite forms, produced by a *universal resentment and indignation against the ancient government;* and whilst *no spirit of party* connected with the changes to be made, or the abuses to be reformed, could mingle its leaven in the operation. The future situations in which we must expect to be usually placed, do not present any equivalent security against the danger which is apprehended.
>
> (*Fed.* 49, 341)

There is no reason to think that the occasions for a constitutional revision to prevent the encroachment of one branch of government upon the others will provide the necessary popular enthusiasm.

The Federalist was not written in a spirit of enthusiasm, nor intended to generate it. It is hard to be enthusiastic about negative measures to limit the impact of passion and interest on political decisions. Self-sacrificial measures usually presuppose a noble goal, "an intense conviction of the worthiness of the object." At the Federal Convention, the most intense conviction was probably fear rather than enthusiasm. As usual, it is hard to tell whether the fear was prudential or visceral. Jefferson seems to have thought the new constitution was written under the influence of visceral fear, or a "security panic." "Our Convention has been too much impressed by the insurrection of Massachusetts," Jefferson wrote William Smith eight weeks after the framers adjourned, "and in the spur of the moment they are setting up a kite [a hawk] to keep the hen-yard in order. I hope in God this article will be rectified before the new constitution is accepted."[32] When Publius refers to the "revolt of a part of the State of North Carolina, the late menacing disturbances in Pennsylvania, and the actual insurrections and rebellions in Massachusetts" (*Fed*. 6, 35), he probably intended to justify prudential fear. However, he may have been the victim of "backward myopia" or of the availability bias when he focused on recent events, ignoring for instance the fact that the hated paper money had functioned well in the colonies prior to 1776 or even 1778.

IV   INTEREST

By interest, Publius mainly had in mind the material (economic) interest of any subgroup of the national community.

> Those who hold and those who are without property have ever formed distinct interests in society. Those who are creditors, and those who are debtors, fall under a like discrimination. A landed interest, a manufacturing interest, a mercantile interest, a moneyed interest, with many lesser interests, grow up of necessity in civilized nations, and divide them into different classes, actuated by different sentiments and views. The regulation of these various and interfering interests forms the principal task of modern legislation.
>
> (*Fed*. 10, 59)

To these interest groups we can add the classes of "mechanics," "manufacturers," and "merchants" whom Publius mentions in *Federalist* 35.

Here "interest" must be understood in an objective sense. The interest of any group comprises all the measures that would benefit it materially. The interest groups may not be subjectively aware of the measures that would benefit them, or not be motivated to take account of known but temporally remote benefits. The *time* dimension constitutes in fact an important source of divergence between objective and subjective interest. The objective interest of a group is the discounted present value of its income stream for the known future. Its members may not, however, look that far into the future, but act on their expectations about short-term benefits. As noted, this truncating of the time horizon may be an effect of passion. Irrational belief formation, due to the urgency and bias induced by passion, is another source of divergence. Finally, the sheer complexity of causal issues may prevent uneducated people from forming an accurate estimate of the measures that would benefit them.

Agents who are unable to identify their own interests can be doubly handicapped: being both ignorant and unaware of the fact they are.[33] Such citizens might therefore choose representatives who fail to promote their real interest. Publius argues, however, that American "mechanics and manufacturers" escape this trap. "They know that the merchant is their natural patron and friend," he observes, and that

> their interests can be more effectually promoted by the merchant than by themselves. They are sensible that their habits in life have not been such as to give them those acquired endowments, without which, in a deliberative assembly, the greatest natural abilities are for the most part useless; and that the influence and weight, and superior acquirements of the merchants render them more equal to a contest with any spirit which might happen to infuse itself into the public councils, unfriendly to the manufacturing and trading interests. These considerations, and many others that might be mentioned prove, and experience confirms it, that artisans and manufacturers will commonly be disposed to bestow their votes upon merchants and those whom they recommend.
>
> (*Fed.* 35, 219–20)

Publius does not usually engage in cant, but here he does. Merchants are the natural *enemy* of mechanics: they want to buy low and mechanics want to sell high. If mechanics vote for merchants it may be not for lack of motive, but for lack of opportunity; if few mechanics stand for office, it may be because they do not satisfy the property require-ments for office-holding imposed in most of the states.

Publius observes that: "[s]tates are distinguished from each other by a variety of circumstances ... And although this variety of interests ... may have a salutary influence on the administration of the government when formed, yet every one must be sensible of the contrary influence, which must have been experienced in the task of forming it" (*Fed.* 37, 238). As was previously observed, the "contrary influence" due to "the spirit of party" can be overcome in extraordin-ary circumstances. The "salutary influence" refers to a central idea of *The Federalist*: "the greater security afforded by a greater variety of parties, against the event of any one party being able to outnumber and oppress the rest" (*Fed.* 10, 64). In normal times, the variety of interests in the extended republic is an obstacle both to change for the better and to change for the worse.

Yet it is difficult to determine whether Publius believes that *ambition* is an interest or a passion. In *Federalist* 4 it seems to be a passion: "absolute monarchs will often make war when their nations are to get nothing by it, but for the purposes and objects merely personal, such as thirst for military glory, revenge for per-sonal affronts, ambition, or private compacts to aggrandize or sup-port their particular families or partisans." Louis XIV and (later) Napoleon did not care about the French, only about the glory of France, which they identified with their own. But in *Federalist* 51 ambition seems to be an interest: "Ambition must be made to counteract ambition. The interest of the man must be connected with the constitutional rights of the place." The *desire for power* may be the common denominator, yet power may be sought either for its own sake or as a means to promote a further end. Of course, many who have sought power as a means to an end have found its exercise so delightful that they forgot about the end. Stories abound about politicians who suffer withdrawal symptoms when they have to step down. The idea of ambition seems too open-ended to be useful for analytical purposes.

V CONCLUSION

In the continuation of a passage cited at the outset of this essay, Albert Hirschman speculates about the emergence in the seventeenth century of *interest* as a separate category of human motivation:

> Once passion was deemed destructive and reason ineffectual, the view that human action could be exhaustively described by attribution to either one or the other means an exceedingly somber outlook for humanity. A message of hope was therefore conveyed by the wedging of interest in between the two traditional categories of human motivation. Interest was seen to partake in effect of the better nature of [both reason and passion], as the passion of self-love upgraded and contained by reason, and as reason given direction and force by that passion. The resulting hybrid form of human action was considered exempt from both the destructiveness of passion and the ineffectuality of reason.[34]

Without attempting to assess the historical accuracy of this account, one can nevertheless conclude that Publius certainly did not see any message of hope in interest as a motivation. As we saw, he was skeptical to the thesis of "le doux commerce." More broadly, he was fully aware that private interest can undermine the public interest by preventing collective action. In the 1780s, the two main authors of *The Federalist* analyzed the main problem of the Confederation as lack of cooperation among the states, in what we could now describe as either a Prisoner's Dilemma or an Assurance Game.[35] In *Federalist* 15, Publius offers a striking analysis of the *unraveling of the cooperation* that had been observed during the Revolutionary War:

> The causes which have been specified produced at first only unequal and disproportionate degrees of compliance with the requisitions of the Union. The greater deficiencies of some States furnished the pretext of example and the temptation of interest to the complying, or to the least delinquent States. Why should we *do more in proportion* than those who are embarked with us in the same political voyage? Why should we consent to *bear more than our*

proper share of the common burden? These were suggestions which human selfishness could not withstand, and which even speculative men, who looked forward to remote consequences, could not, without hesitation, combat. Each State, yielding to the persuasive voice of immediate interest or convenience, has successively withdrawn its support, till the frail and tottering edifice seems ready to fall upon our heads, and to crush us beneath its ruins.

This analysis, which strongly echoes Madison's pre-Convention memorandum on the "Vices of the political system of the United States," suggests that neither the Prisoner's Dilemma nor the Assurance Game captures the full dynamic of self-interest. Rather, the phrases emphasized in the quotation indicate that *selfishness hid behind claims of unfairness.* Each cooperative arrangement would benefit some state more than others, or impose greater burdens on some than on others. The states less favorably treated might refuse to comply, offering an excuse (on Assurance-Game grounds) to the other states for non-compliance as well.

Let us return to the paraphrased metaphor from Hayek invoked at the opening of this essay. Constitution-makers are usually drunk, that is, acting under the influence of passion. The American framers may or may not have been an exception to this proposition. What is certain is that they were not exclusively dominated by reason: the slaveholding and commercial interests played a vital role, as did the interests of the states. Moreover, the framers were not concerned only with the passions of future political agents, but also tried to minimize the destructive impact of their interests. The term "sober", in fact, applies to interest no less than to reason.

NOTES

1 Friedrich Hayek, *The Constitution of Liberty: The Definitive Edition*, ed. Ronald Hamowy (Chicago: University of Chicago Press, 1960, 2011), 268.
2 Albert Hirschman, *The Passions and the Interests: Political Arguments for Capitalism before Its Triumph* (Princeton: Princeton University Press, 1977), 43.

3 Ibid., 29, 30.

4 Morton White, *Philosophy*, The Federalist, *and the Constitution* (New York, Oxford University Press, 1987), 103–04 and more generally, chapters 7–9.

5 *RFC*, I, 376, 381.

6 White, *Philosophy*, The Federalist, *and the Constitution*, 107–08.

7 Jean de la Bruyère, *The Characters of Jean de la Bruyère*, trans. Henri Van Laun (New York: Scribner and Welford, 1885), IV, 77; David Hume, *An Enquiry Concerning the Principles of Morals* (London, 1751), Appendix II.

8 La Bruyère, *The Characters*, III: 87.

9 *DHRC*, X, 1292, 1417.

10 Michael Kwass, *Privilege and the Politics of Taxation in Eighteenth-Century France:* Liberté, Égalité, Fiscalité (New York: Cambridge University Press, 1990), 205.

11 Arthur O. Lovejoy, *Reflections on Human Nature* (Baltimore: Johns Hopkins University Press, 1961).

12 David Hume, "Of the Dignity or Meanness of Human Nature," in idem., *Essays Moral, Political, and Literary*, ed. Eugene F. Miller (Indianapolis: Liberty Fund, 1987), 86.

13 See the title essay in Trevor Colbourn, ed., *Fame and the Founding Fathers: Essays by Douglass Adair* (New York: Norton, 1974), 34; E. Lebègue, *Thouret (1746–1794)* (Paris: Alcan, 1910), 261.

14 Michel de Montaigne, *Essays* (London: Penguin, 1991), 715, 1157–58.

15 Xenophon, *Hellenica*, I.7.

16 Douglas MacDowell, *The Law in Classical Athens* (Ithaca, N.Y.: Cornell University Press, 1978), 74; Martin Ostwald, *From Popular Sovereignty to the Sovereignty of Law: Law, Society, and Politics in Fifth-Century Athens* (Berkeley: University of California Press, 1986), 522, 200.

17 Jon Elster, *Securities Against Misrule: Juries, Assemblies, Elections* (New York: Cambridge University Press, 2013), chapter 3.

18 Alexander Hamilton to James Duane, Sept. 3, 1780, *PAH*, II, 404–05.

19 White, *Philosophy*, The Federalist, *and the Constitution*, 234–35.

20 Jon Elster, *Alchemies of the Mind: Rationality and the Emotions* (New York: Cambridge University Press, 1999), chapter 4; Elster, *Explaining Social Behavior: More Nuts and Bolts for the Social Sciences*, 2nd ed. (New York: Cambridge University Press, 2015), chapter 8.

21 Woody Holton, *Unruly Americans and the Origins of the Constitution* (New York: Hill and Wang, 2007), 155; Roger H. Brown, *Redeeming the*

Republic: Federalists, Taxation, and the Origins of the Constitution (Baltimore: Johns Hopkins University Press, 1993), 80, 128.

22 Dianne Tice, Ellen Braslasvky, and Roy Baumeister, "Emotional distress regulation takes precedence over impulse control," *Journal of Personality and Social Psychology* 80 (2001), 53–67.

23 Paul Ekman, "An Argument for Basic Emotions", *Cognition and Emotion*, 6 (1992), 185.

24 Jeremy Bentham, *Rights, Representation, and Reform: Nonsense upon Stilts and Other Writings on the French Revolution*, ed. Philip Schofield, Catherine Pease-Watkin and Cyprian Blamires (Oxford: Clarendon Press, 2002), 278–79.

25 Elster, *Securities Against Misrule*, 182–83.

26 Hirschman, *The Passions and the Interests*, 31–42.

27 For a summary of these uses, see Elster, *Securities Against Misrule*, 90, 205.

28 Comte de Clermont-Tonnerre, Speech in the National Assembly, *Archives Parlementaires*, Série I: 1787–1799 (Paris 1875–1888), IX, 441.

29 Jon Elster, "A race against time: The making of the Norwegian constitution of 1814", in J. Elster et al., eds., *Constituent Assemblies*, (New York: Cambridge University Press, 2018), 138–60.

30 David Ramsay, *The History of the American Revolution*, ed. Lester H. Cohen (Indianapolis: Liberty Fund, 2011), I, 196–97, 146, 255–56 (emphasis added).

31 Adrian Vermeule, "Libertarian Panics," *Rutgers Law Journal*, 36 (2005), 871–88, and see the brief discussion of the Revolutionary era at 879–80.

32 Jefferson to William Stephens Smith, November 13, 1787, in Julian P. Boyd et al., eds., *The Papers of Thomas Jefferson* (Princeton: Princeton University Press, 1976–), XII, 356–57. By "this article" Jefferson was probably referring to the Republican Guarantee Clause of Article IV.

33 Justin Kruger and David Dunning, "Unskilled and Unaware of It: How Difficulties in Recognizing One's Incompetence Lead to Inflated Self-Assessments," *Journal of Personality and Social Psychology*, 77 (1999), 1121–34.

34 Hirschman, *The Passions and the Interests*, 43.

35 See Keith I. Dougherty, "Madison's Theory of Public Goods," in Samuel Kernell, ed., *James Madison: The Theory and Practice of Republican Government* (Stanford, CA: Stanford University Press, 2003), 41–62; and Jack N. Rakove, *A Politician Thinking: The Creative Mind of James Madison* (Norman, OK: University of Oklahoma Press, 2017), 43–53.

7   Montesquieu, Hume, Adam Smith, and the Philosophical Perspective of *The Federalist*

Paul A. Rahe

In April 1787 James Madison composed for his own use a memorandum entitled "Vices of the Political System of the United States." He did so in preparation for a convention, slated to meet within a few weeks in Philadelphia, which had been called – in part at his urging – for the purpose of proposing amendments to the instrument linking the various American states.

The Virginian had done yeoman service in the 1780s in the Continental Congress. The experience had in time taught him what his fellow congressman Alexander Hamilton had learned much earlier while serving in the Continental Line: that the Articles of Confederation were grossly inadequate to the needs of the fledgling American Union. In September 1786 Madison and Hamilton both attended an abortive gathering in Annapolis, Maryland, aimed at promoting free trade within the United States. There the two had joined forces in an attempt to snatch victory from the jaws of defeat by persuading fellow delegates to issue a joint appeal calling on the Continental Congress to make arrangements for a general convention with broad authority to address all of the defects of the existing confederacy.

Thanks in part to the fears stirred up by Shays' Rebellion, the Continental Congress complied with this request, and a convention was called. Madison's fellow Virginians chose him as a delegate, and he decided to take a stab at seizing the agenda. Prior to 1786, he appears to have thought that amending the nascent Union's instrument of government would suffice. But by the spring of 1787 he had come to the conclusion that Hamilton was right and that the Articles of Confederation would have to be replaced in their entirety. The memorandum that he composed in April was an itemized indictment of the existing order.

Madison's list consisted of twelve items. The first eight focused on the debility of the Union. Their titles tell the tale:

> 1. Failure of the States to comply with the Constitutional requisitions. 2. Encroachments by the States on the federal authority. 3. Violations of the law of nations and of treaties. 4. Trespasses of the States on the rights of each other. 5. want of concert in matters where common interest requires it. 6. want of Guaranty to the States of their Constitutions & laws against internal violence. 7. want of sanction to the laws, and of coercion in the Government of the Confederacy. 8. Want of ratification by the people of the articles of Confederation.

The last four identified defects in government within the states:

> 9. Multiplicity of laws in the several States. 10. mutability of the laws of the States. 11. Injustice of the laws of States. 12. Impotence of the laws of the States.

The penultimate item bothered Madison the most – for, as he readily acknowledged, the propensity of the states for passing unjust laws called "into question the fundamental principle of republican Government," first suggested by Niccolò Machiavelli, "that the majority who rule in such Governments, are the safest Guardians both of public Good and of private rights."[1]

It was Madison's conviction that to remedy the defects he had identified would require a second American revolution – one in which the Articles of Confederation would be discarded, the states would cede extensive powers to the federation, and the federation itself would be reconstituted as a proper, fully articulated government deriving its power from the people. This reconstituted government would be equipped with its own revenues and, endowed with means of coercion enabling it, within a limited scope, to act directly upon the people. In the absence of a more perfect and comprehensive union, he feared that there would soon be no union at all and that the individual states would themselves in time succumb to despotism.

With this in mind, Madison appears to have persuaded the other delegates from his native state to join with him in sketching out a proposal for the establishment of a true national government. In Philadelphia at the end of May, Edmund Randolph, the governor of Virginia, acting on their behalf, presented to the Convention at its opening what came to be called the Virginia Plan. To understand the deliberations that followed and the heated but nonetheless civilized debate that ensued concerning ratification, one must first immerse oneself in the thinking of an analyst rarely studied today. His name was Charles-Louis de Secondat, baron de La Brède et de Montesquieu. His book *The Spirit of Laws* provided late eighteenth-century Americans with an intellectual framework within which to judge the relative propriety of the various political institutions and practices on offer.

THE CELEBRATED MONTESQUIEU

This French aristocrat bestrode the second half of the eighteenth century like a colossus. Every major work that he ushered into print quickly found a wide audience. By 1800, his *Persian Letters*, which first appeared in 1721, had been published in ninety-three editions and had been translated into English, Dutch, German, Polish, and Russian. His *Considerations on the Causes of the Greatness of the Romans and their Decline*, which was first published in 1734, had appeared in sixty-two editions and been translated into English, Italian, Dutch, Swedish, Polish, Russian, and Greek. Neither of these bore comparison with Montesquieu's *Spirit of Laws*. This last work was in a self-evident way serious, and it was enormous as well. One purchased it expecting instruction and not diversion – diverting though it might be. And yet, from the moment of its release in the fall of 1748, it sold like hotcakes. By the end of the century, it had been published in 128 editions, and it had been translated into

English, Italian, German, Latin, Danish, Dutch, Polish, and Russian. In the period stretching from 1748 to 1800, these three books were published together in editions of Montesquieu's complete works no fewer than thirty-six times.

The Spirit of Laws was a publishing phenomenon, and it was much, much more. As the eventful second half of the eighteenth century began, Montesquieu's great work became the political bible of learned men and would-be statesmen everywhere in Europe, and beyond. In Britain, it shaped the thinking of Edmund Burke, Edward Gibbon, William Blackstone, Adam Smith, Adam Ferguson, John Robertson, John Millar, Lord Kames, and Dugald Stewart, among others. In France, it was the starting point for Jean-Jacques Rousseau and all subsequent political thinkers. In Italy, it had a profound effect on Cesare Beccaria, and, in Germany, it was fundamental for Georg Wilhelm Friedrich Hegel.[2]

In North America, Montesquieu reigned supreme. In the period stretching from 1762 to 1800, no one was as often cited in the political tracts and newspapers as he was.[3] Moreover, when his name was mentioned, was nearly always a generous epithet attached. Letters written in 1763 to newspapers in Boston spoke of him as "a great writer," as "this great writer," and as "the great Montesquieu." They termed him "the admired writer" and "the very justly celebrated author of *The Spirit of the Laws*." They called him the "penetrating Montesquieu."[4] Two years later, in a pamphlet published in Newport, Rhode Island, Martin Howard dubbed him "the admired Secondat."[5] As John Dickinson readily acknowledged in his *Letters from a Farmer in Pennsylvania*, the French *philosophe* was "a very learned author."[6] Dickinson's colleagues in the Continental Congress agreed. In an address to the inhabitants of Quebec which he drafted, they spoke of the Frenchman as "an illustrious author of your nation" and termed him "the immortal *Montesquieu*." His is they explained, "a name which all Europe reveres," for he is a "truly great man," a renowned "advocate of freedom and humanity."[7]

Similarly, for Carter Braxton, writing in 1776, the author of *The Spirit of Laws* was "the learned Montesquieu."[8] A contributor to the

Massachusetts Spy that same year called him "the judicious MON-
TESQUIEU" and termed him "a great *authority*."[9] He was, as both
James Madison and Alexander Hamilton took occasion to remark in
The Federalist, "the celebrated Montesquieu" (*Fed.* 47, 324; *Fed.* 78,
523). As such, he was an authority for Federalists and Anti-Federalists
alike.[10] He could even be described as an "oracle" (*Fed.* 47, 324).

Of course, those who cited Montesquieu generally did so for
rhetorical effect, but a great many appear to have studied him with
care as well. In 1763, T. Q. and J., though rival contributors to the
Boston press, agreed on one thing: that a proper interpretation of *The
Spirit of Laws* was the key to understanding whether multiple office-
holding by members of the legislature was a threat to liberty in
Massachusetts.[11] When Benjamin Rush argued against slavery in a
pamphlet penned a decade later, he displayed a detailed knowledge of
Montesquieu's great work.[12] When Worcestriensis wrote to the *Massachusetts Spy* in September 1776 to oppose religious persecution and
yet advocate public support for a religious establishment, he did so as
well.[13] The same can be said for the anonymous South Carolinian
who published his *Rudiments of Law and Government Deduced from
the Law of Nature* in 1783.[14] Even those who found it necessary to
disagree with Montesquieu took it for granted that *The Spirit of Laws*
was the appropriate starting point for reflection on the political question under consideration. On such occasions, even when his name
passes unmentioned, one can often detect his presence.[15] No one did
more to shape American thinking with respect to the constitution of
liberty in modern times.

For Montesquieu's preeminence, there was an obvious reason.
His *Spirit of Laws*, which first appeared in English two years after its
publication in French, is arguably the greatest work in constitutional
prudence penned in modern times, and almost instantly it was recognized as such. In 1749 David Hume informed its author that his book
would be "the wonder of the centuries."[16] Two years later, in his
Enquiry Concerning the Principles of Morals, he alerted the public
to the fact that Montesquieu was "an author of great genius, as well as

extensive learning," and he described *The Spirit of Laws* as "the best system of political knowledge that, perhaps, has ever yet been communicated to the world."[17] In 1750, in his correspondence, Horace Walpole described that work as "the best book that ever was written."[18] Seven years later, in his *Abridgment of English History*, Edmund Burke hailed its author as "the greatest genius, which has enlightened this age."[19] Not since Aristotle composed *The Politics* had anyone so thoroughly surveyed the variety of polities to be found in the known world, examined the conditions under which they thrived, and pondered their virtues, vices, and propensities.[20]

Moreover, Montesquieu took as his principal theme political liberty, understood in terms of the rule of law and the provision for individual security, and the institutions and circumstances conducive to its flourishing, and he singled out as a form of government that had liberty as its direct object the very polity from which the American colonists derived their own institutions. What James Madison said on this subject in *Federalist* 47 was an exaggeration, but there was nonetheless something to the claim:

> The British constitution was to Montesquieu, what Homer has been to the didactic writers on epic poetry. As the latter have considered the work of the immortal Bard, as the perfect model from which the principles and rules of the epic art were to be drawn, and by which all similar works were to be judged; so this great political critic appears to have viewed the constitution of England, as the standard, or to use his own expression, as the mirrour of political liberty; and to have delivered in the form of elementary truths, the several characteristic principles of that particular system.
>
> (*Fed.* 47, 324–25)[21]

Of course, America was not England. It was differently situated. There was no monarch. Not one of the Union's constituent states was endowed with an hereditary aristocracy, and nothing of the sort was likely to emerge. Thanks to the availability of vast tracts of untilled land on the frontier to the west, there were no great, glaring, enduring disparities of wealth in this corner of the New World and none likely to appear in the foreseeable future. Moreover, as a consequence of their quarrel with their mother country and of the war that followed, Americans had abandoned the sentimental attachment to Britain and its institutions that they had once ostentatiously displayed, and in the process they had developed a marked distaste for monarchy and aristocracy. By the 1780s, the newly independent nation's genius had become, as the greatest American admirers of Britain's constitution readily admitted, republican.

This fact notwithstanding, early on the Americans did imitate those institutions. They had no other model ready to hand. These were the forms and formalities with which they were familiar. As Montesquieu had pointed out in his magnum opus, England had given "to the people of her colonies the form of her own government"; "this government" had brought "with it prosperity"; and, in North America, the New World had witnessed "great peoples take form within the very forests that they" had been dispatched "to inhabit."[22] It made sense that, in the immediate aftermath of their Declaration of Independence, the Americans should adjust and not replace the institutions that they had inherited. Without exception, the states eliminated all reference to Great Britain and the crown; and, where governors and other officials had been appointed, they came to be elected. Two of the states thought it sufficient to amend their colonial charters and leave it at that. In the rest, there was a deliberative process, and new constitutions were adopted. In some states, this happened more than once, as the founding generation wrestled with the challenge of governing themselves.[23]

Looking back on all of this, James Madison was anything but sanguine. Some of the states had done better than others. But in his view and in that of many of his compatriots, all of them had fallen short. Thanks to the multiplicity, mutability, injustice, and impotence of the laws passed in these states, there were grounds for concern regarding "the fundamental principle of republican

Government" – grounds for doubting "that the majority who rule in such Governments, are the safest Guardians both of public Good and of private rights." If fledgling American republics were to vindicate this principle, their citizens would have to examine "the vices" to which "the political system of the United States" had given rise, and they would have to devise a remedy consistent with the new nation's republican character.

A REPUBLIC ON AN EXTENDED TERRITORY?

The fundamental question that Madison and his colleagues at the Philadelphia Convention had to tackle was the one posed by Montesquieu: Could a republic be sustained on an extended territory? The French philosopher had devoted the first of the six parts into which he divided his *Spirit of Laws* to the articulation of a novel typology of the various forms of government, supplemented with a description of each and an analysis of its propensities and prerequisites. The account he provided was systematic and comprehensive. It was in this context that he addressed the constraints imposed by different geographical configurations.

Where Aristotle and others had discussed the virtuous and vicious rule of the one, the few, and the many, Montesquieu eschewed moral distinctions and emphasized institutional structures and political psychology. In his estimation, monarchies were distinguished from despotisms by the presence of a hereditary nobility and other intermediary powers. In them, the existence of a complex, entrenched hierarchy gave rise to a sense of pride and propriety and a passion for honor inconsistent with the ethos of abject terror inspired by one-man rule in the absence of a system of ranks and orders; and, though whimsical and arbitrary, the ethos of honor that bound the monarch and his minions was conducive to regularity and the rule of law.

In Montesquieu's opinion, the passions that distinguished the two species of one-man rule and set each in motion were a natural and inevitable product of the structure of each. One could build, as they did, on vanity and fear. They were a reliable part of the human make-up.

The same could not, however, be said regarding "the principle" or passion that set democratic republics in motion. The Frenchman eschewed moral analysis for a reason. He thought man by nature a social but not a political animal. In his judgment, public-spiritedness did not arise in human beings naturally. Nor was it a completion or perfection of human nature. Its exercise was never for human beings a genuine pleasure. The self-sacrifice required was from start to finish a source of pain. Political virtue, the love of equality and the laws, was not, then, as a "principle" an easily acquired taste – off-putting, perhaps, in the beginning, but soon enjoyable and almost addictive. Its acquisition required a distortion of human nature akin to masochism. Republican citizens he compared with monks. If they loved the rules and regulations that imposed on them severe constraints, it was because these constraints left them no pleasures apart from the observance of these same rules and regulations. The most successful of the ancient republics relied on singular institutions, which set their citizens sharply apart in their mores and manners from all outsiders and instilled in them a pride and a xenophobia that powerfully reinforced the sense of fellow-feeling that underpinned the fierce patriotism and the courage for which they were famous.[24]

Montesquieu treated each form of government as a coherent, elaborate system. Over time, each tended to articulate mores, manners, laws, and institutions reflective of its nature and of the political psychology that it inspired or inculcated. It had to do so if it was to survive. He also concerned himself with the preconditions for the flourishing of each of the three political regimes. He devoted the eighth and final book of the first part of his *Spirit of Laws* to a study of what was likely to produce "corruption" in the principle of each of these regimes and thereby, in time, cause its collapse. The fifteenth chapter of this book, which is focused on the preservation "of the three principles," consists of a single sentence: "I shall not be able to make myself understood until the next four chapters have been read."

In these chapters, Montesquieu's chief purpose was to issue a salutary warning to the king of France and his subjects and to the rulers of Europe's other great monarchies and those whom they ruled. To endure, he intimated, monarchies must be of "middling magnitude." If small, such a polity would turn into a republic. If it became "extended to a great degree," the leading men would be out of sight and out of mind; and, if not cowed, they would cease to obey. To survive, therefore, "a great empire" would have to presuppose "in the one who governs a despotic authority."

> Promptness in decision-making is required to compensate for the distance of the places to which orders are sent; fear is required to prevent negligence on the part of the governor or magistrate operating at a great distance; the law must be lodged in a single head; and it must change unceasingly like the accidents, which always multiply within a state in proportion to its magnitude.

It was what he had to say about republics in the first of these four critical chapters that initially arrested the attention of the founding generation in America:

> It is in the nature of a republic that it have a small territory; without that it can hardly subsist. In a large republic, there are great fortunes and, in consequence, little in the way of a moderation of spirit; there are trusts [*depôts*] too great to be placed in the hands of a single citizen. Interests become particular; a man senses that he can be happy, great, and glorious without his fatherland, and soon that he can be great solely on the ruins of his fatherland.
>
> In a large republic, the common good is sacrificed to a thousand considerations; it is subordinated to the exceptions; it depends on accidents. In a small republic, the public good is more fully felt, better known, closer to each citizen. The abuses there are less extensive and, in consequence, less well protected.[25]

The Americans knew something about the quality that Montesquieu called "political virtue." They had just fought a war. It was a heady time. They had warmed to the courage and generosity of some. They had witnessed the cowardice and greed of others. Instinctively, they knew a great deal about the relationship between public-spiritedness and self-sacrifice, on the one hand, and fellow-feeling, on the other. Their experience taught or reconfirmed for them that the requisite ethos could without great difficulty be sustained in a face-to-face community of people closely familiar with one another, and that it could not be sustained in a large society composed of strangers.

The American Union was sizable. By 1787, it was already a great empire, and it promised to be one greater still. Everyone in North America understood as much – which is why Montesquieu's argument had such purchase. The republics of ancient Greece and the early Roman republic fit Montesquieu's description. Because they were small and at odds with one another, the former had succumbed when challenged by Phillip of Macedon; and, although the latter did not give way to a foreign challenger, when it grew into a great empire instead, republican government proved unsustainable and a despotism replaced it via an inexorable process that Montesquieu had traced in detail in his *Considerations on the Causes of the Greatness of the Romans and their Decline*. The question that Madison and his colleagues at the Federal Convention wrestled with, once they admitted to themselves the necessity that America be made a more perfect union, was how to avoid the fate reserved for the Greek *póleis* without incurring that reserved for the Roman *civitas*.

FEDERALISM

With regard to this dilemma, Montesquieu had something to offer. His *Spirit of Laws* was composed as a dialogue of sorts. Each of the parts, subsequent to the first, was a response to and partial correction of what came before. The four chapters in the eighth book of the first part that the French philosopher singled out as central to his argument were by no means his last word on the subject. In the first three chapters of the second part of that work, for example, he takes up the question of self-defense. When viewed from this angle, as he readily admits, monarchies of middling size have a distinct advantage when matched against diminutive republics. But, as he goes on to point out, republics confederated in a league can project power in the manner of a monarchy while retaining their character as republics, avoiding the corruption attendant on territorial extension, and guarding one another against decay. In antiquity, the Lycians had done this, as had the Swiss, the Germans, and the Dutch in modern times.[26]

This, too, astute Americans had noticed. Early in 1786, after he had begun to despair regarding the viability of the Union established under the Articles of Confederation, James Madison had undertaken a study of ancient and modern confederacies. It is telling that, in the extensive notes that he took, the first author mentioned is Montesquieu, whom he may have first encountered while a child under the tutelage of Donald Robertson and whom he had almost certainly read with care while a student at the College of New Jersey, where it was on a list of works recommended by the institution's president John Witherspoon.[27] Alexander Hamilton had also read with care the pertinent chapters in *The Spirit of Laws*, and he rang changes upon them in *Federalist 9*:

> The utility of a confederacy, as well to suppress faction and to guard the internal tranquillity of States, as to increase their external force and security, is in reality not a new idea. It has been practiced upon in different countries and ages, and has received the sanction of the most applauded writers, on the subjects of politics. The opponents of the PLAN proposed have with great assiduity cited and circulated the observations of Montesquieu on the necessity of a contracted territory for a republican government. But they seem not to have been apprised of the sentiments of that great man expressed in another part of his work.
>
> (*Fed.* 9, 52)

To his credit, Hamilton pointed out another defect fatal to the argument of the Anti-Federalists that was no less damaging to his rhetorical appropriation of Montesquieu's defense of republican confederacies. As he intimated, the new Constitution's opponents had failed to consider fully the consequences of "the principle to which they subscribe":

> When Montesquieu recommends a small extent for republics, the
> standards he had in view were of dimensions, far short of the limits
> of almost every one of these States. Neither Virginia,
> Massachusetts, Pennsylvania, New-York, North-Carolina, nor
> Georgia, can by any means be compared with the models, from
> which he reasoned and to which the terms of his descriptions apply.

If the Americans were to take to heart Montesquieu's denial that
republics situated on an extended territory were viable, they would
either have to divide the larger states into small commonwealths or
accept at the state level the inevitability of monarchy (*Fed. 9*, 52–56).

COMMERCIAL REPUBLICANISM

Hamilton could pose this question because it was by no means clear
that the ancient Greek republics and early Rome were appropriate
models. To a careless reader, the political typology articulated in *The
Spirit of Laws* might seem static and timeless.[28] Only once in the first
part of his book does Montesquieu intimate that historical developments might render a particular form of government obsolete. Tell-
ingly, however, the form of government in question is the republic
grounded in virtue. When the virtue of the ancients was in full force,
he reports, "they did things that we no longer see and that astonish
our little souls." If his contemporaries fall short, it is because the
"education" given the ancients "never suffered contradiction," while
"we receive three educations different" from and even "contrary" to
one another: "that of our fathers, that of our schoolmasters, and that
of the world. What we are told in the last overthrows the ideas
imparted from the first two." In short, because Christianity teaches
that men are pilgrims just passing through on the earth, there is now
"a contrast between the engagements" which arise "from religion"
and "those" which "arise from the world" that "the ancients" with
their this-worldly orientation "knew nothing of."[29]

   If, as Montesquieu intimates, virtue on the ancient model can
no longer be inculcated, it follows that there can no longer be

republics "based on virtue." If, however, in his estimation, this fact is not fatal to republicanism as such, it is because there is another species of republicanism – one "based on commerce." In such a polity, where the citizens engage in commerce themselves, he tells us, "it can very well happen that particular individuals have great wealth and that the mores there are not corrupted." This odd and unforeseen result comes about because "the spirit of commerce" often "carries with it a spirit of frugality, economy, moderation, industry, wisdom, tranquillity, orderliness, and regularity."[30] It is the survival of this species of republic in modern times that explains how, after observing that "the Greek statesmen and political writers [*politiques*] who lived under popular government knew of no force able to sustain them other than virtue," Montesquieu can add "[t]hose of today speak only of manufactures, of commerce, of finance, of wealth, and of luxury itself."[31] Montesquieu may not have wholeheartedly embraced the argument articulated by Pierre Nicole, Pierre Bayle, and Bernard Mandeville that what was once considered private vice can give rise to public virtue,[32] but he clearly felt its force. He evidently believed that, within commercial societies, the marketplace tends to impose a modicum of salutary discipline on its participants, and this was, he realized, a matter of considerable political significance. For, in the fourth part of his *Spirit of Laws*, Montesquieu demonstrates that commerce is and has long been a growing force, and there he intimates that polities, such as monarchies, that are incapable of taking full advantage of trade, are already at a decided disadvantage and will in the future be so to an ever greater degree.[33]

The authors of *The Federalist* were commercial republicans. They, too, spoke of manufactures, commerce, finance, and wealth. They rejoiced in the fact that North America was commercial; they were advocates of the scientific project proposed by Sir Francis Bacon; and they embraced the technological and economic dynamism that it promised. Within the constitution that Hamilton and Madison had helped frame, there was a clause providing for the regulation of interstate commerce; another sanctioning tariffs on international trade; and, most telling, a third calling for laws for the protection of intellectual property.

When, in 1791, Hamilton presented to Congress his famous *Report on Manufactures*, he justified his call for the promotion of that particular branch of human endeavor by arguing that it would furnish "greater scope for the diversity of talents and dispositions, which discriminate men from each other." It was, he believed, the task of government to "cherish and stimulate the activity of the human mind, by multiplying the objects of enterprise ... Every new scene, which is opened to the busy nature of man to rouse and exert himself, is the addition of a new energy to the general stock of effort."[34]

Although on other grounds Madison opposed Hamilton's program, he agreed with the sentiments expressed by the man. In *Federalist* 10 he argued that it is from "the diversity in the faculties of men" that "the rights of property originate"; that this diversity forms "an insuperable obstacle to a uniformity of interests"; and that "the protection" of these "different and unequal faculties of acquiring property" is "the first object of government" (*Fed.* 10, 58). If Madison did not favor the establishment of a republic of virtue on American soil, it was not solely or even primarily because he supposed the circumstances uncongenial. It was chiefly because he thought the attempt, mounted most successfully in ancient Sparta, to give "to every citizen the same opinions, the same passions, and the same interests," would prove incompatible with the very purpose of government.[35]

REPRESENTATION AND THE SEPARATION OF POWERS

There was another dimension of Montesquieu's discussion of commercial republicanism that also had a considerable impact on the authors of *The Federalist*. The England that he so admired was, he believed, the modern exemplar of that peculiar form of government. In one passage, he describes the English as "the people in the world who have known best how to take advantage of these three great things at the same time: religion, commerce, and liberty." In another, he speaks of their government as "a republic concealed under the form of a monarchy." What he means by this latter claim he makes clear on the first occasion when he mentions England in his *Spirit of Laws*. There he makes two observations suggesting that England is a democracy dedicated to liberty. If, he writes, you "abolish in a monarchy the prerogatives of the lords, the clergy, the nobility, and the towns," as England's Parliament did, "you will soon have a state popular or, indeed, despotic." Then, he adds that the English, who "in order to favor liberty, have eliminated all the intermediary powers which formed their monarchy, ... have good reason to conserve this liberty," explaining that, "if they should lose it, they would be one of the most fully enslaved peoples on the earth."[36]

In the first part of *The Spirit of Laws*, Montesquieu rarely mentions England. He briefly alludes to the English government's peculiar character; he mentions republics based on commerce; and he leaves both anomalies as puzzles for rumination on the part of careful readers. The commercial republic he does not again discuss until the fourth part of his magnum opus. But when he does, he makes it clear that it is England that fulfills the promise implicit in the ancient examples he mentions.[37] In its second part, where he makes liberty thematic, he describes in detail the English constitution; and in the last chapter of the third part, at the very center of the work, he treats the operation of that constitution and its impact on the character of the English.[38] These two chapters – the longest and arguably the most important in *The Spirit of Laws* – were more widely read in the English-speaking world than anything else that Montesquieu wrote.[39]

The Americans could not simply duplicate the English constitution. The hereditary principle was for them anathema. But, as we have seen, they nonetheless emulated those institutions. Like the English, they embraced the principle of representation, substituting deputies whom they elected for direct popular government on the ancient model; and, after some false starts, they for the most part worked their way around to a unitary executive, a bicameral legislature, and an independent judiciary. While substituting an elected for a hereditary executive and upper house, they self-consciously tried to implement a separation of powers, in which lawmaking was assigned to one power, the execution of the law and the conduct of foreign policy to another, and judging particular cases to a third, with all three powers constituted in such a fashion as to make each independent of the others. And this they did for the reasons laid out by Montesquieu in the sixth chapter of the eleventh book of his *Spirit of Laws*, supposing that the combination of these powers in the hands of a single figure was the very definition of despotism and that the rule of law and liberty understood as personal security could only be established and sustained if the three powers were rendered distinct and independent and thereby kept separate (*Fed.* 51–81, 347–552).

Nowhere did Montesquieu expressly claim that representative assemblies and a separation of powers would, like federalism, enable republican government to cope with the threat to its survival posed by the tendencies inherent in geographical extension. This question he left to his readers to sort out for themselves, commenting, in the last chapter of the book in which he discussed the English constitution, that "it is not necessary to so exhaust a subject that one leaves nothing for the reader to do. The task is not to make him read but to make him think."[40] It should nonetheless have been obvious to anyone who paused to reflect on the matter that the English, whom Montesquieu described as one of "the most fully free peoples that ever existed on earth,"[41] occupied an extended territory and that an institutional arrangement that blocked the concentration of power, deployed self-interest as a check on self-interest, and thereby stood firmly in the way of arbitrary rule must at least in some measure have obviated the danger posed by geographical extension to the unitary "republic concealed under the form of a monarchy" that had emerged on English soil.[42] The Americans instinctively understood this – which explains why, Alexander Hamilton to the contrary notwithstanding, they did not greatly fret about the size of Virginia, Massachusetts, Pennsylvania, New York, North Carolina, and Georgia and why, when they ran into difficulties in the states, they generally turned their attention to correcting defects in their existing institutions on the presumption that the latter had failed to produce a genuine separation of powers.[43]

In defending the proposed federal constitution, the authors of *The Federalist* approached the separation of powers from two perspectives. On the one hand, they followed what Madison called "a policy of supplying by opposite and rival interests, the defect of better motives." As he put it, "Ambition must be made to counteract ambition. The interest of the man must be connected with the constitutional rights of the place ... The constant aim is to divide and arrange the several offices in such a manner as that each may be a check on the other; that the private interest of every individual, may be a centinel over the public rights." To this end, those serving in each of the various branches of the government were to be given "the necessary constitutional means, and personal motives, to resist encroachments of the others" (*Fed.* 51, 349). In the same spirit, Alexander Hamilton noted that "the dissimilar modes of constituting the several component parts of the government" would be such that "there would be little probability of a common interest to cement these different branches in a predilection for any particular class of electors" (*Fed.* 60, 405). When seen from this angle, the American constitution presents itself as a perpetual-motion machine. "To form a moderate government," Montesquieu tells us, "it is necessary to combine powers, to regulate them, to temper them, to make them act, to give, so to speak, a ballast to one in order to put it in a condition to resist another; this is a masterpiece of legislation, which chance rarely produces and prudence is rarely allowed to produce."[44]

On the other hand, Madison and Hamilton concerned themselves with the encouragement of better motives. As they knew, in his *Spirit of Laws*, Montesquieu had singled out monarchy for close examination, observing:

> In monarchies, policy makes great things happen with as little of virtue as it can, just as in the most beautiful machines, art also

employs as little of movement, of forces, of wheels as is possible. The state subsists independently of love of the fatherland, of desire for true glory, of self-renunciation, of sacrifice of one's dearest interests, and of all those heroic virtues which we find in the ancients and know only from hearing them spoken of.[45]

If, in his estimation, virtue was unnecessary, it was because in a monarchy honor took "the place" it had occupied in the martial republics of classical antiquity. The honor that Montesquieu had in mind was artificial: it was, he said, a "false honor," which demanded artificial "preferences and distinctions" and was grounded in "the prejudice of each person and condition." The consequence of this all-pervasive "prejudice" was paradoxical but undeniable. "In well-regulated monarchies," Montesquieu contended, "everyone will be something like a good citizen while one will rarely find someone who is a good man." He compared monarchy to Newton's

system of the universe, where there is a force which ceaselessly repels all bodies from the center and a force of gravity which draws them to it. Honor makes all the parts of the body politic move; it binds them by its own actions; and it happens that each pursues the common good while believing that he is pursuing his own particular interests.[46]

In short, monarchies were ruled by something akin to Adam Smith's "invisible hand."

This particular discussion had a profound impact on the framers of the American constitution, and they put Montesquieu's observation to a use that challenged his attempts to belittle the character of the honor involved. In discussing the separation of powers in *The Federalist*, Madison observed that the elected official's "pride and vanity" would "attach him to a form of government which favors his pretensions, and gives him a share in its honors and distinctions" (*Fed.* 57, 386). Because he and his colleagues represented "the dignity of their country in the eyes of other nations," they would "be particularly sensible to every prospect of public danger, or of a dishonorable stagnation in public affairs" (*Fed.* 58, 395). The congressmen, the senators, the president, and the federal judges would not always be men of virtue, but the exalted character of their separate and distinct stations would have on them the effect which Montesquieu had attributed to the articulation of a monarchy into its various, graded orders and ranks: it would inspire in them a passion for what the French *philosophe* resolutely refused to dignify as more than "false honor," and this artificially induced longing would tend to summon forth from these officials something in its effects indistinguishable from public-spiritedness. In most cases, their sense of their own stature would be a spur adequate to insure the proper performance of their duties, and it would nearly always be a sufficient deterrent to the sacrifice of their rightful prerogatives to the ambitions and material interests of their rivals. Within each branch of government a collegial spirit would develop: each branch could be trusted to exercise a jealous oversight with regard to the others.[47]

FACTION

There was one additional problem that troubled the authors of *The Federalist*. Montesquieu had argued that, in extended republics, the common good was often neglected, and men tended to pursue their particular interests. He had also observed that political liberty "is not present except where there is no abuse of power, and it is an eternal experience that every man who has power is drawn to abuse it; he proceeds until he finds the limits."[48] The consequences Hamilton and Madison had themselves observed in the states, for it was this propensity that accounted for the multiplicity, mutability, injustice, and impotence of the laws adopted therein. It was in reflecting on the challenge this posed to "the fundamental principle of republican Government, that the majority who rule in such Governments, are the safest Guardians both of public Good and of private rights," that they turned to yet another eighteenth-century political analyst rarely studied today: This man's name was David Hume.

Today, Hume is best known for *A Treatise of Human Nature*, which he completed in 1738, when he reached the ripe old age of twenty-eight. To his great dismay, however, that philosophical tome failed to find a large and sympathetic audience. In his own lifetime, he achieved much greater renown for the essays he began publishing at haphazard intervals six years later and for his *History of England*, which appeared in six volumes, one by one, in the years stretching from 1754 to 1762. No one doubted his literary achievement or his penetration, but, from the outset, the skeptical posture Hume assumed was controversial. The devout were put off by his critique of miracles and his evident disdain for religious faith. Englishmen partial to partisan Whig historiography disliked his debunking of their conviction that the Revolution Settlement of 1689 was little more than a reaffirmation of England's ancient constitution.

In North America, where the same misgivings were sometimes voiced, Hume was nonetheless widely read and appreciated in and after the 1760s, and the sympathy he evinced in 1775 for the American cause won him respect.[49] The authors of *The Federalist* were among those intimately familiar with his political and historical works. Although John Witherspoon considered Hume "an infidel" and disliked his moral philosophy, he urged his students at Princeton to read the essays of his fellow Scot, and we can be confident that James Madison, who stayed on for some months after his graduation to study further with Witherspoon, did so.[50] Alexander Hamilton was, from the outset, a pronounced admirer of Hume. In a pamphlet he published in support of the Patriot cause in 1775, when he was eighteen or twenty years in age, he first singled out the Scot as "a celebrated author." Then he quoted at length the first two paragraphs of the essay "Of the Independency of Parliament," in which Hume unpacked a famous claim first advanced by Machiavelli, writing,

> Political writers ... have established it as a maxim, that, in
> contriving any system of government and fixing the several checks
> and controuls of the constitution, *every man* ought to be supposed a

knave, and to have no other end in all his actions, but *private interest*. By this interest, we must govern him, and by means of it, *make him co-operate* to public good, notwithstanding his insatiable avarice and ambition. Without this, we shall in vain boast of the advantages of *any constitution*, and shall find in the end, that we have no security for our liberties and possessions, except the *good will* of our rulers; that is, we should have *no security at all*.

It is therefore a just *political* maxim, that *every man must be supposed a knave*. Though, at the same time, it appears somewhat strange, that a maxim should be true in politics, which is false in fact. But to satisfy us on this head, we may consider that men are generally more honest in a private than in a public capacity; and will go greater lengths to serve a party, than when their own private interest is alone concerned. Honour is a great check upon mankind. But, where a considerable body of men act together, this check is in a great measure removed; since a man is sure to be approved by his own party, for what promotes the common interest, and he soon learns to despise the clamours of adversaries. To this we may add that every court, or senate, is determined by the greater number of voices; so that if self-interest influences only the majority, (as it will always do) the whole senate follows the allurements of this separate interest and acts as if it contained not one member, who had any regard to public interest and liberty.[51]

Twelve years later, when James Madison began drafting "Vices of the Political System of the United States" and the time came for him to ponder the propensity of the states for the adoption of unjust laws, he turned for enlightenment to this same passage from Hume and drew as well on the analysis of interest, principle, and affection as sources of faction articulated in the Scot's essay "Of Parties in General."[52]

"All civilized societies are divided into different interests and factions," Madison observed, echoing Hume,

as they happen to be creditors or debtors – Rich or poor – husbandmen, merchants or manufacturers – members of different religious sects – followers of different political leaders – inhabitants of different districts – owners of different kinds of property &c., &c. In republican Government the majority however composed, ultimately give the law. Whenever therefore an apparent interest or common passion unites a majority what is to restrain them from unjust violations of the right and interest of the minority, or of individuals?

He did not think that "a prudent regard to their own good as involved in the general and permanent good of the Community" would suffice as a restraint. Peoples and even individuals tended to forget that "honesty is the best policy." Nor did Madison think "respect for character" sufficient, and it was here that he most clearly echoed Hume. "In a multitude," he observed, the "efficacy" of character "is diminished in proportion to the number which is to share the praise or the blame. Besides, as it has reference to public opinion, which within a particular Society, is the opinion of the majority, the standard is fixed by those whose conduct is to be measured by it." For similar reasons, Madison doubted the effectiveness of religion as a check: "The conduct of every popular assembly acting on oath, the strongest of religious ties, proves that individuals join without remorse in acts, against which their consciences would revolt if proposed to them under the like sanction, separately in their closets." Moreover, he suspected that, even "in its coolest state," religion "may become a motive to oppression as well as a restraint from injustice."[53]

If it was Hume who had most effectively identified and analyzed the challenge posed by faction within free states, in Madison's opinion, it was he who had also done the most to outline how the challenge might be met. Montesquieu had suggested that, in England, liberty was well served by the spirit of jealousy generated within the larger public by the tension between the legislative and the executive power. Hume agreed. In an essay inspired by James Harrington's tract *Oceana*, entitled "Idea of a Perfect Commonwealth," he acknowledged that "the chief support of the BRITISH government is the opposition of interests." Then he added that "though in the main serviceable," this opposition "breeds endless factions"; and he suggested an elaborate constitutional "plan" by means of which the conflict might do "all the good without any of the harm." In the process, he conceded that it would be "more difficult to form a republican government in an extensive country than in a city." Then he suggested a conclusion contrary to the position taken by Montesquieu, arguing that "there is more facility, once" such a republic "is formed, of preserving it steady and uniform, without tumult and faction." As he explained,

> In a large government, which is modelled with masterly skill, there is compass and room enough to refine the democracy, from the lower people, who may be admitted into the first elections or first concoction of the commonwealth, to the higher magistrates, who direct all the movements. At the same time, the parts are so distant and remote, that it is very difficult, either by intrigue, prejudice, or passion, to hurry them into any measures against the public interest.[54]

In the memorandum he composed for his own use in 1787 in anticipation of the Federal Convention, Madison seized on both parts of Hume's argument. In one passage, he wrote,

> An auxiliary desideratum for the melioration of the Republican form is such a process of elections as will most certainly extract from the mass of the Society the purest and noblest characters which it contains; such as will at once feel most strongly the proper motives to pursue the end of their appointment, and be most capable to devise the proper means of attaining it.

In another, he argued that "an enlargement of the sphere" might actually "lessen the insecurity of private rights," explaining that this would not occur "because the impulse of a common interest or passion is less predominant in this case with the majority, but because a common interest or passion is less apt to be felt and the requisite combinations less easy to be formed by a great than by a small number." Then, to the claim, echoing Hume, that "those who may feel a common sentiment have less opportunity of communication and concert," Madison added an observation of profound importance not found in the Scot's text, writing, "The Society becomes broken into a greater variety of interests, of pursuits, of passions, which check each other." It was on the basis of these three assertions – which he later restated at greater length on the floor of the Federal Convention, in a letter to Thomas Jefferson, and in the tenth *Federalist* – that the Virginian concluded that "the inconveniences of popular States contrary to the prevailing Theory, are in proportion not to the extent, but to the narrowness of their limits."[55]

The last, most original, and perhaps most important of these three observations seems to have derived from Madison's experience in Virginia, where he shepherded Thomas Jefferson's Statute of Religious Freedom through the legislature.[56] David Hume favored religious toleration but vigorously opposed disestablishment. He thought it "vain to think that any free government will ever have security or stability" in the absence of a "dependence of the clergy on the civil magistrates." In his *History of England*, he argued that the "interested diligence of the clergy is what every wise legislator will study to prevent," that zeal gives rise to "superstition, folly, and delusion," and that "each ghostly practitioner, in order to render himself more precious and sacred in the eyes of his retainers, will inspire them with the most violent abhorrence of all other sects" – and there he concluded that "the most decent and advantageous composition" that the authorities could make "with the spiritual guides is to bribe their indolence, by assigning stated salaries to their profession."[57]

In *The Wealth of Nations*, which was published in 1776 and widely read in North America in the years that followed,[58] Hume's close friend Adam Smith took a difference stance. In his *Letter Concerning Toleration*, John Locke had made the wry observation that, where religious sects "have not the power to carry on persecution and to become masters, there they desire to live upon fair terms, and preach up toleration." Smith built on this observation. First, he quoted at length Hume's discussion of the theologico-political problem. He readily acknowledged that "the interested and active zeal of religious teachers can be dangerous and troublesome," but he contended that this condition would obtain "only where there is, either but one sect tolerated in the society, or where the whole of a large society is divided into two or three great sects."

> That zeal must be altogether innocent where the society is divided into two or three hundred, or perhaps into as many [as a] thousand sects, of which no one could be considerable enough to disturb the publick tranquillity. The teachers of each sect, seeing themselves surrounded on all sides with more adversaries than friends, would be obliged to learn that candour and moderation which is so seldom to be found among the teachers of those great sects, whose tenets being supported by the civil magistrate, are held in veneration by almost all the inhabitants of extensive kingdoms and empires, and who therefore see nothing round them but followers, disciples, and humble admirers.

To support his argument, Smith pointed to Pennsylvania, where the establishment of full religious freedom had been "productive of this philosophical good temper and moderation."[59]

James Madison had read both Locke and Smith. He had observed in Pennsylvania and Virginia the ethos of religious moderation they had described; and in pondering the advantages attendant on geographical extension, he had applied their analysis of the consequences of diversity for religious factions to factions based on interest as well.[60] In a letter sent to Thomas Jefferson in late October 1787, which restated the argument outlined in his "Vices of the Political System of the United States," Madison wrote, "The same security seems requisite for the civil as for the religious rights of individuals. If the same sect form a majority and have the power, other sects will be sure to be depressed. Divide et impera, the reprobated axiom of tyranny, is under certain qualifications, the only policy, by which a republic can be administered on just principles."[61] In *The Federalist* he laid out this argument in even clearer terms:

> The society itself will be broken into so many parts, interests and classes of citizens, that the rights of individuals or of the minority, will be in little danger from interested combinations of the majority. In a free government, the security for civil rights must be the same as for religious rights. It consists in the one case in the multiplicity of interests, and in the other, in the multiplicity of sects. The degree of security in both cases will depend on the number of interests and sects; and this may be presumed to depend on the extent of country and number of people comprehended under the same government.
>
> (*Fed.* 51, 351–52)

Madison's solution was not so much an extension of the territory encompassed by the republic as a multiplication of the factions composing it. If, as he hoped, the new federal government could be made a dispassionate and impartial umpire, it was, paradoxically, in part because of the great number and variety of petty parties and factions clamoring for its favor and maneuvering to gain political leverage.[62]

THE AFTERMATH

His contributions to *The Federalist* were not James Madison's last words on the extended republic. In the early 1790s he revisited Montesquieu's argument concerning republics and the extent of territory suitable to them; and, at a time when the nation's territory was much smaller than it is now, and its population was roughly one hundredth of what it is today, he began to worry that the extent of territory encompassed by the United States and the size of its population might be too great. This he did in response to the legislative program proposed by George Washington's secretary of the Treasury, Alexander Hamilton, which he interpreted as a scheme, likely to eventuate in despotism, aimed at subverting federalism and effecting "a consolidation of the States into one government."

In analyzing the likely consequences of such a consolidation, Madison argued that the "incompetency of one Legislature to regulate all the various objects belonging to the local governments, would evidently force a transfer of many of" those objects "to the executive department." Then, he contended that, if the state and local governments were made subject to the federal government, the sheer size of the country "would prevent that control" on the federal Congress, "which is essential to a faithful discharge of its trust, [since] neither the voice nor the sense of ten or twenty millions of people, spread through so many latitudes as are comprehended within the United States, could ever be combined or called into effect, if deprived of those local organs, through which both can now be conveyed." In such circumstances, Madison warned, "the impossibility of acting together, might be succeeded by the inefficacy of partial expressions of the public mind, and this at length, by a universal silence and insensibility, leaving the whole government to that *self-directed course*, which, it must be owned, is the natural propensity of every government."[63]

In time, Madison would drop this argument. In time, he would himself come to favor many of the particulars contained within Hamilton's program, and he does not then appear to have supposed that a general consolidation would result. But the argument that he presented in the early 1790s gained purchase in the course of the last century as just such a consolidation took place and as the legislative power was delegated to an ever-greater degree to regulatory agencies under the direction of the executive, and there are those today who fear that, in consequence, the American government is step by step being abandoned to "that *self-directed course*, which, it must be owned, is the natural propensity of every government."[64]

NOTES

1 James Madison, "Vices of the Political System of the United States," in *PJM*, IX, 345–58, with Niccolò Machiavelli, *Discorsi sopra la prima deca*

di Tito Livio 1.5, 58, in Machiavelli, *Tutte le opere,* ed. Mario Martelli (Florence: Sansoni Editore, 1971), 83–84, 140–42.

2 For the evidence pertaining to the publication history of Montesquieu's various books and to the use to which they were put by his successors, see Paul A. Rahe, *Soft Despotism, Democracy's Drift: Montesquieu, Rousseau, Tocqueville and the Modern Prospect* (New Haven, CT: Yale University Press, 2009), 63–64 (with the attendant notes).

3 See Donald S. Lutz, "The Relative Influence of European Writers on Late Eighteenth-Century American Political Thought," *American Political Science Review,* 78 (1984), 189–97. To date, there is no adequate account of Montesquieu's influence overall. One should begin, however, with Paul Merrill Spurlin, *Montesquieu in America, 1760–1801* (Baton Rouge: Louisiana State University Press, 1940). Regarding his influence on the framers of the American Constitution, more has been done: see Paul Merrill Spurlin, "Montesquieu and the American Constitution," in *The French Enlightenment in America: Essays on the Times of the Founding Fathers* (Athens: University of Georgia Press, 1984), 86–98; James W. Muller, "The American Framers' Debt to Montesquieu," in *The Revival of Constitutionalism,* ed. James W. Muller (Lincoln: Nebraska University Press, 1988), 87–102; and Anne M. Cohler, *Montesquieu's Comparative Politics and the Spirit of American Constitutionalism* (Lawrence: University Press of Kansas, 1988).

4 Letter by T. Q. in *The Boston Gazette and Country Journal,* April 18, 1763; Letter by J. in *The Boston Evening Post,* May 23, 1763; Letter by T. Q. in *The Boston Gazette and Country Journal,* June 6, 1763; and Letter by U. in the *Boston Gazette,* August 1, 1763, in *American Political Writing during the Founding Era, 1760–1805,* ed. Charles S. Hyneman and Donald S. Lutz (Indianapolis: Liberty Press, 1983), I, 19–37 (at 19–20, 23, 25–27, 37).

5 See Martin Howard, Jr., *A Letter from a Gentleman at Halifax* (1765), in *Pamphlets of the American Revolution, 1750–1766,* ed. Bernard Bailyn (Cambridge, MA: Belknap Press, 1965–), I, 541.

6 See *Letters from a Farmer in Pennsylvania to the Inhabitants of the British Colonies* No. VII, in *Empire and Nation,* 2nd ed., ed. Forrest McDonald (Indianapolis: Liberty Fund, 1999), 42.

7 Appeal to the Inhabitants of Quebec, October 26, 1774, *in Journals of the Continental Congress, 1774–1789,* ed. Worthington Chauncey Ford (Washington, DC: US Government Printing Office, 1904–37), I, 107, 110–11.

8 A Native of this Colony, "An Address to the Convention of the Colony and Ancient Dominion of Virginia on the Subject of Government in General, and Recommending a Particular Form to Their Attention," *Virginia Gazette*, June 8 and 15, 1776, in *American Political Writing during the Founding Era*, I, 328–39, at 333.

9 Letter by Worcestriensis No. 4, *Massachusetts Spy*, September 4, 1776, ibid., 449–54, at 450, 453.

10 Cf. *The Complete Anti-Federalist*, ed. Herbert J. Storing (Chicago, IL: University of Chicago Press, 1981): Robert Yates and John Lansing, "Reasons of Dissent" (2.3.7); Luther Martin, "The Genuine Information Delivered to the Legislature of the State of Maryland" (2.4.44); Letters of Cato III (2.6.10–21, 25, 36, 43, 48); Letters of Centinel I (2.7.11, 17–19, 33, 73); Letters from the Federal Farmer II (2.8.15–19, 97, 148); Essays of Brutus (2.9.11–21, 39); Essays of an Old Whig IV (3.3.11, 20); A Review of the Constitution Proposed by the late Convention by a Federal Republican (3.6.8, 16, 19, 23); The Address and Reasons of Dissent of the Minority of the Convention of Pennsylvania To Their Constituents (3.11.16–17, 26, 44–45); Essays by William Penn (3.12.13); Letters of Agrippa IV (4.6.16–17); Letters of a Republican Federalist (4.13.21); Essays by a Farmer (4.17.22); Essays by a Farmer (5.1.13, 68, 93); Address of a Minority of the Maryland Ratifying Convention (5.4.10); Address by John Francis Mercer (5.5.5–6); Letter of Richard Henry Lee to Governor Edmund Randolph (5.6.1); Essays by Cato (5.10.4); Essay by Tamony (5.11.7); Reply to Cassius by Brutus (5.15.1); Speeches of Patrick Henry in the Virginia State Ratifying Convention (5.16.14); Speech of George Mason in the Virginia Ratifying Convention (5.17.1); James Monroe, *Some Observations on the Constitution* (5.21.12–13); Essays by Cincinnatus (6.1.12, 32); Essays by Sidney (6.8.17–19, 31, 35); Speeches by Melancton Smith in the New York Ratifying Convention (6.12.5), with *Fed.* 9, 43, 47, 52–53, 56, 78, 292, 295, 324–26, 328, 523 and with James Wilson, Speeches at the Pennsylvania Convention, November 24 and December 4, 1787; Cato, Poughkeepsie *Country Journal* and *Advertiser*, December 12, 1787; A Citizen of America [Noah Webster], *An Examination into the Leading Principles of the Federal Constitution*, October 17, 1787; and A Foreign Spectator [Nicholas Collin], "An Essay on the Means of Promoting Federal Sentiments in the United States," Philadelphia *Independent Gazetteer*, August 6, 10, 16–17, 24 and September 4, 12–13, 17, 1787, in *Friends of*

the Constitution: Writings of the "Other" Federalists, 1787–1788, ed. Colleen A. Sheehan and Gary L. McDowell (Indianapolis: Liberty Fund, 1998), 74, 212, 237, 346, 386n., 400, 401n., 415, 425–26, 432. In the postscript dealing with the ratification of the Constitution that Bernard Bailyn added to the enlarged edition of his book, Montesquieu plays a considerable role: see Bailyn, *The Ideological Origins of the American Revolution*, enlarged edition (Cambridge, MA: Belknap Press, 1992), 321–79.

11 Letter by T. Q. in *The Boston Gazette and Country Journal*, April 18, 1763; Letter by J. in *The Boston Evening Post*, May 23, 1763; and Letter by T. Q. in *The Boston Gazette and Country Journal*, June 6, 1763, in *American Political Writing during the Founding Era*, I, 19–32.

12 A Pennsylvanian, *An Address to the Inhabitants of the British Settlements in America Upon Slave-Keeping* (1773), in ibid., I, 217–30 (at 218–19n., 225n., 228n.).

13 See Worcestriensis No. 4, Boston *Massachusetts Spy*, September 4, 1776, ibid., 449–54, at 450, 453–54.

14 See *Rudiments of Law and Government Deduced from the Law of Nature* (1783), ibid., 565–605 (esp. 567n., 576n., 577n., 578n., 586n., 592n., 596n., 599n., 603n.).

15 The federalism of John Dickinson is a case in point. First cf. *RFC*, I, 20–22 (May 29, 1787) with ibid., 235–37 (June 13, 1787); note ibid., 242–45 (June 15, 1787); and consider, with care, *Supplement to Max Farrand's The Records of the Federal Convention of 1787*, ed. James H. Hutson (New Haven, CT: Yale University Press, 1987), 84–91. Then, consider *RFC*, I, 85–87 (June 2, 1787), 136 (June 6, 1787), 150, 152–53 (June 7, 1787), II, 114–15 (July 25, 1787), 123 (July 26, 1787), 202 (August 7, 1787), 278 (August 13, 1787), 292 (August 14, 1787), with an eye to *Supplement to The Records of the Federal Convention*, 128–29, 134–39. Finally, see Fabius, "Observations on the Constitution Proposed by the Federal Convention," No. 8, April 29, 1788, *DHRC*, XVII, 246–51 (esp. 246–49), where Dickinson makes it clear that the so-called Connecticut Compromise embodied a set of constitutional principles inspired ultimately by Montesquieu and was no compromise at all.

16 See Louis Desgraves, "Aspects de la correspondance de Montesquieu en 1749," in *Lectures de Montesquieu*, ed. Edgar Mass and Alberto Postigiola (Naples: Liguori Editore, 1993), 66.

17 See David Hume, *An Enquiry Concerning the Principles of Morals* (London: A. Millar, 1751), 54–55, as cited in Robert Shackleton, *Montesquieu: A Critical Biography* (Oxford: Oxford University Press, 1961), 245.

18 Horace Walpole to H. Mann, January 10, 1750, in *Letters of Horace Walpole, Fourth Earl of Oxford*, ed. Paget Toynbee (Oxford: Clarendon Press, 1903–05), II, 419.

19 See Edmund Burke, *Abridgment of English History* (1757), in *Works of the Right Honourable Edmund Burke* (London: H. G. Bohn, 1854–59), VI, 297.

20 One can get a good sense of the work's scope from perusing the essays collected in *Montesquieu's Science of Politics: Essays on The Spirit of Laws*, ed. David W. Carrithers, Michael A. Mosher, and Paul A. Rahe (Lanham, MD: Rowman & Littlefield, 2001). There is much of value as well in *Montesquieu and the Spirit of Modernity*, ed. David W. Carrithers and Patrick Coleman (Oxford: Voltaire Foundation, 2002). For recent attempts at a comprehensive analysis of Montesquieu's masterpiece, see Thomas L. Pangle, *Montesquieu's Philosophy of Liberalism: A Commentary on The Spirit of the Laws* (Chicago, IL: University of Chicago Press, 1973), and Paul A. Rahe, *Montesquieu and the Logic of Liberty: War, Religion, Commerce, Climate, Terrain, Technology, Uneasiness of Mind, the Spirit of Political Vigilance, and the Foundations of the Modern Republic* (New Haven, CT: Yale University Press, 2009). Shackleton's *Montesquieu* is far more valuable for the light it casts on Montesquieu's life than for its analysis of his writings and thought.

21 For Montesquieu's misgivings, see Rahe, *Montesquieu and the Logic of Liberty*, 63–143.

22 Charles-Louis de Secondat, baron de La Brède et de Montesquieu, *L'Esprit des lois*, 3.19.27, which I cite by part, book, and chapter from *Œuvres complètes de Montesquieu*, ed. Roger Caillois (Paris: Bibliothèque de la Pléiade, 1949–51). Unless otherwise specified, all translations are my own.

23 The classic study of this process is Gordon S. Wood, *The Creation of the American Republic, 1776–1787* (Chapel Hill: University of North Carolina Press, 1969), 125–467.

24 Consider Montesquieu, *L'Esprit des lois*, 1.2–5, 7, in light of Rahe, *Montesquieu and the Logic of Liberty*, 65–85.

25 Montesquieu, *L'Esprit des lois*, 1.8.15–19.

26 Ibid., 2.9.1–3.

27 Note James Madison, "Notes on Ancient and Modern Confederacies," April–June, 1786, *PJM*, IX, 3–24, at 4. Robertson had the book in his library: see Editorial Note to "Commonplace Book," *PJM*, I, 4–7 (at 5), and note Dennis F. Thompson, "The Education of a Founding Father: The Reading List for John Witherspoon's Course in Political Theory, as Taken by James Madison," *Political Theory*, 4 (1976): 523–29.

28 See, e.g., Oliver Wendell Holmes, "Montesquieu," in Holmes, *Collected Legal Papers* (New York: Peter Smith, 1952), 250–65.

29 Montesquieu, *L'Esprit des lois*, 1.4.4.

30 Ibid., 1.5.6, 19, 4.20.4–5, 17, 5.21.7.

31 Ibid., 1.3.3 with 4.20.6–14, 21, 21.7.

32 See Paul A. Rahe, "Blaise Pascal, Pierre Nicole, and the Origins of Liberal Sociology," in *Enlightenment and Secularism: Essays on the Mobilization of Reason*, ed. Christopher Nadon (Lanham, MD: Lexington Books, 2013), 129–40.

33 Consider Montesquieu, *L'Esprit des lois*, 4.20–21, in light of Rahe, *Montesquieu and the Logic of Liberty*, 147–238.

34 *Report on the Subject of Manufactures*, December 5, 1791, *PAH*, X, 254–56.

35 Consider Madison, *Fed.* 10, 58, in light of Paul A. Rahe, *The Spartan Regime: Its Character, Origins, and Grand Strategy* (New Haven, CT: Yale University Press, 2016).

36 Note Montesquieu, *L'Esprit des lois*, 4.20.7; consider 1.5.19 in light of 2.12.19 (where, in the title, England is referred to as a republic), and see 1.2.4.

37 Consider Montesquieu, *L'Esprit des lois*, 1.5.6, 19, 4.20.4–5, 17 in light of 4.21.7.

38 Ibid., 2.11.6, 3.19.27.

39 In Edinburgh, almost certainly thanks to David Hume, these two chapters were translated almost immediately after the appearance of the work in French and published separately: see Charles-Louis de Secondat, baron de La Brède et de Montesquieu, *Two Chapters of a Celebrated French Work, Intitled DE L'ESPRIT DES LOIX, Translated into English* (Edinburgh: Hamilton and Balfour, 1750).

40 Montesquieu, *L'Esprit des lois*, 2.11.20.

41 Ibid., 2.12.19.

42 Ibid., 2.11.6.

43 See Wood, *The Creation of the American Republic*, 125–467.

44 Montesquieu, *L'Esprit des lois*, 1.5.14.

45 Ibid., 1.3.5.

46 Ibid., 1.3.6–7, 5.24.6.

47 Consider *Fed.* 57, 386, and 58, 395, in light of Montesquieu, *L'Esprit des lois*, 2.11.9, with 1.3.5–7; and see Cohler, *Montesquieu's Comparative Politics and the Spirit of American Constitutionalism*, 34–169.

48 Montesquieu, *L'Esprit des lois*, 2.11.4.

49 Regarding the reception of Hume, see the admirable study by Mark G. Spencer, *David Hume and Eighteenth-Century America* (Rochester, NY: University of Rochester Press, 2005), 1–153, 188–222, which supersedes all previous publications on this subject.

50 See Thompson, "The Education of a Founding Father," 523–29, and Spencer, *David Hume and Eighteenth-Century America*, 67–69.

51 Cf. David Hume, "Of the Independency of Parliament," in Hume, *Essays Moral, Political, and Literary*, rev. Eugene F. Miller (Indianapolis: Liberty Fund, 1985), 42–46, at 42–43, as quoted by Alexander Hamilton, *The Farmer Refuted* (February 23, 1775), *PAH* I, 94–95, with Machiavelli, *Discorsi sopra la prima deca di Tito Livio* 1.3, in Machiavelli, *Tutte le opere*, 81.

52 See Hume, "Of Parties in General," in Hume, *Essays Moral, Political, and Literary*, 54–63.

53 See Madison, "Vices of the Political System of the United States," *PJM*, IX, 355–56.

54 Note Montesquieu, *L'Esprit des lois*, 3.19.27, and see Hume, "The Idea of a Perfect Commonwealth," in *Essays Moral, Political, and Literary*, 512–29 (esp. 527–29).

55 Note Madison, "Vices of the Political System of the United States," *PJM*, IX, 356–57, and Speech of Madison, June 6, 1787, *RFC*, I, 134–36; Madison to Jefferson, October 24, 1787, *PJM*, X, 212–14; and *Fed.* 10, 56–65, in light of Douglass Adair, "'That Politics May Be Reduced to a Science': David Hume, James Madison, and the Tenth Federalist," in Adair, *Fame and the Founding Fathers: Essays*, ed. Trevor Colbourn (New York: W. W. Norton, 1974), 93–106, and Edmund S. Morgan, "Safety in Numbers: Madison, Hume, and the Tenth Federalist," *Huntington Library Quarterly*, 49 (1986), 95–112. Cf. Theodore Draper, "Hume & Madison: The Secrets of Federalist Paper No. 10," *Encounter*, 58 (1982), 34–47, with Paul A. Rahe, *Republics Ancient and Modern: Classical Republicanism and the American Revolution*

(Chapel Hill: University of North Carolina Press, 1992), III.i.4 n. 69, and Spencer, *David Hume and Eighteenth-Century America*, 188–282.

56 See Lance Banning, *The Sacred Fire of Liberty: James Madison and the Founding of the Federal Republic* (Ithaca, NY: Cornell University, 1995), 84–102, 128–32.

57 David Hume, *The History of England from the Invasion of Julius Caesar to the Revolution in 1688* (Indianapolis: Liberty Fund, 1983), III, 134–36.

58 See Samuel Fleischacker, "Adam Smith's Reception among the American Founders," *William and Mary Quarterly*, ser. 3, 59/4 (October 2002), 897–924.

59 Cf. Hume, "Idea of a Perfect Commonwealth," 525, and David Hume, *The History of England from the Invasion of Julius Caesar to The Revolution in 1688* (Indianapolis: Liberty Fund, 1983), III, 134–36, with John Locke, *A Letter Concerning Toleration and Other Writings*, ed. Mario Montuori (The Hague: Martinus Nijhoff, 1963), 36–37, and see Adam Smith, *An Inquiry into The Nature and Causes of the Wealth of Nations* (Oxford: Clarendon Press, 1976), V.i.g.3–8.

60 See Rahe, *Republics Ancient and Modern*, III.i.4–5.

61 Madison to Jefferson, October 24, 1787, *PJM*, X, and October 17, 1788, XI, 297–98.

62 See Banning, *Sacred Fire of Liberty*, 128–32. Cf. Spencer, *David Hume and Eighteenth-Century America*, 176–87.

63 See Madison, "Consolidation," for *The National Gazette*, December 3, 1791, *PJM*, XIV, 137–39. In this connection, see Rahe, *Republics Ancient and Modern*, III.iii.1–iv.9 (esp. III.iv.9); Colleen A. Sheehan, *James Madison and the Spirit of Republican Self-Government* (New York: Cambridge University Press, 2009); and *The Mind of James Madison: The Legacy of Classical Republicanism* (New York: Cambridge University Press, 2015).

63 See Rahe, *Soft Despotism, Democracy's Drift*, 143–280.

8   Madison's Republican Remedy

The Tenth Federalist *and the Creation of an Impartial Republic*

Alan Gibson

> *When a majority is included in a faction, the form of popular government, on the other hand, enables it to sacrifice to its ruling passion or interest both the public good and the rights of other citizens. To secure the public good and private rights against the danger of such a faction, and at the same time to preserve the spirit and the form of popular government, is then the great object to which our inquiries are directed. Let me add that it is the great desideratum by which this form of government can be rescued from the opprobrium under which it has so long labored, and be recommended to the esteem and adoption of mankind.*
>
> (*Fed.* 10, 60–61)

Since Charles Beard first focused attention upon the tenth *Federalist*, James Madison's famous essay has been rivalled only by the Declaration of Independence and the Constitution itself as the most important political writing of the American founding.[1] A set of specific claims forms the basis of its still-vaunted status. These include uncontested claims for its eloquence and lucidity, its theoretical novelty and brilliance, the uncanny prescience of Madison's depiction of the structure of modern American society, and his farsighted projection of the workings and challenges of the American political system. Nevertheless, these claims also include now deeply disputed assertions about its influence in the adoption of the Constitution, its place at the vital core of Madison's political thought, and its plausibility as an expression of the underlying philosophy or understanding of the original Constitution. This essay elides the specialized debates that have grown up around each of these claims. Its goals instead are to revisit the debate over the meaning of Madison's theory, propose a straightforward reading of *Federalist* 10 that integrates and eclipses previous interpretations, and provide a foundation for future scholarship addressing the numerous disputes that still govern the interpretation of Madison's classic.

The revisionist reading set forth here emerges from locating the intentional structure of Madison's argument in the tenth *Federalist* in his effort to solve what he called the "great desideratum in Government" and from closely following the march of the argument. As it is set forth in *Federalist* 10 and other versions of his argument for an extended republic, Madison's "great desideratum" referred to the peculiar problem faced within republican governments of addressing the threat posed by majority factions without violating the "republican principle" of majority rule (*Fed.* 10, 60–61). It also referred to the general problem faced in *all* forms of government of reconciling and balancing the imperatives of impartiality, on the one hand, and popular control of rulers, on the other.[2] When *Federalist* 10 is interpreted as an effort to address the "great desideratum" understood in this fashion, Madison's argument can be divided constructively into three sections which, taken together, form a seamless defense of the formation of an extended republic as the proper means for promoting the impartial resolution and administration of factional disputes without violating republican principles.

In the first section of his argument, Madison describes the endemic problems that democratic turbulence and factionalism pose in popular governments, sets forth a republican definition of faction, discusses two methods of "curing the mischiefs" of faction, and then settles upon controlling their effects (*Fed.* 10, 58). Madison's preference for controlling the effects of faction, in turn, gives rise to a discussion of the causes of faction, the articulation of a typology of faction, and finally to a remarkably prescient vision of modern American society. In a second section of his argument for an extended republic, Madison focuses upon the peculiar problem posed by majority factions in republics. When this section is carefully read, it can be seen that, contrary to the conclusion of several important scholars, Madison characterizes the "great desideratum" in the tenth *Federalist* much as he had in the other preliminary versions of the theory of the extended republic that he set forth in 1787. Like previous accounts, the "great desideratum" refers here to both the problem of controlling majority factions without violating the "spirit and form of popular government" and of reconciling popular control and impartiality (*Fed.* 10, 61). Once this point is accepted, it can then be recognized that Madison resolved the problem posed as the "great desideratum" in the final third of the argument of the tenth *Federalist* through elections from large districts, but more importantly, extent of territory as means of infusing impartiality into the republican form while remaining consistent with the republican principle of majority rule.

Given the amount of exegetical energy that has been devoted to Madison's theory, it is unlikely that this interpretation or any other will be accepted as dispositive. Nevertheless, this reading sharpens our understanding of the contours of Madison's argument, clarifies the meaning and significance of central passages that are often misinterpreted, incorporates and eclipses insights from previous readings, and provides a foundation for understanding the relative importance of disinterested statesmanship, social diversity, and geographic size within Madison's argument for an extended republic. In particular, it emphasizes extent of territory as the primary means of institutionalizing impartiality in the administration of the government without excessive reliance on enlightened statesmanship. It also emphasizes the importance of extent of territory as the proper means of promoting stability and impartiality in republican governments where integrating a hereditary or self-appointed branch directly into the government is precluded by republican principles and the "unmixed" character of American society (*Fed.* 14, 84). Most broadly, it points the way toward a greater recognition of the importance of impartiality as a presiding principle in Madison's political thought and a better understanding of how Madison saw the creation of an extended republic as integral to the formation of an impartial republic.

DEMOCRATIC TURBULENCE AND THE PROBLEM OF FACTION

Madison's theory of an extended republic is justly celebrated for its conceptual innovations and theoretical novelty. Nevertheless,

Madison's discussion of the problems posed by factions in the American state legislatures and his definition of faction set forth in the initial paragraphs of *Federalist* 10 was purposefully orthodox. Like ancient commentators, Madison identified faction as the pathogen of republics, infecting society and legislative assemblies with the diseases of "instability, injustice, and confusion" (*Fed.* 10, 56). By evoking this familiar narrative, he invited his readers to equate the state governments with the ancient polis. This connection not only established a foundation for rejecting Montesquieu's small republic orthodoxy, it alerted Madison's readers that the pathologies that had destroyed the popular governments of antiquity were now spreading across the American republic. Republican government would have to be redesigned, Madison implicitly suggested even at the earliest stage of his classic essay, lest the American experiment in republican government suffer the fate of short-lived ancient democracies.

If Madison's elite audience, uniformly educated in the writings of classical historians, would have found the echoes of the democratic tragedy in his opening salvo in *Federalist* 10 thoroughly familiar, they would have been no more surprised by the definition of faction that immediately followed. As is well known, Madison defines a faction as "a number of citizens, whether amounting to a majority or minority of the whole, who are united and actuated by some common impulse of passion, or of interest, adverse to the rights of other citizens, or to the permanent and aggregate interests of the community" (*Fed.* 10, 57). Several points about this definition establish its consistency with classical commentary on the phenomena of *stasis* or "the formation of factional associations, the hardening of factional identities, or their mobilization and unleashing in the form of political unrest, disorder, violence, and outright revolution."[3]

Like classical historians and philosophers, Madison treats faction as a "dangerous vice" to be overcome, even though it could not be eliminated without violating liberty (*Fed.* 10, 56). Conversely, contrary to what is still sometimes said by commentators seeking to portray Madison as a modern interest group theorist, this definition is explicitly normative as well as empirical and recognizes no benign forms of faction.[4] Madison held all factions, including those caused by interest, to be opprobrius because of the improper or even wicked impulses and motives that unite and set them in motion, the means of their operation, and their effect. Factions are "united and actuated" by passion and selfish interest rather than reason, said to employ "force" and "violence" as means of achieving their nefarious goals, and are held to be "adverse" to the ends or goals of the political system, namely the protection of rights and the promotion of the "permanent and aggregate interests of the community" (*Fed.* 10, 56–57).

The still sharper difference between the republican understanding of faction Madison sets forth in this definition and the characterization of interest groups given by modern pluralists arises from Madison's identification of a "*permanent* and aggregate interest" (*Fed.* 10, 57). Whereas modern interest group theorists dismiss concepts such as the permanent and collective interest as nonsensical phrases evoking the existence of metaphysical spooks and hold that it is only constructive to think of a collective interest as a residue of negotiations between interests, Madison's definition of faction embraces the idea of an objective, enduring, comprehensive interest. That objective common interest, he clearly believed, could serve as a standard against which factional associations could be determined to be partial and threatening. Thus, while both Madison and modern interest group theorists characterize American society as a collection of competing factions and interests, he embraced what they reject, namely the belief that citizens share a common interest that provides a standard for formulating and assessing public policies and uniting citizens and legislators in concerted action. For Madison, unlike contemporary pluralists, the reality of a multiplicity of competing interests in society did not preclude the existence of a shared common interest.

Having defined faction and identified the problems it posed in republican government, Madison next famously discusses two possible strategies for "curing the mischiefs of faction": removing their causes or controlling their effects. Removing the causes, he argues in this formulation, may be achieved either by abolishing liberty or by "giving to every citizen the same opinions, the same passions, and the same interests." Abolishing liberty is dispatched as "unwise" because it represents a cure worse than the disease. The option of giving to everyone the same opinions, passions, and interests is first dismissed as "impracticable" because faction is "sown in the nature of man," but then quickly rejected as impossible. Both methods of removing the causes of faction are then discarded in favor of controlling their effects (*Fed.* 10, 58).[5]

At this point, Madison's argument for an extended republic takes a decisively modern turn from which it never retreats. As Paul Rahe has observed, Madison's rejection of curing the mischiefs of faction by attempting to give the citizenry the same opinions, passions, and interests amounts to a repudiation of the ancient remedy of *paideia* or comprehensive sets of laws designed to suppress and counteract faction and create a common character among the citizenry.[6] Classical political commentators, Rahe has shown, considered the creation of *homonoia* (political oneness or unity) among the citizenry as a central goal of the polis and *paideia* or laws promoting the moral formation and ultimately the character of the citizenry as the proper means of achieving that goal. Ancient societies, Rahe further observes, practiced numerous remedies for removing the causes of faction and thus lessening divisions within the polis. The most common of these included laws habituating the citizenry toward right opinion, demanding compulsory worship of gods common to the polis, placing restrictions on commerce, equalizing the property holdings of citizens to ameliorate class conflict, and rewarding sacrifice to the city (especially by honouring soldiers killed in battle and providing for their survivors).[7]

Madison's contention in the tenth *Federalist* that representatives will "refine and enlarge the public views" suggests that his rejection of the ancient goal of *homonoia* does not altogether preclude government interventions to, as he later put it, "influence" or even ennoble public opinion (*Fed.* 10, 62).[8] At minimum, however, his repudiation of the option of giving everyone the same opinions, passions, and interests does suggest that he rejected any strong claim that the government either would or even could hope to create *homonoia* among the citizenry by enacting comprehensive plans of moral education or character formation favored by the ancients.[9]

Most important for understanding the march of Madison's argument, this bright line rejection of the ancient goal of *homonoia* and the use of *paideia* to remedy the problem of faction launches Madison's discussion of the causes of faction. This discussion first explicitly identifies "latent" causes of faction that are "sown in the nature of man." These include, by Madison's account, the fallibility of reason, the natural attachments that men have for their interests and the reciprocal influence these have on their opinions, and finally the very protection that government gives to the "different and unequal faculties of acquiring property" (*Fed.* 10, 59). Madison then observes that these latent causes of faction are "brought into different degrees of activity, according to the different circumstances of civil society" and result in three primary types of faction – opinions, passions, and economic interests – with the sweeping caveat that even "the most frivolous and fanciful distinctions" also sometimes give rise to violent factional conflict (*Fed.* 10, 58–59).

The first of these sources or types of faction – those based on opinion – calls attention to what we now might now label political and religious ideologies. Madison's identification of passions creating attachments to factional leaders as a source of division and conflict might have reminded his audience of the factional rivalries between the great dynastic families of colonial and revolutionary America created by personal attachments and alliances. He also clearly had in mind factions led by the charismatic, demagogic "men of factious tempers, of local prejudices, or of sinister designs" and practitioners of the "vicious arts" of persuasion that he calls to the attention of his readers later in the essay (*Fed.* 10, 62–63). However important opinions and passions were to Madison as sources of faction, he nevertheless famously identifies "the various and unequal distribution of property" as the "most constant and durable source of factions" (*Fed.* 10, 59). As Martin Diamond observed, this discussion of the economic sources of faction evident in conflicts between creditors and debtors, those with and without property, and conflicts between different interests based upon trade and industry establishes Madison's recognition of both class and interest group conflict, of conflicts resulting from both "different *degrees* and *kinds* of property" (*Fed.* 10, 58).

More broadly, as two of Madison's most accomplished contemporary interpreters have suggested, this description of the sources and forms of faction that necessarily emerge in "civilized nations" forms a "recognizably modern image of a fluid and diverse society" in which what we now call interest groups have emerged as the "fundamental social force that needs to be controlled" (*Fed.* 10, 59).[10] This modern society composed of "various and interfering interests," these scholars might have added, presents Madison's understanding of the effects of making the protection of "different and unequal faculties of acquiring property" the "first object of government" (*Fed.* 10, 58–59). In this vivid and prescient vision of a commercial republic in America, society is portrayed as bristling with a multiplicity of interest groups arising from the protection that government gives to the diverse faculties of acquiring property. The selfish aims and jostling for advantage among these groups, in turn, creates complex vectors of conflict that ironically threaten the property rights which give rise to interest groups in the first place. The competition between these interests then requires their regulation, which forms the "principal task of modern Legislation" (*Fed.* 10, 59).

In the context in which it was set forth, Madison's vision of American society represented a conceptual innovation in itself and set the stage for his still broader challenge to the small republic thesis. American society, Madison observed explicitly at the Constitutional Convention and implied here, was devoid of the estates and hereditary distinctions that had caused endless conflicts in Europe, but which also set the foundations for the adoption of mixed governments there that were impossible in America. American society also lacked, for now at least, Madison observed, the "extremes of wealth and poverty" that characterized the modern states of Europe. Even in its relative infancy, however, American society was not "one homogeneous mass."[11]

Fortunately for Madison and his fellow Americans, this same depiction of a modern, boisterous, faction-laden commercial society foreshadowed the central insight in his novel effort to address the age-old problems of factionalism and democratic turbulence. The very diversity of interests that Montesquieu and previous philosophers had long suggested made a large republic unworkable, Madison's analysis suggested, might infuse stability and justice into the republican form and thus supply a novel solution to the perennial problems of democratic turbulence and factionalism that republican governments had heretofore lacked.

MAJORITY FACTION AND THE "GREAT DESIDERATUM IN GOVERNMENT"[12]

Madison began the tenth *Federalist* by establishing that the ancient problem of faction had now become alarmingly American and by suggestively prefiguring how that problem might be addressed. He then turned to the necessity of securing a republican solution to the peculiar problem posed by majority factions. Madison's faith in the proposition that the majorities who rule in republics are "the safest Guardians both of public Good and of private rights" waned during the mid-1780s in step with his anger and disgust with the "reiterated oppressions" of factious majorities within the states, but also with the partisan proposals of sectional majorities in the Confederation Congress.[13] In 1786, Madison likened unrestricted rule by numerical majorities no matter what their aim to the reestablishment of "force as the measure of right."[14] Writing the tenth *Federalist* a year later, he continued to characterize majority factions as a "superior force" without moral authority that refused to abide by the rules of justice or to respect the rights of minorities (*Fed.* 10, 57). Rule by factious majorities, he forthrightly told the public that was to adopt or reject the proposed Constitution, marked, in effect, a return to the "anarchy" of the state of nature (*Fed.* 51, 352).

Three characteristics of majority factions were central to Madison's famous but often misunderstood conclusion that they posed a peculiar threat in republican governments. First, he held that majority factions were impervious to traditional moral (or internal or self-)

restraints that militated against improper conduct in ordinary men and often governed the conduct of the most magnanimous individuals. Madison's list of motives that could not restrain an inflamed majority included a prudent regard for the public good as bound up in one's own interests, concern for reputation, and religion. Indeed, Madison not only held that these motives could not restrain the behavior of majority factions, he concluded that they often intensified group passions and catalyzed irrational behavior. As he set forth this understanding of the psychological dynamic of group behavior in the initial formulations of his case for an extended republic, Madison observed that the restraint that a regard for reputation had on the conduct of individuals lost its efficacy as more and more people joined the faction. Once factious opinion became majority opinion, those influenced by a regard for their reputation would be encouraged to behave improperly because of that regard. Similarly, religious principles that might otherwise restrain a single person were inflamed in majority factions by the "sympathy of the multitude" to promote irrational and unjust actions. As the contagion of factious sentiment spread throughout the group, Madison held, men were spurred to improper actions without embarrassment in public that they would have found revolting if presented to them in private.[15]

Second, Madison held that majority factions were so threatening to the stability of the American Union that they might produce a reactionary moment that led to its dissolution. As previously noted, Madison interpreted the agitations, inconstancies, and injustices committed by majority factions in the states during the mid-1780s through the prism of the ancient narrative of democratic turbulence. These exhibitions of democratic turbulence and licentiousness, Madison predicted, would strengthen the case that some of his peers would make for the establishment of a monarchy in the fledgling United States, but would more likely result in the creation of separate confederacies.[16] The "mortal diseases" of the present confederacy, Madison added, had not only "tainted the faith of the most orthodox republicans." They "challenge from the votaries of liberty every concession in favor of stable Government not infringing fundamental principles, as the only security against an opposite extreme of our present situation," namely monarchy.[17] Madison's point here – a corollary of his proposition that men are often spurred by passions to act immorally in large groups – was that excessive liberty or licentiousness would, if left unabated, create a demand for excessive power.[18] Put bluntly, Madison held majority factions to be peculiarly threatening because he believed that if a republican solution could not be found for them, a monarchical one would be.

Third, majority factions posed special difficulties within republican governments because, Madison observed in the tenth *Federalist*, they can "execute and mask" their "violence under the forms of the Constitution," which are based on majority rule. Concretely put, minority factions do not have the votes to enact their wicked, unjust, and ill-conceived policies into law. Majority factions do. More abstractly stated, the "republican principle" of majority rule makes majority factions judges in their own causes and enables them to engage in a form of self-dealing without breaking the rules of the Constitution or violating the fundamental principle of the republican form (*Fed.* 10, 60). The "superior force" of majority factions supplied merely by their numerical advantage ought to be as irrelevant to considerations of justice as the superior physical force of one person or nation over another (*Fed.* 10, 57). A numerical majority of the society is, after all, still only a part of the whole. For justice to be secured, *all* the parties comprising society – whether composed of a major or minor number of its citizens – ought to be subject to the impartial judgment of a third party. But once again in republican governments, the majority, including a factious majority, is both the party affected by the decision and the one making it. In making this important observation in the tenth *Federalist* and other political writings, Madison thus extended the central normative axiom of impartiality in the British legal tradition to the actions of groups of citizens and legislators. The proposition that "no man is allowed to be a judge in his own cause; because his interest would certainly bias his judgment, and, not improbably, corrupt his integrity," Madison wrote in the tenth *Federalist*, applied "with equal, nay with greater reason" to a body of legislators who "are unfit to be both judges and parties at the same time" (*Fed.* 10, 59).

As several of Madison's finest students have emphasized, however, no matter how caustic or probing his indictment of majority factions became, he never abandoned republican government or the republican principle of majority rule.[19] He also never forgot that republican government was the only form acceptable to the American people. Instead, as Madison's opposition to the injustices of majority factions became more pronounced in the years leading up to the Constitutional Convention, so did his resolve to find a way to address those injustices *without* violating the bedrock principles of republican or popular government. Madison called the compelling desire, indeed necessity, for partisans of the republican form to find a republican remedy to the problems posed by majority factions the "great desideratum" and held it out as the "great object" of constitutional reform (*Fed.* 10, 61). The redemption and good name of republican government, he repeatedly announced, depended upon its resolution.[20]

As previously noted, in its several formulations, Madison's "great desideratum" pointed to both a general problem faced by all governments and the specific manifestation of that problem in republican governments. In its general formulation as "the great desideratum *in Government*," Madison described a problem in political architecture of reconciling impartiality in the administration of government with the attachment or connectedness of the people to that government that was necessary to secure the fidelity of rulers to the interests of the people.[21] This formulation amounted to a problem in constitutional or regime design akin to, and overlapping with, the equally vexing one Madison outlined in *Federalist* 37. In that brilliant analysis, Madison highlighted the complexity of the problems of constitutional architecture faced by the delegates at Philadelphia by identifying three essential qualities that all governments needed to possess: stability, energy, and republican liberty. He then observed that the means necessary to achieve any one of these "valuable ingredients" of "good Government" made it more difficult to achieve the others. The bedeviling task of the constitutional architect was thus one of "mingling" the attributes of good government together in their "due proportions" (*Fed.* 37, 233–34).

Analogously, achieving a solution to the "great desideratum" required a similar act of combining and mingling one attribute of good government (impartiality) with another (control) with the understanding that the enhancement of one weakened the other. Enhancing impartiality in any government required giving rulers at least some degree of independence from, perhaps even transcendence over, the many parties composing the society they ruled. This was best achieved in large nations where rulers assumed power through hereditary accession and self-appointment and were given long, indefinite, or even permanent appointments. Of all forms of government, monarchies thus most easily achieved impartiality. Nevertheless, the problem with this form of government, as Americans' experience with the British monarch had illustrated, was that the prince "frequently sacrifices their happiness to his ambition or his avarice."[22]

In contrast, enhancing citizens' attachment to and popular control over the government was best achieved by limiting the geographic area of the nation and by the use of direct and frequent elections in the selection of rulers. In small republics where the people were directly tied to rulers, Madison observed, the interests of the people are rarely sacrificed to those of their rulers. Nevertheless, as both the ancient experience with "pure" democracies where citizens "assemble and administer the Government in person" and the American experience with republics in the states illustrated for Madison, the "small republic" was overly responsive to majority factions and thus insufficiently impartial. In the small republic, majority factions were able to coordinate their activities and oppress the rights of individuals and minorities. Partial toward the majority, small republics could offer "no cure for the mischiefs" of such factions (*Fed.* 10, 61).

As if matters were not complex and difficult enough already, Madison had to confront the particularly vexing form that this problem took as "the great desideratum which has not yet been found for *Republican Governments.*"[23] To elaborate, as previously mentioned, one of the problems with majority factions, according to Madison, was that they can achieve their nefarious aims "under the form of popular government" (*Fed.* 10, 60). In republican governments, then, the same feature that gave the people control over their rulers (the republican principle of majority rule) directly undermined impartiality by potentially granting power to a factious majority (the partisan many with the power to enact its aims). Resolving the "great desideratum" in republican government therefore required that Madison find an institutional arrangement or set of constitutional devices that was consistent with the republican principle of majority rule (leaving the majority a judge in its own cause), but somehow simultaneously blocked majority factions while also promoting the creation of impartial ones.

A republican path to this goal could not easily come from a system of separation of powers or checks and balances among the branches of the government. This was true because if the system of separation of powers and checks promoted impartiality by introducing a monarchical and hereditary order into the government (the mixed government solution), then the government would no longer be "strictly republican" or "wholly popular" (*Fed.* 39, 250; *Fed.* 14, 84). But if the system of separation of powers and checks remained wholly popular and was designed so that one popular branch checked another popular branch, then impartiality would be diminished, if not altogether lost, to the degree that any of the branches was either controlled by a self-judging majority or at least potentially subject to the undue influence from citizens who were subject to its decisions. The greater the degree of connectedness to the people in each branch, in other words, the more likely it was that the people would act as judges in their own causes.

Madison turned to extent of territory as the primary means of bringing together impartiality, on the one hand, and control and fidelity to the republican principle of majority rule, on the other. In particular, Madison's initial means of resolving the "great desideratum" in republican governments addressed the problems posed by majority factions within the state legislatures as well as Congress. As is now well known, this was achieved by the construction of his theory of an extended republic in conjunction with his support for empowering Congress with a universal veto over all state laws.[24] Armed with the universal veto, Congress would serve as a "disinterested & dispassionate umpire in disputes between different passions & interests" within the states, protecting the rights of individuals and minorities from the threat of majority factions. Madison trusted Congress to wield this "Kingly prerogative" in part because, as a republican institution elected by the people, it could be expected not to develop an interest opposed to the American people.[25]

But Madison also had to explain how the "great desideratum" would be resolved at the national level. How would majority factions be prevented from controlling Congress, while maintaining fidelity to the principle of majority rule? Madison's explanation was that majority factions would have to clear the obstacles raised by the extended republic to gain control of that body but that these same obstacles would help promote the development of impartial majorities in Congress. In this system, the "great desideratum" would not be addressed by an appeal to a will independent of the majority in the society. In this sense, the parties composing society, even the majority party or faction, would remain judges in their own causes. Gathering the majority from the numerous citizens and diverse interests encompassed in the extended republic, however, would increase the likelihood that the self-judging majority was not "an interested and over-bearing" one (*Fed.* 10, 57).

Overall, Congress would be under the ultimate control of the people and thus qualified as a republican body to exercise safely the universal veto in umpiring disputes within the states. At the same time, it would be insulated from majority factions by the extended republic and animated by the salutary majorities that formed as the result of being drawn from a large, diverse electorate. As an added guarantee that it would not become tyrannical, Madison consistently insisted that the extended republic would need to be kept within a "practicable sphere" in case it was necessary for the sovereign people to engage in a "defensive concert" against rulers who violated their trust (*Fed.* 14, 83).[26]

Madison's dogged support for the universal veto at the Constitutional Convention, as we know, was not enough to secure its passage. His complex scheme linking the extended republic to the universal veto in a novel federal system was only fully unfolded in his famous October 24, 1787, letter to Thomas Jefferson.[27] In contrast, Madison's case in *Federalist* 10 was limited to how an extended republic might prevent the national government from mirroring the instabilities and injustices introduced by factions into the state governments. Disconnecting his case for an extended republic from the central problem that it had been originally formulated to address (majority factionalism *within the states*) and the specific power that it had been designed to justify (the universal veto), Madison now offered a more modest defense of a large republic based upon the "salutary influence" that the election of representatives from large districts and extent of territory was likely to have in the administration of the national government (*Fed.* 37, 238).

Contrary to the assertions of two of Madison's most important contemporary scholars, however, the loss of the universal veto at the Convention did not lead Madison to abandon his concern to promote the impartial resolution of factional disputes.[28] This was particularly true for his concern that Congress impartially exercise the great powers of taxation and commercial regulation lodged in the national government by the Constitution. Confusion concerning Madison's commitment to impartiality after the loss of the universal veto seems to arise from Madison's insistence in the tenth *Federalist* that the "different classes of legislators" would be "advocates and parties to the causes that they determine" and that the "parties are, and must be, themselves the judges" in the formation of public policies (*Fed.* 10, 59–60).

But once we understand the "great desideratum" as an effort to achieve both impartiality and popular control, then we can recognize the paragraph in the tenth *Federalist* where Madison made these statements as simply another iteration of that problem. In this paragraph, Madison also holds that "no man is allowed to be a judge in his own cause, because his interest would certainly bias his judgment, and, not improbably, corrupt his integrity." He further declares that "justice ought to hold the balance between them [creditors and debtors]" and that the apportionment of taxes requires "the most exact impartiality" (*Fed.* 10, 59–60). His movement back and forth between these seemingly contradictory commitments to impartiality and a popular government in which the parties that compose society must ultimately make the decisions that govern them is simply his way of emphasizing the tension between impartiality and popular control posed in the "great desideratum." Interpreters who hold that Madison abandoned impartiality in favor of turning decision-making over to affected parties fail to see that he was proposing that factional conflicts can be impartially resolved in an extended republic *even though the representatives and parties in society remain judges in their own causes.*

INFUSING IMPARTIALITY INTO THE REPUBLICAN FORM: EXPANDED ELECTORAL DISTRICTS

If the analysis so far is correct, it remains only to be shown that the final third of the tenth *Federalist* defends two distinct strategies – elections from large electoral districts and extent of territory – as proper means for infusing impartiality into the conduct and adminis-tration of the national government without violating the republican principle of majority rule. In the most recent round of debates over Madison's theory, conducted during the 1980s, the highly visible interpretations of Gordon Wood and Garry Wills countered pluralist readings of Madison's argument with interpretations that sought to establish the election of elite representatives from large districts as the primary or even exclusive means that Madison employed to achieve disinterestedness or impartiality. Madison's support for the election of elite representatives from large districts, according to these interpretations, establishes the continuing influence of classical republicanism in his political thought and the importance that a concern for the character of leaders played in the Madisonian political system.[29] The most vivid (and exaggerated) crystallization of this view is set forth by Garry Wills. Wills argues that Madison's argument for an extended republic amounts to the belief that "the people, since *they* were virtuous, would choose wise and virtuous rulers who would exercise power benignly – so long as America remained a republic."[30]

To be sure, like most of his Federalist colleagues, Madison defended elections from large districts as a procedure for securing the election of wise and virtuous representatives. Madison's support for this electoral procedure is hardly surprising. Elections from large districts had long been held to promote the selection of wise and cosmopolitan leaders and Madison had consistently complained about "a defect of adequate Statesmen" at the continental level from the moment that he entered the Confederation Congress.[31] The activities of demagogic leaders and "interested men" engaged in self-dealing plots in the states during the 1780s, had been, if anything, even more troubling.[32]

In general, Madison made three distinct claims in *Federalist* 10 for the virtues of elections from large districts. A fourth emerges when his case for elections from large districts is connected to his discussion of the dynamics of legislative assemblies. Madison's first claim was posed in uncharacteristically convoluted language and expressed as a matter of probability. Madison argued here that elections from large districts would be more likely than those from small districts to result in the selection of wise and virtuous legislators. Concretely put, Madison's point was that if only a "moderate number of representatives" served at the national level under the new Constitution, a scheme of election that forced cosmopolitan elites to compete for the scarce federal offices available would increase the chances that the wisest and most virtuous men in the republic would be selected (*Fed.* 56, 381). Scholars have used several useful metaphors, including skimming, filtering, and distilling, to describe the dynamics and purpose of this electoral procedure.[33] Elections from large districts, Madison held in his most optimistic moments, would "extract from the mass of the Society the purest and noblest characters which it contains."[34]

Madison's second point in favor of elections from large districts examined the competitive advantages that this procedure would give to the great men of extensive reputation in the republic over "unworthy candidates" in securing office (*Fed.* 10, 63). By "unworthy candidates," Madison seems to have meant several kinds of inadequate legislators, including middling men of limited capabilities, state-centered men and provincials with only local knowledge, interested men who sought office for personal gain, and demagogues who sought to beguile the public, obtain public office, and then break the trust of their appointment.[35] Such men, Madison hypothesized, would have greater difficulty practicing the "vicious arts" (including bribery and flattery) by which such candidates too often win elections in contests that took place in large electoral districts than small ones. Conversely, magnanimous men of "diffusive and established characters" or reputations, Madison observed using a Newtonian analogy, were more likely to win elections in large districts because their "attractive merit" would pull voters away from lesser candidates in much the same way as large planets exert a stronger gravitational force than small ones (*Fed.* 10, 63).

The third benefit that Madison identified for elections from large districts pointed to the effect that the size of electoral districts would have on the relationship that representatives would have with their constituents. Electoral districts of the proper size, Madison observed, would be small enough to allow representatives to comprehend the "local circumstances and lesser interests" of their constituents, but large enough that they would not be "unduly attached to these [lesser interests], and too little fit to comprehend and pursue great and national objects" (*Fed.* 10, 63). "The most effectual remedy" for "local bias" in representatives, Madison argued elsewhere in 1788, was to "impress upon the mind" of the representative an attention to a greater part of the society by making them responsible to a greater number of voters.[36] If Madison's second claim had suggested that elections from large electoral districts would point *voters* towards virtuous candidates, this one suggested that elections from districts of the proper size would expand the horizons of *representatives* toward an attention to the aggregate interests of their community, or even nation, by making them the choice of a larger and more diverse constituency.[37]

A fourth claim Madison made for large electoral districts arises by relating this electoral scheme to his observations about the internal dynamics of legislative assemblies. Madison's point is that moderately sized legislative assemblies would increase the chances that laws would be made in a forum that encouraged deliberation and mutual concessions rather than one governed by democratic passions that would, paradoxically, produce an oligarchic spirit in the proceedings. Specifically, Madison argued that excessively large legislative assemblies often produced inconsistent and even contradictory legislation. Containing many members with limited capabilities, they would end up controlled by a few members (usually demagogues). He also held that the larger the assembly, the more it would reflect the factional divisions that were present in the electorate and the more difficult it would be to hold representatives accountable for their actions (because responsibility decreases as the number who share in the praise or blame for an action increases). Conversely, if there were too few representatives in the assembly, the diverse interests of the nation would not be adequately represented, the likelihood that the representatives could be corrupted or would establish an interest independent of the people would increase, and the confidence between the people and their representatives that is necessary to stability in republican governments would be undermined (*Fed.* 55, 374 for quote; *Fed.* 58, 395–97; *Fed.* 63, 423–24).[38]

Against these opposing tendencies, Madison sought to find the correct number of representatives so as to secure information about all the interests of the nation, to prevent the assembly from simply mirroring the divisions of the electorate, to prevent Congress from being dominated by corrupted or bribed politicians, to maintain the confidence of the electorate and responsibility in representatives, and finally to promote "free consultation and discussion" about what policies would best promote the common interest (*Fed.* 58, 374). Here, as in each of the first three claims, Madison was searching for the proper number of representatives to guard against both "the cabals of a few" and "the confusion of a multitude" and to give representatives the proper degree of attachment to and independence from their constituents (*Fed.* 10, 63). In ascertaining the proper number of representatives, as in judging the proper size of the republic itself, he sought to balance connectedness and control on the one hand with independence and impartiality on the other.

Madison's case for the election of representatives from large districts was elaborate and coherent. Expanded electoral districts, however, were not the mechanism Madison believed would be most effective for infusing impartiality into the political system created by the Constitution. The claims that Wood and Wills make for the place of elections from large districts in Madison's constitutional reform program and his theory of an extended republic are betrayed both by what Madison *said* and *did.* In particular, alongside the superlatives he sometimes used to describe the men who would be selected to office under the Constitution, Madison also famously observed that "enlightened statesmen will not always be at the helm" and frequently predicted that a "local spirit" was more likely to prevail in Congress than a national spirit to prevail in the state legislatures (*Fed.* 10, 60; *Fed.* 46, 318). Furthermore, the argument of *Federalist* 10 is clearly not that majority factions will be blocked by representatives who refine or even ignore their constituents' demands. Instead, Madison explicitly emphasized the "greater obstacles" to the formation of majority factions posed by an extended republic as the "circumstance principally which renders factious combinations less to be dreaded" in a large than in a small republic (*Fed.* 10, 63–64). If still more evidence is needed, Madison, in one of the preliminary versions of the argument, called the process of elections from large districts an "auxiliary desideratum" of republican government and identified extent of territory as the "great desideratum" of government.[39]

If we turn to what Madison did, we see that elections from large districts played little role in the development of Madison's constitutional reform program and the proposals that he favored at the Constitutional Convention. As Jack Rakove has observed, proportional representation was far more important to Madison's thoughts and proposals for constitutional reform in the spring of 1787 than elections from large districts.[40] At the Convention, Madison gave a motion to double the number of representatives who would serve in the House of Representatives under the new Constitution and later supported a similar motion.[41] Obviously, this would have cut in half the size of the electoral districts from which representatives were elected. This was hardly the proposal of a statesman pursuing elections from large districts as his central goal.

Extent of territory, not elections from large districts, was the core point of Madison's defense of an extended republic. To understand how extent of territory infuses impartiality into the republican form, we need first to examine what Madison meant by the advantages afforded by an extended republic in its "tendency to break and control the violence of faction" (Fed. 10, 56). This can best be achieved by showing how the barriers established by extent of territory to the concert of majority factions addressed Madison's fears about the threat of democratic turbulence and the dynamics of majority factions. Once we understand how extent of territory impedes and blocks majority factions, serves as a ballast against democratic turbulence, and loosens the pressure that the American people can exert over their representatives, we will be in a position to consider how Madison believed that impartial legislative majorities would be formed in Congress.

Briefly put, extent of territory raises four principal "obstacles" or "impediments" to the formation or consolidation of majority factions and their concert (Fed. 10, 64). These are the greater space or distance (including both the distance between representatives and their constituents and the greater distance between citizens and factions within the large republic), the greater number of citizens in a large republic, the greater variety of interests, and the public or civic consciousness which Madison presupposed would be embedded in public opinion and would act as a barrier to the open communication of factious schemes. Although a full exploration of how each of these barriers helps to neutralize majority factions is not possible here, several observations can be readily made.

First, greater distance as an obstacle to the formation of majority factions refers, in part, to the greater distance *between representatives and their constituents* in an extended than a small republic. In this dimension, the greater extent of territory afforded by the union of the states over any one of them is meant to give representatives the proper degree of independence from their constituents' demands. Placed away from the immediate demands of their constituents and given adequate time in office before they are held accountable for the policies they have supported, representatives are able to formulate policies that relate their constituents' interests to a broader public good.[42] The extended republic remains within acceptable limits as long as representatives are able to assemble as often as is necessary to conduct public affairs and the citizens are able to unite in a "defensive concert" if their rulers become oppressive (*Fed.* 14, 83).[43]

Greater distance as an obstacle to the formation of majority factions also refers to the *distance between factions* created by their dispersion across the extended republic. Here Madison was referring to sheer physical distance as an obstacle to the coalescing of interests into a majority faction and to the balkanization of majority factions within the states. The extended republic is created by the "well-constructed union" of the states, but only for specific policies and limited purposes, such as the regulation of commerce and the imposition of taxes (*Fed.* 10, 56). On these great national questions of policy, the entire citizenry will be affected. Only a national or interstate majority reflected into Congress by representatives will be able to pass legislation.

But with the creation of the extended republic, factious leaders in one state will first have to realize that they are part of a national majority in favor of, for example, paper money legislation to even consider orchestrating a plan to pass such a law. Once they have "discover[ed] their own strength," they will then also have to "act in unison with each other" across the imposing physical distance of the extended republic in the three-mile-an-hour society of eighteenth-century America (*Fed.* 10, 64). The adoption of the Constitution and the creation of an extended republic relocate the decision over key issues to the national government and simultaneously prevent "the existence of the same passion or interest in a majority at the same time" (*Fed.* 10, 61). These reforms isolate factions with the same goals from different states from each other and make it more likely that they remain influential only at the state and local level. As Madison wrote in *Federalist* 10, "the influence of factious leaders may kindle a flame within their particular States, but will be unable to spread a general conflagration through the other States" (*Fed.* 10, 64).

In diffusing or breaking factions in this way and perhaps masking the presence of a factious national majority, extent of territory also helps to prevent the formation and turbulence of majority factions by diminishing the force of passions. Recall our earlier analysis of the psychological dynamics of majority factions and their imperviousness to traditional moral restraints. One of Madison's chief fears about majority factions was their irrationality brought about by the dynamics of opinion and the concerns that members of the faction would have for their reputations. By distancing members of a majority faction from each other, extent of territory serves to invert this dynamic. Factious sentiments that spread by contagion, lead to the formation of unjust majorities, and create a conflagration in favor of ill-conceived and unjust policies in a small geographical area are scattered and their force diminished in the extended republic. In the extended republic, factions flare up but are less likely to ignite a general conflagration. Collective irrationality expressed most prominently as "a rage for paper money, for an abolition of debts, for an equal division of property, or for any other improper or wicked project" is less likely to spread across the whole nation than to pervade any particular state (*Fed.* 10, 64). Conversely, since majority factions are less likely to congeal and act upon their impulses in an extended than a small republic, the public mind is more likely to remain rational in a large nation. Likewise, popular turbulence is less apt to arise and threaten stability and less severe when it does arise.

The most important of the barriers posed by the extended republic – the greater diversity of interests found in the extended republic – provides much the same protection as greater physical space against the formation and influence of majority factions. At this point, we arrive at the foundational proposition of Madison's rejection of Montesquieu's small homogeneous republic of virtue and at what many scholars consider Madison's signature contribution to the history of political thought: the proposition that a diversity of interests in a large republic will promote stability and provide protection for rights.

Several interrelated points are important to Madison's claim. Most importantly, Madison holds that larger nations will *probably* be more diverse than smaller ones. The presence of a multiplicity of interests makes it less likely that any single one will "outnumber and oppress the rest" (*Fed.* 10, 64). Like space, diversity helps prevent a majority faction from becoming aware that it has the numerical strength to pass the unjust and wicked legislation it favors. Unaware of its strength, leaders of majority factions and the citizens within them are discouraged from beginning a scheme of oppression or injustice. If one does begin, the diversity of interests in the extended republic serves as a barrier to its communications and ability to coordinate actions with its members. Even though advancements in communication and transportation will soon bring the nation closer together and factions into more immediate communication with each other, the greater variety of interests in the extended republic acts as a lasting check on the desires of each group to promote the coordinated action of its members in pursuit of the unjust policies it favors.[44] The corporate aggressiveness, the very particularity and selfishness of factions, prevent them from combining for unjust purposes.

The third and fourth barriers erected by the extended republic include the greater number of individuals present in the extended republic and the public or civic consciousness embedded in public

opinion. Both of these obstacles help prevent an open factional conspiracy. Concisely put, Madison refers here to the logistical problems
of coordination and collective action posed by a large number of
individuals. Madison's point here, which he had been exposed to in
John Witherspoon's lectures when he was in college, was that "many
cannot so easily nor so speedily agree upon proper measures, nor can
they expect to keep their designs secret."[45]

Madison also presupposes that these citizens will hold a
common, substantive moral consciousness or, put differently, accept
the contours of a stable public opinion imbued with a sense of justice
and equality. An obscure sentence after the famous one in which
Madison says "extend the sphere, and you take in a greater variety
of parties and interests" provides the key to understanding Madison's
point here. That sentence reads: "Besides other impediments, it may
be remarked that, where there is a consciousness of unjust or dishonorable purposes, communication is always checked by distrust in
proportion to the number whose concurrence is necessary" (Fed. 10,
64). This sentence rests on the submerged metaphor for public opinion – "the public mind" or the "mind of the community." [46] In this
metaphor, Madison envisioned the individual minds in the extended
republic fused into a collective consciousness with a moral content
that would serve as a barrier to the open communications of the
"secret wishes" of an unjust majority (Fed. 10, 64). Thus, if individuals
try to plot and concert a factional conspiracy, their communications
will be checked when they are revealed to other citizens who distrust
them and oppose the conspiracy (Fed. 10, 64). This distrust, Madison
hypothesizes, grows as the number who compose the majority –"the
number whose concurrence is necessary" – increases in the extended
republic (Fed. 10, 64).[47]

FILTERING MAJORITY FACTIONS AND
CONSTRUCTING IMPARTIAL MAJORITIES

So far, this discussion has focused upon the role of extent of territory in
breaking majority factions and addressing the perennial problem of

democratic turbulence without incorporating a hereditary or self-appointed branch into the government. But scholars have also explored how the obstacles presented by extent of territory were not simply negative and how Madison also expected them to facilitate the formation of good or non-factious majorities among the citizenry and in Congress. Like every aspect of Madison's argument for an extended republic, this claim has generated interpretive disputes and questions. How would the extended republic prevent the formation of factious majorities but allow good ones to form? What role did Madison believe that good or non-factious *popular* majorities would have in the formation of public policy? How did he believe that impartial *legislative* majorities would form within the House of Representatives?

Before addressing these questions, we should begin by acknowledging that Madison did not answer them directly. His analyses in *Federalist* 10 and the various versions of his case for an extended republic are concerned explicitly with preventing factious coalitions and only implicitly with the formation of national popular majorities or impartial majorities in Congress. Answers to these questions must thus be addressed indirectly and somewhat speculatively by extrapolating from statements that Madison made about coalitions among the citizens, observations he made about the tendencies and conduct of legislative assemblies, and from his own conduct as a legislative leader. The analysis below is best thought of as a projection of Madison's thinking, based on these sources, about how impartial majorities would be likely to form in Congress even in the absence of enlightened statesmen.

Contrary to the assumption of some scholars, the first of these questions, which might be called the "good majorities/bad majorities problem" or following George Carey the "filter problem," does not pose a stupefying or unanswerable puzzle.[48] The question is really no different than asking how elections from large districts promote the election of elite statesmen and impede the election of unworthy candidates or how separation of powers allows the enactment of wise and just policies but blocks unwise and unjust ones. Each of these cases raises a "filter" problem about how a procedure can facilitate good results and prevent bad ones. As is often the case in addressing questions about how political thinkers have confidence in apparently neutral processes to secure substantive results, the answer lies in some assumption or set of assumptions that are presupposed by the author. In the case of Madison's scheme for the election of elite representatives from large districts, those assumptions are that the people will have the knowledge and virtue to identify and select virtuous statesmen for office and that a "diffusive" or widespread character or reputation will be associated with a cosmopolitan man of virtue (*Fed.* 10, 63).[49] Analogously, Madison's contention with regard to extent of territory is that, while a multiplicity of interests will check the formation of factious majorities in the extended republic, an underlying common interest will facilitate the formation of coalitions among groups pursuing the common interest.[50] Similarly, as noted above, Madison presupposes the existence of a substantive public opinion imbued with a sense of justice that blocks the communication of factious designs. Here, it can be assumed that Madison believes that this same moral consciousness among the citizenry facilitates open communications and coalitions among groups pursuing policies that are consistent with justice and the common interest.

Nevertheless, there are several reasons for concluding that, at least in 1787, Madison did not hope to encourage public policies emanating from popular majorities that were channeled into Congress or expect that this would take place often. Most important, his primary goal in this period was to buffer Congress from the direct influence by the people and give representatives the necessary independence to engage in impartial administration, not to channel citizens' demands to Congress or facilitate the circulation of public opinion. If we turn then to the question of how Madison believed that impartial majorities might be created *within* Congress, we should first realize that there are at least two necessary conditions. First, the formation of impartial majorities requires that the interests and rights of all citizens are "felt and understood in the public councils."[51] This is necessary to give each interest a defensive power to counter attempts to oppress it and to provide influence commensurate with its strength in the community.[52] This condition is met if Congress includes an adequate number of representatives to provide a proper understanding of and sympathy with the claims of the nation's many interests. If adequate representation is provided, then the common or aggregate interest may be visible from the impartial perch of Congress when its members assemble.

Second, if impartial majorities are to form, no majority interest or faction can be present in the national councils. Obviously, if a majority faction gains control of Congress, then it becomes a judge in its own cause and has the power under the forms of the Consti-tution to pass laws that violate individual and minority rights and are contrary to the permanent and aggregate interest of the nation. Fortu-nately, the ability of factious majorities to form, Madison asserts in *Federalist* 51, is rendered "very improbable, if not impracticable" by extent of territory (*Fed.* 51, 351).

When Congress has knowledge of and sympathy toward all the nation's interests and no majority faction is present, then impartial majorities can be formed by less than heroic and disinterested men as a result of several dynamics. First, Madison doubtlessly hoped that what George Carey has called a "mediating group" of impartial legis-lators would be present in Congress on many questions.[53] The impar-tiality of these legislators would be strengthened because the particular issue or legislation being considered had no immediate effect on their constituents. In this scenario, which is a kind of counter-positive to logrolling, representatives who were intensely affected by a specific piece of legislation or provision in a bill might advance the interests of their constituents strongly. Still, the other unaffected representatives – the mediating majority – would form an impartial group to decide the question based on deliberations about its merits and consistency with the public good. Thus, there would be shifting majorities in Congress. But instead of supporting the demands of other congressmen in order to gain future support, representatives would judge claims on the basis of their merit and, in turn, expect that their claims would be judged on their merit.

The way in which this dynamic operated was illustrated in the debate on impost duties in the First Congress. In this debate, representatives discussed – item by item – the allocation of taxes on wine, molasses, whiskey, and other items. When the discussion turned to the items most prominent in their region, representatives became interested parties and several sought (often at the expense of Madison's rebuke) to prevent equal duties from being imposed on the items that most affected their constituents. Nevertheless, an impartial majority was consistently in place to determine the fair amount of tax to lodge on any item and to require that each interest assume its equal share of the public burden.

A second scenario involves a process in which a collection of interested minorities are transformed into an impartial majority during the coalition-building process. In this scenario, representatives would often begin by advancing the partisan interests of their constituents. After all, every interest had some claim in relation to the common interest. Even as they advanced such claims, however, representatives would realize that they did not have the votes to get their way. At this point, deliberations and concessions among representatives would create a broadening of the coalition necessary to form a majority. Aware that they could not successfully advance purely partisan or partial schemes, representatives would be forced to develop a broader understanding of what policies were in the interests of the whole nation based upon a more accurate view of and sympathy for all these interests. In this scenario, the public good or common interest does not emerge as the residue or unintended product of the interactions or negotiations of representatives. Instead, it is *discovered* as representatives gain a full view of all the particular interests in the nation, compare and weigh them against each other, deliberate about what policies are in the common interest, and make "mutual concession[s]" or "equitable sacrifices to the general weal."[54]

Madison's writings also contain evidence that he believed that, at times, what political scientists now call cross-pressures might also promote the adoption of impartial policies. In *Federalist* 54, Madison defended resting both the allocation of representatives and the distribution of taxes on census calculations. If only the allocation of representation rested on census figures, he observed, then the states would have an interest in exaggerating their numbers; if only taxation rested on census figures, then they would have incentives to understate their number of inhabitants. "By extending the rule to both objects," however, "the States will have opposite interests, which will control and balance each other, and produce the requisite impartiality" (*Fed.* 54, 371–72; quote on 372). Such reasoning suggests that Madison would have supported carefully crafted legislation that placed both benefits and burdens on particular interests in ways that cross-pressured representatives supporting them to favor impartial legislation.

Finally, Madison also envisioned situations in which advancing the common interest might require the government to favor one interest or a few interests over others. Madison observed that in such cases representatives would need to be guided by "a sole regard to justice and the public good" (*Fed.* 10, 60). In these cases, the common interest manifesting itself as a vision of the nation's future would serve as a standard for determining which interests to promote. In this scenario, a representative's commitment to impartiality would be measured as an attachment to that vision of collective welfare. Unlike the scenario in which representatives acted as arbiters, partialing out proportional benefits and burdens to each interest, representatives in this scenario could not necessarily expect the interests of their particular constituents to be advanced. Obviously, in this situation, policies consistent with the common good could only be passed if a shared understanding or vision of that good exercised a tight grip on the members of Congress and legislators less qualified to articulate that vision accepted the leadership of those more qualified to do so.

MADISON'S REPUBLICAN REMEDY: EXTENT OF TERRITORY AND THE CREATION OF AN IMPARTIAL REPUBLIC

The interpretation of Madison's theory offered above emphasizes the centrality of extent of territory in addressing the primary practical and theoretical issue raised in *Federalist* 10: the reconciliation of impartiality and popular control in a republican government. Stated differently, Madison saw extent of territory as the primary means by which the self-judging majority that necessarily rules in republican governments could be rendered impartial. To be sure, Madison championed the election of elite representatives from large districts as one means of infusing impartiality into the republican form. Nevertheless, Madison's solution to the "great desideratum" did not unduly emphasize the character and virtue of enlightened public officials as a remedy for the problems posed by democratic turbulence and majority factions. Instead, Madison proposed that extent of territory would help stabilize the government, erect a series of obstacles to the formation and concert of majority factions into the national legislature, and thereby help promote the formation of impartial majorities within Congress.

In infusing stability and impartiality into the political system, extent of territory played the role in Madison's "unmixed and extensive republic" previously played in mixed governments by either the monarch or by the representation of an aristocratic segment of society (*Fed.* 14, 84). Extent of territory allowed Madison to resolve the tension between impartiality and popular control without creating a transcendent and unaccountable power (the monarchical and Hobbesian solution), without introducing an aristocratic or monarchical order in the society into the government (the mixed government solution), and without pursuing an unrealistic plan of civic education to eliminate faction altogether (the solution the ancients had pursued through *paideia*). Extent of territory therefore marked an advance in the science of politics essential for the redemption of the good name of popular governments that was peculiarly suited to the circumstances and composition of American society and Americans' understanding of liberty and republican government.

Previous interpreters of the tenth *Federalist* have fastened onto parts of Madison's argument while simultaneously misreading others. Progressives have been correct to point out that in 1787 Madison sought to insulate the national government from public pressures and disperse majority factions across the extended republic to provide protection for individual rights, especially property rights. They have erred, however, in suggesting that Madison favored relatively long terms of office, a moderate number of representatives, and a large republic in order to advance his own interests or those of his class. Proponents of the pluralist reading have been correct to suggest that the central point of *Federalist* 10 was that an extended republic would contain a multiplicity of economic interests which would help prevent the formation of factious majorities. They have erred, however, in ignoring or dismissing the importance of impartiality in Madison's argument and suggesting that he favored the free interaction of interest groups on the supposition that such competition would somehow miraculously result in policies consistent with the public good. For their part, proponents of the republican reading have established that Madison's goal in the creation of an extended republic was to promote the impartial resolution of factional disputes. They have erred, however, in suggesting that the election of representatives from large districts was Madison's preferred means for promoting impartial administration by the national government.

In contrast to each of these interpretations, the reading set forth here suggests that Madison sought to institutionalize impartiality rather than to rely primarily on the character or virtue of statesmen. Although this essay has not gone beyond Madison's case for an extended republic, it can be shown that Madison also favored power-sharing arrangements within the Constitution including proportional representation and even the three-fifths clause to institutionalize impartiality. Representation based upon population furthered Madison's goal of providing the nation's many economic interests and sections with a defensive power against encroachments by the others and relied upon the strategy of balancing interests to promote impartiality. The system of separation of powers woven into the constitutional framework featured a division of labor among the branches to prevent them from acting as judges in their own causes by executing or judging laws they made or making laws they executed or judged. Madison, it can also be shown, continued to fear the corruption of individual representatives even if they were elected from expanded electoral districts. He thus favored rules of engagement – some included in the Constitution and others adopted by Congress – for public officials to prohibit them from enacting legislation in which they had a personal interest.[55]

So understood, the Madisonian political system (imperfectly embedded in the Constitution) counted upon elite representatives elected from large districts and (perhaps even more) senators to exercise disinterested leadership. Madison's greatest faith for securing impartial administration, however, rested with the dynamics created by the diversity of interests found in the extended republic, by the integration and balancing of interests into the fabric of the constitutional system, and by change-of-venue strategies that allowed representatives who were placed away from the pressures of their constituents and had no immediate interest in the outcome of decisions to formulate public policies. Once the complexity of the Madisonian political system is glimpsed, then we can see that it was premised upon a guarded optimism in elite leadership by virtuous statesmen, but rooted in Madison's famously hard-headed assumptions that the people were naturally factious and quarrelsome and that rulers often become corrupt and tyrannical. This observation, in turn, provides the foundation for understanding how conflicting interpretations of Madison as constitutional architect and realist on the one hand and republican on the other can be brought together. More broadly, this understanding of *Federalist* 10 provides ample reason for returning to Madison's famous essay for how it establishes impartiality as a presiding principle in his political thought, as a key to understanding Madison's normative vision of the American republic, and as a formidable expression of the philosophy underlying the Constitution.

NOTES

1 For a sampling of the praise given to *Federalist* 10 see Douglass Adair, *Fame and the Founding Fathers: Essays by Douglass Adair*, ed. Trevor Colbourn (New York: W. W. Norton & Co., 1974), 97–98; Robert Dahl, *A Preface to Democratic Theory* (Chicago, IL: University of Chicago Press, 1956), 5, 15. See also the collection of comments cited in Larry Kramer, "Madison's Audience," *Harvard Law Review*, 112 (January 1999), 612–13.

2 This formulation of the "great desideratum" is most evident in "Vices of the Political System of the United States," *PJM*, IX, 357.

3 Ronald Weed, *Aristotle on Stasis: A Moral Psychology of Political Conflict* (Berlin: Logos Verlag, 2007), 15–22. Quote on 15.

4 For the normative character of Madison's analysis of faction see Daniel Walker Howe, "The Political Psychology of *The Federalist*," *William and Mary Quarterly*, 44 (July 1987), 502–05. For a tortured effort to establish that Madison recognized a category of non-factious interest groups see James Yoho, "Madison and the Beneficial Effects of Interest Groups: What Was Left Unsaid in 'Federalist' 10," *Polity*, 27 (1995): 587–605. For the error of anachronistically characterizing Madison as a modern pluralist, see Paul F. Bourke, "The Pluralist Reading of James Madison's Tenth Federalist," *Perspectives in American History*, 9 (1975), 269–95.

5 In particular, Madison speaks of the diversity in the faculties of men as an "insuperable obstacle to a uniformity of interests." *Fed.* 10, 58.

6 Paul Rahe, *Republics: Ancient and Modern: Classical Republicanism and the American Revolution* (Chapel Hill and London: University of North Carolina Press, 1992), 59–60, 106, 583–84.

7 Ibid., 28–79.

8 Madison, "Public Opinion," *PJM*, XIV, 170.

9 For a contrary view of this conclusion see Colleen Sheehan, "Public Opinion and the Formation of Civic Character in Madison's Republican Theory," *The Review of Politics*, 67 (Winter 2005), 37–48.

10 Jack Rakove, "James Madison and the Extended Republic: Theory and Practice in American Politics," in *This Constitution: A Bicentennial Chronicle* (Summer 1985), 16; Kramer, "Madison's Audience," 632.

11 Madison, Speech of June 26 *PJM*, X, 76–77.

12 Madison, "Vices of the Political System of the United States," April 1787, *PJM*, IX, 357.

13 Ibid.; *Fed.* 51, 352; Madison to Monroe, October 5, 1786, *PJM*, IX, 141.

14 Madison to Monroe, October 5, 1786, *PJM*, IX, 141.

15 Madison, "Vices of the Political System of the United States," 356.

16 Madison to Edmund Pendleton, February 24, 1787, *PJM*, IX, 295.

17 When he revisited this correspondence late in his life, Madison observed that the reference here was to monarchy. Madison to Thomas Jefferson, March 19, 1787, *PJM*, IX, 318, 322 n. 2.

18 For Madison's complex understanding of the relationship of liberty and power generally see James H. Read, "'Our Complicated System': James Madison on Power and Liberty," *Political Theory*, 23 (1995), 452–75.

19 The scholars who have most consistently emphasized Madison's steadfast commitment to majority rule and republican self-government include Lance Banning, *The Sacred Fire of Liberty: James Madison and the Founding of the Federal Republic* (Ithaca, NY: Cornell University Press, 1995); Martin Diamond, "Democracy and *The Federalist*," *American Political Science Review*, 53 (1959), 52–68; Colleen Sheehan, *James Madison and the Spirit of Republican Self-Government* (New York: Cambridge University Press, 2009); Greg Weiner, *Madison's Metronome: The Constitution, Majority Rule, and the Tempo of American Politics* (Lawrence: University Press of Kansas, 2012); Michael Zuckert, "The Political Science of James Madison," in *History of American Political Thought*, ed. Bryan-Paul Frost and Jeffrey Sikkenga (Lanham, MD: Lexington Books, 2003), 149–66.

20 Madison set forth five formulations of the "great desideratum" from 1786 to 1789. See "Vices of the Political System of the United States," *PJM*, 357; Madison to George Washington, April 16, 1787, ibid., 384; Madison to Thomas Jefferson, October 24, 1787, ibid., X, 214; *Fed.* 10, 61. Madison also lays out this problem in *Fed.* 51, 351–53, but without using the phrase "great desideratum" to describe it.

21 For precise and informative formulations of the problem posed by "the great desideratum" see Michael Zuckert's brilliant essays "The Political

Science of James Madison," 163–65; Zuckert, "A System without Precedent: Federalism in the American Constitution," in *The Framing and Ratification of the Constitution*, ed. Leonard W. Levy and Dennis J. Mahoney (New York: Macmillan Publishing Co., 1987), 145–49.

22 Madison, "Vices of the Political System of the United States," *PJM*, IX, 357.

23 Madison to George Washington, April 16, 1787, ibid., 384. My emphasis.

24 The relationship of the theory of the extended republic to the universal veto was first articulated by Charles Hobson, "The Negative on State Laws: James Madison, the Constitution, and the Crisis of Republican Government," *William and Mary Quarterly*, 36 (April 1979), 216, 225–26, 231–33; and Michael Zuckert, "Federalism and the Founding: Toward a Reinterpretation of the Constitutional Convention," *The Review of Politics*, 48 (1986): 187–99.

25 Madison to Washington, April 16, 1787, *PJM*, IX, 383–84.

26 Madison to Jefferson, October 24, 1787, ibid., X, 214.

27 Ibid., 212–14.

28 See Banning, *The Sacred Fire of Liberty*, 469–70 nn. 52 and 54, and 445 n. 52; Sheehan, *James Madison and the Spirit of Republican Self-Government*, 92–93 n. 26. See also Bryan Garsten, *Saving Persuasion: A Defense of Rhetoric and Judgment* (Cambridge, MA: Harvard University Press, 2006), 199–212.

29 Gordon Wood, "Interests and Disinterestedness in the Making of the Constitution," in *Beyond Confederation: Origins of the Constitution and American National Identity*, ed. Richard Beeman, Stephen Botein, and Edward C. Carter (Chapel Hill: University of North Carolina Press, 1987), 69–109, esp. 91–93; Garry Wills, *Explaining America: The Federalist* (New York: Penguin Books, 1981, 2001), ix–x, 179–265, 270.

30 Ibid., 265.

31 Madison to Jefferson, March 27, 1780, *PJM*, II, 6. For the conventionality of elections from large districts as a means of securing elite leadership see Woody Holton, "'Divide et Impera': *Federalist 10* in a Wider Sphere," *William and Mary Quarterly*, 62 (2005), 175–212.

32 For examples of these activities see Madison to Joseph Jones, October 17, 1780, *PJM*, II, 137; Madison to Washington, December 24, 1787, ibid., IX, 225; Madison, "Vices of the Political System of the United States," ibid., IX, 353–54; Speech of July 26, ibid., X, 117–18; *Fed.* 62, 421–22.

33 For skimming see Akhil Reed Amar, *The Bill of Rights: Creation and Reconstruction* (New Haven, CT, and London: Yale University Press, 1998), 10; for filtration see Wood, *Creation of the American Republic*, 506–18; for distillation see Wills, *Explaining America*, 242–47.

34 Madison, "Vices of the Political System of the United States," *PJM*, IX, 357.

35 See Wood, *Creation of the American Republic*, 471–518; "Interests and Disinterestedness," 93–103.

36 Madison, "Observations on Jefferson's Draft of a Constitution for Virginia," in *PJM*, XI, 286.

37 Madison's point that representatives would be elected from more heterogeneous electoral districts is sometimes misunderstood as his primary claim about the benefits of a diversity of interests in the extended republic. See Wills, *Explaining America*, 218–30, esp. 223.

38 Madison, Speech of June 7, *PJM*, X, 39–40.

39 Madison, "Vices of the Political System of the United States," ibid., IX, 357.

40 Jack Rakove, "The Great Compromise: Ideas, Interests, and the Politics of Constitution Making," *William and Mary Quarterly*, 44 (1987), 429.

41 Madison, Speech of July 10, *PJM*, X, 97. Madison seconded a motion to double the number on September 8. *RFC*, II, 553.

42 It is relevant here that Madison observed that this effect took place for representatives even in the Confederation Congress. In his April 16, 1787 letter to Washington, he observed that "there has not been any moment since the peace at which the representatives of the union would have given an assent to paper money or any other measure of a kindred nature." *PJM*, IX, 384.

43 Madison to Jefferson, October 24, 1787, ibid., X, 214. See also "Public Opinion," ibid., XIV, 170.

44 For how developments will create greater unity in the extended republic see *Fed.* 14, 83–89.

45 See John Witherspoon, *Lectures on Moral Philosophy*, ed. Jack Scott (Newark: University of Delaware Press, 1982), 143.

46 Madison uses these phrases frequently in his writings. See Madison to Jefferson, October 24, 1787, in *PJM*, X, 216–17 for two uses in one letter. The term "mind of the community" is taken from "Location of the Capital," September 4, 1789, ibid., XII, 373.

47 Edmund Morgan, "Safety in Numbers: Madison, Hume, and the Tenth Federalist," *Huntington Library Quarterly*, 49 (1986), 95 –112.

48 George Carey, *The Federalist Design for a Constitutional Republic* (Urbana: University of Illinois Press, 1989), 28–49. Quote on 28. The "good majorities/bad majorities problem" seems to have been first raised by Robert Dahl and then heightened by Garry Wills. Wills apparently sees it as unanswerable and thus turns back to the conclusion that Madison's principal claim in *Federalist* 10 was about the election of virtuous representatives. See Dahl, *A Preface to Democratic Theory*, 29–30; Wills, *Explaining America*, xix, 221–22. For attempts to address this problem see Alan Gibson, "Impartial Representation and the Extended Republic: Toward a Comprehensive and Balanced Reading of the Tenth *Federalist* Paper," *History of Political Thought*, 12 (1991), 289–91.

49 For the assumptions underlying the election of representatives from large districts see Madison's Speech of June 20, 1788 at the Virginia Ratifying Convention, where he announced his commitment to the "great republican principle, that the people will have the virtue and intelligence to select men of virtue and wisdom," *PJM*, XI, 163. See also his contentions that in a republic "personal merit alone could be the ground of political exaltation" and that in "free Governments merit and notoriety of character are rarely separated." Speech of June 6, ibid., X, 35; "Observations on Jefferson's Draft of a Constitution for Virginia," ibid., XI, 286.

50 For how common interests serve as the foundation for the development of coalitions among diverse interests see "Consolidation," *PJM*, XIV, 138–39.

51 Speech of July 26, 1787, ibid., X, 117. This requirement should not be confused with the actual representation of each interest by some member of that group.

52 Speech of June 30, ibid., X, 90.

53 Carey, *The Federalist: Design for a Constitutional Republic*, 38.

54 Quotes are from Madison's Speech of April 9, *PJM*, XII, 70; *Fed.* 58, 397.

55 See Alan Gibson, "Madison's 'Great Desideratum': Impartial Administration and the Extended Republic," *American Political Thought: A Journal of Ideas, Institutions, and Culture*, 1 (2012), 198–203 for more development of this point.

9 The Republicanism of Publius

The American Way of Life

Colleen A. Sheehan

Aristotle conceived of politics as the master science, encompassing both the most practical political concerns and the highest human purpose: the quest for human happiness through the life well-lived. In light of this classical perspective that recognized both the limitations on political life and the nobility of its highest achievements, the renowned scholar Martin Diamond once provocatively asked: How would Aristotle rate America?[1] Diamond's query was not merely an academic exercise, but was intended to prompt his fellow citizens to raise the profoundest of political concerns: Is my country worthy of my allegiance? And am I, as a citizen and human being, worthy of my country – of what it stands for, what it aspires to be?

Diamond's conclusion is direct and disturbing: America is a society that has made mediocrity great. It is a society built on the low but solid foundations of modern political philosophy, which emphasizes security and material prosperity rather than the classical goods of virtue and nobility. The quintessential American who emerges from Diamond's analysis looks a lot like Mark Twain's resourceful Hank Morgan, or maybe Arthur Miller's young and hopeful Willy Loman, but certainly not Aristotle's magnanimous man. He is generally a pleasant fellow, materialistic, opportunistic, perhaps clever, and patently vain about his prosaic talents and traits. This same facileness encapsulates and rounds the edges of his dreams. He is not Achilles, or even Jane Austen's Captain Wentworth. He is a salesman, not a statesman or soldier. If the classical worthy man is concerned with attaining honor and the heights of human excellence, his modern liberal counterpart cares more about the practical, the tangible, the sensible quid pro quo. It would be an understatement to say that these human types have little in common, and indeed, in a certain sense they could neither understand each other nor become fellow citizens.

In Diamond's analysis, while the Achilleses of the world will always be in short supply, a worthy republic will nonetheless have worthy citizens – individuals who have a sense not only of decency, but of honor. From Diamond's perspective, the presence of greatness of soul in the American republic can only be a matter of accident. Should a human being marked by nobility of mind and character arise, he is not likely to be particularly appreciated by his fellow citizen-commercialists, with their flat souls and banal aspirations.

Diamond's less than stellar ranking of America was constructed largely upon his reading of *The Federalist*, and especially on his understanding of James Madison's contributions. In Diamond's interpretation of Madisonian theory, the faculty that elevates humans above the other animals – reasoning or opining – is devitalized and depoliticized. This permits the powerful and more predictable secondary causes of human movement, viz., interests and passions, to be manipulated and controlled by a shrewdly devised, compartmentalized political system. Diamond himself was deeply disappointed with the America he believed the framers created and Publius defended. "Put bluntly," Diamond wrote, "in order to defuse the dangerous factional force of opinion, passion, and class interest, Madison's policy deliberately risks magnifying and multiplying in American life the selfish, the interested, the narrow, the vulgar, and the crassly economic." This is the "substratum on which our political system was intended to rest," he concluded, "and where it rests still." In pronouncing the United States low but solid, Diamond took some solace in the fact that his countrymen prized freedom. The vulgarity of America, he rationalized, is the "cost of Madison's policy, the price to be paid in order to enjoy its many blessings."[2]

Is this the America that Publius envisioned and explicated? What is the purpose of the Constitution and the character of the nation that informed the thought and animated the work of Publius? Indeed, can we speak of the mind and spirit of Publius? After all, the eighty-five essays that constitute *The Federalist* were not produced by a single person, but by three men – Alexander Hamilton, James Madison, and John Jay. A mere four years later, the two chief authors, Hamilton and Madison, became bitter political enemies and led opposing political parties under the new constitutional order. Jay allied himself with Hamilton and the Federalists against the Madison–Jefferson Republican party in the 1790s, drawing the latter's ire as a result of the treaty he negotiated with England in 1794.

Neither Madison nor Hamilton got all of the essential measures that he wanted at the Constitutional Convention. Moreover, while they agreed on the need for a stronger national government and together opposed the New Jersey Plan, they did not agree on the optimal way to control the violence of faction, on the lengths of terms of office befitting republican officeholders, or on many other points of republican political theory and practice. Yet, together with Jay (who was not a delegate to the Convention), they banded together to defend the document that they signed atop Washington's desk at Independence Hall on September 17, 1787.

Five weeks later, Jay invited Hamilton, Madison and a few others for dinner at his home at Katonah, Westchester County, New York. Surely the assembled guests shared with each other a sense of hopefulness, and likely a toast or two, for the success of the ratification project in New York and throughout the American states.[3] One wonders whether the future authors of *The Federalist* stole a few moments to discuss their planned endeavor, for Publius's first essay appeared in the *Independent Journal* less than a week later. Indeed, Hamilton, Madison, and Jay all inscribed their essays with the same allonym, Publius, choosing to speak with one voice under the name of the famed Roman consul, statesman, and founding father of the republic, known for his devotion to the cause of republicanism and guardianship of the people. And so while the triumvirate that constituted the American Publius may have disagreed vociferously in the 1790s, on the pages of *The Federalist* are stamped a general harmony of political principle and consistency of constitutional understanding.

The division of subject matter also contributed to the coherence of the work. According to Hamilton's outline in *Federalist* 1, seven themes were to guide the planned undertaking, though the actual product did not quite follow the original sketch. One of these topics, "[t]he conformity of the proposed constitution to the true principles of republican government," is the general subject of essays 37–51. This topic is also woven into a few subsequent papers on the national legislature and the operation of the representative principle. All of these essays were written by Madison and constitute the bulk of the material he contributed to the project.

In *Federalist* 39 Publius declared the central mission of the American constitutional project. Under the new constitution, the Union of the American states was to be a genuine republic devoted to vindicating the great experiment in self-government. Setting out the question of whether the general form and features of the new government are "strictly republican," Publius ardently declared:

> It is evident that no other form would be reconcilable with the genius of the people of America; with the fundamental principles of the Revolution; or with that honorable determination which animates every votary of freedom, to rest all our political experiments on the capacity of mankind for self-government.
>
> (*Fed.* 39, 250)

Only a genuine republic would answer the call of the generation of Americans who risked their lives during the Revolutionary War. Nothing but the opportunity to govern themselves would satisfy the clarion call of the Declaration of Independence. The "new and more noble course" Americans had chosen to pursue would, he believed, demonstrate to a watchful world, as well as prove to themselves, that mankind is capable of self-government (*Fed.* 14, 89).

What is the import of this republicanism that informed the ideas and animated the genius of Publius?[4] How are we to understand its foundation in the principles of 1776 and the capacity of the people to rule themselves? According to Publius's introduction to the subject, republican principles require that all power is derived directly or indirectly from the people and that the government is administered by persons holding limited terms of office or serving during good behavior.[5] These are minimal qualifying elements of republicanism.

Republican government is part of the genus of popular or democratic government, albeit distinct from pure democracy and the direct exercise of political power by the people. As Publius tells us in the tenth *Federalist*, in a republic the scheme of representation is combined with an enlarged territory and population in order to provide the cure for the diseases that have historically been fatal to popular governments. Most of the popular governments of antiquity were pure democracies administered directly by a small number of citizens who inhabited confined territories. The discovery of the principle of representation is ascribed to modern Europe, though no European nation could claim to have instituted the principle in a large or unmixed republic. This momentous achievement belonged to America.[6]

The purpose of representation is to "refine and enlarge the public views," Publius wrote in *Federalist* 10 (62). The aim is to choose representatives who possess the most wisdom to discern and virtue to pursue the public good (*Fed.* 57, 384). However, since an understanding of human nature and experience of the political world teach us that "enlightened statesmen will not always be at the helm" (*Fed.* 10, 60), Publius tendered the need for "auxiliary precautions." Thus, having constitutionally created representative and administrative offices distinct from the collective people, Publius called for practical precautions, or "inventions of prudence," to limit the scope and check the exercise of governmental power. In *Federalist* 51 he listed four prudential measures to control the government and protect constitutional liberty, viz., separation of powers, checks on power, bicameralism, and federalism.

The supplementary nature of these "auxiliary precautions" coheres with the core message of *Federalist* 51, which declared that the *primary* control on the government is a dependence on the people. Correspondingly, in this essay Publius argued that in republican government there can be no ruling will independent of the society, that is, of the majority, or the people themselves. In republican government, the people are the court of final appeal.

Contrary to the views of other "political authors," Publius argued that mixed government is not republican government.[7] When constitutional authority is not wholly derived from the people, the regime cannot properly be labelled republican. Moreover, the criteria that all authority must be derived from the people, and that the will of the government must be dependent on the will of the people, are necessary but not sufficient conditions of republican government. While only popular governments can be republics, not all popular governments are republics. When the stronger rule the weaker, Publius argued in *Federalist* 51, anarchy may be said to reign as in a state of nature. This is a condition marked by the absence of politics; it is a Hobbesian state of nature in which might makes right and where those in power may freely wield the scepter of violence. Mob rule is one form of anarchy, rule by majority faction is another.

In this same essay, which presents the culminating argument of the string of essays on "the true principles" of republicanism, Publius unequivocally pronounced the purpose of political association:

> Justice is the end of government. It is the end of civil society. It ever has been, and ever will be pursued, until it be obtained, or until liberty be lost in the pursuit.
>
> (*Fed.* 51, 352)

In "Vices of the Political System of the United States," researched and written by Madison in preparation for the Constitutional Convention, he juxtaposed the illegitimacy of mere power, on the one hand, with the standard of substantive justice, on the other. The contrast Madison draws between power and right in "Vices" prefigures the definitive distinction between anarchy and justice that he presented ten months later in *Federalist* 51. In "Vices," Madison claimed that the theory of republican government requires that power be on the side of right. "According to Republican Theory," he contended, "Right and power being both vested in the majority, are held to be synonimous [sic]."[8] In actual experience, however, the majority is not always in the position of greater power vis-à-vis the minority or, if it is, it does not always act in accordance with the principles of justice. Nonetheless, abstractly considered, republicanism can be defined as a government in which the majority rules, and it does so on the basis of a standard of right that is not simply the product of its power or mere will. Rather, republican government presupposes an idea of justice, or right, that is independent of mere will, or in other words, that is established by nature rather than mere human convention. Madison's dichotomy between power and right in "Vices" and between the majority faction and the just majority in *Federalist* 51, then, makes sense only if the "right" or "justice" of which he speaks is constituted by a standard higher than mere numbers or strength. This is the standard set in the Declaration of Independence, to which all governments must conform if they are to be recognized as legitimate and shielded from (at least *de jure*) the right of revolution.

Thus, according to the argument of *Federalist* 51 and its earlier parallel claim in "Vices," government based on a will independent of the society cannot be republican, but neither can a government that is based on the will of the society but contrary to the standard of natural right. As such, Madison's/Publius's conception of republicanism has both procedural and substantive components. The prevention of the rule of majority faction is one part of Publius's plan; the formation of a majority of the whole society whose coalition occurs on the basis of "justice and the general good" is the other. This is Publius's definitive republican response to the challenge of rescuing popular government from its disreputable past. Only by meeting the procedural conditions of majority rule and the substantive conditions of justice can Publius boast that the American republic will preserve both the form and the spirit of republicanism.

Forming a majority that coheres to the republican principles of the Revolution invoked in *Federalist* 39 is the vital work of political and civic life in the new republic envisioned by Publius. These principles are expressed in the Declaration of Independence, whose central tenet is the common nature of all members of the human species.[9] From natural human equality is derived the natural rights to life, liberty, the pursuit of happiness, and the requirement for consent of the governed.

The equality–liberty–consent axis stems from the recognition that human beings possess the opining/reasoning faculty that differentiates them from the other animals. The ability of the human mind to reason is another way to say that the human mind is free. For Madison (and Jefferson as well) the freedom of the mind is the basis of all other liberties and rights. By dint of our very nature, no human being has the right to determine the choices of another of his same and equal species or to rule him without free consent. Accordingly, each person has the right, and indeed the responsibility, to exercise his freedom in a manner that accords with reason. This is the essence of the capacity for self-government, whether it be at the level of the individual or that of society. The rightful exercise of majority rule, then, is described by Publius as the accomplishment of "the cool and deliberate sense of the community," or "the reason of the public" (*Fed.* 63, 425; *Fed.* 49, 343).

The grounding for this conception of self-government is carefully laid out in the tenth essay's treatment of the causes of faction. According to Publius, these causes are opinion, passion, and interest. The self-generating causes of faction, however, are passion and interest, not opinion. In and of itself, opining produces ideas – often erroneous ones – but not actions or even demands. The factious, detrimental political effect of some opinions results when prejudicial passions or narrow interests are attached to them. Conversely, just as passion and interest may influence opinion, the human capacity to opine can also have an effect on our passions and interests, modifying them in light of the standard of reason, or at least the attempt to reason.

It is important to note that Publius does not claim that all passions and interests are disadvantageous or injurious. While some passions are base, others rise to something higher within us – to the better angels of our nature. Although many interests are selfish and harmful to others, Publius also speaks of an aggregate and permanent interest that is akin to the common good. By definition, the self-generating causes of faction include only those passions and interests adverse to the rights of others or to the general good. Nonetheless, Publius is not an idealist; he does not expect most men and women to act primarily on the nobler passions of the soul, though he does recognize the existence of these passions and how critical they may be in the life of a nation. To attain a habitual display of justice in the public square would require something like the nation of philosophers Publius mentions in *Federalist* 49. Such exceptional dedication to the truth coupled with the first-rate capacity to reason would apparently diminish the detrimental (as well as the politically advantageous) effects of passion and interest on human opinion.[10]

Publius's conception of how the human mind works, including particularly his recognition of the independent operation of the opining faculty, distinguishes his understanding of the nature of man from that of Hobbes and present-day moral relativists. This includes most contemporary political scientists, whose professionally-sought standard of value neutrality is grounded in the view that the claim of human "reason" is merely a pretense for personal values, self-interest, male dominance, and/or power.[11] Publius's conception of human nature is anti-Hobbesian and in this regard pre-modern,[12] for Publius recognized that what is distinct about human beings is their capacity to reason about true and false, just and unjust, right and wrong.

The autonomy and freedom of the human mind constitute the essential precondition for the great experiment in self-government. Publius believed that, by nature, human beings possess the capacity to govern themselves, but whether they – or in the present historical case, Americans – would succeed in realizing that potential, was the epochal trial at hand. Distinguished by the virtue of moderation, self-government is the goal sought at both the micro and macro political–ethical levels of human activity; it is the self-restraint employed by the individual in one case, and by the majority in the other, to exercise liberty within the bounds of reason and moral right. Publius's aspiration for self-government in America was the echo of the desire that animates "every votary of freedom" to prove that the people are capable of ruling themselves. Indeed, the "great experiment" in self-government infused the language and the hopes of the men and women of the founding generation, perhaps most memorably Washington in his Inaugural Address. "The preservation of the sacred fire of liberty and the destiny of the republican model of government," the first president reminded his fellow citizens, "are justly considered, perhaps, as deeply, as finally, staked on the experiment entrusted to the hands of the American people."[13]

To give the experiment in self-government a fair trial, Publius advocated a political process that moderated passion and self-interest and promoted the refinement of the citizens' opinions. This could not be accomplished in a direct democracy or small republic, in which the formation of majority faction was all too easy to achieve. To rescue popular government from a history of political notoriety, Publius argued that an extensive federal republic, grounded in the sovereignty of the people and operating on the basis of elected representation, separation of powers, and institutional checks, was necessary. These key features of the proposed constitutional design were intended to prevent the rule by a majority faction or a minority governmental faction; they were also meant to shape a political milieu in which the disposition for self-government was considerably enhanced.

In *Federalist* 10 we learn that two factors are critical to controlling the baneful effects of majority faction in republican government: extension of the territory and representation. In Madison's next essay, *Federalist* 14, the size of the territory is immediately qualified: the republic envisioned by Publius is to be large, but not too large; it is to encompass a "practicable sphere."[14] Had Publius's only objective been to make the formation of majority faction less likely, there would be no reason to delimit the size of the territory. But as he knew from reading Montesquieu's *Spirit of Laws*, a very large territory was generally fit only for despotism, as illustrated by empires such as China, Persia, and Rome. According to Publius, then, both a small republic and a very large empire are unfavorable to liberty. A republic of large but practical extent, which employs the modern mechanical device of representation, offers a more promising prospect.

The reason Publius insisted on a large but demarcated territorial compass is twofold. On the one hand, he wanted a territory large enough to frustrate the easy communication of opinions and views fueled by partial interest and prejudicial passion, thereby thwarting the formation of factious majorities. On the other hand, the practicable sphere places boundaries on the territorial frontier so that the exchange of views throughout the society, while challenging, is nonetheless possible. The natural limits to the size of a republican territory, Publius argued, are set by the ability of the representatives in the most geographically remote states to travel to and from the national capital. This is a continuation of Publius's argument regarding the task of the representatives in *Federalist* 10: to enable them to "refine and enlarge the public views." The practicable sphere provides the effective perimeter to position representatives to listen to the views of their constituents, offer them their own considered views, and then engage in the give and take of debate with their colleagues in Congress. The purpose of representatives traveling back and forth between the national capital and their homes rather than relocating to the capital city, then, is to advance the exchange of ideas both within the Congress and throughout the country. The flow and exchange of opinions reckons the practicable boundaries of republican government. The calculation is contingent not simply on the travel distance, but on the measured flow of communicative activity and the advancement of a refined and deliberate public opinion.

Once the argument for an enlarged but practicable sphere of territory was presented, Publius could take up the subject of federalism. Without a layered system of governance incorporated into the extensive territory of the United States, the Union would be in jeopardy of drifting towards despotism. Publius thus envisioned a crucial

role for the states in the new American republic, including a constitutional division of political authority between the national and state
governments. At the same time, he disavowed the notion of divided
sovereignty.[15] There are four main roles for the states in Publius's
conception of federal government: for the practical purposes of admin-
istering government in a large territory; to provide a structural means
to diffuse authority; to check the power of the national government;
and to provide venues for collecting and conveying the voice and will
of the people spread over an extensive territory. The size and the
structure of the Union are paired features in Publius's vision to preserve both the form and the spirit of popular government in America.

Federalist 39 and 44–46 further examine the federal structure of
the Union, discussing the important role of the states in the politics of
communication over a large nation. States are entities that can counteract unconstitutional acts, preserve the people's liberties, and serve
as networks that "sound the alarm to the people" (Fed. 44, 305).
Federalism is one of the components of the "auxiliary precautions"
that Federalist 51 credits with the ability to assist in maintaining
limitations on the powers of the national government. The other
"auxiliary precautions" are separation of powers, bicameralism, and
the various checks devised to limit the exercise of power. In contrast
to the horizontal separation and checking of power, federalism supplies checks on the national government less by a formal clash of
power and ambition and more by the informal pressure of public
opinion conveyed by state organs.

The "inventions of prudence" that Publius touts as "auxiliary"
are intended to keep the powers of government separate and limited,
thus preventing a minority of politicians from tyrannizing over the
people at large; they also help to prevent a majority faction from
dominating government. Separation of powers, bicameralism, and
federalism produce discrete and rival compartments of authority that
require a process of communication and deliberation with other compartments in order to navigate the system and succeed in the legislative task. Thus, while the prudential devices discussed in Federalist

51 are certainly stopgaps invented to prevent a minority or majority faction from ruling, they also offer means to achieve a more considered public opinion and the deliberate sense of the community.

Nevertheless, Publius does insist that these prudential measures are "auxiliary," and that the "primary" source of control on the government consists in its dependence on the people, through elections, petitions, state resolutions, constitutional amendments, and the general influence of public opinion. This dependence occurs both after *and before* the enactment of national public policy. In other words, public opinion does not act merely as a veto power on pronouncements by government officials. Rather, it is a vital part of the dynamic process of political decision-making. Moreover, prior to the settling of public policy, public opinion is generally more fluid than static, both influencing and being influenced by representatives in government. In the extended republic, any one given interest or view of the larger multiplicity of interests and opinions that are at play must successfully negotiate a complex system of prudentially constructed hurdles in order to remain viable. This commonly requires political give and take, along with the building of coalitions, which is a protracted and laborious endeavor in the large nation.

Accordingly, space and time are utilized to create a political milieu conducive to the refinement and enlargement of the public views, or what might be termed deliberative republicanism. The judiciously designed development of a ruling opinion in the nation is not confined to the halls of Congress, but also involves building a "coalition of a majority of the whole society" on the basis of "justice and the general good" (*Fed.* 51, 353). In the rare instances in which a majority coalition should form on factious grounds, it is the responsibility of representatives "to check the misguided career, and to suspend the blow mediated by the people against themselves, until reason, justice and truth, can regain their authority over the public mind" (*Fed.* 63, 425). It is important to note the deterrent checks Publius places on the will of the majority; it is as important to note that Publius does not make Congress the final arbiter of public decisions in the American republic, even in the lamentable circumstances described in *Federalist* 63, when the public mind is bewitched by "temporary errors and delusions." Instead, the duty of representatives is to act the part of statesmen in a free government, to slow down the legislative process, and to temper the irregular passions and illicit interests of the people, so that "reason, justice and truth, can regain their authority over the public mind" (*Fed.* 63, 425).

In the final analysis, the will of the government remains always dependent on the will of the society, for "in all free governments" the "cool and deliberate sense of the community ... actually will ... prevail over the views of its rulers" (ibid.). Publius's insistence that the will of the government must be dependent on the will of the society is the consistent and logical continuum to Madison's earlier categorical statement in "Vices": "In republican Government," he wrote, "the majority however composed, ultimately give the law."[16] The ultimate republican challenge, then, consists in making the will of the society, which for all practical purposes is identical with the power of the majority, synonymous with the principle of right. Madison's "great desideratum" of a "modification of the Sovereignty" that renders public decisions according to the impartial standard of justice and the general good, comprises more than the achievement of administrative disinterest. It also involves the refinement, enlargement, and modification of the views of the citizenry, that is, of "the people themselves," the ultimate sovereign authority in republican government.

Thus far the focus of this essay has been on the political theory of Publius, bringing in the ideas of Madison qua Madison sparingly, limiting these references to writings or speeches produced before or during the immediate period of the framing and ratification of the Constitution, and eschewing citations to materials Madison penned during the 1790s or later. While Madison did continue to develop his views over the next decade, there is nonetheless a fundamental consistency of thought that spans the 1780s and 1790s, as he further pursued the investigation of themes he treated in *The Federalist*.

Although Madison's conception of republicanism in the 1780s recognized the people as the ultimate rulers and involved the modification of the public views in order to achieve the synchronism between power and right, he did not yet anticipate the need to actively organize public opinion in America. This occurred only after the development of a series of administrative measures that he viewed as contrary to the republican tenets of the Constitution as understood and ratified by the people. In response to this Hamiltonian-led administrative agenda, Madison responded strongly, launching a spate of political criticism under the rubric of the "republican cause." Ultimately, he and Jefferson systematized their political opposition by the establishment of the Republican party. In co-founding this opposition party, however, neither sought to institute a permanent two-party system like that of England.[17] Instead, their aim was to defeat the "anti-republican" Federalist agenda that unjustly benefited particular economic interests, and to make the will of the government dependent on the will of a republican society by gathering and galvanizing public opinion. "The Republican party ... conscious that the mass of the people [are] ... with them," Madison wrote, seeks to banish "every other distinction than that between enemies and friends to republican government," and to promote "a general harmony" and "common cause, ... in spight [sic] of circumstantial and artificial distinctions."[18] In the aftermath of the election of 1800, they succeeded in establishing Republican hegemony in the United States. However, numerous factors typifying the political system of the United States, including the centripetal influence of presidential elections in a large territory, led naturally to the enduring presence of a two-party system in the United States, albeit not the disciplined or highly ideological party system that characterizes the British system.

In the 1790s Madison studied and wrote extensively about the power and authority of public opinion in republican government. A few years earlier, in *Federalist* 49 and 50, however, he forcefully warned against frequent appeals to the people. Given the similarity he draws between such appeals to the people and the toxic problems associated with majority factions that he stressed in *Federalist* 10, as well as the various devices he advocated to multiply and diffuse opinions in the extended republic, it would be easy to conclude that in the 1780s Madison looked upon public opinion as a force to be discouraged rather than encouraged. Just as "every appeal to the people," Publius argued in *Federalist* 49,

> would carry an implication of some defect in the government, frequent appeals would, in a great measure, deprive the government of that veneration which time bestows on every thing, and without which perhaps the wisest and freest governments would not possess the requisite stability.
>
> (340)

The specific context of Madison's argument in this essay is Jefferson's notion of calling constitutional conventions to remedy cases in which one or two departments of government have encroached on the constitutional authority of the other branch(es). Madison clearly challenges the wisdom and effectiveness of appealing to the people to solve breaches of constitutional authority. Such a convention would not solve the problem it was called to fix because the people would tend to choose their representatives as convention delegates (i.e. the public figures with whom they are most familiar). Many of these officeholders would probably be the very culprits engaged in the usurpation of power that needs correction. Thus, the parties to the case would themselves be the judges, and the strongest party would simply carry the day. Publius accordingly gives us an example of how justice can be undermined by a supposed impartial political administration, when, in reality, the lack of checks and filtering devices simply allows might to claim the mantle of right.

In *Federalist* 49 Madison also made known his manifest wariness regarding the kind of direct appeals to the people that calling a constitutional convention necessarily entails. If employed as routine checks on governmental power, such political habits would tend to deprive the Constitution of the respect that time bestows on tried and true laws and institutions. Since all governments rest on public opinion, as Hume had claimed and Publius implicitly agreed with, it would be prudent to keep the favor of the people on the side of the law and the regime.

The topic of *Federalist* 49 concerns ad hoc appeals to the people to control abuses of the government; in *Federalist* 50 Publius discusses periodic appeals to the people to accomplish this same goal. In both cases, such appeals would probably result in the election of men who already have a dog in the fight, and so *"passion,* not *reason"* would preside over the decisions made by the Convention. The majority of convention delegates would likely present opinions actuated by a "common passion" rather than exercise their "reason coolly and freely, on ... questions" before the community (*Fed.* 50, 346). In this scenario, Publius warned his fellow citizens, the passions rather than the "reason ... of the public" would "control and regulate the government," when it is the public reason, alone, that ought to "sit in judgment" (*Fed.* 49, 343).

To draw from these two remarkable essays the conclusion that Publius envisioned the role of the people vis-à-vis the government as passive and reverential rather than active and vigilant, is to neglect the place they occupy within the larger work. Publius presents at least four modes of appealing to or relying on the people. In *Federalist* 49 and 50 the people's role in government concerns the ticklish experiments of constitutional conventions. This is not the same kind of participation by the citizens that is at work in the ordinary process of legislation, as discussed and developed, for example, in *Federalist* 10, 14, 51, 57, and 63. In the ordinary political processes, there are numerous obstacles, checks, and points of delay that work to "refine and enlarge" the public views prior to the final enactment of a law. In these instances, the people's authority is not direct, collective, or immediate; rather, public opinion is the result of a deliberative process of coalescing the views of a large and disparate populace over a wide swath of territory and generally over a substantial period of time.

This is in contrast to the generally time-consuming but none-theless much more direct popular role in the constitutional amend-ment process. Article V allows the people to choose delegates to a convention that can draft the supreme law of the land, requiring only the additional step of ratification by popularly elected delegates in each state. As such, the convention option entails few obstacles and stages of modification of the people's will, especially compared to the ordinary processes of legislation, which involves at least three times the number of check points intended to refine and enlarge the public views.[19] These are two markedly distinctive modes in which the people substantially participate in the ruling element of the polity and which require the will of the government to depend on the will of the society (*Fed.* 51, 351–53).

The Federalist discusses two other kinds of appeals to the people, both of which represent extra-constitutional modes of response to crises in the life of a federal republican polity. One involves state leaders acting in exigent circumstances to "sound the alarm to the people" to redress unconstitutional acts of the national government by effecting a change of federal representatives (*Fed.* 44, 305). This is an example of the "vigilant and manly spirit which actuates the people of America" and checks breaches of trust by the representatives. This spirit also serves as a constant reminder to congressmen of "their dependence on the people" and of the day their power will cease, should they betray the trust of the people (*Fed.* 57, 386–87). In *Federalist* 40, Publius presents the most radical mode of appeal to the people. This is nothing short of the call to the people to rise up in revolution, to be instituted by "some *informal and unauthorized propositions*, made by some patriotic and respectable citizen or number of citizens" (265).

The Kentucky and Virginia Resolutions of 1798 are examples of what Publius meant by sounding "the alarm to the people"; they were intended to signify an urgency that, while not yet at revolutionary pitch, nonetheless required resilient political action outside the rou-tine national legislative processes. The founding of the first political party by Jefferson and Madison earlier in the decade was also accomplished by organizing men and forces both inside and outside the environs of the national government and capital city. The particular type of appeal to the people that accompanied the establishment of the Republican party was neither presaged in the pages of *The Federalist*, nor intended to negate the carefully designed system of political hurdles that must be overcome in order to succeed legislatively. It was, however, meant to serve as a vehicle to facilitate the formation and collection of public opinion in order that it might successfully navigate the challenging political obstacle course designed by the framers.

James Madison did not regard public opinion as monolithic or static. It was not a problem in the 1780s that then became a solution in the 1790s. Rather – in the 1780s and the 1790s – public opinion was both part of the problem and part of the solution. Madison's argument proceeded in three stages: First he distinguished between factious public opinion and reasonable public opinion; next he showed how it is possible to stymie the formation of factious majority opinion; and finally he showed how to achieve the reason of the public while at the same time preserving the republican principle of majority rule, or in other words, the sovereign authority of public opinion. Accordingly, depending on a number of factors, often including the phase of the political process, public opinion can be a detriment or a benefit to the achievement of justice and the common good. The question, then, is what occurs during the political processes that molds and shapes public opinion.

It is true that in the 1780s Madison identified majority or public opinion as the central problem in popular government; or rather, to be more accurate, that he identified a specific kind of opinion, i.e. factious opinion, particularly of the majority, as the problem that most needed to be treated. He held this same view in the 1790s and throughout his life. He never changed his mind about majority faction as the potentially great disease of free governments.[20] In the 1790s he also made clear that he considered public opinion the sovereign authority, and that it must be obeyed by the government. The will of the government must be dependent on the will of the society, he argued, and the will of the society must be dependent on the reason of the society.[21] He made this same essential argument in the 1780s; in "Vices" he declared that public opinion is tantamount to majority opinion, and the majority have the ultimate say in popular government. Further, he contended in *Federalist* 49–51, the will of the government must be kept dependent on the will of the society, and the will of the society is to be based on justice and the general good, or in other words, the reason of the public (338–53, esp. 343, 346, 351–53).

Madison accepted that the latent causes of faction are rooted in man's nature, and thus that politics cannot be based on a homogeneous citizenry (as in Rousseau, whose notion of the general will was "as preposterous as it was impotent").[22] At the same time, Madison rejected the Hobbesian perspective that man is merely self-interested – that his views are merely the product of his desires. Rather, he believed that, despite the robust power of interest and passion within the soul, human beings are capable of being educated and improved. Immediately following the final adjournment of the First Congress in March 1791, Madison hit the books, returning to the foundational philosophic questions about human nature and the challenges of popular government that had been the focus of his research in preparation for the Constitutional Convention and during the ratification period. In fact, he picked up where he left off, referencing his former studies, including "Vices of the Political System of the United States," *Federalist* 10, and his October 24, 1787 letter to Jefferson. Citing Montesquieu, who had emphasized the doctrine of separation of powers to safeguard liberty by creating an equilibrium in the powers of government, Madison retooled Montesquieu's notion of equilibrium and also applied it to the passions and interests of society. He had begun treating this issue in the pages of *The Federalist*; in 1791, he built upon his previous work and further developed his thoughts on the subject. In a section of the 1791 "Notes on Government" titled "Influence of the Size of a Nation on Government," he wrote:

> The best provision for a stable and free Govt. is not a balance in the powers of the Govt. tho' that is not to be neglected, but an equilibrium in the interests & passions of the Society itself, which cannot be attained in a small Society. Much has been said on the first. *The last deserves a thorough investigation.*[23]

Federalist 10 especially, but also *Federalist* 49–51, 57 and 63, address the topic of how the interests and passions of the society can be counterbalanced,[24] whether by way of the extended territory that includes a multiplicity of interests, parties, and sects, by the checking process of a multi-layered system of political institutions, or by the influence of statesmen, whose task is to persuade and elevate, not replace, the opinion of the public.

Publius's commitment to preserving the form and the spirit of popular government is consistent with his declaration in "Vices" that the majority ultimately decides the law, and that power must be placed on the side of right in any genuine republic. This was the challenge Madison set for himself in the 1780s and which he continued to pursue in the 1790s. To this end, he penned the "Notes on Government" and the Party Press Essays, in which he declared that "public opinion sets bounds to every government, and is the real sovereign in every free one."[25] Appealing to the people to be awake, enlightened, and to watch over their government as well as obey its laws, he reiterated the arguments of *Federalist* 49–51, that the will of the government must be dependent on the will of the society, and the will of the society should be grounded in the reason of the society.[26]

Madison saw in the extended territory and representative political system of the United States the potential to refine and enlarge the public views and to achieve what he called the "reason of the society" or "reason of the public." At this stage of refinement, public opinion is substantially more than crude popular views. It is the product of an ongoing process of conversation and deliberation among the representatives, between the representatives and their constituents, and among the people at large, generating a moderated and enlarged view on policy matters. While not every individual will be affected or influenced by this deliberative process, some citizens will be. By its very nature, this salutary process tempers partial interests and weakens prejudicial passions; it softens divisions in society and advances a common interest and general consensus. It reveals a common cause "in spight [sic] of circumstantial and artificial distinctions," and it sows within the citizens a stronger sense of justice and the moral consensus that unites them.[27] Established over an extensive territory and involving representative institutions, inventions of prudence, and various counterbalancing devices both at the level of government and in the society itself, the Madisonian system of communicative and deliberative politics is best understood not as a mechanical process, but as a dynamic political model of opinion formation. It is driven by a process of governance that has the power to transform minds and hearts.

For Madison, public opinion can be constituted by unreflective popular views that are partial and prejudiced, but it can also be the tempered, considered opinion of a republican people. This is the central purpose of the systematically imposed delays and challenges that characterize the complex system of government in the United States. The multifaceted process not only takes substantial time to navigate, but during this time there is, as Buffalo Springfield once observed in song, "something happening here." What is happening is the education of citizens via the commerce, clash, and refinement of ideas. We recall that in *Federalist* 10 Madison expressed serious apprehension about the occasion in which the parties to the case also serve as judges in their own cause. In popular government, the people, that is, the majority – "the most numerous party" – will always prevail.[28] That majority, "however composed," sits in judgment. Madison's project embraced the challenge of forming and educating public opinion, by cultivating a responsible citizenry who understand their mutual "debt of protection" one to another, thereby enabling them to serve capably and honorably as judges in their own cause.[29] Madison's solution was as palpable a requirement as it was, from time past, elusive to achieve: for the parties to the case to act the part of good judges, they must first become republican citizens.

Every political order is constituted by the men and women who actually occupy its environs, who live and work and raise their children upon its land, and whose character reflects its ethos. The words of the American Constitution are not sculpted in alabaster, exempt from tarnish or fading, but are only as strong and clear as the men and women who, at any given time, live their meaning. In America today, some people do resemble fast-talking salesmen and corner-cutters. Others are entrepreneurial and spunky, like Tom Sawyer, or scrappy and "spectable," like Ragged Dick; some are independent and outspoken, like Jo March. Still others are noble and fearless, and set the bar that the rest of us can only hope to aspire to, like Uncle Tom. And most, when asked, will happily engage their fellow citizens, like the New Englander who thrusts his hoe into the mellow earth, "blade-end up and five feet tall," to ramble to the stone wall for a friendly talk with his neighbor.[30]

We recall the question raised by Martin Diamond: How would Aristotle rate America? No doubt it is a long way from the ethos of the classical world to that of the United States of the founding era. In fact, the eighteenth century is separated not only by centuries from classical Greece, it is worlds away in terms of the political, religious, scientific, and economic landscape.[31] Nonetheless, the America Madison envisioned and the regime Aristotle would likely recommend for Americans do not stand in such stark contrast as some might imagine. Madison's dream for America was not one of an association of materialistic, self-interested, vulgar individuals. Rather, he envisioned a nation of self-governing citizens pledged to each other in mutual protection of their lives and liberties, bound together by the ties and pledge of civic friendship.[32]

The America Madison worked to design and establish derives "its energy from the will of the society" and operates "by the reason of its measures, on the understanding and interest of the society." This is "the government," Madison declared, "for which philosophy has been searching, and humanity been sighing, from the most remote ages. Such are the republican governments which it is the glory of America to have invented, and her unrivalled happiness to possess."[33]

How would Aristotle rate *this* Madison's America? We make a good start pondering this question by recalling that Madison's central aspiration for America was to meet the challenge of self-government. In Madison's appreciation of the vigilant spirit that nourishes freedom and animates the work of self-government, as well as in his call to fellow citizens to honor their mutual pledge of civic protection and extend to one another the affection of republican brothers, we come to know something about what Madison's *Americans* look like. In their posture of freedom and pluck of republican pride, they show themselves worthy of their country's cause.

NOTES

1 Martin Diamond, "Ethics and Politics: The American Way," in Robert
   Horwitz, ed., *Moral Foundations of the American Republic*
   (Charlottesville: University of Virginia Press, 1977), 39–72. The
   combination of philosophical richness and sparkling clarity that marks
   Diamond's essay has seldom, if ever, been matched in a single piece of
   contemporary American political science literature.
2 Ibid., 59.
3 John Jay's wife, Sarah, kept excellent records of the dinner parties hosted at
   her home. On this particular occasion, the invitation list included thirteen
   men: "Mr. Gilman, Mr. Irvine, Mr. Madison, Mr. Carrington, Mr. H. Lee,
   Mr. Kean, Mr. Huger, Mr. Few, Mr. Duer, Mr. Hamilton, Chevalier
   [John Paul] Jones, Mr. Varnum, Chief Justice." (There is an "X" before
   Mr. Varnum's name, presumably meaning he was not able to attend.) If
   Mr. H. Lee is Henry Lee III ("Lighthorse Harry" Lee; not the leading Anti-
   Federalist Richard Henry Lee), and Mr. Irvine is William Irvine (not the
   Anti-Federalist James Irvine), then the all-male gathering was hardly
   merely a social occasion, but rather a pro-ratification strategy session of
   Federalist leaders. I am grateful to the John Jay Homestead State Historical
   Site, and particularly to Arthur Benware, Collections Manager, for helping
   me and my graduate assistant, John Guerra, track down Sarah Jay's dinner
   list book, scan it, and send the copy and transcription.

4 In *Federalist* 39 Publius argued that political authors have identified such states as Holland, Venice, Poland, and England as models of the republican forms, which only shows "the extreme inaccuracy with which the term has been used in political disquisitions." Not one of these states is a "genuine republic" (250–51).

5 Publius's minimal republican requirements are similar to those expressed by Hamilton in his day-long speech of June 18 at the Constitutional Convention. *RFC*, I, 282–93.

6 Publius contended that the minimal qualifying elements of republicanism have never been met prior to the American experience; this would deny the mantle of republicanism to the British government, despite Montesquieu's praise of the British constitution as the model republic of the modern age. Hamilton would have disagreed with Madison's assessment of the British government, arguing at the Constitutional Convention that the British government was the best in the world, and he doubted that anything short of it would ultimately succeed in America (ibid., 288–90). In *The Federalist*, however, Hamilton is silent on his ranking of the British government or its status as a republic.

7 Madison almost certainly had in mind here Montesquieu, and probably Alexander Hamilton and John Adams as well.

8 "Notes on *Vices of the Political System of the United States*," in Colleen A. Sheehan, *The Mind of James Madison: The Legacy of Classical Republicanism* (New York: Cambridge University Press, 2015), 198; *PJM*, IX, 350.

9 The looming presence of the principles of the Declaration of Independence in *The Federalist* is sometimes explicit but more often implicit. In *Federalist* 40 Madison quotes the Declaration, and in *Federalist* 39 the reference to the principles of the Revolution means of course the principles of the Declaration of Independence – the principles that inform the genius of the American people and ground their experiment in self-government. The basis of good government in reflective consent is declared in the opening salvo of *Federalist* 1; the operation of reflective consent in the ordinary measures of government is the basis for Madison's distinction between majority faction and the just majority that respects "the rights of other citizens" (*Fed.* 10; cf. *Fed.* 63), between the substantive principles that distinguish legitimate majority rule and the anarchy of the state of nature, as discussed in *Federalist* 51.

10 In Publius's analysis, the causes of faction are synonymous with a particular conception of the human soul and the causes of human movement. Unlike metaphysical philosophy, which is a theoretical science, politics is a practical science that involves choice and action. However, Publius indicates that even the philosopher Socrates was human and not exempt from passion, for if the Athenian assembly had been composed of philosophers like Socrates, it would still have been a mob. On Publius's view of philosophic reason and human passion, compare *Fed.* 49, 340 and *Fed.* 55, 374.

11 In fairness, does not one have to raise the equally scientifically unsubstantiated counterclaim, i.e. that the rejection of the possibility of human reason is merely the façade for personal values, preferences, interests, and perhaps zealous hostility to the tradition of Western civilization and the prominence of natural right doctrine?

12 Martin Diamond pointed out the agreement between Publius and Aristotle on this point in "Ethics and Politics," 51.

13 George Washington, First Inaugural Address, in *George Washington: A Collection*, ed. W. B. Allen (Indianapolis: Liberty Classics, 1988), 462.

14 The very fine work of Lance Banning on Madison's conception of the "practicable sphere" is essential reading on this theme. See "The Practicable Sphere of a Republic: James Madison, the Constitutional Convention, and the Emergence of Revolutionary Federalism," in Richard Beeman et al., eds., *Beyond Confederation: Origins of the Constitution and American National Identity* (Chapel Hill: University of North Carolina Press, 1987), 162–87.

15 In *The Federalist*, Publius argued that attempting to divide sovereignty between two governments is akin to the impracticable idea of an "*imperium in imperio*" or a "sovereignty over sovereigns" (see *Fed.* 15, 93; *Fed.* 20, 128).

16 "Vices," *PJM*, 9:355.

17 In monarchical governments such as Great Britain, the two-party system was thought to reflect the different interests between the king and the people, whereas in republican government there is no such natural distinction between the elected president and the people. See e.g. James Monroe to John Taylor, September 10, 1810 (*The Writings of James Monroe*, ed. Stanislaus Murray Hamilton [New York: G. P. Putnam's Sons, 1901], V, 143–44) .

18 "A Candid State of Parties," *PJM*, XIV, 370–72.

19 First, the people choose representatives to the House of Representatives; they also choose senators, who debate and deliberate within their own chambers and then between the two Houses, producing legislation that must be approved by the president, or if not, then overridden by both Houses of Congress, subject to possible review by the Supreme Court.

20 See letter of Madison late in his life (possibly 1833) to unknown recipient, in *The Mind of the Founder: Sources of the Political Thought of James Madison*, ed. Marvin Meyers (Waltham, MA: Brandeis University Press, 1973), 409–17.

21 See "Universal Peace" and "Spirit of Governments" in *PJM*, XIV, 206–08, 233–34.

22 "Universal Peace," ibid., 206–07.

23 "Notes on Government," *PJM*, XIV, 158–59. Emphasis added.

24 Particularly those passions and interests felt by, or potentially felt by, a majority.

25 "Public Opinion," ibid., 170.

26 See "Who Are the Best Keepers of the People's Liberties?"; "Universal Peace," and "Spirit of Governments," ibid., 426–27, 206–08, 233–34.

27 "A Candid State of Parties," ibid., 370–72; cf. "Consolidation," ibid., 137–39.

28 This is why once a majority faction forms, there is very limited recourse; neither appeals to religion, morality, or respect for character is likely to make any difference once a majority has coalesced on the basis of a harmful passion or selfish interest. Perhaps statesmen can delay and persuade, but it would be much better to prevent the formation of such a majority faction in the first place. This is one reason Madison ultimately supports a bill of rights, which can serve as a kind of republican schoolmaster, educating the people about their rights and responsibilities and instilling within them a kind of republican restraint.

29 See "Property," ibid., 266–68.

30 Robert Frost, "A Time to Talk" in Frost, *Mountain Interval* (New York: Henry Holt and Co., 1920), 33.

31 As Montesquieu noted, the small republics grounded in civic virtue that dotted the classical world are not feasible in the modern, commercial world. Scientific advancements meant new modes of communication, navigation, weaponry, and dominion; the advent of Christianity changed forever the

relationship between church and state. If Aristotle were to evaluate America fairly, these substantial changes would have to be accounted for. What kind of political order, in this changed world of the late eighteenth century, or perhaps today, would Aristotle have recommended? What would he prescribe as the ethos and spirit of its regime, and what would its citizens be like? Ironically, Martin Diamond's analysis of America as seen through the lens of Madison's political philosophy is actually more accurately an interpretation of Montesquieu's assessment of the modern commercial republic. Montesquieu saw the England of his time as a nation of atomistic, self-interested, acquisitive tradespeople, who essentially exchanged their sense of honor for material advancement. In turn, Diamond identified in Madison's and the founders' conception of republicanism the traits Montesquieu identified in the eighteenth-century British political model. Thomas L. Pangle follows Diamond in this regard; see *The Spirit of Modern Republicanism: The Moral Vision of the American Founders and the Philosophy of Locke* (Chicago, IL: University of Chicago Press, 1988). For a vigorous critique of Pangle's work, see William B. Allen's review in *History of Political Thought*, 11 [1990], 551–55. In fact, though, Madison criticized Montesquieu's brand of "republicanism" on more than one occasion, including within the pages of *The Federalist* (see *Fed.* 39, 251). In "Spirit of Governments" he took issue with Montesquieu's praise of the British government, which he accused of substituting "the motive of private interest for that of public duty." Happily, Madison wrote, such a government is "not on the west side of the Atlantic" ("Spirit of Governments," *PJM*, XIV, 233–34).

32 See "Consolidation" and "Property," ibid., 137–39, 266–68.
33 "Spirit of Governments," ibid., 233–34.

10 "The Interest of the Man": James Madison's Constitutional Politics

Larry D. Kramer[*]

A particular understanding of James Madison's constitutional thinking now dominates American scholarship, especially in law.[1] According to this view, Madison was frightened of popular politics and deeply suspicious of majority rule. Having witnessed politics in the states during the critical years just after the Revolution – more, having experienced state government firsthand during an exasperating three-year stint in the Virginia Assembly – Madison had come to see democracy as the problem, particularly as it was practiced in the popularly elected state legislatures. Yet rather than give in to despair, as some of his contemporaries were wont to do, Madison set out to find an answer. And he succeeded brilliantly, shepherding in a new national constitution while helping to create what Gordon Wood has called a fresh "American Science of Politics"[2] – the theoretical framework of which he spelled out in his writings as Publius.

The critical problem, as Madison saw it, was finding a way to choose representatives capable of governing without succumbing to the corrupting influences of faction, insularity, and lust for popularity or power. In his most celebrated essay, *Federalist* 10, Madison famously explained how size could do the trick. A large republic meant large election districts. The sheer number of voters and variety of interests subsumed in such districts would discourage the election of candidates who had parochial views or who were beholden to narrow interests. As broad support became a practical necessity for

[*] An earlier version of this essay was published as "'The Interests of the Man': James Madison, Popular Constitutionalism, and the Theory of Deliberative Democracy," *Valparaiso Law Review*, 41 (2006), 697–754.

office, elections would be "more likely to centre on men who possess the most attractive merit, and the most diffusive and established characters" (Fed. 10, 62). Only the wisest, best educated, and most publicly spirited would be picked to serve: "a chosen body of citizens, whose wisdom may best discern the true interest of their country, and whose patriotism and love of justice, will be least likely to sacrifice it to temporary or partial considerations" (Fed. 10, 62).

Better still, enlarging the republic and embracing a greater variety of interests would make it "less probable that a majority of the whole will have a common motive to invade the rights of other citizens; or if such a common motive exists, it will be more difficult for all who feel it to discover their own strength, and to act in unison with each other" (Fed. 10, 64). In other words, size would also dilute the effects of faction, enabling justice-loving representatives to use their superior wisdom relatively unencumbered by the intense pressure that self-interested groups could bring to bear in distorting government in a smaller society. The result: a deliberative democracy in which elections would sift out an elite who could then deliberate free from the irrationality, unreasonableness, and self-interest that make popular politics such a hazard.[3]

In fact, this conventional reading of Madison misstates his thinking and misrepresents his theory, which were considerably more democratic than the received wisdom recognizes. True, faction and majority tyranny were central preoccupations in his mind, and his anxiety about the hazards of popular government was real. Madison unquestionably saw certain forms of democratic politics as noxious and unjust, and he believed it necessary to engineer the government's internal structure to minimize these. But structural innovations were mere "auxiliary precautions" to a more basic and primary "dependence on the people" (Fed. 51, 349).[4] Madison's whole purpose was to make democratic politics work, not to minimize the extent to which it interfered with a ruling elite. "In bestowing the eulogies due to the partitions and internal checks of power," he wrote in 1791, expressing sentiments acted upon throughout his lifetime, "it ought not the less to be remembered, that they are neither the sole nor the chief palladium of constitutional liberty. The people who are the authors of this blessing, must also be its guardians."[5] Madison was, above all, a committed republican who believed in popular government and believed that the people must control the government and laws at all times.

To set the stage for reevaluating the theory of constitutional government and popular politics that Madison laid out in *The Federalist*, it is essential to grasp the intensely affective nature of his commitment to republicanism, a commitment that was emotional as well as intellectual. It was not always thus. As late as 1774, the twenty-three-year-old Madison was languishing at home, writing self-pitying letters about the emptiness of his life and his expectation of dying young.[6] His despair evaporated abruptly after Britain answered the Boston Tea Party with the Coercive Acts of 1774. Madison caught Patriot fever and was swiftly transformed into a militant Whig.[7] The American Revolution became his life, and politics became his vocation. As his biographer Ralph Ketcham explains, "By the time of the battles of Lexington and Concord, Madison had found the purpose and adopted the ideals that were to motivate and guide him during forty years in public life and twenty years as his country's authentic sage."[8]

What was that purpose? What were those ideals? We sometimes lose sight of what Gordon Wood has aptly called the "radicalism of the American Revolution."[9] Not so the Americans who made it happen. In their eyes, the Revolution "reduc[ed] to practice, what, before, had been supposed to exist only in the visionary speculations of theoretical writers ... exhibiting a political phenomenon unknown to former ages."[10] The idea that a nation could be created and governed based explicitly on the consent of its people was a political novelty and heresy in the 1770s and 1780s. Yet it was precisely this idea on which the American Revolution was staked, and those who embraced it were, in the context of their times, radicals and idealists.

Like radicals and idealists in other ages, moreover, the cause they fought for infused meaning into their lives. The American

Revolution was dedicated first and foremost to the principle that "the people" governed, that "the people" supplied government with its energy and direction, and that monarchical institutions – that is, institutions not controlled by or accountable to the people – needed to be eradicated. Making republican government work was both the reason for the Revolution and its triumph, and it was this ideal that Madison committed his life to achieving.

Equally important is what Madison understood to be the central principle of republicanism, the irreducible condition that defined its existence, namely, popular control. For Federalists, republicanism meant no more than the power of the people to choose their leaders at election time. This view, obscured by events in the 1780s, came into sharp focus only after the Constitution's adoption. "It is often said that 'the sovereign and all other power is seated *in* the people,'" Benjamin Rush complained during his brief period of High Federalism. "This idea is unhappily expressed. It should be – 'all power is derived *from* the people.' They possess it only on the days of their elections. After this, it is the property of their rulers, nor can they exercise it or resume it, unless it is abused."[11] And though not everyone spoke of officeholding as a property right, sentiments like these were pervasive among Federalists. An editorial in the Columbia *Centinel* thus explained how "the *sovereignty of the people* is delegated to those whom they have *freely appointed* to administer [the] constitution, and by them alone can be rightly exercised, save at the stated period of election, when the sovereignty is again at the disposal of the *whole people*."[12] Between elections, however, the people needed only to listen and to obey.

Madison's view – and the view espoused by Jefferson and their followers in what eventually became the Republican party – was very nearly the opposite. The bedrock principle of republicanism, they said, was that "the censorial power is in the people over the government, and not in the government over the people."[13] The American Revolution had not been fought merely to establish a sequence of mini-monarchies, time-limited by elections. The suffrage was a device to secure popular control, but elected officials were responsible to "the sense of the people" at all times.[14]

The need to preserve the paramount authority of the community, particularly on constitutional questions, was a constant theme in Madison's writings, both as Publius and after. As *Federalist* 51 declared, "A dependence on the people is no doubt the primary controul on the government," with structural devices serving only as "auxiliary precautions" (*Fed.* 51, 349). Madison had made the same point, and at greater length, a week earlier in one of his essays on federalism:

> The adversaries of the Constitution seem to have lost sight of the people altogether in their reasonings on this subject; and to have viewed these different establishments [the state and federal governments], not only as mutual rivals and enemies, but as uncontrouled by any common superior in their efforts to usurp the authorities of each other. These gentlemen must here be reminded of their error. They must be told that the ultimate authority, wherever the derivative may be found, resides in the people alone; and that it will not depend merely on the comparative ambition or address of the different governments, whether either, or which of them, will be able to enlarge its sphere of jurisdiction at the expense of the other. Truth no less than decency requires, that the event in every case, should be supposed to depend on the sentiments and sanction of their common constituents.
>
> (*Fed.* 46, 315)[15]

In these essays Madison did not emphasize that popular control was constant or that it would not be surrendered between elections, because in 1788 the issue had not yet been formulated in these terms. That emerged a few years later, when Federalists began denouncing opposition to their measures on the ground that any "appeal to the people" constituted "a gross violation offered to Freedom of Deliberation, in the constituted authorities."[16] But as battle lines formed around this fundamental question of republican government, Madison again took up his pen. Between November 1791 and December 1792, Madison published at least eighteen unsigned essays in the *National Gazette*, virtually all emphasizing the importance of public opinion in controlling the course of government.

The final essay, published in late December 1792, stated some of Madison's key conclusions. In a contrived debate between a fictional character named *"Republican"* and his nemesis, *"Anti-republican,"* Madison apes the Federalist position, but not by much, for the words he puts in *Anti-republican*'s mouth were in fact routinely used by his opponents. *Republican*'s responses reflected Madison's own sentiments. "Who Are the Best Keepers of the People's Liberties?" Madison asks in the essay's title, and *Republican*'s answer is telling:

> *Republican.* The people themselves. The sacred trust can be no where so safe as in the hands most interested in preserving it.
>
> *Anti-republican.* The people are stupid, suspicious, licentious. They cannot safely trust themselves. When they have established government they should think of nothing but obedience, leaving the care of their liberties to their wiser rulers.
>
> *Republican.* Although men are born free, and all nations might be so, yet too true it is, that slavery has been the general lot of the human race. Ignorant they have been cheated; asleep they have been surprized; divided the yoke has been forced upon them. But what is the lesson? That because the people *may* betray themselves, they ought to give themselves up, blindfold, to those who have an interest in betraying them? Rather conclude that the people ought to be enlightened, to be awakened, to be united, that after establishing a government they should watch over it, as well as obey it.
>
> *Anti-republican* ... It is not the government that is disposed to fly off from the people; but the people that are ever ready to fly off from the government. Rather say then, enlighten the government,

warn it to be vigilant, enrich it with influence, arm it with force, and to the people never pronounce but two words *Submission* and *Confidence*.

Republican. The centrifugal tendency then is in the people, not in the government, and the secret art lies in restraining the tendency, by augmenting the attractive principle of the government with all the weight that can be added to it. What a perversion of the natural order of things! to make *power* the primary and central object of the social system, and *Liberty* but its satellite.[17]

This is surprising stuff for scholars who have imbibed the conventional wisdom about Madison, and who might (if not tipped by his choice of pseudonyms) be inclined to assume that Madison identified more with *Anti-republican* than with *Republican*. Perhaps the same discrepancy explains why most of them ignore or slight the *National Gazette* essays.

Yet passages like these surely present a puzzle. After all, the conventional wisdom about Madison does have some basis. Plainly Madison saw risks and dangers in democratic politics; plainly he wanted to temper popular majorities. His essays as Publius are filled with language displaying these efforts and anxieties. One sees hints even in *Republican*'s responses to *Anti-republican*, which acknowledge rather than deny the latter's worries about the people. How, then, do we explain what look like two very different Madisons? Was he confused and self-contradictory? Or did he, in fact, radically change his ideas, as most Madison scholars apparently believe?[18] Did the cautious framer who wanted to put government into the hands of a disinterested elite subsequently shed his worries and become a simple democrat?

In fact, both characterizations are inaccurate. Certainly, Madison was concerned about the harm that could be done by popular majorities, as much so in the decades after ratification as the decade before. The error in that part of the conventional wisdom is in its emphasis and accents: in seeing Madison in the 1780s as more repelled by democratic politics than he was, and, and, as a result, misreading him to embrace positions fundamentally at odds with his deep personal commitment to popular government. Yet Madison always retained the sense (learned in the 1780s) that popular rule could be dangerous and unjust, and the Madison of the 1790s was never a simple democrat. Rather, in both decades, and throughout his life, for that matter, Madison's ideas about popular politics and his conception of republicanism were different and more complex (though also more consistent) than has generally been understood.

We can start the process of reconstructing Madison's thinking with *Federalist* 49–50. This may seem a curious place to begin, because commentators typically read this pair of essays as expressly rejecting the primacy of popular politics.[19] Here Madison went out of his way to criticize a suggestion made by his friend Thomas Jefferson in a 1783 draft of a constitution for Virginia. Jefferson had proposed to enforce the constitution by calling popular conventions whenever "[a]ny two of the three branches of government concur in opinion ... that a convention is necessary for altering this constitution, or correcting breaches of it."[20] Such thinking was characteristic of Jefferson, who wanted direct, popular action to be the first and major line of defense in securing compliance with the constitution. Conventions would enable this, but in a less chaotic and disorderly fashion than the mobbing and extralegal resistance relied on in the British constitutional tradition.[21]

Madison offered three pragmatic reasons in opposition to this direct resort to the people, which most scholars read as confirming his desire to remove constitutional enforcement from popular control. First, Madison worried that a too-frequent appeal to the people would "deprive the government of that veneration, which time bestows on every thing, and without which perhaps the wisest and freest government would not possess the requisite stability" (*Fed.* 49, 340). Second, he said, "[t]he danger of disturbing the public tranquility by interesting too strongly the public passions, is a still more serious objection against a frequent reference of constitutional questions, to the decision of the whole society" (*Fed.* 49, 340). But "the greatest objection of all," according to Madison, was that the community would invariably side with the most popular branch of government, namely, the legislature (*Fed.* 49, 341–42).[22] And it was no answer to this objection that the executive might sometimes be "a peculiar favorite of the people" (*Fed.* 49, 342). Either way, the public decision "could never be expected to turn on the true merits of the question" (*Fed.* 49, 342). Often, the very officials whose actions were at issue would gain election to the Convention and, precisely because they were popular, would dominate it. Still more fatal, the irregular and evanescent nature of popular conventions made them highly susceptible to infection from "the spirit of pre-existing parties, or of parties springing out of the question itself" (*Fed.* 49, 342). As a result, "The *passions* ... not *the reason*, of the public, would sit in judgment" when "it is the reason of the public alone that ought to controul and regulate the government" (*Fed.* 49, 343).[23]

Plainly this reasoning stands in considerable tension with Madison's many statements in his *National Gazette* essays insisting that "[t]he people who are the authors of [the Constitution], must also be its guardians."[24] It is similarly at odds with Madison's reliance in *Federalists* 45–46 on popular enforcement to secure federalism, and with his comment in *Federalist* 51 that the people are meant to provide "the primary controul on the government" (*Fed.* 51, 349). The contradiction is evident even in *Federalist* 49 itself, which begins by recognizing that because "the people are the only legitimate fountain of power" it is "the people themselves[,] who, as the grantors of the [Constitution], can alone declare its true meaning and enforce its observance," and which concludes by insisting that "it is the reason of the public alone that ought to control and regulate the government" (*Fed.* 49, 339, 343).

Statements like these (and numerous others) make clear that Madison, no less than Jefferson, believed the public had a right and a responsibility to interpret and enforce the Constitution. But, then, why did he reject Jefferson's proposal? How could he write in 1792 that "every good citizen will be at once a centinel over the rights of the people; over the authorities of the confederal government; and over both the rights and the authorities of the intermediate governments,"[25] while previously insisting that "appeals to the people" in the form of popular conventions were "neither a proper nor an effectual provision" for safeguarding constitutional limits (*Fed.* 49, 343)?

There is a simple answer to this seeming contradiction. What Madison objected to in Jefferson's proposal was not the principle it embodied, but the way it put that principle into action. Like Jefferson, Madison believed in popular control, believed that "the sense of the people" should ultimately decide what the government did and how the Constitution was interpreted.[26] But Jefferson's approach looked for a *kind* of popular control that would not and could not work in practice because it was too unmediated and direct.

Among the lessons Madison took from his study of history was that popular government could succeed only if decision-making was mediated and refined through a system of democratically accountable representatives. As he explained in *Federalist* 10, the critical distinction between pure democracies, which experience taught were short-lived "spectacles of turbulence and contention," and a well-designed republic was precisely "the delegation of the Government, in the latter, to a small number of citizens elected by the rest" (*Fed.* 10, 61–62). A proper "scheme of representation," thus, "opens a different prospect, and promises the cure for which we are seeking" (*Fed.* 10, 61–62). It did not matter that a question was constitutional in nature: turning directly to "the whole society" for an immediate answer (which is how the founding generation saw popular conventions)[27] was perilous and unnecessary. Not because the public lacked the right to decide, and not because the public would never do so. That right was, in fact, incontestable. But the experience of the ancients – as well as that of Americans themselves – taught that a nation would all too quickly collapse if the public decided too directly, too often, and on too many things. Instead, a proper system of representation was needed: one that would, if carefully constructed, secure popular government while reducing the *need* for direct popular action, which could then be held in reserve for use only on, as Madison put it, "certain great and extraordinary occasions" (*Fed.* 49, 333).

But how would this work? What was Madison's representation-based alternative to Jefferson's direct popular constitutionalism? Having rejected Jefferson's approach, Madison went on to spell out his own version of popular constitutionalism in the next essay, the famous *Federalist* 51.[28]

Madison thought popular government could work only if politics were mediated through representative institutions. But representation was only a start and was not, by itself, sufficient. After all, the popular conventions championed by Jefferson would also consist of delegates chosen by the people. More was necessary to refine and construct a public decision worthy of respect, and that more, Madison explained in *Federalist* 51, consisted of establishing multiple representative institutions within an enlarged polity and setting them in proper relation to one another. Or, in Madison's own words, "the defect must be supplied, by so contriving the interior structure of the government, as that its several constituent parts may, by their mutual relations, be the means of keeping each other in their proper places" (*Fed.* 51, 347–48). This meant, in particular, utilizing a bicameral legislature, an executive veto, federalism, and extensive size.

As with *Federalist* 49–50, comprehending Madison's logic requires avoiding a widely shared misunderstanding. Few passages from *The Federalist* are more familiar than this one, and few have been more consistently and egregiously misread. Conventional wisdom tells us that Madison sought to preserve constitutional limits by devitalizing popular politics and creating a balanced equilibrium within the government, forming "a machine that would go of itself."[29] On this view, the framers complicated the system by establishing separate branches and departments and then giving each a constitutional power to check or obstruct the others. Their hypothesis, supposedly, was that officials within the different institutions could be counted on to protect the powers and prerogatives of their respective offices. They would, as a result, reliably act in the ordinary course of governing to prevent rivals in the other branches from overreaching in violation of the Constitution. Constitutional scholars and political philosophers treat this strategy as nothing less than sheer genius. "[O]fficials would not have to be public-spirited," one commentator observes breathlessly, because "their self-interested defence of the power of their offices would still contribute unintentionally to the maintenance of the constitutional balance."[30]

The problem is that critical aspects of this reading of *Federalist* 51 do not sit well with the content and structure of the essay or even make particular sense. The argument turns, for instance, on the relevant institutions each having a constitutional power to block unconstitutional acts of the others. Yet while some of the devices Madison discussed fit this description, others do not. States have no constitutional power to block the federal government, not after the supremacy clause. So why mention federalism? And extensive size has nothing to do with interbranch or intergovernmental checking. Yet the discussion of these two features takes up more than half of *Federalist* 51, while Madison breezes through bicameralism and the executive veto in a single paragraph.

More damning still, this interpretation of *Federalist* 51 rests on the implausible assumption that officeholders in different branches would make protecting the institutional prerogatives of their respective offices a priority. Even without political parties, why would anyone expect legislators to object to presidential action they supported? Why assume that state governments would oppose federal legislation that did what the states wanted? As Daryl Levinson has pointed out, politicians must normally be expected to put political concerns above institutional ones.[31] Occasionally institutions do act to protect themselves contrary to the immediate political interests of their members. But this is unusual, and that was as true in 1788 as it is today. No thoughtful politician or careful student of politics – and Madison was both – could possibly have thought otherwise.

It is unlikely that Madison would have built his whole theory around such a far-fetched proposition. And, sure enough, the language of *Federalist* 51 supports a different and more sensible reading. In explaining his argument, Madison says that "the great security ... consists in giving those who administer each department, the necessary constitutional means, and *personal* motives, to resist encroachments of the others ... Ambition must be made to counteract ambition. The *interest of the man* must be connected with the constitutional rights of the place" (*Fed.* 51, 349; emphasis added). Madison understood perfectly well that the "personal motives" and "interests" of elected officials would be *political* motives and *political* interests – in other words, that officials would have political agendas they were seeking to advance, agendas that were responsive to the desires and beliefs of their constituents. The key to making the Constitution work then lay in finding a way to harness these political interests, and the power to advance them by using constitutional authority granted to the institutions in which the officials worked, for the benefit of constitutional enforcement.

If this is right, it suggests revisiting the prevailing understanding of Madison's theory of constitutional enforcement, as well as his broader theory of constitutional politics, both of which rest heavily on this (mis)reading of *Federalist* 51. We should do so, moreover, by looking comprehensively at what Madison said and did during the founding period, reading what he wrote as Publius not in isolation, but rather against the background of his earlier and later actions and in conjunction with his writings of the early 1790s. When we do that, a different Madison emerges, with a different theory of popular politics and republicanism.

As we have seen, Madison began from the conviction that a government is republican only if and to the extent that its actions are guided and controlled by public opinion. This point deserves continued emphasis because it has been so widely neglected, and because its importance as Madison's first principle cannot be overstated.[32]

Establishing a republican government meant establishing "a Government of opinion."[33]

This concept of opinion requires some elaboration. When Madison spoke of public opinion, he did not have something abstract or imaginary in mind. Modern political philosophers have tended to flatten the idea of popular sovereignty, to treat it as a disembodied or purely notional justification for government. Not so Madison. He understood public opinion to be "an operationally active and authoritative sovereign," reflecting definite views or positions on public affairs that had been given concrete expression by the people themselves.[34] This is why he saw ignoring public opinion as counter-revolutionary, and why he insisted that true republicans were "naturally offended at every public measure that does not appeal to the understanding and to the general interest of the community."[35] In concrete terms, respect for opinion required elected officials to run their ideas past constituents and to let their reactions determine what the government did.

There is, of course, an important sense in which this sort of public control is inescapable. Government must have the community's acquiescence, if not active support, and no regime can survive if it continuously negates popular will. This was Hume's point about how even the most despotic governments ultimately "have nothing to support them but opinion."[36] Certainly Madison believed this,[37] as did his political opponents. But they drew very different conclusions from it.

For Federalists, who wanted government lodged safely in the hands of gentlemen like themselves, the lesson was to dampen popular politics: to depoliticize public life to the extent possible, and by doing so to foster passive acceptance of government action. Federalists believed in republicanism, but saw themselves as clear-eyed pragmatists with no illusions about the capacity of ordinary citizens to make "disinterested" or "virtuous" judgments about policy. Popular rule needed to be trammeled and hedged in order to ensure that decisions were made only by the most competent and qualified.

Making government remote was one way to achieve this, which is why Federalists preferred national to state power. It is also why they condemned anything that smacked of popular mobilization, and why they relentlessly propagandized the need for submission, obedience, and deference.[38]

Because of his brief alliance with those who held such views, Madison has long been treated as sharing their philosophy and objectives, at least during the period of common partnership in the 1780s. And clearly there were areas of agreement. Madison was perhaps the foremost advocate of using national power to check state politics, and *Federalist* 10 shows how he also believed that government leadership should be in the hands of an elite. But Madison had his own reasons for taking these positions. What agreements existed in the 1780s between him and people like Hamilton, James Wilson, and Gouverneur Morris turned out to be on tactics, obscuring profound differences in philosophy. In critical respects, Madison's beliefs were nearly the opposite of theirs. He thought public opinion *should* control what government did, and he held that creating a republican government meant embracing and maximizing public control, not acting to pacify or divert it. To Madison's way of thinking, the inevitability of popular control gave rise to a corresponding responsibility to refine and improve public deliberations, so as to ensure that the sovereign, controlling public opinion was also reasonable and just.

This last point is crucial, as it draws attention to an important normative qualification in Madison's thinking about opinion. On the one hand, Madison recognized that the will of the majority must rule. "In republican Government," he wrote in his memo on "Vices of the Political System of the United States", "the majority however composed, ultimately give the law." This was, indeed, "the fundamental principle of republican Government."[39] On the other hand, a government could be republican and still be unjust, tyrannical, and not worth serving or preserving. Madison had not dedicated his life to the cause of republicanism without regard for its quality or content.

A republican government *could* be more just, but only if the majority that ruled did not itself become despotic or tyrannical. And the lesson of the 1780s was that this might not be easy and certainly could not be taken for granted. So while republicanism meant subjecting "the will of the government to the will of the society" (meaning the will of the majority), that alone was not enough. It was necessary also to subject "the will of the society to the reason of the society."[40]

In affirming the authority of public opinion, in other words, Madison was preaching majority rule but not simple majoritarianism. Majority opinion would hold sway, but the majority opinion that *should* hold sway had to be more than the fleeting passions or preferences of the moment, more than the unreflective reactions of a transient majority of citizens. Colleen Sheehan explains:

> Madison did not simply equate public opinion with the will of the majority. Public opinion [was] not the sum of ephemeral passions and narrow interests; it [was] not an aggregate of uninformed minds and wills. Rather, public opinion require[d] the refinement and transformation of the views, sentiments, and interests of the citizens into a public mind guided by the precepts of reason, resulting in "the reason ... of the public" or "the reason of the society."[41]

This was Jefferson's point when he urged in his first inaugural address that Americans "bear in mind this sacred principle, that though the will of the majority is in all cases to prevail, that will to be rightful must be reasonable."[42]

Ensuring that the will of the majority was reasonable was, in the first instance, a responsibility of leadership. Those whose situation in life had afforded them the opportunity to elevate their minds had a corresponding obligation to elevate those of their fellow citizens, particularly on matters of politics and government. "The class of the literati," Madison wrote in notes to himself, "are the cultivators of the human mind – the manufacturers of useful knowledge – the agents of the commerce of ideas, – the censors of public manners –

the teachers of the arts of life and the means of happiness."[43] It was the task of this elite to educate and edify, to foster a process of deliberation that refined and enlightened public sentiment in a fashion sufficient for the demands of self-government.

This responsibility lay particularly with elected officials, and Madison emphasized the responsibility of representatives to help shape public opinion where it was "not ... fixed."[44] As Colleen Sheehan notes, precisely because public opinion is sovereign, "the republican statesman is obliged to advance its formation and expression."[45] It was with this in mind, for instance, that Madison emphasized how critical "*Representatives going from, and returning among every part*" of the nation are to securing republican liberty – a safeguard whose importance, he said, is matched only by "a *circulation of newspapers through the entire body of the people.*"[46] Representatives traveling to and from the seat of government act as "agents for the exchange of political ideas among the citizenry. As elected officials whose task is to deliberate on issues of national import, they [could] both attend to the views of their constituents and convey back to them the concerns and interests of the nation at large."[47]

This sort of educative leadership would be effective, however, only if proper leaders were in place. Hence Madison's excitement when he realized how a large republic could foster "a process of elections as will most certainly extract from the mass of the Society the purest and noblest characters which it contains."[48] Madison's objective was not to select an elite that would deliberate *for* the public; nor was it to place this elite at so great a remove from the people that it could work free from their interference. Rather, Madison wanted "the ablest Statesmen & soundest Republicans" to seek positions of leadership so they could teach and inform the public, elevating the discussion, fending off local prejudices, and improving the citizens' minds and morals.[49] Those in office, whoever they were, would necessarily know more about public affairs than ordinary citizens. Public officials were, as a result, in the best position to provide the kind of civic education that was essential to guide the public's thinking. To play their part well, however, these public officials needed to be the sorts of people who would use their superior knowledge and position to move public opinion in the direction of reason, moderation, and justice.

The political process Madison imagined was thus dramatically different from the deferential politics that Federalists wanted (and that Madison has often erroneously been thought to have favored). "Symbolically," explains historian Christopher Grasso, "the 'public' came to be seen, not as a body ruled by a sovereign head, but as a mind that ruled itself."[50] This did not mean the flattening or elimination of all distinctions; neither Madison, nor Jefferson, nor anyone else then alive was quite so modern. But it did embody a profound, if subtle, shift in the nature of politics. Where Federalists emphasized the power and patronage of a wealthy gentry whose superior virtue deserved submission, Madison's politics are better characterized as a conversation in which the elite now led by persuasion an electorate actively engaged in making its own judgments and decisions.

The extended republic served a second critical purpose in Madison's scheme, one that helps explain why he repeated the argument of *Federalist* 10 in *Federalist* 51. Generating reasonable and reasoned public opinions would take time and require a proper forum for deliberation. This was difficult to achieve in a small republic, where the limited range of competing interests made forming a factious majority too easy. Virtuous leaders could, in theory, block this from happening, but in practice one could not depend on it:

> It is vain to say, that enlightened statesmen will be able to adjust these clashing interests, and render them all subservient to the public good. Enlightened statesmen will not always be at the helm: Nor, in many cases, can such an adjustment be made at all, without taking into view indirect and remote considerations, which will rarely prevail over the immediate interest which one party may find in disregarding the rights of another, or the good of the whole.
>
> (*Fed.* 10, 60)

Added safeguards were needed to blunt the process of majority formation: to slow it down long enough to give government officials and
other members of the "literati" an opportunity to lead a proper public
debate. And among the surest of these additional safeguards was
simply to make the republic larger:

> Extend the sphere, and you take in a greater variety of parties and
> interests; you make it less probable that a majority of the whole
> will have a common motive to invade the rights of other citizens; or
> if such a common motive exists, it will be more difficult for all who
> feel it to discover their own strength, and to act in unison with each
> other.
>
> (*Fed.* 10, 64)

The difficulty of forming such majorities would, in turn, create time
and space for the kind of public debate and discussion that was
necessary to refine popular opinion and help it coalesce around a just
decision.

Note how this description of the effects of enlarging a republic
differs from the usual understanding of Madison's famous argument.
The conventional assumption is that, because Madison feared legislators would be too responsive to majorities, he wanted to prevent
majorities from forming, thereby leaving officials free to craft solutions that satisfied an independent and objective notion of "the public
good." But, as we have seen, Madison was committed to the idea of
majority rule and believed in the sovereignty of public opinion. His
actual concern was more focused. It was not majorities that Madison
feared. It was unreflective, factious majorities: the kind that could
form all too easily at the state level. The benefit of extensive size was
that, by making it more difficult for majorities to form, a large republic gave reasoned argument an opportunity to prevail, so that whatever "coalition of a majority of the whole society" eventually emerged
"could seldom take place on any other principles than those of justice
and the general good" (*Fed.* 51, 353).

Yet this still was not enough. For even in a large republic it was dangerous to entrust the role of collecting and acting on public opinion to a small, concentrated set of individuals. There remains the risk that "enlightened statesmen will not always be at the helm." And even if voters did manage to elect only "the most diffusive and established characters" (*Fed.* 10, 63), these representatives would regularly face vexing problems that lacked determinate solutions, for the Constitution was obscure and imprecise in important respects (*Fed.* 37, 231–39).[51] Given such risks and problems, it was not enough merely to elect representatives, even in an extended territory. "The genius of Republican liberty" likewise demanded that "the trust should be placed not in a few, but in a number of hands" (*Fed.* 37, 234).

By "number of hands," Madison did not mean a big government, though he did believe "the Representatives must be raised to a certain number, in order to guard against the cabals of a few" (*Fed.* 10, 62–63).[52] More precisely, Madison meant a *complicated* government that provided "double security ... to the rights of the people" because its powers were "first divided between two distinct governments, and then the portion allotted to each, subdivided among distinct and separate departments" (*Fed.* 51, 351). Structural innovations in the form of federalism and separation of powers thus became the final elements of Madison's theory, indispensable because they provided the means to make the "personal motives" and political interests of elected officials work to advance the cause of republican liberty and popular constitutionalism.

The idea, once understood, really is quite ingenious. We complicate the government by creating several levels, each with multiple branches or departments. All the political departments at each level – that is, the legislative houses and the executive – are then made accountable to the people, but in different ways and to different constituencies. Members of the House of Representatives were directly accountable, for instance, but to small constituencies relative to the other branches. Members of the Senate were accountable to larger statewide constituencies, but only indirectly. The president was still more indirectly accountable, but in his case to the nation as a whole. It was similar at the state level: most of the states also had bicameral legislatures with each house chosen under a different scheme of representation, and most of the states picked their executives by more or less indirect means; some states also had independently elected executive councils, again chosen by various means (*Fed.* 47, 327–31).[53]

These differences in accountability mattered, because they gave members of the different governments and departments different political interests and agendas. This would be true, moreover, no matter how public officers conceived their roles. Perhaps they would put their energy into serving some notion of "the public good," or perhaps they would back whichever measures maximized their chances for reelection. Or, more realistically, they might do a bit of both. It actually would not matter. However elected officials approached their jobs, their perceptions of what the public wanted or needed, or of what furthered their political careers, would necessarily be shaped by the different situations in which they found themselves by virtue of the placement and structure of their office. By then assigning the different offices ways to block or obstruct each other, these varied and various perspectives, with their "opposite and rival interests," could be used to supply "the defect of better motives" in safeguarding the Constitution by securing the sovereignty of public opinion.

How would it work? Suppose the president takes some action, say, unilaterally declaring US neutrality in a war between Britian and France, or initiating a plan to wiretap American citizens without first obtaining warrants. If that action is contrary to the political interests of actors in any part of the system, and a plausible constitutional objection exists or could be made, we can expect to see the issue raised. If, therefore, no one anywhere in this complex system objects, there is as good an assurance as one can ever realistically hope to get that there is no plausible objection.

Obviously, that is not certain; no system is infallible or completely foolproof. One can imagine actions that are unconstitutional but serve the interests of elected officials at every level and in every department. Or there could be moments when potential objectors are not paying attention, or where the stakes for everyone are simply too low to matter. But with so many different institutions, staffed by politicians with so many different potential interests to motivate them, universal acquiescence may be the best possible vote of confidence we can generate.

Conversely, if there is a potential objection, we should expect to see the issue raised by someone in this complex system, and we should expect that individual or institution to use the powers of their office to challenge or obstruct the action in question. This will not end the matter, even if successful. Nor is it supposed to do so. For the use of a constitutional check is not meant to conclude a dispute. It is meant to begin one: to force the kind of public debate needed for "the reason of the society" to emerge and coalesce.

To illustrate, suppose the House debates a bill and concludes that a proposed law reflects good policy and is also constitutional. A majority of the Senate disagrees: they do not like the law, and they believe it unconstitutional for some reason. They refuse to pass it. What happens next? The bill may die, as perhaps it should if members of the House give the law a low priority or have no answer to the Senate's objections. But if they care and have an argument to support their position, the Senate's refusal to act should arouse a response. Recall Madison's admonition about the importance of representatives "going from, and returning among every part of [the people]." Madison assumed that members of the House who supported the bill would go back to their constituents and argue that the Senate was wrong, that the law was both useful and constitutional and that voters needed to put pressure on the Senate to relent. Senators, in the meantime, were not expected to sit idly by. They were supposed to do the same thing: return home, give speeches, write editorials, and make their case that the law was undesirable or unconstitutional. And so we would have a genuine public debate in which, eventually, the community would settle on a view, at which point the political pressure brought to bear would force the losing branch to yield.

Even this might not end the matter. Suppose, for example, that public opinion led the Senate to succumb. There might still be objections from the president, who could exercise a veto, or from politicians in the states, who had at their disposal a variety of devices to challenge federal law (devices Madison fleshed out in *Federalist* 45–46). In either case, the debate would continue to whatever end the public eventually embraced. And in this way, separation of powers and federalism became instrumentalities for generating a robust public discussion, initiated and led by political leaders acting for their own reasons, through which the "reason of the society" could be developed and "the people themselves" retain control.

This is what Madison had in mind when he spoke of connecting the "interest of the man" with "the constitutional rights of the place" (*Fed.* 51, 349). This is how "[a]mbition [could] be made to counteract ambition" (*Fed.* 51, 349) to ensure compliance with the Constitution. But the compliance we get, and the compliance Madison sought, is compliance with the Constitution as understood by the sole, final arbiter of its meaning, "the people themselves; who, as the grantors of the commission, can alone declare its true meaning, and enforce its observance" (*Fed.* 49, 339).

Note how the people's control, while real and substantial, is not direct. It is indirect: mediated through popular responses to arguments and to the action or inaction of representatives in different parts of different governments, representatives who are in turn taking their cues from the public. It is, nevertheless, genuine popular control, a system of political and constitutional regulation that avoids the pitfalls of Jefferson's direct popular constitutionalism without betraying the basic commitment to republicanism.

This revised understanding of Madison's thinking has implications for our understanding of many, if not most, elements of the

Constitution. It even affects the one department about which he had relatively little to say, the judiciary. Judges were largely omitted from Madison's original scheme for interpreting and enforcing the Constitution. Indeed, none of his efforts in the critical years leading up to ratification paid much attention to courts. His letters and private writings make clear that he thought the judicial department too weak to play a meaningful role in constitutional enforcement, unless it was to lend a bit of additional weight to the executive in a Council of Revision.[54] But other than a short passage in *Federalist* 39 suggesting that the Supreme Court might act as an impartial umpire in disputes between the national government and the states (*Fed.* 39, 256), Madison as Publius had essentially nothing to say about the third branch.

Still, the conventional understanding of Madison, which sees him seeking to empower an elite and remove it as far as possible from popular influence, seems eminently compatible with an idea like the modern doctrine of judicial supremacy. If Madison favored minimizing popular control over politics, is it not natural when it comes to the Constitution, the fundamental *law* of the land, to think he might have favored something similar or even more dramatic? Judicial supremacy seems wholly agreeable with this view of Madison's thought, which is why so many defenders and proponents of the Supreme Court's authority have called upon him for support.[55]

Yet once Madison's reasoning is understood properly, he becomes an unlikely ally for a concept like judicial supremacy, which seems wholly at odds with his commitment to a republicanism grounded in public opinion. Madison supported an independent judiciary, of course, like most others at the time.[56] But also like them, his reasons had nothing to do with constitutional enforcement. Instead, he saw the need for independence chiefly through the lens of British and colonial experience, which had no doctrine of judicial review, but which taught that judges needed tenure and salary protection to immunize them from being influenced by the more powerful political branches in ordinary civil and criminal cases.[57] To avoid this, Madison advised his friend Caleb Wallace that the judicial department "merits every care. Its efficacy is Demonstrated in G. Brittain where it maintains private Right against all the corruptions of the two other departments & gives a reputation to the whole Government which it is not in itself entitled to."[58]

Madison wrote this letter in 1785. He did not mention judicial review, though he was already aware of the concept, which had just recently begun to emerge in the states. Indeed, one of the earliest discussions of this newfangled idea arose in a Virginia case, *Commonwealth v. Caton*,[59] decided in 1782. The case achieved a degree of notoriety in the state and was quite controversial, though only two of eight judges argued that courts could review legislation. But letters and newspaper essays fiercely debated what some referred to as "[t]he great constitutional question,"[60] and James Monroe can be found telling Madison as late as 1788 that the Virginia legislature had avoided discussing judicial review as something "calculated to create heats & animosities that will produce harm."

Though controversial at first, the idea continued to gain support, slowly in the beginning, then more rapidly after the Constitution went into effect.[61] A variety of factors help to explain this acceptance, but in part it was simply that the argument for review in its original, modest guise was persuasive and hard to ignore. If the Constitution was supreme law, as everyone agreed it was, then legislative acts contravening its terms were ultra vires and void: not law at all. Judges before whom such acts were brought in the course of ordinary litigation could not ignore this fact. To do so would be to ignore a direct command from "the People" and abet another branch's violation of the people's expressed will. The principle of popular sovereignty, the foundation on which the Constitution and government were supposed to rest, demanded that courts treat such laws as the nullities they were by refusing to enforce them.

Madison was of course willing to allow this much, and he acknowledged during the 1789 debate over the president's removal power that "in the ordinary course of government ... the exposition of the laws and constitution devolves upon the judicial."[62] But, he immediately added, this did not mean that judicial decisions had any special stature or status:

> I beg to know, upon what principle it can be contended, that any one department draws from the constitution greater powers than another, in marking out the limits of the powers of the several departments. The constitution is the charter of the people to the government; it specifies certain great powers as absolutely granted, and marks out the departments to exercise them. If the constitutional boundary of either be brought into question, I do not see that any one of these independent departments has more right than another to declare their sentiments on that point.

Thomas Jefferson, who embraced the same theory throughout his political life,[63] expressed the idea succinctly: "[E]ach of the three departments has equally the right to decide for itself what is its duty under the constitution, without regard to what the others may have decided for themselves under a similar question."

In essence, by recognizing judicial review in this limited form, Madison was simply adding courts to the process of public deliberation described above. The judiciary became an additional voice when it came to constitutional questions: another source of leadership for the community, and one more potential check in the system of constitutional politics built into our complex government. If a bill passed Congress and was signed by the president without protest from the states, it was still possible for the Supreme Court to raise a constitutional objection and ask the public to reconsider by wielding its power of review as what amounted to a judicial veto.

This much is straightforward, at least as a conceptual matter. Someone must have final authority to resolve constitutional conflicts, but in a system based on popular sovereignty that someone can never be the government or any part of it. Government agents, whether legislators, executive officials, or judges, are just that: agents. When it comes to the Constitution, they are the regulated, not the regulators. They must do their best to decide what the Constitution

permits, forbids, or requires them to do, but final interpretive authority always rests with their actual superior, "the people themselves."
Hence, when Madison, Jefferson, and their supporters proffered what
later scholars have called "departmental" or "concurrent" or "coordinate" review,[64] they were not advocating a process in which no one
had final say. They were defending a system in which the people's
different agents, including judges, could articulate their varied understandings of the Constitution in the ordinary course of business and,
in effect, present these to a common superior for judgment. If constitutional conflicts arose, they would in the end be resolved the only
way they could be resolved in a republican government: they would be
decided by the people. As Virginia senator Stevens Thomson Mason
explained in 1802: "All the departments of a popular Government
must depend, in some degree, on popular opinion. None can exist
without the affections of the people, and if either be placed in such a
situation as to be independent of the nation, it will soon lose that
affection which is essential to its durable existence."[65]

Ideally, disputing branches of government would achieve an
accommodation on their own, though Jefferson once observed that
"We have ... in more than one instance, seen the opinions of different
departments in opposition to each other, & no ill ensue."[66] Still,
accommodation by and among the branches was what all the
checking and balancing that Madison had described in *Federalist*
51 was supposed to accomplish. If no compromise was forthcoming,
if different departments insisted on what Senator John Breckinridge of
Kentucky called "[a] pertinacious adherence . . . to their opinions," it
was obvious who would decide. The issue would be answered, in
Madison's words, by "the will of the community, to be collected in
some mode to be provided by the constitution, or one dictated by the
necessity of the case."[67]

This way of thinking about the role of courts supports a system
of judicial review, but one lacking the idea of judicial supremacy. That
is hardly surprising, given what we know of Madison's thinking.
Assigning courts supremacy over constitutional interpretation would

have been flatly anti-republican, because it would have deprived the community of final say over the meaning of their Constitution by giving it to a mere agent of the people, worse, an agent structured and designed to be as *un*accountable as possible. That is something Madison could never accept. The right of the people "to judge whether the [Constitution] has been dangerously violated," he wrote in 1800, "must extend to violations by one delegated authority, as well as by another; by the judiciary, as well as by the executive, or the legislature."[68]

Yet review without supremacy is meaningful only if there is some way for the people to control judicial interpretations, just as they control interpretations of the political branches. Which raised an exceedingly awkward problem, for how are "the people" supposed to repudiate or overturn decisions of the courts on constitutional questions? When it came to the political branches of both the state and national governments, the forms of popular control were obvious. The same devices that created accountability were the tools by which the public registered its agreement or disagreement and ensured that constitutional disputes were resolved according to popular opinion, particularly as these devices fostered a general culture of responsiveness among elected representatives.

But courts were not accountable in these ways and had, in fact, been self-consciously shielded from precisely these sorts of pressures. This was to ensure fair decisions in ordinary cases of "private Right," not because courts were expected to play the part of final arbiter of constitutional meaning (*Fed.* 78).[69] But whatever the reason, judicial independence was a fact, and it created a dilemma in defining the role of courts in a system of popular constitutionalism: how do we secure accountability for constitutional decisions when courts are independent and when, given their other responsibilities, we want them to remain so?

The opportunity to overturn judicial decisions by constitutional amendment was no answer, any more than it would have been an answer to action by the political branches. No one had ever doubted the people's authority to create new constitutional law. But the accompanying power to declare the meaning of the existing Constitution had also always been held by the community, and it remained central to the very idea of republicanism. The unquestioned existence of popular authority to make constitutional law thus did not and could not justify denying popular authority to control its interpretation. The power to amend was situated in a legal and intellectual framework in which interpretive authority remained where it had always been: with the people at large.[70]

That returns us to the same quandary: if judges are not elected and their salaries are protected, and we give them power to obstruct actions by the other branches on constitutional grounds, how do we retain popular control over the Constitution?

Here it is helpful to consider how the major nations of modern Europe have handled the problem. Germany, France, Italy, and Spain (not to mention Russia and the nations of Eastern Europe) have all adopted new constitutions since World War II. As such, they were able to design their governments with our experience in mind, and it has not been missed that all chose for the first time to embrace strong doctrines of judicial review. Less noticed is how these nations structured their judiciaries differently from ours precisely to enable their courts to act while preserving an adequate degree of popular control.

To begin, the nations of Western Europe delegated constitutional adjudication to special courts, which were set apart from the regular legal system in recognition that the Constitution is not just another species of ordinary law and that constitutional litigation is not just another species of litigation.[71] The sole function of these courts is to review constitutional questions. They do not address other matters or issue judgments over whole cases, thus disentangling constitutional review from more conventional legal matters. By this means, independence in constitutional cases could be (and has been) structured and balanced differently than in ordinary cases, enabling the Europeans to take the inherent political nature of constitutional law into account without compromising the need to exclude politics from ordinary litigation.

Given the high political station occupied by constitutional courts, various provisions were then made to ensure an appropriate level of political responsiveness, while still securing the courts' ability to act as an independent counterweight. Once on the bench, the judges are independent. But unlike in other European courts, appointment is political rather than bureaucratic. More important, getting appointed typically requires a supermajority in one or both houses of the legislature, thus guaranteeing that constitutional courts have a mainstream ideology, and the judges serve terms that are limited and staggered to ensure that this remains so through regular turnover.[72] Finally, the constitutions themselves were made more easily amendable than ours.

The combined effect of these structural innovations has been to relieve the pressure a doctrine of supremacy creates, by reducing the likelihood of serious breaches between the constitutional court and the other branches of government and by making political correctives easier to implement when breaches occur. Partly as a result, constitutional courts in Europe have managed successfully to mimic or even exceed American activism without the same controversy.

Structural precautions like these are not found in the United States Constitution because when it was written no one had yet imagined anything even remotely like modern judicial supremacy. Judicial review was first conceived in this country in the context of ordinary litigation, and it matured as an aspect of the normal legal system, intermingling constitutional decisions with other legal questions and conflating constitutional and ordinary law. This meant, among other things, that the robust protection given American judges in ordinary cases, where popular control can be maintained through regular politics, ended up similarly protecting judges from popular control in constitutional cases. As judicial power expanded, and its potential and political importance became clear, supporters and defenders of popular constitutionalism discovered a need to compensate for this mistake in our constitutional design. With no models or prior experience to work from, they and their successors handled the problem of courts as they handled so many other unanticipated problems: by innovating and jerry-rigging a system of political solutions on the fly, as problems arose.

The solutions they crafted are familiar.[73] Thomas Jefferson – with the full support of his secretary of state, James Madison – abolished a lower court, revised Supreme Court procedures, threatened to ignore the Court's mandates, and briefly pursued a strategy of impeaching judges. Andrew Jackson followed Jefferson in threatening to ignore judgments, while Lincoln actually did so (and on more than one occasion). Congresses before and after the Civil War manipulated the Court's size, played with its budget, and stripped it of jurisdiction in controversial areas. Theodore Roosevelt advocated recalling both errant judges and faulty opinions, while his cousin Franklin made a famously brazen effort to pack the bench (one that was rendered unnecessary when the Court backed down first).

This is not the place to examine how these or similar devices could or should work today. The subject is controversial and requires more conceptual depth and analytical detail. Nor can constitutional politics be reduced to this handful of blunt tools. As others have pointed out, there are multiple avenues by which popular will finds its expression in courts.[74] There do, however, need to be mechanisms to clarify and implement the ultimate authority of the people. These devices, or something that can serve their function, are needed to restore the robust democratic constitutionalism that James Madison championed and that remains our nation's best and most distinctive contribution to government and democratic theory.

At the end of *Federalist* 10, Madison exults in what he has accomplished. By enlarging the sphere of the republic, he boasts, "we behold a Republican remedy for the diseases most incident to Republican Government" (*Fed.* 10, 65). Political theorists and constitutional scholars have focused too much on Madison's concern for the *diseases* incident to republican government without paying adequate attention to the first "republican" in that sentence. Certainly, Madison was concerned about the dangers of popular government and what Elbridge Gerry (much later his vice president) called "the excess of democracy."[75] But not just any remedy would do. The remedy had to be *republican*, a remedy consistent with the popular control of government that was the fundamental premise of the Revolution and of Madison's own life and philosophy. And he found his remedy, too, one that is, or rather could be made, as relevant and useful today as it was at our nation's inception.

NOTES

1 One finds this reading, for example, in the introductory materials in leading constitutional law casebooks. See Geoffrey R. Stone et al., *Constitutional Law*, 5th ed. (New York: Aspen, 2005), 12–26. The same understanding is reflected in innumerable articles (see Larry D. Kramer, "Madison's Audience," *Harvard Law Review*, 112 [2001], 611–79, at 612–14 and nn. 2–21), and in the writings of leading constitutional historians. See Jack Rakove, *Original Meanings: Politics and Ideas in the Making of the Constitution* (New York: Alfred A. Knopf, 1996), 35–56; Gordon S. Wood, "Interests and Disinterestedness in the Making of the Constitution," in Richard Beeman et al., eds., *Beyond Confederation: Origins of the Constitution and American National Identity* (Chapel Hill: University of North Carolina Press, 1987), 69–93. It wholly pervades the political science literature.

2 Gordon S. Wood, *The Creation of the American Republic, 1776–1787* (Chapel Hill: University of North Carolina Press, 1969), 593.

3 This by now conventional reading of Madison is most clearly stated and synthesized in Cass R. Sunstein, "Interest Groups in American Public Law," *Stanford Law Review*, 38 (1985), 29–87.

4 Though "experience has taught mankind the necessity of auxiliary precautions," Madison wrote, "[a] dependence on the people is no doubt the primary controul on the government." *Fed.* 51, 349.

5 James Madison, "Government of the United States," *National Gazette*, February 4, 1791, *PJM*, XIV, 217–18.

6 See Larry Kramer, "'The Interests of the Man': James Madison, Popular Constitutionalism, and the Theory of Deliberative Democracy," *Valparaiso Law Review*, 41 (2006), 708–11.

7 Madison to William Bradford, November 26, 1774, *PJM*, I, 129.

8 Ralph Ketcham, *James Madison: A Biography* (Charlottesville: University Press of Virginia, 1990), 67.

9 Gordon S. Wood, *The Radicalism of the American Revolution* (New York: Alfred A. Knopf, 1991).

10 St. George Tucker, "On Sovereignty and Legislature" (1803) in *Blackstone's Commentaries*, appendix A, reprinted in St. George Tucker, *View of the Constitution of the United States with Selected Writings* (Indianapolis: Liberty Fund, 1999), 19.

11 Benjamin Rush, "On the Defects of the Confederation" (1787), in *The Selected Writings of Benjamin Rush*, ed. Dagobert D. Runes (New York: Philosophical Library, 1947), 26–28. See James P. Martin, "When Repression Is Democratic and Constitutional: The Federalist Theory of Representation and the Sedition Act of 1798," *University of Chicago Law Review*, 66, (1999) 166–69.

12 *Columbian Centinel*, September 3, 1794, 1.

13 James Madison, Speech in Congress on "Self-Created Societies" (November 27, 1794), in *James Madison: Writings*, ed. Jack N. Rakove (New York: Library of America, 1999) (hereinafter *Madison: Writings*), 552.

14 Madison to Jefferson, April 2, 1798, *PJM*, XVII,104–05. It was, indeed, this precise understanding that motivated and justified the institutional experiments Republicans essayed throughout the 1790s: the Democratic-Republican Societies, party newspapers, organized petition campaigns, the Virginia and Kentucky Resolves, the formation of a political party with party discipline, and so on, all efforts to keep the government in line with popular opinion, and all opposed and condemned by Federalists (who nevertheless frequently adopted the same tactics).

15 *Federalist* 46 was published on January 29, 1788; *Federalist* 51 came out a week later, on February 6.

16 The quote is from John Fenno, editor of the Federalist newspaper and administration mouthpiece, the *Gazette of the United States*. Fenno was complaining about a petition campaign that had been organized by opponents of the Jay Treaty in an effort to persuade Congress not

to enact enabling legislation. *Gazette of the United States*, May 5, 1796, 3.

17 James Madison, "Who Are the Best Keepers of the People's Liberties?," *National Gazette*, December 20, 1792, *PJM*, XIV, 426–27.

18 See Gordon S. Wood, "Is There a 'James Madison Problem?'," in *Revolutionary Characters: What Made the Founders Different* (New York: Penguin, 2006), 151–55; Douglas W. Jaenicke, "Madison v. Madison: The Party Press Essays v. The Federalist Papers," in Richard Maidment and John Zvesper, eds., *Reflections on the Constitution: The American Constitution after Two Hundred Years* (Manchester, UK: Manchester University Press, 1989), 116–35; Colleen A. Sheehan, "Madison and the French Enlightenment: The Authority of Public Opinion," *The William and Mary Quarterly*, 59(2002), 925–56, at 927 n. 7.

19 See Rakove, *Original Meanings*, 280–82; Jaenicke, "Madison v. Madison," 136.

20 *Draught of a Fundamental Constitution for the Commonwealth of Virginia* (1783), in Thomas Jefferson, *Notes on the State of Virginia*, ed. William Peden (Chapel Hill: University of North Carolina Press, 1954), 209, 221.

21 On constitutional enforcement under the British constitution, see Larry Kramer, *The People Themselves: Popular Constitutionalism and Judicial Review* (New York: Oxford University Press, 2004), 24–29.

22 "The members of the legislative department ... are numerous. They are distributed and dwell among the people at large. Their connections of blood, of friendship and of acquaintance, embrace a great proportion of the most influential part of the society. The nature of their public trust implies a personal influence among the people, and that they are more immediately the confidential guardians of the rights and liberties of the people. With these advantages, it can hardly be supposed that the adverse party would have an equal chance for a favorable issue." *Fed.* 49, 341–42.

23 Madison went on in *Federalist* 50 to explain why these objections were not obviated by holding popular conventions at regular, pre-set intervals.

24 Madison, "Government of the United States," *PJM*, XIV, 217–18.

25 *PJM*, XIV, 179.

26 See also, Madison, "A Candid State of Parties," *National Gazette*, September 22, 1792, *PJM*, XIV, 370–71 (true republicans are "naturally

offended at every public measure that does not appeal to the
understanding and to the general interest of the community"); Madison,
"Consolidation," *National Gazette*, December 3, 1791, ibid., 137–38
(worrying that without state governments "neither the voice nor the
sense" of the people "could ever be combined or called into effect");
Colleen A. Sheehan, "Madison's Party Press Essays," *Interpretation*,
17 (1990), 355–77, at 371–73.

27 Edmund S. Morgan, *Inventing the People: The Rise of Popular Sovereignty
in England and America* (New York: W. W. Norton, 1988). People
"ascribed to one set of elected representatives meeting in convention a
more popular character, and consequently a greater authority, than every
subsequent set of representatives meeting as a legislature" (91); see
Rakove, *Original Meanings*, 93–102; Wood, *Creation*, 306–10, 319,
328–43.

28 Placement alone might have suggested that these three essays (*Federalist*,
49–51) have something to do with one another. Yet with a few notable
exceptions (e.g. Rakove, *Original Meanings*, 280–82), commentators seem
to simply miss the connection. Typical discussions of Madison's ideas in
The Federalist either ignore *Federalists* 49–50 or treat these essays as a
puzzling detour from the analysis of separation of powers Madison had
begun in *Federalists* 47–48. See *James Madison: The Theory and Practice
of Republican Government*, ed. Samuel Kernell (Stanford, CA: Stanford
University Press, 2003); Richard K. Matthews, *If Men Were Angels: James
Madison and the Heartless Empire of Reason* (Lawrence: University Press
of Kansas, 1995); Gary Rosen, *American Compact: James Madison and the
Problem of Founding* (Lawrence: University Press of Kansas, 1999);
Morton White, *Philosophy*, The Federalist, *and the Constitution* (Oxford:
Oxford University Press,1987). This is, I believe, both a cause and an effect
of the general misreading of *Federalist* 51 discussed below.

29 Michael Kammen, *A Machine that Would Go of Itself: The Constitution
in American Culture* (New York: Alfred A. Knopf,1986), 18; see Daryl
Levinson, "Empire-Building Government in Constitutional Law,"
Harvard Law Review, 118 (2005), 915–72, at 950.

30 Jaenicke, "Madison v. Madison," 137.

31 Levinson, "Empire-Building," 950–60.

32 My discussion here owes a great intellectual debt to Colleen Sheehan. See
Sheehan, "Madison and the French Enlightenment"; Sheehan, "Party

Press"; Colleen A. Sheehan, "Public Opinion and the Formation of Civic Character in Madison's Republican Theory," *Review of Politics*, 67 (2005), 37–48; Colleen A. Sheehan, "The Politics of Public Opinion: James Madison's 'Notes on Government'," *William and Mary Quarterly*, 49 (1992), 609–27.

33 Madison to Edward Livingston, July 10, 1822, *PJM, Retirement Series*, II, 544.

34 Sheehan, "Madison and the French Enlightenment," 948; Sheehan, "Politics of Public Opinion," 619; see also Kramer, *The People Themselves*, 3–8.

35 Madison, "A Candid State of Parties," *PJM*, XIV, 370–71.

36 David Hume, *Of the First Principles of Government*, in *Essays: Moral, Political, and Literary*, rev. ed., ed. Eugene F. Miller (Indianapolis: Liberty Fund, 1985).

37 See Madison, "Charters," *National Gazette*, January 18, 1792, in *PJM*, XIV, 191–92 ("All power has been traced up to opinion. The stability of all governments and security of all rights may be traced to the same source. The most arbitrary government is controuled where the public opinion is fixed. The despot of Constantinople dares not lay a new tax, because every slave thinks he ought not.").

38 In essence, Federalists wanted a monarchical social order without a monarch and with an aristocracy based on wealth and accomplishment rather than birth. As Gordon Wood has observed, Federalists believed in democracy, "but not our modern democracy; rather, they believed in a patrician-led classical democracy in which 'virtue exemplified in government will diffuse its salutary influence though the society.'" Wood, "Interests and Disinterestedness", 83.

39 *PJM*, IX, 354–55.

40 James Madison, "Universal Peace," *National Gazette*, January 31, 1792, *PJM*, XIV, 206–07.

41 Sheehan, "Madison and the French Enlightenment," 948.

42 Thomas Jefferson, First Inaugural Address, March 4, 1801, in *Thomas Jefferson: Writings*, ed. Merrill Peterson (New York: Library of America, 1984), 492–93.

43 "Notes for the National Gazette Essays," *PJM*, XIV, 157, 168.

44 See James Madison, "Public Opinion," *National Gazette*, December 19, 1791, *PJM*, XIV, 170 (while public opinion must be obeyed once

it had settled, "where not ... fixed, it may be influenced by the government").

45 Sheehan, "Politics of Public Opinion," 620.

46 *PJM*, XIV, 170. Alongside these devices Madison also listed "good roads, domestic commerce, [and] a free press," that is, "[w]hatever facilitates a general intercourse of sentiments" among the people. Ibid.

47 Sheehan, "Madison and the French Enlightenment," 953.

48 *PJM*, XIV, 357; see also *Fed.* 10, 64.

49 See Jack N. Rakove, "The Structure of Politics at the Accession of George Washington," in *Beyond Confederation*, 261, 271. The quote is from Letter from James Madison to Caleb Wallace (August 23, 1785), in *PJM*, VIII, 350, 354.

50 Christopher Grasso, *A Speaking Aristocracy: Transforming Public Discourse in Eighteenth-Century Connecticut* (Chapel Hill: University of North Carolina Press, 1999), 282, 448–51.

51 Rakove, *Original Meanings*, 156–60.

52 Lance Banning, *The Sacred Fire of Liberty: James Madison and the Founding of the Federal Republic* (Ithaca, NY: Cornell University Press, 1995), 195–233.

53 Madison discussed differences among the states in *Fed.* 47, 327–31. For a more systematic survey, see Willi Paul Adams, *The First American Constitutions: Republican Ideology and the Making of the State Constitutions in the Revolutionary Era* (Lanham, MD: Rowman & Littlefield, 2001), 315–31.

54 Madison to Jefferson, October 24, 1787 *PJM*, 211; Madison, Speech of June 6, 1787, *RFC*, I, 138.

55 See Richard A. Epstein, "Toward a Revitalization of the Contract Clause," *University of Chicago Law Review*, 51 (1984), 705, 711–12; Thomas W. Merrill, "The Economics of Public Use," *Cornell Law Review*, 72 (1986), 115; Frank I. Michelman, "Foreword: Traces of Self Government," *Harvard Law Review*, 100 (1986), 4–77; Norman R. Williams II, "Rising above Factionalism: A Madisonian Theory of Judicial Review," *New York University Law Review*, 69 (1994), 963–1013, at 985.

56 See Gerhard Casper, "The Judiciary Act of 1789 and Judicial Independence," in Maeva Marcus, ed., *Origins of the Federal Judiciary: Essays on the Judiciary Act of 1789* (New York: Oxford University Press, 1992), 281.

57 See Kramer, *The People Themselves*, 18–92. The need for judicial independence was discussed constantly during ratification, but invariably in connection with the ordinary administration of justice.

58 Madison to Caleb Wallace, August 23, 1785, *PJM*, VIII, 350.

59 *Commonwealth v. Caton*, 8 Va. (4 Call) 5, 8 (1782); and see William Michael Treanor, "The Case of the Prisoners and the Origins of Judicial Review," *University of Pennsylvania Law Review*, 143 (1995), 491–570, at 500–40.

60 See Edmund Pendleton to James Madison, November 8, 1782, *PJM*, V, 260–61; ibid., XI, 361.

61 See Kramer, *The People Themselves*, 35–65.

62 Madison, Speech of June 17, 1789, *PJM*, XII, 232, 238.

63 Jefferson to Spencer Roane, September 6, 1819, *Jefferson: Writings*, 1427–28. See David N. Mayer, *The Constitutional Thought of Thomas Jefferson* (Charlottesville: University Press of Virginia,1994), 257–94.

64 See Robert Lowry Clinton, *Marbury v. Madison and Judicial Review* (Lawrence: University Press of Kansas, 1989); Shannon C. Stimson, *The American Revolution in the Law: Anglo-American Jurisprudence before John Marshall* (Princeton, NJ: Princeton University Press, 1990), 100–04; Michael Stokes Paulsen, "The Most Dangerous Branch: Executive Power to Say What the Law Is," *Georgetown Law Journal*, 83 (1994), 217–346, at 228–29.

65 Stevens Thomas Mason, Speech to Congress, January 13, 1802, *Debates and Proceedings in the Congress of the United States* (Washington: Gales and Seaton, 1851), XI, 59.

66 Jefferson, Draft Annual Message to Congress, December 8, 1801, quoted in Jeremy D. Bailey, *Thomas Jefferson and Executive Power* (New York: Cambridge University Press, 2007), 229.

67 "Although ... the courts may take upon them to give decisions which impeach the constitutionality of a law, and thereby, for a time, obstruct its operations," Breckinridge explained: "yet I contend that such a law is not the less obligatory because the organ through which it is to be executed has refused its aid. A pertinacious adherence of both departments to their opinions, would soon bring the question to issue, in whom the sovereign power of legislation resided, and whose construction of the law-making power should prevail." *Annals of Congress*, 59,179–80. By "bring the question to issue," Breckinridge means, of course that "pertinacious

adherence" to conflicting views by different branches would force the public to decide.

68   Madison, Speech of June 17, 1789, *PJM*, XII, 238.

69   Madison, *Report on the Alien and Sedition Acts* (January 7, 1800), in *Madison: Writings*, 608, 613.

70   Only one commentator tied judicial independence to judicial review: Alexander Hamilton, who argued in *Federalist* 78 that judicial independence "is peculiarly essential in a limited constitution" because "the courts were designed to be an intermediate body between the people and the legislature, in order, among other things, to keep the latter within the limits assigned to their authority." *Fed.* 78, 524–25. Although Hamilton was defending only the modest form of review discussed in the text and had not yet pushed the argument to the point of judicial supremacy, he was nevertheless out ahead of everyone else in his reasoning. Of course, *Federalist* 78 was published too late and had too limited a circulation to influence ratification, and no one else at the time made a similar argument. See Kramer, *The People Themselves*, 80–81.

71   Nor did Americans write provisions for amendment into their constitutions with any idea that, in doing so, they were supplanting popular authority to interpret. Rather, formal amendment processes were developed to address problems that could not be solved by interpretation. Americans were aware that their constitutions incorporated numerous untried innovations, and for all their eagerness and enthusiasm, they expected some of these to fail. Problems that arose because of ambiguity or uncertainty in the text could be resolved by a Madisonian process of public deliberation and interpretation. Ibid., 51–54.

72   See Louis Favoreu, "Constitutional Review in Europe," in Louis Henkin and Albert J. Rosenthal, eds., *Constitutionalism and Rights: The Influence of the United States Constitution Abroad* (New York: Columbia University Press, 1990), 38, 40–59 ; Hans Kelsen, "Judicial Review of Legislation: A Comparative Study of the Austrian and the American Constitution," *Journal of Politics*, 4 (1942), 183–200.

73   See the country-by-country surveys in Vicki C. Jackson and Mark Tushnet, *Comparative Constitutional Law* (Victoria Park: Foundation Press, 1999), 489–91; Alec Stone Sweet, "Constitutional Adjudication and Parliamentary

Democracy," in *Governing with Judges: Constitutional Politics in Europe* (Oxford: Oxford University Press, 2000).

74 For a useful survey, see Charles Geyh, *When Courts and Congress Collide: The Struggle for Control of America's Judicial System* (Ann Arbor: University of Michigan Press, 2006).

75 *RFC*, I, 48.

11 Politics Indoors and Out-of-Doors

A Fault Line in Madison's Thinking

Jack N. Rakove

In the winter of 1791–92, James Madison compiled a set of reading notes that scholars long assumed were meant to support the "party press" essays he soon published in the *National Gazette,* the new Republican newspaper edited by his college friend, the poet Philip Freneau. But as Colleen Sheehan has argued, Madison also conceived these "Notes on Government" for a more ambitious project: to draft a treatise on republican government that would apply the lessons of the American experience to problems that had long fascinated political theorists.[1] The table of contents that opens the notebook indicates the outlines of the argument. The treatise, alas, remained unwritten – a reminder of the fact that Madison preferred to do his best political writing for himself, rather than the reading public. Alexander Hamilton, his co-author as Publius, felt fewer inhibitions and proved a more spirited polemicist. Had Madison gone back to Virginia in the fall of 1787, to aid in the ratification struggle in his native state, rather than returning to the Continental Congress, his twenty-nine contributions to *The Federalist* would never have appeared. Without *Federalist* 10 and 51 and a few other essays to guide our thinking, the modern concept of a "Madisonian constitution" might never have formed. Who knows: had Hamilton written nearly all of *The Federalist,* with a little assistance from John Jay, we might have been stuck with a "Hamiltonian constitution" all along.

Near the beginning of his reading notes, Madison inserted this striking comment:

> The best provision for a stable and free Govt. is not a balance in the powers of the Govt. tho' that is not to be neglected, but an

equilibrium in the interests & passions of the Society itself, which can not be attained in a small Society. Much has been said on the first. The last deserves a thorough investigation.[2]

Four years after he wrote *Federalist* 10, the author of the Madisonian Constitution was still ruminating about its core propositions. Madison linked this comment to a second reflection. "Natural divisions exist in all political societies," he observed, echoing the topic sentence of the famous paragraph on faction in *Federalist* 10. ("The latent causes of faction are thus sown in the nature of man.") There was therefore no reason to add further "artificial distinctions," such "as kings & nobles," under the false pretext that these would offer further "checks and balances with each other & with the people."[3] The implicit reference here was to the support that Vice President John Adams and Secretary of the Treasury Alexander Hamilton had already expressed for the British constitution. The famous dinner hosted by Secretary of State Thomas Jefferson where Adams and Hamilton had voiced their admiration for that system had taken place in the spring of 1791. Madison's reading notes demonstrate that the political reverberations of that dinner were still being felt.

The fact that Madison believed that the theory of the extended republic laid down in *Federalist* 10 and reprised in *Federalist* 51 needed further development is fascinating in itself. But it also illustrates a central problem that historians and political theorists need to ask when they engage paradigmatic texts of this kind. Is the critical problem to offer the best interpretation of an authoritative text, as a political theorist might prefer to do? Or is it rather to relate that text to other writings that illuminate but also complicate the progress and uncertainties of an author's thinking, an approach more consonant with the goals of the historian or even the biographer?[4] Once we trace the origins, evolution, and richness of a seminal text, identifying every facet of its development – down to its punctuation – becomes a legitimate, even obsessive scholarly activity.[5] Think of the enormous impact that Peter Laslett's painstaking editing of John

Locke's *Two Treatises of Government* had on the interpretation of his political theory. Or more to the point, consider Mary Bilder's provocative hypothesis that Madison drafted the final passages of his memorandum "Vices of the Political System of the United States," which offers the first version of the factious argument of *Federalist* 10, not in April 1787 but at some later point, perhaps even after the debates at Philadelphia had begun.[6]

There is another reason why Madison's weighing of "a balance in the powers of the Govt." with "an equilibrium in the interests & passions of the Society itself" matters. This comparison reveals a point of tension – even a fault line – in Madison's theory. On one side of this line, he was fascinated by the workings of institutions, especially the representative bodies where he had spent most of his political career. Thinking of ways to improve the quality of their deliberations was one of the two main puzzles that drove his *constitutional* thinking in the mid-1780s. (The other, of course, was his critique of the structural weaknesses of American federalism.) But on the other side of this line, he grew increasingly interested in another problem: not the behavior of legislators, working endogenously within their institutions, but the exogenous influences on their actions exerted by the interests, opinions, and passions of their constituents. This growing concern with popular *political* behavior marked the other main axis of his thought, seeding the pregnant distinction that needed further examination in 1791.

This comparison between the constitutional operations of institutions and the political doings and dealings of interests and factions within society was already present in Madison's thinking in 1787–88. It appears at several noteworthy points in his writings as Publius. In *Federalist* 10 he plays off his belief that factions will neutralize each other within an extended body politic with the prediction that this will help to elevate the quality of legislative deliberations. In *Federalist* 51 he concludes his rather truncated discussion of the separation of powers not by fully explaining how "ambition must be made to counteract ambition" within government, but rather by reprising the argument about faction in *Federalist* 10. Other examples of this way of thinking appear in his analysis of federalism in *Federalist* 45–46, where he juxtaposes the advantage over the national government that the state governments will continue to enjoy with the greater political affection they will command because of their closer connection to the people. A similar argument unfolds in *Federalist* 49–50, where Madison criticized Thomas Jefferson's proposal to allow occasional or periodical conventions of the people to redress violations of the Constitution.

In the late 1780s, then, the dominant fact of republican politics, in Madison's view, was that whichever entity represented the people most directly would also pose the greatest threat to the stability of a polity. This was true for both the competition for power among the institutions of a single government or between two different levels of government. If there were dangers to maintaining a proper separation of powers, they would arise first and foremost from the "impetuous vortex" of the legislature, and especially its most responsive institution, either the lower house of assembly or the federal House of Representatives. If there were threats to the intended redistribution of federal authority, they were more likely to arise from the state governments than from the Union. The true purpose of constitutional design was to improve the deliberations and decisions of government, and there were specific reforms that Madison favored as means to that end. But the true source of the difficulties that most concerned him did not inhere in the defects of institutions. They came instead from "out-of-doors," from the swirling passions, opinions, and, most important, the interests of "the people themselves."

To draw too strong a distinction between Madison's political and constitutional thinking would be an error. What is constitutional thinking, after all, if it is not one important branch of political thinking? And what branch of political thinking could be more important than the study of constitutional mechanisms and decisions? Yet Madison's essays as Publius recognized both themes, and at critical points, his appraisal of exogenous political forces trumped his endogenous account of institutional workings. We are thus left to wonder whether our understanding of the Madisonian constitution depends, finally, more on his political sociology than on his concern with legislative deliberations, checks and balances, and his empirical approach to describing the complexities of the federal system.

It took constitutional commentators an exact century and a quarter to begin to grasp the conceptual significance of *Federalist* 10, and another several decades to recover the proper context for situating its arguments. As every student of historiography knows, Charles Beard's *An Economic Interpretation of the Constitution* (1913) relied on *Federalist* 10 to confirm the importance of a specific set of economic interests in the adoption of the Constitution. Beard had little interest in the argument of the essay per se; he simply treated Madison's account of the sources of faction as evidence for his basic claim. The pluralist scholars, led by Harold Laski, who were writing concurrently with Beard, were more engaged with the content of Madison's ideas, but they imposed anachronistic notions of interest groups on his analysis of factions.[7] Beard remained the dominant figure. Although postwar scholarship found deep flaws in his account of economic influences, his book still exercises a vampirical influence on interpretations of the origins of the Constitution.[8]

Nevertheless, the modern framework for understanding *Federalist* 10 was set by Douglass Adair. In two closely linked articles published in the 1950s, Adair restored the essay, and Madison's thinking more generally, to their original context, demonstrating that the received wisdom Madison was contesting in 1787 was defined by a long-running debate over the essential nature of republics and the traits they required of their citizens.[9] Other essays, notably by Robert Dahl and Martin Diamond, also contributed to this reassessment of the proper context for making sense of Madison's great essay.

In *Federalist* 10, Madison set two criteria for gauging the republican character of the Constitution. The first was institutional. Although his contemporaries often described the lower house of the legislature as the "democratical" branch of government, Madison sought to eliminate democracy (or "pure democracy") from his constitutional equation. Democracy, in his usage, meant the direct administration of government by the citizenry, a formula that historically led to "spectacles of turbulence and contention." By contrast, Madison defined a republic as "a government in which the scheme of representation takes place" (*Fed.* 10, 61–62). The people would elect representatives who would collectively deliberate about and decide the public good, but they would play no direct participatory role.

His second criterion involved an exercise in political sociology. *Federalist* 10 is essentially an essay in comparative politics, weighing the respective merits of national and state-based republics against each other. Which form of republic would prove more capable of withstanding "the violence of faction" that had so often proved fatal to republics, Madison asked: A smaller republic, whether modeled on the city-states of antiquity and early modern Italy, or the state commonwealths of revolutionary America; or a national republic, embracing "a greater variety of parties and interests"?

From this analysis, as all commentators know, Madison offers two sets of cures. The first is constitutional, and rests primarily on improving the conditions for legislative deliberation, so that "the public voice, pronounced by the representatives of the people, will be more consonant to the public good than if pronounced by the people themselves." That result would follow from Madison's main electoral hypothesis: that elections held in large districts "will be more likely to center in men who possess the most attractive merit and the most diffusive and established characters" than in those "unworthy candidates" whose "vicious arts," when applied in a "small republic," too often carried the results (*Fed.* 10, 62–63).

Yet the second and greater security lay elsewhere, in "the greater number of citizens and extent of territory" that favored larger republics over their smaller cousins. "It is this circumstance principally which renders factious combinations less to be dreaded" in larger republics. Madison stated his crucial hypothesis quite succinctly. The larger the society, the "greater the variety of parties and interests" it would contain. That diversity would reduce the probability that a majority would discover "a common motive to invade the rights of other citizens" (*Fed.* 10, 63–64). And if such a motive did exist, it would prove much more difficult for such a latent majority to coalesce to do its mischief.

At first glance – and even, perhaps, upon mature consideration – Madison seems to offer two distinct though complementary solutions to the problem of factious misrule. One involves the nature of legislative deliberation (politics indoors), and the other the ways in which the diversity of interests in the larger society (politics out-of-doors) will prevent the wrong kinds of majorities from forming or collaborating. As his reading notes from 1791 suggest, it was this second solution that Madison found more intriguing and worthy of consideration. Yet the relation between these dual aspects of political action is more complicated than this quick reading would suggest. To understand why this is the case, one has to probe Madison's concept of faction more closely. To do that, it helps to review, as best we can, the evolution of his idea of the problem of faction, the great problem that *Federalist* 10 was written to resolve.

Madison's opening definition of faction is the proper point of departure. "By a faction, I understand a number of citizens, whether amounting to a majority or minority of the whole, who are united and actuated by some common impulse of passion, or of interest, adverse to the rights of other citizens, or to the permanent and aggregate interests of the community" (*Fed.* 10, 57). The concluding passage identifies the dual ends that Madison repeatedly defined as the essential criteria of good governance: private rights and public good. But the critical moves came in the initial clause, where Madison defined faction as "a number of citizens," rather than legislators, and said that a faction could be either "a majority or a minority of the whole." From the vantage point of republican theory, this was a counterintuitive statement. But it was also fundamental to Madison's analysis.

The origins of Madison's concern with factious majorities lies in the 1786 dispute within the Continental Congress over the

Mississippi River. Madison worried that Secretary of Foreign Affairs John Jay's request to relinquish American navigation rights on the river would produce a lasting division between the northern and southern states. "There is no maxim in my opinion which is more likely to be misapplied," he wrote James Monroe, "than the current one that the interest of the majority is the political standard of right and wrong." But in his April 1787 memorandum "Vices of the Political System of the United States," Madison applied this same criticism to the problem of legislative misrule within the individual states. "If the multiplicity and mutability" of state laws discussed in the memorandum's ninth and tenth items "prove a want of wisdom," Madison observed in item 11, "their injustice betrays a defect still more alarming ... because it brings into question the fundamental principle of republican Government, that the majority who rule in such Governments, are the safest Guardians both of public Good and of private rights."[10]

Madison then asked the key analytical question: "To what causes is this evil to be ascribed?" When Madison interposed questions like these in his writings, they were usually substantive, rather than rhetorical in nature. His first answer was inherently institutional: it dealt with the ambitions that brought legislators to office and the circumstances of their deliberations. The second, much lengthier answer began with a strong transitional sentence. "A still more fatal if not more frequent cause lies among the people themselves." Madison first dismissed the various kinds of moral constraints that might discourage the "unjust" behavior of citizens: "a prudent regard to their own good" as it might be affected by "the general and permanent good of the Community"; a "respect for character," which would fall prey to the dominant swing in public opinion; and religion. None of these moral remedies would prove efficacious. The key hypothesis about the benefits of "an enlargement of the sphere" immediately followed.

The exact date of the composition of these observations has come into question. Did Madison complete the final passages on the popular sources of faction in April 1787, as scholars have generally assumed, or some weeks or months later, as Mary Bilder has suggested? But from the vantage point of understanding *Federalist* 10, the answer to this technical question hardly matters. The arguments that Madison developed in item 11 of the Vices reappeared in his lengthy letter to Jefferson of October 24, 1787, which elaborated Madison's rationale for an unlimited congressional negative on state laws.

Federalist 10 was published four weeks later. Its most famous paragraph is the one that Charles Beard so admired, and which anyone who has taken an introductory course in American history or American government well knows. "The latent causes of faction are thus sown in the nature of man," Madison began, and the rest of the paragraph identified the most important sources of division. "A zeal for different opinions" in religion and government comes first, followed by "an attachment to different leaders ambitiously contending for pre-eminence and power," and other "unfriendly passions" that convert even "the most frivolous and fanciful distinctions" into rancorous parties. There are, in other words, sources of political division that do *not* depend on citizens acting as rational economic actors or utility maximizers, and that operate even when "no substantial occasion presents itself." But of course, Madison had a more powerful argument to advance: the existence of "the various and unequal distribution of property" that appears in all "civilized nations," creating the different "interests" that form "the most common and durable source of factions" (*Fed.* 10, 58–59).

Madison concludes this great paragraph with a sentence that seems to state a mere truism. "The regulation of these various and interfering interests forms the principal task of modern legislation, and involves the spirit of party and faction in the ordinary operations of the government." At first glance, this statement merely describes the obvious nature of legislative activity. To take so limited a view, however, involves overlooking the dynamic facets of American governance that concerned Madison in the 1780s. By then he had developed a very modern view of the essential nature of legislative power, and his views of politics indoors – that is, of the desired characteristics of legislative deliberation – reflected that insight.

Prior to the Revolution, conventional constitutional thinking did not view the legislature as the forum where competing interests would develop a political agenda for an entire society. Its dominant role was to ensure that an arbitrary executive did not impose law by fiat or ukase or because *le roi le veut*. The idea that the legislature would henceforth become the main forum where interests would press their views and try to direct public policy was itself a discovery. It was the experience of the Revolutionary War, with the enormous burden of governance that it imposed on the state assemblies, that made that discovery possible, pushing the actual business of legislating into the forefront of Madison's political thinking.

No one else had considered that problem more seriously. Drawing on his service in the Continental Congress (1780–83) and the Virginia legislature (1784–86), Madison went to the Philadelphia Convention armed with a set of proposals for improving the quality of legislative deliberation and decision at both the state and national levels of government. Three proposals in particular stand out. First, his attachment to an unlimited congressional negative on state laws rested on the conviction that there was no obvious cure to the mischiefs of faction within the individual states. Their legislatures would remain vulnerable to faction precisely because the states were less diverse and extensive than the national republic. Second, Madison's fondness for a joint executive–judicial council of revision reflected his belief that it would be better to improve the quality of laws prior to their enactment, even if that involved giving judges an advisory role in lawmaking. Third, Madison believed that a well-constituted upper house would remain an essential instrument of sound legislation – a source of *"wisdom* and steadiness."[11]

When he wrote *Federalist* 10 in November 1787, Madison had no reason to discuss either the negative on state laws or the council of revision. Neither was part of the Constitution, and Publius was hardly going to disclose his experience as one of its framers. Nevertheless, Madison had every reason to develop his ideal of national lawmaking, and to explain why the process of legislative deliberation within Congress would mark a significant improvement over the equivalent procedures within the states.

Why would "the spirit of party and faction" become a necessary part of the "ordinary operations of the government"? Madison expected representatives to act as delegates for their constituents. That was the main point of the intriguing though neglected paragraph of *Federalist* 10 that follows the famous paragraph on faction. Representatives emerging from a district-based system of elections would have to act as "both judges and parties at the same time." That dual character is inherent in the nature of the representative enterprise. "What are the different classes of legislators," he asked, "but advocates and parties to the causes which they determine?" The constituencies each represented would possess some dominant set of interests, he supposed, and legislators would naturally seek to advance those concerns. Whenever acts of public policy affected economic interests, *any* decision a legislature took would affect rights of property, either positively or adversely. All of those decisions, over paper money or duties or taxes, would create winners and losers. Because the preservation of property remained a preeminent constitutional value, the differential impact of economic decisions necessarily involved matters of distributive justice: "what are many of the most important acts of legislation, but so many judicial determinations, not indeed concerning the rights of single individuals, but concerning the rights of large bodies of citizens?" (*Fed.* 10, 59–60).

It is one of those nice technical questions of scholarship to ask whether Madison was more intent on describing certain categories of *legislation* as being inherently (or even ontologically) judicial in their very nature, or whether he simply wanted *legislators* to act more judiciously (or even judicially) in their deliberations. Gordon Wood, in his interesting discussion of "the Madison problem," prefers the latter interpretation. Far from being a "practical pluralist" or an early

advocate "of modern interest group politics," Wood argues, Madison
wanted American lawmakers to act as their colonial predecessors had
done. Much of their work *had* been judicial in nature, because colonial assemblies repeatedly received petitions asking them to resolve
legal controversies. What Madison envisioned, Wood argues, was a
Congress composed of "liberally educated, rational men" who would
"decide questions of the public good in a disinterested adjudicatory
manner."[12] Or one could argue, conversely, that it was the process of
collective deliberation, rather than the individual orientation of lawmakers, that would have to produce more judicious results. As Madison noted in the next paragraph of *Federalist* 10, "It is in vain to say
that enlightened statesmen will be able to adjust these clashing interests, and render them all subservient to the public good," because
such "statesmen will not always be at the helm." Madison expected
such parties as would form – representatives speaking for the commercial towns or the planter elite of the southern states – to act in
their "immediate interest" while "disregarding the rights of another
[party] or the good of the whole." Nor was Madison naïve about the
character of his likely brethren in Congress. Scanning the roster of the
first House of Representatives, he found only "a very scanty proportion who would share in the drudgery of business" with the same
enthusiasm Madison felt.[13]

Yet the model of congressional deliberation he sketched in *The
Federalist* still provides a better conception of Madison's expectations. Madison rightly expected most members of Congress to be
short-timers, amateur lawmakers who would serve a term or two and
then go home, either to resume their private occupations or to seek
some other office.[14] In *Federalist* 53 he justified the two-year terms of
the House as a device designed less to insulate representatives from
their constituents than to enable members to learn their jobs and
acquire the knowledge needed to make informed decisions. The conventional wisdom about annual elections (usually stated: "where
annual elections end, tyranny begins") worked well for the state level
of governance (though even there Madison thought that a three-year

term would be fine.[15]) But the same diversity of interests that would promote the stability of an extended republic would also challenge the wisdom of its legislators. One could only gain the knowledge to legislate through the very process of deliberation. "No man can be a competent legislator who does not add to an upright intention and a sound judgment a certain degree of knowledge of the subjects on which he is to legislate," Madison observed in *Federalist* 53, and that could only be "thoroughly attained, by actual experience in the station which requires the use of it" (*Fed.* 62, 419).

To a perceptive modern reader – especially one concerned with the vices of the political system of the United States in our own age of hyper-partisan impasse – this account of legislative duty wholly ignores one critical factor. At no point does Madison invoke an incumbent's desire for reelection as an influential factor in political behavior. That desire, which today forms the dominant fact of congressional ambition, plays no role in Publius's account of legislative politics. A desire for reelection does figure in Hamilton's account of presidential power, notably in *Federalist* 72. And, of course, in *Federalist* 51, Madison famously declared that "Ambition must be made to counteract ambition" for the separation of powers among the departments to work. But that ambition was a matter of institutional loyalty rather than personal advancement. Madison's account of legislative behavior accurately reflects the assumptions of a prior age, when public service was far more of an avocation than a profession.

Federal representatives, as Madison portrayed them, would thus have to act in two capacities. Individually they would have to convey to Congress a reasonably detailed knowledge of the laws and conditions of their states and constituencies and to absorb what their colleagues in turn were reporting. There was no obvious number available to prove how many representatives were needed to fulfill the first task, but in *Federalist* 56 Madison explained how "a very few intelligent men, diffusively elected within the State" would provide the information their colleagues would have to learn. The likelihood that they would have previously served in their state legislatures would offer other data Congress would need. It would take representatives some time to master this knowledge, as it related to pending subjects of legislation. Every Congress would constitute its own learning cycle.

There was, therefore, an idealized model of deliberation that Madison hoped the House could fulfill. But he doubted whether every session of Congress would prove equally qualified. When Madison discussed the Senate in *Federalist* 62–63, his final two essays, he implied that an unchecked House of Representatives would repeat the misdeeds of the state legislatures.

> It is not possible that an assembly of men called for the most part from pursuits of a private nature, continued in appointment for a short time, and led by no permanent motive to devote the intervals of public occupation to a study of the laws, the affairs, and the comprehensive interests of their country, should, if left wholly to themselves, escape a variety of important errors in the exercise of their legislative trust.
>
> (*Fed.* 62, 419)

Madison was no enthusiast for the Convention's key decisions about the Senate. The election of senators by the state legislatures was his least favorite mode of appointment. As Publius, however, he could still have borrowed many of the arguments his colleagues had made to support that decision; instead he dismissed the whole subject with three cursory sentences at the opening of *Federalist* 62. The equal state vote in the Senate deserved better treatment; he gave this topic a full three paragraphs. Yet here, too, he balked at defending the decisions on its merits, or replaying the claims of state equality he had worked so hard to deny and disparage at Philadelphia. There was no point defending the equal state vote as a matter of constitutional theory, Madison concluded, when it was only "the lesser evil" the Convention had adopted.[16]

Yet these disparaging comments notwithstanding, Madison still believed that the Senate would have an essential role to play in reinforcing the deliberative capacity of Congress. His remaining comments in *Federalist* 62 and 63 echo concerns he had been voicing since 1785, when he ranked the lack of effective senates as the most conspicuous vice of the state constitutions.[17] His analysis of the function of the Senate reiterated his criticisms of the failings of the state legislatures before 1787. He still fretted over the impulsiveness of legislative proceedings; the lack of acquaintance most lawmakers would have with public affairs; the embarrassing task of "repealing, explaining, and amending laws, which fill and disgrace our voluminous codes"; and the harmful effects of "a mutable government" and "a mutable policy" (*Fed.* 62, 419–23). These were exactly the vices a senate was meant to check or correct.

Arguments like these are essentially institutional and constitutional in nature. They concern the basic nature of legislative deliberation, the expected qualifications of lawmakers, the virtues of bicameralism, and the calamities that will arise when the best procedures of discussion and decision are not followed. These opinions directly reflected Madison's experience since 1776 in national and state government. This is what politics indoors was all about. If the multiplicity of interests worked as Madison envisioned it would, discouraging the formation of factious majorities, a space would be cleared for congressional deliberation. The sources of faction would not disappear: interest, passion, and fallible opinion would still swirl through society. But their effects would be moderated, perhaps even cured.

Yet when one pushes Madison's analysis beyond these ideals of constitutional deliberation, other factors come to the fore. His very last sentence as Publius, the concluding judgment of *Federalist* 63, emphasized the political weakness of the Senate. "Against the force of the immediate representatives of the people," he warned, "nothing will be able to maintain even the constitutional authority of the Senate, but such a display of enlightened policy, and attachment to the public good, as will divide with that branch of the legislature the affections and support of the entire body of the people themselves" (*Fed.* 63, 431). For the Senate to be *politically* successful, it would have to do its very best to fulfill its constitutional duties, to act as the best senate it could possibly be. Only then, only when it could attract the attachments of the body of the citizenry, would the Senate be able to withstand the superior force of the House, the real "impetuous vortex" whose errors and excesses needed checking.

This concern with identifying the true sources of political "force" or "power," conceived in almost physical terms, appears in other passages of Madison's writings in 1787–88, sometimes overtly, sometimes latently. Consider the lone paragraph midway through *Federalist* 51, where Madison explicitly addressed the institutional separation of powers created by the Constitution. Here Madison somewhat obliquely defended the limited legislative veto of the president by emphasizing the "qualified connection between this weaker department and the weaker branch of the stronger department" (*Fed.* 51, 350). By "weaker department," Madison clearly meant the presidency; "weaker branch of the stronger department" obviously meant the Senate; and "qualified connection" referred to their joint role under the two "advice and consent" clauses. Yet why would Madison call the Senate the weaker department? It possesses the same legislative powers as the House, other than the authority to initiate revenue measures – a distinction that Madison had dismissed as inconsequential when it was proposed at Philadelphia.[18] Senators would serve longer terms in a smaller chamber, where they would be better able to concert their aims and tactics. And its "qualified connection" would give the Senate a quasi-executive authority in appointments and foreign relations that the House lacked. By these measures the Senate clearly seems the stronger house. Most Anti-Federalists reached the same conclusion, for with its concentration of legislative, executive, and judicial (as the court of impeachment) powers, the Senate posed the greatest threat to maintaining a separation of powers. But to Madison's way of thinking, the House would be the superior, more potent branch because it alone could claim to speak directly for the people.

Madison's lengthy October 1788 letter to Jefferson, explaining his evolving position on adding a declaration of rights to the

Constitution, illustrates the same mode of analysis. There were a variety of arguments that could be made for or against such a statement, Madison conceded. But the decisive reservation – the one that best indicated why even a well-drafted statement of rights would remain a "parchment barrier" – again revealed his underlyingly political concerns. "Wherever the real power in a Government lies, there is the danger of oppression," he observed.

> In our Governments the real power lies in the majority of the Community, and the invasion of private rights is *cheifly* [sic] to be apprehended, not from acts of Government contrary to the sense of its constituents, but from acts in which the Government is the mere instrument of the major number of the constituents.

Then Madison added another observation that Jefferson needed to hear. "This is a truth of great importance, but not yet sufficiently attended to, and is probably more strongly impressed on my mind by facts, and reflections suggested by them, than on yours which has contemplated abuses of power issuing from a very different quarter."[19] That "different quarter" was the *ancien régime* monarchy of Louis XVI, now entering its final months, that Jefferson had been observing the past four years, while Madison was contemplating the homegrown vices of American republicanism.

When Madison sent this letter, his days as Publius were already seven months in the past. Yet the concerns he summarized for Jefferson marked only the most recent statement of a line of analysis that strongly informed his contributions to *The Federalist*. At key moments, his political sociology trumped his constitutional theory. Madison's political thinking in the late 1780s was driven by his desire to identify the locus of "real power" within the polity. That search was less concerned with the relative authority of institutions than with the swirl of interests and passions in society that determined the life force of republican politics. It was, in other words, a matter of politics out-of-doors.

Three critical segments of *The Federalist*, all falling within essays 45–51, best illustrate this mode of thinking. The first involves his comparison of national and state authority in *Federalist* 45–46. The second concerns his discussion of the separation of powers in *Federalist* 48 and 51. And the third emerges in the curious digression of *Federalist* 49–50, where Madison considered but rejected Jefferson's proposal, laid out in his *Notes on the State of Virginia*, to allow popularly elected conventions to operate either occasionally or periodically as constitutional monitors.

Federalist 45 and 46 culminate Madison's discussion of federalism, which began in *Federalist* 37, where Madison explained why "the task of marking the proper line of partition between the authority of the general and that of the State Governments" was so inherently difficult (*Fed.* 37, 234). *Federalist* 37 is a uniquely epistemological reflection on the problem of accurately classifying political phenomena. For Madison there could be no substitute for describing the character of political institutions in exact detail, reasoning inductively from both the text of a constitution and the evidence of experience to map their design and operations. Madison first applied this lesson in the second part of *Federalist* 39, where he provided a fivefold analysis of the "federal" and "national" features of the proposed Constitution. Although *Federalist* 39 offers yet another example of Madison's fondness for drawing distinctions, it is better interpreted as a specific application of a Madisonian approach to political reasoning.[20]

Having characterized the federal system in this way, Madison suggested that "two important questions arise" when one considered the federal properties of the Constitution. *Federalist* 41–44 answered the first of these questions: "Whether any part of the powers transferred to the general government be unnecessary or improper" – a curious inversion of the Necessary and Proper Clause, which the concluding paragraphs of *Federalist* 44 had analyzed at some length (*Fed.* 41, 268). These essays have a formal, even predictable character, as Madison justifies each of the legislative powers enumerated in Article I, Section 8 in terms of their general reasonableness.

With *Federalist* 45 and 46, however, the tenor of Madison's language changed as he turned to his second important question:

"Whether the whole mass" of powers granted to the general government would prove "dangerous to the portion of authority left in the several States"? Madison began his response with a robust restatement of the true criterion for judging the Constitution: "the public good, the real welfare of the great body of the people, is the supreme object to be pursued." Against that standard, neither abstract claims for the supremacy of the Union nor for the sovereignty of the states could prove decisive. The real problem to pursue was whether "the unsacrificed residue" of state powers "will be endangered" by the creation of a stronger union (*Fed.* 45, 308–09).

Madison's first answer to this problem, in *Federalist* 45, was to compare the formal allocation of authority between the Union and the states. Drawing on his pre-Convention historical reading, Madison argued that the dominant tendency of federal systems was to favor the authority of member states over any consolidation of power in a central government. The states would enjoy other formal advantages. Their governments would employ many more officials, whose duties would be essential to daily life. The national government would likely rely on import duties, which implied that its revenue officers would be concentrated on the Atlantic coast. Its main duties would involve either foreign relations or the management of interior territories. It could exercise only the enumerated powers of Article I, Section 8, while the plenary legislative authority of the states was limited only by the modest restrictions of Article I, Section 10. In some respects, notably in the regulation of commerce, the Constitution clearly enlarged the jurisdiction of the national government. But in other areas, even including the power of taxation, its real change was to give the national government the means to discharge responsibilities it already possessed.

In the next essay, *Federalist* 46, Madison moved beyond this comparison of the relative authority of the two levels of government to develop his second answer, which pivoted on "the predilection and support of the people," that is, on the popular political resources that states and the nation would attract. Here, again, "the first and most natural attachment of the people will be to the governments of their respective States." The states would enjoy a deeper connection with the "domestic and personal interests of the people" and with "the ties of personal acquaintance and friendship, and of family and party attachments." A similar disparity would operate institutionally should national and state governments come into conflict. "A local spirit will infallibly prevail much more in members of Congress, than a national spirit will prevail in the legislatures of the particular States," he observed, tacitly reflecting on his own experience in the Virginia Assembly in the mid-1780s (*Fed*. 46, 315–16). There was a deep localism and provincialism in American attitudes that it would take some time to overcome. Madison certainly hoped that the experience of national governance would moderate these attitudes, but given the expected high rates of rotation in Congress, this process would require repeated renewal. Forming and maintaining a "consolidationist" outlook within the national government would be a daunting enterprise. Should that unlikely outcome ever occur, the states collectively would still retain powerful advantages, fortified in no small measure by the existence of the state-run militias as a check against national military power.

Yet embedded within this calculation of all the political advantages favoring the states was one further consideration that illustrated a more profound understanding of the logic of federalism. Imagine that "the people should in future become more partial to the federal than to the State governments," Madison supposed; "the change can only result from such manifest and irresistible proofs of a better administration, as will overcome all their antecedent propensities" (meaning their innate fondness for local and provincial institutions) (ibid.). The real dynamic of American federalism would not inhere in the formal division of authority between nation and states, nor would it be determined by the *initial* attachments of the people at large. It would flow instead from the changing sentiments of the American people, the real force of republican politics. Ultimately those sentiments would rest, not on a principled loyalty to either the nation or the states, but on the specific ways in which institutions of government would respond to the interests, opinions, and passions of the people, the independent variables of *Federalist* 10. These were the real factors that would determine the course of popular political action, rather than an abstract belief in some ideal structure of federalism – a factor that Madison never considered. For now, the existing attachments of Americans would favor the states. But circumstances, or rather political developments, could well alter those loyalties.

With *Federalist* 47, Madison turned his attention to the other great subject of constitutional design, "the particular structure of this government, and the distribution of this mass of power among its constituent parts" (*Fed.* 47, 323). Madison began his discussion of the separation of powers by again applying the epistemology of constitutional analysis laid down in *Federalist* 37. The first challenge was to produce a proper definition of the concept, to develop a precision and consistency in usage that the rhetorical conventions of political argument often muddied or obscured. Madison was a strong Lockean. Distilling Book 3 of the *Essay Concerning Human Understanding*, he noted that "no language is so complex as to supply words and phrases for every complex idea, or so correct as not to include many equivocally connoting different ideas" (*Fed.* 37, 236). One had to obtain as much accuracy or "perspicuity" – a word we no longer use – as possible in the use of political terms.[21]

Separation of powers offered a preeminent example of the difficulty of this enterprise. As Madison further observed in *Federalist* 37, in an oft-cited passage,

> Experience has instructed us that no skill in the science of government has yet been able to discriminate and define, with sufficient certainty, its three great provinces the legislative, executive, and judiciary; or even the privileges and powers of the different legislative branches. Questions daily occur in the course of practice, which prove the obscurity which reigns in these subjects, and which puzzle the greatest adepts in political science.
>
> (*Fed.* 37, 235)

Madison certainly numbered himself among those adepts, and with his colleagues in this field, he ranked "the celebrated Montesquieu" atop the authorities who had shaped this idea. Locke, too, had discussed separation of powers in the *Second Treatise*, but in accord with conventional English practice, he collapsed judicial and executive power while treating "federative" power – the authority to deal with foreign nations that could not be bound by domestic law – as a distinct category, generally (but not necessarily) subsumed by the executive. Montesquieu's great claim to fame in this area was to make judicial power a third independent branch of domestic governance.

But how did Montesquieu and his American acolytes – including the authors of the first state constitutions – actually understand the concept? "Because the British constitution was to Montesquieu what Homer had been to the didactic writers on modern poetry," (*Fed.* 47, 324), Madison observed, the best way to decipher Montesquieu's meaning involved asking how (or how far) British practice in fact did separate the various powers. So, too, with the Americans: It was not enough to cite the various clauses in the state constitutions that treated the three departments as hermetically enclosed entities, never the trio to meet. One also had to reason inductively from observed practice. From these observations of the British and American cases, Madison reasoned, the eighteenth-century notion of separation of powers meant little more than avoiding a situation where the authority of one entire branch of government essentially subsumed the authority of another. That was as limited a definition as one could provide, and it left open a vast field for a scheme of checks and balances in which authority would be effectively shared.

Definition marked the first but only preliminary stage of this analysis. The next and more important task was "to provide some practical security for each" branch "against the invasion of the others." To create a "practical security" meant identifying the real sources of encroachment, and to Madison's experience-driven mode of thinking, having collected "vouchers in abundance" from the states, it was obvious that this danger lay in the legislature, which "is everywhere extending the sphere of its activity, and drawing all power into its impetuous vortex." This was a danger that the authors of the state constitutions had never foreseen. They assumed that the executive was the great threat. "But in a representative republic" the legislature enjoyed two advantages over the other branches: "the intrepid confidence" it felt because of its influence over the people; and the superiority it wielded from its rulemaking authority, which allowed it to "mask, under complicated and indirect measures, the encroachments which it makes on the coordinate departments" (*Fed.* 48, 332–35). Here, again, Madison combined two modes of analysis, one resting on the assertive attitudes that legislators gained from their direct *political* ties to the people, the other deriving from their *legal* superiority in the enactment of legislation, the great concern that had driven Madison's constitutional thinking since 1785.

Yet this analysis left two important questions unasked. First, on what basis would a bicameral legislature collaborate in encroachments on the weaker two departments? In the ratification debates of 1787–88, Anti-Federalists argued that the preeminent threat to maintaining a proper separation of powers would emanate not from the House but from the Senate, the one institution that possessed all three forms of power.[22] Madison did not address this question directly. Second, what would be the real source of legislative misbehavior: the improper ambitions and ends of lawmakers, colluding *in camera*; or the pressure that representatives would experience from their constituents out-of-doors?

Madison could have answered these questions immediately. But instead *Federalist* 49 and 50 diverted his readers to consider a topic no one else was discussing: Jefferson's proposal, in his draft of a revised constitution for Virginia, to make violations of the separation of powers subject to review by popularly elected conventions. In effect, Madison was dragging from literary obscurity a proposal that would operate as a popular alternative to an institutional separation of powers enforced by checks and balances. The conventions could meet either occasionally, when a crisis warranted, or periodically, like the Pennsylvania council of censors. In either case, such conventions could claim one sovereign virtue. They would represent "the people themselves," the original source of republican sovereignty, and thus the body that "can alone declare its true meaning and enforce its observance" (*Fed.* 49, 339). But that claim to authority did not outweigh the prudential calculations that cut in the opposite direction. The people could never act as the best guardians of a constitution, Madison argued. Some working scheme of checks and balances among the departments was the only mechanism available for preserving the Constitution.

Madison's repudiation of Jefferson's proposal was both respectful yet vigorous. He began by reminding readers that the stability of a constitution would often depend on its popular "veneration." The more frequently Jefferson's proposal was used, he warned, the less constitutional veneration the people would feel. But this loss of veneration would also reflect the lack of confidence individual citizens would feel in their own judgment. Popular opinion would fall prey to the passions of the masses. Americans had to recall the favorable circumstances that had converged to make their first acts of constitution writing, a decade earlier, a relatively harmonious enterprise. Those conditions might not exist in the future. Indeed, the quarrels that were likely to generate the need for a revisionary convention might well illustrate the prior existence of disruptive factions.[23]

Yet beyond these general cautions lay "the greatest objection of all," which again involved identifying the most likely source of danger. If the dominant "tendency of republican government is to an aggrandizement of the legislative at the expense of the other departments," then the most likely source of "appeals to the people" would come from the politically weaker executive and judiciary. In the ensuing competition to sway public opinion, all the political advantages would fall to the legislature. They were more numerous, enjoyed many more ties to their constituents, and naturally appeared to act as "the confidential guardians of the rights and liberties of the people" (*Fed.* 49, 341–42). Here, again, the vector driving the debate would be the close political connection between the people and their elected representatives.

Admittedly, there could be occasions when the abuse of legislative power would produce an appeal to the people from a popular executive. Yet even then this procedure would be subject to fatal flaws. In Madison's harsh judgment, the resolution of questions of this kind "could never be expected to turn on the true merits of the question." This whole mechanism of constitutional deliberation would be too politicized from the outset, too tied to "the spirit of pre-existing parties, or of parties springing out of the question itself," or to the doings of influential individuals, to produce a reasoned resolution. "The *passions* therefore not the *reason*, of the public, would sit in judgment. But it is the reason of the public alone, that ought to controul and regulate the government" (*Fed.* 49, 342–43). In this view of things, political reason, as it applied to constitutional questions, could only be the product of institutional deliberations, which needed as much insulation as possible from popular passions. The moment would never recur, it seemed, when the people could exercise their sovereign constitutional authority.

Over the course of the next decade, Madison's views on this matter did change. When he wrote the "party press" essays in 1791–92, he began to view the electorate as political monitors of constitutional landmarks. As party competition escalated during the rest of the decade, he and Jefferson realized that elections could serve as decisive tests of constitutional beliefs. But the Madison who wrote as Publius in 1787–88 operated under different assumptions. Then his dominant concern still lay with the potential abuse of legislative power, and his dominant fear was the role that the people themselves would play in fomenting that misuse.

When Madison returned to his main subject in *Federalist* 51, there were many more things he could have said about the constitutional scheme of separated powers. At the Convention, he had preferred the idea of an *ex ante* judicial role in the council of revision as a mechanism for improving the quality of legislation to an *ex post* judicial review of the constitutionality of laws already enacted. As with his negative on state laws, he had no motive to discuss that now. But Madison certainly knew the arguments for judicial review well enough to have restated them in *Federalist* 51. The same could be said for the presidential veto on legislation, which got a cursory treatment in the lone paragraph of *Federalist* 51 that explicitly discussed the separation of powers. There was much more he could have written about how separation would work in practice. Instead readers are left with the famous motivational statement that "Ambition must be made to counteract ambition" and the puzzle of understanding why the Senate is actually "the weaker branch of the stronger department." Explaining how the separation of powers would actually work was, in the end, a subject that almost bored Madison, even if these essays do contain some memorable quotes. If indeed "questions daily occur in the course of practice, which prove the obscurity which reigns in these subjects," as *Federalist* 37 had stated, why bother to spend too much time worrying about them here?

Federalist 51 is thus remarkable for how little it says about its ostensible subject – except that its final paragraphs, restating the argument of *Federalist* 10, still indicate why these two essays remain the *locus classicus* of the concept of the Madisonian constitution. Beyond the institutional division of power within the national government, Madison observed, "two considerations particularly applicable to the federal system of America" also bear emphasis. The first he dispatched quickly in a paragraph that echoes *Federalist* 46. "In the compound republic of America," the division of authority between the nation and the states, each composed of the new trinity of departments, will provide "a double security" protecting "the rights of the people" that does not exist in other governments (*Fed.* 51, 350–51). The essential facts of federalism will compensate for the ambiguities of separated powers.

The critical second consideration follows, for it does nothing less than invert the discussion of this whole series of essays by returning to the central thesis of *Federalist* 10. "It is of great importance in a republic not only to guard the society against the oppression of its rulers, but to guard one part of the society against the injustice of the other part." For Madison, the second half of this sentence, not the first, defined the true problem of rights in a republic. The political force that really mattered, the power that had to be checked, belonged less to the government than to the people out-of-doors, or rather to the dominant interests and potentially factious majorities within society. As republicans, Americans could not erect a "power independent of the society" – a hereditary aristocracy or monarchy – to mediate their disputes. They had to rely instead on the diversity of interests and classes that would characterize "the federal republic." Should too many small new states be formed, akin to notorious Rhode Island, the security of rights would be weakened as "factious majorities" flourished within their provincial boundaries. But "In the extended republic of the United States, and among the great variety of interests, parties, and sects which it embraces," this danger would diminish, for legislative majorities would "seldom take place on any other principles than those of justice and the general good," the two normative lodestars of Madison's thinking (*Fed.* 51, 351–53). The true solution to the problem of separated powers did not require further exercises in constitutional engineering among the branches of government, but rather grasping the benefits to be derived from the diversity of interests out-of-doors, in that extensive and expanding society. Three years later, when drafting his "Notes on Government" with the putative ambition of writing a treatise on republican government, this was the matter that Madison still deemed worthy of a "thorough investigation."

Yet that treatise regrettably remained unwritten, and after 1792 Madison's constitutional thoughts followed a different trajectory. From Washington's second administration on, he was increasingly concerned with issues of foreign relations and the political dimensions of presidential power, a matter he had not taken that seriously in the late 1780s. In 1787 it had been difficult, even impossible, to grasp the political potentiality of the presidency. Once foreign relations began to dominate the agenda of government, as they manifestly did after 1793, Madison came to realize that control of the government depended on control of the presidency. That concern naturally led him to revisit the problem of separated powers, especially when the wielding of the powers that John Locke had called "federative" by Washington and John Adams sparked points of friction with the American constitutional system. Equally important, the capacity of the Federalist and Republican parties to identify two national candidates for the presidency in 1796 demonstrated that the calculus of political competition had changed, to an extent that none of the framers of the Constitution ever imagined. Here were "vouchers in abundance" of new political facts that Madison spent much of the 1790s exploring, and reminders, to his later commentators, that Madison's best political thinking was always empirical in nature.

NOTES

1 The editors of the Madison papers give the heading "Notes for the National Gazette Essays," but I follow Colleen Sheehan in believing that "Notes on Government" makes more sense. Sheehan reprints these notes and other related documents, with excellent scholarly annotation, in *The Mind of James Madison: The Legacy of Classical Republicanism* (New York: Cambridge University Press, 2015), 127, 129.

2 *PJM*, XIV, 158–59.

3 Ibid., 160.

4 I pursue this distinction at some length in Jack Rakove, *A Politician Thinking: The Creative Mind of James Madison* (Norman: University of Oklahoma Press, 2017).

5 Consider, for example, the interpretations of the Declaration of Independence presented in Danielle Allen, *Our Declaration: A Reading of the Declaration of Independence in Defense of Equality* (New York: Liveright, 2014), which pivots in part on the punctuation of its Preamble; Jay Fliegelman, *Declaring Independence: Jefferson, Natural Language, and the Culture of Performance* (Stanford, CA: Stanford University Press, 1993); and Pauline Maier, *American Scripture: Making the Declaration of Independence* (New York: Alfred A. Knopf, 1997).

6 Mary Bilder, *Madison's Hand: Revising the Constitutional Convention* (Cambridge, MA: Harvard University Press, 2015), 158–59, 288–89 n. 8, 308–09 n. 13.

7 Paul Bourke, "The Pluralist Reading of James Madison's Tenth Federalist," *Perspectives in American History*, 9 (1975), 271–95.

8 See Woody Holton, *Unruly Americans and the Origins of the Constitution* (New York: Hill and Wang, 2007), and Michael Klarman, *The Framers' Coup: The Making of the United States Constitution* (New York: Oxford University Press, 2016).

9 Douglas Adair, "The Tenth Federalist Revisited," and "'That Politics May Be Reduced to a Science': David Hume, James Madison, and the Tenth Federalist," reprinted in Trevor Colbourn, ed., *Fame and the Founding Fathers: Essays by Douglas Adair* (Chapel Hill: University of North Carolina Press, 1974), 75–106. The essays were originally published in 1951 and 1957.

10 Madison to James Monroe, October 5, 1786, in *PJM*, IX, 140–41; Madison, Vices of the Political System, *PJM*, IX, 353–57 (for this and the following paragraph).

11 Madison to Caleb Wallace, August 23, 1785, ibid., VIII, 350–51.

12 Gordon S. Wood, "Is There a 'James Madison Problem'?" in Wood, *Revolutionary Characters: What Made the Founders Different* (New York: Penguin, 2006), 161–64; and see Christine Desan, "The Constitutional Commitment to Legislative Adjudication in the Early American Tradition," *Harvard Law Review*, 111 (1997–98), 1381–503.

13 Madison to Edmund Randolph, March 1, 1789, in *PJM*, XI, 453; and see Jack Rakove, "The Structure of Politics at the Accession of George Washington," in Richard Beeman et al., eds., *Beyond Confederation: Origins of the Constitution and American National Identity* (Chapel Hill: University of North Carolina Press, 1987), 286–88.

14 Ibid., 271–73 and sources cited in nn. 21–22.

15 Madison to Caleb Wallace, August 23, 1785, in *PJM*, VIII, 354.

16 Jack N. Rakove, "A Model for Deliberation or Obstruction: Madison's Thoughts about the Senate," in Benjamin Wittes and Pietro Nivola, eds., *What Would Madison Do? The Father of the Constitution Meets Modern American Politics* (Washington, DC: Brookings Institution, 2015), 124–27.

17 Madison to Caleb Wallace, August 23, 1785, in *PJM*, VIII, 350–51.

18 *RFC*, I, 527.

19 Madison to Jefferson, October 17, 1788, *PJM*, XI, 297–99.

20 Rakove, *A Politician Thinking*, 138–45.

21 See Hannah Dawson, "Locke on Language in (Civil) Society," *History of Political Thought*, 26 (2005), 398–425.

22 Jack Rakove, *Original Meanings: Politics and Ideas in the Making of the Constitution* (New York: Alfred A. Knopf, 1996), 268–75.

23 For a more skeptical view of Madison's thoughts about veneration, see Jeremy D. Bailey, *James Madison and Constitutional Imperfection* (New York: Cambridge University Press, 2015), 15–37.

12 "The Cool and Deliberate Sense of the Community"

The Federalist *on Congress*

Greg Weiner

The American civic canon holds that the Constitution creates three branches of government that are both separate and "equal." Publius's essays on Congress cast serious doubt on this supposition, at least with respect to the extent of each branch's influence on the workings of the national regime. It is no mistake that both the Constitution and *The Federalist* treat Congress as the first branch of government. It is "justly regarded" as such, Louis Fisher says, primarily because of the appropriations power elucidated in *Federalist* 58.[1] *The Federalist* understands Congress, George W. Carey writes, "to be the heart of the proposed system."[2] Even the doubts and concerns that Publius expresses about Congress reflect regard for its authority. *Federalist* 51, for example, acknowledges that the legislature "necessarily predominates" (*Fed.* 51, 350) in a republic, but it also seeks a remedy for the "inconveniency" this poses to the separation of powers. Institutionally, Congress has the power both to constitute and discipline the other branches, which have no comparable authority over it.[3] Even when defending executive energy, Publius describes it as secondary to legislative deliberation.[4] The centrality of the legislative branch is demonstrable not only institutionally but also theoretically, for it is here that Publius places his greatest hopes for solving one of his most fundamental problems: the reconciliation of a government with sufficient authority and energy on the one hand, with the preservation of both public and personal liberty, on the other – a concern that Hamilton and Madison respectively expressed in *Federalist* 1 and 37.

The answer to that problem is to construct a regime in which majorities rule but are likeliest to behave in a manner most consistent with "the rights of other citizens" and "the permanent and aggregate interests of the community" (*Fed.* 10, 57). That is not the only problem that Publius faces, but it is a paramount one, and the legislature necessarily lies at the center of its resolution. Publius's solution to this problem is bound by his fidelity to the "fundamental principle of free government," majority rule (*Fed.* 58, 397). The challenge is to find ways to discipline majority rule from within the confines of a majoritarian system. Publius does so by erecting a prime mover in government – the legislature – that is institutionally prone to deliberation and the seasoning effects of delay, which diffuses popular passions, and which enables the people to favor their long-term interests over their immediate appetites.

The comprehensive vision of Congress portrayed in *The Federalist* is best understood through the collective eyes of its pseudonymous author, Publius. This is partly because *The Federalist* is not intended to express the private intentions of its authors. On the contrary, its particular value lies in its presentation of a political understanding of the Constitution, one that reflected the compromises and accommodations of diverse and powerful minds. The principal authors of the essays on Congress, Alexander Hamilton and James Madison, agreed neither wholly with each other nor each privately with what they wrote in *The Federalist*. Their essays reflect a rough division of labor according to which Hamilton wrote many of the papers on the powers of Congress, while Madison's themes tended toward assuring that those powers were reasonably exercised. Even within this division, there is overlap: Hamilton in *Federalist* 15 emphasizes the value of "deliberations" over "hurry[ing] into improprieties and excess" (*Fed.* 15, 96) a theme that also preoccupies Madison. Madison, by contrast, observes in *Federalist* 41 that "necessary" powers must be granted, especially since all powers are subject to abuse (*Fed.* 41, 268–69). It is generally the case that Publius unifies Hamilton and Madison behind the conclusion that the legislature must have adequate powers, and because it must, those powers must be channeled toward thoughtful uses.

POWERS OF CONGRESS

That Congress is such a prime mover is evident through the powers Publius accords to it. According to *Federalist* 15, government itself is associated with "the power of making laws" (*Fed.* 15, 95) while Publius indicates in *Federalist* 40 that the resolution of the Continental Congress authorizing the Philadelphia Convention of 1787 called for a government "adequate to the exigencies of the union" (*Fed.* 40, 258). This government's sphere will be limited, but within it, its powers will be extensive; indeed, some will, like the exigencies themselves, be incapable of "precise bounds." This Constitution accords adequate power for "every possible contingency ... somewhere in the government" (*Fed.* 26, 156).

The succeeding essays, 41 through 43, explore those powers in detail. Jack Rakove notes that these essays assert unlimited national power with respect to defense and taxation while emphasizing the limited ends of national authority in other areas.[5] These authorities are typically vested in the Congress, so much so that Publius often refers to the powers of the national government and the powers of the Congress interchangeably. *Federalist* 41 is entitled "A General view of the powers proposed to be vested in the union," but the analysis that follows refers almost exclusively and specifically to the powers of Congress. Publius indicates that the Union will have six classes of powers: security, international commerce, maintaining harmony among states, "miscellaneous objects of general utility," restraining states from abuse, and, finally, "[p]rovisions for giving due efficacy to all these powers" (*Fed.* 41, 269).

Each of these categories largely addresses a power of Congress. Even the heading "[s]ecurity against foreign danger" refers immediately to the power to declare war before proceeding to the clearly legislative responsibilities to raise and equip armies and navies and call forth the militia. Of the remaining powers, the only ones not obviously legislative are the restraints on the states that appear in Article 1, Section 9 of the Constitution. Their inclusion in the legislative article is thus highly suggestive. Publius's discussion of the

Guarantee Clause of Article IV is the only exception to this rule, and even in that case, the Supreme Court in *Luther v. Borden* ultimately ruled that it was for Congress to decide whether a state's government was republican.[6] By the end of *Federalist* 44, James Burnham notes, Publius pronounces his discussion of the powers of the federal government complete even though he has only discussed the powers of Congress at this point.[7]

Publius asserts repeatedly that Congress has only the powers specifically enumerated for it. *Federalist* 56, for example, denies that representatives need a comprehensive acquaintance with every interest of their constituents because they will have to be familiar only with those affecting "objects within the purview of [Congressional] authority" (*Fed.* 56, 379). Yet *within* that purview, he is equally clear that the limits of those powers themselves are difficult to specify, so that *where* the Congress has the power, the working extent of its authority is not easily defined. These powers are laterally but not vertically enumerated. Publius specifically contrasts the nature of legislative with executive and judicial power by saying the latter two can be clearly bounded while the first is "less susceptible of precise limits" (*Fed.* 48, 334). The clearest example of this broad nature is the power to provide for defense, which must be unlimited because potential dangers to national security are unlimited, too (*Fed.* 23, 148–49). The "direction" of the forces is of course an executive function, but their formation and support are plainly legislative. *Federalist* 31 denies the possibility of carefully defining all powers: "I repeat here what I have observed in substance in another place, that all observations, founded upon the danger of usurpation, ought to be referred to the composition and structure of the government, not to the nature and extent of its powers" (*Fed.* 31, 197).

The centerpiece of this "composition and structure" is the separation of powers, and far from seeking to cramp congressional powers, Publius says they are a vital part of the system's maintenance. This is especially true of the power of the purse, which *Federalist* 58 calls the most potent weapon for preventing executive aggrandizement. "This power over the purse may, in fact, be regarded as the most complete and effectual weapon, with which any constitution can arm the immediate representatives of the people, for obtaining a redress of every grievance, and for carrying into effect every just and salutary measure" (*Fed.* 58, 394).

Yet Publius also frankly recognizes the potential abuse of legislative powers: "[I]n every political institution, a power to advance the public happiness, involves a discretion which may be misapplied and abused" (*Fed.* 41, 269). The real question, he explains, is whether the powers are necessary.

> It cannot have escaped those, who have attended with candour to the arguments employed against the extensive powers of the government, that the authors of them have very little considered how far these powers were necessary means of attaining a necessary end. They have chosen rather to dwell on the inconveniencies which must be unavoidably blended with all political advantages; and on the possible abuses which must be incident to every power or trust, of which a beneficial use can be made.
>
> (*Fed.* 41, 268)

This analysis merits careful notice. If the powers are necessary, the risk of their abuse appears to be worthwhile. The passage illustrates the primacy Publius places on the public good. How to restrain authority is a vital yet derivative question, which is to say that once society determines it requires a set of authorities for the public good, the question is how to encourage their responsible use. Publius provides several reasons to believe Congress will do so: the device of representation, bicameralism, the size of the respective bodies, the length of their terms, and the tools with which the executive is empowered to check the legislature.

REPRESENTATION

In *Federalist 9*, Publius ranks "the representation of the people in the legislature, by deputies of their own election" as one of the improvements in "the science of politics" that make republican government more practicable in modern than in ancient times (*Fed.* 9, 51). Representation, he further explains in *Federalist* 63, was not wholly unknown to the ancients, but the key innovation, reflecting modern improvements on classical practice, is the *"total exclusion of the people, in their collective capacity,* from any share" in American government (*Fed.* 63, 428, emphasis in original). That power would be exercised solely through the mediating device of representation.

Yet the nature of that representation was hotly disputed. Anti-Federalists generally hewed to what may be best understood as a "reflective" model of representation according to which the legislature should mirror the people in both composition and views. The Federal Farmer thus asserted that "a full and equal representation, is that which possesses the same interests, feelings, opinions, and views the people themselves would were they all assembled."[8] Publius, by contrast, specifically denies in *Federalist* 35 that it is necessary for the House of Representatives to mirror the people in composition (*Fed.* 218–21). *Federalist* 57 emphasizes that everyone is equally eligible for service in the House – "[n]ot the rich, more than the poor; not the learned, more than the ignorant; not the haughty heirs of distinguished names, more than the humble sons of obscure and unpropitious fortune" – but it is not important that elections produce an exact simulacrum of the populace (*Fed.* 57, 385). It is more important that the "interests and feelings" of the people be "understood" and "attended to" – "sympathy," in Publius's Scottish terminology – a task of which representatives will be capable. He thus explains that "[t]he aim of every political constitution is, or ought to be, first, to obtain for rulers men who possess most wisdom to discern, and most virtue to pursue, the common good of the society; and in the next place, to take the most effectual precautions for keeping them virtuous, whilst they continue to hold their public trust." It bears observation that part of virtue is maintaining one's trust to the people, but this also clearly includes exercising judgment as to the "common good," which comes "first" and is "common," not "personal." These representatives will be "distinguished by the preference of their fellow citizens" and thus presumably will exhibit the qualities that "entitle them to" that preference (*Fed.* 57, 384–85).

This understanding of representation is best understood as "refractive" as opposed to "reflective" because its purpose is to focus rather than reflect the public views. In Daniel W. Howe's phrase, representation is a "refining process in which higher faculties ... [are] sorted out, concentrated, and strengthened."[9] This conception is most clearly expressed in the well-known prediction of *Federalist* 10 that an extensive republic will yield representatives best able to "refine and enlarge" the public views. The public views remain the raw material, so to speak, with which the representative works to fashion coherent policy. This is not a fundamentally anti-democratic or anti-majoritarian point of view. Contrast this with, for example, Edmund Burke's famous view of representation, which held that the representative's judgment is ultimately independent from the views of his constituents because he owes his judgment to an independent and objective moral good it is up to him to ascertain. This notion of refinement and enlargement might be compatible with either Colleen Sheehan's understanding that Publius (as James Madison) seeks the formation of public opinion into a dedication to the common good or Alan Gibson's emphasis on impartiality in representation. Both conceptions seek to focus rather than merely reflect the public views.[10]

The question, then, is how institutionally to assure, first, these representatives' fidelity and, second, their deliberativeness. These problems and the solutions to them are linked, beginning with bicameralism.

BICAMERALISM

Bicameralism – the practice of dividing the legislative authority into two chambers – was almost universally practiced in the American states. Publius explains that the first reason for bicameralism is to protect the public against faithless representatives: The Constitution "doubles the security to the people, by requiring the concurrence of two distinct bodies in schemes of usurpation or perfidy, where the ambition or corruption of one would otherwise be sufficient" (*Fed.* 62, 418). Publius means no more here than that it will take, so to speak, two keys to launch a missile. He had said in *Federalist* 51 that a purpose of bicameralism was to divide the legislative authority because it was the strongest and thus the likeliest to encroach on the other branches. Here his point is that it is likeliest to encroach on the people.

Publius proceeds to say that the dissimilar composition of the two chambers, which are chosen by different mechanisms, makes their cooperation in perfidious schemes even more difficult. However, they should be distinguished only "by every circumstance which will consist with a due harmony in all proper measures, and with the genuine principles of republican government" (*Fed.* 62, 418). The capacity of the legislature to do what legislatures need to do – which complies with the republican principle according to which majorities should be able to work their deliberate will – superintends the concern about abuse. Publius claims in the succeeding essay that "[t]he people can never wilfully betray their own interests: But they may possibly be betrayed by the representatives of the people; and the danger will be evidently greater, where the whole legislative trust is lodged in the hands of one body of men, than where the concurrence of separate and dissimilar bodies is required in every public act" (*Fed.* 63, 426–27).

Bicameralism also facilitates deliberation. Publius warns in *Federalist* 62 of "the propensity of all single and numerous assemblies, to yield to the impulse of sudden and violent passions, and to be seduced by factious leaders into intemperate and pernicious resolutions" (*Fed.* 62, 418). Publius's concern with passion offers important clues to his ideals of deliberation, which is needed to reconcile the turbulence of majority rule with the task of securing the public good and private rights. The temptation for deliberative assemblies is "passion," which Publius describes in terms of its "sudden" and also "violent" shifts, often producing resolutions that are not only "pernicious" but also "intemperate."

The solution to this is to constitute legislative bodies that are small enough and serve for sufficient terms that passions do not spread or, if they do, have time to dissipate. Publius specifies that large assemblies are more prone to passion, apparently because of the relative anonymity of their members. The terms of Congress play a central role in slowing these passions by giving members of Congress time to cast controversial votes while still having time – as emotions cool – to recover their popularity before they face reelection. This is the keystone of Publius's institutional architecture for Congress. It is what will distinguish it from a direct democracy, which is incapable of deliberation.

INSTITUTIONAL ARCHITECTURE: THE HOUSE

Publius is tasked first with defending the Constitution's departure from the almost sacred American tradition of annual elections. He begins his discussion of the two-year terms for representatives by explaining that the House in particular "should have an immediate dependence on, and an intimate sympathy with the people" (*Fed.* 52, 355). This sympathy – initially obtained by the Constitution's specification that the House will be chosen by the same voters who choose the lower house of state legislatures – can be secured only by "[f]requent elections." These frequent elections "support in the members an habitual recollection of their dependence on the people," such that before power can go to their heads, they must "anticipate the moment when their power is to cease, when their exercise of it is to be reviewed, and when they must descend to the level from which they were raised; there for ever to remain, unless a faithful discharge of their trust shall have established their title to a renewal of it" (*Fed.* 57, 386).

Citing *Federalist* 52, David Mayhew regards reelection as the only dependable tie between representatives and constituents for purposes of either empirical analysis or accountability, but Publius writes that there is no "precise calculation" that can indicate how frequent these elections must be.[11] Significantly, Publius rejects abstract reason in favor of historical exploration: "Let us consult experience, the guide that ought always to be followed whenever it can be found" (*Fed.* 52, 355). He finds that relevant examples of representatives' terms, including the experience of the American colonies prior to the Revolution, range as high as seven years, which suggests that two-year terms are amply safe. Reminding his reader of the aphorism that "where annual elections end, tyranny begins," Publius replies that it would be absurd to connect the "sun or the seasons" with "the period within which human virtue can bear the temptations of power." Instead of being "confined to any single point of time," liberty "lies within extremes, which afford sufficient latitude for all the variations which may be required by the various situations and circumstances of civil society" (*Fed.* 53, 359–60).

Publius surmises that the eagerness for one-year terms arises from an assumption that the House can alter its own power, yet – and here Publius most clearly distinguishes fundamental and statutory law – this will not be the case under the proposed Constitution. "The important distinction, so well understood in America, between a constitution established by the people, and unalterable by the government; and a law established by the government, and alterable by the government, seems to have been little understood, and less observed in any other country." Lacking a written constitution and thus any permanent security for freedom, one's natural tendency is to keep representatives on a short leash. In the United States, the fact that representative terms cannot be changed by "the ordinary power of the government" makes them safer than those in governments in which terms are shorter but alterable (*Fed.* 53, 360–61).

Moreover, since "the federal legislature will possess a part only of that supreme legislative authority" that the British Parliament and colonial assemblies exercised completely, it can be trusted with longer terms: "It is a received and well founded maxim, that, where no other circumstances affect the case, the greater the power is, the shorter ought to be its duration; and, conversely, the smaller the power, the more safely may its duration be protracted" (*Fed.* 52, 358). Biennial elections are not only safe, they are also "useful," one reason being that a legislator acquires skill by means of both "information" and "experience," both of which require time, especially when one is unfamiliar with the more diverse objects of federal legislation.

Another reason, perhaps less obviously stated, for these two-year terms is to assure an appropriate constitutional distance between the legislators and the people so as to facilitate deliberation. For the same reason, the House should be relatively small. Well before proceeding to the design of the chamber, Publius has already identified the challenge in *Federalist* 10: "In the first place, it is to be remarked, that however small the republic may be, the representatives must be raised to a certain number, in order to guard against the cabals of a few; and that, however large it may be, they must be limited to a certain number, in order to guard against the confusion of a multitude" (*Fed.* 10, 62–63). In *Federalist* 55, defending the initial constitution of the House at sixty-five members – a number that opponents of the Constitution assailed as insufficient to represent the diversity of the country – Publius denies that one can "found our political calculations on arithmetical principles." Bigger is not necessarily better. One of the most famous passages from Publius's pen follows. The size of assemblies should occupy a mean between being too small – in which case there might be too few individuals and ideas present for meaningful deliberation to occur – and too large, which might lead to chaos. "Had every Athenian citizen been a Socrates, every Athenian assembly would still have been a mob" (*Fed.* 55, 374).

According to this robust assertion about human nature, we appear to be all but incapable of retaining our wits in large groups, even those "fit characters" whom Publius had predicted in *Federalist* 10 would naturally rise to the top of an extensive republic. The reason seems to be a combination of the close contagion of passions and the faceless anonymity that operates in such settings. Moreover, Publius explains in *Federalist* 58, "in all legislative assemblies, the greater the number composing them may be, the fewer will be the men who will in fact direct their proceedings" (*Fed.* 58, 395). The reason for this is both what we have already seen – that passion gains the advantage over reason in large assemblies – but also a sort of converse of *Federalist* 10's prediction that a large republic would produce more high-quality representatives. The larger the assembly, he explains, the larger the number of "members of limited information and of weak capacities," who will naturally be the dupes of their eloquent and manipulative colleagues (*Fed.* 58, 396).

This suggests that Publius wants power diffused through the representative body rather than controlled by a handful of elite leaders, which arises from his basic commitment to majority rule. Add to this Publius's striking answer to the question of how Americans can be confident that the sixty-five House members elected will not be tyrants. Publius – contrary to the portraits of him by, among others, American Progressives like the historian Charles Beard as an aristocrat seeking to enchain the populace – trusts the people. Significantly, excessive caution about abuses appears in this passage as a "passion":

> The sincere friends of liberty, who give themselves up to the extravagancies of this passion, are not aware of the injury they do their own cause. As there is a degree of depravity in mankind, which requires a certain degree of circumspection and distrust: so there are other qualities in human nature, which justify a certain portion of esteem and confidence. Republican government presupposes the existence of these qualities in a higher degree than any other form.
>
> (*Fed.* 55, 378)

For this reason, Publius makes a seemingly un-Publian declaration: "I am equally unable to conceive, that there are at this time, or can be in any short time in the United States, any sixty-five or an hundred men, capable of recommending themselves to the choice of the people at large, who would either desire or dare, within the short space of two years, to betray the solemn trust committed to them" (*Fed.* 55, 376). Accordingly, Publius not only trusts the people, he trusts those whom they elect. One of the assurances he provides is that these representatives will have to abide by the laws they pass, a principle "that has always been deemed one of the strongest bonds by which human policy can connect the rulers and the people together" (*Fed.* 57, 386). Yet that leaves the reader to wonder what will compel them to do so. Publius answers: "the genius of the whole system; the nature of just and constitutional laws; and, above all, the vigilant and manly spirit which actuates the people of America; a spirit which nourishes freedom, and in return is nourished by it" (*Fed.* 57, 387). This, again, is striking, as it seems more a political than an institutional solution. Of course, "the genius of the whole system" includes the separation of powers and bicameralism. But Publius recalls that the Constitution ultimately relies on a vigilant public even to maintain mechanisms such as that. "If this spirit shall ever be so far debased, as to tolerate a law not obligatory on the legislature, as well as on the people, the people will be prepared to tolerate anything but liberty" (*Fed.* 57, 387).

INSTITUTIONAL ARCHITECTURE: THE SENATE

One reason for confidence about his commitment to majority rule is that Publius accords popular authority space in which to operate. Thus six-year Senate terms – and the Senate more broadly – serve a particular purpose, a substantial part of which is stabilizing the political system. While this may seem at first blush like an anti-republican function, Publius does not see it that way. He notes on several occasions the propensity of the American legislatures to change laws frequently at the behest of immediate majorities, but he explains in *Federalist* 62 that this operates to the detriment of settled majorities, who will not be comforted "if the laws be so voluminous that they cannot be read, or so incoherent that they cannot be understood: if they be repealed or revised before they are promulged, or undergo such incessant changes, that no man who knows what the law is to-day, can guess what it will be to-morrow" (*Fed.* 62, 421). Under such circumstances, no one will "hazard his fortunes" in investment or entrepreneurial activity. Worse still, evoking Aristotle and reinforcing a point he had made in *Federalist* 49, Publius explains that constantly changing laws induce "that diminution of attachment and reverence, which steals into the hearts of the people, towards a political system which betrays so many marks of infirmity, and disappoints so many of their flattering hopes" (*Fed.* 63, 422).

He goes further: Not only does mutable legislation harm majorities, it also empowers minorities. Allowing the people to insist on as many laws or changes in laws as they like may seem democratic, but Madison argues it will have the opposite effect. Only "the sagacious, the enterprising, and the moneyed few" can monitor and exploit the changes, which gives them an advantage "over the industrious and uninformed mass of the people... This is a state of things in which it may be said, with some truth, that laws are made for the few, not for the many" (*Fed.* 62, 421).

Six-year Senate terms are Publius's steadying answer: the foundation of an institution that will "blend stability with liberty" (*Fed.* 63, 426). There are other stabilizing influences in the Senate – members must be older, and, as Gary C. Jacobson and Jamie L. Carson emphasize, only a third of the body turns over with each election, a device so important that Publius says the Senate would be more stable with terms a third of the length, or two years, yet only gradually turning over, than with triple the length, or eighteen years, but with the entire body changing at once (*Fed.* 61, 413–14).[12] Publius writes that, ironically, these terms increase dependence on the people by making one body responsible for the long-term consequences of legislation. This may raise the concern that they will permit an aristocracy to entrench itself, but Publius's answer to this concern is suggestive: "To this general answer, the general reply ought to be sufficient; that liberty may be endangered by the abuses of liberty, as well as by the abuses of power; that there are numerous instances of the former, as well as of the latter; and that the former, rather than the latter, is apparently most to be apprehended by the United States"

(*Fed.* 63, 428–29). The underlying concern here is the protection of liberty, not the protection of power; the question is merely what endangers it in this particular political culture. He proceeds to explain that a senate, to accomplish such a "revolution," would have to "corrupt itself"; corrupt the state legislatures, which elect it; corrupt the House, whose authority is coordinate with it; and, significantly, "must finally corrupt the people at large," who remain the ultimate safeguard for liberty.

Most importantly, these six-year terms permit the dissipation of public passions. This mechanism works because passions are, by their very nature, transient. Thus *Federalist* 63 avers that the Senate will help defend "the people against their own temporary errors and delusions":

> As the cool and deliberate sense of the community ought, in all governments, and actually will, in all free governments, ultimately prevail over the views of its rulers: so there are particular moments in public affairs, when the people, stimulated by some irregular passion, or some illicit advantage, or misled by the artful misrepresentations of interested men, may call for measures which they themselves will afterwards be the most ready to lament and condemn. In these critical moments, how salutary will be the interference of some temperate and respectable body of citizens, in order to check the misguided career, and to suspend the blow meditated by the people against themselves, until reason, justice, and truth, can regain their authority over the public mind?
>
> (*Fed.* 63, 425)

This passage in many ways encapsulates Madison's democratic theory.[13] First, its empirical and normative elements converge. The sense of the community *should* prevail in *all* governments, but it is particularly the case in free governments that it *will* prevail regardless. Second, it is a particular kind of sense: the "cool and deliberate" one, which – again, note the temporal overtones – "ultimately," as opposed to immediately, prevails. Next, there are "particular" moments when things go awry, which is not the normal course of affairs because Publius notes that the people are then induced by an "irregular passion." Evidently the default tendency, then, is a sensible disposition of public affairs.

When these unusual moments arise, it will be useful for a "temperate" group to "suspend the blow" the people have struck "against themselves." This idea of "suspension" suggests that legislators cannot permanently block the public will, and indeed it is not their job to do so, because the public sense inevitably prevails "ultimately." The idea of suspension is to provide time and space for "reason, justice, and truth" to "regain" their authority, a formulation that suggests they had authority to begin with but simply lost it "temporar[ily]." Because passions are by their very nature fleeting, time bears a substantial burden for dissipating them.[14] So do the "fit characters" of *Federalist* 10, who perform a pedagogical function in encouraging reconsideration of unreasonable public demands – something that is, of course, likelier to succeed if passions cool.

Consequently, the Senate operates as a fail-safe mechanism for the extensive-republic theory Publius previously elucidated in *Federalist* 10. It may appear that this theory has rendered a mechanism like the Senate unnecessary since "a people spread over an extensive region, cannot, like the crouded inhabitants of a small district, be subject to the infection of violent passions; or to the danger of combining in the pursuit of unjust measures" (*Fed.* 63, 425). Yet in the only instance in which *The Federalist* qualifies that theory, Publius specifies that the Senate operates as an "auxiliary precaution" that is necessary because the same extensiveness that makes contagious passions unlikely will also make them harder to cure if they spread (*Fed.* 63, 425–26).

The Senate of course exhibits the anti-majoritarian feature of the equality of state representation. Publius has already betrayed some degree of concern about this feature in *Federalist* 58, which describes as "a peculiarity in the federal constitution" the fact that one chamber will represent "citizens" and the other "the States." It may, he allows, be inferred that the Senate, leaning toward the interests of smaller states, will resist augmenting the size of the House when population growth justifies increases. But Publius allays this concern by reassuring readers that the House, being more numerous and drawing its power directly from the people, will enjoy a natural advantage over the Senate in institutional combat, especially given its power over appropriations (*Fed.* 58, 392).

Still, the equality of state representation in the Senate is not an insignificant departure from the Constitution's normal commitment to seasoned majority rule. But what is striking from the perspective of *The Federalist* is that Madison, who elsewhere in the book defends measures he did not support at the Constitutional Convention, declines to apologize for this one. At the Convention, Madison had bitterly opposed the equality of state representation, calling its anti-majoritarian character "confessedly unjust."[15] By the time of *The Federalist,* he seems not to have yielded in that opinion. "It is," he declares, proceeding to quote George Washington's circular to the states accompanying the proposed Constitution, "superfluous to try, by the standard of theory, a part of the constitution which is allowed on all hands to be the result, not of theory, but 'of a spirit of amity, and that mutual deference and concession which the peculiarity of our political situation rendered indispensable.'" The suggestion is that the equality of state representation was a necessary concession to obtain the imperative of "[a] common government, with powers equal to its objects" (*Fed.* 62, 416).

CONTROLLING CONGRESS

Publius places both institutional and political controls on Congress. The institutional controls are the checks exercised by other branches and levels of government and by the two branches of the legislature on each other. The political controls on which Publius ultimately relies are the checks provided by public opinion, manifest in elections.

In extraordinary cases, which Publius means clearly to discourage, the extra-constitutional remedy of rebellion is available.

The case for institutional checks begins with Publius's observation in *Federalist* 48 that Congress is especially prone to exploit its power. The reason is that it occupies a middle position for abuse: It is large enough to be in contact with and thus to draw energy from "all the passions which actuate a multitude," yet not too large "to be incapable of pursuing the objects of its passions" by using reason. Moreover, although the countervailing executive and judicial powers are carefully circumscribed, the boundaries of the legislature's power are inherently blurred. The legislature in a republic is "inspired by a supposed influence over the people" and is fueled by "an intrepid confidence in its own strength" (*Fed.* 48, 334). This intriguing expression – "influence over the people" – indicates that the contamination of passions works in both directions: they can be communicated from the people to their representatives, but also the other way around.

Consequently, the legislature should be the great object of institutional jealousy. Yet in the end, the only institutional check Publius provides within the national government is the executive veto, which he describes in defensive terms – it is "the natural defence with which the executive magistrate should be armed" – and implies is to be directed mainly against the House, since the Senate's institutional link with the presidency will help to strengthen the use of the negative and inhibit its abuse (*Fed.* 51, 350). Because the state legislatures will also keep watch on the Congress, the institutional checks are intergovernmental as well as interdepartmental. *Federalist* 52 assures readers that "the federal legislature will not only be restrained by its dependence on the people, as other legislative bodies are; but that it will be moreover watched and controled by the several collateral legislatures, which other legislative bodies are not" (*Fed.* 53, 359). Similarly, the federal government could never manipulate elections "without causing an immediate revolt of the great body of the people, headed and directed by the state governments" (*Fed.* 60, 404). In fact, encroachments of the federal government would pit "one set of representatives" against "thirteen sets of representatives," and the "whole body" of the people would side with the latter (*Fed.* 46, 320).

Publius also mentions checks internal to the legislature. Since the legislature "necessarily predominates" in a republic and it is "not possible" to equip each branch equally – a formulation that implies that the branches are not intended to be equal in power – Publius's first response is "to divide the legislature into different branches; and to render them by different modes of election, and different principles of action, as little connected with each other as the nature of their common functions, and their common dependence on the society, will admit" (*Fed.* 51, 350). These institutional controls are limited, then, by the twin principles of the common functions of the houses – that is, they need to be able to do what they need to do – and the republican principle of dependence on the majority.

Ultimately, though, Publius relies on the people to check the legislature. In an instance of Hamilton endorsing republican controls, *Federalist* 31 thus concludes that the balance between the national and state governments "must be left to the prudence and firmness of the people" (*Fed.* 31, 198). In *Federalist* 59, Publius again soothes concerns regarding federal control of elections by noting that an abuse of such a trust could only proceed from "a fixed and rooted disaffection in the great body of the people; which will either never exist at all, or will, in all probability, proceed from an experience of the inaptitude of the general government to the advancement of their happiness; in which event, no good citizen could desire its continuance" (*Fed.* 59, 401). This argument rests on several points. One is that the security of the system ultimately depends on the sense of the people, and what matters is their "fixed and rooted" sense, not their transient feelings. Finally, and strikingly, a government so inept as to produce a fixed and rooted sense of corruption would have no claim to continue existing. Lest there be any doubt what Publius means, *Federalist* 60 clarifies it: federal interference in elections would "occasio[n] a popular revolution" (*Fed.* 60, 404).

CONGRESS IN RELIEF

The Congress that Publius theorizes is, in many senses, not the vastly larger Congress we have today. The Senate, the great chamber of deliberation, is half again larger than the original House of Representatives. The House, capped at 435 members, consists of districts in which the number of electors would have stunned the framers and panicked their opponents. Its approval rating is the stuff of late-night comedy television shows even though the reelection rate of incumbents who wish to return is near universal. Congress legislates sometimes ploddingly and sometimes sporadically, but rarely with any consistency according to the measures of legislative "productivity" that appear incessantly in press coverage, which focuses on the number of bills enacted. Meanwhile, against all the predictions in *Federalist* 51, Congress has willingly spun off powers and deferred to the presidency. Whereas *Federalist* 73 describes the executive veto as "a salutary check upon the legislative body, calculated to guard the community against the effects of faction, precipitancy, or of any impulse unfriendly to the public good, which may happen to influence a majority of that body," Congress today sees itself as a brake on the executive rather than the other way around (*Fed.* 73, 495).

The most dramatic result of this has been a surge not only in presidential but also in administrative governance. Congress has delegated wide swaths of authority to agencies, often with hardly any standards for their execution. As a result, administrative governance poses a dual problem: First, the combination of policymaking, executive and judicial authority in violation of the separation of powers, and second – because Congress does not prescribe rules, only objectives – the vulnerability of these agencies to capture by the very entities they are supposed to regulate.

Collective-action problems alone do not explain Congress's abdication, but polarization might. Since the "McGovern reforms" of the 1970s, which were designed to make parties more transparent and democratic, candidates have generally been nominated by the most partisan voters – those who participate in primaries – rather than by party leaders whose interest is not ideological purity but rather appealing to the broader electorate. Members now fear facing primaries from their right or left, a phenomenon that has contributed to the intense polarization in Congress since moderates of either party must contend with challenges from the extremes. The sorting-out of party identification that has led conservative Democrats to become Republicans and liberal Republicans to become Democrats has further undermined the legislature's capacity to stand up for itself against the presidency. This is especially so in the Senate, which operates on informal consensus. Meanwhile, gerrymandering certainly contributes to this partisanship in the House, but it cannot explain the same phenomenon in the Senate. Moreover, not even changes to the McGovern regime might solve polarization, as growing evidence suggests the Congress simply reflects a polarized electorate.

The Federalist provides scant guidance for such problems. Publius, especially in Madison's essays, generally assumes that durable ideological parties will not exist, yet Madison himself helped to theorize and create the first party system. One sense in which Publius can illuminate the problem is that *Federalist* 10 says there is a point of diminishing returns on the extended republic theory. If electoral districts are too large, voters do not know candidates for office; if they are too small, officeholders are beholden to parochial interests (*Fed.* 10, 63). The essay had similarly explained that the "vicious arts" of politics, by which Publius seems to mean bribery and the notorious practice of "treating" voters to whiskey and other indulgences before they cast their ballots, could not be practiced in large districts. But another mean may apply here, according to which new vicious arts – demagoguery, superficial campaigns that give scant attention to meaningful issues, and the like – take over once electoral districts become too large.

But in other ways, Publius might help show us the way forward by taking the route back. That would begin with an appreciation of

Congress as the First Branch and an understanding of its task, which is not merely to legislate in volume but rather to represent its constituents and to deliberate about justice and the general good. Measures of legislative productivity that simply gauge output presume that the job of Congress is to pass legislation. William G. Howell and Terry M. Moe, for example, see Congressional dysfunction as a reason to transfer authority to the executive. "*To act,*" they write, "*governments must pass laws.*"[16] But government should not necessarily act in every situation. Sometimes it should; other times it should refrain. A member of Congress who has deliberated extensively and reasonably on a piece of legislation, taken his constituents' genuine interests and views into account, and then opposes its passage has done his or her job as much as one who seeks its passage. That is, there is no inherent reason bills should be passed; there may be inherent reasons they should be opposed, not the least of which are Madison's warnings about the "multiplicity" of legislation. Legislation itself is value-neutral. The value for Publius is the public good, and the devices for attaining it are representation and deliberation. An emphasis on change for its own sake would make an equally important function of regimes – their own maintenance and the conservation of customs and mores – difficult and may even dismiss these goals as dysfunctional.

Ever since Andrew Jackson warred with Congress over the National Bank, presidents have claimed a superior right to represent the public views because they are said to represent all the people. Yet this diminishes one of Congress's foremost contributions to representation, which Publius emphasizes: the multiplicity of views it encompasses. The presidency is a unitary institution. One who votes for the president finds his or her views represented for four years; one who was on the losing side of an election is on the outs. Yet Congress is large and diverse enough to encompass a broad spectrum of views. Virtually everyone within the mainstream of American politics will find his or her views accommodated in the legislative process, even if not necessarily by his or her own representative. Congress has a superior claim to representation precisely because it is virtually impossible in an extensive republic to speak of a single, undifferentiated public will.

Still, critics complain that the American legislative process is ill-suited to contemporary political life. As Willmoore Kendall argued, the executive branch has acquired an aura of scientific expertise, whereas Congress is viewed as parochial.[17] Eric A. Posner and Adrian Vermeule, both executive supremacists, say legislatures cannot govern the administrative state.[18] It is true that if the state is to be primarily administrative, Congress may be too plodding to conduct its business, but two cautions are in order. One is that, as Theodore J. Lowi has written, Congress can still delegate authority to the executive branch while retaining its legislative nature by doing so with specific standards attached.[19] Second, these accounts tend to arise from a politics of instant gratification according to which the deliberate pace of Congress is unfitted to the lightning speed of contemporary political life. Such complaints are hardly new. Woodrow Wilson voiced them as early as 1885: "*Power and strict accountability for its use* are the essential constituents of good government. It is, therefore, manifestly a radical defect in our federal system that it parcels out power and confuses responsibility as it does."[20]

Yet the slow pace of Congress, whose purpose was to diffuse passions and facilitate deliberation, was an intended feature of the legislature.[21] The very diffusion of power that Wilson indicted is a benefit rather than a defect of Congressional government. It is also sometimes said that Congress is incapable of acting because of the collective-action problems endemic to a large body. But Congress was also large enough to trigger collective-action problems when Wilson complained about its dominance over a century ago.

But the separation-of-powers theory of *Federalist* 51 also indicates that the only motive, or "ambition," in the argot of that essay, that will impel a restoration of Congress is the desire of its members to exercise their power. Institutional reforms may help here. Suggestions have included reclaiming its taxing, spending and borrowing powers, utilizing sunset provisions for delegations of authority to the executive, and term limitation.[22] These suggestions all merit serious reflection, but Publius also says that the ultimate safeguard both for Congressional authority and for public liberty is the republican character of the people. In *Federalist* 38, Publius wonders that the ancient Greeks were driven to entrust their liberty to a single "illustrious citizen" like Solon or Lycurgus rather than "a select body of citizens, from whose common deliberations more wisdom, as well as more safety, might have been expected" (*Fed.* 38, 240–41). The ultimate reason to see Congress as the First Branch is that the primary controls on it are internal and political rather than imposed from without. This is inevitable in a republican system in which the legislative authority "necessarily predominates" and should be preeminent because of its "sympathy" with the people. The challenge, and responsibility, it imposes is that the same authority – that is, the republicanism of the people – is the only ultimate force that can restore Congress when, as is now the case, it has eroded.

NOTES

1 Louis Fisher, *Constitutional Conflicts between Congress and the President*, 6th ed. (Lawrence: University Press of Kansas, 2014), 215.

2 George W. Carey, *The Federalist: Design for a Constitutional Republic* (Urbana, IL: University of Illinois Press, 1994), 32.

3 See George W. Carey, *A Student's Guide to American Political Thought* (Wilmington, DE: ISI Books, 2014), and Garry Wills, *A Necessary Evil: A History of American Distrust of Government* (New York: Simon and Schuster, 2002).

4 "In the legislature, promptitude of decision is oftener an evil than a benefit. The differences of opinion, and the jarring of parties in that department of the government, though they may sometimes obstruct salutary plans, yet often promote deliberation and circumspection; and serve to check excesses in the majority. When a resolution too is once

taken, the opposition must be at an end. That resolution is a law, and resistance to it punishable" (*Fed. 70*, 475). That is, the executive function is swiftly and firmly to execute resolutions of the legislative body.

5 Jack N. Rakove, *Original Meanings: Politics and Ideas in the Framing of the Constitution* (New York: Alfred A. Knopf, 1996), 198.

6 *Luther v. Borden* 48 US 42 (1849).

7 James Burnham, *Congress and the American Tradition* (New Brunswick, NJ: Transaction Publishers, 2003), 94–95.

8 Federal Farmer II, in *The Complete Anti-Federalist*, ed. Herbert J. Storing (Chicago, IL: University of Chicago Press, 1981), I, 230.

9 Daniel W. Howe, "The Political Psychology of *The Federalist*," *William and Mary Quarterly*, 44 (1987), 506.

10 Colleen Sheehan, *James Madison and the Spirit of Republican Self-Government* (New York: Cambridge University Press, 2009) and *The Mind of James Madison: The Legacy of Classical Republicanism* (New York: Cambridge University Press, 2015); Alan Gibson, "Madison's Republican Remedy: The Tenth *Federalist* and the Creation of an Impartial Republic," Chapter 8 above.

11 David Mayhew, *Congress: The Electoral Connection* (New Haven, CT: Yale University Press, 2004), 17.

12 See Gary C. Jacobson and Jamie L. Carson, *The Politics of Congressional Elections* (Lanham, MD: Rowman & Littlefield, 2016), 9.

13 Some controversy persists as to whether Madison or Hamilton wrote this essay, but it bears the unmistakable imprint of Madison's democratic thought more generally, especially in this passage and in its general commitment to the rule of deliberate majorities.

14 See Greg Weiner, *Madison's Metronome: The Constitution, Majority Rule and the Tempo of American Politics* (Lawrence: University Press of Kansas, 2012).

15 Constitutional Convention, June 29. *PMF*, X, 86–87.

16 William G. Howell and Terry M. Moe, *Relic: How Our Constitution Undermines Effective Government, and Why We Need a More Powerful Presidency* (New York: Basic Books, 2016), 16 (emphasis in original).

17 Willmoore Kendall, "The Two Majorities," in *Willmoore Kendall Contra Mundum* (New Rochelle, NY: Arlington House, 1971).

18 See, generally, Eric A. Posner and Adrian Vermeule, *The Executive Unbound: After the Madisonian Republic* (New York: Oxford University Press, 2010).

19 Theodore J. Lowi, *The End of Liberalism: The Second Republic of the United States* (New York: W. W. Norton and Company, 2009).

20 Woodrow Wilson. *Congressional Government: A Study in American Politics* (Mineola, NY: Dover Publications, 2006), 186–87.

21 On the importance of Congressional deliberation, see Burnham, *Congress and the American Tradition*, esp. 28–33, where Burnham associates support of Congress with what he calls the conservative "syndrome" in American politics.

22 See Christopher DeMuth Sr., "Reviving a Constitutional Congress," *Imprimus: A Publication of Hillsdale College*, 44 (2015), esp. 4–5. See also Josh Chafetz, *Congress' Constitution: Legislative Authority and the Separation of Powers* (New Haven, CT: Yale University Press, 2017), 61. On the case for term limitation generally, see George F. Will, *Restoration: Congress, Term Limits and the Recovery of Deliberative Democracy* (New York: The Free Press, 1992). The idea is that term limitation might attract a type of lawmaker whose sole interest is exercising power for a brief interval rather than entrenching him- or herself for the sake of careerism. William Kristol, endorsing term limitation, argues that the case for the device entails a refutation of Publius, who considered and rejected it. See William Kristol, "Debate: *The Federalist* and the Contemporary Debate on Term Limits – Term Limitations: Breaking Up the Iron Triangle," *Harvard Journal of Law and Public Policy*, 16 (1993), 95–100.

13 Publius on Monarchy

Eric Nelson

I

The eleven essays published by "Publius" between March 11 and April 4, 1787 jointly constitute the most famous defense of presidential power in the American constitutional tradition. It is here that Alexander Hamilton extols "energy in the executive," along with the canonical litany of "decision, activity, secrecy, and dispatch." Such energy, for Hamilton, requires "unity" in the chief magistracy, the focus and coherence of a single mind (*Fed.* 70, 471–472). But it equally demands "firmness" – a readiness to exert oneself in defense of the "constitutional powers" of one's office – which can only be expected from those whose "duration in office" is sufficiently long. "It is a general principle of human nature," Hamilton explains, "that a man will be interested in what he possesses, in proportion to the firmness or precariousness of the tenure, by which he holds it." Only a magistrate who regards his office as truly his own will subject himself to danger or opprobrium in order to secure the system of which it is a part – and this he must routinely do. For while "it is a just observation that the people commonly *intend* the PUBLIC GOOD," they do not, alas, always "*reason right* about the means of promoting it." An effective, energetic executive must accordingly wield his prerogatives to tame their episodic folly; to "withstand the temporary delusion, in order to give them time and opportunity for more cool and sedate reflection." The republican principle may require deference to "the deliberate sense of the community," but it "does not require an unqualified complaisance to every sudden breeze of passion, or to every transient impulse which the people may receive from the arts of men, who flatter their prejudices to betray their interests" (*Fed.* 71, 481–82).

These passages will be familiar to any student of American politics and jurisprudence, but far less familiar is the broader argument of which they are a part. For Hamilton is not merely analyzing "the proposed executive" in *Federalist* 67–77; he is, rather, offering a distillation of his views on monarchical government in general, and on the British monarchy in particular. Indeed, this series of essays has deep roots in a text that Hamilton published years before the drafting of the new federal Constitution.

In 1775, when he was still an undergraduate at King's College in New York, he took up his pen to answer an attack on the Continental Congress that had been written by the Loyalist Samuel Seabury. *The Farmer Refuted*, as Hamilton entitled his rejoinder, primarily addressed itself to Seabury's argument that Parliament, as the supreme legislature of the British Empire, must naturally have jurisdiction over America. Seabury rested his case on a reputable understanding of the English constitution:

> In every government, there must be a supreme absolute authority lodged somewhere. In arbitrary governments this power is in the monarch; in aristocratical governments, in the nobles; in democratical in the people; or the deputies of their electing. Our own government being a mixture of all these kinds, the supreme authority is vested in the King, Nobles and People, i.e. the King, House of Lords and House of Commons elected by the people. This supreme authority extends as far as the British dominions extend. To suppose a part of the British dominions which is not subject to the power of the British legislature, is no better sense than to suppose a country, at one and the same time, to be and not to be a part of the British dominions.[1]

"This argument," Hamilton thundered in reply, "is the most specious of any, the advocates for parliamentary supremacy are able to produce."[2] In truth, the American colonies were not at all "subject to the power of the British legislature," but it did not follow from this fact that they were not "British dominions." The colonies were instead connected to Britain solely through "the person and prerogative of the King." The monarch alone "conjoins all these individual societies, into one great body politic. He it is, that is to preserve their mutual connexion and dependence, and make them all co-operate to one common end the general good. His power is equal to the purpose, and his interest binds him to the due prosecution of it."[3] On this view, Parliament had no more authority over British America than the Massachusetts General Court enjoyed over Great Britain. "The several parts of the empire, though, otherwise, independent on each other, will all be dependent on" the crown.[4]

So far, Hamilton had not asserted anything remotely idiosyncratic. By the late 1760s and early 1770s, most Patriot theorists had embraced the view that the king alone wielded just authority over America and that he should revive long defunct prerogatives of the crown (among them the royal "negative," or veto) in order to become the "pervading" and "superintending" power of the empire. These opposition leaders thereby committed themselves to a radical critique of the eighteenth-century Whig constitutional consensus. The settlement that followed the Glorious Revolution had definitively subjected the king to Parliament, drastically curtailing his prerogatives and recasting him as a pure "executive." Those powers of state that legally remained with the crown were no longer wielded by the person of the king, but rather by ministers who were required to command a parliamentary majority (and who themselves sat in one of the two houses). Patriots were thus effectively proposing to turn back the clock on the English constitution by over a hundred years – to separate the king from his Parliament and his British ministers, and to install him as an independent king and emperor, wielding prerogative powers that his Hanoverian predecessors had never claimed.[5] The great Patriot complaint, as Benjamin Franklin put it, was that the Lords and Commons "have been long encroaching on the Rights of their and our Sovereign, assuming too much of his Authority, and betraying his Interests."[6]

Hamilton, however, went a good deal further in 1775. Virtually every other Patriot theorist would have accepted in principle Seabury's claim that, within Great Britain itself, "the supreme authority is vested in the King, Nobles and People, i.e. the King, House of Lords and House of Commons elected by the people." They would have dissented from Seabury only in insisting that the king *also* enjoyed an independent political existence outside Parliament, by virtue of which he wielded imperial authority over his American dominions – and in asserting that the royal negative and other prerogative powers still rightfully belonged to the king himself, rather than to a parliamentary ministry. Hamilton, in contrast, flatly rejected the claim that, under the English constitution, sovereign power is shared among king, Lords, and Commons. Having initially accused Seabury merely of "losing sight of that *share* which the King has in the sovereignty, both of Great-Britain and America,"[7] he went on to make clear that, in fact, the error runs deeper. If we wish to speak with "propriety," Hamilton observed, we will hold instead "that the King is the *only* Sovereign of the empire. The part which the people have in the legislature, may more justly be considered as a limitation of the Sovereign authority, to prevent its being exercised in an oppressive and despotic manner: Monarchy is universally allowed to predominate in the constitution."[8]

It is difficult to overstate the radicalism of this claim. Hamilton was endorsing a particularly strident variant of seventeenth-century Royalist thought. Seabury, after all, was merely quoting as doxa a claim about the character of the English constitution that Charles I himself had introduced in the *Answer to the Nineteen Propositions* (1642). In the course of defending the royal negative and other prerogatives against the pretensions of the Commons, Charles had famously characterized England as a "mixed monarchy":

> There being three kinds of Government amongst men, Absolute Monarchy, Aristocracy and Democracy, and all these having their particular conveniencies and inconveniencies. The experience and wisdom of your Ancestors hath so moulded this out of a mixture of

> these, as to give to this Kingdome (as farre as humane Prudence can provide) the conveniencies of all three, without the inconveniencies of any one, as long as the Balance hangs even between the three Estates, and they run joyntly on in their proper Chanell (begetting Verdure and Fertilitie in the Meadows on both sides) and the overflowing of either on either side raise not deluge or Inundation ... In this Kingdome the Laws are joyntly made by a King, by a House of Peers, and by a House of Commons chosen by the People, all having free Votes and particular priviledges.[9]

The most conservative Royalists of the 1640s, while agreeing that England was a limited monarchy, objected that Charles had conceded too much in this passage. As Henry Ferne put the complaint: while it is true that the Lords and Commons must consent "to certain Acts of Monarchical Power, and this makes a Mixture," the two houses technically "have no share in the very power, but concurre to the exercise of it only."[10] The king, on this view, is not one of three co-equal estates amongst which "the Balance hangs even"; rather "the Prelates, Lords, and Commons are the three Estates of this King-dome, under his Majesty as their Head."[11] The constitution places salutary *limits* on the sovereign authority, but it does not *divide* that authority among king, Lords, and Commons. The king is above the estates of the realm, and he alone is sovereign.

It is this position that the young Hamilton endorses.[12] There is, on his account, only one sovereign in each of the personal domin-ions of George III: the king himself. This power is not shared with the legislature, either in Britain or its colonies. Rather, "the part which the people have in the legislature, may more justly be considered as a limitation of the Sovereign authority, to prevent its being exercised in an oppressive and despotic manner." The people rightfully play a constitutional role in each dominion of the crown, but, *pace* Seabury, they do not partake in any way of "the supreme authority." For Hamilton, monarchy "predominate[s] in the constitution," and he assures his reader that this axiom is "universally allowed." In fact, it was allowed by almost no one in the eighteenth-century Atlantic world. On the contrary, it was a high Royalist constitutional heresy.

In Hamilton's juridical imagination, the crown was therefore spectacularly powerful. As an empirical matter, however, he believed that the monarchy had become lamentably weak in recent decades. In this respect, he straightforwardly associated himself with a distinctive view of English constitutional decline that we have come to know (problematically) as "Tory." The basic historical facts were not in dispute. All agreed that no British monarch had vetoed a parliamentary bill for generations (indeed most British Americans – including Hamilton – believed, mistakenly, that no monarch had done so since before 1688[13]) and that the executive powers of the crown in relation to war and peace, appointment to office, and the regulations of trade had long been exercised, not by the king himself, but rather by ministers who were required to maintain the support of a parliamentary majority. Whigs explained these facts by asserting, counterintuitively, that the crown had secured an iron grip on the legislature: it now used patronage to obtain the support of a majority of MPs, with the result that it invariably got its way in the Commons without employing the negative. Likewise, the fact that the king allowed his ministers to wield the prerogatives of the crown without interference demonstrated, not that the will of the sovereign no longer held sway in these areas of government, but rather that the Parliament to which the ministry answered was filled with the monarch's "creatures."

But this "Country" or "real" Whig narrative of constitutional decline had its committed opponents. Beginning in the 1730s, a series of theorists began to argue that, in fact, the British monarchy had been largely absorbed by the legislature – that it had become too weak, not too strong. The most eloquent spokesman for this rival position was David Hume. In his essay "Of the Independency of Parliament" (1742), Hume announced that the latter-day Whigs had gotten things precisely backwards. "The share of power, allotted by our constitution to the house of commons," he declared, "is so great, that it absolutely commands all the other parts of government."[14] In particular, the practice of seeking the royal assent for parliamentary bills had become a mere pantomime: "The king's legislative power is plainly no proper check to it [the House of Commons]. For though the king has a negative in framing laws; yet this, in fact, is esteemed of so little moment, that whatever is voted by the two houses, is always sure to pass into a law, and the royal assent is little better than a form."[15] On this rival account, no monarch had vetoed a bill in generations because no monarch would dare to do so. Nor would any monarch attempt to wield the other prerogatives of the crown without parliamentary approval.

But Hume's proposed solution to "this paradox" of royal weakness was unexpected. He did not suppose that the king could revive his negative voice and other defunct prerogatives. Rather, he focused his hopes on the patronage power of the crown.[16] The unending crusade of the Commons to subjugate the executive could be "restrained," Hume believed, by the self-interested behavior of individual legislators seeking royal favor. "The crown has so many offices at its disposal, that, when assisted by the honest and disinterested part of the House, it will always command the resolutions of the whole, so far, at least, as to preserve the ancient constitution from danger." Others may call this "influence" by "the invidious appellations of *corruption* and *dependence*," but in truth "some degree and some kind of it are inseparable from the very nature of the constitution, and necessary to the preservation of our mixed government."[17] In a world of unbridled parliamentary supremacy, patronage would have to replace prerogative.

A great many Patriot theorists of the 1770s and 1780s came to share Hume's diagnosis of what had gone wrong with the English constitution, but Hamilton was again virtually alone in embracing Hume's remedy. While he had already quoted Hume extensively in *The Farmer Refuted*, it was in the Constitutional Convention that he nailed his colors most firmly to the mast. During the debate over what would become Article I, Section 6 of the Constitution – which provides that "no Person holding any Office under the United States, shall be a Member of either House [of Congress] during his

Continuance in Office" and bars senators and congressmen from being appointed to any office created during their terms – Pierce Butler of South Carolina declared in Whiggish tones that "this precaution ag[ain]st. intrigue was necessary" and "appealed to the example of G[reat] B[ritain]. where men got into Parliament that they might get offices for themselves or their friends."[18] "This," Butler announced, "was the source of the corruption that ruined their Gov[ernmen]t." Hamilton, by contrast, objected to the measure. He cited instead "[one] of the ablest politicians (Mr Hume)," who "had pronounced all that influence on the side of the crown, which went under the name of corruption, an essential part of the weight which maintained the equilibrium of the Constitution."[19] The crown's prerogative control of the "many offices at its disposal," Hamilton agreed with Hume, constituted the last remaining bulwark against abject legislative tyranny. The English monarch might well be "the only Sovereign of the Empire" as a legal and constitutional matter, but his political position had in fact become exceedingly precarious. This distinctive combination of Royalist constitutional theory and Humean political sociology would animate Hamilton's remarkable performance as Publius in the months to come.

Publius's discussion of executive power formally begins in *Federalist* 67, but Hamilton actually launches his own exploration of this subject much earlier, in *Federalist* 17, where he addresses the Anti-Federalist anxiety that the government of the "Union" would overwhelm those of the states under the proposed Constitution.[20] Hamilton argues in response that "the experience of all federal constitutions" shows quite the reverse: that the central government will always be in constant danger of assault from the periphery (*Fed.* 17, 107–08). In support of this claim, he offers a somewhat surprising example: the history of "feudal systems" in medieval European monarchies. While these were "not, strictly speaking, confederacies," Hamilton insists nonetheless that they "partook of the nature of that species of association (*Fed.* 17, 108)." In particular, as he goes on to explain, the great pathology of feudal systems was the weakness of the monarch:

There was a common head, chieftain, or sovereign, whose authority extended over the whole nation; and a number of subordinate vassals, or feudatories, who had large portions of land allotted to them, and numerous trains of *inferior* vassals or retainers, who occupied and cultivated that land upon the tenure of fealty or obedience, to the persons of whom they held it. Each principal vassal was a kind of sovereign, within his particular demesnes. The consequences of this situation were a continual opposition to authority of the sovereign, and frequent wars between the great barons or chief feudatories themselves. The power of the head of the nation was commonly too weak, either to preserve the public peace, or to protect the people against the oppressions of their immediate lords. This period of European affairs is emphatically styled by historians, the times of feudal anarchy.

(*Fed.* 17, 108)

Hamilton continues by observing that "in general, the power of the barons triumphed over that of the prince; and in many instances his dominion was entirely thrown off, and the great fiefs were erected into independent principalities or states" (*Fed.* 17, 109).[21] And, as he explains in *Federalist* 84, "Magna Carta" was merely one such encroachment on royal power, "obtained by the barons, sword in hand, from King John" (*Fed.* 84, 578).[22] At long last, when

the monarch finally prevailed over his vassals, his success was chiefly owing to the tyranny of those vassals over their dependents. The barons, or nobles equally the enemies of the sovereign and the oppressors of the common people were dreaded and detested by both; till mutual danger and mutual interest effected a union between them fatal to the power of the aristocracy.

(*Fed.* 17, 109)

Hamilton returned to precisely the same material in his speech to the New York Ratifying Convention, offering this description of "the antient feudal governments":

It has been proved, that the members of republics have been, and ever will be, stronger than the head. Let us attend to one general historical example. In the antient feudal governments of Europe, there were, in the first place a monarch; subordinate to him, a body of nobles; and subject to these, the vassals or the whole body of the people. The authority of the kings was limited, and that of the barons considerably independent. ... The history of the feudal wars exhibits little more than a series of successful encroachments on the prerogatives of monarchy. ... I may be told, that in some instances the barons were overcome: But how did this happen? Sir, they took advantage of the depression of the royal authority, and the establishment of their own power, to oppress and tyrannise over their vassals. As commerce enlarged, and as wealth and civilization encreased, the people began to feel their own weight and consequence: They grew tired of their oppressions; united their strength with that of the prince; and threw off the yoke of aristocracy.[23]

Here again, the disorder of feudal government is monarchical weakness and baronial hegemony, and this pathology is ultimately resolved only when king and people forge a momentous alliance in favor of liberty.

The first point to stress about this account is that it has an identifiable source: book 3, chapter 3 of Adam Smith's *Wealth of Nations*, "Of the Rise and Progress of Cities and Towns, after the Fall of the Roman Empire." In feudal societies, Smith had likewise argued, "the authority of government" was always "too weak in the head, and too strong in the inferior members; and the excessive strength of the inferior members was the cause of the weakness of the head."[24] Even "after the institution of feudal subordination, the king was as incapable of restraining the violence of the great lords as before. They still continued to make war according to their own discretion, almost continually upon one another, and very frequently upon the king; and the open country still continued to be a scene of violence, rapine, and disorder." This period is therefore most properly described as "the times of feudal anarchy."[25] It was brought to its merciful conclusion only when king and people united against their baronial oppressors: "The burghers naturally hated and feared the lords," who "plundered" them mercilessly, and "the king hated and feared them too; but though, perhaps, he might despise, he had no reason either to hate or fear the burghers. Mutual interest, therefore, disposed them to support the king, and the king to support them against the lords."

The fact that Hamilton took his account almost verbatim from Smith is not, however, a mere matter of antiquarian interest. In describing feudalism in these terms, Smith and Hamilton were each straightforwardly setting themselves against the crucial historiographical underpinnings of Whig political theory. Whigs located in the remote Saxon past an "ancient constitution" of balanced, free government, in which elected monarchs merely executed laws approved by their independent, landowning subjects in a primeval parliament. This republican idyll, they believed, was then tragically interrupted by the Norman Conquest of 1066, which introduced feudal tenures and, consequently, absolute monarchy. The great constitutional watersheds of English medieval and early modern history – chief among them Magna Carta – were celebrated in the Whig canon for restraining the power of the crown and thereby reconfirming the ancient liberties enjoyed by Englishmen before the arrival of the Conqueror.[26]

Royalist historians of the seventeenth century, by contrast, had emphatically rejected this narrative. For Sir Henry Spelman, Robert Brady, and their disciples, the pre-feudal constitution of liberty was pure myth. They insisted that in its origins Parliament was a fundamentally feudal institution and that the House of Commons had not existed in any form until the high medieval period. More importantly, these historians rejected the Whig conceit that feudalism was pathological because it amounted to monarchical tyranny. On the contrary, they argued, the distinctive perversity of feudalism was its tendency to weaken the king at the expense of "Factious barons," who (in Brady's words) "when they had secured their own Liberties, rather made use of them to Oppress, than Relieve their Tenants and Neighbours."[27] Magna Carta itself could only properly be understood as an episode in this disturbing narrative of creeping aristocratic hegemony and perilous royal retreat – yet another encroachment by "incorrigible Norman rebels against their own Norman princes."[28] This revisionist account returned to prominence with the publication of Hume's *History of England* (1754–61), in which readers learned that, under feudalism, the great danger was "that the community would every where crumble into so many independant baronies, and lose the political union, by which they were cemented" (Hume cites Brady directly on this point) and that the system only achieved equilibrium when the king "assumed the salutary office of general guardian or protector of the commons."[29] Adam Smith merely developed and intensified the Royalist thrust of his friend Hume's earlier narrative.

It was this tradition that Hamilton wholeheartedly embraced in 1788. The great political danger in modern states, he believed, was not royal power, but monarchical weakness. Feudal history, rightly understood, reveals that the monarch is the natural champion of popular rights, bound to the Commons by "mutual interest." The great enemy of the people is instead the aristocracy. In making this case, Hamilton was essentially echoing his argument from the *Farmer Refuted* that the colonists could depend upon the king because he "is under no temptation to purchase the favour of one part of his dominions, at the expense of another; but, it is his interest to treat them all, upon the same footing. Very different is the case with regard to the Parliament. The Lords and Commons have a separate interest to pursue."[30] Seen in relation to British America, Parliament itself had become a kind of aristocracy – a body of men not derived from the people, who were happy to plunder and oppress their fellow-subjects across the sea. As Thomson Mason of Virginia put the point in 1774, his fellow Americans sought merely "to check the growing power of aristocracy [i.e. Parliament] in *Great Britain*, and to restore your Sovereign to that weight in the National Councils which he ought to possess." Mason could accordingly assure his readers that "the general opinion, that the great defect in the present Constitution of *Britain* is the enormous power of the Crown" ought to be dismissed as "a vulgar errour."[31]

By the late 1770s, an influential group of American theorists had emerged as champions of this distinctive account of modern politics. These men had pioneered the Patriot defense of the royal prerogative only several years earlier, and they now used the same arguments to defend a sweeping conception of executive power.[32] Benjamin Rush fretted in 1770 that it is in the nature of legislative bodies to be "filled in the course of a few years with a majority of rich men," whose "wealth will administer fuel to the love of arbitrary power that is common to all men" – eventually yielding "aristocracy," a noxious regime in which there are "only two sorts of animals, tyrants and slaves."[33] Only a prerogative-wielding chief magistrate, constituting a full third of the legislative power, could resist the forces of aristocratic despotism in the name of liberty. John Adams was making the very same point as early as 1779: "we have so many Men of Wealth, of ambitious Spirits, of Intrigue, of Luxury and Corruption, that incessant Factions will disturb our Peace, without [the chief magistrate's negative voice]."[34] Writing to Jefferson in December 1787, he repeated his basic conviction: "You are afraid of the one – I, of the few. We agree perfectly that the many should have a full fair and perfect Representation. – You are Apprehensive of Monarchy; I, of Aristocracy."[35]

Adams accordingly insisted that the wealthy few should be quarantined in their own legislative chamber, thus preventing them from coming to dominate the popular chamber.[36] The "many" would then find their crucial support against the encroachments of the aristocratic house in the prerogatives of the chief magistrate:

> it is the true policy of the common people to place the whole
> executive power in one man, to make him a distinct order in the
> state, from whence arises an inevitable jealousy between him and
> the gentlemen; this forces him to become a father and protector of

the common people, and to endeavor always to humble every proud, aspiring senator, or other officer in the state, who is in danger of acquiring an influence too great for the law, or the spirit of the constitution.[37]

James Wilson likewise defended both an independent chief magistrate and a weak senate on the grounds that the president would naturally be "the man of the people," their ally against the aristocratic few.[38] He would "stand the mediator between the intrigues & sinister views of the Representatives and the general liberties & interests of the people."[39]

With Adams posted overseas, Wilson and Hamilton led the campaign in favor of a strong executive in the Philadelphia Convention (although the latter left Philadelphia on June 29 and did not return until the end of the proceedings). It was Wilson who moved that the new federal executive should "consist of a single person," a proposal he defended on the grounds that "the people of America Did not oppose the British King but the parliament – the opposition was not against an Unity but a corrupt multitude."[40] And it was largely thanks to their combined efforts (along with those of Gouverneur Morris) that Article II of the Constitution created a single president, independent of the legislature, armed with a veto and vested with the authority of commander-in-chief. But it is essential to recognize that Hamilton and Wilson (along with Adams, *in absentia*) had wished to go even further. Each had argued strenuously in favor of giving the president an "absolute" rather than "qualified" negative (that is, a veto that could not be overridden by a legislative supermajority), and insisted that the chief magistrate should have plenary power to make appointments to executive offices (without the consent of the Senate).[41] Moreover, in his famous speech of June 18, Hamilton broke with Wilson in proposing that the president should serve a life term "on good behavior" – a proposal supported by four state delegations, as well as by Madison and Washington himself.[42]

Hamilton made no secret of the motivating idea behind these proposals. He believed "that the British Gov[ernmen]t. was the best in the world: and that he doubted much whether any thing short of it would do in America." If his fellow citizens could not be persuaded to adopt a proper hereditary monarchy, "we ought to go as far in order to attain stability and permanency, as republican principles will admit." As for the objection "that such an Executive will be an elective Monarch,"[43] Hamilton answered that "Monarch is an indefinite term. It marks not either the degree or duration of power. If this Executive Magistrate w[oul]d. be a monarch for life – the other prop[ose]d. by the Report from the Committee of the whole, w[oul]d. be a monarch for seven years." The president, in short, would be a "monarch" whether given an absolute negative or a qualified veto; whether elected for seven years or for life. The question was not whether to have a monarch, but, rather, what kind of monarch to have. And Hamilton's answer to this question was perfectly clear: a British monarch, or the closest available thing to it.

But the British monarch that Hamilton had in mind was not the beleaguered, empirical figure described by Hume, reduced to using patronage to compensate for the erosion of his rightful prerogatives. This figure could not possibly serve as the sort of transcendent champion of the Commons that Hamilton had desired since 1775. Hamilton wanted the new American chief magistrate to resemble instead the British monarch of his high Royalist constitutional imagination: the "only Sovereign of the Empire," vested with sweeping prerogatives that no actual English king had wielded for a hundred years. Yet Hamilton did not quite get his way. The executive that emerged from the Convention was far more powerful than many would have wished, but a good deal less powerful than Hamilton himself had hoped. It is this fact above all that explains the peculiar character of Publius's essays on the executive.

II

While Hamilton believed that the new president was insufficiently monarchical, he confronted a mass of Anti-Federalist opinion that took precisely the opposite view. Many Americans would have agreed with

Edmund Randolph of Virginia that the proposed single executive amounted to a "foetus of monarchy."[44] Thus, Mercy Otis Warren fumed that the Constitution established a "Republican *form* of government, founded on the principles of monarchy," investing "discretionary powers in the hands of man, which he may, or may not abuse."[45] Luther Martin of Maryland, one of the dissenting delegates to the Convention, likewise declared that the new president "as here constituted, was a king, in every thing but the name" and that he would be able "to become a king in *name*, as well as in substance, and establish himself in office not only for his own life, but even, if he chooses, to have that authority perpetuated to his family"[46] – a point seconded by "Montezuma," who wrote in the *Independent Gazetteer* (posing satirically as a Federalist) that "president" was merely a name adopted "in conformity to the prejudices of a silly people who are so foolishly fond of a Republican government, that we were obliged to accommodate in names and forms to them, in order more effectually to secure the substance of our proposed plan; but we all know that Cromwell was a King, with the title of Protector."[47] The anonymous author of the "Tamony" letters agreed: in truth, he observed, "though not dignified with the magic name of King," the president "will possess more supreme power, than Great Britain allows her hereditary monarchs."[48]

Hamilton's task in *Federalist* 67–77 was to answer this charge. He sought, on the one hand, to defend a strong executive vested with significant prerogative powers; but, at the same time, he attempted to assuage concerns about the monarchical tendencies of the Constitution by stressing the *weakness* of the president relative to the king of Great Britain. Rather than applauding the degree to which the new Constitution borrowed from the British original, Hamilton's tactic in this context was to accentuate its distance from that model. This approach required two highly rhetorical series of maneuvers. First, Hamilton had to defend as virtues of the Article II presidency all of the features that he had assailed as its vices in the Convention itself: the lack of a life term, the absence of an absolute negative, the partial character of the chief magistrate's appointment power and so on. Second, and even more importantly, he had to paint a wholly outlandish picture of the powers of the British monarch, as they actually existed in 1787. That is, in order to make the presidency look weak in relation to the British monarchy, he had to contrast the former to a radically idealized, parchment version of the latter.[49] Hamilton knew perfectly well that the prerogative powers that he attributed to the crown in these essays had not in fact been wielded by English kings for generations; indeed, as we have seen, this had always been his great lament. His performance in *Federalist* 67–77 was, therefore, disingenuous in the extreme, but it was not simply that. The rhetorical imperative to make the British monarchy seem stupendously powerful gave Hamilton a final, grand opportunity to reaffirm his own radical conception of the *proper* role of the British sovereign, one that he had been defending since the *Farmer Refuted*.[50] The result was perhaps the most stridently Royalist account of the British constitution to appear in the eighteenth century.

Hamilton began his performance by complaining that no aspect of the proposed Constitution "has been inveighed against with less candor or criticised with less judgment" than its vision of the chief magistrate. "Here the writers against the Constitution seem to have taken pains to signalize their talent of misrepresentation. Calculating upon the aversion of the people to monarchy, they have endeavored to enlist all their jealousies and apprehensions in opposition to the intended President of the United States; not merely as the embryo, but as the full-grown progeny, of that detested parent" (here Hamilton was clearly recalling Randolph's charge that the president would be a "foetus of monarchy," *Fed.* 67, 452). He proceeded to offer an elaborate satire of Anti-Federalist anxieties:

> To establish the pretended affinity [with monarchy], they have not scrupled to draw resources even from the regions of fiction. The authorities of a magistrate, in few instances greater, in some instances less, than those of a Governor of New-York, have been

magnified into more than royal prerogatives. He has been decorated
with attributes superior in dignity and splendor to those of a King of
Great Britain. He has been shown to us with the diadem sparkling
on his brow and the imperial purple flowing in his train. He has
been seated on a throne surrounded with minions and mistresses;
giving audience to the envoys of foreign potentates, in all the
supercilious pomp of majesty. The images of Asiatic despotism and
voluptuousness have scarcely been wanting to crown the
exaggerated scene. We have been taught to tremble at the terrific
visages of murdering janizaries, and to blush at the unveiled
mysteries of a future seraglio.

(*Fed.* 67, 452–53)

Drawing perhaps from the opening of Book II of *Paradise Lost* – where
we encounter Satan seated "High on a throne of royal state, which
far / Outshone the wealth or Ormuz and of Ind, / Or where the gorgeous
East with richest hand / Showers on her kings barbaric pearl and gold"
(II.1–4)[51] – Hamilton lampooned his opponents for imagining the new
president as an Asiatic Grand Signor, "decorated with attributes superior in dignity and splendor to those of a King of Great Britain."

His refutation of the charge takes the form of a point-by-point
comparison of the powers of the president and the British monarch,
designed to show the relative weakness of the former.[52] The discussion begins innocently enough, by stating the obvious: although both
the British constitution and the proposed American one vest the
"executive authority" in "a single magistrate," in the latter "that
magistrate is to be elected for four years; and is to be re-eligible as
often as the People of the United States shall think him worthy of
their confidence," whereas the king of Great Britain serves for life
as a hereditary prince. Hamilton had bemoaned this asymmetry in the
Convention, but here it served his purpose. Where the president can
be removed by impeachment, the king is immune from such proceedings and his person is deemed "sacred and inviolable" (*Fed.* 69, 463).
Likewise, the king presides over an established church and may

"confer titles of nobility," prerogatives the president lacks. And, whereas the "the President is to nominate, and, *with the advice and consent of the Senate*, to appoint Ambassadors and other public Ministers, Judges of the Supreme Court, and in general all officers of the United States established by law," the king "appoints to all offices" without the formal consent of a legislative body (*Fed.* 69, 468). Once again, Hamilton had desperately sought to assign the president an analogous prerogative of appointment, but now this failure is presented as a virtue of the scheme.

So far, all of this is relatively unremarkable.[53] But Hamilton does not leave matters here. "The President of the United States," he continues, "is to have power to return a bill, which shall have passed the two branches of the Legislature, for re-consideration; and the bill so returned is to become a law, if, upon that reconsideration, it be approved by two thirds of both houses. The King of Great Britain, on his part, has an absolute negative upon the acts of the two houses of Parliament." (*Fed.* 69, 463–64) The royal negative, as Hamilton well knew, had not been exercised for generations, but here he insists that

> the disuse of that power for a considerable time past does not affect the reality of its existence; and is to be ascribed wholly to the crown's having found the means of substituting influence to authority, or the art of gaining a majority in one or the other of the two houses, to the necessity of exerting a prerogative which could seldom be exerted without hazarding some degree of national agitation.
>
> (*Fed.* 69, 464)

In order to make the British monarch appear as strong as possible (and the American president correspondingly weak), Hamilton deploys the Whig explanation for the "disuse" of the negative: the king has simply felt no need to wield the negative because he is powerful enough to control both houses of Parliament by means of corruption. This was a view of the British constitutional predicament that Hamilton had always rejected; he had instead followed Hume in regarding "corruption" as a wholly inadequate, but still essential, *replacement* for prerogative powers (chiefly, the negative voice) that now, regrettably, existed only as a matter of form. Like "Centinel," he bemoaned the fact that "the king of England ... enjoys but in *name* the prerogative of a negative upon the parliament" and "has not dared to exercise it for near a century past."[55]

Moreover, Hamilton would shortly argue in *Federalist* 73 that the qualified negative of the president should be preferred to the absolute negative because it would *strengthen*, rather than weaken the prerogative: "in proportion as it would be less apt to offend, it would be more apt to be exercised; and for this very reason it may in practice be found more effectual" (*Fed.* 73, 498). But in this polemical context Hamilton is happy to emphasize the weakness of the president's qualified negative in relation to what he had regarded for two decades as a lamentably defunct prerogative of the sovereign. As one Anti-Federalist complained, "touching on the President" ("more properly, our new KING"), Hamilton and his allies were aiming "to conceal his immense powers, by representing the King of Great Britain as possessed of many hereditary prerogatives, rights and powers that he was not possessed of." In particular, the president, unlike the British monarch *in fact*, is to have "a negative over the proceedings of both branches of the legislature: and to complete his uncontrouled sway, he is neither restrained nor assisted by *a privy council*, which is a novelty in government."[56]

Next, we read that "the President is to be the 'Commander-in-Chief' of the army and navy of the United States. In this respect his authority would be nominally the same with that of the king of Great Britain, but in substance much inferior to it," for "that of the British king extends to the declaring of war and to the raising and regulating of fleets and armies – all which, by the Constitution under consideration, would appertain to the Legislature" (*Fed.* 69, 465).[57] This was an extraordinary claim. Although the making of war and peace formally remained prerogatives of the crown, in reality decisions of this kind had long been taken by cabinet ministers. These ministers were in turn required to maintain the support of a majority in the House of

Commons, and they themselves sat in one of the two Houses.[58] Indeed, George III had only recently shown himself powerless to assume any personal control over the waging of the Revolutionary War, and in 1779 had nearly provoked a constitutional crisis simply by choosing to summon and address his own cabinet (no monarch since Queen Anne had done so).[59] Moreover, while it remained a prerogative of "the crown" (read: ministers of the crown) to raise and equip armies and fleets, monarchs since the Glorious Revolution had lacked the authority to do so in the absence of an annual "Mutiny Act" passed by the House of Commons – and, in any event, required supply from the Commons in order to pay their troops.[60]

Hamilton's Anti-Federalist opponents eagerly seized upon these facts. The still unidentified author of the letters of "Cato" could distinguish no important respects in which "this president, invested with his powers and prerogatives, essentially differ[s] from the king of Great Britain (save as to name, the creation of nobility, and some immaterial incidents, the offspring of absurdity and locality)." "Cato" pointedly observed that "though it may be asserted that the king of Great-Britain has the express power of making peace or war, yet he never thinks it prudent so to do without the advice of his parliament from whom he is to derive his support – and therefore these powers, in both president and king, are substantially the same."[61] William Lancaster likewise rose in the North Carolina Ratifying Convention to insist that "a man of any information knows that the king of Great Britain cannot raise and support armies. He may call for and raise men, but he has no money to support them."[62] The author of the "Tamony" letters went even further, observing that the new president "will possess more supreme power, than Great Britain allows her hereditary monarchs, who derive ability to support an army from annual supplies, and owe the command of one to an annual mutiny law. The American President may be granted supplies for two years, and his command of a standing army is unrestrained by law."[63] Hamilton registered these objections, but replied in the language of a strident Royalist: "TAMONY, has asserted that the king of Great–Britain owes his prerogative as commander-in-chief to an annual mutiny bill. The truth is, on the contrary, that his prerogative, in this respect, is immemorial, and was only disputed, 'contrary to all reason and precedent' ... by the Long Parliament of Charles I" (*Fed.* 69, 465n.). In truth, Hamilton declared (quoting Blackstone's *Commentaries*, but badly misrepresenting the position of his source[64]), "the sole supreme government and command" of armies and navies "EVER WAS AND IS the undoubted right of his Majesty and his royal predecessors, kings and queens of England, and that both or either house of Parliament cannot nor ought to pretend to the same."

The crucial thing to note is that Hamilton had made precisely the same argument in *The Farmer Refuted* over a decade earlier. Then he was responding to Seabury's claim that British Americans owed allegiance to Parliament in return for "the protection we have received from the mother country."[65] "Nothing is more common," he lamented, "than to hear the votaries of parliament" defending this assertion, but, in truth, "they entertain erroneous conceptions of the matter." Parliament could never have protected the American colonies, because it had no rightful share of the sovereign prerogatives of war and peace. "The King himself," Hamilton insisted, "is regarded by the constitution, as the supreme protector of the empire. For this purpose, he is the generalissimo, or first in military command: in him is vested the power of making war and peace, of raising armies, equipping fleets and directing all their motions. He it is that has defended us from our enemies, and to him alone, we are obliged to render allegiance and submission."[66] The fact that his British contemporaries had regrettably "los[t] sight" of the king's sovereign authority in no way altered this constitutional reality.[67]

Hamilton's argument in *Federalist* 69 proceeds in much the same vein. "The President," he continues, "is to have power, with the advice and consent of the Senate, to make treaties, provided two thirds of the senators present concur. The king of Great Britain is the sole and absolute representative of the nation in all foreign transactions. He can of his own accord make treaties of peace, commerce, alliance, and of every other description." (*Fed. 69*, 467). Opponents of the Constitution scoffed once again. "It is contended," observed Patrick Henry in the Virginia Ratifying Convention, "that, if the king of Great Britain makes a treaty within the line of his prerogative, it is the law of the land." But

> can the English monarch make a treaty which shall subvert the common law of England, and the constitution? Dare he make a treaty that shall violate Magna Charta, or the bill of rights? Dare he do any thing derogatory to the honor, or subversive of the great privileges, of his people? No, sir. If he did, it would be nugatory, and the attempt would endanger his existence.[68]

Even some Federalists were prompted to concede as much. Wilson Nicholas of Virginia mocked the notion that "the king of Great Britain can make what treaties he pleases." "But, sir," he countered, "do not the House of Commons influence them? Will he make a treaty manifestly repugnant to their interest? Will they not tell him he is mistaken in that respect, as in many others? Will they not bring the minister who advises a bad treaty to punishment? This gives them such influence that they can dictate in what manner they shall be made." Francis Corbin added that "if the king were to make such a treaty himself, contrary to the advice of his ministry," a constitutional crisis would ensue.[69] Moreover, a number of Anti-Federalists pointed out that treaties in Britain were in fact frequently laid before Parliament – not least the Peace of Paris that had ended the Revolutionary War.[70]

Hamilton once again stuck to his Royalist guns. "It has been insinuated," he wrote, "that his authority [i.e. the king's] in this respect is not conclusive, and that his conventions with foreign powers are subject to the revision, and stand in need of the ratification, of Parliament." But, Hamilton insisted,

> I believe this doctrine was never heard of, till it was broached upon the present occasion. Every jurist of that kingdom, and every other

man acquainted with its Constitution, knows, as an established
fact, that the prerogative of making treaties exists in the crown in
its utmost plentitude; and that the compacts entered into by the
royal authority have the most complete legal validity and
perfection, independent of any other sanction.

(*Fed.* 69, 467)[71]

James Iredell, who simply paraphrased Hamilton's comparative argument in the North Carolina Convention, agreed: "A gentleman from
New Hanover has asked whether it is not the practice, in Great
Britain, to submit treaties to Parliament, before they are esteemed as
valid. The king has the sole authority, by the laws of that country, to
make treaties." To be sure, "after treaties are made, they are frequently discussed in the two houses, where, of late years, the most
important matters of government have been narrowly examined." But
"the constitutional power of making treaties is vested in the crown;
and the power with whom the treaty is made considers it as binding,
without any act of Parliament."[72]

Hamilton had no compunction about carrying his argument
through to its logical conclusion. He confidently attributed to the
person of the king an effective prerogative to "prorogue or even dissolve
the Parliament," to select his ministers at pleasure, to "make denizens
of aliens," to "erect corporations with all the rights incident to corporate bodies," to "serve as the arbiter of commerce," "establish markets
and fairs," "regulate weights and measures," "lay embargoes for a
limited time," "coin money," and "authorize or prohibit the circulation of foreign coin" (*Fed.* 69, 470). And although the sovereign was
duty-bound to seek advice from his ministers, Hamilton insisted that
"the king is not bound by the resolutions of his council, though they
are answerable for the advice they give. He is the absolute master of his
own conduct in the exercise of his office and may observe or disregard
the council[sic] given to him at his sole discretion" (*Fed.* 70, 478).
Again, as a description of the British monarchy as it actually functioned
in the late eighteenth century, this was mere burlesque. But as a
defense of a particular conception of what the monarchy *should* be like

under the proper construal of the English constitution, it was perfectly continuous with what Hamilton and other Patriots of similar views had been arguing since the imperial crisis. At that time, even Jefferson had implored the king to separate himself from his "British counselors" – who were dismissed as intruding "parties" – and to "think and act for yourself and your people."[73] But this high Royalist understanding of the kingly office was as reactionary in 1787 as it had been in 1775.

In other contexts, it suited Hamilton's purpose to acknowledge this fact. In *Federalist* 71, he developed a subtle a fortiori argument designed to reassure critics who might remain anxious about the prerogatives assigned to the chief magistrate. In Britain, the argument goes, the king is vested with hereditary power and other "splendid attributes," but even these advantages of the crown had spectacularly failed to prevent the House of Commons from achieving complete supremacy during the course of the previous century. How much less, then, should we fear that the far weaker president, as imagined in Article II, would come to dominate the legislature? This argument, in short, attempted to strike yet another delicate balance: it once again sought to emphasize the strengths of the British monarch, relative to those of the president, but, at the same time, to demonstrate that the monarchy had been gradually but utterly subjected to the legislature despite these advantages (thus directly contradicting the carefully wrought account of sweeping royal power in *Federalist* 69).

> If a British House of Commons from the most feeble beginnings, *from the mere power of assenting or disagreeing to the imposition of a new tax*, have, by rapid strides, reduced the prerogatives of the crown and the privileges of the nobility within the limits they conceived to be compatible with the principles of a free government, while they raised themselves to the rank and consequence of a coequal branch of the Legislature; if they have been able, in one instance, to abolish both the royalty and the aristocracy, and to overturn all the ancient establishments, as well in the church as State; if they have been able, on a recent occasion,

> to make the monarch tremble at the prospect of an innovation
> attempted by them [Charles James Fox's India Bill[74]], what would
> be to be feared from an elective magistrate of four years duration,
> with the confined authorities of a President of the United States?
>
> (*Fed.* 71, 485–86)[75]

Here the king of Great Britain, depicted in *Federalist* 69 as master of
all he surveys, is shown "trembling" before an all-powerful legislature. We are finally allowed to glimpse the Humean reality lurking
behind the Royalist idyll.

III

Fifteen years after the Constitution was ratified, the Virginia jurist St.
George Tucker revisited Hamilton's influential comparison of the
presidency and the British monarchy in his 1803 annotated edition of
Blackstone's *Commentaries*. The occasion was apposite: Hamilton had
festooned his analysis of royal power in *Federalist* 69 with references
and direct quotations drawn from Blackstone, plainly hoping that the
appearance of agreement with England's greatest constitutional authority would lend credibility to his account. Tucker, for his part, was no
committed defender of the new American chief magistracy: he openly
mused that the presidency might perhaps be replaced with a "numerous executive," on the model of the French Directory, and fretted in his
commentary that "if a single executive do not exhibit all the features
of monarchy at first, like the infant Hercules, it requires only time to
mature it's [sic] strength, to evince the extent of it's [sic] powers."[76]
But he was nonetheless fully prepared to explore and acknowledge the
ways in which the American executive might be seen to perfect the
British original. His project, however, required emphasizing the degree
to which Hamilton had, in fact, deployed a caricature of Blackstone's
constitutional analysis in 1788. For, while Blackstone had admittedly
been a Tory who was eager to minimize the extent of the century-long
transition from royal to ministerial government, Tucker recognized
that he had also been a lucid observer of British political reality. The

great jurist had indeed supplied a list of what remained, as a matter of law, the prerogatives of the crown (although he took a far narrower view of these than Hamilton suggested[77]), but he had also immediately reminded his readers that many of these powers were no longer at the effective disposal of the king.

"The powers of the crown are now to all appearances greatly curtailed and diminished since the reign of King James the first," Blackstone had observed, to the extent that "we may perhaps be led to think that, the balance is enclined pretty strongly to the popular scale, and that the executive magistrate has neither independence nor power enough left, to form that check upon the lords and commons, which the founders of our constitution intended."[78] Blackstone argued that this conclusion was overly hasty, but not because he had any illusions that British monarchs could exert their prerogative powers in government as they had before the parliamentarian revolutions. Instead, like Hume, he identified "influence" as a substitute for prerogative, although he was both far more confident in its efficacy than was Hume, and far more anxious about the dangers of the substitution (in this respect, he came rather close to endorsing the standard Whig theory of English constitutional corruption).[79] "The instruments of [royal] power are not perhaps so open and avowed as they formerly were," on Blackstone's telling, "but they are not the weaker on that account." The rise of what we now call the eighteenth-century fiscal–military state had placed the monarch in control of an extensive patronage network and thereby assigned the "executive power so persuasive an energy ... as will amply make amends for the loss of external prerogative." "Whatever may have become of the *nominal*, the *real* power of the crown has not been too far weakened by any transactions of the last century ... the stern commands of prerogative have yielded to the milder voice of influence."[80] On Blackstone's account, if the king remained strong, it was *despite* the fact that he no longer wielded the legal powers of the crown; the latter were now the effective possession of ministers accountable to Parliament.

Armed with this recognition, Tucker concluded that, although it is certainly true that "many of the most important prerogatives of the British crown, are transferred from the executive authority, in the United States, to the supreme national council, in congress assembled," in a very real sense the Constitution had assigned the American president powers far *greater* than any enjoyed by the king of Great Britain.[81] In the English constitution, the "unity of the executive" and its attendant "dispatch" were, in truth, illusory:

> If such are the real advantages of a single executive magistrate, we may contend that they are found in a much greater degree in the federal government, than in the English. In the latter it exists, only theoretically, in an individual; the practical exercise of it, being devolved upon ministers, councils, and boards. The king, according to the acknowledged principles of the constitution, not being responsible for any of his acts, the minister upon whom all responsibility devolves, to secure his indemnity acts by the advice of the privy council to whom every measure of importance is submitted, before it is carried into effect. His plans are often digested and canvassed in a still more secret conclave, consisting of the principal officers of state, and stiled the cabinet-council, before they are communicated to the privy council: matters are frequently referred to the different boards, for their advice thereon, previously to their discussion, and final decision, in the council. Thus, in fact, the unity of the executive is merely ideal, existing only in the theory of the government; whatever is said of the unanimity, or dispatch arising from the unity of the executive power, is therefore without foundation.[82]

Here was the great fact about the eighteenth-century British monarchy that Hamilton had deplored for all of his adult life, the same fact that he had been forced to occlude in order to make his rhetorical case in *Federalist* 69. While the crown retained its "prerogatives," the king enjoyed most of them only in name.[83] Under the Constitution of the United States, in contrast, "we find a single executive officer substituted for a numerous board, where responsibility is divided, till it is entirely lost, and where the chance of unanimity lessens in geometrical proportion to the number that compose it."[84] Moreover, "as every executive measure must originate in the breast of the president, his plans will have all the benefit of uniformity, that can be expected to flow from the operations of any individual mind."[85] The president of the United States does in reality what the king of Great Britain does only in theory.

But if the new president was, for this reason, more powerful than any British monarch had been for almost a century, he was nonetheless weaker than the splendid, revivified sovereign that Hamilton had begun to imagine in 1775. At least one of his fellow delegates at the Convention registered and appreciated this fact. Years later, Thomas Hart Benton of Missouri recalled a conversation with the aged Rufus King of New York "upon the formation of the constitution in the federal convention of 1787." On this occasion, he explained, King "said some things to me which, I think ought to be remembered by future generations, to enable them to appreciate justly those founders of our government who were in favor of a stronger organization [i.e. executive] than was adopted."

> He said: "You young men who have been born since the Revolution, look with horror upon the name of a King, and upon all propositions for a strong government. It was not so with us. We were born the subjects of a King, and were accustomed to subscribe ourselves 'His Majesty's most faithful subjects'; and we began the quarrel which ended in the Revolution, not against the King, but against his parliament."[86]

Publius himself could not have said it any better.

NOTES

1 Samuel Seabury, *A View of the Controversy Between Great Britain and her Colonies* (New York, 1774), 9.
2 Alexander Hamilton, *The Farmer Refuted: or, A More Impartial and Comprehensive View of the Dispute between Great-Britain and the Colonies* (New York, 1775), 15. Hamilton quotes in full Seabury's characterization of the English constitution.

3 Ibid., 16.

4 Ibid., 17.

5 See Eric Nelson, *The Royalist Revolution: Monarchy and the American Founding* (Cambridge, MA: Harvard University Press, 2014), esp. ch. 1.

6 Benjamin Franklin to Samuel Cooper, June 8, 1770, in *The Papers of Benjamin Franklin*, XVII, ed. William B. Willcox (New Haven, CT: Yale University Press, 1973) (hereafter *PBF*), 163.

7 Hamilton, *The Farmer Refuted*, 16. My italics

8 Ibid. My italics.

9 Charles I, *His Maiesties Ansvver to the XIX Propositions of Both Houses of Parliament* (London, 1642), 11–12.

10 See Henry Ferne, *A Reply unto Severall Treatises* (London, 1643), 17–18. For Ferne's position on the far right (as it were) of Royalist discourse, see Corinne Comstock Weston, *English Constitutional Theory and the House of Lords, 1556–1832* (New York: Routledge and Kegan Paul, 1965), 23–24.

11 Ferne, *A Reply*, 32.

12 For the closest thing to a second contemporary American endorsement of this view, see Benjamin Franklin, "Marginalia in *An Inquiry*, an Anonymous Pamphlet," in *PBF*, XVII, 345 ("the King ... alone is the Sovereign").

13 It was, for example, taken as an uncontroversial statement of fact in the Constitutional Convention that "the King of G[reat] B[ritain]. had not exerted his negative since the Revolution [i.e. 1688]." See *The Records of the Federal Convention of 1787*, 3 vols., ed. Max Farrand (New Haven, CT: Yale University Press, 1911), I, 98–99 (note that Hamilton and Franklin agreed on this point). British Americans were not alone in making this error. See e.g. Jean-Louis Delolme, *The Constitution of England* (London, 1775), 398–99.

14 David Hume, *Political Essays*, ed. Knud Haakonssen (Cambridge: Cambridge University Press, 1994), 25.

15 Ibid.

16 For the views of the "Court Whigs" whose thoughts prefigured Hume's, see Simon Targett, "Government and Ideology during the Age of the Whig Supremacy: The Political Arguments of Sir Robert Walpole's Newspaper Propagandists," *The Historical Journal*, 37 (1994), 289–317 (esp. 307–13).

17 Hume, *Political Essays*, 26.

18 *Records of the Federal Convention*, I, 376.

19 Ibid. On Hamilton's use of Hume, see Paul Rahe, *Republics Ancient and Modern*, 3 vols. (Chapel Hill: University of North Carolina Press, 1994), III, 115–16; Forrest McDonald, *The American Presidency: An Intellectual History* (Lawrence: University Press of Kansas, 1994), 94–97; and Gerald Stourzh, *Alexander Hamilton and the Idea of Republican Government* (Stanford, CA: Stanford University Press, 70–87). This was the aspect of Hamilton's thought that Jefferson later bowdlerized for polemical purposes (see Jefferson, "The Anas, 1791–1806," in *The Works of Thomas Jefferson*, ed. Paul Leicester Ford [New York: G. P. Putnam's Sons, 1892], I, 167–80). "Hamilton," Jefferson announced, "was not only a monarchist, but for a monarchy bottomed on corruption" (179). For a discussion of Jefferson's use of "political gossip" in constructing this account of Hamilton's constitutionalism, see Joanne B. Freeman, "Poison, Whispers, and Fame: Jefferson's 'Anas' and Political Gossip in the Early Republic," *Journal of the Early Republic*, 15 (1995), 25–57 (esp. 36–39, 55). Wilson likewise came quite close to endorsing Hume's position in remarks to the Pennsylvania Ratifying Convention: "The reason why it is necessary in England to continue such influence [i.e the king's patronage power], is, that the crown, in order to secure its own influence against two other branches of the legislature, must continue to bestow places; but those places produce the opposition which frequently runs so strong in the British Parliament." *DHRC*, II, 498.

20 While I shall use the established terminology of "Federalist" and "Anti-Federalist" throughout the remainder of this essay, I do so with a deep sense of its inadequacy. To label opponents of the Constitution as "Anti-Federalists" is to beg the very question that the parties were debating: namely, whether the unamended Constitution provided the only plausible route to an effective federal union of the states. Virtually all the participants in the ratification debates accepted that the Articles of Confederation had proved gravely deficient and that a series of new powers should accordingly be conferred on the federal government. All of them were "federalists" in this sense.

21 Hamilton adds that, in this period, "when the sovereign happened to be a man of vigorous and warlike temper and of superior abilities, he would acquire a personal weight and influence, which answered, for the time, the purpose of a more regular authority." This comment also adapts a remark by Hume: "where [the king] was possessed of personal vigour and abilities

(for his situation required these advantages) he was commonly able to preserve his authority, and maintain his station as head of the community, and the chief fountain of law and justice." Compare John Adams, *Defence of the Constitutions of Government of the United States*, 3 vols. (London, 1787–88), I, 75: "When the prince was an able statesman and warrior, he was able to preserve order; but when he was weak and indolent, it was common for two or three barons in conjunction to make war upon him."

22 Hamilton may have taken this phrase from Hume, who writes that, immediately after the signing of Magna Carta, "those generous barons, who first extorted these concessions, still held their swords in their hands" (David Hume, *The History of England* (Indianapolis: Liberty Fund, 1983), I, 445–46).

23 *DHRC*, XXII, 1958.

24 Adam Smith, *An Inquiry into the Nature and Causes of the Wealth of Nations*, 2 vols., ed. R. H. Campbell, A. S. Skinner, and W. B. Todd (Indianapolis: Liberty Fund, 1981), I, 418. Madison was clearly paraphrasing the same passage in his well-known October 24,1787 letter to Thomas Jefferson: "[The new Constitution] presents the aspect rather of a feudal system of republics, if such a phrase may be used, than of a Confederacy of independent States. And what has been the progress and event of the feudal Constitutions? In all of them a continual struggle between the head and the inferior members, until a final victory has been gained in some instances by one, in others, by the other of them." *James Madison: Writings*, ed. Jack N. Rakove (New York: Library of America, 1999), 146–47. Cf. *Federalist* 45, 310–311.

25 Ibid., I, 386. Writing several years before Smith (although probably influenced by his Edinburgh lectures of 1748–50), William Robertson referred to "the universal anarchy" of feudalism (Robertson, *History*, 16). Hume, for his part, had seen within this form of political life "a mixture of ... order and anarchy, stability and revolution" (Hume, *The History of England*, I, 456). Gibbon likewise later referred to the "feudal anarchy of Europe" and "the days of feudal anarchy." See Edward Gibbon, *The History of the Decline and Fall of the Roman Empire*, ed. J. B. Bury, 12 vols. (New York: Fred de Fau and Co., 1906), VII, 323, 361. Chapter 53, in which this phrase appears, was not published until 1788. For Robertson's debts to Smith, see Nicholas Phillipson, "Providence and Progress: An Introduction to the Historical Thought of William Robertson," in *William*

Robertson and the Expansion of Empire, ed. Stewart J. Brown (Cambridge: Cambridge University Press, 1997), 55–73 (esp. 59–60).

26 J. G. A. Pocock, *The Ancient Constitution and the Feudal Law: A Study of English Historical Thought in the Seventeenth Century* (Cambridge: Cambridge University Press, 1957).

27 Robert Brady, *A Complete History of England, from The First Entrance of the Romans under The Conduct of Julius Caesar, Unto the End of the Reign of King Henry III* (London, 1685), B1r.

28 Ibid., B2r.

29 Hume, *The History of England*, I, 464.

30 *Farmer Refuted*, 18.

31 [Thomson Mason], "The British American" (1774), Letter 6, in *The American Archives*, ed. Peter Force (Washington, D.C.: St. Clair Clarke and Peter Force, 1837), 4th series, I, 519. See also William Strahan to David Hall, April 7, 1766, in "Correspondence between William Strahan and David Hall, 1763–1777," *Pennsylvania Magazine of History and Biography*, X (1886), 86–99 (esp. 97–98). "The Crown, even upon the ablest Head, is now hardly able to retain its just and proper Weight in the Legislature."

32 For a full discussion, see Nelson, *The Royalist Revolution*, ch. 4.

33 "Ludlow," Letter 2, *The Pennsylvania Journal*, May 28, 1777, 1.

34 Adams to Elbridge Gerry, November 4, 1779, in *Papers of John Adams*, ed. Robert J. Taylor (Cambridge, MA: Harvard University Press, 1977), VIII, 276.

35 Adams to Jefferson, December 6, 1787, in *The Adams–Jefferson Letters*, ed. Lester J. Cappon (Chapel Hill: University of North Carolina Press, 1988), 213. Compare Adams's later claim that "cities have advanced liberty and knowledge by setting up kings to control nobles ... Since the existence of courts, the barons have been humbled and the people liberated from villainage." Adams, Annotations to Mary Wollstonecraft, *Historical and Moral View of the Origin and Progress of the French Revolution* (1796), reprinted in Zoltán Haraszti, *John Adams and the Prophets of Progress* (Cambridge, MA: Harvard University Press, 1952), 232–33.

36 Adams, *Defence*, III, 299. Compare Delolme, *The Constitution of England*, 210–11.

37 Adams, *Defence*, III, 460.

38 *Records*, I, 523. For Wilson's impassioned rejection of hereditary aristocracy, see his "Lectures on Law" (1790), in *The Works of James*

Wilson, ed. Robert Green McCloskey, 2 vols. (Cambridge, MA: Belknap Press of Harvard University Press, 1967), I, esp. 314–15.

39 *Records*, II, 30.

40 Ibid., I, 71 (King).

41 For Wilson's endorsement of these proposals, see ibid., I, 98; II, 73–74 (on the negative); I, 119; II, 538–39 (on the appointment power). For Hamilton's, see ibid., I, 98; I, 291–93.

42 Ibid., 1:290–91. The sheet in Madison's Notes recording this vote and its circumstances is among the most extensively revised in the manuscript. Madison was eager, in retrospect, to cast his support of the motion as purely tactical in character, as opposed to Hamilton's. See Mary Bilder, *Madison's Hand: Revising the Constitutional Convention* (Cambridge, MA: Harvard University Press, 2015), 114–15.

43 *Records*, I, 290.

44 Ibid., I, 66.

45 Mercy Otis Warren, *Observations on the New Constitution, and on the Federal and State Conventions* (Boston, MA, 1788) in *Pamphlets on the Constitution of the United States*, ed. Paul Leicester Ford (New York: Da Capo Press, 1968), 7, 15. Compare William Grayson's comment of June 11, 1788 in the Virginia Ratifying Convention: "What, sir, is the present Constitution? A republican government founded on the principles of monarchy, with the three estates. Is it like the model of Tacitus or Montesquieu? Are there checks in it, as in the British monarchy? There is an executive fetter in some parts, and as unlimited in others as a Roman dictator." *DHRC*, XI, 1169.

46 Luther Martin, "Mr. Martin's Information to the General Assembly of the States of Maryland," in *The Complete Anti-Federalist*, ed. Herbert J. Storing (Chicago, IL: Chicago University Press), II, 67–68.

47 "Letter from Montezuma," *Independent Gazetteer* (Philadelphia), October 17, 1787. The author continues by attributing to the president all of the prerogatives of the crown, as enumerated by Blackstone.

48 "Tamony," *The Virginia Independent Chronicle*, December 20, 1787.

49 See the wise remark on this subject in Frank Prochaska, *The Eagle and the Crown: Americans and the British Monarchy* (New Haven, CT: Yale University Press, 2008), 14. See also Ray Raphael, *Mr. President: How and Why the Founders Created a Chief Executive* (New York: Alfred A. Knopf, 2012), 151; and Josep M. Colomer, "Elected Kings with the Name of

Presidents. On the Origins of Presidentialism in the United States and Latin America," *Revista Latinoamericana de Política Comparada*, 7 (2013), 79–97.

50 Scholars have tended to take Hamilton's description of the powers of the crown at face value. See, most recently, Michael P. Federici, *The Political Philosophy of Alexander Hamilton* (Baltimore, MD: Johns Hopkins University Press, 2012), 135.

51 *John Milton*, ed. Stephen Orgel and Jonathan Goldberg (Oxford: Oxford University Press, 1991), 376.

52 Hamilton also compares both to the governor of New York, with the aim of demonstrating that the president is far more similar to him than to the king.

53 I say "relatively," because even here Hamilton's account is significantly exaggerated. Legally, all appointments to office were indeed a matter of the royal prerogative – and eighteenth-century monarchs did retain the discretionary power to create peers and bishops – but, in practice, the king was not at liberty to select ministers at pleasure (any minister was required to command the support of the House of Commons). Moreover, it was an accepted norm that he would not dictate appointments to executive departments below the ministerial level. On this, see John Brooke, *George III: A Biography of America's Last Monarch* (New York: McGraw-Hill, 1972), 241; John Brewer, "Ministerial Responsibility and the Powers of the Crown," in *Party Ideology and Popular Politics at the Accession of George III* (Cambridge: Cambridge University Press, 1976), 112–36.

54 Compare with *Fed.* 73, 496–97.

55 "Centinel," Letter 2, in *Complete Anti-Federalist*, II, 150–51. On this issue, see William E. Scheuerman, "American Kingship? Monarchical Origins of Modern Presidentialism," *Polity*, 37 (2005), 24–53 (esp. 41).

56 [Benjamin Workman,] "Philadelphiensis," Letter 12, in *Complete Anti-Federalist*, III, 137.

57 Compare "Philadelphiensis," Letter 10, ibid., 131–32.

58 See, in general, Jeremy Black, *Parliament and Foreign Policy in the Eighteenth Century* (Cambridge: Cambridge University Press, 2004), 1–12.

59 On this, see Andrew Jackson O'Shaughnessy, "'If Others Will Not be Active, I Must Drive': George III and the American Revolution," *Early American Studies*, 2 (2004), 1–46 (esp. 33). When forced to accept the principle of American independence in 1782, George went so far as to draft

a letter of abdication, lamenting that "one Branch of the legislature" had "totally incapacitated Him" from "conducting the War with effect" (quoted in O'Shaughnessy, *The Men Who Lost America: British Leadership, the American Revolution, and the Fate of the Empire* [New Haven, CT: Yale University Press, 2013], 42–43). For a more general account, see Brewer, *Party Ideology and Popular Politics*, 112–36.

60 The Act of Settlement had likewise imposed a requirement of parliamentary consent for any war fought for non-British interests – although this limitation was not invoked during the eighteenth century. See Jeremy Black, *A System of Ambition? British Foreign Policy 1660–1793*, 2nd ed. (Stroud: Sutton, 2000), 14; and Jack Rakove, "Taking the Prerogative out of the Presidency: An Originalist Perspective," *Presidential Studies Quarterly*, 37 (2007), 85–100 (esp. 88–91).

61 "Cato," Letter 4, in *DHRC*, XIV, 10.

62 Elliot, *Debates in the Several State Conventions*, IV, 214. Iredell, for one, acknowledged this fact (*Pamphlets on the Constitution of the United States*, 363).

63 "Tamony," *The Virginia Independent Chronicle*, December 20, 1787. Madison conceded this point. See *Fed.* 41, 273.

64 See Sir William Blackstone, *Commentaries on the Laws of England*, 4 vols. (London, 1765–69), I, 254.

65 *Farmer Refuted*, 9 (paraphrasing Seabury, *A View of the Controversy*, 15–16).

66 Ibid., 9.

67 Ibid., 16.

68 *DHRC*, X, 1384–85.

69 Ibid., XII, 1251. Roger Sherman likewise conceded that "the king of Great Britain has by the constitution a power to make treaties, yet in matters of great importance he consults the parliament" (Ford, *Essays on the Constitution of the United States*, 155).

70 *DHRC*, X, 1392.

71 See, for example, Patrick Henry's remarks of June 19, 1788, *DHRC*, X, 1394–95.

72 It is worth noting that, even at the level of pure theory, the crown was required to seek parliamentary approval for any treaty requiring expenditures of money or changes to British law. See Black, *Parliament and Foreign Policy*, 2, 10, 102. James McHenry raised this point in the Federal Convention (see *RFC*, II, 395).

73 Elliot, *Debates in the Several State Conventions*, IV, 128. Iredell heaped praise on *The Federalist* in his response to George Mason's objections, calling it "a work which I hope will soon be in every body's hands" (*Pamphlets on the Constitution*, 363).

74 [Thomas Jefferson], *A Summary View of the Rights of British America* (Williamsburg, VA, 1774), 22. See Gerald Stourzh's perceptive remark that Hamilton's mature constitutional thought "was influenced by the peculiar predicament of the final stage of the British–American contest before independence, from 1774 to 1775 ... the period when leading colonial advocates like John Adams, Thomas Jefferson, James Wilson, and Alexander Hamilton himself espoused a dominion theory of the British Empire. While they now denied the supremacy of the British Parliament ... they continued to see in the king of England their sovereign ruler." Stourzh refers to this period as "an Indian summer of virtual Tory philosophy" (Stourzh, *Alexander Hamilton and the Idea of Republican Government*, 26, 43).

75 George III vehemently opposed this bill (drafted by Edmund Burke), which would have nationalized the East India Company. It passed the House of Commons, raising the prospect that the king might be left with the unpalatable choice of either accepting the bill or else attempting to revive the defunct royal negative. Instead, when the bill reached the House of Lords, the king let it be known that "whoever voted for the India Bill were not only not his friends, but he should consider as his enemies." The bill was defeated on December 17, 1783. Hamilton is stressing the fact that the king feared to wield his negative power. For this episode, see Brooke, *George III*, 250–55.

76 Compare Hamilton's remarks of June 21, 1788 in the New York Ratifying Convention *DHRC*, XXII, 1789.

77 *Blackstone's Commentaries: with Notes of Reference to the Constitution and Laws of the Federal Government of the United States*, ed. St. George Tucker, 5 vols. (Philadelphia, PA, 1803), I, 349. Tucker was particularly worried about the president's power of appointment to offices: "The influence which this power gives him, personally, is one of those parts of the constitution, which assimilates the government, in its administration, infinitely more nearly to that of Great Britain, than seems to consist with those republican principles, which ought to pervade every part of the federal constitution" (ibid., 321).

78 To take one important example, although Blackstone agreed that the crown is empowered to act on behalf of the nation "in foreign concerns," he never supposed that this category embraced "imperial" concerns. It was for this reason that he utterly rejected the Patriot Royalist position during the 1760s and 1770s. In the Commons debate over repeal of the Stamp Act on February 3, 1766, Blackstone insisted that "all the Dominions of G. B. are bound by Acts of Parl[iamen]t" – not dependent only on the crown. See *Proceedings and Debates of the British Parliaments respecting North America*, ed. Leo Francis Stock (Washington, DC: Carnegie Institution of Washington, 1924), II, 148. He likewise readily conceded that, although the king retained a legal prerogative to raise and equip armies, such forces were in fact now "kept on foot it is true only from year to year, and that by the power of parliament" (Blackstone, *Commentaries*, 1:325). Many other examples could be offered.

79 Ibid., I, 323.

80 Blackstone notes approvingly that when the conditions requiring the operation of what scholars now call the fiscal–military state are relaxed, "this adventitious power of the crown will slowly and imperceptibly diminish, as it slowly and imperceptibly rose" (ibid., 326).

81 Ibid., 326–35. Tucker's comments on this section of Blackstone make clear that he regarded this as a profoundly unwelcome development (ibid., II, 335n., 337).

82 Ibid., II, 280n.

83 Ibid., I, 316–17. Tucker may well have drawn this argument from Wilson. The latter had made precisely the same observation in his "Lectures on Law" (1790). See McClosKey, ed., *Works of James Wilson*, I, 318–19.

84 In relation to treaties, Tucker points out that, while the crown possesses "plenitude of authority in this respect," Blackstone had laid considerable stress on the fact that "the constitution hath interposed a check by means of parliamentary impeachment, for the punishment of such members as from criminal motives advise or conclude any treaty, which shall afterwards be judged to derogate from the honor and interest of the nation." Tucker, *Blackstone's Commentaries*, I, 335.

85 Ibid., 319.

86 Ibid., 318–19. Thomas Hart Benton, *Thirty Years' View, Or A History of the Working of the American Government for Thirty Years, from 1820–1850*, 2 vols. (New York, 1858), I, 58.

14　The Genius of Hamilton and the Birth of the Modern Theory of the Judiciary

William M. Treanor[1]

In late May 1788, with *The Federalist*'s essays on Congress and the executive now completed, Alexander Hamilton turned finally to Article III and the judiciary. His six essays on the judiciary, *Federalist* 78–83, had only a limited effect on ratification. No newspaper outside New York reprinted them,[2] and they appeared very late in the ratification process – after eight states had ratified. But, if these essays had little immediate impact – essentially limited to the ratification debates in New York and, perhaps, Virginia – they were a stunning intellectual achievement. Modern scholars have made Madison's political and constitutional theory the great story of the *Federalist*, and *Federalist* 10, in particular, has long been "in the center of constitutional debate."[3] But careful study of essays 78–83 reveals that Hamilton had an innovative and consequential vision of the law and the judicial role that deserves at least as much attention as Madison's contributions.

As he championed the Constitution's provision on the judiciary, Hamilton had a worthy intellectual opponent – the Anti-Federalist writing under the pseudonym Brutus – and Brutus's critique provided Hamilton's analytic framework. The power of the challenges posed by Brutus was immediately evident. Shortly after Brutus's first essay appeared in the *New York Journal*, James Madison wrote to Edmund Randolph that "a new Combatant ... with considerable address & plausibility, strikes at the [Constitution's] foundation."[4] Brutus's most compelling arguments appeared in essays 11–15, where he attacked the proposed federal judicial system. Brutus forcibly advanced a basic theme: "nothing could have been better conceived to facilitate the abolition of the state governments than the constitution of the judicial."[5]

For Hamilton, Brutus was not only a worthy opponent; he was, apparently, a consistent opponent. Most scholars believe Brutus was Melancton Smith, a New York lawyer who had served in the Continental Congress. Hamilton and Smith had already engaged in a historically significant debate. When Alexander Hamilton in 1784 made his path-breaking argument in favor of judicial review as an attorney in the case of *Rutgers v. Waddington*, Smith wrote the revolutionary era's most significant critique of judicial review, a pamphlet arguing that the position that a court could invalidate a statute was "absurd."[6] And Smith was to be Hamilton's primary antagonist at the New York State ratifying convention in the summer of 1788, where he was the leading critic of the Constitution, and their debates were to be one of the intellectual high points of the ratification conventions.

Scholars have paid close attention to Hamilton's arguments, particularly his famous description of the judiciary as the "least dangerous" branch and his seminal defense of judicial review in *Federalist* 78, the most complete justification of the doctrine before *Marbury*. While this close analysis is merited, it is also essential to view Hamilton's essays through a broader lens, to study these six essays as a whole. When one carefully examines the debate between Publius and Brutus, one sees that *Federalist* 78–83 offer a systematic and novel response to the competing vision of the judiciary and juries advanced by Brutus. Hamilton developed a new theory of the judiciary and legal decision-making that gave coherence and logical force to Article III. While the drafters of Article III had departed from revolutionary era precedent, Federalists prior to Publius had not explained that departure. Hamilton offered a new vision that made sense of Article III.

Overwhelmingly, Brutus eloquently championed a traditional point of view, one that reflected faith in juries and legislative decision-making, suspicion of judges, and confidence in the states. By contrast, Hamilton developed the case for federal courts and their role in establishing uniform laws, and he challenged deeply settled practices and the principles that had guided the treatment of the judiciary in the state constitutions. Hamilton offered a recognizably modern view of the law that combined profound respect for the considered judgments of "the people" as they engaged in constitution-making, faith in judicial expertise and the judiciary's commitment to the rule of law, suspicion of juries and ephemeral legislative majorities, and the need for uniformity in the proposed constitutional system. Specific legal doctrine – his broad conception of the scope of judicial review, the need for lower federal courts, the importance of the supremacy of the Constitution, and the establishment of the judiciary as a wholly independent branch of government – were derived from this larger conception. His tacit debate with Brutus thus reflects a broader transition in the ways in which Americans conceived the power of judges and juries and even the role of law. The significance of Hamilton's path-breaking and deeply coherent contribution has likely been underestimated because so much of what was novel in 1788 has evolved into the common wisdom. Hamilton's conception of the judicial role in the federal system and his vision of the law reflected an insight and an intellectual power that can fairly be described as genius. His contemporaries and near contemporaries lauded the extraordinary power of his legal thinking. Justice Story remembered, "I have heard [Secretary of War and Treasury] Samuel Dexter, John Marshall, and Chancellor Livingstone say that Hamilton's reach of thought was so far beyond theirs that by his side they were schoolboys – rush tapers before the sun at noon day."[7] The praise was well-merited. Examination of the six essays on the judiciary reveals that brilliance.

BACKGROUND TO THE FEDERALIST PAPERS

Responding to the perceived legislative excesses of the revolutionary era, the drafters of the Constitution decisively broke with the framework established under the state constitutions by elevating the judiciary to the status of a co-equal and wholly independent

branch of government. They also broke with the structure established by the Articles of Confederation by making the judiciary a
separate branch of the national government and by expanding its
jurisdiction dramatically. While traditional views celebrated juries,
the drafters did not guarantee jury trials in civil cases. Finally, to a
remarkable extent, they accepted judicial review, a concept that
had already provoked controversy in a handful of cases by revolutionary era courts. Yet even as they re-created the judiciary, the
framers gave this topic little attention. They were guided by an
emerging consensus, rather than by an articulated rationale. On
the other side of the ratification debate, Anti-Federalists had similarly not developed a sophisticated justification for their position on
Article III – even though it was a focus of their attack – until
Brutus's essays appeared. As a result, Brutus and Publius were not
simply championing conventional Anti-Federalist and Federalist
causes; they were creating a larger theoretic framework that made
sense of their compatriots' views.

While the idea that there are three separate branches of government is now a bedrock principle of Constitutionalism in the United
States, the notion that the judiciary was a separate branch of government was controversial at the time of independence. Blackstone's
Commentaries treated the judiciary as a part of the executive.[8] That
conception had its American adherents. John Adams, for example,
wrote in 1766: "the first grand division of constitutional powers is,
into those of legislation and those of execution." The judiciary was
part of the executive: "[H]ere the King is by the constitution, supreme
executor of the laws, and is always present in person or by judges, in
his courts, distributing justice among the people."[9] In contrast, it was
Montesquieu who first articulated a conception of the British constitution as composed of three branches and declared that "there is no
liberty, if the judiciary power be not separated from the legislative and
executive."[10] But, when Montesquieu spoke of the judiciary, his focus
was on juries, not judges, which made it hard to conceive of the
judiciary as a separate department of government.[11]

Moreover, in many practical respects the judiciary *was* subordinate to both the legislature and the executive. Colonial legislatures often exercised judicial functions. They resolved private petitions, which were often disputes between parties; they tried cases in equity; they granted new trials. This exercise of authority was popular among colonists – decisions were being made by representative assemblies rather than crown-controlled judges. Colonists were sharply critical of the judiciary because, unlike in Great Britain, their judges served at the pleasure of the Crown. In addition, governors and councils were courts of appeals in civil cases in the colonies, and, even though it no longer heard appeals from English common law courts, the English Privy Council heard appeals from governors and councils.[12] This system of appeals and the lack of tenure protection supported the belief that the judiciary was part of the executive.

The Declaration of Independence illustrates how concerned Americans were about executive interference with courts and juries. Five of the twenty-nine "injuries and usurpations" it listed involved courts or juries. In particular, the Continental Congress attacked George III because "[h]e has made Judges dependent on his Will alone, for the tenure of their offices, and the amount and payment of their salaries."

Following Montesquieu, most of the first state constitutions proclaimed that there were three branches of government. As the Virginia Constitution of 1776 stated, "[T]he legislative, executive, and judiciary departments shall be separate and distinct, so that neither exercises the powers properly belonging to the other."[13] But, despite such assertions, judicial powers and independence remained severely limited. Legislatures increasingly resolved private disputes.[14] New Jersey's and South Carolina's constitutions provided for Privy Councils that would have ultimate judicial authority.[15] More significant, the judiciary was subject to legislative control. In most states the legislatures, not the governor, played a critical role in the selection of judges. Except in Maryland and Pennsylvania, they either appointed the judges themselves or shared the appointment power with the executive. Judicial tenure protection was weak. Five states gave judges only fixed terms, and they were sometimes quite short – a year in Connecticut and Rhode Island.[16] While in the remaining eight states constitutional provisions stated that judges would hold office during good behavior, five of the eight provided for judicial removal upon recall by the legislature, and in New York judges had to retire at sixty.[17] While precise provisions varied from state to state, judges ultimately were dependent on the legislature, since no state guaranteed both lifetime tenure and a fixed salary. The drafters of the state constitutions thus made the court *more* dependent on the legislatures than they had been in the colonial era. As they created courts, state constitution makers were motivated by hostility to crown (or executive) control, rather than a principled embrace of judicial independence.

As legislatures began to govern, they inevitably acted in ways that advanced some interests in the states at the expense of others. As historian Jack Rakove has written, "[T]he Revolution... created the first sustained impulse to legislate, and under pressing conditions that required stopgap measures that were burdensome, intrusive, and often hastily adapted under adverse circumstances."[18] Confronted with the reality of exercises of legislative power (particularly statutes that disadvantaged creditors or curtailed the rights of loyalists), prominent Americans began to re-examine their faith in popular assemblies and to reconsider the role of courts. Madison and others came to focus on the importance of judicial independence as essential to checking legislative abuse.[19] Even more notably, the infant doctrine of judicial review became an important manifestation of this new conception of the judiciary as constraining the legislature, and judicial review became closely linked to the emerging concept of a written constitution as fundamental law, superior to normal legislative acts. Scholars debate whether a handful of seventeenth century and early eighteenth century British cases – the most prominent being the *Bonham's Case*[20] – reflect exercises of the power of judicial review or are better understood as exercises of statutory construction. But, regardless of whether British courts had once very occasionally engaged in judicial review, by the time of the American Revolution, the doctrine of parliamentary supremacy was well-established in Great Britain. As Blackstone asserted, "[I]f the parliament will positively enact a thing to be done which is unreasonable, I know of no power in the ordinary forms of the constitution, that is vested with authority to control it ... ."[21]

Thus, as the revolutionary era began, the idea that courts could invalidate statutes defied legal convention. Nonetheless, in a small group of cases in the years after independence, parties asked courts to do just that. In an even smaller number, courts accepted that invitation.[22] The most prominent cases in which courts were asked to invalidate statutes – the Rhode Island case of *Trevett v. Weeden*,[23] Virginia's *Case of the Prisoners*,[24] and New York's *Rutgers v. Waddington*[25] – involved assertions of legislative authority that affected groups that were disadvantaged in the legislative process: loyalists and creditors. While each case shows that judicial review was an issue with which courts were starting to grapple, they also show that it was controversial.

In *Trevett*, a Rhode Island court invalidated a statute that denied a jury trial to creditors who refused to accept the state's paper money as equivalent to the gold or silver provided for in their contracts. A furious legislature summoned the judges to appear before it to explain their decision. Four of the five judges offered explanations for their action, and all were replaced. Only the judge who was silent retained his position. *Trevett* illustrates not only that judicial review was controversial in Rhode Island, but that judicial independence was limited.

The issue in the *Case of the Prisoners* was the validity of a pardon of three loyalists that arguably satisfied the requirements of the state constitution but that clearly did not satisfy the requirements imposed by statute. Of the eight judges on the Virginia Court of Appeals, two ruled in favor of the prisoners and six ruled against them. The opinions reflect a full range of positions on the validity of judicial review. Only three of the eight judges asserted that they had the power to invalidate unconstitutional statutes. The case is particularly noteworthy, not simply because it gives an early instance of consideration of judicial review, but because it introduced a range of important Virginians to the issue. Edmund Randolph, as Attorney General, argued that the court did have the power to invalidate the statute but should choose to uphold it. Madison followed the case and asked Randolph and one of the judges for their notes. The case was also known to a young John Marshall, whose future law teacher, George Wythe, while ruling against the prisoners, nonetheless asserted that courts had the power to invalidate statutes. Legend has it that Marshall was present when the decision was announced.

The most important case from the vantage point of *The Federalist* was *Rutgers v. Waddington*, a case in which a young Alexander Hamilton, appearing as an attorney for one of the parties, urged the state court to exercise judicial review. Hamilton, representing a British merchant who had operated a tavern in New York City during the British occupation, argued that the court should invalidate a statute barring the merchant from introducing into evidence the military order authorizing him to operate the tavern. He made two claims, both reflecting a sophisticated approach to the exercise of judicial review. First, he argued that the statute violated the law of nations and was unconstitutional because the state constitution contained a provision adopting "the common law of England."[26] Although the constitution did not explicitly refer to the law of nations, Hamilton broadly interpreted the common law by invoking English authorities who had relied on the law of nations in cases concerning the wartime capture of property. Second, he argued that the statute violated the Treaty of Paris, which had been ratified pursuant to the national powers implicit in the Declaration of Independence. The Declaration, Hamilton asserted, "is the fundamental constitution of every state."[27] When the state statute and an exercise of national authority conflicted, the latter controlled: "When two laws clash that which relates to the most important concerns ought to prevail."[28]

Hamilton's arguments reflected a structural approach to judicial review. There was no clear textual conflict between the statute and the state constitution, and Hamilton did not invoke natural law. Rather, he argued that the statute was unconstitutional because it was at odds with broad constitutional principles – the state constitution's implicit embrace of international law and the primacy of the Declaration. In other words, the statute was unconstitutional because it was inconsistent with the basic structure of governance established by the state constitution.

Despite the sophistication of this argument, Hamilton achieved only limited success as an advocate for judicial review. Although the Mayor's Court largely ruled in his favor on the matter of statutory interpretation, its opinion carefully avoided the question of the legitimacy of judicial review.[29] Nonetheless, the opinion was widely read as an exercise of judicial review. The New York Assembly adopted a resolution attacking the court for having "dispense[d] with" a statute.[30] Melancton Smith wrote a pamphlet that read the decision as an exercise of the power of judicial review and sharply attacked the legitimacy of this idea, and his work was the most complete critique of judicial review produced in the revolutionary era.[31]

Foreshadowing the arguments of Brutus, Smith attacked judicial review on several grounds. Judicial review was at odds with popular government, he argued: it "render[ed] abortive the first and great privilege of freemen, the privilege of making their own laws by their representatives."[32] Second, judicial review threatened individual rights: "For if the power of abrogating and altering [statutes] may be assumed by our courts, and submitted to by the people, then, as far as liberty, and the security of property are concerned, they become useless as other opinions which are not precedents, and from which judges may vary."[33] Finally, the judicial independence created by the constitutional grant to judges of tenure in office during good behavior exacerbated the risks created by judicial review: "[P]ower is ... transferred to judges who are independent of the people."[34] Thus, for Smith, as it would be for Brutus, judicial review was dangerous because it would place courts above the legislature, enable them to act without control, and allow them to threaten popular sovereignty and individual liberty.

Thus, the three landmark cases – *Trevett,* the *Case of the Prisoners,* and *Rutgers* – reflect a move towards a greater judicial role than had been evidenced in revolutionary era state constitutions; they also show how controversial that increased role was. Given this background, the Federal Constitution's provisions on the judiciary and the relevant debates in Philadelphia are both striking and surprising.

The Constitution has notably strong guarantees of judicial independence. Indeed, as legal scholar Gerhard Casper has observed, it reflects the "[e]xtreme solution – an appointed judiciary guaranteed salary for life, subject only to impeachment. No state offered this combination."[35] The Constitution also goes farther than Great Britain had, where both houses of Parliament could remove judges by petition.[36] Not only is the conclusion the drafters reached surprising in historical context, it is surprising how uncontroversial it was at the convention. There was a consensus that federal judges should serve during good behavior, and Connecticut was the only delegation that favored qualifying making judges removable by Congress. The framers also readily agreed that judicial salaries should not be subject to decrease.[37]

The drafters also designed a federal court system of broad jurisdiction. The Continental Congress (a legislative body) exercised both executive and judicial powers. Before the adoption of the Articles of Confederation, Congress had the power to resolve disputes between states, and it had created a Court of Appeals in Cases of Capture.[38] Under the Articles, Congress had the power to set up tribunals "for the trial of piracies and felonies committed on the high seas" and "for receiving and determining finally appeals in all cases of captures."[39] It was also empowered to act as "the last resort on appeal in all disputes and differences ... between two or more States" and to appoint temporary "commissioners or judges to constitute a court for hearing and determining the matter in question ... ."[40] Thus, Congress had control over the nation's judicial functions; also significantly, those functions were distinctly limited.

The weakness of this structure had long concerned Hamilton. In 1783 he decried the fact that under the Articles "the most approved and well-founded maxims of free government, which requires that the legislative, executive and judicial authorities should be deposited in distinct and separate hands ... [and] the want of a federal juridicature, having cognizance of all matters of general concern in the last resort."[41] He objected to the national government's lack of enforcement authority for its decisions and its need to rely on the states to implement its acts.[42] As Hamilton observed in *Federalist* 21, the Confederation presented the "striking absurdity" of "a government destitute even of the shadow of constitutional power to enforce the execution of its own laws" (*FED.* 21, 130).

With little discussion, the drafters decisively rejected the limited judicial powers of the Articles and created an independent national judicial system with final authority to decide "Cases" of national importance and certain enumerated categories of "Controversies." They also required jury trials in all criminal cases except for impeachments. The most significant controversy among the drafters was whether a set of lower federal courts should complement the Supreme Court. Strong nationalists like James Madison and James Wilson sought to mandate the establishment of such courts, while other delegates (led by John Rutledge and Roger Sherman) sought to empower state courts to decide federal rights of action in the first instance. Ultimately, the drafters settled on a compromise fashioned by Madison that authorized Congress to create lower federal courts but also left it free to empower state courts to act as lower federal courts.[43]

Just as the drafters departed from state constitutions in creating strong protections for judicial independence, so their views of judicial review also reflected dramatic change. Judicial review is not explicitly recognized in the constitutional text, and most of the discussion of judicial review at the convention arose in the context of debate over a Council of Revision, a joint executive-judicial body unsuccessfully championed by Madison and Wilson that would have had the power to veto legislation.[44] Eight of the framers who reflected a broad range of views on other matters – Madison, Wilson, Gouverneur Morris, Luther Martin, Elbridge Gerry, George Mason, Hugh Williamson, and Sherman – all spoke in favor of judicial review. In contrast, only John Dickinson and J. F. Mercer spoke against it.[45] This apparent support for judicial review reflected the growing acceptance of the view that courts had the power to invalidate statutes they deemed unconstitutional. In the first Congresses that followed ratification, senators and representatives repeatedly asserted that courts would review statutes for constitutionality.[46] Although many legal scholars still wrongly portray the decision in *Marbury* as the "establishment" of judicial review, before 1803 there were thirty-one cases in which a statute was invalidated and seven more in which at least one dissenting judge ruled a statute unconstitutional.[47]

Yet the limited extent of this discussion of the judiciary is just as noteworthy as the drafters' striking departure from earlier conceptions of the judiciary. As Forrest McDonald has observed, "The delegates devoted less time to forming the judiciary – and less attention to careful craftsmanship – than they had expended on the legislative and executive branches."[48] The need for a federal judicial system (comprising at least a Supreme Court) and for judicial independence is largely assumed, as is the legitimacy of judicial review. As a result, while the conception of the judicial role at the convention was novel and the apparent subject of an emerging consensus among the participants, the theoretical justification for that new approach was left undeveloped. It was stipulated rather than articulated.

If the drafters had reached a general consensus about the judiciary, it soon became apparent that Anti-Federalists did not share their view. Article III quickly became a main object of their repeated and forceful attacks. A look at the substantive provisions of the Bill of

Rights illustrates how central these concerns were: five of the first eight adopted amendments were principally concerned with courts or juries.[49]

Yet even as Anti-Federalists challenged specific provisions of the Constitution, no one initially stepped forward to offer a coherent framework for their critique of the judiciary. In late January 1788, Melancton Smith noted that "very little has yet been written" about the judicial power. Smith bemoaned the failure of the Anti-Federalists to pursue this question. "It appears to me this part of the system is so framed as to *clinch* all the other powers, and to extend to them in a silent and imperceptible manner to any thing and every thing, while the Court who are vested with these powers are totally independent, uncontroulable and not amenable to any power in any decisions they may make."[50]

A week later, Brutus launched an attack on the Constitution's plan for the judiciary in his eleventh essay. The identity of Brutus has long been a matter of debate. For many years, most scholars focused on Robert Yates, one of the two New York Anti-Federalist delegates to leave the constitutional convention.[51] More recent scholars, however, have shown that both the literary style and the types of argument advanced indicate that Yates was not the author, and they have convincingly argued that the essays were either written by Melancton Smith[52] or someone with whom he was closely connected.[53] The timing of Essay 11 – following shortly after Smith's letter to Yates – provides additional support for the thesis that Smith was Brutus.

Essay 11 begins innocuously enough: "The nature and extent of the judicial power of the United States, proposed to be granted by the constitution, claims our particular attention."[54] Over the next two months, Brutus published five strong and thoughtful essays challenging the Constitution's plan for the judiciary. He focused on the dangers of judicial independence and the ways in which federal courts' exercise of judicial review and construction of the Constitution would cripple the states. He ended Essay 16 with a dire warning about the Constitution's framework and the people's inability to control federal courts: "[W]hen this power [of construing the language of the Constitution and of exercising judicial review] is lodged in hands of men independent of the people, and of their representatives, and who are not, constitutionally, accountable for their opinions, no way is left to controul them but *with a high hand and an outstretched arm.*"[55]

In *Federalist* 78–83, Hamilton responded to Brutus's challenge by articulating a comprehensive theory of the role of the federal judiciary. But these essays were not the first occasion on which Publius discussed the federal judiciary. A wide variety of judicial issues were discussed in earlier papers. In *Federalist* 16, for example, Hamilton indicated that the Constitution contemplated judicial review, asserting that federal courts would have the power to "pronounce the resolutions of [Congress] ... to be contrary to the supreme law of the land, unconstitutional, and void."[56] Hamilton and Madison each wrote of the need for a federal court to resolve controversies authoritatively and to impose uniformity. In *Federalist* 22, Hamilton had asserted that "[a] circumstance which crowns the defects of the Confederation remains yet to be mentioned, the want of a judiciary power. Laws are a dead letter without courts to expound and define their true meaning and operation" (*Fed.* 22, 143). In making the case for a federal judiciary, he gave particular emphasis to the consistent interpretation of treaties: "The treaties of the United States, under the present Constitution, are liable to the infractions of thirteen different legislatures, and as many different courts of final jurisdiction, acting under the authority of those legislatures. The faith, the reputation, the peace of the whole Union, are thus continually at the mercy of the prejudices, the passions, and the interests of every member of which it is composed" (*Fed.* 22, 144). Madison in *Federalist* 39 had stressed the need for an ultimate federal judicial authority to resolve conflicts between the state and national governments and suggested that the Constitution's guarantees of judicial independence ensured that disputes would be fairly resolved.[57] In *Federalist* 44, Madison also suggested that federal courts would have the power to review congressional statutes for their constitutionality."[58]

Madison's observations on the judiciary reflected three main points. First, as he argued at the close of *Federalist* 39, the Supreme Court would bear the responsibility of adjudicating the boundaries of federalism, acting "impartially" as a disinterested observer. Second, judges had to be made as independent of legislative control and manipulation as possible. But third, and of critical importance, all the political advantages in a republic would flow to the legislature, which enjoyed the most direct connection to the people. The judiciary and the executive were the inferior departments, and the great challenge of the separation of powers in a republic, as Madison famously remarked in *Federalist* 48, was to protect these weaker institutions against the "impetuous vortex" of the legislature.

Thus, before *Federalist* 78, Publius had touched on most of the salient issues involving the judiciary. Publius had discussed the importance of judicial checks on legislative abuses, recognized the significance of judicial independence, acknowledged the weakness of the judiciary (in comparison to Congress), stressed the need for uniformity in the federal legal system, and assumed the existence of judicial review. But the treatment of the judiciary was limited. *Federalist* 78–83 did not depart from the positions previously advanced. Rather, these essays expanded the prior positions and, unlike the previous papers, developed a theory of the federal judicial role.

Hamilton's essays on the judiciary systematically confronted the full range of issues raised by Article III, and his analysis merits reconstruction at some length. *Federalist* 78 is by far the most significant essay.[59] Its ostensible purpose was to explain why the judiciary should be an independent branch of government, but here Hamilton also developed both a justification for judicial review and a description of its proper scope. *Federalist 78* establishes the framework of Hamilton's conception of the federal judiciary and informs the spirit of the more tightly focused essays that follow. *Federalist* 79 defended the Constitution's guarantees of judicial independence through tenure in office and compensation. *Federalist* 80 justified the grant of jurisdiction to federal courts. *Federalist* 81 explained the Supreme Court's establishment as the court of last resort, the capacity of Congress to create lower federal courts, and the Supreme Court's jurisdiction. *Federalist* 82 analyzed the relationship between state and federal courts. Finally, the longest essay, *Federalist* 83, answered one of the Anti-Federalists' most persistent criticisms by defending the Constitution's failure to guarantee jury trials in civil cases.

Brutus and Publius were engaged in enterprises that mirrored each other. Anti-Federalists had harshly attacked many provisions of Article III, but without articulating a general theory to support their attacks. Brutus formulated that larger analytic framework; he built on traditional notions of the judicial role and contended that the new federal courts would undermine state authority. In contrast, the drafters at the convention had moved decisively away from the traditional notions espoused by Anti-Federalists, embracing judicial independence and judicial review and fashioning a role for federal courts that preserved the proposed constitutional order. But they had not conceptualized an overarching justification for their positions. Publius brilliantly developed a theory to defend this new conception of the judicial role in general and the function of federal courts in particular.

FEDERALIST 78

Federalist 78 establishes the overall framework for the ensuing essays and implicitly responds to Brutus's critiques. Developing a rationale for the judicial role reflected in the Constitution, Publius argues that respect for the rule of law, liberty, and popular decision-making all require that the judiciary be a separate and independent branch of government and that judicial independence requires lifetime tenure. Articulating a justification for the acceptance of judicial review, he contends that courts need the power to invalidate statutes in order to protect the Constitution's supremacy over statutes, and the essay reflects a structural concept of judicial review. Responding to the challenge that the vast powers of the federal judiciary would threaten the states, Publius develops a concept of the judiciary as the "least dangerous" branch and as guided by expertise, not politics.

Brutus had argued that "nothing could have been better conceived to facilitate the abolition of the state governments than the constitution of the judicial."[60] His contention that the federal judiciary would eviscerate the states rested on a vision of how federal courts would exercise judicial review. Brutus argued that federal courts would review congressional statutes, particularly those trenching on state authority, deferentially. They would interpret the Constitution "not only according to its letter, but according to its spirit and intention; and having this power, they would strongly incline to give it such a construction as to extend the powers of the general government, as much as possible, to the diminution, and finally to the destruction, of that of the respective states."[61] Conversely, they would scrutinize state statutes quite strictly: "In proportion as the general government acquires power and jurisdiction, by the liberal construction which the judges may give the constitution, will those of the states lose its rights, until they become so trifling and unimportant, as not to be worth having."[62] Brutus implicitly assumes that federal courts will use a structural approach to judicial review: they will look to broad principles of constitutional structure in deciding which statutes to uphold (congressional statutes) and which to strike down (state statutes).

As the Supreme Court learned how to exercise its power of judicial review, it would grow uncontrollable. Brutus noted that British judges were subject to oversight: "In England the judges are not only subject to have their decisions set aside by the house of lords, for error, but in cases where they give an explanation to the laws or constitution of the country, contrary to the sense of the parliament, though the parliament will not set aside the judgment of the court, yet, they have authority, by a new law, to explain a former one, and by this means to prevent a reception of such decisions."[63] The United States Supreme Court would escape such limitations. It "would be exalted above all other power in the government, and subject to no controul" Brutus warned.[64] "I question whether the world ever saw, in any period of it, a court of justice invested with such immense powers, and yet placed in a situation so little responsible."[65] Brutus bemoaned the fact that the Constitution gave judges tenure during good behavior and prohibited reductions in their salaries. They "are to be rendered totally independent, both of the people and the legislature, both with respect to their offices and salaries. No errors they may commit can be corrected by any power above them, if any such power there be, nor can they be removed from office for making ever so many erroneous adjudications."[66]

In predicting that federal judges would expand national power and cripple the states, Brutus made two types of basic arguments. First, he focused on those clauses that would enable courts to expand national power and curtail the authority of the states. Federal courts would read the Constitution's preamble to "give latitude to every department under it [the national government], to take cognizance of every matter, not only that affects the general and national concerns of the union, but also of such as relate to the administration of private justice, and to regulating the internal and local affairs of the different parts."[67] Second, the self-interest of judges would further incline them to create a powerful national government: "Every body of men invested with office are tenacious of power; ... this of itself will operate strongly upon the courts to give such meaning to the constitution in all cases where it can possibly be done, as will enlarge the sphere of their own authority."[68] In addition, Brutus raised the possibility that expanded judicial powers would increase judicial business and, hence, judicial fees.[69] Thus, the federal judiciary would have incentives to expand national powers and curtail state powers.

Congress would in turn build on these judicial decisions to expand the scope of national power, and it would do so with greater success than if it had been operating without the assistance of the federal courts. Brutus wrote that Congress "might pass one law after another, extending the general and abridging the state jurisdictions, and to sanction their proceedings would have a course of decisions of the judicial to whom the constitution has committed the power of explaining the constitution."[70] In the absence of federal courts, Congress "would have explained it [the Constitution] at their peril; if they exceed their powers, or sought to find, in the spirit of the constitution, more than was expressed in the letter, the people from whom they derived their power could remove them, and do themselves right."[71] But the federal judiciary would shield Congress from this danger. The formal separation of powers would not ensure that the branches would check each other, Brutus warned. Instead, Congress and the judiciary would naturally collaborate to expand their authority.

Implicitly responding to Brutus, in *Federalist* 78 Publius offers a dramatically different conception of the judicial role. In Hamilton's account, federal judges will be making decisions based on the law, not on self-interest, and guarantees of judicial independence are necessary to enable judges to act as they should, rather than yielding to political pressure or personal interest.

At the outset of *Federalist* 78, Hamilton observed that it "is not disputed" that the lack of a federal judiciary was a manifest weakness of the Confederation. The critical issue was not whether federal courts should exist at all, but how to appoint federal judges, determine their tenure and settle "[t]he partition of the judiciary authority between different courts, and their relations to each other." The method of appointment followed the procedure for other federal officers and therefore needed no separate analysis. Turning to the issue of judicial tenure, Hamilton accurately noted that this had been a focus of Anti-Federalist criticism. Federal judges would hold office during "good behavior," following the famous precedent set by the parliamentary Act of Settlement of 1701. This was the same tenure established by many state constitutions, including New York's, and Hamilton praised its wisdom: "[I]n a republic it is ... [an] excellent barrier to the encroachments and oppressions of the representative body. And it is the best expedient which can be devised in any government, to secure a steady, upright, and impartial administration of the laws" (*Fed.* 78, 522). These over-arching goals – preventing legislative "encroachments and oppressions" and preserving the rule of law – informed the conception of the judicial role Hamilton advanced.

Hamilton then moved to the larger issue of separation of powers, emphasizing both the judiciary's status as one branch of government and its place as "the weakest of the three departments of power." As he explained in a famous passage:

> Whoever attentively considers the different departments of power
> must perceive, that, in a government in which they are separated
> from each other, the judiciary, from the nature of its functions, will
> always be the least dangerous to the political rights of the
> Constitution; because it will be least in a capacity to annoy or
> injure them ... The judiciary ... has no influence over either the
> sword or the purse; no direction either of the strength or of the
> wealth of the society; and can take no active resolution whatever. It
> may truly be said to have neither Force nor Will, but merely
> judgment; and must ultimately depend upon the aid of the
> executive arm even for the efficacy of its judgments.
>
> (*Fed.* 78, 522–23)

Thus, the judiciary is the "least dangerous" branch. It is limited both because it has no enforcement power – only the executive can enforce judgments if the losing party refuses to follow the court's decision – and because judicial decision-making is constrained. The court is simply exercising "judgment," not giving effect to its "will." Courts are bound by the rule of law. As Hamilton had described their role in *Federalist* 78, they "secure a steady, upright, and impartial administration of the laws." Because the judiciary is doubly constrained by its lack of independent power and by its obligation to judge according to the law, "liberty can have nothing to fear from the judiciary alone." In contrast, if the judiciary is not a separate and independent branch, liberty is at risk.

Invoking Montesquieu on the importance of separating "the power of judging ... from the legislative and executive powers," Hamilton argued that "from the natural feebleness of the judiciary, it is in continual jeopardy of being overpowered, awed, or influenced by its co-ordinate branches." To secure the judicial independence that the security of liberty required, "nothing can contribute so much to its firmness and independence as permanency in office" (*Fed.* 78, 504).

Hamilton's description of the judiciary as "the least dangerous branch" has profoundly influenced modern constitutional theorists. Perhaps most notably, it provided the title for Alexander Bickel's classic work, *The Least Dangerous Branch*,[72] which argued for a constrained judicial role. But *Federalist* 78, viewed in historical context, is not a plea for judicial restraint. The concept of the judiciary as a separate branch was itself controversial prior to the drafting of the Constitution.

Thus, in making his strong case for judicial independence, Hamilton was identifying a novel structural element of the Constitution that departed from standing norms and practice. He also stressed that the judiciary's status as a separate and independent branch was essential to liberty. "[T]he general liberty of the people can never be endangered" by the judiciary, he argued, "I mean so long as the judiciary remains truly distinct from both the legislature and the Executive." The threat to the proper separation of the branches and judicial independence was ongoing: "The Judiciary is in continual jeopardy of being overpowered, awed, or influenced by its co-ordinate branches." Judicial independence was particularly significant in a "limited Constitution" because the Constitution "specified exceptions to the legislative authority; such, for instance, as that it shall pass no bills of attainder, no ex-post-facto laws, and the like." Only courts could police those limitations: "Limitations of this kind can be preserved in practice no other way than through the medium of courts of justice, whose duty it must be to declare all acts contrary to the manifest tenor of the Constitution void. Without this, all the reservations of particular rights or privileges would amount to nothing" (*Fed.* 78, 523–24).

Like its treatment of judicial independence, the discussion of judicial review in *Federalist* 78 has great significance. British legal theory had rejected judicial review, the handful of judicial review cases in this country during the revolutionary era had been controversial, and, while most of the framers seemed to favor it, the topic received only peripheral attention at Philadelphia.[73] The analysis of judicial review in *Federalist* 78 became the most significant discussion of the subject in the years before the Court invalidated part of the Judiciary Act of 1789 in the 1803 case of *Marbury v. Madison.*

Federalist 78's treatment of judicial review is significant for other reasons, particularly in describing the circumstances when this authority should be exercised. Here, again, the connection to Brutus matters. Strikingly, just as Melancton Smith's arguments against Hamilton in *Rutgers* anticipated Brutus's critique, so the structural approach Hamilton employed in *Rutgers* was a template for the interpretive approach he adopted in *Federalist* 78. Some scholars have argued that *Federalist* 78 embraced a broad conception of judicial review enabling courts to review statutes for their consistency with unwritten natural law.[74] Others have held that Hamilton thought courts should invalidate only statutes that were clearly unconstitutional.[75] The most accurate reading of *Federalist* 78, however, falls into neither camp.

Brutus had argued that federal courts would use judicial review to expand national authority and constrain the powers of the states and that federal judges asserting this authority would be uncontrollable. Hamilton, in contrast, stressed the constraints under which courts would operate, and he emphasized the distinction between law and politics. Courts were to decide cases on the basis of law. "The interpretation of the laws is the proper and peculiar province of the courts. A constitution is, in fact, and must be, regarded by the judges as a fundamental law. It therefore belongs to them to ascertain its meaning, as well as the meaning of any particular act proceeding from the legislative body." Judicial review involved a court's consideration of two laws: a statute and the Constitution. "If there should happen to be an irreconcilable variance between the two, that which has the superior obligation and validity ought of course to be preferred; or in other words, the constitution ought to be preferred to the statute, the intention of the people to the intention of their agents" (*Fed.* 78, 525). The court, Hamilton made clear, was not superior to the legislature. It was simply giving controlling effect to the will of the people. As Hamilton had observed at the outset of *Federalist* 78, courts exercised neither "Force nor Will, but merely judgment."

The exercise of judgment was not merely mechanical invalidation of clearly unconstitutional statutes. Hamilton used the word "tenor" as he described the inconsistency between a statute and the Constitution that necessitated invalidation. "[S]pecified exceptions to the legislative authority ... can be preserved in practice in no other way than through the medium of the courts of justice, whose duty it must be to declare all acts contrary to the manifest tenor of the constitution void" (*Fed.* 78, 524). "There is no position which depends on clearer principles, than that every act of a delegated authority, contrary to the tenor of the commission under which it is exercised, is void" (*Fed.* 78, 524). The term "tenor" connoted underlying principles: in John Ash's dictionary, "tenor" is "a general drift, the general sense."[76] Similarly, Samuel Johnson defined the term as "general course or drift." Thus, much as he had done as an advocate in *Rutgers*, when he invoked the law of nations and the federal treaty power without a clear basis in constitutional text for relying on either, Hamilton was contending that a statute at odds with the "general drift" of the Constitution should be invalidated by courts.

Implicitly responding to Brutus, Hamilton carefully explained why judicial review was necessary. Because the Constitution created the government, it was superior to any legislative act: "No legislative act therefore contrary to the constitution can be valid. To deny this would be to affirm that the deputy is greater than his principal" (*Fed.* 78, 524). The legislature could not be assumed to be "the constitutional judges of their own powers" nor could the Constitution "intend to enable the representatives of the people to substitute their *will* to that of their constituents" who had adopted the constitution. Courts exercising judicial review were simply choosing which of two laws was superior – the constitution or the statute. In exercising judicial review, courts would necessarily gave precedence to that fundamental law.

Responding to another argument of Brutus, Hamilton contended that judicial review did not make the courts superior to legislatures. Judicial review, he wrote, "only supposes that the power of the people is superior to both [the legislature and the courts]; and that where the will of the legislature, declared in its statutes, stands in opposition to that of the people, declared in the Constitution, the judges out to be governed by the latter rather than the former" (*Fed.* 78, 525). Where Brutus had argued that federal courts would be political and unconstrained, Hamilton countered that the exercise of judicial review was consistent with normal exercises of judicial authority. He analogized the assertion of judicial review with the judicial determination to follow a later statute rather than an earlier one. Preference for the later statute "is a mere rule of construction, not derived from any positive law, but from the nature and reason of the thing." Similarly, judicial review was appropriate because "the nature and reason of the thing ... teach us that the prior act of a superior ought to be preferred to the subsequent act of an inferior and subordinate authority." The argument that "the courts on the pretence of a repugnancy, may substitute their own pleasure to the constitutional intentions of the legislature." would be equally applicable to constitutional adjudication as to adjudication involving two statutes and, indeed, "every adjudication upon any single statute." In all these circumstances, courts had an obligation to judge according to the law, not to impose their views: "The courts must declare the sense of the law; and if they should be disposed to exercise WILL instead of JUDGMENT, the consequence would equally be the substitution of their pleasure to that of the legislative body" (*Fed.* 78, 526).

The importance of judicial review, in turn, necessitated judicial independence, and, in developing his argument for judicial independence, Hamilton also recognized the importance of judicial protection of groups of people in society who might be harmed by majorities. Hamilton stated that "ill humours ... disseminate[d] among the people themselves ... [might] occasion dangerous innovations in the government, and serious oppressions of the minor party in the community." Such attacks on "the Constitution and the rights of individuals" reflected "ill humors" that would "speedily give place to better information, and more deliberate reflection" (*Fed.* 78, 527). Unless these beliefs became part of the Constitution, courts should reject the statutes that reflected those beliefs. Judicial independence was necessary to ensure that courts would protect the Constitution and "minor part[ies]" against temporary majorities. "[I]t would require an uncommon portion of fortitude in the judges to do their duty as faithful guardians of the Constitution, where legislative invasions of it have been instigated by the major voice of the community" (*Fed.* 78, 528).

Judicial independence was also important when courts confronted statutes that, while not unconstitutional, harmed particular groups in society. "[T]he independence of the judges may be an essential safeguard against ... the injury of the private rights of particular classes of citizens, by unjust and partial laws." So, too, "the firmness of the judicial magistracy is of vast importance in mitigating the severity of such laws" (*Fed.* 78, 528).

Hamilton did not explain exactly what he meant by the "serious oppressions of the minor party in the community," but his argument is consistent with the types of cases in which revolutionary courts had exercised judicial review. As previously noted, the most prominent of these cases involved legislation that adversely affected politically unpopular groups, such as loyalists or creditors.[77] In *Federalist* 78, Hamilton sees judicial review as protecting the considered judgment of the majority that adopted the Constitution against temporary legislative majorities, and it protects individual liberty. The references to legislation affecting particular minorities evidence another argument in favor of judicial review: it protects segments of the polity that legislatures seek to deprive of their rights. This argument accords well with Madison's concern with protecting the rights of minorities and individuals. It reflects a larger shift in rights thinking in which the critical problem was no longer seen as protecting the people against the concentrated power of the state, but, rather, as protecting the minority against a majority.

In the early republic, federal courts were to review the constitutionality of state legislation disadvantaging political minorities. The supremacy clause, which made the Constitution "the supreme Law of the Land,"[78] superior to state (and federal) legislation, provided a textual basis for such review. Notably, the first occasion on which the Court overturned state legislation – the 1796 case of *Ware v. Hylton* – involved a revolutionary era statute that discriminated against loyalists, much like the statute in *Rutgers*. The statute provided that payment into the Virginia loan office of a debt owed to a loyalist extinguished that debt. The Supreme Court invalidated the statute, finding that it ran afoul of the Treaty of Paris, and two Justices explicitly relied on the Supremacy Clause in their opinions.[79]

Yet, while the Supremacy Clause provided a textual basis for federal court review of state statutes, *Federalist* 78 does not invoke the clause. Similarly, Hamilton does not cite the "arising under"[80] clause, the other clause that scholars and courts have focused on as a textual basis for judicial review. His focus is, instead, on the larger theoretical justification for judicial review as following from the separation of powers. In *Federalist* 81, Hamilton makes this point more directly. He asserts:

> I admit, however, that the constitution ought to be the standard of construction for the laws, and that wherever there is evident opposition, the laws ought to give place to the constitution. But this

> doctrine is not deducible from any circumstances peculiar to the
> plan of the convention. . . .
>
> (*Fed.* 81, 543)

Hamilton is here making (somewhat) explicit a point that is implicit in his approach in *Federalist* 78. Judicial review is not "deducible from any circumstances peculiar to the plan of the convention." Rather, it follows from the enforcement of a popularly adopted written constitution by an independent judiciary.

Hamilton closed *Federalist* 78 by attempting to justify the Constitution's decision that judges would hold office during good behavior. "Periodical appointments, however, regulated, or by whomsoever made, would, in some way or other, be fatal to their independence." The act of judging required "long and laborious study" and lifetime tenure would be necessary to encourage lawyers to become judges. Hamilton ended *Federalist* 78 by appealing to the British practice of tenure during good behavior: "The experience of Great Britain affords an illustrious comment on the excellence of the institution" (*Fed.* 78, 529–30). Hamilton's position on tenure reflects the overall disagreement *Federalist* 78 has with Brutus. Brutus saw federal judges as driven by self-interest to expand national power and to limit state power. External checks are necessary to keep judges from abusing their power. But for Hamilton, federal judges operate within a legal system that calls for their "judgment," not their "WILL." They check legislatures through the exercise of judicial review, but their power is limited. Indeed, judges need protections such as lifetime tenure to gain the independence requisite to carrying out their role faithfully.

FEDERALIST 79

Federalist 78 presented a broad framework for Hamilton's conception of the judicial role under the Constitution and Article III. *Federalist* 79 turned to specific elements of the first section of Article III: tenure in office and compensation. In analyzing the elements of the

Constitution that (improperly) made the judiciary superior to the other branches of government, Brutus had expressed particular concern about were its provisions on salary and removal from office. "There is no authority that can remove them from office for any errors or want of capacity, or lower their salaries," Brutus complained, "and in many cases their power is superior to that of the legislature."[81] *Federalist* 79 rebutted that argument. The constitutional provision that barred diminution of judicial salaries was essential to judicial independence, Hamilton asserted. "Next to permanency in office, nothing can contribute more to the independence of the judges than a fixed provision for their support," Hamilton observed in opening the essay. "In the general course of human nature, *power over a man's subsistence amounts to a power over his will*" (*Fed.* 79, 531). Similarly, any provision allowing for removal from office for lack of ability would be unwise because it would be exploited for political reasons: "An attempt to fix the boundary between the regions of ability and inability, would much oftener give scope to personal and party attachments and enmities, than advance the interests of justice, or the public good" (*Fed.* 79, 533). Where Brutus saw protections for the judiciary as a flaw because they enabled judges to engage in a self-interested pursuit of power, Hamilton offered arguments that reflected a faith in the integrity of judicial decision-making and a belief that the Constitution established the protections necessary to protect that integrity. Hamilton closed by objecting to mandatory retirement, such as New York's age limit of sixty. He wrote, "In a republic, where fortunes are not affluent, and pensions not expedient, the dismission of men from stations in which they have served their country long and usefully, on which they depend for subsistence, and from which it will be too late to resort to any other occupation for a livelihood, ought to have some better apology to humanity than is to be found in the imaginary danger of a superannuated bench" (*Fed.* 79, 533–34).

FEDERALIST 80

In its opening provision, Article III, Section 2 of the Constitution declares, "The judicial power shall extend to all cases, in law and equity, arising under this Constitution, the laws of the United States, and treaties made, or which shall be made, under their authority."

Brutus construed this provision as broad and dangerous. His analysis pivots on his interpretation of the word "equity" in the grant to federal courts of power over "all cases in law and equity, under this Constitution, the laws of the United States and treaties." The word "equity" has a non-technical meaning: its synonym is "fairness." But "equity" also has a technical legal meaning. In the English legal system, there were two sets of courts with overlapping jurisdiction. As James E. Pfander and Nassim Nazemi have recently written, "Courts of law heard suits for damages, among other things, and entered judgments enforceable through seizure of person or property. Courts of equity, by contrast, did not award damages as such but issued orders that compelled the parties, on pain of contempt, to comply with the court's conception of what equity and good conscience required." Unlike courts of equity, "courts of law did not recognize equitable defenses, such as fraud, mistake, and unconscionability, and they did not make discovery available to the parties."[82]

In interpreting the jurisdictional grant, Brutus drew on the non-technical meaning of "equity" and argued that the Constitution problematically gave federal courts the power to decide cases based on their idea of what was fair. Federal courts "would be authorized to explain the Constitution, not only according to its letter, but according to its spirit and intention; and having this power, they would strongly incline to give it such a construction as to extend the powers of the federal government, as much as possible, to the diminution, and finally to the destruction, of that of the respective states."[83] They could "explain the constitution according to the reasoning spirit of it, without being confined to the words or letter."[84] Inspired by the "reasoning spirit" of the Constitution, judges would view federal powers expansively. They will give "latitude to every department under it to take cognizance of every matter, not only that affects the general and national concerns of the union, but also of such as relate to the administration of private justice, and to regulating the internal and local affairs of different parts."[85] Conversely, "the states will lose [their] rights, until they become so trifling and unimportant, as not to be worth having."[86]

Implicitly responding to Brutus's argument that these jurisdictional grants would eviscerate the authority of the states, Hamilton carefully examined the precise ways in which federal courts would affect the states, and he contended that those powers were both limited and necessary elements of a federal system. For example, discussing "cases arising under the Constitution," he focused on the need to enforce the explicit constitutional prohibition on emitting paper money. In discussing jurisdiction over territorial disputes, he argued that "[w]hatever practices may have a tendency to disturb the harmony between the states, are proper objects of federal superintendence and control" (*Fed.* 80, 537). "From this review of the particular powers of the federal judiciary, as marked out in the constitution," Hamilton concluded, "it appears, that they are all conformable to the principles which ought to have governed the structure of that department, and which were necessary to the perfection of the system" (*Fed.* 80, 541). Where Brutus had portrayed the grants as open-ended, Hamilton held them as constrained and as necessary to resolve particular categories of legal disputes.

The linchpin of Brutus's argument was his expansive interpretation of "equity" as a permissive device allowing federal courts to decide cases in conformity to the "spirit and intention" of the Constitution. Hamilton focused on the technical meaning of the word, arguing that it actually had a narrow meaning grounded by prior judicial practice. "There is hardly a subject of litigation between individuals, which may not involve those ingredients of *fraud, accident, trust* or *hardship*, which would render the matter an object of equitable rather than of legal jurisdiction, as the distinction is known and established in several of the States" (*Fed.* 80, 539). Invoking New York "practice," he said there is a "formal and technical distinction between LAW and EQUITY" (*Fed.* 80, 540). The countervailing positions of Brutus and Hamilton with respect to the Constitution's grant of judicial authority mirror their positions with respect to judicial review: Brutus portrayed judicial decision-making as open-ended and political; for Hamilton, judicial decision-making was constrained and governed by legal principles.

FEDERALIST 8 1

Hamilton used the next essay to return to Article III, Section 1: "The judicial Power of the United States, shall be vested in one Supreme Court, and in such inferior Courts as the Congress may from time to time ordain and establish." In this essay, he covered a range of Anti-Federalist criticisms concerning "the partition of the judiciary authority between different courts, and their relations to each other" (*Fed.* 81, 541). He justified the Supreme Court's establishment as the court of last resort, and defended the discretionary power of Congress to create lower federal courts. Significantly, he indicated that, because of the nature of sovereignty, states could not be sued in federal court for revolutionary era debts, a position that the Court was to reject in the 1793 case *Chisholm v. Georgia*, but that the Eleventh Amendment was to adopt. Finally, he rebutted Anti-Federalist concerns that the Court's appellate jurisdiction would lead to the "*abolition* of the trial by jury" (*Fed.* 81, 552).

Hamilton began by discussing the general authority of the Supreme Court. This was the essay where Hamilton addressed Brutus most directly. Without citing Brutus by name, Hamilton presented, in quotations, an extensive paraphrase of his equity-based argument that the Supreme Court would be "uncontrollable and remediless" because it will "constru[e] the laws according to the *spirit* of the Constitution" and because the Constitution gave the Supreme Court ultimate authority; whereas in Great Britain "the judicial power, in the last resort, resides in the House of Lords, which is a branch of the legislature" (*Fed.* 81, 542).[87]

Hamilton dismissed the concern that the Supreme Court would interpret statutes according to the Constitution's spirit by observing that the Supreme Court would have no "greater latitude ... than may be claimed by the courts of every State" in construing their constitutions. In addition, while the Supreme Court had the power to invalidate a statute "wherever there is evident opposition" between the statute and the Constitution, "this doctrine is not deducible from any circumstance peculiar to the plan of the convention, but from the general theory of a limited Constitution; and as far as it is true, it is equally applicable to most, if not all the State governments" (*Fed.* 81, 543). As in *Federalist* 78, Hamilton was again championing judicial review, explaining that it follows from the general principle of a limited constitution rather than being a distinctive attribute of the proposed constitution. Nothing in the Constitution would lead the Supreme Court to adopt a different approach to constitutional interpretation than any state court would follow.

Hamilton forcefully rebutted Brutus's argument that the final decision in legal cases should belong "to a part of the legislature." Judges were better positioned to decide cases because, unlike legislators, they would be selected for their legal expertise and given the independence provided by tenure during good behavior. Unlike judges, legislatures would reflect "the pestilential breath of faction" and be prone to decisions based on passions: "From a body which had even a partial agency in passing bad laws, we could rarely expect a disposition to temper and moderate them in the application" (*Fed.* 81, 543–44).

Again, as in *Federalist* 78, Hamilton was contrasting judicial and legislative decision-making and suggesting that judges will decide based on reason, rather than because of the influence of passion and faction. The constraints on judicial power would be effective:

> Particular misconstructions and contraventions of the will of the legislature may now and then happen; but they can never be so extensive as to amount to an inconvenience, or in any sensible degree to affect the order of the political system. This may be inferred with certainty from the general nature of the judicial

power; from the objects to which it relates; from the manner in which it is exercised; from its comparative weakness, and from its total incapacity to support its usurpations by force.

(Fed. 81, 545)

Hamilton then turned to Congress's power to create lower federal courts. As previously discussed, during the constitutional convention, after considering Wilson and Madison's proposal to create lower federal courts and Sherman and Rutledge's proposal to have state courts act as lower federal courts, the delegates adopted a compromise under which Congress could create lower federal courts but could also choose instead to authorize state courts to act as lower federal courts.[88] In *Federalist* 81, Hamilton's allegiance clearly lies with the earlier Wilson–Madison proposal. Hamilton acknowledges, almost grudgingly, the alternative option of having state courts operate as federal courts.[89] But he quickly explains why that would be unwise: state judges might reflect "local spirit"; without secure tenure in office, they "will be too little independent to be relied on for an inflexible execution of the national laws"; state judges' weakness in deciding federal issues might necessitate "in practice ... [an] unrestrained course to appeals," and allowing a broad right of appeal would be "a source of public and private inconvenience" (Fed. 81, 547).

Hamilton then offered his own plan for the potential design of lower courts: between four and six federal districts should be created and "[t]he judges of these courts, with the aid of the State judges, may hold circuits for the trial of causes in the several parts of the respective districts" (Fed. 81, 547). Hamilton thus addressed Anti-Federalist concerns that lower federal courts would be distant from the parties – which would make litigation time-consuming and expensive – and that states would be removed from judicial decision-making under the Constitution.

Hamilton next considered the division of authority within the federal court system. The scope of the Supreme Court's original jurisdiction was clear: "cases affecting ambassadors, other public ministers, and consuls, and those in which A STATE shall be a party" (*Fed.* 81, 548). "[T]he original jurisdiction of the Supreme Court would be confined to two classes of causes, and those of a nature rarely to occur" (ibid.). Lower federal courts would have original jurisdiction over all other matters heard in federal court.

In the midst of this discussion, Hamilton embarked on a "digression" of significance. In Essay 13, Brutus raised the specter that individuals from one state would be able to sue another state in federal court to collect on revolutionary war debts. "Every state in the union" he wrote, "is largely indebted to individuals. For the payment of these debts they have given notes payable to the bearer. At least this is the case in this state. Whenever a citizen of another state becomes possessed of one of these notes, he may commence an action in the supreme court of the general government; and I cannot see any way in which he can be prevented from recovering."[90] Hamilton dismissed this fear as groundless, noting that "[i]t is inherent in the nature of sovereignty, not to be amenable to the suit of an individual *without its consent*" (*Fed.* 81, 548).

Hamilton's argument also suggests, however, that states would be suable for actions they took *after* ratification. He wrote, "The contracts between a nation and individuals are only binding on the conscience of the sovereign, and have no pretensions to a compulsive force. They confer no right of action independent of the sovereign will" (*Fed.* 81, 549). In other words, once a state is no longer a separate "nation" – because, with ratification of the Constitution, it has become part of a nation – it would be suable.[91]

The question whether states could be sued in federal courts was a significant one in the ratification debates. In Virginia, in particular, Patrick Henry and other Anti-Federalists followed Brutus in attacking the Constitution as allowing individuals, under diversity jurisdiction, to bring suit in federal court to collect on Revolutionary War debts. Like Hamilton, Madison and Marshall responded that states would not be suable in federal court (although, in contrast, Randolph said that states could be sued in federal court for pre-existing debts).[92]

In 1793, in *Chisholm v. Georgia*,[93] the Supreme Court (with Justice Iredell dissenting) held that it had jurisdiction to hear a suit against Georgia brought by a citizen of another state who was seeking to collect on a revolutionary era debt. The Eleventh Amendment was adopted in the aftermath of *Chisholm*. Modern Supreme Court case law has asserted that the Eleventh Amendment followed *Federalist* 81 and established a principle of state sovereignty immunity against suit by individuals.[94] But *Federalist* 81 did not stand for this broad proposition. It stood for the more limited proposition that Article III did not permit suit against states on debts incurred *prior* to the Constitution. The question whether the Eleventh Amendment incorporated that narrower principle is a separate one, but close reading of *The Federalist* shows that Hamilton's concern was with revolutionary war debts.[95]

Following his "digression" about state suability, Hamilton discussed the Supreme Court's appellate jurisdiction – "both as to Law and Fact, with such Exceptions, and under such Regulations as the Congress shall make"[96] – and addressed the Anti-Federalist argument that the clause was "an implied supersedure of the trial by jury" (*Fed.* 81, 549–50). Anti-Federalists repeatedly asserted that, if the Supreme Court could determine facts, it could readily disregard the jury's factual determinations. Hamilton countered that the Supreme Court had to be able to review facts in certain types of appeals, such as cases in which the trial did not involve a jury. (He noted that this was the practice in New York in admiralty, probate, and chancery cases.) There were some cases in which the Supreme Court should not review facts: most cases tried before a jury would fall into this category. Yet given the diverse range of state practices concerning the role of juries, it would be impossible to fashion a constitutional standard about when the Court could appropriately review facts. The Constitution therefore appropriately delegated to Congress the power to create "exceptions" to the Court's appellate jurisdiction; Congress could be trusted to use that power to bar the Court from reconsidering facts whenever it would be inappropriate for the

Court to do so. "[A]n ordinary degree of prudence and integrity in the national councils will insure us solid advantages from the establishment of the proposed judiciary, without exposing us to any of the inconveniences which have been predicted from that source" (*Fed.* 81, 552).

FEDERALIST 82

While the previous essays on the judiciary were largely framed as responses to Anti-Federalist arguments, *Federalist* 82 explores the relationship of the state and federal courts without reference to Anti-Federalist critiques. Hamilton was writing on almost a blank slate, since the concept of interconnected state and federal courts was novel. His analysis on this topic had a sophistication and completeness that no other writing from the founding era rivalled. It is, like so much else in these essays, a tour de force.

Following the general principle of *Federalist* 31 regarding state powers under the Constitution, Hamilton held that "the state courts will *retain* the jurisdiction they now have, unless it appears to be taken away in one of the enumerated modes" (*Fed.* 82, 554). Because the Constitution left the existing jurisdiction of state courts intact, "the most natural and the most defensible construction" was that they would retain concurrent jurisdiction in such cases (although appeal would lie to the Supreme Court). Similarly, since the state and federal courts were "parts of ONE WHOLE, the inference seems to be conclusive, that the State courts would have a concurrent jurisdiction in all cases arising under the laws of the Union, where it was not expressly prohibited" (*Fed.* 82, 555).

Thus, unless Congress prohibited it in specific instances, state courts could hear the same types of cases that could be heard in federal courts. But the logic of the constitutional system meant that state courts could not have the final word in such cases. "The evident aim of the plan of the convention is that all the causes of the specified classes, shall for weighty public reasons receive their original or final determination in the courts of the United States"

(*Fed.* 82, 556). The Constitution did not, however, address the question whether appeals had to go to the Supreme Court or whether state court decisions could be appealed to a lower federal court. Hamilton argued that, in the absence of such a determination, there was no "impediment to the establishment of an appeal from the State court to the subordinate national tribunals." There would be "many advantages" to giving federal district courts the final word on appeal from state courts. In particular, it would allow state courts to hear a broad range of "federal causes" in the first instance without burdening the Supreme Court by requiring it to resolve them on appeal (*Fed.* 82, 557).

The most significant element of the essay is Hamilton's conclusion that, even in cases initially brought in state courts, federal courts would have the final word over matters involving federal laws and the Constitution. The issue was later to be the center of national controversy. In the landmark 1816 case of *Martin v. Hunter's Lessee*,[97] Justice Joseph Story held that Congress could constitutionally give the Supreme Court appellate jurisdiction over state courts in cases involving a federal issue, and the decision provoked heated critique by champions of states' rights, most prominently Spencer Roane of the Virginia Court of Appeals (whose decision Story and the Supreme Court had overturned).[98] But Story was not proclaiming a new idea. Hamilton had recognized long before that the supremacy of federal courts was implicit in the Constitution's structure.

FEDERALIST 83

By far the lengthiest essay concerning the judiciary is the final one, *Federalist* 83, which addresses the Constitution's failure to guarantee juries in civil trials. (It is almost twice the length of *Federalist* 78.) Although largely overlooked today, the essay's subject was one of pressing concern to Anti-Federalists.[99] Hamilton notes at the outset that the absence of a requirement for juries in civil trials was "[t]he objection to the plan of the convention, which has met with most success in this

State, and perhaps in several of the other States" (*Fed.* 83, 558). In Brutus's words, "the trial by jury, which has so justly been the boast of our fore fathers as well as ourselves is taken away under them."[100]

Despite its length, *Federalist* 83 presented a simple argument: because different states have different practices concerning jury trials, it was impossible to fashion a constitutional standard on the subject. "The great difference between the limits of the jury trial in different states is not generally understood" (*Fed.* 83, 558), Hamilton stated, and he offered a survey of the types of cases heard by juries in the different states and how they differed. He drew two conclusions from that survey: "First, that no general rule could have been fixed upon by the convention which would have corresponded with the circumstances of all the states; and secondly, that more, or at least as much might have been hazarded, by taking the system of any one state for a standard, as by omitting a provision altogether, and leaving the matter as it has been left, to legislative regulation" (*Fed.* 83, 566–67).

The most notable aspect of the essay is not Hamilton's technical argument about the impossibility of fashioning a workable national rule. What is more striking is the profound gap between his view of juries and the common Anti-Federalist perception. The fact that the lack of a provision for civil juries trials was, by Hamilton's estimate, the most common objection to the Constitution in New York "and perhaps in several of the other States," is evidence of a profound faith in jury decision-making. Anti-Federalists treated jury trial "as the very palladium of free government" (*Fed.* 83, 562). Brutus saluted "the inestimable right of trial by jury."[101] It has "so justly been the boast of our fore fathers."[102]

In marked contrast, Hamilton repeatedly stressed the limited competence of juries, observing "there are many cases in which the trial by jury is an ineligible one." Juries could not decide prize cases, for example, because their members lacked "a thorough knowledge of the laws and usages of nations" (*Fed.* 83, 568). Similarly, matters considered by courts of equity were "too complicated" for trial by jury (*Fed.* 83, 570).

"[T]he establishment of the trial by jury in *all* cases would have been an unpardonable error in the plan" (*Fed.* 83, 572).

Hamilton fundamentally disagreed with the Anti-Federalists' faith in juries as legal decision-makers. The very structure of his essays reflects a fundamental shift in perspective. For Anti-Federalists, jury decision-making was of central importance. For Hamilton, it was not, and he relegated it to the end of his discussion of the judiciary. After five essays celebrating judges and their expertise, he dealt with juries in one essay, and it was a highly critical essay. Anti-Federalists like Brutus did not portray legal reasoning as the product of distinctive expertise. Judges would be guided by self-interest and had to be checked. Juries could be trusted to reach proper decisions. Hamilton, in contrast, championed the legal expertise of judges.[103]

CONCLUSION

As a lawyer and as a legal thinker, Hamilton was a prodigy. He began his legal studies in 1782 and chose to instruct himself, rather than follow the traditional clerkship route. Within six months, he had been admitted to the bar, and the study manual he prepared, *Practical Proceedings in the Supreme Court of the State of New York*, "was so expertly done, its copious information so rigorously pigeonholed, that it was copied by hand and circulated among New York law students for years," biographer Ron Chernow reports.[104] Still only somewhere in his mid- to late-twenties – his birth year is a matter of dispute – he soon was one of the leading lawyers in New York City, and he made his landmark judicial review argument in *Rutgers* only two years after he began his legal studies.

And his profound contributions to the law only grew as his career unfolded. He was one of the leading figures at the Philadelphia convention (although not as significant as Madison and Wilson), a major force for nationalism. He was the intellectual leader of the Federalists at the crucial New York Ratifying Convention, as the Federalists, despite being the overwhelming minority at the start of the debates, eked out by a three-vote victory.

(Melancton Smith also played a key role. The intellectual leader of the Anti-Federalists, he declared his support for the Constitution after the news of Virginia's ratification arrived.) As secretary of the treasury, he played the critical role in constitutional interpretation during the Washington administration, establishing an enduring legacy. His memorandum to Washington supporting the constitutionality of the Bank of the United States convinced the president to sign the Bank Bill, and it laid the groundwork for Chief Justice Marshall's 1819 decision in *McCulloch v. Maryland*. That memorandum created a lasting framework for a broad reading of the Constitution's grants of national power, both by offering an expansive interpretation of the "necessary and proper clause" and by championing the doctrine of implied powers. His Pacificus Essays of 1793, defending Washington's Neutrality Proclamation, articulated a capacious view of executive power generally and in the foreign affairs area in particular, and they continue to shape constitutional debate, serving as the touchstone for advocates of presidential power. When the Supreme Court first considered the constitutionality of an act of Congress in *Hylton v. United States,* he argued on behalf of the United States in support of a carriage tax adopted when he was secretary of the treasury, and the Court followed his expansive conception of the federal taxing authority and upheld the statute.

And of course he served, with Madison and Jay, Publius. In his remarkable contributions to the *Federalist*, essays 78 through 83 stand out because of their intellectual and historic significance. The framers had abandoned the faith in legislative decision-making that informed the early state constitutions. They were creating a system of governance that involved the primacy of a written constitution adopted by "We the People" and a dramatically changed and expanded judicial role. But they had not developed a theory that made sense of this emerging consensus. Hamilton offered a path-breaking theoretical framework that justified that new role, and he explicated with insight and care the specific legal doctrine implicit and explicit in the Constitution.

Scholars have long focused on the Madisonian constitutional and legal vision in *The Federalist*, and particularly *Federalist* 10. Hamilton's vision of the judiciary deserves equivalent attention – and perhaps more. By defending judicial independence and the concept of the judiciary as a separate and co-equal branch, articulating a structural concept of judicial review, criticizing juries, conceptualizing both concurrent state and federal jurisdiction and a strong role for federal courts in the new constitutional system, and championing the rule of law, he was developing a linked set of principles that have become so familiar that we have missed how original they were when Hamilton proclaimed them. A conceptual tour de force, *Federalist* 78–83 developed a modern theory of the judicial role.

The contribution of Hamilton's essays is even clearer when their influence at the founding is contrasted with that of *Federalist* 10 and Madison's theory of the virtues of an extended republic. While scholars have longed assumed that the influence of *Federalist* 10 was powerful, legal scholar Larry Kramer has convincingly shown that "[t]he theory of the extended republic, particularly those aspects that are important to theorists today, played essentially no role in shaping the Constitution or its aftermath."[105] *Federalist* 10 was ignored until it was discovered (and vilified) by Charles Beard.

Thus, the contribution of *Federalist* 10 is fundamentally different from the contribution of Hamilton's essays on the judiciary. In developing the idea that an extended republic addressed the problem of factions and self-interested majorities, Madison offered a brilliant explanation for the way in which the Constitution resolved a fundamental problem, but he did not shape his contemporaries' understanding of the Constitution. Hamilton's insights were not merely brilliant and creative, they transformed the way in which courts and the law were understood. When this difference is recognized, Hamilton's contributions to *The Federalist* are even more deserving of celebration than Madison's. While both Madison and Hamilton were path-breaking political thinkers, Hamilton created a path that others followed.

Moreover, Hamilton's contribution operated not only at the level of grand constitutional theory; it also shaped the articulation of a series of critical legal doctrines. Hamilton wrote at a time in which judicial review and constitutional interpretation were in their infancy, and *The Federalist*, particularly *Federalist* 78, offers a very specific and influential approach to the role courts should play in the exercise of the power of judicial review. He also confronted a series of complex legal issues that the Constitution gave rise to – such as the suability of states, the concurrent jurisdiction of state and federal courts, the merger of equity and common law, whether federal courts were to be the final decision-maker in matters involving federal laws and the Constitution – and presented thoughtful analyses of what he saw as the Constitution's answers. Thus, Hamilton offered not only a broad vision of the role of courts, but also a coherent analysis of how particular legal doctrines fit into that vision, and, writing before ratification, he anticipated and cogently analyzed the issues that the Court was to grapple with in such landmark cases as *Chisholm, Marbury*, and *Martin v. Hunter's Lessee.*

It is a breathtaking contribution, but what almost defies belief is that he wrote *The Federalist* essays on the judiciary a mere six years after he began studying for the bar. Law is an accretional discipline, unlike, say, math or music. It is mastered (if at all) only after years of study, experience, and reflection. Law, famously, has no prodigies. But a look at the *Federalist Papers* indicates that there was an exception to this rule, a legal thinker who produced a work of genius when new to the profession. Our Hamilton, the figure our culture knows best today, is prominently associated with Lin-Manuel Miranda's fabulous rap musical.[106] But the closest musical counterpart to Hamilton is a composer of classical music. Hamilton was the law's Mozart.

NOTES

1 This essay has benefitted from the thoughtful comments of Randy Barnett, Maeva Marcus, John Mikhail, Jim Pfander, Larry Solum, and Derek Webb

and from the research support of the Georgetown University Library team, and particularly Christine Ciambelle. Colleen Sheehan and Jack Rakove made comments that greatly strengthened this essay. Any lack of clarity in the essay is the product of Professor Rakove's ruthless editing.

2 Elaine Crane, "Publius in the Provinces: Where was The Federalist Reprinted Outside New York City?," *William and Mary Quarterly*, 21 (1964), 289–92.

3 Garry Wills, *Explaining America: The Federalist* (Garden City, N.Y.: Doubleday, 1981), xv.

4 James Madison to Edmund Randolph, Oct. 21, 1787, *PJM*, X, 199.

5 Herbert Storing, ed., *The Complete Anti-Federalist* (Chicago and London, 1987), 2.9.195

6 Melancton Smith et al., Pamphlet on *Rutgers v. Waddington*, in Michael Zuckert and Derek Webb, eds., *The Anti-Federalist Writings of the Melancton Smith Circle* (Indianapolis, 2009), 3, 9.

7 Charles Warren, *The Supreme Court in United States History* (Boston: Little, Brown, 1923), I, 149.

8 According to Blackstone, the King "has alone the right of erecting courts of judicature; for, though the constitution of the kingdom hath intrusted him with the whole executive power of the laws, it is impossible, as well as improper, that he should personally carry into execution this great and extensive trust: it is consequently necessary that courts should be erected to assist him in executing this power; and equally necessary that, if erected, they should be erected by his authority. And hence it is that all jurisdictions of courts are either mediately or immediately derived from the crown, their proceedings run generally in the king's name, they pass under his seal, and are executed by his officers."1 Blackstone Commentaries *267. See also Forrest McDonald, *Novus Ordo Seclorum: An Intellectual History of the Constitution* (Lawrence KS: University Press of Kansas, 1985), 210 (for Blackstone, "the judicial power was a subordinate of the executive"). Locke's conception of separation of powers resembled Blackstone's in that the judiciary was part of the executive. He divided government into the legislative, the executive (which included the judiciary), and the federative (which involved dealings with foreign powers). See John Locke, *The Second Treatise of Government*, in *Two Treatises of Government* §§ 143–48, at 382–84 (Peter Laslett ed., 1960) (first published 1690).

9 John Adams, Clarendon, no. 3 (January 27, 1766), reprinted in Philip
 Kurland and Ralph Lerner, eds., *The Founders' Constitution* (Chicago and
 London, 1987), I, 630–32. On the acceptance of this view in the colonies,
 see Gordon S. Wood, *The Creation of the American Republic, 1776–1787*
 (Chapel Hill, N.C., 1969), 159–60.

10 Montesquieu, *The Spirit of the* Laws, book 11, in *Founders' Constitution*,
 I, 624–28.

11 See id. ("The judiciary power ought not to be given to a standing senate; it
 should be exercised by persons taken from the body of the people at certain
 times of the year, and consistently with a form and manner prescribed by law,
 in order to erect a tribunal that should last only so long as necessity requires."
 Ibid., 625) Montesquieu's focus on the jury, as opposed to judges, in his
 description of the exercise of judicial power was, however, inconsistent with
 the increasing power that eighteenth century British judges were exercising.
 See Jack N. Rakove, The Original Justification for Judicial Independence, 95
 Geo. L.J. 1061, 1063 (2007) ("Being French, Montesquieu tended to be long on
 theory and short on practice. . . .") [hereinafter Rakove, Judicial Independence].

12 Wood, *Creation of the American Republic*, 155, 159; Christine A. Desan,
 The Constitutional Commitment to Legislative Adjudication in the Early
 American Tradition, 111 Harv. L. Rev. 1381 (1998). Tenure during good
 behavior had been established in Great Britain by the Act of Settlement of
 1701.

13 Virginia, Va. Const. of 1776, 5, reprinted in Francis Newton Thorpe, ed.,
 Constitutions, Colonial Charters, and Other Organic Laws of the States,
 Territories, and Colonies Now or Heretofore Forming the United States of
 America. (Washington: Government Printing Office, 1909), VII, 3812–13.
 For similar provisions, see Md. Const. of 1776, art. VI, reprinted in ibid., III,
 1687; N.C. Const. of 1776, art. IV, reprinted in ibid., V, 2787; Georgia, Ga.
 Const. of 1777, art. I, reprinted in ibid., II, 778; Mass. Const. of 1780, art.
 XXX, reprinted in ibid., III, 1893; New Hampshire, N.H. Const. of 1784,
 art. XXXVII, reprinted in ibid., IV, 2457. In New Jersey and South Carolina,
 however, the judiciary was not treated as a separate and independent
 branch. See Willi Paul Adams, *The First American Constitutions:*
 Republican Ideology and the Making of the State Constitutions in the
 Revolutionary Era (Chapel Hill: University of North Carolina Press, 1980),
 264–65.

14 Wood, *Creation of the American Republic*, at 155–56, 454.

15 S. Car. Const. Art. V, XVI (1776) (creating Privy Council from members of executive and legislature that would operate as a Court of Chancery); N.J. Const. IX (1776) (Governor and the Legislative Council to be court of last resort).

16 Wood, *Creation of the American Republic*, 148, 160–61.

17 Gerhard Casper, *Separating Powers: Essays on the Founding Period* (Cambridge MA: Harvard University Press, 1997), 136.

18 Rakove, Original Justification, at 1066.

19 Wood at 454; Rakove, Original Justification at 1066.

20 (1610) 77 Eng. Rep. 646, 652 ("[I]t appears in our books, that in many cases, the common law will controul Acts of Parliament, and sometimes adjudge them to be utterly void . . . ."). This statement was cited with approval in Day v. Savage, (1614) 80 Eng. Rep. 235, 237, and in City of London v. Wood, (1701) 88 Eng. Rep. 1592, 1602.

21 Blackstone Commentaries *91. See also id. at 160.

22 William Michael Treanor, Judicial Review before Marbury, 58 Stanford L. Rev. 455, 473–96 (2005). My discussion of the early judicial review cases in this essay follows the discussion in the Stanford article.

23 There was no published opinion in *Trevett*. The principal record is a pamphlet written by James Varnum, Weeden's attorney, who argued for the exercise of judicial review. James M. Varden, The Case, Trevett v. Weeden, reprinted in Bernard Schwartz, ed., *The Bill of Rights: A Documentary History* (New York: Chelsea House Publishers, 1971), vol. I.

24 Commonwealth v. Caton, 8 Va. (4 Call) 4 (1782). The published opinion is incomplete and often in error. For a fuller discussion of the case, drawing on the papers of the participants, see William Michael Treanor, The Case of the Prisoners and the Origins of Judicial Review, 143 U. Pa. L. Rev. 491 (1994).

25 While the opinion in *Rutgers* was not published, it was printed in Julius Goebel, Jr., *The Law Practice of Alexander Hamilton: Documents and Commentary* (New York: Columbia University Press, 1964–81), I, 393. For a recent account of the case focusing on the way in which the legal system mediated competing claims of Loyalists and Patriots, see Peter Charles Hoffer, *Rutgers v. Waddington: Alexander Hamilton, the End of the War for Independence, and the Origins of Judicial Review* (Lawrence KS: University Press of Kansas, 2016).

26 New York Constitution of 1777, Article XXXV.

27 Hamilton, Brief, in Goebel, ed., *Law Practice of Hamilton*, I, 374.

28 Ibid., 381 (quoting Cicero).

29 For the opinion in the Mayor's Court, see Ibid., 399–417. For an analysis of the decision, see Treanor, "Judicial Review before *Marbury*," 484–87.

30 New York Assembly Resolution, *New York Assembly Journal*, October 4–November 29, 1784, reprinted in Goebel, ed., *Law Practice of Hamilton*, I, 312.

31 Melancton Smith and Others, "To the People of the State of New York," reprinted in *The Antifederalist Writings of the Melancton Smith Circle*, 3. Smith is listed as the lead author and is generally thought to have written the essay. See ibid.

32 Ibid., 9.

33 Ibid.

34 Ibid.

35 Casper, *Separating Powers*, 138–39.

36 Act of Settlement, 1701, 12 & 13 Will 3, ch 2. See James E. Pfander, Removing Federal Judges, 74 U. Chicago L. R., 1227, 1235 (2007).

37 The only controversial matter with respect to compensation was whether salaries could be increased. Madison had moved to prohibit increase of salaries – but this was rejected on the grounds that the approach did not take into account the possibility of inflation. See McDonald, *Novus Ordo Seclorum*, 53.

38 Robert Pushaw, Article III's Case/Controversy Distinction and the Dual Functions of Federal Courts, 69 Notre Dame L. Rev. 447, 468–69 (1999).

39 Articles of Confederation, Article IX, sec. 1.

40 Articles of Confederation Article IX, sec. 2.

41 Hamilton, Unsubmitted Resolution Calling for a Convention to Amend the Articles of Confederation, *PAH*, III, 421.

42 Pushaw, Article III's Case/Controversy Distinction, 469.

43 James E. Pfander, *One Supreme Court: Supremacy, Inferiority, and the Judicial Power of the United States* (New York: Oxford University Press, 2009), 6. See also Max Farrand, *The Framing of the Constitution of the United States* (New Haven: Yale University Press, 1913), 79–80. ("The most serious question was that of the inferior courts. The difficulty lay in the fact that they were regarded as an encroachment upon the rights of the individual states... . The matter was compromised: inferior courts were not required, but the national legislature was permitted to establish them."); Amanda Frost, Overvaluing Uniformity, 94 Va. L. Rev. 1567, 1620 (2008) ("This was the compromise, orchestrated by James Madison, between

those who wanted to establish lower federal courts and those who thought they were unnecessary. The two camps split the difference by leaving the creation of the lower federal courts to Congress' discretion.").

44 *RFC*, II, 21–36, 71–83.

45 *RFC*, I, 97 (Gerry); II, 27 (Sherman), 28, 92, 299 (Gouverneur Morris); 73 (Wilson, Mason); 76 (Martin); 376 (Williamson); 420 (Madison). It should be noted that Madison's position on judicial review was complex and not consistent. See Larry Kramer, *The People Themselves: Popular Constitutionalism and Judicial Review*, (New York: Oxford University Press, 2005), cha. 4, 6. For the statements in opposition to judicial review, see *RFC*, 11, 298 (Mercer), 299 (Dickinson).

46 Maeva Marcus, "Judicial Review in the Early Republic," in Ronald Hoffman & Peter J. Albert eds., *Launching the "Extended Republic": The Federalist Era* (Charlottesville VA: University Press of Virginia, 1996) 25, 33–35.

47 William M. Treanor, Judicial Review before Marbury, Stanford Law Review, 58 (2005) 497–554 (surveying cases).

48 McDonald, *Novus Ordo Seclorum*, 253

49 Casper, *Separating Powers*, 133.

50 Letter from Melancton Smith to Abraham Yates, Jan. 23, 1788, *DHRC*, XX, 638–39.

51 Paul Leicester Ford, ed., *Essays on the Constitution of the United States* (Brooklyn NY: Historical Printing Club, 1892), 295; Cecelia M. Kenyon, ed., *The Antifederalists* (Indianapolis: Bobbs-Merrill, 1966), 323; Julius Goebel, Jr., *History of the Supreme Court of the United States*, vol. I, *Antecedents and Beginnings to 1801* (New York: Macmillan, 1971), 292–93, 308–12; Terence Ball, ed., *The Federalist with Letters of "Brutus"* (New York: Cambridge University Press, 2003), 436. Bernard Bailyn has suggested that Brutus was either Robert Yates or Abraham Yates, Jr. Bernard Bailyn, ed., *The Debate on the Constitution* (New York: Library of America, 1993), I, 1149. Saul Cornell has written that "the identit[y] of Brutus ... remains a mystery." Saul Cornell, *The Other Founders: Anti-Federalism and the Dissenting Tradition in the United States, 1788–1828* (Chapel Hill: University of North Carolina Press, 1999), 96 n.23.

52 See, e.g., William Jeffrey, Jr., The Letters of 'Brutus' – A Neglected Element in the Ratification Campaign of 1787-88, 40 U. Cin. L. Rev. 643, 645 (1971); David Siemers, *The Antifederalists: Men of Great Faith and*

Forbearance (Lanham MD: Rowman & Littlefield, 2003), 121 ("Brutus' identity is uncertain, but speculation has centered on Melancton Smith); John Burrows, "The Authorship of Two Sets of Anti-Federalist Papers: A Computational Approach in The Antifederalist Writings of the Melancton Smith Circle," in Zuckert and Webb, eds., *Smith Circle*, 418–19. (computational analysis of vocabulary provides "compelling" evidence that Melancton Smith was Brutus).

53 Michael Zuckert and Derek Webb, Introduction, ibid., xxix. Zuckert and Webb offer strong evidence that Smith was the Federal Farmer and that he was Brutus, largely because both the Federal Farmer and Brutus advanced arguments that Smith made elsewhere. At the same time, they point out that it was unlikely that the same person wrote both sets of essays: they differ significantly too much in style and it is unlikely that one person would write two different series "overlapping in time and topic." Id. at xxviii. Thus, they postulate that one was likely written by Smith and the second by someone strongly influenced by Smith.

It should be noted that Federal Farmer, like Brutus, voiced deep suspicion of the federal judiciary, although he devoted much less attention to the subject. Federal Farmer expressed particular concern that the federal judiciary would be able to abuse power because its actions, typically only affecting one person, would escape popular attention. See Federal Farmer, Essay 15, storing, 2.8.183–185. Both Brutus and Federal Farmer expressed concern about the Constitution's failing to protect the jury trial right, Federal Farmer celebrated the jury more than Brutus, applauding its importance as a representative decisionmaking body. See Federal Farmer, Essay 15, Storing, 2.8. 190–194. For further discussion of Federal Farmer's criticism of Article III, see Cornell at 89–90.

In this essay, I take the view that Brutus was Smith, rather than someone influenced by Smith. That conclusion accords with the weight of recent scholarship. Perhaps of greater importance, where Federal Farmer devotes comparatively little attention to the judiciary, the judiciary is of central concern to Brutus. As Zuckert and Webb observe, "It is of more than passing interest that *Federal Farmer* 's treatment of institutions is weak just where *Brutus*'s is strong – on the judiciary." *Smith Circle*, xxxi. In particular, Smith's concern with judicial review, as reflected in his memo in the aftermath of *Rutgers*, support the idea that he was Brutus, since Brutus also focused extensively on judicial review (and Federal Farmer did not).

54 Essay 11, ibid., 233.

55 Essay 16, ibid., 262.

56 "But if the execution of the laws of the national government should not require the intervention of the State legislatures, if they were to pass into immediate operation upon the citizens themselves, the particular governments could not interrupt their progress without an open and violent exertion of an unconstitutional power....The success of it would require not merely a factious majority in the legislature, but the concurrence of the courts of justice and of the body of the people. If the judges were not embarked in a conspiracy with the legislature, they would pronounce the resolutions of such a majority to be contrary to the supreme law of the land, unconstitutional, and void." (*Fed.* 16, 104–5).

57 Madison wrote: "It is true that in controversies relating to the boundary between the two jurisdictions [state and federal], the tribunal which is ultimately to decide, is to be established under the general government. But this does not change the principle of the case. The decision is to be impartially made, according to the rules of the Constitution; and all the usual and most effectual precautions are taken to secure this impartiality." *Fed.* 39, 256.

58 "In the State Constitutions and indeed in the Federal one also, no provision is made for the case of a disagreement in expounding them [the law]: as the Courts are generally the last in making their decisions, it results to them by refusing or not refusing to execute a law, to stamp it with a final character. This makes the Judiciary Dept. paramount in fact to the Legislature, which was never intended and can never be proper." Madison, Observations on the "Draught of a Constitution for Virginia," Oct. 15, 1788, *PJM*, XI, 293.

59 It is, for example, the *Federalist* essay on the judiciary most frequently cited in law reviews, and by a wide measure. A search in the Lexis database on September 16, 2016 found that it had been cited 3149 times. The other essays were cited 254 times (*Federalist* 79), 660 times (*Federalist* 80), 841 times (*Federalist* 81), 285 times (*Federalist* 82), and 480 times (*Federalist* 83). It is also the most cited in Supreme Court decisions, though here the citation count is much closer: *Federalist* 78 (48 citations); *Federalist* 79 (12 citations); *Federalist* 80 (28 citations); *Federalist* 81 (35 citations); *Federalist* 82 (21 citations); *Federalist* 83 (11 citations).

60 Storing 2.9.195.

61 Storing 2.9.145.

62 Storing at 2.9.158.

63 Storing at 2.9.193.

64 Storing at 2.9.186.

65 Storing at 2.9.186.

66 Storing at 2.9.130.

67 Storing 2.9.150.

68 Storing 2.9.142.

69 Storing 2.9.142.

70 *Smith Circle*, 261–62.

71 ibid.

72 Alexander Bickel, *The Least Dangerous Branch: The Supreme Court at the Bar of Politics* (Indianapolis: Bobbs-Merrill, 1962).

73 See Treanor, Judicial Review before Marbury, 469–71 (discussion of statements about judicial review in the federal convention and during the ratifying debates).

74 Benjamin F. Wright, *The Growth of American Constitutional Law* (Boston: Houghton Mifflin, 1942), 25.

75 Sylvia Snowiss, *Judicial Review and the Law of the Constitution* (New Haven: Yale University Press, 1990), 90.

76 John Ash, *The New and Complete Dictionary of the English Language* (London: Vernor and Hood, 1795).

77 For further discussion see Treanor, Judicial Review before Marbury, 473–96.

78 "This Constitution, and the Laws of the United States which shall be made in Pursuance thereof; and all Treaties made, or which shall be made, under the Authority of the United States, shall be the supreme Law of the Land; and the Judges in every State shall be bound thereby, any Thing in the Constitution or Laws of any State to the Contrary notwithstanding." Article VI, cl. 2.

79 3 U.S. at 236 (Chase, J.); id. at 284 (Cushing, J.).

80 "The judicial Power shall extend to all Cases, in Law and Equity, arising under this Constitution, the Laws of the United States, and Treaties made, or which shall be made, under their Authority ..." Art III, sec. 2, cl. 1.

81 Essay 15, March 20, 1788, Storing, 2.9.191.

82 James E. Pfander* and Nassim Nazemi, The Anti-Injunction Act and the Problem of Federal State Jurisdictional Overlap, 92 Tex. L. Rev. 1, 11 (2013).

83 Storing 2.9.145.

84 Storing 2.9.137.

85 Storing 2.9.150.

86 Storing 2.9.158.

87 Scholars have previously pointed out that the unattributed quote is, in fact, a paraphrase of Brutus. See Goebel, *Supreme Court*, I, 316; Ball, ed., *The Federalist*, 393 n.2. For the original in Brutus, see Storing, 2.9.138 and 2.9.193.

88 For further discussion, see Pfander, *One Supreme Court*, 6.

89 "To confer the power of determining such causes upon the existing courts of the several States, would perhaps be as much 'to constitute tribunals,' as to create new courts with the like power" (*Fed.* 81, 427).

90 Storing 2.9.162.

91 This argument is developed in James Pfander, History and State Suability: An "Explanatory" Account of the Eleventh Amendment, 83 Cornell L. Rev. 1269, 1304–06 (1998).

92 *DHRC*, X, 1405 (Mason); 1414 (Madison); 1422–23 (Henry); 1433 (Marshall); 1453 (Randolph). For further discussion, see Pfander, History and State Suability, 1309–13.

93 2 U.S. 493 (1793).

94 See Seminole Tribe v. Florida, 517 U.S. 44, 54 (1996).

95 Pfander, History and Statue Suability, 1276.

96 Article III, sec. 2.

97 14 U.S. (1 Wheat.) 304 (1816).

98 See F. Thornton Miller, "John Marshall versus Spencer Roane: A Reevaluation of Martin v. Hunter's Lessee", *Virginia Magazine of History and Biography*, 96(1988), 297.

99 See Akhil Reed Amar, *America's Constitution: A Biography* (New York: Random House, 2005), 233–35 (discussing Anti-Federalist opposition to Constitution on the grounds that it "undermined the good old jury").

100 Storing 2.9.179.

101 Storing 2.9.184.

102 Storing 2.9.179.

103 Jack N. Rakove, *Original Meanings: Politics and Ideas in the Making of the Constitution* (New York: Alfred Knopf, 1996), 328. ("[B]y placing the subject of the jury last in the six essays he devoted to Article III, [Hamilton] illustrated a shift in emphasis that did distinguish Federalist and Anti-Federalist perceptions of judicial power.").

104 Ron Chernow, *Alexander Hamilton* (New York: Penguin, 2004), 168.

105 Larry Kramer, Madison's Audience, 112 Harv. L. Rev. 611(1999).

106 Lin-Manuel Miranda, *Hamilton: An American Musical* (Los Angeles: Warner/Chappell, 2016).

15 Publius's Political Science

John Ferejohn and Roderick Hills

INTRODUCTION

How does Publius's treatment of politics in *The Federalist* measure up as "political science"? On one hand, the purpose of the essays was more polemical than scientific. *The Federalist* sought to persuade New Yorkers to adopt the proposed Constitution rather than to evaluate it from an entirely dispassionate stance. Yet Publius's rhetorical method necessarily required predictions about the ways in which the new institutions would work. *The Federalist* necessarily made use of positive (empirically based) political science to ground normative political arguments to defend the novel constitutional scheme.

The modern discipline of political science has two aspects. First, it claims to possess some substantive principles or generalizations, either induced or derived, that are useful in making and criticizing political choices. The content of these propositions necessarily depends on history and context. Second, it uses empirical methods as the best way to gain and revise such generalizations. Like any other science, political science is dynamic: its substantive content can be expected to change with experience.

In this essay we characterize Publius's essays as "political science," focused on the solution of collective action problems – that is, problems of coordination among large numbers of agents with diverse interests. While both Alexander Hamilton and James Madison, writing as Publius, revealed substantive beliefs about how institutions would work, they also shared an intellectual commitment to revisit and update their beliefs based on experience. Both saw the new nation as embarked on an *experiment* to determine whether the United States could maintain an effective republican government.[1] Both saw the proposed Constitution as the best attempt to establish such a government on an uncharted political terrain. *The Federalist* presents the constitutional project in this light and asks its readers to understand the new design and to see that it does not threaten their attachments to liberty and self-government, while emphasizing that the Constitution would remain open to modification if things did not work as they expected.

Two interconnected issues might interfere with our project. First, we must ask whether Publius can usefully be understood as a "person" with coherent beliefs and a commitment to rational discourse. We assume that, whatever their differences in beliefs and expectations, during the ratification process Hamilton and Madison shared the overarching goal of securing the strong national government that the Constitution proposed – and that this belief indeed enabled them to write coherently in support of that project as "Publius."

The second issue is whether either author's beliefs changed after ratification in ways that would make it dubious to use subsequent information to make inferences as to what Publius (as a person) "believed" during the ratification debates. One famous version of this problem has been called the "Madison question": Did Madison change his views substantially after 1790 (as Hamilton and other Federalists believed he did) or did later events give Madison substantive reasons to infer new conclusions from his stable premises? One could ask the same question about Hamilton. Obviously the two took different political positions after 1790 on various issues. It seems unlikely, however, that either really changed his underlying normative objectives or his beliefs about human psychology. On the contrary, the best way to understand their divergent post-ratification positions lies in examining their changing empirical beliefs about how the Constitution would work, what political problems the new nation would face, and how public opinion would evolve. In other words, such changes in their empirical beliefs – their political science – account for their shifting political positions over time.

After 1790, domestic and foreign policy issues put pressure on Congress to adopt massive new legislative projects and on the executive to act with dispatch. The powers conferred on the executive by Congress and inferred by the executive from the Constitution itself turned out to be much more formidable than the essays of *The Federalist* had predicted. Publius was forced to adjust the original assumptions of *The Federalist* in light of this new evidence. Even as Hamilton and Madison drew opposite normative conclusions about this expansion of executive power, it was precisely their (largely shared) evolving empirically based beliefs about politics that drove them to different political conclusions.

As "experimentalists," neither Hamilton nor Madison could take all of his beliefs as equally open to revision in light of new evidence. Like any experimental scientist, each would retain certain beliefs as fixed or "maintained hypotheses" while revising others. Neither Madison nor Hamilton would have been prepared to conclude that his foundational theory of human nature was wrong even if the proposed institutions did not work as expected. Instead, each held constant their shared fundamental principles about the problems of collective action that constitutions were supposed to solve. Madison and Hamilton parted ways instead on their normative assessments about how well state officials, Congress, and voters could control executive power: Madison systematically revised Publius's assessment in light of the post-1790 operation of the presidency, while Hamilton – a primary author of such presidential behavior – retained his confidence in the benefit of relatively broad implied presidential powers.

Our argument proceeds in four parts. Part 1 examines some of Publius's design principles for a constitution rooted in his beliefs about human nature and predictions about institutional behavior based on those beliefs as well as the study of classical and contemporary republics. Parts 2 through 4 focus on Madison rather than Hamilton, because the emerging evidence as to how the Constitution worked largely corresponded to Hamilton's expectations. Part 2 examines *Federalist* 10 and asks how Madison revised his theory of representation in light of the perceived failure of Congress to impose adequate curbs on Hamilton's financial program. Madison's response to this failure was constitutional: he tried to devise interpretive canons that would ameliorate the newly revealed weaknesses in the text. Part 3 shows how Madison's naïve understanding of the presidency proved deficient and how he tried, in line with his response to the predictive failure of *Federalist* 10, to devise interpretive canons to cabin newly claimed executive authority. Part 4 examines how Madison tried other constitutional moves to counter the Alien and Sedition Acts, seeking to enlist other states to block or interpose enforcement of these laws. Following the disappointing response to this initiative, he and Thomas Jefferson launched a political campaign to appeal to "The People Themselves" in a "constitutional" campaign that culminated in what was called the Revolution of 1800. The key aspect of that campaign was the appeal to the "people" as the "guardian of the Constitution." Madison's move away from formal constitutional institutions to the people themselves as the mechanism for enforcing the Constitution bears an analogy to the Weimar-era controversy between Hans Kelsen, who argued that a constitutional court standing outside normal politics was the most reliable guardian of the Constitution, and Carl Schmitt, who responded that only a democratically accountable president can fulfill that function.[2] In some sense, Madison during the 1790s reformulated Publius's original position in a Schmittian direction.

In each case, the key event was the failure of an empirical prediction as to how constitutionally designed institutions would work, causing Madison to revise Publius's assumptions about executive power and adopt a new reading of the document that would curb the power that he, as Publius, had once defended. Hamilton would not have seen, in any of these events, any reason to change his views about executive power and certainly no reason to attempt to curb it.

PUBLIUS'S POLITICAL THEORY

Publius's normative recommendations depend on, first, the domestic and international context in which the new government would operate, and, second, on the broad goal of designing a government capable of dealing effectively with anticipated challenges while honoring the commitment to popular or republican government.

Publius's Normative Commitments

We assume that Hamilton's and Madison's normative views, about which *The Federalist* is somewhat informative, bracket those of other framers of the Constitution.[3] Roughly speaking, Hamilton wanted the new republic to be powerful enough, both militarily and financially, to match up to European powers on land and sea and to secure internal social order. Such a government needed the capacity to raise revenues and troops independently of the state governments, to be able to borrow on favorable terms, and to be led by a decisive (energetic) president in order to exercise its power effectively.[4] It also needed a productive legislature capable of sustaining economic and foreign policies in a treacherous world. Hamilton thought that a powerful republic had to be economically robust, with a flourishing industry and commerce, and that the national government should be committed to supporting these interests.

However different their normative commitments, the two main authors *of The Federalist* agreed on certain principles of constitutional design. Six of the essays – *Federalist* 10, 49, 51, and 63, written by Madison, and two of Hamilton's most important pieces, *Federalist* 70 and 78 – collectively provide a summary statement of the characteristics of a stable republican constitution. Each of these papers articulates a practical norm of republican constitutional design, and each rests on some underlying proposition of political science, drawn from classical and early modern examples of popular governments, which are then used to justify some aspect of the Constitution or some critique of the Articles of Confederation or the revolutionary state constitutions. Here is a short list of the controlling propositions:

1. The republic ought to be large and diverse; this will make it difficult for factions to form and capture governmental institutions (*Federalist* 10).

2. Stability and rule of law require that the powers of the departments ought to be separated to some extent and that the weaker departments of the executive and judiciary be given the means to defend themselves against encroachments by the legislature, which is the strongest and most dangerous department in a republic (*Fed.* 51, 78).

3. Government should be conducted by elected representatives and their appointees, because a well-structured election process will assure high-quality representatives; the people themselves should have no direct role either in the operation of the government or the revision of the Constitution, because "the people" acting together (as a mob) will prove vulnerable to appeals to their particular interest and passions rather than to the public interest (*Fed.* 49, 51, and 63).

4. The executive authority ought to be exercised by a single person holding office for a fixed and lengthy period, because otherwise the laws will be badly executed and have little effect on the conduct of public or private affairs (*Fed.* 70).

5. Constitutional norms ought to be enforced by independent judges: otherwise the constitution would be no constraint on the conduct of government (*Fed.* 78).

These practical "design" norms pervade other numbers of *The Federalist*, although in different ways. Generally speaking these essays justify the creation of a representative government with stably separated powers, on a large scale, with large election districts, and regular but not very frequent elections.

Publius's Political Psychology

The Federalist abounds with generalizations about human nature that are deployed to expound on and justify features of the proposed Constitution. In his overview of checks and balances in *Federalist* 51, for example, Madison starts from an Augustinian description of humans after the Fall: People are, he thought, powerfully motivated to pursue their material interests despite their (usually weaker) attraction to larger public purposes. This frailty explains why we accept government with coercive powers over us: "what is government itself but the greatest of all reflections on human nature," Madison opined, noting that, "[i]f men were angels there would be no need for government" (*Fed.* 51, 349).[5]

In *Federalist* 70, Hamilton paints a similarly pessimistic picture of human nature, though with more emphasis on men's vanity and passion than on their material self-interest:

> Men often oppose a thing, merely because they have had no agency in planning it, or because it may have been planned by those whom they dislike. But if they have been consulted, and have happened to disapprove, opposition then becomes, in their estimation, an indispensable duty of self-love. They seem to think themselves bound in honor, and by all the motives of personal infallibility, to defeat the success of what has been resolved upon contrary to their sentiments.
>
> (*Fed.* 70, 474–75)

Like Madison, Hamilton thought that a smart constitutional engineer could harness personal vices to serve the public good: a single executive, knowing he would be held responsible whatever he did or failed to do, would be amply motivated by vanity to take responsibility for giving effect to the laws and protecting the nation from internal and external threats.[6]

Collective Action: Problem and Opportunity

Starting from these pessimistic generalities about human nature, Publius offered three more specific generalizations about organizational and institutional behavior. First, partly because people are self-seeking, collective action is difficult to achieve. Second, the tendency of the popular and powerful legislative branch to encroach on other departments (or on personal liberties) needs to be curbed. Third, the main difficulty in establishing stable republican rule is the psychology of the people themselves, requiring that the mass of citizens be prevented from playing an active role in both day-to-day and constitutional politics.

Start with the obstacles to collective action. According to Publius, it is hard for both the people and the states to coordinate their actions to pursue public goods and so such goods will tend to be undersupplied.

> There was a time when we were told that breaches, by the States, of the regulations of the federal authority were not to be expected; that a sense of common interest would preside over the conduct of the respective members, and would beget a full compliance with all the constitutional requisitions of the Union. This language, at the present day, would appear as wild as a great part of what we now hear from the same quarter will be thought, when we shall have received further lessons from that best oracle of wisdom, experience.
>
> (*Fed.* 15, 96)[7]

This principle, stated in its familiar or positive form, is presented as a justification for giving Congress the authority to make laws binding directly on the people. Hamilton presents the case:

> The great and radical vice in the construction of the existing Confederation is in the principle of
> LEGISLATION for STATES or GOVERNMENTS, in their CORPORATE or COLLECTIVE CAPACITIES, and as contradistinguished from the INDIVIDUALS of which they consist ... the United States has an indefinite discretion to make requisitions for men and money; but they have no authority to raise either, by regulations extending to the individual citizens of America. The consequence of this is, that though in theory their resolutions concerning those objects are laws, constitutionally binding on the members of the Union, yet in practice they are mere recommendations which the States observe or disregard at their option.
>
> (*Fed.* 15, 93)

The same principle was invoked in other papers, including the essays that explained why federal taxation would be more efficient than that of the states and why the federal government is more likely than the states to build a navy to protect American commerce.

The collective action problems confronted by citizens, however, are not only a bug to be overcome but also a feature to be employed. Like Publius's defense of a unitary executive, Madison's defense of the large republic in *Federalist* 10 harnesses individual vice – that is, individuals' predilection for shirking in collective enterprises – to protect the public interest. "Extend the sphere, and you take in a greater variety of parties and interests," Madison notes, making it "more difficult for all who feel it to discover their own strength, and to act in unison with each other." The case for the large republic, in short, rests on public benefits of collective action problems that Publius elsewhere decries as vices. In that respect, the principle of collective action plays two roles in justifying the constitutional design: as a problem to be overcome, it supports the expansion of congressional powers to create public goods; as a beneficial vice to be exploited, it justifies the formation of a large and heterogeneous republic.

Publius's second institutional assumption is that the legislature would be the most powerful and dangerous branch. For this reason, its powers needed to be carefully regulated in order for the executive and judicial departments to do their jobs. This regulation required that the legislative power be divided and checked and subjected to review. By contrast, few such checks were needed on the powers of the weaker but no less essential executive and judicial branches. The point of having a distinct executive was to create an official who could detect dangers to the republic and act expeditiously without going to Congress or the people and thus be subjected only to *ex post* accountability. The point of having judges was to apply the laws evenhandedly, no matter what members of Congress thought, according to their expert judgment, and to maintain the superiority of the Constitution over ordinary statutes.

Publius's final institutional assumption was that excessive responsiveness of republican governments to public opinion would make the republic tumultuous and unstable. Madison and Hamilton both believed that the republican principle required that the legislature be open to the people's control through popular elections and the operation of public opinion. The new Constitution recognized this necessary dependence in various ways. But this dependence was appropriately modulated by bicameralism, by relatively long terms of office for the House and especially the Senate, by making the election of senators indirect, and in other ways as well. Even with these checks on public opinion, however, Madison believed that the legislature would remain excessively powerful and dangerous. He hoped that the citizenry would elect representatives who would be older, more experienced, better educated, and generally more likely to be guided by public purposes than ordinary voters. In addition, the Constitution imposed checks on Congress in Article I, Sections 8 and 9, that were far more detailed than those imposed on other departments in order to resist its tendency to draw other matters into the "legislative vortex."

THE CONSTITUTION IN ACTION

By the end of the Convention, both Madison and Hamilton thought that the institutions agreed to in the proposed Constitution were reasonably well adapted to the ends each of them sought – however different these ends may have been.[8] The Constitution provided ample new legislative powers to the national government, a single executive, and an independent judiciary, while allowing the states to retain a great degree of control over local affairs. It also provided protections against congressional intrusions on the other powers and, to an extent, against the states, too. If the states ratified the Constitution, the authors of The Federalist would have an opportunity to learn from experience about how their proposed institutions worked and seek to change them if they did not work as anticipated. To the extent that institutions did not work as expected, they could learn which of their beliefs were false. This would be a matter of testing the design adopted in Philadelphia and agreed to in the state conventions and seeing how it worked in the laboratory of experience.

Failures of Federalist 10

The first test came early, with Hamilton's proposal that Congress confer a charter of incorporation on a private bank with which the United States would deposit all of its revenues while holding only 20 percent of its shares. Hamilton believed that the national government's use of such a fiscal agent would provide a ready source of funds for large-scale capital projects, thus promoting economic development. Private subscribers to the Bank's stock would support the new nation's taxing powers, thereby becoming an interest group in favor of import duties, excise taxes, higher prices for the public domain, and other sources of federal revenue. Because the proposed Bank would enjoy the exclusive privilege of holding deposits of federal revenue without paying interest, it would have ample reserves from which to make loans to private entrepreneurs and thereby create a de facto federal currency of circulating banknotes.

The proposal, however, immediately mobilized gentry opponents of finance capital. It also provoked a rupture between Hamilton and Madison that transformed a cordial working alliance into bitter political and personal enmity. The proposed Bank seemed to confer special privileges on merchants and manufacturers who owned stock or received loans from the federally favored corporation. Virginians like Madison, Jefferson, and Attorney General Edmund Randolph had a visceral revulsion against merchants and creditors to whom southern planters were perennially in debt.[9] Beyond this sectional worry, however, lay the legacy of the larger Country party ideology that worried about the corrupting effects that commerce and finance could inflict on a republic.

The success of Hamilton's proposal, once it was enacted, suggested to Madison that the Anti-Federalists had been nearer to the truth about the effects of scale on a republic than *Federalist* 10. In the eyes of the Anti-Federalist opponents of the Constitution, the larger geographic and demographic constituencies of the new national government would increase the power of merchants and bankers. As the size and diversity of the electorate increased, farmers' and small producers' networks rooted in land and local markets would fade in importance, while the influence of financial and commercial networks rooted in liquid, mobile assets unmoored to any particular physical space would increase. Being less deeply involved in trans-Atlantic commerce and finance than the Constitution's supporters, Anti-Federalists were alarmed over the domination of the national government by commercial interests lodged in the coastal ports.[10]

Back in 1787–88, well before Congress authorized the First Bank of the United States, Publius had placated these Country party worries by arguing that the electoral connection between voters and representatives would prevent domination of Congress by a self-interested minority. "If a faction consists of less than a majority," *Federalist* 10 reassured its readers, then "relief is supplied by the republican principle, which enables the majority to defeat its sinister views by regular vote" (*Fed.* 10, 60). Madison did not dispute the Anti-Federalist argument that the Constitution strengthened the influence of such a cosmopolitan elite. In his phrase, legislative office would go to "men who possess the most attractive merit and the most diffusive and established characters," that is, gentlemen holding reputations for literary fame, military service, legal skill, or commercial success. But, as Publius noted elsewhere, the election of such "diffusive" men would not mean the subordination of the landed to the monied interest, because the latter simply lacked the numbers to carry elections: "In a country consisting chiefly of the cultivators of land, where the rules of an equal representation obtain, the landed interest must, upon the whole, preponderate in the government" (*Fed.* 60, 406). To the extent that high-flying lawyers and merchants were disproportionately represented in Congress, this would simply be the result of the voters' freely electing the most competent representatives, it being "altogether visionary" that "each occupation should send one or more members" (*Fed.* 35, 219).

The creation of the First Bank, however, shook Madison's optimistic faith that majority voting would produce genuine majority rule. The adoption of Hamilton's bank proposal, with the imprimatur of President Washington, cast some doubt on this confidence in the electoral connection as a sufficient antidote to domination by "natural aristocrats." Madison apparently concluded that *Federalist* 10 had overestimated the electorate's power to overcome the costs of organizing on a continental scale. Soon after he lost the vote on the bank, Madison endorsed the Anti-Federalist idea that popular opinion could not be rallied on a continental scale: "neither the voice or the sense of twenty millions of people, spread through so many latitudes as are comprehended within the United States, could ever be combined or called into effect" by national elections alone, Madison asserted in "Consolidation," a short essay published for Philip Freneau's *National Gazette*, the newly founded Republican Party's chief newspaper. Unable to act together at a national scale, citizens would soon cease to make the futile effort: "[T]he impossibility of acting together, might be succeeded ... at length by a universal silence and insensibility," Madison warned, "leaving that whole government to that *self-directed course*, which, it must be owned, is the natural propensity of every government."[11] Scale thus threatened to eliminate the expression of public opinion altogether: "The larger a country, the less easy for its real opinion to be ascertained, and the less difficult to be counterfeited," Madison wrote in a second essay in the *Gazette*. Large scale also demoralized potential opposition to the national government, because "the more extensive the country, the more insignificant is each individual in his own eyes," a psychological state of impotence "unfavorable to liberty."[12]

In short, Madison seemed to flip his argument in *Federalist* 10 on its head. He continued to maintain that demographic heterogeneity and large population impeded the mobilization of majorities, but now he regarded this impediment as a fault to be remedied, not "a republican remedy for the diseases most incident to republican government." Publius had mocked the idea that Congress could be corrupted into betraying the interests of the majority by noting the implausibility of a majority of Congress being bribed either by "foreign gold" or executive places: the "people of America" would not stand for it, and the state legislatures would sound the alarm (*Fed.* 55, 376). Madison's *Gazette* essays, however, suggested that the people might not hear the alarm or, if they did, prove incapable of acting on it. The suggestion borne out by the disappointing experience of having seen Congress approve the plainly unconstitutional Bank provoked these essays. The problem was that federal resources could be used to counterfeit public opinion. Jefferson had complained that the permanent funded debt "enabled Hamilton so to strengthen himself by corrupt services to many that he could afterwards carry his bank scheme and every measure he opposed in defiance of all opposition," deploying "that speculating Phalanx" of bondholders "in and out of Congress."[13] Jefferson was simply echoing familiar Country party rhetoric that Hamilton's opponents had been using as early as 1790, even before Madison's break with Hamilton.[14] Commercial ties and corrupt influences could create a "multitude" that could overcome the obstacles to political organization that a national republic could erect,[15] while the opponents of these networks would be silent and cowed by the difficulties of rallying public opinion.

Interpretative Strategy

Experience had, in sum, seriously challenged Publius's confidence that "the republican principle" of regular elections sufficed to safeguard majority control of the federal government. Based on this experience, Madison offered a new constitutional principle by which to supplement electoral control: the idea of what we would now call "strict scrutiny" of especially suspicious exercises of Congress's implied powers. Madison incorporated this principle into his speeches on the floor of the House of Representatives opposing the Bank, one of three leading Virginian politicians' constitutional expositions (the other two being memos by Attorney General Randolph and Secretary of State Jefferson).[16] All three opinions started from the textual premise that the enumeration of congressional powers in Article I, Section 8 implicitly barred additional implied powers that strayed too far from the express powers, because such powers by implication would lead to "consolidation," meaning the aggrandizement of all legislative power by the federal government. Madison supplemented this simple textual position with a canon of constitutional construction requiring the interpreter to resolve textual ambiguities by closely considering the effects of interpretation.

In particular, Madison argued that the "importance" of an implied power should weigh against its being accepted as "necessary and proper" for the execution of enumerated powers, because "the degree of [a power's] importance" determines "the probability or improbability of its being left to construction." The power to charter a corporation like the First Bank was "a great and important power" because private banks were dangerously corrupting institutions. Madison invoked all of the Country party's fears of financial corporations, "dilat[ing] on the great and extensive influence that incorporated societies had on public affairs in Europe." "They are powerful machines," Madison declared, "that have always been found competent to effect objects on principle in a great measure independent of the people." Madison saw special danger in the Congress's proposed grant of land-purchasing authority and exclusive banking privileges to the First Bank. "Congress themselves could not purchase lands within a state without the consent of its legislature," Madison noted: "How could they delegate a power to others which they did not possess themselves?" The power to act as the United States' exclusive fiscal agent for twenty years "takes from our successors, who have equal rights with ourselves, and with the aid of experience will be more capable of deciding on the subject, an opportunity of exercising that right for an immoderate term." Moreover, the proposal "involves a monopoly, which affects the equal rights of every citizen."[17]

Madison's attempt to constitutionalize a canon of strict construction of "important" powers failed in the Bank debate, and this failure suggested the need for what Madison (in *Federalist* 51) had called "auxiliary precautions" – the checks and balances embedded in the Constitution that were supposed to defend the separation of powers – which looked by 1792, to be the main impediment to an encroaching national government.

THE UNDERRATED EXECUTIVE POWER

Publius's views on the value of the separation of powers were essentially identical to the orthodox eighteenth-century viewpoint most famously expressed by Montesquieu[18] in Book XI of *The Spirit of the Laws*. On this view, the exercise of judicial, executive, and legislative powers by the same decision-maker was (in Madison's words) "the very definition of tyranny" (*Fed.* 47, 324).[19] Unfortunately, such assertions, without more elaboration, are also the very definition of tautology. Although the principle favored by Montesquieu and Publius was plain enough, their reasons for this insistence on functional specialization by different bodies of officials was lost in the brevity of their Augustan style.[20]

Behind Montesquieu's elegantly oracular aphorisms, however, it is possible to disentangle three distinct ideas, all related to the virtues of functional specialization. First, a multi-member body designed to reach consensus among different social classes (the "licentious" multitude and the aristocracy) was incapable of acting with the "dispatch" needed for executive business.[21] Second, a body that simultaneously enacted and interpreted laws would twist the interpretation to defeat the notice provided by the enactment. Montesquieu was admittedly not as plain as Locke in laying out this idea that lawmakers had too much incentive to favor allies and punish enemies when acting as judges. But the idea is sufficiently conveyed by Montesquieu's condemnation of "Italian republics" for vesting "[t]he same body of magistrates with power to act as both "executors of the laws" and "legislators," because the former becomes, in effect, "the whole power" of legislation, such that "every private citizen may be ruined by their particular decisions."[22] Finally, in defending the tedious legalisms of the French *Parlements*, Montesquieu hinted at the idea that the adjudicative process of determining whether a law has been violated should be slower and more deliberate than the executive process of dealing out justice writ large. Again, the idea was conveyed elliptically through a sarcastic compliment for the expeditiously unified executive and adjudicative functions of Turkish magistrates "where little regard is shewn to the honour, life, or estate, of the subject" but "all causes are speedily decided," because "[t]he method of determining [disputes] is a matter of indifference, provided they be determined" such that "[t]he bashaw, after a quick hearing, orders which party he pleases to be bastinadoed, and then sends them about their business."[23]

Separating functions among different types of officials, in short, protects what Jeremy Waldron calls "articulated governance" – that is, the distinct skills and virtues needed for the different stages of making and executing the law (where execution embraces adjudication as well as administration).[24] Initial general policymaking should reflect broad community consensus, while adjudication should focus on accuracy in applying that general policy, and execution should focus on efficiency and dispatch in carrying out those adjudications. Montesquieu may have been cavalier about laying out systematically the idea that distinct virtues were necessary for distinctive stages of government, because he assumed that his readers would be familiar with the idea of a Ciceronian "balance" of rival and complementary virtues of the one, few, and many in a classical republic.

The constitutional problem of achieving such a "balance" turned on assuring that each set of officials had incentives and powers to "check" rivals who refused to stay in their proper realm of governance. "Checks," in this sense, were distinct from, and perhaps unnecessary to maintain, this "balance" of functions. It was possible, for instance, that even authoritarian monarchs had incentives to protect the power of an independent parliament as a useful device to deflect the blame they might receive for unpopular decisions favoring one social class or another.[25]

Despite that possibility, both Montesquieu and Publius started from the presumption that the legislature, in particular, would have both the incentive and the ability to trespass on the powers of judges and executive magistrates. Montesquieu makes this point (as usual) rather obliquely, asserting that executive officials were more in need of checks against the legislature than vice versa.[26] Publius, however, made the defense of checks on the legislature a central pillar of his defense of the proposed Constitution.

For Publius, the problem of legislative dominance derived from the character of the House of Representatives as a multi-member body elected from districts no larger than a single state, a characteristic that would make it more directly accountable to the people than either the president or federal judiciary. The House of Representatives would be elected by constituencies that would closely monitor its performance and reward its members for following the popular will. Because it was obliged to win the affection of the people in frequent elections from relatively small districts, the House would have a built-in advantage over rival institutions – and an electoral incentive to use this advantage to undermine their functions. Therefore, the people "ought to indulge all their jealousy and exhaust all their precautions" against the House of Representatives, because "a representative republic ... inspired by its supposed influence over the people" would have "an intrepid confidence in its own strength" and be "sufficiently numerous to feel all the passions which activate a multitude; but not so numerous as to be incapable of pursuing the objects of its passions" (Fed. 48, 333–34). The advantage of the House of Representatives over the Senate, president, and Supreme Court was suggested by drawing an analogy to the advantage allegedly enjoyed by the state legislatures over Congress. Because both the House of Representatives and state legislatures were elected more frequently from smaller constituencies than their rivals, both would be able, and indeed impelled by electoral incentives, to usurp their rivals' powers.

To counteract these electoral incentives, Publius called for a constitution that defined legislative powers more meticulously than executive powers and saddled the Congress with a bicameral process subject to presidential veto. "As the weight of the legislative authority requires that it should be thus divided," Publius argued in Federalist 51, "the weakness of the executive may require that it should be fortified" (*Fed.* 51, 350). The interests of the Congress would be sufficiently vindicated by what could be called the principle of institutional self-interest according to which the occupants of any office, whether legislative or executive, would identify their own self-interest with the powers of the position they currently held, and therefore defend those prerogatives. Driven by such institutional self-interest, members of Congress and presidents would compete on a constitutionally leveled playing field, with no need for any judicial review to redress the balance of power between them. In this sense, the distribution of powers given in the Constitution appeared to be self-enforcing, almost mechanical, with no need to rely either on the internal self-restraint of officials or on an external enforcement mechanism (such as judicial review).

The assumption of legislative dominance influenced not only the design of the written Constitution but also the post-enactment strategies for its interpretation. To the extent that this original plan was ambiguous, both Madison and Hamilton were initially united in resolving such ambiguities with anti-legislative canons of construction drawn from Montesquieu's and Publius's idea of inherent legislative advantage. The first such ambiguity surfaced around the question of whether the president enjoyed the inherent power to remove high officials. Did the power to appoint ministers with the advice and consent of the Senate imply that the president must also consult the Senate before such officials can be fired? The natural implication of Article II's language was that hiring and firing should be symmetrical, with the Senate's participation in both processes. So Hamilton argued in *Federalist* 77. Madison, however, rejected that natural implication on the practical ground that the president, as the most responsible officer in government, could be stuck with ministers with whom he could not work and for whom he could not be responsible. Moreover, he thought that placing this authority in the Senate could keep it in continuous session, which he believed was both impractical and dangerous. Behind this practical worry lay the institutional assumption that the Congress would always enjoy an inherent advantage over the president that should be counterbalanced with a canon of construction favoring presidential power. When in doubt, Madison still thought, it was better to construe the prerogatives of the president broadly, because "if the Federal Government should lose its proper equilibrium within itself, I am persuaded that the effect will proceed from the Encroachments of the Legislative department."[27]

As with the idea that state powers would be sufficiently safeguarded by federal electoral accountability, Publius's idea of inherent congressional advantage over the president was soon cast into doubt by the Washington administration's conduct of foreign policy. The outbreak of a general war between Revolutionary France and monarchical Europe in 1792 placed the United States in the position of having to decide whether to honor its commercial and mutual defense treaty with France, dating to 1778, that assured France of most favored nation treatment and entitled it to America's aid if France were attacked. Madison and Jefferson were particularly sympathetic to a pro-French American policy and were bitterly disappointed by President Washington's proclamation of strict neutrality that favored British control of Atlantic trade and implicitly undercut the 1778 treaty. In their view, the Proclamation was not merely unwise but unconstitutional: Jefferson had argued in cabinet that the president could not constitutionally declare neutrality without involving Congress, because the proclamation of neutrality was essentially a "legislative" act.

The ensuing pamphlet debate over this question between Hamilton (writing under the pseudonym "Pacificus") and Madison (writing as "Helvidius") marked Madison's full retreat from his call for robust executive power in *The Federalist*. Hamilton proposed a narrow construction of the Senate's power to approve treaties and Congress's power to declare war, because both "are exceptions out of the general executive power, vested in the President [by Article II], they are to be construed strictly."[28] In effect, Hamilton took a page from Madison's own 1789 playbook, when Madison defended the exclusivity of the president's implied power to remove executive officers on the ground that the Senate's express power to advise and consent to the appointment of executive officers should be construed narrowly. Like Hamilton, Madison (in 1789) had treated the Senate's express powers of advice and consent as an exception to Article II's default rule that "executive" powers otherwise be vested in the president.[29] Madison likewise offered (again in 1789) the gloss that all such exceptions should be read narrowly to maximize the president's "executive" powers. Hamilton, as Pacificus, offered precisely the same argument, simply substituting the Senate and Congress's express diplomatic powers for the Senate's removal powers.

Despite Madison's protests to the contrary,[30] it is difficult not to view Madison's "Helvidius" essays as adopting reasoning almost exactly opposite to his 1789 argument for an implied presidential removal power. According to "Helvidius," the Proclamation of Neutrality trespassed on Congress's powers over foreign affairs, because the respective express powers of the Senate to ratify treaties and of both houses to declare war carried along with them implied and exclusive powers to construe treaties and therefore the power to proclaim (or not) neutrality. Against Hamilton's argument that the president's power to "take care that the laws be faithfully executed" implied a concurrent power to announce and enforce a particular interpretation of treaty law, Madison insisted that the express grant to Congress of the power to declare war necessarily carried with it an equally exclusive power to declare peace.[31]

Madison's insistence on the legislative character of this treaty-construing power sat oddly with his own concession that the "federative power" – the power to enter into treaties – was neither unambiguously "executive" nor "legislative."[32] Why did not this ambiguity invite a canon of construction drawn from the logic of *Federalist* 51? "As the weight of the legislative authority requires that it should be thus divided, the weakness of the executive may require, on the other hand, that it should be fortified" (*Fed.* 51, 350). When in doubt about the "executive" character of an ambiguous power, why should not the principled interpreter favor the reading that "fortified" the president? Even if one believed that the federative power was in some sense less essential to the executive function of the president than the president's unencumbered power to fire subordinates, there was a powerful traditional case that, in Locke's words, diplomacy "must necessarily be left to the prudence and wisdom of those, whose hands it is in, to be managed for the public good," because diplomatic maneuvers were "much less capable to be directed by antecedent, standing, positive laws" than ordinary domestic powers.[33] Given that the unitary executive alone possessed the "perfect *secrecy* and immediate *despatch*" required for international relations (*Fed.* 64, 434), the case for a broad construction of the presidential power to construe treaties seemed comparable to a broad construction of the presidential removal power. Why, then, adopt an opposite canon of construction disfavoring presidential power where treaties were concerned?

The answer to this question lies in Madison's reassessment of Publius's view of the relative power of the president and Congress. That view was based on the idea that legislators, having been elected more frequently from smaller constituencies, would be "closer" to the people, and therefore more capable of rallying them to the support of legislative prerogatives. But such a theory of institutional power did not reckon on the agenda-setting power of a highly visible single executive with powers to take quick and detailed actions in the absence of specific legislation. Such agenda-setting authority gave the president powers to redefine the status quo in ways that a sluggish bicameral legislature would find difficult to reverse. Those powers to redefine the status quo, in turn, allowed the president to build a political coalition from anyone benefiting from his exercise of political discretion. To Madison and his fellow Republicans, this discretion was the very essence of corruption.

The driving engine for Madison's argument against the neutrality proclamation was therefore not technical hair-splitting about whether the "federative power" was "executive" or "legislative" in character, for, as Madison conceded, it was both. Instead, suspicion of presidential discretion in foreign affairs – even discretion to proclaim neutrality and peace – was rooted in the vintage Country party rhetoric of *Helvidius No. 4.* "War is in fact the true nurse of executive aggrandizement," Madison declared: "In war the public treasures are to be unlocked, and it is the executive hand which is to dispense them. In war the honors and emoluments of office are to be multiplied; and it is the executive patronage under which they are to be enjoyed."[34] These worries about the president's mobilizing veterans like the Society of the Cincinnatus to champion presidential positions echoed Madison's fear of the First Bank and its "phalanx" of subscribers and paper holders. The proto-military-industrial complex of officers, veterans, government contractors, and bond underwriters was simply the diplomatic and military version of the alliance of stockjobbers and creditors held together by the commercial paper of the First Bank of the United States. *Federalist* 51's idea of relative departmental power had been inverted by the political reality that the executive discretion to deal specific benefits to particular persons was a more effective way to create a political coalition than the enactment of general rules. Thus, by 1793, Madison believed that it was the authority of Congress, rather than that of the president, that needed to be "fortified" with implied powers.

The president's institutional advantage was not merely that he could direct specific benefits to particular supporters but also that his power to set the agenda quickly made it difficult for Congress to overturn any presidential choice of policy. The advantage of presidential agenda-setting was powerfully illustrated by the Washington administration's suppression of the Whiskey Rebellion and its negotiation of the Jay Treaty. In both cases, the administration placed before Congress a take-it-or-leave-it package that Jefferson, Madison, and their followers intensely disliked but could not overturn, precisely because, as unpopular as the packages were, they were better than the status quo ante.

The dispute over the controversial Jay Treaty revealed other advantages of executive power. After the treaty was ratified by the Senate in August 1795 and finally signed by Washington in February

1796, the Republican majority in the House of Representatives asked the president to turn over the papers relating to the negotiations so that the House could decide whether to appropriate money for the various fact-finding commissions required by the treaty. Washington's refusal to disclose the documents placed the Republicans in a dilemma. Refusal to approve any funds containing an appropriation for the challenged commissions would place the entire budget in jeopardy. But acquiescence gave the Senate and president alone the power to use the treaty power to determine spending priorities that had been formally delegated to the House of Representatives.[35] As Madison noted, treaties creating obligations to spend money effectively obviated the House's constitutionally guaranteed powers over revenue, because failure to appropriate money for agreements to engage in military operations already approved by the Senate and president would amount to a species of treason. The president's agenda-setting power would reduce the House to "mere heralds for proclaiming [war]."[36] Madison's complaint about the president's first-mover advantage anticipates Thomas Romer's and Howard Rosenthal's later argument that the executive who proposes can defeat the interests of the legislature that disposes, simply because the latter can only dispose of that which the executive has put on the agenda.[37]

The president's "first mover" advantage was even more pronounced in the suppression of the Whiskey Rebellion. When Secretary of the Treasury Hamilton's excise tax on liquor inspired resistance from whiskey-distilling (and drinking) farmers in western Pennsylvania, Hamilton persuaded Washington to suppress the insurrection with an overwhelming force of over 12,000 militiamen provided by the governors of Virginia, Maryland, New Jersey, and Pennsylvania, led personally by the president himself.[38] The rebellion quickly melted away, but that result was overshadowed by another and more important triumph in public relations – the Federalists' successful tarring of the Democratic-Republican Societies as instigators of the insurrection. Formed mostly by small farmers on the western frontier and urban artisans in coastal cities, these societies supported the

French Revolution, opposed Hamilton's financial program, and generally attacked the Federalists' corrupting the nation through the blandishments of stock in federally chartered companies and the emoluments of federal office.[39] Because the societies in western Pennsylvania had been particularly vocal in attacking the whiskey excise tax, Washington excoriated them in his November 1794 address to Congress as "certain self-created societies" who incited "a few counties" in western Pennsylvania "to frustrate" tax collection. All of Madison's efforts in the House of Representatives could not erase this stain of subversion, and the societies quickly disbanded or became inactive as a result of the reputational blow. As Madison explained to James Monroe, "the game was to connect the Democratic Societies with the odium of insurrection," and, in this game, the Federalists controlled the trump card of the president's bully pulpit.[40]

Madison's experience of fighting off a House resolution joining the president and the Senate in condemning "self-created societies" exploded the assumptions of *Federalist* 49 and 51 that the House would enjoy an advantage over the president in the battle for public opinion. That assumption was rooted in the alleged "closeness" of the tie between politicians elected from small electoral districts and their constituents, closeness that a president, with a nationwide constituency, could never enjoy. That "closeness" indeed reduced the costs of constituents' communicating with their representatives. But these same factors increased the costs of the House of Representatives' communicating collectively with their constituents: the House faced collective action problems that the president, working alone, did not confront. Presenting his version of events saliently in a national address that was immediately visible even to inattentive voters, Washington easily outflanked the House of Representatives, which, divided among multiple members proposing multiple resolutions and amendments, could not so quickly and unequivocally provide a rival version of events to "rouse the people completely from their lethargy."[41] "If the people of America are so far degenerated already as not to see with indifference, that the Citadel of their liberties is menaced by the precedent before their eyes," Madison complained, then there was little that Democratic Republicans could do to sound the alarm.[42] The public's inattentiveness to politics automatically gave the most visible and quick-acting politician an advantage in the battle for public opinion.

Interpretive Strategy Redux

As with the battle over the First Bank, Madison invoked a constitutional canon of construction to redress these imbalances of power. The power of the president and Senate to enter into treaties must be construed narrowly because this authority was "substantially of a legislative, not an executive nature," and thus required the participation of both houses of Congress.[43] Madison argued that the treaties could not be self-executing: where treaties ratified by the Senate cover topics within the legislative power of Congress as a whole (such as treaties requiring expenditures of revenue), Congress must retain its authority to legislate with respect to those latter topics, regardless of the treaty's terms. Madison dismissed the notion that this view of the treaty power would emasculate the nation's capacity to form stable agreements with other nations, asserting that "the several powers vested in the several Departments form but one Government; and the will of the nation may be expressed thro' one Government, operating under certain checks."[44]

The perfunctory character of Madison's statement conceals the distance that he had traveled since Publius in *Federalist* 64 argued that the treaty power could not be committed "to a popular assembly, composed of members constantly coming and going in quick succession." Such a body would not sit long enough to attain "those great objects, which require to be steadily contemplated in all their relations and circumstances" that are the topics of international diplomacy (*Fed.* 64, 433–34). Although this essay was written by Jay, not Madison, the idea that frequency of elections reduces legislators' expertise was a common theme for their joint persona of Publius. That Madison would simply ignore the institutional differences between the Senate and the House in defending the authority of the latter suggests how radically he had revised his assessment of the dangers of presidential power since 1788.

A NEW ROLE FOR THE PEOPLE

Facing unified Federalist opposition and a president who was ever more closely allied with Hamilton, Madison's constitutional canon failed with foreign policy just as the analogous canon failed with the Bank. By 1798, the presidency, now held by John Adams, had successfully claimed all of the powers that Madison characterized as "legislative." Things were about to get much worse as hostilities between the British and French escalated, leading both sides to attempt to drag Americans into their conflict. Faced with a hostile Republican press, the president's congressional allies thought his neutrality policy could not succeed without restricting certain domestic liberties. The Federalist-dominated Congress pushed through the Alien and Sedition Acts criminalizing criticism of the government and exposing noncitizens to deportation.

The Alien and Sedition Acts posed a new problem for Madison, because now both the legislative and judicial branches seemed to be aligned with President Adams against Madison's understanding of the Constitution. During the ratification debates Madison had famously rejected Jefferson's idea that the "people" (in the form of occasional or periodic conventions) should be called upon to settle constitutional disputes, arguing that frequent appeals to such conventions would deprive the Constitution of popular veneration and empower conniving politicians purporting to act in the name of We the People. After a frustrating decade of political defeats had convinced Madison that powerful financial interests were using war and debt to enlarge their powers, Madison was prepared to rethink his earlier skepticism of popular constitutional interpretation.

In the Virginia Resolutions, Madison used state legislatures rather than constitutional conventions as the device for rallying popular sentiment against what he regarded as unconstitutional legislation to which all three federal branches had acquiesced. The Virginia Assembly declared that the "states," as "parties" to the constitutional "compact ... have the right, and are in duty bound, to interpose for arresting the progress of the evil, and for maintaining within their respective limits, the authorities, rights and limits appertaining to them." In speaking on behalf of "the good people of this commonwealth" and their "feelings of the most scrupulous fidelity to that constitution," the Virginia Assembly was not engaged in ordinary politics. As Madison later explained, by referring to the "the states" as "parties" to the "compact," the Virginia Assembly referred to "the people composing those political societies, in their highest sovereign capacity."[45]

By what right did the Virginia Assembly assume this role as the mouthpiece for the "sovereign" people of Virginia? The claim seemed in tension with *Federalist* 49's list of "insuperable objections against the proposed recurrence to the people" in resolving disputes about constitutional meaning. Among those objections was the worry that members of any such convention would simply be politicians with a stake in the dispute about the federal branches' powers and, hence, "parties to the very question to be decided by them." Such deliberations "could never be expected to turn on the true merits of the question" but instead "would inevitably be connected with the spirit of pre-existing parties, or of parties springing out of the question itself" such that "[t]he *passions*, therefore, not the *reason*, of the public, would sit in judgment" (*Fed.* 49, 342–43).

Although *Federalist* 49 imagined that members of Congress would dominate the Constitutional Convention proposed by Jefferson, its attack on that idea applied with even greater force to the Virginia Assembly's claim to speak on behalf of the people of Virginia in their sovereign capacity as parties to the constitutional compact. After all, these state legislators were opining about the balance of power between Congress and the state legislatures, such that they were "parties to the very question to be decided by them" – indeed, "parties springing out of the question itself" to the extent that the Republicans defined themselves in terms of their opposition to an expansive interpretation of federal powers. *Federalist* 49 had attributed the success of the conventions that drafted the first state constitutions in the mid-1770s to the "enthusiastic confidence of the people in their patriotic leaders, which stifled the ordinary diversity of opinions on great national questions" and insured that "no spirit of party ... could mingle its leaven in the operation" (*Fed.* 49, 341). The Virginia Resolutions, by contrast, were suffused with the "spirit of party." Although written as an appeal to other states to oppose the Alien and Sedition Acts, Madison surely foresaw the adverse response of the New England state legislatures, dominated as they were by orthodox Federalists. There was no "enthusiastic confidence of the people in their patriotic leaders" here to stifle "the ordinary diversity of opinions on great national questions." Instead, there was a largely sectional division about the Adams administration in which one section (the South) inveighed against a New England president's legislative agenda, while another (New England and some mid-Atlantic states) told the Virginians to mind their own business. When the Massachusetts legislature responded to Virginia by noting that "the people ... have not constituted the state legislatures the judges of the acts or measures of the federal government," it was apparently humming Publius's own tune in *Federalist* 49.[46]

Why had Madison changed his mind about the people's participating in the process of resolving constitutional disputes? His changing views on popular constitutionalism were closely connected to another change of heart: his view, developed during the 1790s, on the necessity of partisan organization to counteract the influence of financiers and other "aristocrats" on the federal government. The problem was that the heterogeneity of interests celebrated by *Federalist* 10 as a brake on majority faction had somehow empowered a minority faction of bondholders, military veterans, and others who profited from federal power. Madison, therefore, embraced the idea of a political party that could unite otherwise disorganized constituents across the United States, transcending geographic and occupational divisions. The idea of party organization underlay the Democratic-Republican Societies championed by Jefferson and

Madison in 1793. Madison's endorsement of the idea of party, however, transcended these short-lived societies. The more basic idea was that the enemies of Hamilton's program should place their common opposition above any other geographic or occupational interests that might divide them. "The antirepublican party" will try to multiply the dimensions of politics, Madison warned, "by reviving exploded parties, and taking advantage of all prejudices, local, political, and occupational, that may prevent or disturb a general coalition of sentiments." To counteract this effort to divide the majority by multiplying the issue environment, the Bank's opponents needed to bury "all antecedent questions" and banish "every other distinction than that between enemies and friends to republican government, and in promoting a general harmony among the latter."[47] The call for party loyalty was essentially an effort to work around what *Federalist* 10 described as the "greater variety of parties and interests" in a nationally scaled democracy that made it "more difficult for all who feel [a common motive] to discover their own strength, and to act in unison with each other."

Described by *Federalist* 10 as "a republican remedy for the diseases most incident to republican government," such coalition-defeating diversity was now a threat to republican government. Partisan unity, by contrast, would prevent Hamilton from prying apart an anti-Bank majority coalition with distributional goods – say, more Bank branches in the South or loans on easy terms for western farmers. By framing the case against the First Bank as a matter of constitutional principle to galvanize a unified majority, Madison was seeking to foster precisely what *Federalist* 10 had hoped the national scale of American democracy would thwart: a unified, programmatic popular opposition to a legislative program. This idea of an organized people out of doors by the mid-1790s had evolved into the idea of a popular political party.

By promoting partisan organization as an antidote to federal corruption, Madison was also endorsing a much more direct role for the popular policing of constitutional boundaries. The whole point of parties in the electorate was to focus public opinion on a few critical questions to prevent the enemies of republican government from counterfeiting public opinion by distracting it from what really mattered. If the anti-republicans managed to capture all three branches of the federal government through such counterfeit popularity, then mobilizing the people against the federal government through partisan advocacy was not merely legitimate but essential. The Virginia Resolutions' invocation of the "sovereign" power of the people to overturn an unconstitutional regime was completely consistent with this new vision of how large-scale partisan organization was needed to redress the failings of continental-scale democracy.

It is tempting to paper over the differences between Publius's thoughts in 1787–88 with Madison's stance on popular constitutionalism in the 1790s by noting how Madison consistently endorsed a role for active "public opinion" in monitoring elected officials. Larry Kramer offers such a harmonizing account of *Federalist* 49 and Madison's *National Gazette* essays, arguing that the former did not reject a role for the people in construing and enforcing the Constitution but merely cautioned against popular control that was too "unmediated and direct."[48] According to Kramer, Madison consistently envisioned a constitutional politics in which rival federal representatives educated public opinion by contesting parochial or factional views, thereby insuring a role for the public in enforcing the Constitution more sophisticated than a simple up-or-down vote in a constitutional convention. Colleen Sheehan similarly argues that Madison consistently defended the sovereignty of public opinion throughout the 1780s and 1790s.[49]

All of these efforts to harmonize Madison's attitudes, however, founder on his defense of partisan democracy in the 1790s. Such an idea is wholly missing from the *Federalist*, which is replete with denunciations of "party spirit." It is one thing to embrace the general idea that the educated public ought to guide the actions of elected representatives, guided by literati and channeled through the elite jockeying between federal branches. It is another thing altogether to call on the public to stand behind a party platform that contradicts the views of all three federal departments, form local organizations to pursue that platform (the Democratic-Republican Societies), and, when those societies collapse as a result of a Federalist smear campaign, whip up public sentiment through the alternative mechanism of state legislative pronouncements in the teeth of obvious hostility from sister states. Madison's adoption of the latter program was not a continuation of the gentlemanly populism of Publius. It was instead a radical departure from the suspicion of mass populism so evident in *Federalist* 10, 49, and 50

In addition to supporting a more active and *pugnacious* role for public opinion, Madison also favored a more robust role for state legislatures in enforcing the Constitution. The reference in the Virginia Resolutions to the states' "interposing" their authority was ambiguous, and Madison's later report defending that power of "interposition" did little to clarify exactly the type of constitutional authority that he was claiming on behalf of the states. Again, it is tempting to smooth over the radical character of the Virginia Resolution's claim of a power of "interposition" by citing Publius's earlier defense of a state role in sounding the "general alarm" against federal usurpations in *Federalist* 45 and 46. Publius's arguments for a state role in *The Federalist*, however, did not envision a formal constitutional role for state legislatures in curbing the federal government's unwarranted assertions of powers. Instead, Publius predicted merely that, because of "the predilection and probably support of the people," state politicians would successfully rally the public to oppose federal overreaching: a correspondence would be opened," "[p]lans of resistance would be concerted," and, unless the federal government backed off, an "appeal to a trial of force" would be made (*Fed.* 46, 320).

The claim in the Virginia Resolution that the state legislatures had a power of "interposition" as a consequence of their being original parties to the constitutional compact seems more legal and less prepolitical than such a right of revolution. Madison was coy about explaining precisely how the state legislature could "arrest the progress of the evil." Perhaps, by sounding the "clarion" call that he had anticipated in *Federalist* 45–46, the Virginia and Kentucky legislatures were merely asking their sister legislatures to amend the Constitution pursuant to Article V. On this view, the reference in the Kentucky Resolutions to "a nullification, by those [state] sovereignties, of all unauthorized acts" could be construed as a *collective* nullification through an amendment properly ratified by three-quarters of those state "sovereignties." Virginia's and Kentucky's opponents apparently construed "interposition" and "nullification" to mean a more robust remedy to be exercised by individual states. In a cautionary letter to Jefferson, Madison complained that the Virginians' "zeal may forget some considerations which ought to temper their proceedings" – in particular, that only a state constitutional convention could be "the ultimate Judge of infractions" to the Constitution and that the Virginia legislature's claiming a greater power could "invite the charge of Usurpation in the very act of protesting agst the usurpations of Congress."[50] Even this claim on behalf of state conventions, however, left ambiguous the question of whether such state conventions could individually interpose their authority without using the collective procedure of Article V. Neither Jefferson nor Madison resolved this ambiguity, and it lingered on throughout the nineteenth century as the "spirit of '98," invoked to justify South Carolina's attempted "nullification" of the "tariff of abominations" in 1832 as well as anti-slavery advocates' calls for the "interposition" of state authorities between federal power and the kidnapping of black residents under the 1850 Fugitive Slave Act.

The debate over the precise content of "nullification" or "interposition," however, obscures a less dramatic, yet more lasting idea of sub-national governments forming an institutional home for party organization. Virginia's and Kentucky's calls for united state opposition to the incumbent national administration went nowhere, because state officials, divided among Federalists and Republicans, did not form any sort of united interest. Such calls formed a rhetorically and organizationally effective way to rally voters against the

Adams administration by demonstrating that its opponents had officially recognized electoral support. Virginia and Kentucky were constitutionally recognized representatives of their constituents and,
therefore, were not vulnerable to the accusation leveled against the
Democratic-Republican Societies that they were merely "self-created
societies" with no legitimate right to speak for the "people" against
duly elected constitutional officers. *Federalist* 51 had envisioned officials aligning their ambitions with the defense of the prerogatives of
their office. This idea of institutional balances, however, had collapsed under the weight of partisan and sectional differences dividing
state officials. Instead, state officials played the role of party leaders,
rallying their rank and file on behalf of a partisan agenda only loosely
tied to any particular institutional arrangement.

CONCLUSION

The point of this chapter has been to distinguish Publius's contributions to government and political science from his normative political
commitments. We have argued that Publius was committed to a
political science based on historical and contemporary experience
which evolved as new lessons were learned. Madison and Hamilton
would have agreed on the propositions of the new political science at
each historical moment: in 1787–88 writing as Publius, and later on,
as they learned how the Constitution worked in practice. The substantial difference between the two men concerned two issues: the
nature of the domestic and international challenges that the new
government would face; and the ways in which the powers of the
constitutional departments actually worked. Hamilton envisioned a
hostile international environment for the new nation and thought it
imperative to build its industrial and military capacities to deal with
dangerous foreign powers. Building those capacities required an active
executive and a Congress able to initiate big legislative projects.
Hamilton also thought that the executive had to retain a firm hold
on power at all times. The way to deal with internal commotions was
to mobilize force to crush it: to appear as a "Hercules" and intimidate

any who would challenge governmental authority. He articulated this view repeatedly from the early 1780s to the end of his life. Madison seemed to envision a more benign environment both internationally (where he believed the Americans would trade peacefully with European powers and avoid clashes) and domestically. He thought the protections built into the Constitution would resist the passage of bad laws and limit popular discontent of the kind that might require a coercive response.

Publius's lasting contribution, an achievement that both Hamilton and Madison could embrace, was a vision of institutional design that was based on a realistic, if pessimistic, view of human nature – one that regarded a competent and well-structured government as a means to pursue genuinely common interests. From this viewpoint, it is a virtue of a set of institutions that they are stable or self-enforcing and, given his view of human nature, it seemed natural to seek to obtain this stability by enlisting man's lesser capacities – ambition, jealousy, inflated self-regard, self-dealing – to accomplish these necessary tasks. Institutions, so designed, seem well suited to work among individuals who must be taken largely as they are found. This vision of institutional design still inspires modern political scientists.

After 1789, we must abandon the authorial personality of Publius and consider the political science of Madison and Hamilton. We doubt that, as rational men, they would have differed very much on matters of fact. They both learned almost immediately that republican rule on a large scale did not prevent well-financed and highly motivated (minority) factions from capturing governmental powers, but they drew very different lessons from this. While Madison was alarmed at this prospect – seeing in it the failure of what he had called the "republican principle" – Hamilton was probably pleased that, despite the difficulty of forming majorities, it was not impossible for public-spirited men to form congressional majorities to pursue big public projects. He was probably neither surprised nor disappointed by the success of urban banking and commercial interests in getting favorable policies enacted.

Madison learned soon afterwards, in the fights over the Bank and neutrality, that the presidency was far more powerful than he had imagined. There were few constitutional checks capable of limiting the authority of an imaginative and energetic executive. Hamilton learned that, too, but no doubt concluded that presidential powers had evolved largely in ways he had hoped and anticipated. Finally, Madison learned, in the reaction to the Alien and Seditions Acts, that the carefully designed federal institution could not be counted on to resist the temptation to impose what he thought were plain violations of the First Amendment.

Thus, there was no real difference in the positive political beliefs of the two men. They disagreed, of course, with Publius, who had not had the benefit of the experience of the 1790s. Publius was wrong in *Federalist* 10 in thinking that the republican principle would limit the influence of minorities. He was wrong in *Federalist* 51 in thinking that the checks he described there would be adequate to maintain the departments within their "proper sphere." Or perhaps he was half right. He was correct in arguing (in *Federalist* 10) that it would be hard for majorities to form; but this meant that majorities had a hard time resisting capture by interested minorities. And he was right that the checks cited in *Federalist* 51 would be effective against Congress; but that meant that Congress could not effectively limit executive adventures. By 1800, both Hamilton and Madison could have appreciated these failures of Publius's political science.

Despite his decade of frustration, Madison ended up with the last and lasting word. As it became clear that the ordinary constitutional mechanisms had failed to prevent tyrannical laws, it was left to these two leaders to craft a role for the people to interpose their authority against those laws in ways that could be situated within the Constitution. This they accomplished by running an electoral campaign aimed at asserting, through ordinary electoral processes, that the people refused to accept the conduct of the national government. Historians writing of the 1800 campaign generally fixate on the peculiar mechanism by which the vice president was chosen (as the candidate with the second highest vote total in the electoral college). Because presidential electors could, constitutionally, be chosen either by direct election or appointed by the state legislatures, the way was open for the Federalists, who controlled most of the legislatures, to act on short-run political considerations, picking the system that they expected to benefit them the most. As a result, only two states chose direct election, forcing the Republican campaign to develop a ticket and state-level organizations that would win state legislative campaigns.

The 1800 election, in other words, involved a full-scale partisan campaign in which the people themselves had been asked to interpose against the enactment of unconstitutional laws not through popular conventions but rather through ordinary state legislative elections. By removing the Federalists from executive and legislative power, the people responded positively to this partisan plea to enforce a particular vision of the Constitution

Using party organization and party appeals to provide a popular role as "guardian of the Constitution" in the course of ordinary electoral politics was diametrically opposed to Publius's position in *Federalist* 49. Such a mechanism was never articulated in the high constitutional discourse of the Virginia Resolution nor, indeed, in interpretations of various clauses of the Constitution. Such debates were carried out in the old ways: arguments about the "meanings" of texts or by appeal to "first principles" of social contracting. In the end, however, the constitutional balance was reconfigured at the hustings, through an electoral appeal in the most ordinary kind of electoral politics.

Ironically, the result of such popular constitutional politics was that Republican control of the elected branches and Federalist control of the judiciary led to the gradual development of a judicial role in the enforcement of separation of powers. This evolution, timid at first, eventually blossomed into the system that we have today, for better or worse. Madison as a constitutional theorist had objections to this development. But Madison as a political scientist ought to have been able to appreciate how far it was driven by the actual experience of the new republic.

NOTES

1 We do not doubt that normative beliefs may also be rationally revised in light of experience. We may always question what it makes sense to want or aim at as well as how best to attain what we want. Could either of us rationally pursue a career in theoretical physics?

2 While the debate is much older, its modern origin may found in efforts to attribute authorship of various Federalist papers. Douglass Adair, "The Authorship of the Disputed Federalist Papers." *William and Mary Quarterly*, 1 (1944), 97–122, 235–64. Alpheus Mason, "The Federalist – A Split Personality," *American Historical Review*, 57 (1952), 625–43.

3 The classic texts of this momentous debate between two great constitutional theorists is now available for the first time in English translation. Hans Kelsen and Carl Schmitt, *The Guardian of the Constitution*, ed. Lars Vinx (Cambridge: Cambridge University Press, 2016).

4 Banning has argued that "[i]n 1787 as in 1798 Madison desired a well-constructed federal republic – not as Hamilton did, because nothing better could be secured – but because no other form of government seemed consistent with the American Revolution … [Madison's] starting point for constitutional reform and his conception of the finished Constitution were never anything but incompatible with Hamilton's." Lance Banning, "The Hamiltonian Madison: A Reconsideration," *The Virginia Magazine of History and Biography*, 92 (1984), 9. As a statement of normative aspirations we can agree with this. But we think that they may well have shared certain empirical beliefs in 1787–88 that they no longer shared in 1791.

5 Hamilton's early views on some of these issues can be found in his *Continentalist* essays which were published in 1781, where he emphasizes the need for the new nation to develop strong financial institutions, a sound currency, to pay its debts, and to avoid expropriating Royalist properties.

6 Nowadays scholars doubt that the Constitution's design actually accomplished what Madison claimed. We agree. But that only means that the framers fell short as constitutional designers; not that the task itself is impossible or unattractive.

7 Ironically, modern political science has tended to give better marks to Hamilton's design ideas than to Madison's. As we shall see, the

constitutional scheme gives the president ample incentive to act responsibly – at least it did until the adoption of the Twenty-Second Amendment which incentivized a second-term president only through his care for his legacy and for his party's fortunes.

8 Hamilton helpfully connected the problem of state governments' misbehavior to his view of individual human nature: "It at all times betrayed an ignorance of the true springs by which human conduct is actuated, and belied the original inducements to the establishment of civil power. Why has government been instituted at all? Because the passions of men will not conform to the dictates of reason and justice, without constraint. Has it been found that bodies of men act with more rectitude or greater disinterestedness than individuals? The contrary of this has been inferred by all accurate observers of the conduct of mankind; and the inference is founded upon obvious reasons. Regard to reputation has a less active influence, when the infamy of a bad action is to be divided among a number than when it is to fall singly upon one. A spirit of faction, which is apt to mingle its poison in the deliberations of all bodies of men, will often hurry the persons of whom they are composed into improprieties and excesses, for which they would blush in a private capacity" (Fed. 15).

9 See generally Stanley Elkins and Eric McKitrick, The Age of Federalism: The Early American Republic, 1788–1800 (Oxford and New York: Oxford University Press, 1995), 113–14, 133–61.

10 James H. Hutson, "Country, Court, and Constitution: Antifederalism and the Historians," William and Mary Quarterly, 38 (1981), 337, 340; Jackson Turner Main, Political Parties before the Constitution (Chapel Hill: University of North Carolina Press, 1973), 358, 388 (noting that Anti-Federalists tended to be "agrarian-localist" rather than "commercial cosmopolitan" leaders). Donald Lutz notes that Main's anti-cosmopolitan explanation for Anti-Federalist opposition to the Constitution cannot explain the Constitution's support from the inhabitants in some frontier areas of the states. See Donald S. Lutz, "Federalist versus Antifederalist," in Popular Consent and Popular Control: Whig Political Theory in the Early State Constitutions (Baton Rouge: Louisiana State University Press, 1980), 171, 175–86.

11 James Madison. "Consolidation," The National Gazette, December 5, 1791, PJM, XIV, 138.

12 James Madison. "Public Opinion," *The National Gazette*, December 19, 1791, ibid., 170.

13 Thomas Jefferson, "Memorandum on the Compromise of 1790," in *Liberty and Order: The First American Party Struggle*, ed. Lance Banning (Indianapolis: Liberty Fund, 2004) 64–65.

14 Walter Jones, a Virginia Republican, complained to Madison that Hamilton had the backing of "strong auxiliaries" – "system-mongers and fund jobbers," in Jones's phrase – that the "landed interest" could not easily match. Walter Jones to Madison, March 25, 1790, *PJM*, XIII, 118–21.

15 See also George Lee Turberville to Madison, April 7, 1790, ibid., 143–45.

16 Jefferson's legal opinion can be found in *Papers of Thomas Jefferson*, XIX (1974), 275 (279–80). Randolph's opinion can be found in H. Jefferson Powell, *The Constitution and the Attorneys General* (Durham, NC: Carolina Academic Press, 1999), 3–9. For a general account of the debate, see Elkins and McKitrick, *The Age of Federalism*, 229–34.

17 See especially Madison's speeches of February 2 and 8, [1791], *PJM*, XIII, 372–87. In Jefferson's words, "to take a single step beyond the boundaries thus specially drawn around the powers of Congress is to take possession of a boundless field of power, no longer susceptible of definition." Jefferson, Opinion on the Constitutionality of the Bill for Establishing a National Bank, February 15, 1791, in Julian P. Boyd, ed., *The Papers of Thomas Jefferson* (Princeton: Princeton University Press, 1950–), XIX, 276.

18 We are not claiming that Montesquieu could be ideologically identified as a republican but only that he offered a "positive theory" of republican government that was largely accepted by Madison among others. This theory stressed the importance of maintaining a separation of legislative and executive from judicial powers, if republican liberties are to be preserved. He also anticipated later writers in defending something like checks and balances in order to preserve adequate separation of powers. See M. J. C. Vile, *Constitutionalism and the Separation of Powers* (Indianapolis: Liberty Fund, 1998), 83–106.

19 Montesquieu's plainest statement of the idea is found near the beginning of *The Spirit of Laws*, bk VI, ch. 2. "When the legislative and executive powers are united in the same person, or in the same body of magistrates, there can be no liberty; because apprehensions may arise, lest the same monarch or senate should enact tyrannical laws, to execute them in a tyrannical manner. Again, there is no liberty if the judiciary power be not separated from the legislative and executive. Were it joined with the

legislative, the life and liberty of the subject would be exposed to arbitrary controul; for the judge would be then the legislator. Were it joined to the executive power, the judge might behave with violence and oppression." Charles Louis de Secondat, Baron de Montesquieu, *The Complete Works of M. de Montesquieu*, (London: T. Evans, 1777), I, 199. Madison offers his restatement of the principle in *Federalist* 47: "The accumulation of all powers, legislative, executive, and judiciary, in the same hands, whether of one, a few, or many, and whether hereditary, self appointed, or elective, may justly be pronounced the very definition of tyranny."

20 Jeremy Waldron, "Separation of Powers in Thought and Practice," *Boston College Law Review*, 54 (2013), 433–68, at 455.

21 Montesquieu, *The Complete Works of M. de Montesquieu*, 4 vols. (London: 1775), I, 205 ("The executive power ought to be in the hands of a monarch, because this branch of government, having need of dispatch, is better administered by one than by many: on the other hand, whatever depends on the legislative power, is oftentimes better regulated by many than by a single person").

22 Ibid., 198–99.

23 Ibid., 95.

24 Waldron, "Separation of Powers," 459–66.

25 For an argument to this effect, see Niccolò Machiavelli, *The Prince*, trans. Tim Parks (London: Penguin, 2011), 75.

26 "If the executive does not have the right to check the enterprises of the legislative body, the latter will be despotic." But "the legislative power must not have the reciprocal faculty of checking the executive. As execution has limits of its own nature, it is useless to restrict it" (Montesquieu, *The Complete Works of M. de Montesquieu* ,162).

27 Madison to Edward Pendleton, June 21, 1789, *PJM*, XII, 252–53.

28 *Pacificus No. 1*, June 29, 1793, in *The Pacificus–Helvidius Debates of 1793–1794: Toward the Completion of the American Founding*, ed. Morton J. Frisch (Indianapolis: Liberty Fund, 2015), 16.

29 James Madison, Removal Power of the President, June 17, 1789, *PJM*, XII, 233.

30 *Helvidius No. 1*, in *Pacificus–Helvidius Debates*, 62–63.

31 *Helvidius No. 2*, ibid., 66.

32 *Helvidius No. 1*, ibid., 64.

33 John Locke, *Second Treatise of Government*, in *Two Treatises of Government*, ed. Peter Laslett (Cambridge: Cambridge University Press, 1988), §147.

34 *Helvidius No. 4*, in *Pacificus–Helvidius Debates*, 87.

35 A dispute of this kind had arisen earlier in treaty negotiations with the Barbary powers. Those treaties were agreements to pay ransom for American hostages or to purchase free passage for American ships. As such, these treaties were concerned with money and nothing else. The Americans had, at that point, no way of actually threatening to retaliate against the Barbary states.

36 Madison's Speech, March 10, 1796, *PJM*, XVI, 259.

37 Thomas Romer and Howard Rosenthal, "Bureaucrats Versus Voters: On the Political Economy of Resource Allocation by Direct Democracy," *Quarterly Journal of Economics*, 93 (1979), 563. In Romer's and Rosenthal's model the voters play the role of the legislature, but the analogy *mutatis mutandis* stands.

38 William Hogeland, *The Whiskey Rebellion: George Washington, Alexander Hamilton, and the Frontier Rebels Who Challenged America's Newfound Sovereignty* (New York: Simon & Schuster, 2006).

39 See generally Eugene Perry Link, *Democratic-Republican Societies, 1790–1800* (New York: Columbia University Press, 1942).

40 Madison to James Monroe, December 4, 1794, *PJM*, XV, 406.

41 Ibid., 407.

42 Madison to Jefferson, November 30, 1794, ibid., 397–98.

43 *Helvidius No. 1*, in *Pacificus and Helvidius Debates*, 60.

44 Madison, Speech on Jay Treaty, March 10, 1796, *PJM*, XVI, 262.

45 Report of 1800, *PJM*, XVII, 308, 347, 306.

46 Herman V. Ames, ed., State Documents on Federal Relations: The States and the United States (Philadelphia: University of Pennsylvania Department of History, 1906), 18–20.

47 Madison, "A Candid State of Parties," *The National Gazette*, September 22, 1792, *PJM*, XIV, 371–72.

48 Larry D. Kramer, "'The Interest of the Man': James Madison's Constitutional Politics," supra, 337.

49 Colleen Sheehan, "Madison versus Hamilton: The Battle over Republicanism and the Role of Public Opinion," *American Political Science Review*, 98 (2004), 415.

50 Kentucky Resolution, December 3, 1799, at http://avalon.law.yale.edu/18th_century/kenres.asp; Madison to Jefferson, December 29, 1798, *PJM*, XVII, 191–92.

16 The Republican Form of Government in *The Federalist*

Harvey C. Mansfield

The wisdom of *The Federalist* brings the politics of liberalism to a height it had not reached before and was not to keep. To sustain this lofty claim, I shall first briefly compare its political science – the form of its wisdom – both backward to its sources in liberalism and republicanism and forward to its unwitting heir, the political science of today. *The Federalist* made liberalism popular and republicanism viable, on the one hand refashioning Locke and Montesquieu to accommodate the American "republican genius" (*Fed.* 66, 448; also *Fed.* 37, 234; *Fed.* 70, 471) and on the other, giving lessons in prudence to naïve republicans in thrall to utopian theory and unable to learn from sad experience. Looking forward, we shall see that our political science repeats the formula we have from Publius (apparent author of *The Federalist*), as it criticizes formal theory and then proceeds to recreate a formal theory of its own. But our political science does this unconsciously and incompletely, so that it loses the capacity to give advice. To recover the wisdom of *The Federalist* – still available to us – I shall examine its reform of the republican form and try to show how we can recover its sage and subtle advice. To follow Publius will require a study of the use and abuse of forms in politics.

Today one sees political science in thrall to anti-utopian theory as if it had been taught to be practical, or as it would say "pragmatic," by Publius. Yet it is held back by a strange but nearly universal professional ethic of belief in the fact/value distinction, which says that science (for it the only true "wisdom") is confined to facts and never extends to values, none of which can be validated by science. Lacking knowledge of values, this political science cannot give advice, as did Publius in supporting ratification of the new Constitution. If it could give advice, it would declare that having a constitution makes no difference. Dutifully confined as it is to describing or "modeling" the facts of behavior, it becomes impatient when confronted with the formalism of the Constitution. Yet the Constitution is necessarily a formal document, as it is intended for a free people and consists of institutional powers and procedures rather than specifying what a free people must do through them. These institutions are forms that set limits to "constitutional" behavior but, in accordance with the "value" of freedom, do not describe what actually happens. The constitutional principle of separation of powers, for example, on which Publius sets great store, is said by Robert Dahl, the late kingpin of anti-constitutional political science, to be no help in describing the behavior of the three branches of government but merely supplies a false impression of "separation" to actual, factual negotiation and persuasion between the branches, which are not really separate in their behavior.[1] Today's political science, whether calling itself "behavioral" or "formal," seeks the informal, factual reality that is not revealed, but masked, by the Constitution. Although it cannot in good conscience give advice, it has left its mark in the prevailing hostility to constitutional formalism in the understanding of politics.

To defend the particular formalism advocated by The Federalist, one may begin with a major instance of it in the pseudonym of its very author, Publius, actually concealing three men writing in 1787–88 – Alexander Hamilton, James Madison, and John Jay. Hamilton and Madison in the 1790s became bitter political enemies, Hamilton defending and Madison attacking the administration of George Washington. Yet under the name of Publius they thought alike and even wrote in styles so much the same, that when a dispute arose after Hamilton's death as to who wrote certain of the papers, it became a feat of scholarship to decide which claim was correct.[2] Much of the scholarship on The Federalist brushes aside the authorship of "Publius" and tries to identify what in it is Hamiltonian, what Madisonian – an act that ignores their cooperation and the text's coherence as a whole, in favor of their earlier views at the Constitutional Convention or their later partisan division.[3] But we learn the full wisdom of

The Federalist from its formal author, Publius, with Hamilton and Madison speaking together in one voice.

That wisdom consists in a significant departure from both liberal theory, as it had been in Locke and Montesquieu, and republican theory, in both cases for the sake of greater adaptability to political reality. Locke and Montesquieu were republicanized, their vestiges of aristocracy and monarchy removed, and the government made "wholly popular." In America, the republican genius was dominant, and republicanism was practically necessary even more than it may have been politically or morally desirable. It is true, and we shall see, that the aristocratic and monarchic vestiges were removed by being republicanized rather than expunged, and improved rather than abolished, so that Locke and Montesquieu, and even Aristotle, could take satisfaction in the permanence of their insights in the work of Publius. But the explicit institutional reservations of these philosophers against unmixed popular government were abandoned. This was not to be a mixed regime, certainly not Aristotle's mix of popular and oligarchical principles nor with Locke's and Montesquieu's accommodations to existing monarchies.

Republicanism, however, was not left as it had been in previous republican theory. Its whole character was transformed from wishful utopianism to sophisticated realism. What Publius did to republicanism ought to impress our political scientists, for their critique of his work repeats his transformation but mistakes his correction of republican formalism for more unsophisticated, unrealistic formalism. Instead of dismissing Publius, our political science could recognize its kinship to his and try to learn from him.

Publius's correction of republicanism begins with an analysis of choice and moves to the problem of the republican form. In the first paragraph of *The Federalist* Publius says that the American people are deciding the question whether societies of men can establish "good government" by "reflection and choice" or must depend on "accident and force" (*Fed.* 1, 3).[4] Good government by reflection and choice has to be republican, because otherwise it would depend on the accident of a good monarch or aristocracy to rule the people, which they would probably do against their will, by force. Yet good government requires more than the people's will behind it; it calls for a choice, a deliberate choice informed by reflection. When held to the standard of good government, a non-arbitrary standard of reason external to it, republican government is shown to need reason in addition to will. The element of will in choice grounds it in the universal human insistence on having things one's own way, but if will were not accompanied by reason, it would bring anarchy (= accident) and tyranny (= force). Reason supplies direction and solidity, so that the will of the people rises to an "honorable determination" to succeed in this "experiment" (*Fed.* 14, 88; *Fed.* 39, 250).[5] Reason teaches the will, refining out its inconsistencies and whims, so that government by choice is stable; when it changes, it does so by design and for a purpose. The passions of the people will not be suppressed, but "controlled and regulated by the government."

Government will elicit reason from the people, not impose it on them, as it is "the reason of the public," not some individual's reason, that will control and regulate (*Fed.* 49, 343).[6] In making their choices they must be made aware of the limits of choice; above all, choice can rise above but cannot abolish the influence of accident and force in human affairs. In the pairing presented by Publius in his opening paragraph, it is "reflection" on the necessities arising from accident and force that makes "choice" successful, as opposed to the wishing away of necessity characteristic of republican theory. "We have it in our power to begin the world over again," said Tom Paine in *Common Sense* (1776), comparing the situation of America to that of Noah, appropriating the power of God and illustrating republican enthusiasm of the kind reproved by Publius. Publius denounces the "utopian speculations," "idle theories," "theories of the wildest projectors," "theoretic reasoning," to cite but a few instances of a theme he holds to in rebutting the version of republican theory held by his opponents, the Anti-Federalists (*Fed.* 6, 28–35; *Fed.* 10; *Fed.* 14, 88; *Fed.* 43, 293).[7]

These theorists ignore facts of politics arising from the necessities of chance and human nature, of which Americans have present
experience, bringing dangers in both foreign and domestic affairs that
have come to a "crisis" (*Fed.* 1, 3).[8] The Constitution is a response to
this crisis, and in defending it Publius puts necessity to the fore, and
begins with the dangers from war (*Fed.* 3–5), moves to domestic
dangers (*Fed.* 6–8) and deals with domestic factions (*Fed.* 9–10). It is
faction that presents the greatest danger and requires the greatest
attention. Faction is republican choice gone wrong, and the danger
from it has been wrongly identified in the republican tradition. Republicans had previously understood faction as coming from a minority,
an individual or an oligarchy, opposed to the will of the majority. But
the greater danger comes from a *majority* that wants to do wrong,
because the majority's actions and demands appear to accord with the
republican principle of majority rule and the republican maxim that
power is safer in many hands. A faction is defined by Publius as a
number of citizens, whether a minority or majority, united or actuated by a passion or interest contrary to the rights of other citizens or
against the permanent and aggregate interests of the community (*Fed.*
10, 57; *Fed.* 58, 396). This definition, be it noted, nicely comprises the
rights-based and utilitarian concepts often thought to be incompatible
by political theorists today. One could consider it famous if today the
same disregard of majority faction were not typical of republican or
democratic theory. These theorists and publicists waste their indignation, energy and ingenuity against their enemies and do not see the
menace within. Publius, however, deploys a remarkable faculty of
introspection to reveal the danger of majority faction in the very
quality of choice in republican government that honors it and distinguishes it from monarchy and aristocracy. As he says in defending
"the necessity of a well-constructed Senate," "liberty may be endangered by the abuses of liberty as well as by the uses of power" (*Fed.* 63,
424, 428).

Our political science is unable to recognize the problem of
majority faction because Publius's definition of it is not value-free or

beyond dispute; it contains and requires a value judgment as to what is against others' rights and for the public good. Making such judgments is what citizens do every day but what political scientists today, keeping a safe distance from citizens, believe they must never do. With this modesty – or is it obtuseness? – they forswear the possibility of becoming as relevant, important, and beneficial to their country as were the authors behind Publius. They also fail to appreciate that in considering the problem of majority faction, Publius was addressing, if indirectly, the greatest and most obvious instance of it, slavery (*Fed.* 54; *Fed.* 42, 281–82).[9] For a value-free political science cannot say that slavery was not deserved or that America had a problem.

Majority faction has been a danger in previous republics, above all "the petty Republics of Greece and Italy," says Publius with a flourish dismissing the ancient polis, and has in fact resulted in the "perpetual vibration between the extremes of anarchy and tyranny." This means that the republican form of government "needs to be rescued from the opprobrium under which it has so long labored" – which Publius proceeds to do. The republican form is so far from a remedy for majority faction that it gives credit to any majority and does "nothing to check the inducements to sacrifice the weaker party, or an obnoxious individual" (*Fed.* 9, 50; *Fed.* 10, 61; *Fed.* 51, 352).

Here Publius, speaking as a behavioralist would today, shows that the form does not explain what actually happens and does not produce the behavior it desires and promises. He can do this because he holds the republican form to the higher standard of "good government," for which it is necessary to prevent anarchy and tyranny. The baleful history of republics might not matter so much if there were not also "theoretic politicians" who "patronize this species of government" because they want to reduce mankind to "a perfect equality in their political rights." When the republican form is made theoretically perfect by being made simple,[10] the chances for majority faction are enhanced. The remedy will be not to abandon the republican form but to frame it anew so that it is complicated and in a sense at odds, even in conflict, with itself, and thus more in accord with the facts of human behavior. First, it is necessary to *behavioralize the formal*, so as to see what the republican form actually produces, then to *formalize the behavioral* so as to adjust the form to the facts.[11]

The new Constitution is the form adjusted to the deplorable facts of previous republics, summarized in the danger of majority faction. Publius does not turn against all constitutions, but only against constitutions far removed from fact, those that provide only "parchment barriers" against corruption, especially usurpation by the legislature, always the likely governmental instrument of majority faction (*Fed.* 48, 333).[12] His "republican remedies" for the ills of republics do not wave aside all formalities just because the simplistic form of theory does not work. His remedies reform and complicate the old-fashioned republican form of a homogeneous people, small size, and common virtue, with government close to the people, that Montesquieu had found in the ancient republics and that the Anti-Federalists more or less adopted as their standard. The new form was for a large republic with diversity of interests and sects, based on a certain virtue in the people but encouraging the interests, ambition and talents of the enterprising few, matched with a new federalism in which state governments could remain close to the people while the new federal government was at a distance, with separate powers fashioned so as to remain separate. Yet with all its complexity, the new form, unlike the old one, would be as capable of energetic action and long-term planning as a monarchy. The Anti-Federalists had two contradictory criticisms of the Constitution: that it was too complex and too consolidated – defects which were rightly its virtues according to Publius.

In John Locke's political science, the term "constitution" is a verbal noun for the result of constituting, related to the emphasis on human design without reference to its object (as in the Greek *politeia*, regime).[13] "Constitution of what?" is the question unanswered by this usage. With the term "constitution" one finds "establishment" and "institution" used frequently in *The Federalist*, referring to the making of governmental forms. Publius is one of the founders of what is known today as "institutional political science," describing that disposition of modern political science to rely on normal or predictable behavior rather than virtue for the functioning of government. Yet the forms of institutions, as forms, do not simply reproduce the facts; though they do not demand self-sacrifice they do attempt to channel self-interest in useful directions. They offer the bait of incentives (though Publius does not use our economic term) leading not to wealth or mastery but to the satisfaction of a job well done and well received in popular esteem. Institutions with their expectations normalize in form what is otherwise merely factually or behaviorally or statistically normal; they put virtue within reach of ordinary citizens and those of typical ambition, "fit characters," as Publius describes them. "Enlightened statesmen will not always be at the helm," he says to the reader's amusement and instruction, yet with the confidence that enlightened statesmen do not need to be there (*Fed.* 10, 60, 63). "Good government" apparently does not require enlightened statesmen, unless perhaps to institute it.

Publius discusses the Constitution through its clauses, explaining the reasoning behind each and answering the objections of opponents or his own. Those clauses grant powers and define limits of age and term. Consistent with the character of a free constitution that leaves the people to govern as they see fit, the clauses do not state the purposes that the powers and officers should aim at: not stating the substance of government, they are formal descriptions of institutions that are thereby, with this forbearance, formal institutions. Publius fills out the actual expectations that the framers had from these formal provisions in glowing terms promising the best results. Under the new Constitution "fit characters" with "enlightened views and virtuous sentiments" will go to work to "refine and enlarge the public views." This general description – or is it praise? – is distributed to the parts of the Constitution. The House of Representatives is said to be "open to merit of every description," which might include open to merit rarely found or open to demerit as well, yet as Publius continues, he warms to the task and claims that its members will be "safe and competent guardians" whose "merit will recommend" them (*Fed.* 52, 355; *Fed.* 56, 383; *Fed.* 57, 385).[14] The Senate as a "temperate and respectable body of citizens" "must be in all cases a salutary check on the government" so as to ensure that "the cool and deliberate sense of the community" will prevail (*Fed.* 62, 418).[15] Turning to the executive, Publius's promising reaches a crescendo as he declares that the new electoral college "affords a moral certainty" that a man lacking eminent qualifications will seldom become president, indeed, that "it will not be too strong to say" that there will be "a constant probability" of "characters pre-eminent for ability and virtue" in that office (*Fed.* 68, 460–61). At the end the judiciary will supply steady administration as well as "firmness and independence" despite the fact that it will have "neither force nor will but merely judgment" (*Fed.* 78, 523).

In this way Publius promises that through the forms of the Constitution its effect will be the vast improvement over the Articles of Confederation that is needed. Political science today with its deprecation of forms would mock these promises, which with hindsight do seem excessive. The electoral college, praised as "if not perfect, at least excellent" (an A minus), though soon found ineffectual, seems particularly egregious (*Fed.* 68, 458). Yet some sort of form abstracted from behavior seems necessary to political science so that a constitution constituted of "institutions" can function as a guide for free citizens to desired behavior. If political science attempted merely to describe, rather than guide, behavior, it would have to discover mechanisms of behavior that leave nothing to chance or virtue and work as dependably as a machine, like turning a key to start a car. The Constitution has indeed been described as a mechanism, its political science likened to Newtonian mechanics.[16] But human beings have by nature a certain freedom of action that prevents them from operating as dependably and necessarily as a machine yet enables them to behave more nobly as well (*Fed.* 10, 58).[17]

Publius certainly provides an "institutional" political science that relies on more dependable motives of interest (including ambition, as will be seen) than virtue, which is rare at its best and inconstant even when ordinary. *The Federalist* is speckled with verbal nouns like *institution, constitution,* and *establishment,* referring to forms drawn from behavior. But it does not speak of determinate mechanisms that work by necessary causes or toward necessary ends (*Fed.* 14, 84).[18] However institutional, political science functions on "reflection and choice," and not only in the founders but also in the politicians and citizens who are actors. A mechanism would require motives in its moving parts that are petty enough to be universal, and so unfailing. According to Publius, however, an institution like the Constitution works with motives that are inclinations rather than necessarily determined motions, and which are above the average of virtue rather than below it. So in describing the working of the constitutional offices, he touts them while describing them, using the language of aspiration as opposed to that of an operating manual. He speaks in the optative mood so as to describe a reasonable expectation or at least a responsible hope. Overall, his political science reflects not the calculation of interest and the satisfaction of a puzzle solved but "that honorable determination, which animates every votary of freedom, to rest all our political experiments on the capacity of mankind for self-government" (*Fed.* 39, 250).[19] In honorable determination we see the alternative to determinate interest and a well-directed, forceful will rather than one directed by the force of necessity.

Necessity itself has a notable, but complex, character in *The Federalist*. As we have seen, Publius appeals to necessity in order to correct wishful republican theory, forcing it to face the hard facts of defending the Union against its enemies, both foreign and domestic. The Union of the United States cannot be taken for granted, and its necessity must be addressed first so that it can be guaranteed and the American republic can be the first successful republic. Although the Anti-Federalists agreed with Publius on the goal of union, they did not see its necessity or appreciate the changes necessary to secure the Union. In foreign policy they underestimated the cunning of European powers seeking to divide the Union, and in their traditional republican conservatism they railed against a standing army. In domestic policy they could not grasp the necessity above all else of executing the powers of the Union (*Fed.* 15, 92–94).

The *Federalist* is divided in two parts, papers 1 to 36 on the necessity of union, and 37 to 85 on the new republicanism based on meeting that necessity and incorporating it in the Constitution. In the second half of the book – for *The Federalist*, though published serially, is a book with parts that make a whole – Publius turns from necessity in the face of danger, an overbearing necessity against the republican wish for liberty in peace, to a necessity to provide opportunity for virtue, not a constraining but a liberating necessity. The "good government" standard on the first page of *The Federalist* proves to comprise both the necessity to be confronted and the necessity to be welcomed that goes beyond meeting danger to the noble task of "honorable determination."

Confronting necessity compels Publius to abandon the simplicity of republican theory, but also the simplicity of a mechanistic behavioral science. Such a science knows no honorable determination, requiring the free cooperation of the politician and citizen; it knows only causal determination that leaves no room for doubt, hence none for virtue. A behavioral science that can prove every effect as the consequence of a cause producing it has no need, and no room, to recognize the form of an office: the office will necessarily produce a certain result. In Aristotle's terms, an office would be an efficient cause, necessarily preceding its effect and so predicting the effect. A formal office, however, such as Publius presents in his defense of the Constitution, is a formal cause in Aristotle's sense, causing only an inclination, a probable effect, and not preceding but accompanying the action it causes. An example would be the capacity of the constitutional office of the presidency to produce, or better to say, call forth, behavior that people today call "presidential." It is true that not every president is presidential, and also that the word is vague, but it is *constitutionally* vague. The vagueness is inevitable and arises from two causes: the first is that a human being can aspire to more virtue than can be expected of him, which in turn is more than can be guaranteed from him – while what can be guaranteed is sometimes or often not enough for a republic to survive and prosper. The other cause is the desire for freedom in a republic, for freedom requires both defense against enemies, hence provision for emergencies, and room for excellence, hence opportunity to excel, which necessarily risks the chance of failure. A republic needs its guarantees of survival, as well as its promises, necessarily optimistic, to survive with honor, as opposed to behavioral political science, which is so optimistic as to try to survive solely with guarantees, as if hope were superfluous to a rational actor. Institutional political science tries to achieve a certain level of behavior through its institutions, and it is always tempted either to assume that the virtue required will appear or to suppose that one can do without it, through a minimal substitute such as self-interest. To assume the virtue is to suppose like Plato that a philosopher can be a king (a possibility Publius jokingly invokes in *Fed.* 49, 340[20]), or like republican theorists that a citizen can be a statesman. To try to do without virtue is to suppose that cunning and stupidity will rule the world; in the manner prescribed by Machiavelli, through "accident and force."

Publius differs from Aristotle in a way useful to clarify. Aristotle identifies the formal cause of a regime with its end, the final cause: a republic has as its end the making of republicans because good citizens are republicans.[21] But Publius believes that the identification of republicanism with good government conceals the main problem of republican government, which is majority faction. Aristotle would agree, but he would address that problem through a change in the republican form in the direction of mixed government with a large middle class, combining the advantages of popular government with those of monarchy and aristocracy. Publius is subtly different. He proposes a distinction between the formal cause and final cause, that is, the republican form and its end, "good government." Formalism of this kind, keeping form and end separate, is the very essence of the political science of liberalism because liberals do not want to dictate to a free people how it must exercise its freedom to a prescribed end. "Good government" must be the end of a republican people by choice and not contained necessarily in the very definition of republican form, which, as given to majority faction, is ambivalent. Thus, liberal formalism is the protection and security of what is today called liberal pluralism, and in Publius's day, popular government. "Good government" in Publius's usage, becomes to a certain degree, not value-free because it is good, but impartial among regimes rather than identified with republics, enabling it to be an independent standard.

Good government requires the effectual use and distribution of power, which means "power" in the modern sense, first conceived by Thomas Hobbes, of power to act generally to do anything, power without an end, as opposed to the Aristotelian definition of power as always power to do some particular thing, power with an end.[22] "Power" in the new sense is borrowed from modern science and applied to politics. Its minimal character, enabling its use for any end, is an aid to the liberal freedom to choose; it is value-free science in support of human liberty. Power in the people is not to be assumed good, as it might be by the people's "republican genius," but it is not generally bad either, as Aristotle with his general disposition to aristocracy supposed. So, Publius goes about his new task, in accordance with his praise of the improved modern science of politics (*Fed.* 9, 51; cf. *Fed.* 31, 194; *Fed.* 37, 235; *Fed.* 47, 324), of conceiving a denuded power, shed of its end, which can yet accomplish the end of good government in two ways that are compatible with republican liberty, even if not spontaneously agreeable to it. The first is by defining power as action given to "encroachment," and the second is by erecting the system of constitutional powers calling for responsible exercise of power to justify the high hopes, seemingly excessive, that Publius claims for it. The duality of good government corresponds to the duality of necessity – necessity for survival and necessity for good – with which Publius criticizes the republicanism that he wants to make old-fashioned, the system of the Articles of Confederation and its embarrassed defenders, the Anti-Federalists. Publius changes the form of republicanism, as Aristotle would advise, but not in his way. Nor does he set forth a totally behavioral science that would do away with forms and constitutions altogether. His political science is behavioral insofar as it consults the behavior of previous republics in order to found a better republic, and in so doing criticizes the republican form as previously held to. But it is also Aristotelian because it insists on a standard above what can be found in average behavior. This is a revised republican form, now consonant with the minimal "constitution of human nature" in its all-too-human "love of power," that despite these concessions to human imperfection, institutes expectations of good behavior well above the minimum (*Fed.* 15, 97). The result is an unmixed republic that has found republican remedies for the republican disease, yet follows "a new and more noble course" (*Fed.* 10, 65; *Fed.* 14, 84, 89).

The combination of modesty and hope can be found at its height, and in its profundity, in *Federalist* 37, which begins the second half of the book. Here a new republicanism must be set forth to replace the old republicanism which has been torpedoed in the first half. The demonstration of the necessity of union, in effect of the necessity of necessity, must be followed by a demonstration that necessity is not fatal to republics. Having shown "the absolute necessity for an entire change in the first principles of the system [of the Articles]," Publius turns to caution as he sets forth the formal structure of the new Constitution (*Fed.* 23, 148).[23] By contrast to the "manly spirit" in favor of "novelty" called for in *Federalist* 14, he now raises five difficulties, the very first of which is "the novelty of the undertaking" (*Fed.* 14, 88; *Fed.* 37, 233). The most interesting difficulty is the third, what one might call a question of epistemology, "the faculties of the mind," presented by Publius as a question of constitutional form. Drawing a line between the national and the state governments makes him think of the general difficulty in drawing lines in nature, as reflected in the particular difficulty of defining the powers of the three constitutional branches, "which puzzle the greatest adepts in political science." Besides the obscurity of objects in nature, human language is obscure, and the ideas expressed in language are inadequate. Publius takes up the skepticism of modern epistemology, and rather than using it to set aside difficulties in philosophy in order to promote certainty in politics, as did Locke and David Hume, Publius cites his skepticism to support "the necessity of moderating ... our expectations and hopes from the efforts of human sagacity" (*Fed.* 37, 235). Instead of enthusiasm for novelty and his earlier advice not to try to "reconcile contradictions but firmly embrace a rational alternative," he counsels combining opposites in a spirit of moderation (*Fed.* 23, 151).

The second difficulty cited in framing the Constitution illustrates the opposites to be combined: first stability and energy as opposite features of power, then the need for power so combined within "good government" to be combined with liberty and the "Republican form." To refute the "theoretic politicians," Publius needs some theory of his own. He imagines "good government" as having no form itself but rather stating features that any form of government must have, namely stability and energy. Stability is "essential to national character" and to "repose and confidence" in the people, whereas energy is essential to meeting dangers and executing laws. Of these two, securing "energy" has to be the special care, for under the Articles the United States had been "destitute of energy," and those who had felt an "enlightened zeal" for energy had been stigmatized as hostile to liberty (*Fed.* 15, 93; *Fed.* 1, 5). Stability and energy are two modes of power, and although energy is needed for the sake of stability, the people appreciate stability more than energy. These are terms in physics, only just entering political science and political discourse with *The Federalist*, presented as "the effects of good government" rather than the republican form (*Fed.* 37, 234).[24] Energy is not virtue; it is neutral as to its good or bad use. Coming from outside politics, it avoids the name of monarchy while abstracting from monarchy a neutral version of its virtue, now made available to a well-advised republic.

Abstract power in good government, unconnected to any form of government, has no end that limits it; this is power understood as one thing. As such, power has a constant tendency to "encroach," a frequent term in *The Federalist*, because, power being endless and fungible like money, one never can be sure of holding enough of it. The encroaching nature of power provides the first of Publius's two arguments for the separation of powers. Their separation is needed as a precaution against the ambition common to those holding power, and this argument does not need to examine sorts of powers or paths of ambition. It is satisfied if power is checked by power, and its concern is negative, protection against tyranny. In the famous statement of *Federalist* 47: "The accumulation of all powers in the same hands, whether of one, few or many, and whether hereditary, self-appointed or elective, may justly be pronounced the very definition of tyranny." This does not mean that all men necessarily desire power after power, but it does assume that absolute power will be abused. Here Publius, holding to republican suspicion of power, departs from the classical tradition that holds open the possibility of a wise man who would not abuse absolute power.[25] Strangely enough, *abstract* power, conceived by modern political science and not directed to a specific end, is the protection against *absolute* power, which would be directed or justified by some claimed good. For an abstract quantity of power can be divided up for the sake of safety in contrast to the absolute quality of the supposed best power, which cannot. The protection, be it noted, appeals to the minds of republican citizens. For his definition of tyranny resulting from violation of the separation of powers, Publius claims as his "oracle" the "celebrated Montesquieu," whose "maxim" has its source in the British constitution. What the British constitution was to Montesquieu, Homer was to epic poetry – the "perfect model" or standard from which to judge. Publius takes over from Montesquieu and Homer, combining political science and poetry by adopting a standard not taken directly from human nature but mediated through republican opinion.[26]

The second argument for the separation of powers is less obvious and quite different. Its possibility is deprecated in *Federalist* 37, which denies the power of political science to discriminate and define "the three great provinces" of legislative, executive and judicial power, yet implied in *Federalist* 48 by the mention of the "regular" distribution of power that would make the powers work better. In *Federalist* 47 and 48 Publius refutes the simplistic republican doctrine of separating powers that each power should be located and isolated in its own branch away from the other powers. This doctrine overlooks the very encroaching nature of power that republicans believe ought to be feared. Because power encroaches, each branch of government must be given means of self-defense against the other branches if they are to be kept separate. One cannot rely on mere definition inscribed on fancy paper – "parchment barriers" – and one must resort to mutual checks that necessarily involve the three branches with one another, such as the president's veto that makes him part of the legislative process and the Senate's consent to executive appointments and treaties that bring it into the executive power. Without such means of self-defense, the legislative power will dominate, "drawing all power into its impetuous vortex," and reinforcing rather than remedying the danger of majority faction. Republican suspicion of power as such contradicts itself when it forgets the power of the majority, reflected in the dominance of the legislature. The same could be said today when the danger has perhaps shifted from the legislature to the executive. Popular government must not forget the encroaching power of the people.

Publius uses two motives to drive his remedy against encroachment that are often taken as one: interest and ambition (*Fed.* 57, 387).[27] In *Federalist* 51 he sets forth "a policy of supplying by opposite and rival interests, the defect of better motives," a policy that induces the remark that "if men were angels, no government would be necessary" (*Fed.* 51, 349).[28] The interest of humans, by contrast to bodiless messengers, is to have greater power. But greater power might lead to more stability with less energy, and one cannot assume that rival interests will promote rivalry rather than withdrawal into the role of "free rider," as we say today, or the baneful "individualism" that Tocqueville decries. So, Publius turns from the people with their suspicion of power to the class of the ambitious with their love of power to engage a stronger motive, the very spirit of encroachment. In the justly famous phrase epitomizing the spirit of American politics (and society), "Ambition must be made to counteract ambition."

The ambitious will defend against the ambitious, as they know better what the ambitious are up to, and it is they, not ordinary citizens, who love rivalry with their kind and whose interest it is to be ambitious. Publius shows republicans that they can trust those they distrust, precisely to oppose and not simply deplore ambition, using its ways to defeat its ways. Ambition becomes useful by counteracting itself. It is in a sense republican to the extent that it despises fixed, hereditary classes, and although the ambitious constitute a class, it is a class that helps maintain diversity. Ambitious people distinguish themselves by leading others to do new and different things. Thus, the forms of the separated powers create their own social support in the spirits of the ambitious. Unlike simplistic republicans and the Anti-Federalists, Publius does not frown upon ambition.

Publius goes further than show the use of ambition. In the rest of *The Federalist* he gives ambition in the separate powers separate things to do. In effect, and despite the skepticism he avowed earlier, he describes the three powers in different tasks or functions to which the ambitious, or the "fit characters" among the ambitious, are called. The merits required in each branch are presented as the expected consequences of its merely formal requirements: the relatively lengthy term of two years and small size of the House of Representatives (relative to the annual term and larger size of republican tradition and Anti-Federalist objections, seeking a body more intimate with the people); the number and term of senators and of the president; and the lifetime tenure of judges. All constitutions seek probable qualities from certain quantities,[29] but Publius is careful not to identify the result as anything other than "wholly popular," derived from the people, but all of it representative, hence none of it directly popular. His argument moves first from what is necessary to any government to what is congenial to republicans, as we have seen, but then from what is congenial to what is good for republics, leaving it to be inferred that "the more permanent branches" – the Senate, the executive and the judiciary – are not the ones republicans would claim as their own, though they enable republics to be more permanent.

For the popular branch, Publius makes a point of choice by merit when the people elect their representatives. He replies to the Anti-Federalists, who insist on trusting the people, that to trust the people is to trust their choice of representatives – that is, their choice of those they enable to choose for them. Legislators need to know their locality but must also have a capacity to generalize through combining diverse interests. In the Senate, with a longer term, they will be a force for stability, possessing "great firmness" against the evils of mutable government that easily arise in popular legislatures. The executive will be the source of energy because he is one rather than plural, and of firmness because of the length of his term and his eligibility for indefinite reelection. In contrast to legislators, who in making laws deliberate for the medium term, his capacity will be both short-term and long-term: to make immediate decisions in emergencies and to plan, undertake and coordinate "extensive and arduous enterprises." Since republican legislation is notoriously both slow and volatile, executive energy quickens it and executive firmness makes it lasting and coherent.

In the descriptions of what behavior to expect from the formal terms of legislative and executive offices may be discerned the less visible positive side to the obvious negative checking function of the separation of powers. A bicameral legislature is not merely divided so that each chamber can check the other, but also unified so that each makes its contribution to wise legislation. The executive veto too is not merely a check on the legislature but also an addition to its capabilities. These expectations also improve the checking function by providing some sense of what encroachment would actually arise from these branches and why it is unreasonable to go beyond its constitutional rights. "Parchment barriers" are not enough to stop encroachment, but they are an aid to real barriers because they permit the three branches to defend themselves from defensible positions. As a whole, the separation of powers is, Publius says, one of the "auxiliary precautions" of the Constitution, auxiliary to its accountability to the people in elections. It goes beyond keeping government responsive *to* the people to making it "responsible" *for* them, acting for their good with a view to their approval.[30] "Responsibility" and "energy" are new terms coined or made current by Publius, now familiar and indispensable in the American vocabulary, made originally to improve our understanding of what makes republics work. Both imply powers that are separated from the people as well as from one another, so as to maintain what one might call a "constitutional distance."[31] At a distance, first set forth in *The Federalist* and still best understood there, government can serve the people responsibly without being merely their instrument, and the people can hold it to account without hindering it from governing with energy.

What is the place of the judiciary? It is hardly mentioned in the first, negative account of the separation of powers in *Federalist* 47 to 51, though it is singled out for the "peculiar qualifications" of its members in *Federalist* 51. In *Federalist* 49 Publius rejects a proposal of Thomas Jefferson to submit breaches of the Constitution to conventions of the people for judgment. This leaves the judiciary for the task, the branch declared by Publius in *Federalist* 78 to be the "least dangerous," meaning least able to injure or annoy the other two branches, thus not a factor in the system of ambition counteracting ambition. It checks the other two branches but not in the way that they check each other. It has "neither Force nor Will, but merely Judgment," even though it was said in *Federalist* 51 to be "evident that each department should have a will of its own" (*Fed.* 51, 348; *Fed.* 78, 523). Judging, as distinct from legislating and executing, is the measuring of laws and actions against a pre-existing standard, the Constitution (which is a law) or an ordinary law and includes interpreting the standard. If the judiciary is to be separate, it must be independent, and its judging must reach to judicial review of the rest of the government. With this task the judiciary passes from one power among three, and the least dangerous, to the one above the others, the only one with its eye steadily on the whole, monitor of the separation of powers and guardian of the Constitution. The separation of powers does not work automatically like a mechanism but rather requires two of them to yield to the supremacy of the judiciary, which acts on its judgment, not by reactive will. To do so is not unrepublican because it puts "the intention of the people" in establishing a constitution above the intention of their agents in the other branches that have force and will. Judicial review will not even seem unrepublican, despite its high authority, lifetime tenure and unelected character, because it offers possible relief from the injustices of government to individuals.

The use of ambition by Publius brings up another fundamental change he makes to the republican form of government not yet considered – which is size. Of the two republican remedies for the republican disease of majority faction set forth in *Federalist* 10 representation has been discussed but not the extended sphere. The "proper structure" of the Union, containing both the national and the state legislatures, will give form to its large extent, and the new federalism in the Constitution is elaborated in *Federalist* 39. There we learn that the Union will be "federal" in a new sense that abandons the form of a league of republics, ineffectual because it makes the national government dependent on the constituent states, for a new type, previously unknown, that confers power over individuals to both state and national governments and subordinates state sovereignty to the newly empowered central government still called by the old name of federal. *The Federalist* steals its name from the traditional *confederal* league of republics and applies it to a novel form. Then in *Federalist* 51, Publius adds the new federal structure of the American republic to the refashioned separation of powers to assert the general principle that a society "broken into so many parts" by its form will meet the danger of majority faction. In such a society a coalition majority "could seldom take place on any other principles than those of justice and the general good." Under the direction of Publius republican safety tends to excellence in the "republican cause" (*Fed.* 51, 353).

The result of the auxiliary precautions both within and between governments is to establish a formal distance between government and people that leaves room for ambition to operate without "micro-management" as we say. But the use of ambition calls for a worthy object of ambition so as to inspirit rather than frustrate the ambitious. A worthy object would be holding office in a republic of a size that enables it to aim for greatness. And Publius is not bashful about America's ambition to choose a Constitution that will set an example for mankind, proclaimed on his first page. Not to do so would give America "reason to exclaim, in the words of the Poet, 'Farewell, A Long Farewell, To All My Greatness'" (*Fed.* 2, 13).[32]

American greatness would be prevented by dissolution of its Union, but this is not the reason given in support of extending the sphere in *Federalist* 10, where the advantage of a large republic is to bring safety from majority faction. The old republican theory looked for trust between government and people, assured by homogeneity of opinion, which requires small size. The new theory of Publius brings in conflicting interests to fragment opinion so as then, through repre-sentative government, to create from heterogeneous opinion "the cool and deliberate sense of the community." Heterogeneity of interest and opinion will calm the zeal behind majority faction because a majority has to be collected by representatives of the people rather than surging out of the people as a "general conflagration" in the raw form of democracy (*Fed.* 63, 425).[33] Then in *Federalist* 23, the "extent of the country" is shown to be "the strongest argument in favor of an energetic government," and Publius has it both ways: safety against majority faction, requiring large size, and energy to face republican necessities, given large size (*Fed.* 23, 151). After the republican form has been set against the standard of the necessities of "good govern-ment," the form is new-modeled (*Fed.* 49, 339)[34] to absorb those necessities.

No part of the Constitution is more welcoming to greatness than the executive office.[35] The Constitution establishes the first republic with a strong executive consistent with republicanism and not an exception from it like the Roman dictator, the Venetian doge, or the Cromwellian Protector. To defend it Publius had to refute "the idea ... that a vigorous executive is inconsistent with the genius of republican government" (*Fed.* 70, 471).[36] This idea had its "advocates" in the republican tradition as well as among Anti-Federalists, who held to the advantage of greater safety they supposed would result from a plural executive subordinate to the legislature. Publius advanced the contrary view that a single executive is more responsible because he is unable to escape criticism by deflecting it to his colleagues; as to the legislature, he must be equal in power with the legislature if he is to be independent. Executive independence in the new, expanded realm of executive power is necessary in the two stages of its use, emergency and long-term. Together, they illustrate the value to be gained from what Publius in this context calls "the love of fame, the ruling passion of the noblest minds." It is the presidency that "will always bid fair to be filled" by men of wisdom and integrity. "The sole and undivided responsibility of one man will naturally beget a livelier sense of duty and a more exact regard to reputation." These formulations reveal the highest reach of aspiration in Publius's republican forms (*Fed.* 75, 506; *Fed.* 76, 510).

Together, the presidency and the large extent of the country become available to serve as the ground for America's greatness. Wary of republican suspicion, Publius does not wave the flag of "greatness" before his readers. He has his own cause, the Constitution, which offers *republican* greatness based on reflection and choice, not conquest. He does stir the desire of Americans to compete with "European greatness" if only for self-defense (*Fed.* 11, 73),[37] and he proclaims that "the Roman Republic attained to the utmost height of human greatness" (*Fed.* 34, 210).

The Roman Republic reached that height by having two coexisting legislatures for the patrician and plebeian interests, combining the few and the many as was sought by classical political science. The modern political science of Publius begins, instead, from a state of nature in which all men are equal rather than divided into the few and the many. In accordance with this beginning, he says that government arises from a contract of equals rather than from rule by a part, and the meaning of "wholly popular" is that the "people" are not divided from the few. Yet Publius makes room in his forming of the republic, not for New World patricians but for the ambitious few, showing respect for the fact of their existence despite the supposed equality of men by nature. The few in their modern form – "the sagacious, the enterprising and the moneyed few" – can stir up trouble when "mutable policy" gives them opportunity, but the remedy is not to suppress them or ignore their existence (*Fed.* 62, 421). Properly formed in institutions like the Senate, which abstract the benefit of stability from the frosty spirit of patrician oligarchy, ambitious energy can serve public stability and make American republican novelty respectable. Publius expects the American Constitution to gain "veneration" – as it has (*Fed.* 49, 340).[38]

"Veneration" for the Constitution that Publius endorses would appear to bring it into the lives of Americans, improving their "national character" (*Fed.* 37, 234; *Fed.* 62, 420, 422; *Fed.* 63, 423; *Fed.* 64, 437) specifically by endowing it with greater "responsibility" and "energy," and generally by sustaining their pride in a founding based on "reflection and choice" and governing themselves successfully thereafter as a republic. At the same time, such veneration would seem to limit in practice the right "to alter or to abolish" any form of government as a whole, stated in the Declaration of Independence. In effect, this right is now to be exercised under the Constitution, in accordance with Article V rather than against the Constitution as a whole. The American people are sovereign over the Constitution for having ordained and established it – as "We the People" in its preamble – and yet subject to it not only in the laws they obey but also in the lives they lead. The republican form produces a republican people with "the republican genius." Better to say, the American republic reproduces the republican genius on which it is based.

The Federalist is a partisan document written under pressure of time to win ratification of the Constitution in the state of New York. Yet its immediate purpose comprises the ambition and argument of high partisanship in the general cause of republican government. That cause has to deal with the tradition of republicanism that is misconceived in theory and has proved unsuccessful in its ancient history and its recent experience. Publius's new theory maintains a distance between government and people, creating a new form to replace the old one of closeness to ensure responsive obedience of republican government to the people.

This constitutional distance is the essential quality of the republican form according to Publius. It gives scope to the ambitious among the people and makes possible the use of their energy to act responsibly and their firmness to resist acting responsively. It "establishes" and "institutes" – two characteristic expressions of Publius – the power of government as both preventive and productive, the former to address the tendency of power to encroach, the latter to satisfy the need for good performance in administration. Preventive power is divided, dispersed and competitive; performing power is mixed, combining, and cooperative. Whereas the first is elaborated in modern political science, which includes "all" in the people, the second is the ancient mixed regime, which divides the "all" into three parts and combines the advantages of government by one, few, and many. Because both one and few are motivated by honor or "the love of fame," the mixed regime can be said to represent the few and the many as a whole with parts, as opposed to a republican whole without parts. So the Constitution is both modern and ancient, both "wholly popular" and based on the difference between the people and the ambitious (today, the elite). The republican form is both opposed to its enemies, monarchy and aristocracy, and refashioned to include them in republicanized versions, rather than merely oppose them. It differs from the ancient mixed regime by forswearing a principle of rule that might threaten the republican spirit, and by substituting the principle of separation of powers, leaving no sovereign power except, as a last resort, the benign and inconspicuous judiciary without will.

It almost goes without saying that Publius did not conquer his adversary, the old republicanism of responsive government supported by "theoretic politicians," nor did he abolish the bane of republican-ism, majority faction. That term now sounds antique and the distinc-tion it requires between republic and democracy is no longer in use. Almost from the beginning the American republic was democratized by popular election of the president and the appearance of political parties. The undemocratic features of monarchy and aristocracy in the British constitution that Publius republicanized began to be democra-tized in the progress toward ever-greater democracy. "Demagogues" – the rogues of democracy – still exist, but they are now likely to be regarded as responsive leadership rather than execrated as they were by Publius for "paying an obsequious court to the people."

Today, political science pays court to the people: with the universal practice of surveying and polling the people political science does its best, without quite knowing what it is doing, to reduce the constitutional distance that Publius found and justified – in order to return to the constitutional responsiveness that he thought wrong and irresponsible. Yet if Publius did not conquer his adversary, he won the battle he entered when the Constitution was ratified. Since then, despite the wearing away of his prize inventions, despite new circum-stances suggesting that legislative usurpation is no longer the main danger, despite the loss of understanding that attends veneration, and despite the hostility of some scholars, the Constitution remains mainly intact. One cannot blame Publius for later changes that depart from the advice he gave in his arguments against excessive democracy unless those arguments are wrong. We still need to know whether majority faction is the danger and, if so, how to handle it. To understand American politics as of now, hardly a single better source exists than the fictive author of *The Federalist*.

NOTES

1 For an analysis of Robert Dahl's influential critique of *The Federalist* and his attempt to replace it, see Harvey C. Mansfield, *America's Constitutional Soul* (Baltimore, MD: Johns Hopkins University Press,

1991), ch. 11. Imitating Publius, Dahl replaced the formalism of the Constitution with a form or model of his own, meant to be more realistic, called "polyarchy."

2 For a summary see Robert Scigliano's Introduction to the Modern Library edition of *The Federalist* (New York: Random House, 2000).

3 For a recent example, see Quentin Taylor, "The Mask of Publius: Alexander Hamilton and the Politics of Expediency," *American Political Thought*, 5 (2016), 55–79, esp. 66–67. Publius not merely has a mask but as author of *The Federalist* is a mask as real as Hamilton and Madison apart from each other.

4 Thomas Paine: "The cause of America is in great measure the cause of all mankind." *Common Sense*, in Ian Shapiro and Jane E. Calvert, eds., *Selected Writings of Thomas Paine* (New Haven, CT: Yale University Press, 2014), 10.

5 "Experiment" occurs forty-four times in *The Federalist*, an indication of its modern scientific pretension.

6 See William Kristol, "The Problem of the Separation of Powers: Federalist 47–51," in Charles R. Kesler, ed., *Saving the Revolution; The Federalist Papers and the American Founding* (New York: Free Press, 1987), 117.

7 Paine, *Common Sense*, 46. Fed. 6, 28–35; *Fed.* 10; *Fed.* 14, 88; *Fed.* 43, 293. On Anti-Federalist republican theory, see Herbert J. Storing, *What the Anti-Federalists Were For*, in Herbert Storing, ed., *The Complete Anti-Federalist*, 7 vols. (Chicago, IL: University of Chicago Press, 1981), I. On pre-Federalist republican theory, see the summary in Michael Zuckert, "The Political Science of James Madison," in Bryan-Paul Frost and Jeffrey Sikkenga, eds., *History of American Political Thought* (Lanham, MD: Lexington Books, 2003), 153–55, developing the distinction between "short-leashed republicanism" and "free constitution" or long-leashed.

8 Publius uses the word, *Fed.* 1, 3. On its use by others at the time, see Storing, *What the Anti-Federalists Were For*, in *The Complete Anti-Federalist*, 25–26.

9 *Federalist* 54, full of irony, discusses slavery in regard to the notorious 3/5 compromise by which the House of Representatives was to be apportioned. Here Madison, speaking as Publius, defends the compromise by imagining the argument in its favor from "one of our Southern brethren," as if he were not among them, and then allowing himself to be reconciled to it (367, 371). The compromise requires slaves to be held both

as "moral persons" to be represented (of course without the right to vote) and as property, a contradiction that leaves it, Publius admits, "a little strained." Cf. *Fed.* 42, 281–82 on the "unnatural traffic" of the slave trade. The delicacy shown reflects the obvious fact that part of America at the time was laboring under a majority faction with a perverted view of the republican genius.

10 See Paine, "the more simple anything is, the less liable it is to be disordered, and the easier repaired when disordered." Paine, *Common Sense*, 10. On the hostility of the Anti-Federalists to "complex government," see Storing, *What the Anti-Federalists Were For*, 53–63.

11 See Mansfield, *America's Constitutional Soul*, 151–53.

12 See Kristol, "The Problem of the Separation of Powers," 109–10.

13 See Harvey C. Mansfield, *Taming The Prince; The Ambivalence of Modern Executive Power*, 2nd ed. (Baltimore, MD: Johns Hopkins University Press, 1993), 187–90.

14 For the development of "cool and deliberate sense" see Greg Weiner, *Madison's Metronome; The Constitution, Majority Rule, and the Tempo of American Politics* (Lawrence: University Press of Kansas, 2012).

15 See Michael Kammen, *A Machine that Would Go of Itself. The Constitution in American Culture* (New York: Alfred A. Knopf, 1987). On the influence of Woodrow Wilson, see Mansfield, *America's Constitutional Soul*, 5–6, 126, 213.

16 "Liberty ... is essential to political life ..." *Fed.* 10, 58.

17 Publius comes close to mechanism in the one reference to representation as "this great mechanical power" by which will is concentered and its force directed. *Fed.* 14, 84. But in what direction?

18 For an extensive appreciation of the phrase "honorable determination" see David F. Epstein, *The Political Theory of The Federalist* (Chicago, IL: University of Chicago Press, 1984), ch. 4, the best book overall on *The Federalist*.

19 In the context of the need for prejudice in addition to reason, see also the reference to Socrates, which jokingly supposes the nation of philosophers denied in the reference to Plato; *Fed.* 55, 374. Epstein nicely observes: "*The Federalist* distinguishes between an assembly of Socrateses, which would be ruled by passion, and a nation of philosophers, which would not." Epstein, *Political Theory of The Federalist*, 196.

20 Aristotle, *Politics*, 3:3, 7–9.

21 Thomas Hobbes, *Leviathan*, chs. 10, 11; Aristotle, *Politics*, 4:14–15.

22 See Gary Rosen, *American Compact; James Madison and the Problem of Founding* (Lawrence: University Press of Kansas, 1999), 101–07.

23 The form judged by its effects reminds us of Machiavelli's "effectual truth" (*The Prince*, ch. 15) as well as of the laws of Newtonian physics.

24 Aristotle speaks of seeking honor rather than power, and he considers ambition (*philotimia*, or love of honor) to be a moral virtue. But he notes that the virtue of "right ambition" as it were, between too much and too little, has no name, as it is often not clear how much is the right amount. *Nicomachean Ethics*, 4: 4.

25 Kristol's discussion of Publius's subtlety here is not to be missed; "The Problem of the Separation of Powers," 104–05.

26 Note that interest and ambition are listed separately in *Fed.* 57, 387.

27 Aristotle, *Politics*, 4:11–13.

28 On responsibility, see Colleen A. Sheehan, *James Madison and the Spirit of Republican Self-Government* (New York: Cambridge University Press, 2009), 100; Epstein, *Political Theory of The Federalist*, 179–82; Charles R. Kesler, "Responsibility in The Federalist," in Mark Blitz and William Kristol, eds., *Educating the Prince* (Lanham, MD: Rowman & Littlefield, 2000), 219, 237; Harvey Flaumenhaft, *The Effective Republic: Administration and Constitution in the Thought of Alexander Hamilton* (Durham, NC: Duke University Press, 1992), 285 n. 5.

29 Cf. the distinction between "free constitution" and "short-leash republicanism" by Zuckert, "The Political Science of James Madison," 153–55.

30 The Poet is Shakespeare and his unnamed character is Cardinal Wolsey, lamenting his own fall from counselor to King Henry VIII, not a likely republican hero for Publius to adopt. But Wolsey gets his comeuppance in *Fed.* 6, 29–30.

31 Note that the opinions promoted by "theoretic politicians" (*Fed.* 10, 61–2) become "a greater variety of parties and interests" (*Fed.* 10, 64) as Publius's diagnosis of the problem becomes a remedy. At the end "variety of sects" appears as a needed addition to "interest" in cooling zealous opinion. Republican theory, but not Publius, forgets the danger of sectarian violence to republican peace and quiet.

32 See *Fed.* 49, 339, for this word, redolent of the republican New Model Army in seventeenth-century Britain.

33 See Mansfield, *Taming the Prince*, ch. 10.

34 "Let Americans disdain to be the instruments of European greatness!" – leaving it uncertain whether greatness is merely European, and as such a threat, or necessary to avoid being an instrument of someone else's greatness, and thus a worthy goal. *Fed.* 11, 73.

35 This is "that veneration, which time bestows on everything," a gift to humanity, not always a reward. See Storing, *What the Anti-Federalists Were For*, 75. Critics of *The Federalist* cannot abide the shift from damning "a blind veneration for antiquity" (*Fed.* 14, 88) to endorsing veneration of the Constitution: see Garry Wills, *Explaining America: The Federalist* (New York: Penguin, 1982), 24–41; Sanford Levinson, *An Argument Open to All: Reading The Federalist in the 21st Century* (New Haven, CT: Yale University Press, 2015), 52–54, 183–85.

36 On energy see *Fed.* 1, 5; *Fed.* 15, 93; *Fed.* 23, 148; *Fed.* 37, 233; *Fed.* 70, 471; *Fed.* 73, 494; on firmness, see *Fed.* 71, 484–5; *Fed.* 78, 523. The absence of both is "servile pliancy," *Fed.* 71, 492.

37 For the character of one, see "single man" in *Fed.* 70, 471; for that of a "few," see *Fed.* 47, 324; *Fed.* 56, 381; *Fed.* 62, 421; *Fed.* 73, 493; *Fed.* 78, 529; for "wholly popular" see *Fed.* 14, 84. See Kristol, "The Problem of the Separation of Powers," 119.

38 *Fed.* 1, 6. "Leader" is not a complimentary, nor even a neutral, term for Publius; see *inter alia Fed.* 6, 33; *Fed.* 10, 64; *Fed.* 62, 418; *Fed.* 70, 479. See James Ceaser, *Designing a Polity; America's Constitution in Theory and Practice* (Lanham, MD: Rowman & Littlefield, 2011), ch. 5.

Index